W9-CXL-767

MAGILL'S
LITERARY ANNUAL
2009

MAGILL'S
LITERARY ANNUAL
2009

Essay-Reviews of 200 Outstanding Books
Published in the United States During 2008

With an Annotated List of Titles

Volume One
A-Lib

Edited by
JOHN D. WILSON
STEVEN G. KELLMAN

SALEM PRESS
Pasadena, California   Hackensack, New Jersey

Cover photo: © Warren Rosenberg/Dreamstime.com

Copyright ©2009, by SALEM PRESS
All rights in this book are reserved. No part of this work may be used or reproduced in any manner whatsoever or transmitted in any form or by any means, electronic or mechanical, including photocopy, recording, or any information storage and retrieval system, without written permission from the copyright owner except in the case of brief quotations embodied in critical articles and reviews or in the copying of images deemed to be freely licensed or in the public domain. For information address the publisher, Salem Press, P.O. Box 50062, Pasadena, California 91115.

∞ The paper used in these volumes conforms to the American National Standard for Permanence of Paper for Printed Library Materials, Z39.48-1992 (R1997).

LIBRARY OF CONGRESS CATALOG CARD NO.
ISBN (set): 978-1-58765-547-0
ISBN (vol. 1): 978-1-58765-548-7
ISBN (vol. 2): 978-1-58765-549-4

FIRST PRINTING

PRINTED IN CANADA

028.1
M1945
2009
v.1

CONTENTS

CONTENTS

PUBLISHER'S NOTE

Magill's Literary Annual, 2009, is the fifty-fifth publication in a series that began in 1954. Critical essays for the first twenty-two years were collected and published in the twelve-volume *Survey of Contemporary Literature* in 1977; since then, yearly sets have been published. Each year, *Magill's Literary Annual* seeks to evaluate critically 200 major examples of serious literature, both fiction and nonfiction, published during the previous calendar year. The philosophy behind our selection process is to cover works that are likely to be of interest to general readers, that reflect publishing trends, that add to the careers of authors being taught and researched in literature programs, and that will stand the test of time. By filtering the thousands of books published every year down to 200 notable titles, the editors have provided the busy librarian with an excellent reader's advisory tool and patrons with fodder for book discussion groups and a guide for choosing worthwhile reading material. The essay-reviews in the *Annual* provide a more academic, "reference" review of a work than is typically found in newspapers and other periodical sources.

The reviews in the two-volume *Magill's Literary Annual, 2009*, are arranged alphabetically by title. At the beginning of both volumes is a complete alphabetical list, by category, of all covered books that provides readers with the title, author, and a brief description of each work. Every essay is approximately four pages in length. Each one begins with a block of reference information in a standard order:
- Full book title, including any subtitle
- *Author:* Name, with birth and death years
- *First published:* Original foreign-language title, with year and country, when pertinent
- Original language and translator name, when pertinent
- Introduction, Foreword, etc., with writer's name, when pertinent
- *Publisher:* Company name and city, number of pages, retail price
- *Type of work:* (chosen from standard categories)

Anthropology	Essays	Literary criticism
Archaeology	Ethics	Literary history
Autobiography	Film	Literary theory
Biography	Fine arts	Media
Current affairs	History	Medicine
Diary	History of science	Memoir
Drama	Language	Miscellaneous
Economics	Law	Music
Education	Letters	Natural history
Environment	Literary biography	Nature

Novel	Psychology	Sociology
Novella	Religion	Technology
Philosophy	Science	Travel
Poetry	Short fiction	Women's issues

- *Time:* Period represented, when pertinent
- *Locale:* Location represented, when pertinent
- Capsule description of the work
- *Principal characters* [for novels, short fiction] or *Principal personages* [for biographies, history]: List of people, with brief descriptions

The text of each essay-review analyzes and presents the focus, intent, and relative success of the author, as well as the makeup and point of view of the work under discussion. To assist the reader further, essays are supplemented by a list of additional "Review Sources" for further study in a bibliographic format. Every essay includes a sidebar offering a brief biography of the author or authors. Thumbnail photographs of book covers and authors are included as available.

Four indexes can be found at the end of volume 2:

- Biographical Works by Subject: Arranged by subject, rather than by author or title. Readers can locate easily reviews of biographical works—memoirs, diaries, and letters in addition to biographies and autobiographies—by looking up the name of the person covered.
- Category Index: Groups all titles into subject areas such as current affairs and social issues, ethics and law, history, literary biography, philosophy and religion, psychology, and women's issues.
- Title Index: Lists all works reviewed in alphabetical order, with any relevant cross references.
- Author Index: Lists books covered in the annual by each author's name.

A searchable cumulative index, listing all books reviewed in *Magill's Literary Annual* between 1977 and 2009, as well as in *Magill's History Annual* (1983) and *Magill's Literary Annual, History and Biography* (1984 and 1985), can be found at our Web site, **www.salempress.com**, on the page for *Magill's Literary Annual, 2009*.

Our special thanks go to the editors for their expert and insightful selections: John D. Wilson is the editor of *Books & Culture* for *Christianity Today*, and Steven G. Kellman is a professor at the University of Texas at San Antonio and a member of the National Book Critics Circle. We also owe our gratitude to the outstanding writers who lend their time and knowledge to this project every year. The names of all contributing reviewers are listed in the front of volume 1, as well as at the end of their individual reviews.

COMPLETE ANNOTATED LIST OF TITLES

VOLUME 1

COMPLETE ANNOTATED LIST OF TITLES

COMPLETE ANNOTATED LIST OF TITLES

COMPLETE ANNOTATED LIST OF TITLES

COMPLETE ANNOTATED LIST OF TITLES

VOLUME 2

COMPLETE ANNOTATED LIST OF TITLES

COMPLETE ANNOTATED LIST OF TITLES

COMPLETE ANNOTATED LIST OF TITLES

COMPLETE ANNOTATED LIST OF TITLES

COMPLETE ANNOTATED LIST OF TITLES

CONTRIBUTING REVIEWERS

Michael Adams
*City University of New
York Graduate Center*

Richard Adler
*University of
Michigan-Dearborn*

Thomas P. Adler
Purdue University

M. D. Allen
*University of
Wisconsin-Fox Valley*

Emily Alward
*Henderson, Nevada,
District Libraries*

Andrew J. Angyal
Elon University

Charles F. Bahmueller
*Center for Civic
Education*

Barbara Bair
Duke University

Dean Baldwin
*Penn State Erie, The
Behrend College*

Carl L. Bankston III
Tulane University

Milton Berman
University of Rochester

Cynthia A. Bily
Adrian, Michigan

Margaret Boe Birns
New York University

Franz G. Blaha
*University of
Nebraska-Lincoln*

Pegge Bochynski
Salem State College

Steve D. Boilard
*California Legislative
Analysts' Office*

Harold Branam
*Savannah State University
(retired)*

Peter Brier
*California State
University, Los
Angeles*

Jeffrey L. Buller
*Florida Atlantic
University*

Thomas J. Campbell
*Pacific Lutheran
University*

Edmund J. Campion
University of Tennessee

Henry L. Carrigan, Jr.
Northwestern University

Dolores L. Christie
*Catholic Theological
Society of America
(CTSA)
John Carroll University*

Marc C. Conner
*Washington and Lee
University*

Richard Hauer Costa
Texas A&M University

Mary Virginia Davis
*University of California,
Davis*

Frank Day
Clemson University

Francine A. Dempsey
College of Saint Rose

M. Casey Diana
Arizona State University

Robert P. Ellis
*Worcester State College
(retired)
Northborough Historical
Society*

Thomas L. Erskine
Salisbury University

Thomas R. Feller
Nashville, Tennessee

Rebecca Hendrick
Flannagan
*Francis Marion
University*

Roy C. Flannagan
*South Carolina Governor's
School for Science and
Mathematics*

Robert J. Forman
*St. John's University, New
York*

Kathryn E. Fort
*Michigan State University
College of Law*

Donald R. Franceschetti
*The University of
Memphis*

Jean C. Fulton
Landmark College

Ann D. Garbett
Averett University

Janet E. Gardner
*University of
Massachusetts,
Dartmouth*

Leslie E. Gerber
*Appalachian State
University*

Sheldon Goldfarb
*University of British
Columbia*

Karen Gould
Austin, Texas

Lewis L. Gould
*University of Texas,
Austin*

Hans G. Graetzer
*South Dakota State
University*

Jay L. Halio
University of Delaware

Diane Andrews
Henningfeld
Adrian College

Carl W. Hoagstrom
*Ohio Northern University
(retired)*

William L. Howard
Chicago State University

Jeffry Jensen
*Glendale Community
College*

Kyle Keefer
Converse College

Fiona Kelleghan
University of Miami

Steven G. Kellman
*University of Texas,
San Antonio*

Howard A. Kerner
Polk Community College

Grove Koger
*Boise, Idaho, Public
Library*

Margaret A. Koger
Boise, Idaho

James B. Lane
*Indiana University
Northwest*

Eugene Larson
*Los Angeles Pierce
College*

Leon Lewis
*Appalachian State
University*

Thomas Tandy Lewis
St. Cloud State University

R. C. Lutz
Madison Advisors

Janet McCann
Texas A&M University

Joanne McCarthy
Tacoma, Washington

Andrew Macdonald
*Loyola University,
New Orleans*

Gina Macdonald
Nicholls State University

S. Thomas Mack
*University of South
Carolina-Aiken*

David W. Madden
*California State
University, Sacramento*

Lois A. Marchino
*University of Texas at
El Paso*

Charles E. May
*California State
University,
Long Beach*

Laurence W. Mazzeno
Alvernia College

Vasa D. Mihailovich
*University of
North Carolina*

Timothy C. Miller
Millersville University

Robert Morace
Daemen College

Daniel P. Murphy
Hanover College

Robert Niemi
St. Michael's College

John Nizalowski
Mesa State College

Holly L. Norton
*University of
Northwestern Ohio*

Robert J. Paradowski
*Rochester Institute of
Technology*

David Peck
Laguna Beach, California

Marjorie J. Podolsky
*Penn State Erie, The
Behrend College*

Cliff Prewencki
Delmar, New York

CONTRIBUTING REVIEWERS

Maureen J. Puffer-
Rothenberg
Valdosta State University

Edna B. Quinn
Salisbury University

Thomas Rankin
Concord, California

R. Kent Rasmussen
*Thousand Oaks,
California*

Rosemary M. Canfield
Reisman
*Charleston Southern
University*

Mark Rich
Cashton, Wisconsin

Carl Rollyson
*City University of New
York, Baruch College*

Joseph Rosenblum
*University of North
Carolina, Greensboro*

John K. Roth
*Claremont McKenna
College*

Marc Rothenberg
*National Science
Foundation*

Elizabeth Sanders
Nicholls State University

R. Baird Shuman
*University of Illinois,
Urbana-Champaign*

Thomas J. Sienkewicz
Monmouth College

Charles L. P. Silet
Iowa State University

Carl Singleton
*Fort Hays State
University*

Roger Smith
Portland, Oregon

Maureen Kincaid Speller
*University of Kent at
Canterbury*

Theresa L. Stowell
Adrian College

Gerald H. Strauss
Bloomsburg University

Paul Stuewe
Green Mountain College

Paul B. Trescott
Southern Illinois University

William L. Urban
Monmouth College

Sara Vidar
Los Angeles, California

Ronald G. Walker
*Western Illinois
University*

Shawncey Webb
Taylor University

Twyla R. Wells
*University of
Northwestern Ohio*

Bob Whipple
Creighton University

Thomas Willard
University of Arizona

John Wilson
Editor, Books & Culture

Scott D. Yarbrough
*Charleston Southern
University*

Author Photo Credits

Kwame Anthony Appiah: *Greg Martin*; Paul Auster: © *Jerry Bauer*; Julian Barnes: © *Isolde Ohlbaum*; Eavan Boland: *Library of Congress*; Jennifer Finney Boylan: *James Bowdin/Courtesy, Random House*; Geraldine Brooks: *Randi Baird/ Library of Congress*; William F. Buckley, Jr.: *Courtesy, Carnegie Library of Pittsburgh*; Michael Chabon: © *Patricia Williams/Courtesy, Random House*; Michael Connelly: *Courtesy, Allen & Unwin*; Scott Douglas: *Diana Le Counte/Courtesy, Perseus Books*; Louise Erdrich: *Michael Dorris/Courtesy, HarperCollins*; Dominique Fabre: *Courtesy, Archipelago Books*; Robert Frost: *Library of Congress*; John Grisham: *Courtesy, Doubleday & Co.*; Amy Laura Hall: *Courtesy, Wm B Eerdmans Publishing*; P. D. James: *Courtesy, Allen and Unwin*; Ha Jin: *Kalman Zabarsky*; Stephen King: *Tabitha King*; Ursula K. Le Guin: © *Marion Wood Kolisch/Courtesy, Harcourt Books*; Dennis Lehane: *David Shankbone*; Alexander McCall Smith: *Tara Murphy/Library of Congress*; Alexander McCall Smith: *Chris Watt/Courtesy, UCLA*; Toni Morrison: *Lynda Koolish/Courtesy, University Press of Mississippi*; Joyce Carol Oates: © *Norman Seeff*; Frank O'Hara: *Worcester Polytechnic Institute, Archives & Special Collections/George C. Gordon Library/Courtesy, George Montgomery*; Cynthia Ozick: *Nancy Crampton/Courtesy, Houghton Mifflin Company*; Grace Paley: *Courtesy, New York State Writers Institute, State University of New York*; Richard Price: *Ralph Gibson/Houghton Mifflin*; Anne Rice: *Courtesy, Random House*; Philip Roth: © *Nancy Crampton*; John Updike: © *Davis Freeman*; Mario Vargas Llosa: © *Jerry Bauer*; Gore Vidal: © *Jane Bown*; Kurt Vonnegut: © *Jill Krementz*; Steven Waldman: *Christine Austin/Courtesy, Random House*; Simon Winchester: © *Marion Ettlinger/Courtesy, Picador USA*; Larry Woiwode: © *Nancy Crampton*; Tobias Wolff: © *Jerry Bauer*

MAGILL'S
LITERARY ANNUAL
2009

ACEDIA AND ME
A Marriage, Monks, and a Writer's Life

Author: Kathleen Norris (1947-   )
Publisher: Pantheon (New York). 334 pp. $25.95
Type of work: Memoir
Time: 1947-2007
Locale: South Dakota and Hawaii

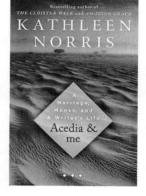

Norris examines the concept of acedia from its ancient understanding in monastic spirituality through its more recent role in philosophy, psychology, literature, and American culture and also in her spiritual, marital, and writing life

Kathleen Norris, a poet and nonfiction writer, has written earlier about her life and her spirituality in *Dakota: A Spiritual Geography* (1993), *Cloister Walk* (1996), and *Amazing Grace: A Vocabulary of Faith* (1998). In these and in *The Virgin of Bennington* (2001), an account of her college and early professional years, Norris alludes to the bouts of despondency and the resistance to commitment that marked her life. She maintained that she had found professional help for her depression, but she had no name for or understanding of the latter affliction. In *Cloister Walk*, written after two residencies at a Benedictine monastery, she devotes a few pages to acedia, and she credits a lecture that became *The Quotidian Mysteries: Laundry, Liturgy, and "Women's Work"* (1999) with inspiring her to do a full-length study based on her belief in the usefulness of the literature of monasticism for herself and her world.

In *Acedia and Me: A Marriage, Monks, and a Writer's Life*, Norris focuses on this belief. She found that those in monastic life, going back to the fourth century, understood acedia best, identifying it as the "noonday devil," a spiritual temptation to weariness unto giving up that may be felt by a monk after his first fervor, at a time when he is facing the reality of his day-by-day life committed to prayer. It was at noon that a monk felt most acutely the temptation to lose his belief that he could live a life completely devoted to prayer. In the first chapter, "Somewhere," the writer acknowledges that in discovering the term "acedia" she felt "a weight lift from [her] soul." For Norris, throughout her life, making any commitment was difficult, since the thought of having to follow through on commitments was wearying.

Discovering acedia was life-changing for Norris, giving her an understanding of the feeling she had suffered from childhood and still suffers. After this discovery, she spent years in research to broaden and deepen this understanding, and the result is *Acedia and Me*, which describes the connections between acedia and her nearly thirty-year marriage, her ongoing spiritual journey, and her successful writing life. Norris first briefly recounts the understanding of acedia in early monastic literature. She points to the inclusion of the term "acedia" with spelling variations in editions

~
Kathleen Norris is an award-winning poet, and three of her nonfiction titles have been national best sellers and New York Times *Notable Books of the Year. She has received grants from the Bush and Guggenheim Foundations, and she is an editor-at-large of* The Christian Century.
~

of the *Oxford English Dictionary* from the fourteenth century though the 1989 edition. This persistence of the word, says Norris, is "like the lexicon's version of a mole, working on us while hidden from view." The persistence even while obscure means, Norris adds, that acedia has always been and remains a human affliction. The opposite of acedia, she suggests, is caring, and to illustrate the importance of caring she gives her text an underlying foundation of her battles with acedia, moving easily in the text from an essayist's discussion of acedia to a story-teller's presentation of its role in the different phases of her life.

In her earlier texts, Norris connected her spirituality to her Presbyterian roots in rural South Dakota and her sojourns at the Benedictine St. John's Abbey in Collegeville, Minnesota. She grounded these narratives in the landscape of the midwestern plains and in the rhythms and images of scriptural and liturgical hymns and prayers of her religious roots. Though Norris's spiritual language is also part of *Acedia and Me*, this style is often overwhelmed by her research. The text is replete with definitions and quotes, valuable to the reader but lacking useful bibliographical citation. "I can hear scholars howling with some justification," she writes, "that I am mixing it all up, failing to make the necessary and proper distinctions." Perhaps to make up for her freewheeling style, in the final chapter she gives the reader "Acedia: A Commonplace Book," forty-five pages of quotations, arranged chronologically, that give or imply a definition of acedia. These alone make rich reading.

Norris asserts her right to her chosen writing style in the "Author's Note": What she is attempting is a lengthy "meditation on the subject of acedia." Meditation as method seems to give the writer license to discuss acedia in the way that works for her. The text meanders, looking at the main topic from every angle: depression, faith, hope, illness, love, prayer, marriage, theology, monastic life, suffering, caregiving, writer's block, and more. Norris quotes rich material from every age, genre, and spiritual tradition. Numerous insights of great value appear within her presentation of these source materials, as if Norris the poet is trying to share in another way the epiphanies that are the heart of the rigidly concise forms of poetry. If sometimes her insights seem to be buried in the breadth and depth of her prose, much enlightenment does come to the reader.

Some of the richest sections in Norris's study of acedia relate the story of its role in her marriage to the poet David Joseph Dwyer (1946-2003), to whom she dedicates this book. Throughout this marriage, as she dealt with the mysterious malady she now calls acedia, her husband suffered from psychological problems, alcoholism, serious illnesses, and in the end terminal cancer. Perhaps in *Acedia and Me* the writer found a safe way to express honestly the ongoing pain and enduring love in her marriage and to face the seventh decade of her life as a widow. The narrative sections make a sometimes overly informative text a richer reading experience, and traveling with Norris on her spiritual journey is always worthwhile.

Norris's stated intention of rescuing the lost term "acedia" and restoring it in contemporary language, psychology, and spirituality effectively holds the text together. Although it is difficult to define because it is a complicated syndrome, properly understood, acedia is, she asserts, what the third millennium needs to heal "much of the restless boredom, frantic escape, commitment phobia, and enervating despair" she has found in herself and seen in her contemporaries. One difficulty is that dictionary definitions of acedia by the end of the twentieth century, when they did appear, were so broad as to confuse or hide what the word meant. She finds many terms and phrases: "heedlessness, torpor . . . [a] non-caring state"; "the deadly sin of sloth," "spiritual torpor and apathy"; "a mental syndrome, the chief features of which are listlessness, carelessness, apathy, and melancholia." None captures as well as monastic literature about acedia the mental, emotional, and spiritual impact that she has suffered during her lifetime.

Some distinctions that Norris makes are useful to understanding acedia. Though some confuse clinical depression and acedia, Norris asserts that the former implies a certain level of anguish, while in the latter it seems a matter of indifference. "Despair" is not an adequate synonym, either: "For despair, participation in the divine nature through grace is perceived as appealing, but impossible; for acedia, the prospect is possible, but unappealing." Better to understand acedia as the monks did: that it is a "bad thought," meant to be replaced by another thought, a good thought. At one time Christianity defined acedia as one of the "eight bad thoughts" that were part of one's being but could and should be rejected in favor of good thoughts, lest they lead to sinful acts. Norris agrees that acedia comes as a bad thought, and she is surprised that at some point in church history the eighth bad thought, acedia, disappeared into the term "sloth," and the remaining seven bad thoughts became the "seven deadly sins." Acedia is not in her mind a sin, such as sloth, but bad thinking that might lead to sinful acts, such as walking out on one's commitments. According to Norris, the cure is humility, knowing that one is weak but also knowing that with God's grace one can be strong. Her poet self helps Norris explain that looking at one's own smallness with humility gives one "fresh eyes" to see that impasses or blocks are "not merely the cause of the symptom of . . . misery but also as places where the light of promise shines though."

Though "Abbas" and "Ammas," wisdom figures in ancient Christian monastic life, are her primary sources for understanding acedia, Norris finds other helpful teachers across the ages. One is the sixteenth century spiritual leader John of the Cross (1542-1591). When this Carmelite mystic and monk describes spiritual aridity, he means acedia, Norris says, that which is felt by anyone who reaches a mental impasse, "whether in writing, art, prayer, marriage, or parenting." The defeating thought is that the impasse or block one faces cannot be overcome because no tactic one can think of will work, so why bother? All is futile, hopeless. Norris, who has faced both writer's block and spiritual emptiness many times, notes how appropriate it is that John of the Cross is the patron saint of poets. Similar is the statement by philosopher Søren Kierkegaard (1813-1855) that it is presumptuous to think "that there is no way out for God because I cannot see any." For a twentieth century view, Norris calls on playwright Wendy Wasserstein (1950-2006), who, in writing on sloth was really referring to acedia. Wasserstein wrote that, like "traditional" sloths, "New Age [sloths look] at the possibility of real thought" and reject it.

Norris's spiritual journey with acedia, with its integral connection with monastic texts and Benedictine men and women religious, has led her to many epiphanies about her writing life. For example, when St. Benedict (480-547) writes about sloth, he says, "Every time you begin a good work, you must pray to [God] to bring it to perfection." Benedict, she finds, sees all who follow the Benedictine rule as beginners, and she contrasts this attitude with our culture's view that beginners are those at the bottom of the heap. Better are those who leap forward, quickly, impatient with any delays. Like the pilgrim on a spiritual journey, beginning again and again, Norris as a writer begins over and over, facing again the feared blank page. "Beginning requires that I remain willing to act, and to summon my hopes in the face of torpor . . . rejecting that self-censurious spirit that will arise to scorn my efforts as futile."

Another important definition of acedia helpful to her writing life came from an essay by Aldous Huxley (1894-1963) called "Accidie." Huxley traces the term from medieval times through nineteenth century Romantic literature where it assumed a "deadly form, a mixture of boredom, sorrow, and despair, [that became] an inspiration to the greatest poets and novelists, and it has remained so to this day."As a young writer in New York during the 1960's, like many younger poets, Norris was tempted to believe that writing poetry required such ennui. Huxley's essay, Norris says, taught her that one could be a poet and have faith. These words define accurately the Norris known through her totally human and deeply spiritual writings.

Francine A. Dempsey

Review Sources

America 199, no. 10 (October 6, 2008): 31.
The Atlantic Monthly 302, no. 4 (November, 2008): 140-141.
Booklist 104, no. 21 (July 1, 2008): 27.
Christianity Today 52, no. 8 (August, 2008): 59.
Kirkus Reviews 76, no. 14 (July 10, 2008): 80.
Library Journal 133, no. 19 (November 15, 2008): 44.
Publishers Weekly 255, no. 23 (June 9, 2008): 44.

THE AGE OF REAGAN
A History, 1974-2008

Author: Sean Wilentz (1951-   )
Publisher: HarperCollins (New York). 564 pp. $27.95
Type of work: History
Time: 1974-2008
Locale: Washington, D.C.

A fast-paced, well-documented analysis of the rise of Ronald Reagan, his presidential administration, and his impact on American politics

Principal personages:
RICHARD NIXON (1913-1994),
    U.S. president, 1969-1975
GERALD FORD (1913-2006),
    U.S. president, 1975-1977
JIMMY CARTER (1924-   ), U.S. president, 1977-1981
RONALD REAGAN (1911-2004), U.S. president, 1981-1989
GEORGE H. W. BUSH (1924-   ), U.S. president, 1989-1993
BILL CLINTON (1946-   ), U.S. president, 1993-2001
GEORGE W. BUSH (1946-   ), U.S. president, 2001-2009

Sean Wilentz, who teaches American history at Princeton University, has a well-deserved reputation as both an outstanding scholar and a strong partisan for the Democratic Party in contemporary American politics. His was a leading voice, for example, against the effort to impeach President Bill Clinton in 1998. Because of Wilentz's involvement in contemporary politics, this new study, *The Age of Reagan*, on the impact of Ronald Reagan on recent national politics will surprise Wilentz's critics and disconcert some Democrats. In this lengthy but lively treatment of the last four decades of public affairs, Wilentz takes Reagan seriously and examines his effect on the political scene with a shrewd sense of the president's genuine importance. From that interpretive point of view, Wilentz then proceeds to analyze Reagan's impact on subsequent presidents and American politics in general.

Wilentz's scholarly field has been the United States in the mid-nineteenth century, about which he has published important books about Jacksonian democracy and for which he has received prizes for his substantial accomplishments. Wilentz brings his strong capacity to do extensive research in primary sources and to write compelling prose to his study of Reagan and his times. His in-depth explorations in the archival collections of the Gerald R. Ford Library and the Jimmy Carter Library are among the genuine strengths of this study. Wilentz offers a timely reminder that extensive research in primary sources is still one of the hallmarks of excellence in an historian.

Readers will find an abundance of fresh information about the major players in the time period covered by Wilentz's book. He has useful things to say about the

Sean Wilentz is a member of the history faculty at Princeton University. His book The Rise of American Democracy *(2004) won the Bancroft Prize in 2005.*

deeper meaning of the Iran-Contra episode of Reagan's second term. Few writers have provided more intelligent treatments of Clinton's trials at the hands of the president's political enemies during the 1990's. Throughout, Wilentz has an eye for the appropriate quotation to illustrate his arguments and to illuminate the character of the public figures that he discusses. Wilentz has mastered the facts of innumerable now-forgotten controversies, and he sets the record straight on such questions as *The New York Times* and its questionable role in promoting the bogus Whitewater flap of the Clinton era.

The narrative begins with the resignation of Richard Nixon in August, 1974, and the launch of the administration of Gerald R. Ford, and Wilentz provides an insightful analysis of Ford's brief tenure in the White House. He emphasizes the importance of such figures as Donald Rumsfeld and Richard Cheney to the decision making of the president in the run-up to the 1976 presidential election. The displeasure with Congress that Rumsfeld and Cheney experienced at that time influenced their disdain for Congress during the administration of George W. Bush. Ford emerges as an underrated president who suffered from the legacy of Nixon and his inability to overcome the negative public reaction to his pardon of the former president in September, 1974.

The Carter administration comes in for a tart appraisal from Wilentz. The president's political ineptitude in office and the contradiction between his lofty campaign rhetoric and his maladroit governing style are developed in rich detail. Carter overmanaged the details of his presidency and failed to connect with the public as economic conditions worsened. This chapter recaptures the difficulties of the Carter years and the consequent decay of the Democratic Party as a governing coalition.

The key to the book, however, is the enigmatic personality and enduring political appeal of Reagan. Wilentz describes how Reagan's star rose in California politics during the mid-1960's and why the governor became the darling of Republican conservatives in the 1970's. Reagan had a winning style that avoided the stridency of Barry Goldwater and the moral squalor of Nixon. With his team of savvy media advisers, Reagan used the techniques of Hollywood stardom to package conservatism in a way that addressed the fears of Americans in the turbulence of the post-Watergate era. Wilentz is especially good on Reagan's ability to adapt to changing political circumstances, even when his tactical shifts conflicted with his philosophical creed. In California and in Washington, the tax-cutting Reagan proved able to raise revenues when it was politically necessary.

Reagan's inscrutable character has defied the efforts of biographers such as Edmund Morris to explain what made this disengaged executive so successful and popular for most of his eight years in office. Reagan was not a leader who revealed his inner thoughts on paper or to his closest associates. The memoirs of those who worked in the Reagan White House are filled with episodes in which aides try to decipher what the chief executive was thinking or how he exerted himself to achieve his ends. Not since Franklin D. Roosevelt, who was president from 1933 to 1945, had there been so opaque a leader who hid from view the way he arrived at conclusions and decided issues. While there have been volumes published of Reagan's speeches, his letters, and his personal diaries of the White House years, the core of the man remains a mystery that has eluded biographical examination.

Wilentz stresses Reagan's genuine commitment to arms control and his antipathy to the prospect of nuclear war as key elements in driving his willingness to negotiate with the Soviet Union and its leader, Mikhail Gorbachev. Wilentz shows how Reagan rebounded from the reverses associated with the Iran-Contra scandal to end his administration on a high note and with his popularity restored. At the same time, the author resists giving Reagan too much credit for the decline and breakup of the Soviet Union.

Wilentz is an expert and evenhanded guide through the complexities of the Reagan years in power. He recalls the difficult first two years, when the economic program associated with tax cuts and increased defense spending resulted in a brief, sharp recession. He then shows how the economic stimulus of the Reagan tax cuts restored prosperity in the middle of the 1980's and propelled the president to his sweeping triumph in the 1984 election. Time after time, the president escaped the Democratic efforts to paint him into a corner in political terms. Wilentz's balanced account will be a keystone for genuine revisionism about Reagan's record as president.

In his effort to be fair to Reagan, Wilentz sometimes overstresses the positive argument for the president. The accumulated deficits impaired the economy and started a process of economic unraveling that has yet to end. Reagan was a divisive force on the race issue, as Wilentz shows, with his presidential suspicions about Dr. Martin Luther King, Jr., and his willingness to pander to the worst tendencies of Southern Republicans.

Wilentz gives Reagan credit for his turnaround after the Iran-Contra scandal in 1986 and 1987. With a new leadership team in the White House led by former Senator Howard Baker, Reagan pursued serious arms agreements with the Soviet Union that accelerated the collapse of that political system. As a result, Reagan renewed his popularity with the American people.

The accounts of the Bush and Clinton administrations carry forward Wilentz's contention about the key role Reagan played in modern American politics. In the case of George H. W. Bush, the effort of the president to soften the Reagan policies and make them more acceptable resulted in an administration that outraged the right wing of the Republicans without producing corresponding electoral gains among moderate Democrats. The economic downturn of the early 1990's doomed Bush's chances for reelection in 1992.

Clinton's election in 1992 ushered in a turbulent decade in national politics. The Republicans never accepted Clinton as a legitimate chief executive, and the president faced a series of campaigns to oust him from office. Wilentz traces the evolution of these right-wing efforts to find grounds for impeachment in Clinton's pre-presidential career and in his conduct as president. There are few better brief treatments of the Clinton "scandals" and the resulting impeachment trial of the incumbent in 1999. Wilentz acknowledges Clinton's moral lapse in his affair with Monica Lewinsky and the political trial that grew out of that mistake, but he underscores how much politics rather than genuine conviction lay behind the Republican drive for impeachment.

There is an abbreviated examination of the presidency of George W. Bush, a chief executive for whom Wilentz has little regard. The conclusion of the narrative comes down to the 2008 primary election season and seems somewhat tacked on for contemporary relevance. However, the rather hasty conclusion of Wilentz's story should not detract from the merits of his larger argument. This study is one of the first to endeavor to place Reagan in historical context and to weigh his record with dispassionate evaluation. Few will doubt Wilentz's conclusion about Reagan's historical importance, whatever one might think about the president's performance in office.

Only in passing does Wilentz examine an important element in the reshaping of American politics under Reagan. The former film star, with his sure sense of how to handle the television and print media, came into power during a key shift in how Americans received news about public affairs. With the emergence of cable television during the early years of Reagan's presidency, entertainment values, especially the relentless drive for ratings, dominated the news business. Reagan and his advisers understood that attractive visual images and a well-constructed daily narrative trumped hard news every time. In the process, American politics was "dumbed down" to the lowest common denominator of what would grab the attention of the viewing public. That development was another key legacy of Reagan and the show-business ethos he embodied. Journalists who read this book with close attention will get a needed lesson in how their professional practices declined during the years of Reagan's ascendancy in American politics.

Writing contemporary history is no easy assignment. The absence of primary sources that reveal the motivations of the participants is one handicap. Modern journalism, often unreliable, makes establishing basic facts a formidable challenge. Misinformation clouds the Internet, and urban legends about politicians proliferate on blogs and in the resulting commentary. That is what makes Wilentz's achievement here so impressive. He has navigated through the intricacies of the Reagan era and the decades that followed with a sure hand. Interested readers will find in his annotations guides to all the important issues of the period and information about where to locate more relevant data. This is a resource that historians and their students will be mining for years.

While Wilentz has written a book that scholars can use, he has also well served the reading public. His account of the Reagan era will stimulate debate and provoke useful dialogue. He has achieved his purpose of opening up the Reagan presidency and its consequences for serious discussion. In that sense, a historian of liberal Democratic beliefs has done for Reagan what conservative apologists for the president have failed to accomplish. Wilentz has placed Reagan in historical context and made his career in American politics a centerpiece of how the late twentieth century in the United States will be understood in the future.

Lewis L. Gould

Review Sources

Booklist 104, no. 15 (April 1, 2008): 19.
Commonweal 135, no. 21 (December 5, 2008): 22-24.
Kirkus Reviews 76, no. 3 (February 1, 2008): 141.
Library Journal 133, no. 4 (March 1, 2008): 97.
The New York Times Book Review, May 18, 2008, p. 50.

AJAX

Author: Sophocles (496-406 B.C.E.)
Translated from the Greek by John Tipton
Foreword by Stanley Lombardo
Publisher: Flood Editions (Chicago). 112 pp.
   Paperback, $13.95
Type of work: Drama, poetry
Time: The final year of the Trojan War (c. 1184 B.C.E.)
Locale: The Greek encampment outside the walls of Troy

A *fast-paced contemporary rendering of Sophocles'* tragedy

Principal characters:
   ODYSSEUS, the Greek warrior who has
      received the armor of Achilles
   AJAX, the Greek warrior denied Achilles'
      armor, then inflicted with madness by Athena
   ATHENA, daughter of Zeus and Metis ("Wisdom"), born of Zeus's head
   TECMESSA, Ajax's bride by capture
   TEUCER, Ajax's brother, entrusted with his burial
   MENELAUS, Greek warrior who awarded Achilles' armor to Odysseus
   AGAMEMNON, Menelaus's brother who refuses Ajax burial

Modern medicine would classify Ajax's problem as battle fatigue or as post-traumatic stress. In Sophocles' play, Athena is to blame, or be praised, since by sending a fit of madness to Ajax she saves her champion Odysseus. The immediate result is the mass slaughter of the Greek army's herd animals. The ultimate outcome is the suicide of the disgraced Ajax.

Ajax has reason for his anger. Agamemnon and Menelaus have denied him the armor of the dead Achilles and awarded it instead to Odysseus, the great strategist of the Trojan horse. Odysseus is the hero most beloved by Athena, the goddess who masterminds the Olympian strategies that keep Zeus in power. Usually, Athena is protrayed as a benign and comforting deity who reassures everyone that order in the cosmos is possible. Sophocles' Athena, however, has a sadistic streak. She encourages Ajax in the delusion that he is killing the Greeks who slighted and ridiculed him, even to the point of admiring the ram he plans to kill last and believes to be Odysseus. His suicide at the play's climax places him literally and figuratively among the animals that he has slaughtered.

John Tipton's textual realization of Sophocles' play is not so much a translation as it is a modern rendering. In verse, it employs what Tipton calls the "counted line." By this he means that each line of dialogue represents his choice of six words that render the parallel Greek line. The immediate effect is to shorten and simplify diction and sometimes to create poetic shorthand that preserves the narrative while rewriting Sophocles' poetry.

An example of this technique is worthwhile. When Ajax's wife Tecmessa realizes that her husband has awakened from his fit and realizes what he has done, she says:

> At least while he was sick
> he was happy in his havoc;
> I was the one in pain.
> But after he could breathe again
> the ugly truth poured over him.
> I'm no better now than before
> and his problems have just doubled.

Ian Johnston's translation, which is closer to the Greek text, reads:

> That man in there, when he was still so ill,
> enjoyed himself while savage fantasies
> held him in their grip, but we were sane,
> and, since he was one of us, we suffered.
> But now there is a pause in his disease,
> he can recuperate and understand
> the full extremity of bitter grief,
> yet everything for us remains the same—
> our anguish is no milder than before.
> This is surely not a single sorrow,
> but a double grief?

Tipton's rendering reduces twelve lines of Greek to seven. More significant, he changes the emphasis of Tecmessa's speech. He makes her a character independent of the collective identity of the Greek forces and a pained wife rather than a captive woman among sympathizing onlookers. What Tipton's text loses in fidelity to Sophocles it gains in immediacy and humanity. A reader might object to this, but it is hard to argue that Tipton departs from Sophocles' larger intention to describe human transcendence. Tipton's immediate influence is the poet Louis Zukofsky, who employs the counted line in his anthology *80 Flowers* (1978).

Tecmessa is a bride by capture who becomes a willing spouse. Teucer is an initially diffident brother who argues for Ajax's right to burial and ultimately performs that ritual scrupulously. Even Odysseus, the warrior who receives the armor by judgment of Agamemnon and Menelaus, argues for Ajax's honorable burial. While even Menelaus recognizes the necessary justice of this, Agamemnon does not. In fact, Agamemnon becomes a paradigm of the leader who refuses to acknowledge a disastrous mistake. The mistake extends beyond awarded armor to prosecution of the Trojan War itself. Agamemnon had be-

∾

John Tipton is an experimental poet working in Chicago. Flood Editions also published his earlier book, Surfaces *(2004). He prides himself on being considered a nonacademic poet, works for Morningstar, Inc., and has had previous work published in the* Chicago Review *and on the Internet in* Cordite Poetry Review, Fascicle, *and* MiPOesis. *With Louis Zukofsky, he has pioneered use of the counted line as a creative technique.*

∾

gun this enterprise by sacrificing his daughter Iphigenia, what one could reasonably characterize as a mad act performed by a man the world judges as sane. He remains unconverted to the last.

Sophocles' *Ajax* is, thus, a deceptively subtle play that contrasts small-minded brutality and generous forgiveness. Ajax sacked Tecmessa's city and tore her from her father, yet she comes to love him as her husband. Odysseus is the ally who becomes, after receiving the armor, Ajax's most hated enemy. Odysseus forgives Ajax and argues for his burial; this is a request Agamemnon grants with mean reluctance.

Tipton takes even greater liberties with the Chorus than he does in translating the dialogue. The choral odes become abstractions of the Greek rather than translations. This is by design. Tipton eliminates all first-person references. He further abstracts syntactical elements to make the Chorus's words those of a psychologically distressed human being. After Ajax leaves the stage, intent on his suicide, the Chorus, which consists of sailors rather than soldiers, compares the dull pain of wielding oars to the formless ache it feels for Ajax's disgrace. Alliteration merges with repetition in the words

> hurt heaps hurt here
> left right
> left where it will
> will it learn the place?
> dropped it
> dropped can't find it be found
> half a boat's oars in sync
> with what?

These changes create a dynamically contemporary play. They underscore its symmetry in the sense that the initial frenzy that results in Ajax's slaughter of the herds parallels the ten-year slaughter of the Trojan War. The dead Ajax among the herds becomes another senseless corpse among the other corpses, leveling the value of warriors and the animals that sustain them. In essence, Tipton has written another play. It extends the myth to an apocalypse, a bare landscape that is timeless, and such, after all, was the goal of Sophocles. In Tipton's realization, the ancient world merges with the modern. Tipton has no problem having Ajax describe his sword, a "gift" he received through Hector "who was my most hated enemy—planted in the angry Trojan ground," as though it were a gun "cocked and ready . . . " The zeugma describes both the sword that Ajax will plant upright in order to fall upon it and Hector himself, for whom his city has become his burial place. Tipton's Chorus wonders about "where it will end/ the count of years wandering/ the toll the statistics of missiles." It concludes that it is "better [to be] hurled into space/ or into the crowd in hell/ than to be a bomb maker/ and share your results/ the Los Alamos boys knew what they'd done."

None of this is Sophocles. It has an anger that one never finds in that playwright. Tipton still does manage a powerful realization of the mythic idea implicit in the Ajax myth. That myth, in the final analysis, is about endless war, brutalizing by its nature, and the power of the human heart to generously forgive. In doing this, Tipton continues in the tradition of the ancient playwrights who created neither their characters nor the plots of their plays. The originality of Sophocles, just as the originality of Aeschylus, Euripides, or Tipton, lay in his ability to emphasize an aspect of personality or an element of the theme that is appropriate to a historical period.

Ajax was a great hero, but he was never the greatest hero. The decision of Agamemnon and Menelaus to award the armor of Achilles to Odysseus makes logical sense. Odysseus had masterminded the scheme through which the Greeks stole the statue of Athena from the Palladium, the temple that stood on the Trojan citadel. This achievement, which fate had decreed necessary if Troy were ever to fall, would have been enough to ensure Odysseus's fame. The deep-seated fear of Ajax, then, is his realization that while he is a hero, he is not one of the first rank.

Ajax's achievement, such as it first seems to him to be, is that he has slain and imprisoned his enemies, his fellow warriors who brought him to Troy, allowed him to fight there for ten years, and then would not recognize his service. Athena encourages this delusion. Ajax's achievement, such as it is in reality, is that he has proved that though everyone considers that killing the herds proves Ajax's insanity, Agamemnon's pursuit of a ten-year war and the death of thousands of soldiers is proof of courage and perseverance.

Tipton's rendering allows the audience to realize that those Ajax perceives as his enemies, his fellow warriors, may be so in actuality. Agamemnon had led him into war and maintained the war for ten full years. After madness that Ajax cannot control causes him to kill the herds, Agamemnon becomes Ajax's declared enemy.

Nearly a third of the play follows Ajax's suicide. This is a definite indication that Sophocles intends something more for his audience to consider. It can only be the debate over Agamemnon's refusal of burial. Both in Sophocles' text and in Tipton's vision of the play, this passage shows maturity in the character of Teucer, generosity on the part of Odysseus, and sullen stubbornness in the character of Agamemnon. Only Odysseus's appeal to Agamemnon as a friend causes the latter to relent, though he remains ungracious to the end and refuses participation in the rites. The world at large would judge Agamemnon a great leader. Sophocles' audience, and certainly Tipton's, might easily question that hero's sanity.

Robert J. Forman

Review Sources

Bryn Mawr Classical Review 44 (August, 2008).
The Nation 287, no. 3 (July 21, 2008): 41-44.
Publishers Weekly 255, no. 20 (May 19, 2008): 37.

ALFRED KAZIN
A Biography

Author: Richard M. Cook (1941-   )
Publisher: Yale University Press (New Haven, Conn.).
    Illustrated. 452 pp. $35.00
Type of work: Literary biography, literary history
Time: 1915-1998
Locale: New York City; Roxbury, Connecticut;
    Wellfleet, Massachusetts; California; Italy

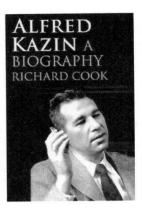

This first comprehensive literary biography of one of the most notable literary critics of his age chronicles Kazin's emergence while still in his twenties as a critic of considerable note, and it relates this emergence to the intellectualism that abounded in New York during the 1930's

Principal personages:
> ALFRED KAZIN (1915-1998), a prominent literary critic
> GITA FAGELMAN KAZIN (d. 1990), Alfred's mother
> GEDAHLIA "CHARLES" KAZIN (d. 1970), Alfred's father
> ANN BIRSTEIN (1927-   ), Kazin's third wife
> JUDITH DUNFORD (1933-   ), Kazin's fourth wife
> MICHAEL KAZIN (1948-   ), Kazin's son
> CATHRAEL "KATE" KAZIN (1955-   ), Kazin's daughter
> HANNAH ARENDT (1906-1975), a notable intellectual and Kazin's friend
> RICHARD HOFSTADTER (1916-1970), a historian and Kazin's friend
> CARL VAN DOREN (1884-1950), Kazin's friend who encouraged him to write *On Native Grounds*

Richard M. Cook might well have subtitled his biography of Alfred Kazin "An Anatomy of Loneliness." Throughout his eighty-three years, Kazin was never able to relate easily to people nor did he find in any of four marriages the kind of closeness that marriage usually involves. His first marriage to Natasha Dohn in 1938 was annulled in 1944. His marriage in 1947 to Carol Bookman ended in divorce after three years and one child. His tumultuous sixteen-year marriage to Ann Birstein was terminated in 1978. Finally, in 1983, he wed Judith Dunford, eighteen years his junior, to whom he remained married for the rest of his life.

The son of Eastern European immigrants to New York, Kazin was brought up in the Brownsville section of Brooklyn, living there with his parents from birth until he had completed a bachelor's degree at New York's City College in 1935 and a master's degree at Columbia University in 1938. He shared the values found in many immigrant families of the period. His parents, like those of many Jewish American children who grew up during the Great Depression, sacrificed substantially with the expectation that their children would become the first college graduates in the family and would devote themselves to worthwhile endeavors.

Kazin's mother, Gita Fagelman Kazin, was a seamstress who worked at home making fashionable clothes for a circle of devoted customers. Gita had a dominant personality and doted on her son and his sister, Pearl,

~

Richard M. Cook, a professor of American literature at the University of Missouri at St. Louis, knew Alfred Kazin. Cook talked in depth with Kazin about his contributions to American literature as a field of study.

~

seven years Kazin's junior. Kazin's father, Gedahlia Kazin, who Americanized his name to Charles, was born in Minsk. After living in New York in the early 1890's, he had returned to Europe with his mother, who, remarried and unable to care for him, placed him in an orphanage at age nine. The boy grew up feeling unwanted and was extremely shy. Kazin viewed his father as someone who felt abandoned and incredibly lonely. Charles returned to the United States in his twenties, holding various jobs around the country until he married Gita and settled into life as a painter.

Kazin's notion of marriage was based on his mother's dominance and on his father's virtual withdrawal from family interaction. The couple was not demonstrative with each other, but they did lavish love on their two children. Although withdrawn and virtually unable to communicate verbally with his children, Charles, did take them across the Brooklyn Bridge to the magic city of New York, exposing them to museums, theater, and music on a regular basis.

Kazin always felt drawn to the cultural excitement of New York City, yet he felt anchored in Brownsville. On the first anniversary of his death, his son, Michael, and his widow, Judith, took a box containing his ashes to the center of the Brooklyn Bridge and dropped it into the water, believing it to be a symbolic gesture Kazin would have appreciated.

Like his father, Kazin was shy and had difficulty reaching out to other people. Throughout his years in elementary and secondary school, he was afflicted by a stutter, made worse when he was under pressure. He did not like school, although he loved learning and read voraciously, as did his sister. Both children gained fluency in Yiddish because their parents' ability in English was quite limited. Yiddish was the language in which they usually communicated at home.

It was expected that first-generation Jewish American children in the Brownsville ghetto would strive to do well in school, fearing the shame that their parents would suffer should they not excel in their studies. Cook reports that Kazin, at age ten, bought a bottle of iodine he could ingest to kill himself if he failed to meet his mother's expectations.

It was also a given that the children, particularly the male offspring, of these Eastern European immigrants would enjoy the free education offered to all local citizens at City College, in which Kazin enrolled at age sixteen. When he completed his bachelor's degree in 1935 at age twenty, he had little idea of what he wanted to do with his life, so he embarked on a career as a freelance writer, often writing for the "Books" section of the *New York Herald Tribune*, whose editor was Irita Van Doren, the wife of literary critic and Columbia University professor Carl Van Doren. Irita gambled on hiring an unknown to write critical articles, but she was well rewarded by the scope and vitality of Kazin's literary writing.

Still uncertain about where he was headed, Kazin thought he might become a secondary-school teacher, so he enrolled in a master's degree program at Columbia University. He knew that the life of a freelance writer did not offer the financial stability that he needed, especially after his marriage to Dohn shortly after he completed the master's degree.

It was at this point that Carl Van Doren suggested to Kazin that he might write a serious study of American literature. Kazin had been looking for a job, but jobs were scarce during the Great Depression. Carl told Kazin that if he would write such a book, Carl would encourage the publishing house of Reynal and Hitchcock, for which he was an adviser, to publish it, liberating Kazin from having to worry about finding a job.

Still only twenty-three years old, Kazin decided to do what Carl suggested. The result, four years later, was the publication of Kazin's *On Native Grounds* (1942), one of the most influential books of literary history and criticism produced in the twentieth century. At age twenty-seven, Kazin unexpectedly became a celebrity, for which he paid a high price when his neglect of Dohn during the feverish writing of his book resulted in the annulment of their marriage.

Cook has a keen appreciation of the strong influence that Kazin's family had on him. His relationship with his father, a loner who made small attempts to expose his children to the finer things in life, was never warm. Injured emotionally in his youth, Charles never recovered from being consigned to an orphanage when it was inconvenient for his mother to care for him. Similarly, Kazin was alienated from his children, Michael and Cathreal, during their formative years, although, as a divorced father, he saw them regularly if not always enthusiastically. He helped them to attend good schools, but he did not feel close to them, although in his later years, he grew closer to his son, especially after Michael married Beth Horowitz, a physician who won Kazin's heart.

Reflecting on his father's death in 1970, Kazin "often worried about the traits they shared, particularly the penchant for self-preoccupation and self-pity." Kazin wrote, "One looks for one's father—one looks—one looks and one realizes I *am* my father." As penetrating as it was, this insight was not comforting to Kazin, who in actuality was more like his mother than his father.

The Kazin that Cook presents is a mass of contradictions, as perhaps any complex person is. For example, Kazin longed for stable relationships with women, but once he achieved stability, he strayed and had affairs outside his marriages. Always good looking, he usually gave in to the temptations that his handsome looks threw into his pathway. He opposed the establishment of Israel, but he rejoiced when it finally proved viable.

Kazin used his celebrity to obtain visiting professorships at prestigious universities, among them Harvard, Princeton, Stanford, and Brown. Once appointed, however, he did little to endear himself to his academic colleagues, generally treating them with condescension and contempt. Cook does not attempt to analyze the reasons for this, but it seems obvious that Kazin was unsure of himself, which caused him to act defensively.

The condescension Kazin showed in many academic situations carried over into his relationship with Michael, whose political radicalism went far beyond his father's. As Cook notes, "He strongly disputed Michael's easy assumption that socialism offered the best answer to every national problem." Kazin told Michael, "You ought to think about . . . concrete situations in themselves. What continued *dumbness* on your part not to recognize that each country, each situation, has its historical past, its specific traditions." Some of his reaction to Michael's political postures was obviously tongue-in-cheek, such as calling Michael "comrade." Underlying much of it, however, was a deep-seated condescension.

Kazin's tour de force, *On Native Grounds*, did a great deal to rescue American literary studies from the oblivion that it faced in much of the academic community during the first four decades of the twentieth century, when it was viewed as something of a stepchild by serious literary scholars. Vernon Parrington had paved the way for broadening the scope of literary criticism in 1927 with the publication of his monumental *Main Currents in American Thought*, a book that greatly influenced Kazin, as had F. O. Matthiessen's *American Renaissance* (1941), published one year before *On Native Grounds* was released. No book could have been more right for its time than Kazin's.

The late 1940's and the 1950's saw the establishment of cross-disciplinary programs in American civilization and in American studies at many of the most prestigious universities in the United States, including Harvard, Brown, Princeton, and Yale. Kazin's book was, in part, the motivating force behind such developments.

Cook, who interviewed scores of people and who used Kazin's journals extensively in creating this biography, notes that of the dozen books Kazin published, *On Native Grounds*, for which he is best known, was his only work of pure criticism. Some of his later books are collections of critical essays, but it was his first book that focused exclusively on the broad presentation of the American literary canon.

Kazin wrote with singular vigor and verve about American literature, and Cook quotes Kazin as saying that he "fell in love with it [American literature] because in a sense this literature was mine—I felt at home with it. . . . I responded [to the writers and their texts] with intellectual kinship and pleasure. I knew the modulations of their language." Kazin captured many of these modulations in his own writing, notably in *A Walker in the City* (1951) and in *Starting out in the Thirties* (1965), both works that drew heavily on his Brownsville background and on his family experiences. Brownsville and the alluring metropolis across the Brooklyn Bridge came to symbolize the yin and the yang of Kazin's personality.

R. Baird Shuman

Review Sources

Booklist 104, nos. 9/10 (January 1, 2008): 34.
Commentary 125, no. 4 (April, 2008): 61-64.
Journal of American History 95, no. 2 (September, 2008): 579.
Library Journal 133, no. 5 (March 15, 2008): 72.
London Review of Books 30, no. 12 (June 19, 2008): 11-14.
New England Quarterly 81, no. 3 (September, 2008): 525-527.
The New Republic 238, no. 5 (March 26, 2008): 43-47.
The New York Review of Books 55, no. 10 (June 12, 2008): 54-56.
The New Yorker 83, no. 44 (January 21, 2008): 81.
The Times Literary Supplement, May 2, 2008, pp. 10-11.
The Wall Street Journal 251, no. 10 (January 12, 2008): W9.

ALGERIA
Anger of the Dispossessed

Authors: Martin Evans (1964-   ) and John Phillips
Publisher: Yale University Press (New Haven, Conn.).
    352 pp. $35.00
Type of work: History
Time: 1830 to the present
Locale: Algeria

A thoughtful and well-researched study that explains clearly why Algerian governments, since independence from France in 1962, have failed to meet the expectations and needs of the vast majority of Algerian Muslims

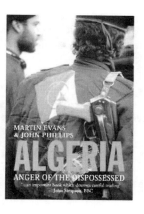

Principal personages:
    CHARLES DE GAULLE, president of France,
        1958-1969
    AHMED BEN BELLA, president of Algeria, 1963-1965
    HOUARI BOUMEDIÈNE, president of Algeria, 1965-1978
    CHADLI BENDJEDID, president of Algeria, 1979-1992
    MOHAMMAD BOUDIAF, president of Algeria, 1992; assassinated on
        June 29, 1992
    ABDELAZIZ BOUTEFLIKA, president of Algeria, 1999 to the present
    ABASSI MADANI, leader of the Islamic Salvation Front
    ALI BELHADJ, number two in the Islamic Salvation Front

With the subtitle *Anger of the Dispossessed*, Martin Evans and John Phillips evoke well in their book *Algeria* the tragic fact that, since the French invasion and occupation of Algeria in 1830, most Algerians have been effectively excluded from any meaningful involvement in determining the economic, political, social, and religious policies of their country. This marginalization quite naturally caused deep feelings of bitterness, especially because Algerian Muslims, who remained faithful to Islam, recognized all too clearly their powerlessness to create a society in which the basic tenets of Islam determined governmental policies and the rule of law in Algeria.

Evans and Phillips do an excellent job describing the humiliating nature of the French domination of Algeria, which lasted 132 years, from 1830 until 1962. This was far longer than French colonial rule in any other African country. Further insults to Algerian Muslims were manifested when France annexed Algeria, sent French immigrants to settle in the country, and showed contempt for the well-known Muslim prohibition against alcohol by planting vineyards and making wine in Algeria. France made a mockery of its supposed commitment to liberty, equality, and fraternity, three values affirmed in the motto of the French Republic, by offering French citizenship to those Algerians who renounced Islam. Apostasy is an unforgivable sin for Muslims.

~

*Martin Evans is a history professor at
the University of Portsmouth in
England. He has published extensively
on colonial and postcolonial Algerian
history. John Phillips was a reporter in
Algeria from 1991 to 1997 for the
London newspaper* The Times. *He has
published extensively on recent wars in
the former Yugoslavia.*

~

Algerian Muslims understood all too well that they would be exploited for as long as they remained under French domination.

Although many Algerian soldiers fought bravely with Free French Forces under the command of General Charles de Gaulle and helped to liberate France from Nazi occupation, nothing really changed in Algeria after France and Algeria were freed from Nazi rule. In November, 1954, Algerian Muslims saw no alternative to overt resistance to continuing French domination in Algeria. Under the general leadership of the National Liberation Front, Algerian Muslims began a civil war that French soldiers and police officers could not suppress. In 1958 the French Fourth Republic came to an end, and French voters turned to De Gaulle to extract France from the seemingly endless violence in Algeria. Although De Gaulle had favored preserving the French empire during and immediately after World War II, he was a realist: He realized that the modern world was rejecting colonialism. Starting in 1960, he began granting independence to French colonies throughout Africa, while at the same time offering financial and technical assistance to new democracies. In Algeria, rebel French army officers undertook military action against Algerian Muslims in a vain effort to prevent De Gaulle from granting their country independence, but De Gaulle handled effectively this disobedience to the rule of law. He went on French television and denounced military officers who had committed treason by disobeying lawful orders from their commander in chief. His speech followed several attempts by French traitors in the Secret Army Organization led by General Jacques Massu to assassinate De Gaulle. De Gaulle skillfully persuaded people in both Algeria and France that France could remain faithful to its ideals of liberty, equality, and fraternity only by granting these same values to all people, no matter where they might live. Hepresented French and Algerian people a simple choice: order or chaos. Order meant a peaceful transition in Algeria from colonial domination to independence; chaos meant endless violence fomented by the Secret Army Organization under the traitorous Massu against Algerian Muslims or violence by the National Liberation Front against French citizens in Algeria that had been occurring since 1954. On March 18, 1962, Algerian and French negotiators signed the Evian Treaty, granting Algeria independence, and submitted it to Algerian and French voters. In both countries, support for the independence of Algeria was more than 90 percent. This permitted a peaceful transition to independence, and both countries were understandably hopeful.

Things, however, quickly deteriorated in Algeria. The leaders of the National Liberation Front promptly transformed Algeria into a one-party dictatorship in which socialism and not Islam inspired all significant political, social, and economic decisions. The new Algerian government made numerous decisions that hurt Algeria economically. Its new president, Ahmed Ben Bella, undertook an absurd and costly war in a vain attempt to seize land in eastern Morocco. Ben Bella also forced French residents in Algeria to leave the country in order to completely eliminate French influence in Algeria. The immediate result was that Algeria lost the expertise of thousands of well-educated technicians and professionals. Algeria has vast amounts of petroleum, but without technical experts, the petroleum remained in the ground. In addition, Ben Bella and other leaders in the National Liberation Front ignored Muslim leaders who wanted Islam to have a significant influence in the newly independent Algeria. Ben Bella created a sharp separation between religion and politics, alienating influential imams. Algerian Muslims soon concluded their government was no more responsive to their needs than were the French colonial administrators.

Although Algerian generals overthrew Ben Bella in a 1965 coup and replaced him with Houari Boumediène, nothing really changed. Like Ben Bella before him. Boumediène spoke repeatedly about the supposedly positive values of Russian and Cuban communism. He invited thousands of Cuban and Russian advisers into Algeria, where they drank alcohol publicly in clear violation of the Muslim prohibition against the presence or consumption of alcohol in a Muslim country. In the minds of practicing Muslims, who constitute a vast majority of Algerian citizens, atheistic communists had simply replaced French administrators. The new Algerian government appeared as unsympathetic to Islam as was the French government. Although Algeria did earn a great deal of money by selling petroleum to other countries, almost all of this money was used to pay down debts to the Soviet Union and to enrich the generals who ruled Algeria with iron fists. Very little was spent on education, health care, and infrastructure. Average Algerians continued to live in abject poverty while generals lived in luxurious villas in fancy neighborhoods to which ordinary Algerians came as domestic servants.

Although significant increases in the price of petroleum in the 1970's enriched the Algerian government that had nationalized the oil fields, this wealth was not distributed fairly. Basic needs such as housing, health, clean water, and education were not met, and unemployment remained distressingly high in a country that was receiving massive amounts of money from the sale of petroleum. Algerian Muslims, observing that things were going badly in their country, demanded change. However, no significant change was forthcoming from the National Liberation Front. After President Boumediène's death from natural causes on December 27, 1978, the generals appointed Chadli Bendjedid as the new president of Algeria. His government continued its Soviet-style planned economy that prevented economic innovation and flexibility, making the Algerian economy even worse.

The National Liberation Front was unwilling to change a corrupt system that had enriched a privileged few at the expense of a suffering majority. Several influential Muslim clerics under the leadership of Abassi Madani and Ali Belhadj argued that a return to the purity of Islamic traditional practices would eliminate the overt corruption that had denied Algerians basic human dignity. Together, Madani and Belhadj created a political movement called the Islamic Salvation Front. Preachers in mosques in Algeria called upon faithful Muslims to participate in peaceful protest marches against political corruption among Algerian military and political leaders. By the fall of 1988, the Islamic Salvation Front had a huge following, and Algerian generals viewed supporters of the Islamic Salvation Front as a threat to their wealth. They feared that if the Islamic Salvation Front were ever to attain political power, it would audit bank accounts of leading Algerian military and political leaders, who might then end up in prison. In October, 1988, Algerian generals overreacted by firing on peaceful demonstrators in the streets of Algiers, turning the Algerian people en masse against Algerian military leaders.

In an effort to restore calm, President Bendjedid tried to appease alienated Algerians by permitting multiparty participation in free elections. He mistakenly thought that he could somehow control the righteous anger of "dispossessed" Algerians, but he underestimated the depth of their mistrust of the National Liberation Front that had ruled Algeria since independence in 1962. He scheduled the two rounds of parliamentary elections for December 26, 1991, and January 16, 1992. In the first round, 231 members of the Algerian parliament would be elected, and the remaining 199 seats would be determined in the second. Much to the surprise of President Bendjedid, the Islamic Salvation Front won 188 of the 231 seats in the first round, and it was expected to do as well in the next round. The Algerian generals were unwilling to accept the loss of their absolute power. On January 11, 1992, Bendjedid was forced to resign, and just three days later Algerian generals canceled the second round of elections, imprisoned the leaders of the Islamic Salvation Front, and installed an aged businessman named Mohammed Boudiaf as the puppet president of Algeria. This "putsch" enraged the Algerian public and contributed to active resistance and violence against the usurpers who had transformed Algeria into an overt military dictatorship. Several resistance groups that came to be known by the French acronyms GSPC (Salafist Group for Preaching and Combat) and the GIA (Armed Islamic Group) carried out violent attacks throughout Algeria, and the Algerian soldiers retaliated with similar violence to all attacks against the Algerian governments.

Political assassinations were common, and President Boudiaf was assassinated on June 29, 1992. Evans and Phillips, who lived in Algeria for many years, confirm that most Algerians believe that Algerian generals had Boudiaf killed because they believed that the president was about to arrest high-ranking military officers for corruption. Murders of simple workers and apolitical religious leaders were frequent occurrences in Algeria throughout the 1990's. Abdelaziz Bouteflika won a fairly honest presidential election in 1999 and was then reelected in 2004 to a second five-year term. Although Algerians generally admire President Bouteflika for his personal integrity, it will take a succession of ethical leaders for Algerians to begin to trust their political and military leaders.

Edmund J. Campion

Review Sources

Foreign Affairs 87, no. 1 (January/February, 2008): 192.
History Today 58, no. 12 (December, 2008): 70.
International Affairs 84, no. 2 (March 2008): 394.
Publishers Weekly 254, no. 44 (November 5, 2007): 59.
The Spectator 306 (January 5, 2008): 26-27.
The Times Literary Supplement, October 10, 2008, p. 24.

ALL OF IT SINGING
New and Selected Poems

Author: Linda Gregg (1942-   )
Publisher: Graywolf Press (St. Paul, Minn.). 213 pp.
  $24.00
Type of work: Poetry

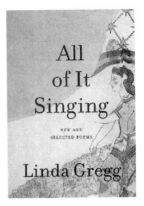

This collection of Gregg's older and new poems incorporates elements of classicism, nature, and contemporary life

The older poems in *All of It Singing* are drawn from Linda Gregg's collections *Too Bright to See* (1987), *Alma* (1989), *The Sacraments of Desire* (1992), *Chosen by the Lion* (1995), *Things and Flesh* (1999), and *In the Middle Distance* (2006). This collection spans a landscape of love, loss, and redemption. Beginning with poems from *Too Bright to See*, Gregg starts small in "We Manage Most When We Manage Small," with an image of hair, which "falls before you./ Fragile and momentary, we continue." In fact, the two lovers in the poem are so vulnerable and ethereal that they are only "Managing as thin light on water" and "love a little, as the mice huddle." From this small moment, Gregg's poetry expands.

Through personification, Gregg gives elements of nature a mythical quality, as in her depiction of the sun and the moon in "Different Not Less": "The sun, bull-black/ and ready to return, holds back so the moon,/ delicate and sweet, may finish her progress." In this description, the strength of the sun and the translucence of the moon interplay to create a kind of eclipse, coming close but not quite touching, like the lovers in the poem who "look into the night, or death, our loss,/ what is not given." The speaker describes how she and her lover "see another world alive/ and our wholeness finishing." This observation of wholeness and detachment from it is also portrayed in "Classicism," a three-line poem describing how "The nights are very clear in Greece./ When the moon is round we see it completely/ and have no feeling." In "Whole and Without Blessing," this wholeness becomes a self-contained autonomy where the speaker renounces her attachment to people and announces her detachment from earthly things: "I proclaim myself whole and without blessing,/ or need to be blessed. A fish of my own/ spirit. I belong to no one. I do not move." Even the sun that warms her is "indifferent." In "Safe and Beautiful" from *Alma*, the moon is personified again, but this time "lying around in pretty satin," her "hair fixed all careful like a widow," playing "safe, safe, beautiful and safe," as if to preserve herself from pain.

The matter-of-fact tone with which the speaker of Gregg's poems describes her isolation continues in "Summer in a Small Town," where the speaker explains, "When the men leave me,/ they leave me in a beautiful place." With this acceptance comes irony, the speaker walking "back across the mown lawn/ loving the smell and the houses/ so

completely it leaves my heart empty." Perhaps it is the familiar smells and sights of
summer that comfort this woman after feelings of abandonment and of being "alone no
loneliness in the dream in the quiet" that is repeated like a chant in "Alma to Her Sister." In
"New York Address," there is a marked contrast to this, with the speaker "walking three
miles to get home" and wanting to die. Rather
than an empty heart, she doesn't "seem to
have a heart at all." In "Eurydice" Gregg describes the loss after Eurydice and Orpheus
have been reunited, only to be separated again
forever because Orpheus looked back at her,
not trusting that she was there. It is more painful for Eurydice to have had a brief glimpse of
Orpheus after resigning herself to being without him: "I did not cry as much in the dark-
ness/ as I will when we part in the dimness."
Orpheus and Eurydice reappear in "The Ninth

*Among Linda Gregg's awards are a
Guggenheim Fellowship, a Lannan
Literary Foundation Fellowship, a
National Endowment for the Arts grant,
a Whiting Writer's Award, and multiple
Pushcart Prizes. She won the Sara
Teasdale Award in 2003 and the PEN/
Voelcker Award for Poetry in 2006.
Gregg teaches at Princeton University.*

Dawn" from *Chosen by the Lion*. The gods are "willing to have/ the lovers destroyed .
. . pulsing around their perishing." This alliteration mimics the heartbeat that is threatened to be silenced because Eurydice "went too far into the woods and after/ lived
with the darkness around her forever." One can hear her voice in "The Terrifying
Power of Darkness Is Inseparable from the Redemptive Power of the Sacred": "If you
do this to me, if you/ do this to me, if you take your love away, if you take,/ if you go
away, you will make my heart blind in me."

In poems from this collection, Gregg also confronts middle age, coming "prepared
to answer questions, because it said there would be questions." It's as if the speaker
sees herself in "The Shopping-Bag Lady" who has a way of getting money, "Never
asking. Sideways and disconcerting" or the women who are "asleep on the floor/ on
pieces of cardboard." The detachment continues with "Dry Grass & Old Color of the
Fence & Smooth Hills," where "All life is beautiful/ at a distance" from the women in
a California town with their "mess and canning and babies crying." Gregg also confronts mortality in her poems depicting the brutality that can exist in nature and relating it to humanity, as in "The Men Like Salmon," in which she describes how "The
flesh falls off like language,/ bruised and sick." "Sick with the bones. Rotten with sorrow," it leaves "everything good or loved behind." This brutality continues with "The
Copperhead," where "Almost blind he takes the soft dying/ into the muscle-hole of
his haunting./ The huge jaws eyeing, the raised head sliding/ Back and forth, judging
the exact place of his killing." This copperhead "knows the fastness/ of his mouthing"
but "does not see the quickness collapsing" and "does not see at all what he has done."

In poems such as these, Gregg shows how nature is not only beautiful but unfor-
giving and will not hesitate to do whatever it takes to survive. This violence in nature

continues in the title poem from *Chosen by the Lion*, where the speaker is "the one chosen by the lion at sundown/ and dragged back from the shining water./ Yanked back to the bushes and torn open, blood/ blazing at the throat and breast of me./ Taken as meat. Devoured as spirit by spirit."

The Sacraments of Desire begins with a more celebratory tone in "Glisten," where the speaker knows that no one is there to see her glistening when she returns "naked to the stone porch." The "almond tree with its husks/ cracking open in the heat" contrasts the moisture that is lying on her skin. She notices how the earth is "moving slowly" as she stands there drying in the light. This appreciation of the body continues in "The Small Thing Love Is," with the speaker describing how her body is "filled by a summer of lust" and how she "can't tell the difference between desire,/ longing, and all the sweet speeches/ love hoards." She marvels at "the wet couple undone/ by a power only the earth could love," the earth perhaps represented by an unnamed woman in "All the Spring Lends Itself to Her." The speaker entreats, "We will lie in the humming fields/ and call to Her, coaxing Her back. We will lie/ pressed close to the earth, calling Her name,/ wondering if it is Her voice we are whispering."

Resignation and even relief for being alone reappear in this section with "Grinding the Lens." "In the middle of my life," the speaker says, she is "Alone and happy." In "Singing Enough to Feel the Rain," she is "alone writing as quickly as [she] can,/ dulled by being awake at four in the morning,/ Between the past and future, without a life." In another reference to midlife, she is "writing on the line [she walks] between death/ and youth, between having and loss." Perhaps she is writing poetry to capture "the voice of what has no voice," to which she refers in "There Is No Language in This Country." Perhaps it is also her duty to "live in the suffering and desire of what/ rises and falls. The terrible blind grinding/ of gears against our bodies and lives," as described in "It Is the Rising I Love."

Yet even choosing to be in a relationship is a resignation in "I Thought on His Desire for Three Days," with the speaker explaining, "I chose this man, consciously, deliberately,/ I thought on his desire for three days/ and then said yes" despite his being married. In fact, she says, "I am here/ to tell you I did not mind." Even when the man's wife calls and says she's a whore, the speaker says, "I was quiet, but inside I said, 'perhaps.'" She cannot bring herself to see the relationship as tawdry, viewing herself and her lover as "innocent in purity and magnificent disorder" ("The Clapping") and even describing how they "could have been mistaken for a married couple" in "Asking for Directions." Perhaps she is referring to her lover's marriage when she says, "Let the tower in your city burn" ("The Resurrection"). Yet after this operatic exhortation, the speaker calmly observes her lover's forehead, cheek, and lips in "Winter Light." In contrast to the brutality of nature portrayed in other poems by Gregg, nature and God become complicit when the lovers make love in a "collision that makes His face shine./ Makes the sap rise. God squeezes and relents/ like winter ending, and the sap rising." Nevertheless, the speaker of "A Bracelet of Bright Hair About the Bone" (a line from John Donne's "Relic") wants something more permanent, a material memento of the relationship, "Dirt and corpses even." This sequence of poems ends with an exultation in "Let Birds," where the speaker pledges to "never give up longing" and let her hair stay long. In the repetition of lines that begin with "Let," such as "Let birds, let birds./ Let leaf be passion./ Let jaw, let teeth, let tongue be/ between us," she opens herself to all possibilities and accepts whatever may come, including whatever repercussions she may have in this tumultuous relationship.

The poems of *Things and Flesh*, however, take a more modest approach, as in "Precision," where the speaker observes, "There is a modesty in nature, where The leaf moves/ just the amount the breeze indicates/ and nothing more." In an ironic comparison she sees this in "the power of lust, too," where "there can be a quiet and clarity, a fusion/ of exact moments." She describes this stillness as profound in how "There is a silence of it/ inside the thundering. And when the body swoons,/ it is because the heart knows its truth." In yet another paradox, though, "There is a hunger for order,/ but a thirst against" ("A Thirst Against"). "The Limits of Desire" gives human form to Love, who comes along and says, "I know,/ I know. Abandoned after all/ those promises./ But I can't help. I traffic/ in desire, passion, and lust."

People who lose their moorings are one of Gregg's recurrent themes, as in the woman in "Downsized" who thinks to herself, "I am less/ and less part of the world, even though/ I live closer to it than ever," and the woman in "Hephaestus Alone," whose "heart is like a boat that sets forth alone,/ on the ocean and goes out far from him." Yet this feeling of aloneness is also cherished in Gregg's poems, as in "Staying After," where the speaker describes living "alone in a kind of luxury," echoing Alfred Lord Tennyson's line about it being better to have loved and lost than never loved at all when she states, "I fell in love./ I believed people." There are no regrets in these lines, just as there are no regrets in lines that range from startlingly brutal to achingly gentle, from complete detachment to complete immersion. In describing how people connect with and are separated from each other and nature, Gregg shows how people are all essentially alone, how "Each person has a secret world" ("Getting Down") but still feels the need to be in the world and with others.

Holly L. Norton

Review Sources

Library Journal 133, no. 13 (August 15, 2008): 89.
Los Angeles Times, September 14, 2008, p. F9.
Poetry 193, no. 2 (November, 2008): 162-168.
Publishers Weekly 255, no. 33 (August 18, 2008): 44-45.

ALL SHALL BE WELL; AND ALL SHALL BE WELL; AND ALL MANNER OF THINGS SHALL BE WELL

Author: Tod Wodicka (1976-   )
Publisher: Pantheon Books (New York). 272 pp. $21.95
Type of work: Novel
Time: The present day
Locale: New York state, Germany, and the Czech Republic

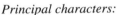

Burt Hecker, a widower who has lived his entire life out of step with his family and his surroundings, attempts to find peace as he journeys across Europe in search of his lost son

Principal characters:
> BURT HECKER, founder of the Confraternity
>> of Lost Times Regained, reenactor,
>> husband of Kitty, father of Tristan and June
> KITTY HECKER, wife of Burt and owner of the Mansion Inn
> ANNA BIBKO, Kitty's mother, a partisan for the rights of the Lemko
>> people
> TRISTAN HECKER, son of Burt and Kitty, talented musician and
>> instrument builder, who leaves home after his mother's death to live
>> among the Lemkos and learn their music
> JUNE HECKER, daughter of Burt and Kitty, who rejects her father and
>> refuses to speak to him
> LONNA KATSAV, Burt Hecker's friend and lawyer

As Tod Wodicka's *All Shall Be Well; and All Shall Be Well; and All Manner of Things Shall Be Well* opens, Burt Hecker is taking part in celebrations for the nine-hundredth anniversary of the birth of Hildegard of Bingen, nun, prophet, and composer. Members of the group with which he is traveling are reenacting the hermetic life of an anchorite, sequestered for a few days in an isolated tent. Although Hecker is on the outside, shutting the other members away from the world, he is, for all intents and purposes, an anchorite in the twentieth century. His beloved wife, Kitty, has died of cancer, compounding the disarray of his life. Tolerant and loving, Kitty had been his anchor in a modern world where Hecker has never really belonged. Founder of the Confraternity of Lost Times Regained, Hecker has attempted to live in medieval times, wearing the clothes, eating the food, making and using the artifacts of that era, all while obsessively striving not to be out of period (OOP). He has gathered around him a small group of equally dedicated reenactors, who meet periodically to live as fully as possible a medieval life.

The irony is that Hecker has spent most of his adult life OOP, with Kitty acting as his bulwark against the modern world. Kitty ran a successful period hotel, the Man-

sion Inn, while Hecker lurked in the background, having abandoned his training as a
high school history teacher. Instead, he devoted himself to recovering the lost skills and
arts of the medieval period, assisted in this by
Tristan, his son and initially eager follower.
His daughter, June, on the other hand, had long
since rejected everything her father stood for,
striving to be as modern as possible, becom-

Tod Wodicka was born in Glen Falls,
New York, and raised in nearby
Queensbury. He studied at the
University of Manchester in England
and moved to Berlin, Germany. All
Shall Be Well . . . *is his first novel.*

ing an obsessive fan of the television series *Star Trek* and all forms of science fiction.
As an adult, she marries a dull but modern man and moves across the United States, as
far from her father as possible. She refuses to speak to him, and she encourages her
children to fear their crazy grandfather.

As he grew older, Tristan came under the influence of his grandmother, Anna
Bibko, mother of Kitty. Daughter of Polish immigrants who originally embraced all
things American, she has gradually turned back to her roots, among the neglected
Lemko people from the Carpathian Mountains. From her and from his travels to her
ancestral land, Tristan has learned the music and the customs of the Lemko. Just as his
father lives in the Middle Ages, Tristan vigorously embraces all things Lemko, until
finally he flees the family home and disappears in Europe.

Completely unhinged by Kitty's death, Hecker finally finds himself in court,
agreeing to take a plainchant workshop to deal with his anger-management issues. It
is then he hatches a grand plan, breathtaking in its scope and seemingly out of character for him. The Mansion Inn has been sold, and Hecker is traveling to Germany with
the plainchant workshop members to celebrate the nine-hundredth anniversary of the
birth of Hildegard of Bingen. However, no one knows that his ticket is one way and
that he is going to try to find his missing son.

Hecker's journey from the New World to the Old World is, in fact, a journey from
the past into the present, as he recalls his life—from his first meeting with Kitty, his
strained relationship with her mother Anna, and his attempts to be a good father to his
children. All this is set alongside his experiences at the anniversary celebrations and
the performances of his workshop group, which are, he realizes, unpolished but utterly sincere.

Hecker's memories bring back to life his daughter's increasing disenchantment
with her father's behavior and his son's increasing preoccupation with his grandmother's heritage. Hecker strongly suspects that his mother-in-law's intense relationship with Tristan is a means of getting back at him for not being the financially successful all-American husband she imagined for her daughter, even though Hecker and
Kitty were clearly a love match. The most poignant memory involves the time when
Burt was shut out of the house while his wife was dying because of his erratic behavior and forced his way in to spend the precious final hours with her.

Traveling deeper into Europe, revisiting his own life and his own struggle with being in and out of period, Hecker finally arrives in Prague, where, according to a tipoff
from Lonna, his son Tristan is now working as a musician. Hecker assumes that

Tristan is still performing traditional folk music, and it comes as a shock to discover that his son, now calling himself Tim, is more aggressively in period with the present day than Hecker could ever have imagined. He finds himself in a club, watching his barely recognizable son perform music Hecker can barely comprehend. Their first meeting is tense and unsuccessful. However, finally, with the help of Tim's girlfriend, Lenka, and Lonna, who has followed Hecker to Europe, the family gathers again, joined, unexpectedly, by June, who is in the process of divorcing her husband, and unbelievably Anna, who speaks only in her native tongue and glares malevolently at Hecker.

This is no happy reunion. June demands that Hecker buy back the Mansion Inn because she has set her heart on living in it, and Tim, having finally escaped his father's orbit, does not know how to respond to his reappearance. The attempted reconciliation disintegrates, and Hecker finds himself sitting in the stairwell of his son's apartment block, in the dark, listening to the music of Hildegard of Bingen pouring out of the flat. Despite everything that has gone wrong, Hecker becomes convinced that there is still hope for him and for his family. It is impossible to tell if he is just deluding himself, yet, uncertain of his future, Hecker conjures a vision of the anchorite Hildegard that bolsters his hope. At this point, it is not difficult to understand why, despite all of Hecker's infuriating ways, Kitty loved him.

Maureen Kincaid Speller

Review Sources

Booklist 104, no. 8 (December 15, 2007): 23.
Kirkus Reviews 76, no. 1 (January 1, 2008): 14.
Library Journal 133, no. 1 (January 1, 2008): 91.
New Criterion 26, no. 8 (April, 2008): 71-73.
New Statesman 136 (July 30, 2007): 57-58.
The New Yorker 83, no. 45 (January 28, 2008): 83.
Publishers Weekly 254, no. 46 (November 19, 2007): 36.
The Times Literary Supplement, September 21, 2007, p. 20.

ALL THE WORLD'S A GRAVE: A TRAGEDY
A New Play by William Shakespeare

Author: John Reed (1969-   )
Publisher: Penguin (New York). 197 pp. $12.00
Type of work: Drama
Time: The early seventeenth century
Locale: Bohemia and Aquitaine

A conflation of parts of several of Shakespeare's trage-dies formed into a new tragedy with additional dialogue

Principal characters:
  HAMLET, prince of Bohemia
  JULIET, princess of Aquitaine
  KING LEAR, Juliet's father
  IAGO, Hamlet's lieutenant
  ROMEO, a general under Hamlet
  THE QUEEN OF BOHEMIA, Hamlet's mother
  MACBETH, the queen's lover and later king
  OLD HAMLET (and HIS GHOST), Hamlet's father
  THREE WEIRD SISTERS, witches
  ROSENCRANTZ and GUILDENSTERN, Hamlet's friends
  POLONIUS, the speaker for the Senate

Textual conflation has long been a problem for editors of Shakespeare's plays, those with two or more substantive texts that do not completely agree. A famous example involves the two texts of *King Lear*, the quarto text of 1608 and the Folio text of 1623. Each version of the play omits lines found in the other and includes lines unique to itself. Until recently, editors—not wishing to lose any of Shakespeare's language—engaged in combining the two texts into a single text of the play that Shakespeare never saw performed. A long play, *King Lear* in the conflated text is even longer. An even more extreme example is *Hamlet*, which has three different texts: the first quarto of 1603, a second quarto of 1604, and the Folio version. Not only do these texts have lines unique to each (the first quarto even has a unique scene in act 4), but often their readings have variant words or phrases, making the job of the modern editor still more difficult and problematic.

What John Reed has done is to take conflation to a further extreme. His play, *All the World's a Grave*, subtitled *A New Play by William Shakespeare*, combines large chunks of dialogue from several of Shakespeare's tragedies into what is indeed a "new play." Despite the fact that Shakespeare is the author of about 80 percent of the text, one might well question whether it deserves to be called a new play "by Shakespeare," for Reed has transformed his sources, rearranged much of the plot and structure, and added a good deal of his own dialogue. He has borrowed extensively from Shakespeare's *Hamlet*, *King Lear*, *Romeo and Juliet* (pb. 1597), *Henry V* (pb. 1600),

∼

*John Reed graduated from Columbia
University's program in creative
writing with an M.F.A. A novelist, he is
currently working on his fifth book.
Among his novels are* A Still Small
Voice *(2000) and* Snowball's Chance
(2002), a critique of George Orwell's
Animal Farm *(1945).*

∼

and *Othello* (pb. 1622), along with scraps of verse from several other plays when it suited his purposes. What results is something new and strange, amusing (and occasionally a little baffling) to those who know Shakespeare's original works and entertaining—to say the least—to those who are less acquainted with the originals but enjoy seeing them in a new light.

As if to demonstrate Hamlet's martial prowess, but mostly to fuse his character with Othello's, Reed starts the play with the prince on the field of battle in Aquitaine against the forces of King Lear. Iago has the opening lines, borrowed from the first Chorus of *Henry V* ("O for a muse of fire"), appropriately modified to introduce the new situation; hence, after referring to "the swelling scene," he says: "Then should the warlike Hamlet, all for love,/ Assume the cost of blood." Readers soon understand that Hamlet is battling against the forces of Aquitaine to gain his love, Juliet, whom he presumably has met earlier and with whom he has fallen in love. Before the battle begins, he speaks Romeo's lines, fearing "some consequence yet hanging in the stars." Iago urges him on to claim his bride, and Hamlet responds with more lines from *Henry V* (act 3, scene 1, lines 3-17) on the proper countenance and behavior of the warrior. In the next scene, Hamlet lightly paraphrases Henry's "St. Crispin Crispian" lines (act 4, scene 3, lines 18-67), converting it to a St. Valentine's Day speech. The battle ensues, and a herald later confirms that the day is Hamlet's: King Lear has lost.

In scene 3, Hamlet/Othello/Henry V assumes a Romeo-like role, knocking on the door of a parish church, as Juliet comes to meet him. Reed here adapts lines from *Romeo and Juliet* (act 2, scenes 2, 3, and 6), taking a few lines out of context from *Hamlet* (act 1, scene1), before the pastor (not a friar) agrees to marry the young couple. The dialogue in the following scene is quite unlike the aubade in *Romeo and Juliet* (act 3, scene 5), though the situation is roughly similar. It ends with more lines taken out of context as Juliet, not Romeo, asks if her lover will leave her "so unsatisfied," and Romeo replies, "What satisfaction canst thou have, dear love?" This role reversal is an "in" joke, and it is clear by now that Reed's play is a spoof of Shakespearean tragedy.

The last scene of act 1 is set outside the Boar's Head tavern, where Hamlet and Juliet are celebrating their wedding night. Not content with adapting lines from Shakespeare's plays, Reed has Iago begin by reciting Sonnet 129 ("Th' expense of spirit in a waste of shame") directly to the audience. Soldiers are loading corpses onto a wagon, while inside the tavern General Romeo and his surviving soldiers carouse. They drink to the health of the prince and princess, oblivious of anything tragic that will follow.

Act 2 opens in Bohemia with the weird sisters chanting their diabolical charm around a bubbling cauldron from act 4, scene 1 of *Macbeth* (pb. 1623), when Macbeth enters as if summoned by them. They hail him as "king hereafter." Since no Banquo character accompanies Macbeth, he speaks some of Banquo's lines. The witches vanish, leaving him amazed. The next scene opens with the queen of Bohemia, and although Reed does not name her, she is a composite of Hamlet's mother Gertrude and Lady Macbeth. She complains about being married to "a poor, infirm,/And despised old man" (Old Hamlet) and spurs her lover, Macbeth, to murder him. Most of the action and the lines here and in the rest of act 2 are taken directly from the plot to murder Duncan in *Macbeth*.

In act 3 Hamlet returns home to Bohemia to find that his mother and her paramour, now the king, have murdered his father. However, the first scene opens with Iago's soliloquy about how he hates Hamlet, who has appointed Romeo general instead of him. The *Othello* plot is thus introduced, although it is not until act 4 that Iago's machinations are fully developed. Act 3 is chiefly concerned with King Macbeth's attempt to deal with King Lear, who tries to regain his daughter, much as Brabantio does in *Othello*, and with young Hamlet's meeting with the ghost of his father. The news of the Ghost is brought to him not by Horatio and Marcellus (as in *Hamlet* act 1, scene 2), but by Rosencrantz and Guildenstern. Meanwhile, Iago secretly allies himself with King Lear to take revenge on the prince, who has put on an antic disposition. The act ends again with Iago's soliloquy, largely taken from *Othello* (act 1, scene 3, lines 392-404), in which he foments his plot against Hamlet, Romeo, and Juliet. It is curiously preceded by his speaking Ophelia's lines in *Hamlet* (act 2, scene 1, lines 84-97), describing the prince's strange visitation to her in her chamber.

Act 4 is the longest in the play; in fact, each act up to this one gets longer. It includes the banquet scene from *Macbeth*, where the ghost of Old Hamlet substitutes for the ghost of Banquo; Hamlet's greeting of Rosencrantz and Guildenstern from *Hamlet* (act 2, scene 2, lines 222-379), despite the fact that they have been together earlier in act 3; a version of the Players Scene (*Hamlet*, act 2, scene 2, lines 421-605), in which lines 145-170 from act 3, scene 2, of *Richard II* (pb. 1600) substitute for Aeneas's Tale to Dido; Romeo's attempt to comfort Juliet, who complains about Hamlet's mad disposition, glimpsed by Iago and Hamlet; the play within the play—*The Pantomimi of Murder*, not *The Murder of Gonzago*, but essentially the same—immediately followed by Iago's deception of Hamlet regarding his wife's infidelity with Romeo, as in *Othello* (act 3, scene 3, lines 90-329), including the dropped handkerchief (but no Emilia); Hamlet's confrontation with his mother, taken almost verbatim from *Hamlet* (act 3, scene 4), except that the Ghost materializes here naked and does not speak; Hamlet's "to be or not to be" soliloquy after Gertrude exits followed by an adaptation of the Nunnery Scene and then Iago's further goading of Hamlet (as in *Othello*, act 3, scene 3, lines 335-480); King Macbeth's prayer scene and Hamlet's abortive attempt to kill him (as in *Hamlet*, act 3, scene 3); Hamlet's abuse of Juliet about her missing handkerchief (as in *Othello*, act 3, scene 4, lines 35-45 and 51-97 and act 4, scene 1, lines 240-249), with Juliet's pathetic pleas taken from Helena's dialogue with Demetrius from lines 195-212 of act 2, scene 1 in *A Midsummer Night's Dream* (pb. 1600).

The final scenes of act 4 include the weird sisters (but no Hecate) around their cauldron once again, invoking for Macbeth the apparition of the bloody infant wearing a crown who warns Macbeth that the prince will doom him to death, but he need not fear any man born of woman. Reed's lines occupy most of scene 7, in which the queen, unlike Gertrude in *Hamlet*, curses her "revolting" son and King Macbeth sympathizes not with her but with Hamlet! They welcome Rosencrantz and Guildenstern, who agree to discover the cause of Hamlet's affliction.

Act 5 opens with the sleepwalking scene adapted almost wholly from *Macbeth* (act 5, scene1), except that the queen enters naked. Without a scene break, the location shifts to Hamlet digging a grave and singing lines from the dirge in *Cymbeline* (pb. 1623), "Fear no more the heat o' the sun." He throws up various skulls, commenting on them somewhat as the First Gravedigger does in *Hamlet* (act 5, scene 1), but interspersing his monologue with lines from the dirge, when Iago enters and further antagonizes Hamlet about his wife's infidelity with Romeo, as in *Othello* (act 4, scene 1, lines 3-47). Hamlet here does not fall into a trance, though his strange cry, "Baaaa! Baaaa!" may signify something of the sort.

Elsewhere in act 5 Reed intersperses more of Shakespeare's lines, including some dialogue from lines 270-278 in act 5, scene 3, of *All's Well That Ends Well* (pb. 1623), but changes several salient aspects of the plot. For example, Hamlet does not, like Othello, smother Juliet; he orders Romeo to do so, and, faithful soldier that he is, Romeo does. However, that awakens in Hamlet the awareness of Romeo's innocence and Juliet's infidelity. Nevertheless, Hamlet kills Romeo, who falls into the grave that Hamlet has dug. Meanwhile, King Lear advances on Bohemia with his army, when King Macbeth gets the news of his queen's death, delivered by the Doctor in Gertrude's description of Ophelia's death (*Hamlet*, act 4, scene 7, lines 166-183). While trying to guard Macbeth against Lear, Rosencrantz is killed by Iago, who also kills Guildenstern, who sings more lines from the dirge in *Cymbeline* as he dies. Finally, Macbeth confronts Lear, a man not born of woman but untimely ripped from his mother's womb. He drops his weapon, and Lear kills him. The play ends with this scene, Lear speaking lines mostly from the last scene of Shakespeare's *King Lear* but also some from Romeo's apostrophe to Juliet in *Romeo and Juliet* (act 5, scene 3, lines 101-115) as he mourns the death of his daughter, Juliet.

In an afterword he calls "Gist," Reed justifies his approach and explains how he has modernized Shakespeare's language. He sums up his justification with: "[I]t is precisely because Shakespeare's plays were monsters assembled from other monsters that a fresh monstrosity can be assembled from Shakespeare. And because of Shakespeare's use of stock players and storylines, a new Shakespearian narrative is equally possible." Not everyone will agree that Shakespeare's plays are "monsters," though whether Reed's play is one may be a subject of debate.

Jay L. Halio

Review Sources

Booklist 104, no. 22 (August 1, 2008): 25.
New York Post, July 8, 2008, p. 11.

ALPHABET JUICE
The Energies, Gists, and Spirits of Letters, Words, and Combinations Thereof . . .

Author: Roy Blount, Jr. (1941-   )
Publisher: Farrar, Straus and Giroux (New York).
    364 pp. $25.00
Type of work: Language

Underlying this eclectic, hilarious consideration of language is the author's conviction—with examination and examples—that the meanings of words and their constructions are not arbitrary

Roy Blount Jr.

The full subtitle of *Alphabet Juice: The Energies, Gists, and Spirits of Letters, Words, and Combinations Thereof; Their Roots, Bones, Innards, Piths, Pips, and Secret Parts, Tinctures, Tonics, and Essences; With Examples of Their Usage Foul and Savory*—peculiar, expansive, begging to roll off the tongue—is a fitting appetizer for what follows. The author has explained it as a tribute to his ancestor Sir Thomas Blount, who in 1656 published a dictionary with an unusual subtitle. However, it could also be the author poking a bit of fun at academia, where titles—and subtitles—tend to twist and turn with studied abandon. It is difficult to be sure with Roy Blount, Jr. He seems to be a down-home Georgia country boy, except that he graduated from Vanderbilt University magna cum laude, Phi Beta Kappa, and he earned a master's degree in English from Harvard University. He is best known as a humorist, compared by many to Garrison Keillor and Will Rogers. However, he has also made his living as a sportswriter, lecturer, novelist, poet, essayist, performer, dramatist, anthologist, and storyteller

Like its author, *Alphabet Juice* is also hard to classify. Its focus is language, and readers can certainly learn much about usage, grammar, punctuation, and more. In addition, the author's idiosyncrasies share center stage. For example, in elucidating the subjunctive tense, Blount uses the title of O. J. Simpson's book *If I Did It* (2007), explaining that it would be grammatical only if Simpson did not know whether or not he had committed the homicide for which he was acquitted in criminal court but found in civil court to be responsible. Blount says that if Simpson had not done it, he would have titled his book—subjectively—"If I Had Done It." However, if Simpson did do it, he would "certainly not be above going with *If I Did It,* which is catchier, in a loathsome sort of way." Blount suggests that "with the rising tides of uncertainty and unthought-out assertiveness in Western civilization today . . . , the subjective often blends with the indicative to create a syntactical can of worms."

Alphabet Juice comprises its own can of worms, in the best sense, as linguistics cavorts with ingenuity and erudition meets horse sense to create an unconventional reality. Similar to a dictionary, the entries in this book are formatted *A* to *Z,* giving readers

~

Roy Blount, Jr., is the author of twenty-one books, and his work has appeared in many publications. Among other affiliations, he is a contributing editor to The Atlantic Monthly, *a long-term member of the* American Heritage Dictionary *Usage Panel, and a regular panelist on National Public Radio's quiz show "Wait, Wait . . . Don't Tell Me."*

~

something familiar to hold on to as Blount twirls his language loves—and occasional pet peeves—like Möbius strips. A few reviewers have noted that Blount's personal associations may lose his readers in places, yet most critics seem to consider this part of the charm. All the entries will probably not resonate with all readers, and some may even begin to feel slightly exasperated in places. However, Blount seems to be having too much fun to care, and his glee—and originality—are contagious.

As with traditional dictionaries, readers can learn from *Alphabet Juice* how to pronounce "divisive" correctly and appreciate that "tango" does not derive from the Latin *tangere* (to touch), but rather from American Spanish, perhaps of Niger-Congo origin. Blount offers word definitions, and many of the terms he includes—such as "chic" and "mnemonic"—would also be found elsewhere. Nevertheless, how many examinations of "mnemonic" would begin with a confession that, although the author would prefer to appreciate rather than criticize words, one such as "mnemonic" should be easier to keep in mind? Similarly, not many dictionaries—after tracing the derivation of "chic"—would add that none of it had anything to do with the etymology of the chewing gum Chiclets. Blount concludes this entry with the news that Chiclets "comes from chicle" (quoting the *American Heritage Dictionary* definition: "the coagulated milky juice of the sapodilla, used as the principal ingredient of chewing gum"), which he says in turn comes from the "even chewier Nahuatl word *chictli*," and then he announces that chiclets meaning teeth ("in particular knocked-out ones") derive from physical likeness alone.

Digressions aside, there are other features that make this book distinctive. For example, Blount offers introductory remarks to each letter before delving into its entries. Some prologues are scholarly; others are barely there. However, each gives readers an opportunity to catch their breath and take a particular angle before entering into a relationship with the next unit of the alphabet. Some, such as *A*, are fun to read aloud as Blount lists "denotative upbeat long-*a* words" that include "*May, lei, play, gravy, pay* (assuming you're receiving), *gay, way* (as opposed to *no way*, and as in 'Where there's a way, there's a will'), and *ray* (of hope, of light, of sun, of Charles)." The remarks about *H* also demand enunciation, such as where Blount lists "a heap of effortful words," forty-one, to be exact, beginning with "hack, haggle, hammer, handle, hard, harness, harry, harsh . . . . " Other introductions offer tidbits as diverse as the reason why capital *Q* extends below the line; a joke about an aging Leonid Brezhnev, former leader of the Soviet Union, beginning his opening speech at the Moscow Olympics by reading the Olympic symbol as O! O! O!; and the result of a university research study that "S would seem to be monkeys' favorite letter."

Another peculiarity of this book concerns the entries themselves. In addition to words that might be predicted, Blount offers items such as "of a," noting erroneous usage on the sports page of *The New York Times*. The entry that follows "chicken" is "children's classic, in verse, all I have so far" (just four short lines). A pithy entry is "has-been": "A bee that is over the hill." Unhampered by dictionary expectations, Blount suits himself, tendering items such as "Bossom/Bottum" (about an editor for *The Weekly Standard* whose name was routinely misspelled and what he decided to do about it); "death, coolest euphemism for" (attributed to Louis Jordan, considered one of the most successful African American musicians of the twentieth century); and "syntax collie" (Blount's invention, inspired by a *New Yorker* cartoon). It would be a mistake for readers to come to *Alphabet Juice* looking for a specific word. Still, trying to find something in particular would be as good an entry point as any into this array. Nothing is really left out, considering the assortment of what is included. Similarly, nothing is really included, given the spaces within and around the extraordinary leaps that Blount makes.

Alphabet Juice has been well received by critics. In seeking to capture and expound upon Blount's stream-of-consciousness vision, they tend to cite their own favorite entries, often quoting at length. The book has been variously termed a language elixir, the ultimate browser's dictionary, and word play on steroids. Blount presents himself as a word lover meandering at will, illuminating particulars that strike his fancy, occasionally getting in little digs at things that may have bothered him for a while. In fact, Blount explained in an interview that he has been making little notes about items included in this book for fifty years. Due to its dictionary structure, he did not have to maintain any narrative and thus felt free, he says, to hop around considerably as he wrote, calling it a very self-indulgent undertaking.

Readers are also likely to navigate this book by their own paths. Those who read dictionaries for sport may devour *Alphabet Juice* in one or two sittings. For most people, however, it is probably best appreciated a few bites at a time. Ian Frazier, American writer and humorist, says this book is as much fun to read backward as forward. Blount advises that he would read it the way he wrote it, "thumbing back and forth, without ever being sure you've read it all." In addition to encouraging connections among ideas within entries, Blount also creates a simulated, low-tech Google experience across items. Words in the text that appear in boldface are themselves entries, he explains, something his readers "might want to check out."

Alphabet Juice offers readers options in terms of approach and subject matter as well as irreverent wit, yet this is a book of consequence. The introduction gives a glimpse of the knowledge base upon which it rests. Blount is well acquainted with dictionaries and other reference volumes, he has a working knowledge of Latin, French, and Greek, and he holds his own views about language. Considering himself a "shade-tree etymologist" (like a shade-tree mechanic), he sets up shop at the side of the road and knows what he is doing. Regarding the relationship between how a word sounds and what it means, which linguistic scholars say is arbitrary, Blount's position is clear: "arbitrary, schmarbitrary." Acknowledging that "linguisticians" would probably allow him onomatopoeia (like "snap," "crackle," and "pop"), Blount asserts it goes much beyond that. Each language, he says, has its own "deep aesthetic network of sonic correspondences." What runs through the veins of language is alphabet juice:

"the quirky but venerable squiggles which through centuries of knockabout breeding and intimate contact with the human body have absorbed the uncanny power to carry the ring of truth."

Blount coins the term "sonicky" to describe "a word whose sound doesn't imitate a sound, like *boom* or *poof*, but does somehow sensuously evoke the essence of the word: *queasy* or *rickety* or *zest* or *sluggish* or *vim*." In this book, many sonicky examples are woven through Blount's opinions, assorted bits of quirky information, and a wealth of language nuggets. However, as some critics have emphasized even as they acknowledge Blount's argument, this book is not designed to make a case, least of all to a scholarly audience. Blount says simply that he hopes it will be useful to anyone who wants to write better, including himself. Whenever "disinterested" is used instead of "uninterested," he explains, an angel dies, and each time "very unique" appears, "thousands of literate people lose yet another little smidgen of hope." Blount considers himself the kind of person who "realistic latitudinarians" think of as a crank; still, his tongue seems firmly planted in cheek. He offers insight in *Alphabet Juice* but does not prescribe. He cites established language sources but also such references as urbandictionary.com (where he has contributed a top definition). In the entry "voyeur," Blount's elegantly spare comments on the thinning effects of television may reverberate in readers' minds for some time, even gaining momentum, but will probably not cause defensiveness. This is a book of intelligence and energy, likely to be appreciated by those who love language, those who value humor, and those just looking for something singular to read.

Jean C. Fulton

Review Sources

Booklist 104, no. 22 (August 1, 2008): 2.
The Buffalo News, October 5, 2008, p. F9.
The Columbus Dispatch, November 2, 2008, p. O4E.
Fortune 158, no. 7 (October 13, 2008): 82.
The New York Times, November 16, 2008, p. L9.
Publishers Weekly 255, no. 33 (August 18, 2008): 53.
The Seattle Times, October 30, 2008, p. 14.
Sports Illustrated 109, no. 24 (December 15, 2008): 24.
The Washington Post Book World, October 12, 2008, p. BW10.

AMERICA AMERICA

Author: Ethan Canin (1960-   )
Publisher: Random House (New York). 458 pp. $27.00
Type of work: Novel
Time: 1971-2006
Locale: Saline, a small town in upstate New York near
   Lake Erie

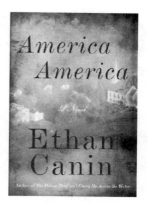

   A young man from a working-class family becomes involved with a wealthy landowner and the senator he is supporting for president in 1972

> *Principal characters:*
> HENRY BONWILLER, a New York state
>   senator who runs for president
> LIAM METAREY, a wealthy patriarch and
>   Bonwiller's financial supporter and campaign manager
> COREY SIFTER, teenage protégé of Liam; he later publishes a newspaper
> JOELLEN CHARNEY, a young female campaign worker who has an affair
>   with Bonwiller
> TRIESTE MILLBURY, a high school intern on Sifter's newspaper
> JUNE METAREY, Liam's wife
> CLARA METAREY, Liam's daughter, Corey's wife
> CHRISTIAN METAREY, Liam's daughter
> GRANGE SIFTER, Corey's father
> ANNA BAINBRIDGE SIFTER, Corey's mother

   The novel *America America* begins in 2006. Corey Sifter, a middle-aged newspaper publisher, describes attending the funeral of Henry Bonwiller, eighty-nine, a New York state senator and a resident of the small town of Saline, New York. Sifter recalls thirty-four years earlier when Bonwiller was running for the Democratic nomination for the presidency as "the best friend the working men of this country have ever had"—a man who would beat Richard Nixon and bring the troops home from Vietnam. At that time, Sifter was the protégé of Liam Metarey, a wealthy businessman supporting Bonwiller's bid for the nomination, and he was Bonwiller's junior aide and driver during the campaign. After the funeral, Sifter, seeing a man kneel and weep at the graveside, recalls his involvement with Metarey and Bonwiller and the death of a young campaign worker that the two men had covered up and in which Sifter, perhaps innocently, played some part.

   Sifter is the son of a plumber who sometimes works on Aberdeen West, the estate of Liam Metarey. As he works with his father on a plumbing job on the grounds, his conscientious effort not to injure the roots of an ancient oak that have clogged the underground pipes sparks the admiration of Metarey who offers him a position doing odd jobs on the estate.

   Metarey is the descendant of Scottish migrant Eoghan Metarey, a hard-nosed, and

Ethan Canin is the author of six books of fiction, including his highly praised debut collection of stories, Emperor of the Air *(1988). He is on the faculty of the Iowa Writers' Workshop at the University of Iowa.*

sometimes unscrupulous, pioneer who rose from impoverished circumstances to become a mining and lumber magnate. At one point, he was blamed by union officials for the deaths of five men trapped in a collapsed mine shaft. The Metareys are almost wholly responsible for building the town of Saline and still own much of it. Liam is a milder man than his ruthless father and, perhaps feeling responsible for his father's aggrandizing acts in the past, serves as a benevolent patriarch of the town. His decision to try to get Bonwiller, a populist friend of the workingman who has vowed to bring the troops home from Vietnam, elected president is also perhaps part of his effort to compensate for his father's callousness.

In the novel's outset, Sifter is a middle-aged man recalling the days when, as a sophomore in high school, he began working for Metarey and trying to justify his involvement with Metarey and Bonwiller's cover-up of a scandal. This is a traditional bildungsroman, a coming-of-age novel, and it is also a political novel, with a message, sometimes laid on too heavy-handedly by Canin, in which the boy's lost idealism is a reflection of a nation's lost idealism. As the title suggests, and Canin's sympathetic treatment of Metarey and Sifter indicate, this book intends to be an American Dream epic, a Great American Novel, in the classic sense. Perhaps for this reason, the characters, although larger than life, are two-dimensional, and the plot moves with a predictable inevitability.

Metarey is a rich man who tries to wear his wealth lightly. Although he lives in a twenty-four-room brick and stone Edwardian mansion on a huge estate covered with ancient oaks, he dresses modestly, spends little, saves much, and tries to remain in the background. His wife gets her clothes in a local shop, and his children attend public school. Although he owns his own airplane, which his wife often recklessly and sometimes drunkenly flies, he putters around in his workshop and saves parts and pieces of old machinery that he files away carefully. Perhaps because Metarey sees in Sifter a reflection of his own youthful idealism, he takes the boy under his wing, securing him a scholarship at a fancy boarding school and supporting him through college. Metarey seems to be a wise, honest man, more an inhabitant of a novel from the nineteenth century than of the twentieth. These characteristics make his fall from grace at the end of the novel all the more tragic, yet all the more predictable.

As a young man, Sifter was idealistic, hardworking, respectful, polite, and scrupulously honest, and he narrates the story from his position as the aging owner of a small-town newspaper, recalling his past involvement in American politics with a mixture of guilt and justification. He still insists that Metarey was a generous, civic-minded, and "altruistic patron" of the community. His tendency to make excuses for the politicians in his past are tempered by his somewhat cynical high school intern, Trieste Millbury, who challenges his gullibility. As a young man, Sifter is often in awe of the powerful political figures with whom he rubs elbows, marveling that while his father is a poor plumber, he is the driver for a man who could become president.

Bonwiller, the liberal senator who aspires to be president, is less clearly delineated. Although he is saluted for doing more for the causes of civil rights and labor than anyone in congressional history, Bonwiller never becomes anything more than a shadowy and distant figure in the novel. In spite of his devotion to abstract liberal values, he is a drinker and a womanizer. Conscientious in public, he is careless in his personal life. What continues to torment Sifter is how Bonwiller combined public idealism with personal ruthlessness.

The novel places fictional characters in the midst of real-life politicians, such as Richard Nixon, Edmund Muskie, and the Democratic presidential candidate in 1972, George McGovern. A huge party at the Metarey mansion is attended by George Meany, Carl Stokes, Averell Harriman, Senator Edward Kennedy, Senator Mike Mansfield, and Senator Hubert Humphrey. Sifter also describes seeing Arthur Schlesinger, Betty Friedan, David Halberstam, Daniel Patrick Moynihan, and Shirley Chisholm. Later, Sifter recalls that even as a young man, he sensed that there was a new sort of stature in the room.

When Bonwiller has an auto accident while out drinking with his intern JoEllen Charney, he staggers away, leaving her in the snow. Metarey covers it up and Sifter lies to the authorities, saying he has never seen Bonwiller take a drink. Even worse, he helps Metarey crash the car to conceal the damage done in the drunken accident. Bonwiller's liberal leanings and his womanizing make it impossible to ignore that Canin bases him on Ted Kennedy and his involvement in the death of a young aide at Chappaquiddick in 1969, a scandal disastrous to Kennedy's ambitions to be president.

In the last part of the novel, Sifter, now middle-aged, helps to care for his aging father, who is in a convalescent home after suffering a stroke. The older man spends much of his time reading and talking with his son about his involvement with Metarey and Bonwiller. He insists that Metarey was a better father to Sifter than he had been and that, regardless of what happened, Bonwiller was the best friend the workingman has ever had. His father tells Sifter that there is always something half criminal about progress. After Metarey's death in a plane crash, Bonwiller reads W. H. Auden's famous poem "Museé des Beaux Arts" at his funeral, about Pieter Breughel's painting of Icarus, in which a ploughman in the foreground does not seem to notice the death of the young man in the background. The novel ends, predictably, with the loss of the old world, as bulldozers tear down the great Metarey mansion and destroy the majestic oaks that surround it to make room for a shopping center and housing development. All that is left is an iconic image of an oak at the entrance to the shopping center.

When he published his first book in 1988, the collection of short stories entitled *The Emperor of the Air*, Ethan Canin at the age of twenty-seven amazed his readers with his sensitive ability to penetrate the mysteries of motivation in the minds of both teenagers and elderly men. Although the stories could be interpreted as being about the tension between hope and hopelessness and between great expectations and disappointment, these abstract categories were so skillfully embodied in the complexities of Canin's characters that they could not be directly stated but rather could only be intuited and emotionally felt. *America America*, because of its ambitions to be a Great

American Novel, embodying youthful idealism and adult disillusionment, is much less subtle. Although this may be because Canin is a better short-story writer than a novelist, it may also be due somewhat to basic differences between the two narrative forms. The great Italian novelist Alberto Moravia once argued that the difference between the short story and the novel is the difference between their ground plan or structure. The novel, he says, has a bone structure of ideology, whereas the short story is boneless. Thus, while the short story is more like a lyric, the novel is similar to the essay or the philosophical treatise. A comparison between the title story of *The Emperor of the Air* and *America America*, both told from the point of view of an aging man, supports Moravia's distinction. What makes characters act in Canin's short story is mysteriously embedded in their secret lives, whereas the motivations of the characters in his novel seem obvious and abstract, more a result of the conventions of the political novel than the complexities of the characters. In *America America*, Canin faced the challenge of writing a political novel, which deals with the conventional clash between idealism and reality, yet endowing it with originality and psychological complexity. No matter how hard the writer may try, the pull of the abstract theme of such a novel is often so strong that characters become mere ciphers, puppets dominated by the power of the political theme.

Thus, *America America*, in spite of its ambitions to be an epic political novel, seems to be more a skeleton of concepts, abstractions, and ideas. The result is a certain flatness and predictability. Such a story may have been more compelling if handled by a historian rather than a fiction writer, who runs the risk of falling into the trap of clichés posed by the Great American Novel.

Charles E. May

Review Sources

Booklist 104, no. 17 (May 1, 2008): 4-5.
The Boston Globe, July 13, 2008, p. C6.
Elle 23, no. 11 (July, 2008): 88.
Entertainment Weekly, June 20, 2008, p. 69.
Kirkus Reviews 76, no. 9 (May 1, 2008): 449.
Library Journal 133, no. 12 (July 1, 2008): 60.
The New York Times Book Review, July 6, 2008, pp. 81-83.
O, The Oprah Magazine 9, no. 7 (July, 2008): 139-140.
Publishers Weekly 255, no. 16 (April 21, 2008): 31.
The Times Literary Supplement, August 1, 2008, p. 20.
USA Today, July 8, 2008, p. 5D.
The Washington Post Book World, June 29, 2008, p. BW07.

AMERICAN LION
Andrew Jackson in the White House

Author: Jon Meacham (1969-   )
Publisher: Random House (New York). 483 pp. $30.00
Type of work: Biography
Time: 1824-1837
Locale: Washington, D.C., and Tennessee

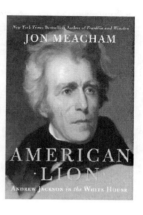

Meacham explores the character of one of America's early heroes during the years that Jackson served as president of the United States, examining his role in redefining the office of president

Principal personages:
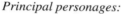

ANDREW JACKSON, seventh president of the United States
ANDREW JACKSON DONELSON, nephew of Jackson and secretary to the president
EMILY DONELSON, niece of Jackson and his hostess at the White House
JOHN C. CALHOUN, vice president and Jackson's rival
HENRY CLAY, senator from Kentucky and a Jackson rival
NICHOLAS BIDDLE, president of the Second Bank of the United States
JOHN HENRY EATON, Jackson's first secretary of war
MARGARET EATON, wife of Jackson's secretary of war and controversial Washington, D.C., socialite
MARTIN VAN BUREN, Jackson's secretary of state and vice president

There is no dearth of books about Andrew Jackson, America's seventh president. He is a towering figure in American history. Born in colonial North Carolina, orphaned as a teenager, captured by the British during the Revolutionary War, he grew up to be an ardent patriot and public servant. Lacking formal education, he worked tirelessly both to improve his own prospects (he became a lawyer and eventually a judge) while accepting every opportunity presented him to serve his fellow citizens in his new home, Tennessee, where he became its first representative in the U.S. Congress in 1796 and later a U.S. senator. He served in his state's militia, then in the U.S. Army, and in 1815 he secured his place in history as leader of the American forces that defeated the British in the Battle of New Orleans. Lionized as the greatest military leader since George Washington, he used his fame as a drawing card to gain popular support in national politics. Although he lost his bid for the presidency in 1824, to the surprise and dismay of many who had long been involved at the top levels of the government, he was elected to the country's highest office in 1828. Despite his advanced age and sometimes questionable health, he managed to serve two terms, during which he transformed the presidency from its traditional role as the chief executive for Congress into the undisputed representative of the people at

~

Jon Meacham is editor of Newsweek *magazine. He is the author of the best-selling historical studies* Franklin and Winston: An Intimate Portrait of an Epic Friendship *(2003) and* American Gospel: God, the Founding Fathers, and the Making of a Nation *(2006) and editor of* Voices in Our Blood: America's Best on the Civil Rights Movement *(2001), a collection of nonfiction about struggles against Jim Crow laws.*

~

large, equal to (and sometimes surpassing) Congress in determining the fate of the nation.

That Jon Meacham would undertake a new study of such a powerful figure whose career has been well documented speaks to his own temerity and skills. Rather than produce another standard biography, however, in *American Lion* Meacham focuses on Jackson's presidency, providing readers only a brief summary of Old Hickory's career from his birth in rural North Carolina through the tumultuous years in which he rose to prominence as a lawmaker and military leader. Meacham's central thesis is that Jackson was first and foremost a family man. Orphaned as a child, he came to value the concept of "family" in both his personal and political lives. His long-time marriage to Rachel Donelson gave him the stability and comfort to face the rigors of life in the field with his troops and in the halls of state and federal legislatures. Her death just months before he left Tennessee for Washington, D.C., to assume the presidency drove him to fill that void by creating a new family for himself, taking under his wing his nephew and niece, Andrew and Emily Donelson, who went to the capital with him as his personal secretary and as his hostess, respectively. Jackson's relationship with these two and with his small group of confidants (the majority outside his official cabinet) provided him the kind of family circle, Meacham says, on which he depended in his efforts to transform the presidency. At the same time, Meacham argues, Jackson saw the entire country as his family—with himself serving as a benevolent father figure whose principal responsibility lay in serving their best interests, not the wishes and whims of the Congress.

Relying on published research and newly discovered documents, Meacham outlines the major battles Jackson waged in his efforts to reshape the role of the president. While all of these have been written about before, Meacham's focus on Jackson's motives makes his account particularly engaging. Unlike his six predecessors, Jackson had little use for what he perceived as the untitled aristocracy that had ruled America since the revolution. He entered office as a sworn enemy of patronage, moving swiftly to dismiss hundreds of government workers who had been appointed by previous presidents to positions they had assumed to hold for life. Although he was a devout (but not churchgoing) Protestant, he held strong beliefs about the separation of church and state, and he fought efforts by a coalition of clergymen to push the country toward adopting legislation that would make it the exclusive privilege of white Protestant Christians to hold public office.

Jackson was active in promoting treaties that would remove the Native American population from all lands east of the Mississippi River. Having been a major force in securing Florida as a U.S. territory while he was still serving as a general in the U.S.

Army, he was a committed expansionist who was delighted to lend his tacit support to Americans mounting a rebellion in Texas. He almost took the country to war against France when that nation refused to honor a debt for damages inflicted on U.S. shipping during the Napoleonic wars, claiming that the snub was an affront to national honor and that to allow the French to behave with such disdain for America would weaken the United States' position on the international stage.

Meacham concentrates much of his narrative on Jackson's struggles against those who sought to challenge his ideology and thwart his policies. From the start of his presidency, Jackson had to contend with powerful opponents, including Kentucky Senator Henry Clay, a perennial rival for the presidency who thought Jackson was seeking to turn the office into a virtual dictatorship. Chief among those who sought to check Jackson at every turn was his first vice president, John C. Calhoun. A man with his own presidential ambitions, Calhoun was a states' rights supporter who worked actively with politicians in his home state of South Carolina to promote the concept of nullification, the right of an individual state to declare federal laws invalid within its borders. The immediate cause for Calhoun and his fellow South Carolinians' concern were the high tariffs imposed in 1829 to protect American manufacturing. Many Southern states thought the tariffs unfairly favored those in the North and, for several years, tried in Congress to have them repealed. When that failed, South Carolina's leaders at home and in Washington began championing the idea of nullification—and hinting that the state might be forced to secede from the Union if its demands were not met. Jackson, a strong Unionist, thought this was one step on the road to secession, and events proved him right. For all of his first term and part of his second, he battled against the nullifiers in the press and in the legislature, eventually getting Congress to grant him extraordinary powers to take military action against any state that might attempt to nullify a law or secede from the Union. Not until well into his second term did he finally quell this crisis.

Jackson's struggle against the Second Bank of the United States is often cited as the most notable incident in his years as president. Meacham presents this story as a traditional conflict of personal wills, pitting Jackson against the bank's president, Nicholas Biddle. The charter for the bank, a private corporation in which all federal funds were deposited, was to expire during Jackson's term, and the president was adamant that it not be renewed. Jackson's argument against the bank was that, by consolidating all federal funds in a single institution, Congress was giving the bank's president inordinate power to influence national politics. With millions of dollars at his disposal, Biddle could—and did—make money available to those who supported efforts for rechartering, usually in the form of loans to their pet projects. Jackson's behind-the-scenes efforts to remove the federal government's deposits and invest them in various state banks, and his public relations campaign in which he appealed directly to the American people to gain support for dissolution of Biddle's bank, ushered in a new era of political maneuvering that changed the way politics in Washington was conducted.

Curiously, one crisis that plagued Jackson during his early years in office, and which led to the breakup of his first cabinet, was something instigated by his stubborn refusal to separate himself from loyal friends. As his first secretary of war, he appointed John Eaton, a fellow Tennessean who had recently married Margaret Timberlake, a notorious socialite whose scandalous behavior caused her to be ostracized by almost all of Washington society (including Jackson's niece Emily). Jackson insisted that his cabinet members support the Eatons and accept them socially. Few would do so, and Jackson ended up diverting much time from matters of government to resolving disputes over the treatment the Eatons received from both elected and appointed officials. The only person to benefit from the Eaton affair, Meacham suggests, was Secretary of State Martin Van Buren, who befriended Mrs. Eaton and thereby ingratiated himself with the president. Van Buren soon became Jackson's closest adviser in the cabinet. Eventually he became Jackson's vice president and succeeded him in the White House in 1836.

In nearly every encounter between Jackson and his political foes, Meacham takes pains to paint Jackson in a favorable light. At the same time, however, Meacham is not shy about discussing the darker side of Jackson's character. He had a quick temper that, coupled with his conviction that he always knew what was best for both his political future and that of the nation, made him a formidable presence, difficult for friends and enemies alike to deal with. He was, Meacham admits, a man of his time who believed that slavery was acceptable. He owned slaves, his family owned them, and he was committed to the preservation of the South's "peculiar institution," even though the idea seemed to run counter to his professed belief in the equality of all people. He held only slightly less patronizing views toward Native Americans, believing that it was in their best interests to be separated from white Americans—preferably in lands away from those which white Americans wished to have for themselves. Jackson was far from perfect, Meacham admits, but his courage in forging ahead with his agenda and his unwavering commitment to the idea that the president owes his allegiance to the people of America and not to Congress transformed the nature of politics in the country forever. Such accomplishments must be acknowledged and admired despite Jackson's shortcomings.

Meacham weaves together these stories of Jackson's public life with accounts of his relations with various relatives, especially the Donelsons, further highlighting the seamless nature of Jackson's vision of himself as head of a family that extended in concentric circles from his blood relations outward to include the entire nation. Whether he is relating the account of Jackson's struggles to eradicate the Second Bank of the United States or the lingering illness and untimely death of Emily, Meacham has the ability to convey the emotional impact of the events he describes. He writes with a flair for the dramatic, but his scholarship is sound and his ability to extract from events long past the character and motives of his subject make *American Lion* a book of significant value to anyone interested in Jackson or the evolution of the American presidency.

Laurence W. Mazzeno

Review Sources

Booklist 105, no. 6 (November 15, 2008): 14.
Entertainment Weekly, December 5, 2008, p. 75.
Kirkus Reviews 76, no. 19 (October 1, 2008): 1054-1055.
National Review 60, no. 22 (December 1, 2008): 53-54.
The New York Times, November 11, 2008, p. C1.
The New York Times Book Review, November 6, 2008, p. 16.
Newsweek 152, no. 19 (November 10, 2008): 36-39.
Publishers Weekly 255, no. 37 (September 15, 2008): 57.

ANTOINE'S ALPHABET
Watteau and His World

Author: Jed Perl (1951-   )
Publisher: Alfred A. Knopf (New York). Illustrated.
   207 pp. $25.00
Type of work: Fine arts

Perl explores history, artistic creation, symbols, and the human condition by examining Antoine Watteau's paintings. The book, in the form of an alphabet primer or dictionary, elucidates the influence of Watteau and his work

By choosing the form of an alphabet book or dictionary for *Antoine's Alphabet*, Jed Perl has produced a text that can be read as a single entity or consulted as a reference book with attention given only to specific topics. From the prologue to the last page of the book, Perl extols Antoine Watteau's greatness as an artist and adeptly explains why Watteau is his favorite painter. He also uses Watteau's paintings as a springboard into an exploration of the influence of art and creativity in the shaping of human history and also as a reflection of the sensory and sentimental realities experienced in living.

The book is subtitled *Watteau and His World*. Through the alphabetical entries, Perl takes the reader into Watteau's world, which has no boundaries, neither geographical nor temporal. Watteau's is the world of the human spirit and of the human life experience, filled with uncertainties, hesitations, and ambiguities and yet totally and vitally alive.

Preceded by an illustration of Watteau's painting of *Mezzetin*, the prologue begins with a literary portrait of the character portrayed in the painting. Perl describes his attitude of abandonment, his fanciful attire, his energetic pose, and his elusive thoughts. Perl's discussion is reminiscent of the descriptions of paintings written by the eighteenth century philosopher Denis Diderot in *Les Salons* (1759-1781). Both writers create stories suggested to them by the paintings. With this introduction, Perl unabashedly announces that Watteau, a French artist of the early eighteenth century, is his favorite painter. The rest of the prologue previews what is to be found in the text. Thirty-six entries are devoted to Watteau and his paintings or are closely linked to Watteau; five treat art in general; and twenty-one discuss topics more or less related to Watteau.

In the various entries about Watteau, Perl discusses specific paintings by the artist; themes and characters painted by Watteau; Watteau's methods of working; and his friendships with and his influences on later artists, writers, musicians, dancers, and filmmakers. The two Watteau paintings that receive the most elaborate treatment are *Gersaint's Shopsign* and *The Pilgrimage to Cythera*. Perl sees Watteau's paintings as having an immense power of attraction, of symbolism, and of ambiguity. For him, the men and women depicted are never static or easily categorized. They are individuals subject to ever-changing emotions and indecision. With his detailed verbal descriptions, Perl draws the reader into the world of the painting just as Watteau draws the observer into the painting with his visual imagery.

~

Jed Perl has been the art critic for The New Republic *since 1994. He has also written* Paris Without End: On French Art Since World War I *(1988),* Eyewitness: Report from an Art World in Crisis *(2000), and* New Art City: Manhattan at Mid-Century *(2005).*

~

In his entry *Gersaint's Shopsign*, Perl describes the luxury items sold by the store and the elegant aristocratic shoppers, and he discusses the way in which Watteau shifts the symbolism of desire back and forth from desire for beautiful objects to sexual desire. Perl succeeds in enticing the reader to enter the shop and participate in the action of the painting. Then he incorporates William Cole's description of Madame Dulac's shop in Paris in 1760 and a scene from Henry James's *The Golden Bowl* (1904) into his discussion in order to illustrate further the many suggestions that Watteau makes in this painting.

In his entry on *The Pilgrimage to Cythera*, Perl discusses how Watteau uses ambiguity. Upon viewing the painting, the spectator is overcome with uncertainty as to exactly what is happening. Are the men and women leaving for Cythera or are they returning? Are they falling in love or have they been in love? Illuminating this point, in the entry on "Soldiers," Perl emphasizes Watteau's predilection for painting scenes in which the characters are about to do something of importance or have just finished doing something.

Watteau peopled his paintings with men and women who are often in ambiguous relationships but who always draw the attention of the spectator. What are these men and women like? Did Watteau create a Watteauesque man and a Watteauesque woman? Perl believes the artist did and defines each of these characters. Preceding the entry for an illustration of a print taken from one of Watteau's drawings of a man, Perl describes men who are at ease, completely relaxed, and doing exactly what they want to do, reflecting what Perl calls an understated masculinity. The men that Watteau created and portrayed in his paintings have a certain air of mystery about them, and they are at home in Watteau's world.

Perl examines the concept of women in terms of Watteau's depiction of them in the entry "Women." He begins his discussion by stating that Katharine Hepburn in the film *Bringing Up Baby* (1938) is an example of the Watteau woman, beautiful and sexy with a capacity for being funny. She is also independent yet feminine. She is not overly concerned about her looks, and she is not fettered by social convention. She is above all else the incarnation of indecisiveness; for her, everything as a possibility. Perhaps she is ready to embark for Cythera, perhaps she is not. She is ambiguous and mysterious like her male counterpart.

Although few biographical facts are known about Watteau, Perl does include in the various entries information about Watteau's life as an artist and about his personal life. He mentions that Watteau was friends with Edme-François Gersaint, the shopkeeper for whom he painted *Gersaint's Shopsign*, and with Jean de Julienne, who was in charge of the weaving and dying processes at the Gobelins tapestry works. Perl tells the reader that Watteau was accepted as a member of the Royal Academy in 1712 and was given the privilege of choosing the subject of the presentation piece he was required to paint. Watteau neglected to paint the piece and was finally told that he had six months to produce the painting and submit it if he wished to be a member of the Royal Academy.

Perl's book explores the world created in Watteau's paintings in the entry "Party." Perl visualizes a party to which Watteau has invited all the artists, writers, musicians, dancers, and other creative individuals that he has influenced. The painter Giorgione and the writer Colette are there as well as the poets Paul Verlaine, Guillaume Apollinaire, and Wallace Stevens, the painters Henri Matisse and Pablo Picasso, and the dancer Vaslav Nijinsky. In this way, Perl elucidates the tremendous influence that Watteau has had.

Perl devotes a considerable number of entries to the importance and influence of the characters Harlequin and Pierrot. These two characters place the painter in a long artistic tradition, related to commedia dell'arte, to actors, to illusion, to shifting emotions, and to mystery, all elements important in Watteau's paintings. These two characters also bring about a rediscovery of Watteau's world long after he had created it in his paintings. The entry "Impresario" takes as its subject Sergei Diaghilev and his Ballets Russes. After discussing Diaghilev's skills as an entrepreneur and his relationship with his dancers, especially with Léonid Massine and Nijinsky, Perl describes Nijinsky dancing Harlequin and Massine dancing Pulcinella (Pierrot) and sees in their performances and in their relationship with Diaghilev a reincarnation of Watteau's world, with its masks, its mysterious characters, its exuberance, and its ephemeral quality.

In "Cezanne," Perl tells the story of Cezanne painting Harlequin and Pierrot. Inspired by a Harlequin costume hanging in his studio, Cezanne decides to ask his son Paul to pose in it. Then, Paul's friend Louis is asked to wear the Pierrot costume and pose with Paul. Once the painting is finished, Cezanne sits looking at it and realizes that all of the uncertainties that he had experienced while painting it have somehow combined into one uncertainty. Once again, Watteau's world has reappeared. The reader begins to feel that any appearance of Harlequin and Pierrot will, almost magically, re-create Watteau's world.

In the entry "Verlaine," Perl writes about how Watteau's world was re-created in a different medium when Verlaine published *Fêtes galantes* (1869), a book of poems in which he treated the themes that Watteau had portrayed in his paintings.

In the five entries treating art in general, Perl shares some of his personal viewpoints in regard to art. In "Art-for-Art's Sake," Perl discusses the modernists' desire to free beauty from any requirement to possess meaning, permitting beauty to be equated to an emotional state or to an act resulting from feeling. The entry "New" presents Perl's concept that new is not synonymous to evolutionary or progressive but rather to individual, to that which is uniquely the artist's, which imbues the work with the emotions of the artist. His concept of "New" also insists that the artist's feelings must be freed to exist in the work independently of the artist. In "Qualities," Perl reveals his personal need for a work to contain a wide range of different and, at times, unexpected qualities, which, he asserts, gives the work a wholeness. These entries reveal why Watteau is Perl's favorite painter.

Perl's book includes forty-three illustrations, most of which are reproductions of prints of Watteau's paintings. These illustrations are an integral part of his discussion of the quality and of the attributes of Watteau's works, especially for the reader who may not be familiar with Watteau's paintings. Upon reading an entry such as "Actor" or "Backs" or "Kleist," the reader is drawn to look closely at the illustrations accompanying the entry. In this way, the reader reaffirms what Perl has presented in his entry.

Antoine's Alphabet: Watteau and His World is an affirmation of Watteau as a talented and important painter. Perl convincingly argues that Watteau's impact ranges across the full spectrum of artistic creation, influencing artists, poets, musicians, and dancers from the eighteenth century to the present.

Shawncey Webb

Review Sources

Art & Antiques 31, no. 10 (October, 2008): 138.
Booklist 105, no. 1 (September 1, 2008): 23.
The New Yorker 84, no. 33 (October 20, 2008): 93.
Publishers Weekly 255, no. 26 (June 30, 2008): 169.

THE APPEAL

Author: John Grisham (1955-   )
Publisher: Random House (New York). 355 pp. $27.95
Type of work: Novel
Time: 2007
Locale: Mississippi

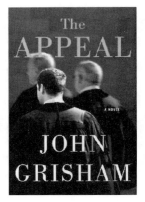

After a Mississippi jury returns a verdict against Krane Chemical for dumping toxic waste into the town of Bowmore's water supply, the company appeals to the Mississippi Supreme Court, whose newest member has been hand-picked by Krane Chemical

Principal characters:
MARY GRACE PAYTON, popular small-town
    trial lawyer, good wife, and mom
WES PAYTON, her partner in law, good husband, and dad
CARL TRUDEAU, Wall Street tycoon and CEO of Krane Chemical
RON FISK, clean-cut attorney picked by Krane Chemical to run for the
    Mississippi Supreme Court
SHELIA McCARTHY, incumbent Mississippi Supreme Court judge
BARRY RINEHART, behind-the-scenes political consultant
TONY ZACHARY, Rinehart's man who runs rigged elections
JEANNETTE BAKER, plaintiff in the Krane Chemical trial
DENNY OTT, supportive pastor
BRIANNA TRUDEAU, billionaire Carl Trudeau's trophy wife

Now that husband-and-wife attorney team Wes and Mary Grace Payton have won a forty-one-million-dollar verdict in the seventy-one-day *Baker v. Krane Chemical* trial, they can take their children out for pizza. As recounted in John Grisham's *The Appeal*, it has been four long years since the couple had taken the case that was to cast them into bare-bones poverty. They are deeply in debt, living in a run-down campus apartment, practicing law in a shabby office whose rent has not been paid in months, employing a courageous staff that has gone without wages, and dreading the appearance of the banker to whom they owe four hundred thousand dollars. Before the trial, their life had been replete with a luxury home and sports cars. Luckily, they have a friend in minister Denny Ott, who also provides spiritual sustenance to the victims of Krane Chemical's toxic dumping in the water supply of Bowmore, Mississippi.

After hearing the "guilty" verdict, the primary victim, Jeannette Baker, who lost her husband and young son to cancer, finally stops crying. Although her grief provided her with courage throughout the lengthy and excruciating trial, she nevertheless has no faith that she will ever see a penny of her enormous verdict and continues to live in her trailer so she can visit the graves of her loved ones. The other victims, many in advanced stages of cancer, are eager to finalize the case in order to experience a modicum of personal satisfaction in the just verdict and to have some much needed financial relief.

Simultaneously, Wall Street billionaire Carl Trudeau, the chief executive officer of Krane Chemical, is apoplectic about Krane's plummeting stock and his loss of the case. He never pauses to think about the cancer rate in Bowmore, which has skyrocketed to fifteen times the national average and which has been caused by his company's illegal dumping of chemical waste into the town's water supply. He simply carries out his luxurious lifestyle with his bubble-headed, anorexic trophy wife, Brianna. On the evening of the punishing verdict, he attends a highbrow party at which he buys a hideous piece of dubious art for twenty million dollars. After all, he will never give the others on the *Forbes* world's wealthiest list the satisfaction of seeing him cringe over his enormous financial losses. Trudeau fully realizes if the verdict is not overturned, all the other victims will come forward for a bite of what he considers his exclusive pie. On a balcony overlooking New York City, Trudeau

John Grisham graduated from the University of Mississippi law school and set up a legal practice in Southaven. He was elected to the Mississippi House of Representatives in 1983. After his enormous success with The Firm *(1991), he moved to Oxford, Mississippi, to concentrate on his writing. Grisham is a highly prolific writer;* The Appeal *is his twentieth novel.*

vows to win back his money and gain much, much more—after the appeal.

Another player in these legal and financial high jinks is Barry Rinehart, a nefarious, behind-the-scenes fixer who, in a secret meeting with Trudeau, promises him a bought-and-paid-for judge to be elected to the Supreme Court of Mississippi. Rinehart's man, Tony Zachary, has located a squeaky-clean, churchgoing, baseball-coach local attorney who can easily be elected with a campaign chest of three million dollars funded by various special-interest groups in Washington, D.C., who are intent on crippling trial lawyers by bringing about legislation that places limits on monetary awards in lawsuits. Trudeau jumps at Rinehart's bait. After all, this is Trudeau's opportunity to recoup his loss and make billions more by purposely causing Krane Chemical's stock to fall. He will buy as much stock as possible at deflated prices and sit back and watch his bottom line grow bigger and bigger after his own newly elected judge overturns the *Baker v. Krane Chemical* verdict.

Meanwhile, attorney Ron Fisk has been approached by Zachary, Rinehart's henchman, promising Fisk a seat on the Mississippi Supreme Court. Zachary assures Fisk, a conservative, that he has been selected to run against the incumbent judge Shelia McCarthy because he is a family-values type of guy, with no skeletons in his closet. After all, McCarthy, Zachary confides, is much too liberal. It does not matter in the slightest that Fisk has no judicial experience. Leave the business aspects of the election to him, Zachary tells Fisk. Just get out there, look good, and say the things the voters want to hear. Fisk, who cannot believe his good luck, is whisked off to Washington in a private jet to meet the bigwigs who will finance his campaign.

In addition, Zachary has rounded up a red-herring candidate, a highly unelectable shady alcoholic lawyer named Coley Clete, to run against Fisk and McCarthy. Clete's candidacy serves to generate negative headlines that will make Fisk look much better by comparison.

While the appeal to the forty-one-million-dollar verdict is proceeding, shyster lawyers invade Bowmore for a piece of the pie that is sure to come about if the verdict is not overturned. Wes and Mary Grace, who study the sixteen-thousand-page trial transcript and continue to battle the opposing lawyers' myriad objections, manage to attract more clients. Their financial situation improves, although they are not making much progress in paying down their bank loans. They hold their breath, waiting for an outcome on the appeal in their favor or a rich settlement from Krane Chemical, which could turn them overnight into millionaires and bring great financial relief to their suffering friends and neighbors. In this regard, the Krane lawyers set up a meeting, bogusly holding out bait for a large settlement—all of which serves to lower the price of Krane stock when the settlement falls through.

A nasty election ensues for the seat of the Mississippi Supreme Court judge who will be instrumental in determining the fate of the appeal. McCarthy is sideswiped by the millions of dollars poured into her opponent Fisk's campaign. In campaign advertisements, she is painted as a liberal, a supporter of gun control, and an advocate for same-sex marriage—issues traditionally not viewed favorably in that region of the United States. Despite her best efforts and an infusion of funds from the state's Trial Lawyers' Association, McCarthy loses and Fisk takes her seat. He has managed to look good and speak well on the stump, but he has remained clueless about the underhanded operation of his campaign.

All the while, behind the scenes, the strings of the puppet people are being pulled by Rinehart, whose company specializes in rigging elections, and Wall Street tycoon Trudeau, who sits back gleefully watching the price of Krane stock tumble and waiting to buy large quantities of Krane stock at bargain-basement prices. He is safe in the knowledge that Krane stock will turn around and skyrocket, and he will gain billions after the judge he just bought overturns the verdict. Meanwhile, in a vindictive move, Trudeau arranges to buy the bank where Wes and Mary Grace have their long-overdue loans, forcing the couple into bankruptcy. None of those ignorant people, Trudeau swears emphatically, will ever get one thin dime of his money.

Although the stage is set for Trudeau to make a financial comeback, a glitch upsets his plans. Fisk's son is injured in a baseball accident and rushed to the local hospital. After an examination, he is given a clean bill of health and returns home, shaken but apparently okay. As time goes on, however, it appears that in fact he did suffer a serious injury when the ball hit his head, and he slips into a coma. An investigation determines that the hospital was negligent because the overworked physician read the wrong X-rays. Sadly, the son suffers permanent brain damage, and the newly elected Fisk is left with a serious dilemma. While he is certainly free to engage a trial lawyer, sue the hospital, and win a large monetary verdict, he realizes that he will become a laughingstock if he chooses this path—after all, he won the election based on the premise that trial lawyers were hurting corporations, and thus causing employees to lose jobs, because of enormous verdicts. Ultimately, while Fisk, as expected, votes to overturn the huge Krane Chemical verdict, he does so with a heavy heart and a statement decrying the process of his decision. This does not help the victims in Bowmore, but Trudeau is catapulted to financial heaven.

Unlike the traditional legal thriller, which usually ends with a trial, Grisham's *The Appeal* begins with a trial and goes on to focus, for three hundred pages, on the event that is usually overlooked—the subsequent appeal. Indeed, after the plot machinations of a meaty legal thriller, readers often blow a sigh of relief at the completion of the trial, when traditionally the corporate lawyers get their comeuppance for harming the disenfranchised victims. However, in *The Appeal*, readers must wait to see if any of the victims and their struggling lawyers ever get a dime of the juicy forty-one-million-dollar verdict, although the outcome is not surprising. After reading about the corporate and legal shenanigans behind fixed elections, they know there is no happy ending.

Although Grisham has been criticized for his weak characterization—his characters appearing like paper-doll cutouts—there is little doubt that he is a fine storyteller. In *The Appeal*, he surpasses his reputation as a story-meister. Indeed, this powerful and shocking tale opens readers' eyes to the wheelings and dealings behind what appear to be benign local elections. In short, Grisham's book shows how elections can be bought and paid for and how any candidate, regardless of experience, can be elected if he or she has enough money to attract voters through negative thirty-second sound bites that sling mud and assassinate reputations. No doubt Grisham, who admits to being an election addict and who spent two terms in the State of Mississippi House of Representatives, is deeply aware of how big money controls political races.

M. Casey Diana

Review Sources

Booklist 104, no. 16 (April 15, 2008): 61.
Entertainment Weekly, no. 976 (February 1, 2008): 78.
Forbes 181, no. 6 (March 24, 2008): 38.
The New York Times, January 28, 2008, p. 48.

ARMAGEDDON IN RETROSPECT
And Other New and Unpublished Writings on War and Peace

Author: Kurt Vonnegut (1922-2007)
Introduction by Mark Vonnegut
Illustrations by Kurt Vonnegut and Edie Vonnegut
Publisher: G. P. Putnam's Sons (New York). Illustrated. 234 pp. $24.95
Type of work: Short fiction, memoir
Time: 1067; 1918; May, 1945; 1951; February, 2000; the future
Locale: Dresden, Germany; Floyd City, Indiana; Chateau-Thierry, France; Stow-on-the-Wold, England; Peterswald, Czechoslovakia; Beda, Czechoslovakia; Verdigris, Oklahoma

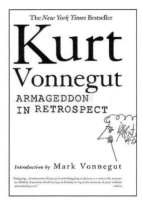

A collection of short works, primarily fiction, relating to issues surrounding the endings of wars, with special focus on the firebombing of Dresden, Germany, in 1945

Principal characters:
GREAT DAY, private in a future Army of the World
CAPTAIN PORITSKY, officer in charge of a time-traveling operation
PRIVATE DONNINI, gourmet-minded prisoner of war in Germany
PRIVATE KNIPTASH, gluttony-minded prisoner of war in Germany
CORPORAL KLEINHANS, German prison-camp guard
OLD MAN, undocumented civilian in a war-ruined city
BOY, undocumented orphan cared for by the old man
LOUIS GIGLIANO, collaborationist prisoner of war in German camp
ELMER, eleventh century English woodcutter
IVY, the woodcutter's wife, who yearns for courtly life
ETHELBERT, their son
ROBERT THE HORRIBLE, friend of William the Conqueror
BABY GIRL, first child born January 1, 2000, in New York City
PAUL, prisoner of war in Sudetenland taking victor's spoils
SAM KLEINHANS, German American prisoner of war liberated by Russians
GEORGE FISHER, German American prisoner of war and collaborationist
POP, English-speaking cabinet maker in Beda, Czechoslovakia
MARTA, his daughter
MAJOR LAWSON EVANS, war-hardened American overseeing occupation of Beda
CAPTAIN PAUL DONNINI, the major's assistant in the occupation of Beda
DR. SELIG SCHILDKNECHT, theorizer of a unified theory of mental illness
JESSIE L. PINE, oil millionaire obsessed with Schildknecht's theory
DR. GORMAN TARBELL, scientist who assists Pine
DR. LUCIFER J. MEPHISTO, Pine's business manager

Kurt Vonnegut was unusual among American novelists for his frequent return, in his fiction, to an incident early in his life that profoundly affected him. *Armageddon in Retrospect*, the first planned posthumous collection of his unpublished works, is a remarkably fitting capstone on a career that stretched for more than fifty years—for not only does that recurring incident reappear here, but it provides the unifying thread for the entire volume.

Kurt Vonnegut earned a reputation as a darkly sardonic humorist with his early novels, including The Sirens of Titan *(1959) and* Cat's Cradle *(1963). His 1969 novel* Slaughterhouse-Five *became a best seller and was turned into a film, making him a literary celebrity. He wrote fourteen novels and four plays.*

The formative event took place near the end of World War II, in Dresden, Germany. Vonnegut, a private in the U.S. Army's 106th Infantry Division, was captured by the Germans in mid-December, 1944, and imprisoned in Dresden, a city famed for its beauty where many noncombatant Germans sought safety. Two months after Vonnegut's capture, he witnessed Dresden's destruction by an Allied firebombing. As a surviving prisoner, he gained firsthand knowledge of the carnage, being assigned to a work crew disinterring victims, many of them women and children.

Vonnegut revisited this incident in several important works, most famously in his novel *Slaughterhouse-Five* (1969). Although the historical incident remained the same, from work to work, successive works were varied in their approaches to the theme of individual responsibility. For Vonnegut, an individual may act as if innocent and may feel innocent of wrongdoing. Nevertheless, in the face of universal culpability for the horrors of war, the sensitive individual must confront the issue of personal responsibility in some way.

Armageddon in Retrospect takes the reader back to Vonnegut's Dresden experiences with a strikingly effective summary, written by him only months after the events, as a letter to his family. The letter's dry, sardonic style anticipates his later fiction, as in this brief note on the firebombing: "On about February 14th the Americans came over, followed by the R.A.F. Their combined labors killed 250,000 people in twenty-four hours and destroyed all of Dresden—possibly the world's most beautiful city. But not me."

Earlier in this letter, Vonnegut had written about the captured Americans who died from shock in the delousing showers, after days of starvation, thirst, and exposure; then he added, "But I didn't." In echo, the phrase "But not me" appears several times, prefiguring the author's later use of repeated phrases in his novels.

This typewritten document, "Letter from PFC Kurt Vonnegut, Jr., to his family, May 29, 1945," is presented in facsimile form. The subsequent short memoir,

"Wailing Shall Be in All Streets," provides more details and relates incidents from the liberation of Dresden that have their own echoes in the short stories to follow:

> The occupying Russians, when they discovered that we were Americans, embraced us and congratulated us on the complete desolation our planes had wrought . . . but I felt then as I feel now, that I would have given my life to save Dresden for the World's generations to come. That is how everyone should feel about every city on Earth.

To describe the book's structure in musical terms, *Armageddon in Retrospect* is a theme-and-variations composition. Vonnegut's letter of May 29, 1945, and the short memoir state the thematic elements, while the subsequent stories provide artistic variations. Consistent with his own varied literary background, Vonnegut treats his theme through the approaches of science fiction, semiautobiographical fiction, historical fiction, fable, and even semireligious fantasy.

No notes accompany these stories to indicate if they are of older or of recent vintage, or whether perhaps all were written in the last years before Vonnegut's death. The quality of writing, however, is consistently high throughout.

Among the most memorable short stories, for the bleak notes they strike, are "Great Day" and "Happy Birthday, 1951." The former is a science-fiction story involving time travel, and the latter is fablelike in presenting unnamed characters living in the wreckage of an unspecified city.

In "Great Day," an Indiana soldier with a full store of hick expressions, who acquires the nickname Great Day, lives in a future where there is an Army of the World, with "everbody like brothers everwhere, peace everlasting, nobody hungry, nobody ascared." His commanding officer, Captain Poritsky, hungers for real war to such a degree that he leads a party backward in time to Europe in 1918, to witness a World War I battle in which American soldiers were counterattacking German forces. Great Day and Poritsky become stranded in 1918, and Great Day emerges a celebrated hero. When he maintains he is no such thing, others tell him, "We'll all swear we seen you killing Germans with your bare hands."

The sardonic bitterness of "Great Day," in which inhabitants of a peaceful world are drawn back into disastrous war, whether by inner need or by external circumstances, is surpassed by the quiet pessimism of "Happy Birthday, 1951." In this fable, an old man without proper documents lives in a ruined city. Soldiers patrolling the area have just forced him to fill out papers for himself and the boy he has been caring for. Having to choose a birthdate for the boy, the pair decide to celebrate it the next day. The old man hopes to observe it in a way that reflects his distaste for all matters military. The boy slips away on his "birthday," however, making the old man go in search. Nearing the wreck of a tank, he hears the word "Bang!" cried out by a small voice from within. With the story's last sentences, Vonnegut underlines the futility of the old man's hopes: "The boy raised his head from the turret triumphantly. 'Gotcha!' he said."

In some cases, successive stories in *Armageddon in Retrospect* employ similar elements and situations. The short stories "Spoils" and "Just You and Me, Sammy" depict events on May 8, 1945, when Peterswald, Czechoslovakia, is being liberated by the Russian army. Both involve American prisoners nervous about their new status; both revolve around the spoils being claimed by the victors. The aims, techniques, and thematic developments of the two stories, however, are distinct. Despite the reiterations of fact and the repetition of situations and character types, each story has its internal integrity; and the strength of Vonnegut's narrating voice keeps the experience surprisingly fresh for the reader, as remains true throughout the volume. The impact of these closely related stories, in fact, may be deepened by their being presented together.

The Peterswald stories deal with the remorse felt even by the lowliest of victors—the captured prisoners, upon their release. In "Spoils," when a freed American named Paul tentatively engages in spoils-taking, he is so forcefully struck by remorse he can partake no further. That he returns to the United States with a single piece of rusty metal, not the valuables other soldiers take home with them, becomes a defining element of his character.

In "Just You and Me, Sammy," two released American prisoners, Sam Kleinhans and George Fisher, become engaged in a conflict over Kleinhans's dogtags. Fisher, who collaborated with the German guards during imprisonment, plans to return to the United States disguised as the similar-looking Kleinhans. The response of "Sammy" to the situation generates his remorse, although the sharpness of his feelings is mitigated by a later revelation about Fisher's real motive.

The title story, "Armageddon in Retrospect," is an unusual fantasy utilizing religious elements. Vonnegut's wartime-born perspective is satirically embodied in the character of the late Dr. Selig Schildknecht, of Dresden, Germany, who "believed that the mentally ill were possessed by the Devil." The theory inspires oil tycoon Jessie L. Pine of Verdigris, Oklahoma, to set up an institute for eradicating all mental ills, including the inclination toward violence. With the help of a business manager, who is the narrator, and a scientist, Gorman Tarbell, Pine undertakes to ward off the Devil's influence over several Oklahoma counties and then to capture the Devil himself in a force-field container, an act that might prove to be Biblical Armageddon. Describing Tarbell as "the living martyr of Armageddon," the narrator reveals his character in such a way as to underline the futility of attempting to remove humankind's inner evils.

Along with recurring locations, times, and events, recurring characters may be found in *Armageddon in Retrospect*. While the characters appearing in different stories under the names Paul, Private Donnini, and Major Paul Donnini may or may not be exactly the same individual, they play similarly sympathetic roles. The unnamed first-person narrator who seems to be Vonnegut also appears, as in the story "Brighten Up."

The constant and powerful focus brought to those moments surrounding the ending of war, however, provides the main unitary element, making this work cohere in a way unusual for story collections. With his clear, humane voice steadily refreshing the memory of the Dresden firebombing and of other devastating and inhumane acts of war, Vonnegut in this posthumous collection ably demonstrates the artistic skill that won him high standing in American letters.

The collection includes graphic works, many incorporating pithy statements by Vonnegut, and an introduction by Vonnegut's son, Mark. Included also is Vonnegut's last speech, "At Clowes Hall, Indianapolis, April 27, 2007." The speech was to kick off a "year of Kurt Vonnegut" in the city of his birth. Although Vonnegut died before that date, the speech was delivered by his son. Even in print, it offers a fine example of yet another form in which this unconventional American humorist excelled.

Mark Rich

Review Sources

Booklist 104, no. 14 (March 15, 2008): 8.
The Boston Globe, April 13, 2008, p. C6.
The Hartford Courant, March 30, 2008, p. G4.
Kirkus Reviews 76, no. 3 (February 1, 2008): 141.
Library Journal 133, no. 7 (April 15, 2008): 85.
Los Angeles Times, April 6, 2008, p. R2.
The New York Times Book Review, May 4, 2008, p. 16.
Publishers Weekly 255, no. 8 (February 25, 2008): 66.
The Village Voice 53, no. 13 (March 26, 2008): 44.

ATMOSPHERIC DISTURBANCES

Author: Rivka Galchen (1976-   )
Publisher: Farrar, Straus and Giroux (New York).
   240 pp. $24.00
Type of work: Novel
Time: The early 2000's
Locale: New York, Buenos Aires, Patagonia, and Argentina

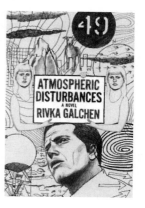

Galchen's debut novel chronicles what happens when a psychiatrist becomes convinced that his wife has been replaced by a double

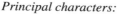

   Principal characters:
       DR. LEO LIEBENSTEIN, a delusional fifty-one-year-old psychiatrist
       REMA, Leo's young wife from Argentina
       DR. TSVI GAL-CHEN, a fellow of the Royal Academy of Meteorology
       HARVEY, one of Leo's patients who thinks he can control the weather
       MAGDA, Rema's mother who lives in Buenos Aires

   Rivka Galchen's *Atmospheric Disturbances* concerns Dr. Leo Liebenstein and his quest to find his wife, Rema, who, he believes, has been replaced by a double. There is no particular reason for the reader to accept that Rema has been substituted by what he calls a "simulacrum," and once the reader learns to doubt Leo's perspective, much of the novel's tension comes from trying to tease out what is real and what is delusion. Written in the unreliable first-person narrative tradition of Fyodor Dostoevski's *Zapiski iz podpolya* (1864; *Letters from the Underworld*, 1913; better known as *Notes from the Underground*), *Atmospheric Disturbances* alerts the reader to Leo's bizarre theory in the novel's first sentence: "Last December a woman entered my apartment who looked exactly like my wife." As a "fifty-one-year-old male psychiatrist" with no previous history of mental illness, Leo is used to analyzing his patients' crazy behavior, but he has a humorously hard time distinguishing his own. In an interview, Galchen has admitted, "I'm not that interested in the medical side of the narrator's condition—did he get hit on the head with a board? Is it dementia? I'm more concerned with the emotions behind it." Through the lens of Leo's highly intellectual but distorted point of view, Galchen creates a novel of the mind enlivened by the scientific and psychological mysteries as well as anything happening externally in the novel's plot.

   Once the reader starts to see through Leo's presumed discovery, the novel raises the question "Why would he think that his wife has been replaced?" Perhaps the answer has something to do with her being so much younger than he is. In addition, her "double" brings home a puppy, and he's certain that Rema would never do that, since she does not like dogs. His alienation from her might have something to do with how

~

*Raised in Tulsa, Oklahoma, Rivka
Galchen has received an M.D. from the
Mount Sinai School of Medicine and an
M.F.A. from Columbia University. In
2006, she won the Rona Jaffe
Foundation Writers Award.*
Atmospheric Disturbances *is her first
novel.*

~

their relationship has changed over time. Leo also betrays insecurities about Rema that may have led to his theory of her supposed disappearance. He constantly fears male competition for her affection. When he first leaves the home to go check about a patient, Harvey, Leo notes how many of Rema's colleagues are devoted to her. When he tells a colleague that there may be something "off" about Rema, the man abruptly replies: "You used to just be jealous. Now you've converted your jealousy into a psychological gain, some narcissistic pleasure in believing that everyone else wants what you have, wants to sleep with your wife. You should grow up. It's not healthy." Every now and again, reality almost intrudes upon Leo's delusions in this fashion, but he's good at finding evidence to refute it. In another scene, he considers that even though the "simulacrum" looks very much like Rema as she leans against the counter in the kitchen, he worries that he may be falling into "post hoc reasoning" of the "psychotic," when "all evidence [is] interpreted under the shadow of an axiomatic belief." Therefore, she must not be Rema. In other scenes, he even considers "analyzing" his situation as if it were a "patient's," but ultimately his psychiatrist's detachment helps keep him from ever correctly diagnosing himself. He continues to find external clues to help support his crazy deductions. Through this process, Galchen meditates on how the most familiar person (such as one's spouse) can become alien through a small shift in perspective, and in the tradition of Argentine writer Jorge Luis Borges, the characters' identities become opaque and fragment during the remainder of the novel.

As the novel's title implies, Galchen uses the weather both metaphorically and scientifically. Leo has a patient with "schizotypal personality disorder," the aforementioned Harvey, who believes that, as a member of the Royal Meteorological Society, he can control the weather. After receiving directives from clues buried in the *New York Post*, Harvey sometimes leaves New York to encounter some storm or weather front in different places in the United States. To stop Harvey from making these dangerous trips, Rema persuades Leo to pretend to be an official of the Royal Meteorological Society at a level superior to Harvey so that Leo can order his patient to stay in New York City. Leo has serious problems with her proposal, but he goes along with the duplicity, in part to get along with her. When they are obliged to mention another member of the society as a colleague, they arbitrarily find a member's name—Tsvi Gal-Chen—to firm up the deception. Their ruse works very well, but it also leads Leo to assume other identities with greater ease later in the novel.

Ironically and poignantly, Tsvi Gal-Chen is also the name of Galchen's father, a professor of meteorology who died in 1994. As Leo gradually becomes obsessed with Gal-Chen, the author plays in a postmodern fashion with her relationship with her father and, by implication, with her grief over his loss. Galchen includes in the novel a photograph of her family that Leo analyzes at length after Rema attaches it to the refrigerator. The author therefore allows a small, realistic image to assume a mystery in her narrative. Galchen also begins the novel with Tsvi Gal-Chen's epigraph that "we cannot tell what the weather will be tomorrow (or the next hour) because we do not know accurately enough what the weather is right now." The quote perfectly summarizes Leo's problems with self-knowledge. He can continue to look around for Rema indefinitely, but he will not find her as long as he remains blind to his conflicted impulses. Ultimately, Tsvi Gal-Chen hovers over all of the goings-on of the novel like a scientific deity, the man who unites the characters with their creator.

Galchen also frequently alludes to Franz Kafka's techniques in using analysis as means to give ironic transparency and exactitude to a dream narrative. Leo's early visit to a hospital to check up on Harvey leads to a Kafka-esque moment when a male nurse guffaws at him for no apparent reason. The scene echoes the one in Kafka's *Der Prozess* (1925; *The Trial*, 1937) when the guards first laugh at Joseph K. In both cases, the protagonists are too caught up in their own interpretations to be able to clearly see why they are appropriate subjects for ridicule. In addition, *Atmospheric Disturbances* shares with *The Trial* an opening sentence that launches the novel into an extended inquiry that the novelist deliberately does not ever fully answer. Just as Joseph K. must try to decipher the reason for his arrest, so does Leo have to determine what happened to his wife. In neither case is the author interested in solving the riddle. Last, as in Kafka's *Das Schloss* (1926; *The Castle*, 1930), Galchen likes to have the protagonist engage in mysterious communications with officials, such as Tsvi Gal-Chen, that fuel contradictory interpretations as to what's going on. Leo corresponds with Gal-Chen by e-mail several times over the course of the novel. Later, he learns that Gal-Chen may be deceased. When he asks him about getting the "impression that he was not alive," Gal-Chen responds, "Oh. Yes. That is true, in most senses."

Part inverted love story, part psychological intrigue, the novel follows a mock detective story line as Leo searches for the original Rema when he's not stopping by coffee shops for refreshment or attending to his Blackberry for recent e-mail. After investigating Rema's absence at the New York Public Library, Leo arbitrarily decides to leave for Buenos Aires, Argentina, to search for her. Once there, he meets up with Rema's estranged mother, Magda, whom he has never before seen. The forged-identity lies that Leo started with Harvey continue when Magda thinks that he is actually Rema's lover and not her husband, and Leo goes along with it. Leo also blithely tells her that he is a meteorologist, and once again he retires to a nearby coffee shop to pursue his investigations over coffee and cookies. The novel's imagery tends to repeat in more elaborate ways that reflect Leo's free associations. Rema's puppy leads him to notice multiple dogs in Argentina. The waitress in the Argentine coffee shop looks like Rema, so Leo leaves a lovingly large tip. Since his suitcase was lost en route, Magda lets Leo borrow some clothes that look suspiciously like Tsvi Gal-Chen's clothes in the photograph. Increasingly, much of what Leo sees reflects and refracts his delusions.

Concerned, Rema flies to Argentina to try to talk some sense into Leo. Many of Leo's conversations with people end up at cross purposes because he's so preoccupied with his theories, he's often not listening, and increasingly he finds Rema crying because he's acting strange. After her arrival, he leaves her again for Patagonia—to take on a job for his new assumed identity as a meteorologist for the Royal Academy. Since Rema has characterized Patagonia as the "wild, uncultivated unconsciousness of Argentina," the reader gets a sense that Leo retreats further and further into his own mind the more he eludes his family and his practice. Pretty soon, Harvey joins him to cross-fertilize his crazy theories with the psychiatrist's, thereby relating Rema's disappearance with a weather war: "Harvey worked out that the Rema swapping most likely had been an early move to harvest chaos from our world to bring to a nearby one, that the dog was likely an essential determining agent, that the Patagonian crop-destroying winds—they weren't after sheep, just fruit—would be deployed soon . . . and that nevertheless it was essential to understand this not as a minor skirmish but as a pivotal battle that might be the tipping point in the full determination of our . . . world." Humorously, Leo has only one small quibble with this outlandish theory.

Galchen also alludes to Thomas Pynchon's *The Crying of Lot 49* (1966) and its conspiracy theories when Leo and Harvey worry about the 49 Quantum Fathers, an underground organization seeking to undermine the Royal Meteorological Society. Conspiracy theories often give a spurious sense of order to random occurrences, and, besides, both Harvey and Leo enjoy attaching cosmic significance to their personal concerns.

By the last portion of the novel, Galchen has created such a hall of mirrors that the plot basically stops. Leo admonishes himself to not "*get metaphysically and metaphorically extravagant*," but that ends up happening as the narrative becomes burdened with crisscrossing analytical speculations. Still, by constantly having Leo almost realize how crazy he is, and by maintaining such an intellectual investigation into the roots of his denials, Galchen dramatizes how the mind eludes self-understanding. In addition, there is always some truth to Leo's theories. Rema has changed over time, and she is not the same person that he first fell in love with. His alienation from her reflects the fragmentation of his own identity. He claims that "I've always thought of my own mind as an unruly parliament, with a feeble leader, with crazy extremist factions, and so I don't look down on others for being the same." By allowing Leo to betray himself obliquely through his lies, his investigation, and his insecurities, Galchen explores the geography and the atmosphere of her main character's psyche.

Roy C. Flannagan

Review Sources

Booklist 105, no. 6 (November 15, 2008): 65.
The Economist 387 (June 28, 2008): 92-93.
Kirkus Reviews 76, no. 8 (April 15, 2008): 383.
Library Journal 133, no. 8 (May 1, 2008): 55.
The New York Times Book Review, July 13, 2008, p. 4.

The New Yorker 84, no. 18 (June 23, 2008): 79-80.
Publishers Weekly 255, no. 6 (February 11, 2008): 47.
Time 171, no. 22 (June 2, 2008): 62.
The Village Voice 53, no. 24 (June 11, 2008): 47.
The Wall Street Journal 251, no. 122 (May 24, 2008): W1-W6.

AUSTERITY
Britain, 1945-51

Author: David Kynaston (1951-   )
Publisher: Walker (New York). 704 pp. $45.00
Type of work: History
Time: 1945-1951
Locale: Britain

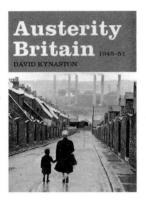

The first volume of Tales of a New Jerusalem, *a history of
Britain from VE Day to the election of Margaret Thatcher
in 1979, focuses on the way in which the victorious 1945
Labour government shaped Britain over three decades*

On May 8, 1945, a Mass Observation investigator over-
heard two women complaining about the way in which the
end of the war in Europe had been announced the previous
day. The peace declaration had been signed at 2:40 A.M., but it had not been announced in Britain until sixteen hours later. At that point, legend has it, the country
went wild, and the citizens of London poured into the streets to celebrate—or at least
some of them did. As the opening chapters of the first volume of David Kynaston's
magisterial new history of postwar Britain, *Austerity*, show, most people stayed qui-
etly at home or expressed disappointment at the nature of the boisterous celebrations
in their local area. As Mass Observation's research revealed, "riotous abandon was
the exception rather than the rule." In fact, many were apprehensive about what the
future would bring. Already people were starting to remember the aftermath of World
War I, when, not twelve months after it ended, men were out of work and desperate to
scrape out some sort of living. As it turned out, they were right to be concerned,
though unemployment would be less of an immediate worry than the lack of housing
and the continued rationing of practically everything. For anyone who had imagined
that the end of the war would mean an immediate return to prewar normality, there
was a rude awakening.

In postwar Britain, there were so many problems to be tackled, it was difficult to
know where to begin. Nearly a million houses had been destroyed or severely damaged by bombing, while public services were suffering under the strain. Britain had a
national debt of 3.5 billion pounds, a record sum. However, many of Britain's problems were far older. Life expectancy had risen and many diseases, formerly killers,
were coming under control, but access to medical services was at best patchy. Many
people lived in appalling conditions, with no running water, indoor sanitation, or adequate heating, and indeed many shared houses with parents and grandparents. After
the economic slump of the 1930's, poverty was endemic. Britain needed a plan, and
during the war people had begun to work on one. The Beveridge Report of 1942 had
effectively formulated a plan for a welfare state, attacking "the five giant evils" of
"want, disease, ignorance, squalor, and idleness." As war came to an end, the Labour

Party produced a manifesto for the election that must surely follow called "Let Us Face the Future."

When the election did come and, as seemed inevitable, the Labour Party did win, a new and, for many, worrying era of British life began. For the conservatives and the Conservative Party, the Labour Party was simply the acceptable face of communism, and they feared a Labour victory, assuming that the old ways would immediately be overturned. As it happened, change proceeded slowly, more slowly than many ardent Labour supporters might have wished, and the old guard found less to complain about than they might have expected. Those with enough money and black market contacts could still maintain a decent lifestyle, although the "servant problem" was a constant topic of conversation.

〜

David Kynaston has been a professional historian since 1973. He has published fifteen books, including the widely acclaimed four-volume The City of London *(1995-2002). He has been a visiting professor at Kingston University in London.*

〜

For the middle and working classes, basic survival was a more urgent problem. Rationing, a bone of contention throughout the war itself, remained in place and, in fact, became more severe as the government poured all of its resources into earning money through exports. For the first time, bread was rationed, which did not sit well with a nation that, although well nourished, was tired and desperate for novelty and excitement. Although the government understood this, it frequently seemed at a loss to know how to respond. As Mass Observation's many inquiries showed, people, particularly the women who were still fighting on the "home front," were less interested in national strategies and more interested in knowing how the government would re-house them and help them get a decent meal on the table. Of equal concern was the fact that although Labour was the professed party of the people, its grand schemes too often failed to take into account what "the people" really wanted.

Perhaps the biggest debate concerned the regeneration of towns and cities. As Kynaston shows, what people wanted and what town planners thought they should have were two entirely different things. Most people wanted a little house with a bit of garden, putting things back as they had been before the war. However, planners thought in terms of grand schemes, many involving the total razing of districts and the introduction of blocks of flats, and they imposed these ideas, insisting that ordinary people did not know what they really wanted. It took fifty years to prove that people knew exactly what they wanted, and many towns and cities are still coping with the legacy of those lofty, out-of-touch plans.

Likewise, the government's education plans were less well received than anticipated. Raising the age of leaving school to fifteen did not prove popular with some parents, who wanted their children out earning as soon as possible. For brighter working-class children, a place at grammar school was as much a curse as a blessing, and many suffered greatly at the hands of better-off schoolmates. Nationalization of the railways and the coal mines was not as successful as the government had hoped.

The great success was the creation of the National Health Service in 1948 (although many doctors protested against its formation), in spite of the fact that portions of the institution revealed staggering ignorance on the part of officials of the health needs of ordinary people. To take but one example, the demand for spectacles was twice that anticipated in the first year, simply because so many people had been making do with cheap glasses from stores such as Woolworth's.

Nevertheless, as Kynaston's history shows, little by little, things did begin to improve. He draws heavily on Mass Observation surveys and private letters and journals to illustrate how, gradually, as items came off ration and the country's debts began to decrease, people's lives improved. Holidays became possible once again, and families began to dream of owning a home and a car. What is also striking in the accounts he uses is how insular people were. Myths abound about Blitz spirit, about a greater sense of community, yet it is quite clear that many people did not engage with the world around them. They did not belong to clubs or political parties, they played little part in their local communities, and women in particular remained firmly at home, apparently by choice. They worried about the influx of immigrants, especially from the West Indies. They worried about changes in industrial practice, about women working outside the home. For every innovator, four other people were ready to step forward and argue for a return to the good old prewar days. For those pressing for social change, it was still an uphill battle.

Kynaston draws on a wide range of accounts and personal testimonies to paint a vivid portrait of postwar Britain that is by turns thrilling and disturbing, showing how people struggled to come to terms with a new political and social landscape. The confidence of the Elizabethan era is yet to come, and many people are puzzled by the world in which they find themselves. They know they cannot go back, and yet, on the threshold of a new Britain, they hold back nervously, waiting. The first volume of Kynaston's new history perfectly catches this uncertainty.

Maureen Kincaid Speller

Review Sources

The Atlantic Monthly 301, no. 5 (June, 2008): 89-93.
Booklist 104, no. 18 (May 15, 2008): 17.
History Today 57, no. 7 (July, 2007): 64.
Kirkus Reviews 76, no. 4 (February 15, 2008): 183-184.
Library Journal 133, no. 12 (July 1, 2008): 94.
London Review of Books 30, no. 8 (April 24, 2008): 30-31.
New Criterion 27, no. 1 (September, 2008): 68-71.
New Statesman 136 (May 28, 2007): 55-56.
Publishers Weekly 255, no. 7 (February 18, 2008): 145.
The Spectator 303 (May 5, 2007): 53-54.
The Times Literary Supplement, June 15, 2007, pp. 7-8.
The Wall Street Journal 251, no. 117 (May 19, 2008): A13.

THE BALL IS ROUND
A Global History of Soccer

Author: David Goldblatt (1965-   )
First published: The Ball Is Round: A Global History of
    Football, 2006, in Great Britain
Publisher: Riverhead Books (New York). 974 pp. $24.00
Type of work: History
Time: The early 1800's to 2006
Locale: Primarily Europe and Latin America

   Goldblatt's comprehensive book intertwines the history
of soccer with the general political and social history of the
countries around the world where soccer has been an im-
portant popular sport

         Principal personages:

            PELÉ, born EDSON ARANTES DO NASCIMENTO, charismatic Brazilian
               soccer player
            DIEGO MARADONA, Argentine soccer player
            JOAO HAVELANGE, president of the Federation Internationale de Football
               Association (FIFA), 1974-1998
            MATTHIAS SINDELAR, Austrian soccer player
            SEPP BLATTER, FIFA president beginning in 1998
            JOHAN CRUYFF, Dutch soccer player
            SILVIO BERLUSCONI, Italian media magnate, politician, and owner of
               soccer club AC Milan
            JOSEF "SEPP" HERBERGER, German national soccer coach, 1936-1964

    David Goldblatt's *The Ball Is Round* is much more than a history of soccer. Rather, it is an epic depiction of how soccer developed within the political and social history of different countries and societies around the world for the last 150 years. Goldblatt's broad historical scope is deliberately opposed to a narrow focus on sports alone, such as that exemplified by the 361 notebooks of legendary German national team coach Josef "Sepp" Herberger that never mention anything but soccer, even though they cover the momentous years of World War II. Ironically, it is Herberger's famous quip about the basic fact of soccer that Goldblatt chose as title for his sweeping historical work.

    Since *The Ball Is Round* was published first in the United Kingdom in 2006, Goldblatt added a foreword to his American edition of 2008. Here, the author alerts his readers that, except for the subtitle and this foreword, he did not substitute the term soccer for a game known outside the United States as football. For the next nine hundred pages, American readers must remind themselves that football in Goldblatt's book does not mean the American version of the game. The American edition is virtually identical to the first English one, ending just prior to the 2006 World Cup in Germany without an update.

~

*A British sociologist, David Goldblatt
is coeditor of* Global Transformations
*(1999; revised edition, 2009) and
author of books on the social sciences
such as* Knowledge and the Social
Sciences *(2004). He wrote the British
Football Yearbook for three soccer
seasons, 2002-2003, 2003-2004, and
2004-2005. In 2008 he became a
lecturer at Open University in the
United Kingdom.*

~

Throughout *The Ball Is Round*, Goldblatt's central thesis is that there is a strong correlation between a nation's social and political conditions and its sports, particularly its soccer games. For this reason, Goldblatt places the birth of soccer in the modern period in Great Britain, when social and economic forces favored team sports and discipline. While briefly describing other forms of people playing with balls, such as China's cuju or kickball popular from about 200 B.C.E. to its extinction in 1644, Goldblatt dismisses as "utterly vacuous" the claim that football is as old as human history. This claim was made by Sepp Blatter, president of the Federation Internationale de Football Association (FIFA) since 1998, whom at the end of the book Goldblatt charges with gross mismanagement.

Instead, Goldblatt convincingly shows that modern football developed in the early to middle 1800's when the game became popular in English public schools. Eventually, schools wrote down their rules, and when graduates from different schools wanted to play against each other, they had to agree on shared rules. In November, 1863, the Football Association (FA) was founded in London and published rules that would lay the foundation for the development of association football, called soccer in the United States and known as football everywhere else. Goldblatt maps out the ensuing development of the referee system, the play for the first FA Cup won by the Wanderers 1-0 in 1871, and the formation of an English league in 1888.

Tantalizing the reader, Goldblatt mentions the first international soccer match, England versus Scotland in 1872, but does not give its score. Maybe this demonstrates that *The Ball Is Round* is more interested in soccer's connection to society rather than mere scores and statistics. Throughout, Goldblatt inserts whimsical descriptions of some historical matches but gives no tables or lists.

Always, Goldblatt strongly ties his narrative to the development of the societies in which soccer is played. As to the nature of this relationship, Goldblatt writes that in the late 1800's, "industrialization underpinned the emergence of British working-class football in a number of direct and material ways." He thus chooses the term "industrial football" to characterize the game in England and Scotland before World War I. "Early-twentieth-century industrialization would spawn the same connections in much of Europe and Latin America," to where the focus of the book shifts.

Here, Goldblatt shows the apparent irony that soccer failed to catch on in the countries of the British Empire and its former colony, the United States. Instead, the game made great progress wherever contact with England was more casual. In Europe, soccer became the sport of the liberal Anglophile elite before encompassing the working classes. In Latin America, contact with British sailors and expatriates popularized the game. In 1867, the FA rules were published in Buenos Aires, and a Spanish translation appeared there in 1903 as the sport spread to the working class and the recent European immigrants.

Contemplating the early success of soccer in Europe and Latin America, Goldblatt adds to the sociological explanations a deeply felt emotional one, stating that "people played because they just loved to play" soccer. Here and elsewhere in his magisterial book, Goldblatt does acknowledge that there are always national exceptions to major economic, social, and political trends. While industrialized France hosted the foundation of FIFA in 1904, for instance, soccer enjoyed only regional interest there. In Germany, gymnastics competed with soccer for mass participation in sport. The Ottoman Empire faced Islamic opposition to the game.

Discussing the global development of soccer after World War I, Goldblatt looks again at larger social shifts as well as at changes to the game itself. He discusses internal changes in the national organization of the game in England, continental Europe, and Latin America, as well as development of new tactics and strategies. However, narrative space is also devoted to a tangential discussion of the Viennese coffee house, for example. Relatively rare are such passionate portrayals as that of the Austrian anti-Nazi striker Matthias Sindelar, called "the wafer." An innovative force on the playing field, Sindelar was "found . . . dead in his flat" in 1939 after Hitler's takeover of Austria. His death remains one of soccer's great mysteries.

As Goldblatt's narrative passes through the decades of the twentieth century, *The Ball Is Round* addresses the major issues in the development of soccer. The rise of professionalism, the improved coaching, the international competitions, the impact of mass media (such as sports magazines and radio, later television) which increased the base of supporters, as fans are known in England, and the darker issues such as racism, violence, and scandals are portrayed and related to society at large. Fascist, National-Socialist, and Communist attempts to co-opt the sport are detailed, and Goldblatt shows soccer's relationship to international politics.

The Ball Is Round does justice to the importance of soccer in Latin America. The period of 1935 to 1954 is seen as "The Road to El Dorado," when soccer was played with passion in countries that slowly emerged from the Great Depression. As political and economic conditions deteriorated in South America, Goldblatt sees a time of "Demons and Angels," from 1955 to 1974. The book juxtaposes the situation in Brazil, where soccer was played both for serious competition and for pleasure, in an atmosphere of relative freedom. This style was exemplified by Pelé, a young Brazilian striker who made his national debut in the 1958 squad that won the World Cup. He repeated that feat with his team in 1962 and 1970. Goldblatt reminds readers that Pelé, like his teammates, "were products of their time" and the result of a "social production line," although some readers may take exception to this Socialist interpretation.

In Argentina, Goldblatt argues, social repression created a brutal soccer game focused on destroying the opponent's game and lurking for swift counterattacks. When *The Ball Is Round* discusses Argentine soccer in the 1970's, the reader will learn as much about Argentine generals running the country as about Diego Maradona, Argentina's star player of the period.

As soccer develops further, Goldblatt looks at the work of João Havelange, who transformed FIFA during his long presidency from 1974 to 1998. Havelange is depicted as a master politician and network specialist who modernizes FIFA and turns the World Cup tournament into the most-watched global sporting event. The postwar rise of European soccer is highlighted as benefiting from television as well as the 1954 formation of the Union des associations européens de football (UEFA) that brought annual competitions of the best European clubs. In the context of the Cold War, Goldblatt credits UEFA as being one of the few institutions in which Communist Eastern and Free Western Europe worked well together.

As an organizing principle, each chapter focuses on a particular region and time period, and Goldblatt generally goes from country to country looking at soccer and society together. Thus the emergence of Dutch star player Johan Cruyff, whose team bitterly lost the 1974 World Cup final to Germany, is related to social changes in Dutch society that altered the way soccer was played in the Netherlands. At times, going from country to country inevitably leads to some duplication of soccer's international events, yet this books shows them from a unique perspective each time.

When Africa decolonizes after World War II, *The Ball Is Round* looks at soccer in the emerging countries. Predictably, the underdeveloped economies and instable political situation of many African nations of the 1960's and 1970's are reflected in the difficulties soccer teams face there. Goldblatt tells of the indomitable spirit of African players and spectators who manage to hold matches against considerable odds. In the 1990's, many African talents migrate to European clubs.

The Ball Is Round honestly chronicles the crisis of European, and particularly English, soccer in the 1980's. Hooliganism becomes a serious problem, and attendance falls. Goldblatt fixes as low point the tragedy of Heysel Stadium in Belgium on May 29, 1985, when thirty-nine people die after a dilapidated wall is crushed by fans. Now, Goldblatt states, "football was rescued from its predicament by the forces of the market," and "unalloyed commercialism" turns soccer into "one of the central collective cultural experiences of the new millennium." The market overcame hooliganism as it threatened its precious product, which became "sanitized entertainment" instead.

Goldblatt identifies as one exponent of commercial soccer Silvio Berlusconi, an Italian media mogul and later politician who bought and restructured AC Milan in 1986, though not without allegations of match fixing and corruption. Yet as Goldblatt's subsequent chapters show, soccer rises again in Europe, flourishes in Latin America, begins to blossom in Africa, and takes Asia by storm in the 1990's. As the world readied for the 2006 World Cup, Goldblatt shows, soccer was a global event with very few, but notable, exceptions, such as India and the United States.

About half of *The Ball Is Round* contains descriptions of larger political events with a varying degree of their link to soccer history. As a result, at times Goldblatt's book reads like a work on soccer's place in world history. Yet his book has been quite popular in the United States, despite Goldblatt's insistence on the term football for the game. His work follows the tradition of Simon Kuper's *Football Against the Enemy* (1994), graciously acknowledged by Goldblatt, that strongly linked soccer to politics. About one-third the size of Goldblatt's work, Kuper's American edition, *Soccer*

Against the Enemy (2006), not only translated football consistently as soccer in the text but also updated the book.

At times, a stronger focus on soccer and some judicious cuts could have tightened *The Ball Is Round*. It does not mention some recent innovations in soccer rules, such as the change to award three instead of two points to the match winner or experiments with golden and silver goals in international games. After compiling three yearbooks on soccer for a British publisher covering the seasons of 2002-2003 to 2004-2005, British sociologist Goldblatt obviously desired to write a book that would place the special history of soccer in the larger context of the historical development of the societies where the game has been played. The result, *The Ball Is Round*, makes for compelling reading.

R. C. Lutz

Review Sources

History Today 57, no. 4 (April, 2007): 62.
Library Journal 133, no. 12 (July 1, 2008): 38.
Sports Illustrated 107, no. 26 (December 31, 2007): 19.
Times Literary Supplement, January 19, 2007, p. 32.

THE BEAUTIFUL SOUL OF JOHN WOOLMAN,
APOSTLE OF ABOLITION

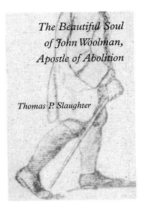

Author: Thomas P. Slaughter (1954-   )
Publisher: Hill and Wang (New York). 449 pp. $30.00
Type of work: Biography, religion, ethics
Time: 1720-1772
Locale: Colonial America and England

This biography of Quaker saint and social reformer Woolman traces his spiritual development, analyzes the roots of his activism, documents the changes he helped bring about, and recognizes his continuing relevance to issues such as racism, economic justice, cruelty to animals, and simple living

Principal personages:
JOHN WOOLMAN, tailor, traveling minister, and author
SARAH ELLIS WOOLMAN, his wife
MARY WOOLMAN, their daughter
SAMUEL WOOLMAN, John's father
ELIZABETH BURR WOOLMAN, John's mother
JOHN SMITH, a friend from a wealthy Quaker family
BENJAMIN FRANKLIN, a Philadelphia publisher
BENJAMIN LAY, a radical Quaker reformer
SLAVE WOMAN, for whom young John writes a bill of sale
JOHN PAPUNHANK, an Indian spiritual leader and prophet
ABNER WOOLMAN, John's brother and fellow writer
JAMES PEMBERTON, a friend from a wealthy Quaker family
JOHN PEMBERTON, a friend from a wealthy Quaker family
JOHN COMFORT, Woolman's son-in-law
STEPHEN COMFORT, his father, Woolman's executor
SAMUEL EMLEN, a friend and fellow Quaker minister
SARAH MORRIS, a traveling minister in England
DEBORAH MORRIS, her accompanying niece
WILLIAM TUKE, Woolman's final host in England

Early New Jersey Quaker John Woolman (1720-1772) was an eccentric who dressed all in white, sometimes walked rather than rode his horse, refused to drink from silver cups, and declined inoculations against smallpox, from which he eventually died. He was also a saintly man who resisted war taxes, opposed cruelty to animals (and humans), and led the fight to abolish slavery. These two sides of Woolman have a common explanation: A deeply religious person, Woolman cultivated the life of the spirit and the moral actions that flowed from it. For the same reasons, he undertook a traveling ministry that led him to leave his wife and daughter at home for long periods and journey through the colonies and to England preaching his messages.

Woolman also wrote pamphlets and left his *Journal* (1774), which has never been out of print.

For these clear explanations of the strange and saintly Woolman, readers are indebted to historian Thomas P. Slaughter's biography *The Beautiful Soul of John Woolman, Apostle of Abolition.* Slaughter's well-performed task was doubly difficult not just because of Woolman's complex personality but because that personality had to be reconstructed, sometimes with sparse information, for a modern audience alien to the frame of mind and to the many beliefs that moved Woolman. Slaughter's biography is like an archaeological excavation of psychology, history, and religion.

~

Thomas P. Slaughter is a professor of history at the University of Rochester. His other books include Bloody Dawn: The Christiana Riot and Racial Violence in the Antebellum North *(1994),* Exploring Lewis and Clark: Reflections on Men and Wilderness *(2004), and* The Natures of John and William Bartram *(2005).*

~

One might think that Woolman's *Journal* would have supplied most of the answers that Slaughter needed. but *Journal* is a spiritual autobiography, a genre much favored by the Religious Society of Friends (Quakers) but reaching back to antiquity. Such autobiographies focus on the inner life of the spirit, the state of the soul, and typically record outer events only as they influence the inner life. For example, Woolman does not specify the activities of his youthful friends that repulsed him, says little about his courtship of and marriage to Sarah Ellis, says nothing about their infant son who died, and seems oblivious to the beauty of the natural landscapes he traveled through. However, he does record his dream visions and his spiritual crises as a child and young adult: the time he talked back to his mother, the time he killed a mother robin and her nest of young, and the time he made out a bill of sale for a female slave.

Woolman began writing his *Journal* in his thirty-sixth year, so this raises questions about how well he remembered his childhood and young adulthood, what he left out, and how he interpreted what he remembered. The sparse information forces Slaughter to speculate at times, but he stays close to what can be documented from the journal and from other sources, such as meeting records. Woolman also wrote several drafts of the journal, and a Quaker committee edited the first published version (deleting all of the dream visions). Slaughter traces the changes and deletions closely to glean additional information. (The authoritative modern edition, taking the various drafts into account, is *The Journal and Major Essays of John Woolman*, published in 1971 and edited by Phillips P. Moulton.)

Most importantly, Woolman's *Journal* reveals his overall frame of mind, the mind-set of a sensitive soul immersed in religious belief. Even in his own religious age, Woolman was something of a throwback: He admired the Old Testament prophets, the early Christian martyrs, and the Quaker martyrs of the seventeenth century, thousands of whom had been thrown into prison in England and persecuted with Calvinistic zeal in New England. The Religious Society of Friends recognized Woolman's unusual spiritual gifts, appointing him a minister at the age of twenty-two, endorsing his travels, and publishing his writings—even though the moral beliefs emerging from his spirituality put him in opposition to many of the common practices of the time, including among the Quakers. Slaughter supplies the historical contexts that make Woolman's spirituality and his preaching of reforms understandable.

The saintly Woolman was always a work in progress, so that the story of his life reads somewhat like the archetypal journey of Christian in John Bunyan's *The Pilgrim's Progress* (1678). Even at a young age, Woolman showed a precocious tendency to cultivate his inner life, preferring around the age of seven to leave his playmates and go off by himself to read Revelations. As a teenager, he disapproved of his friends' worldly ways, but some of them belonged to rich New Jersey and Philadelphia Quaker families that had libraries he desired to use. These same families offered him access to the prosperous business world when he became an adult, but after working in a Mount Holly shop for several years and turning down other business opportunities, Woolman withdrew to the more solitary occupation of a lowly tailor and later of a farmer. The crucial incident that turned him away from the business world was making out a bill of sale for a black female slave.

During Woolman's time, slavery was widespread in the colonies, including the Northern ones, and even Quakers owned slaves. When Woolman visited Quaker homes that had slave servants, he felt uneasy, and making out a bill of sale for a slave provoked a major spiritual crisis that Woolman never forgot. He felt complicit in a business world built on slavery and exploited laborers, on cruelty to animals, on unjust dealings with the displaced Indians, on the sale of shoddy and unneeded goods, and on the encouragement of a vain, luxurious, materialistic way of life. Woolman looked around him at William Penn's green promised land of Pennsylvania and of New Jersey and saw his fellow Quakers living in Bunyan's Vanity Fair.

Like his reasons for seeking reforms, Woolman's methods of achieving them flowed from his saintly temperament: He always worked nonviolently from within the Religious Society of Friends. Some earlier abolitionists had resorted to harsher methods, such as the dwarfish radical Quaker Benjamin Lay (1681-1759), who "spattered pokeberry juice on [meeting] worshipers" and "kidnapped a slaveowner's son." Run out of meeting, Lay moved to a cave near Philadelphia from which he made his attacks. Some later abolitionists resorted to guerrilla warfare, such as the militant martyr John Brown (1800-1859).

In accordance with Woolman's subtle nonviolent methods, he was first of all scrupulous to relieve his own mind but also to set an example by disassociating himself from any connection with slavery, however indirect. He stopped making and wearing clothes that were dyed, eventually wearing all white, because the manufacture of dyes involved slave labor. He stopped riding horses on his traveling ministry because they were often fed and groomed by slaves. He refused to use anything made out of silver because South American Indian slaves mined it, even refusing to drink from silver cups when he was a guest in someone's house.

Woolman's behavior as a guest illustrates how he subtly worked inside Quaker homes, including those of his rich friends, to make slavery a moral issue. He discussed the issue personally with meeting members, friends, customers, acquaintances, and strangers. If a slave served him in a Quaker home, he would pay the slave for services rendered, maybe embarrassing the slave's owner. After making out that first bill of sale, he refused to process other sale transactions involving slaves and agonized over serving as coexecutor of an estate that included slaves. In some instances, Woolman's influence resulted in the freeing of slaves.

Most prominently, Woolman preached (strictly speaking, Quaker silent meetings do not have preachers, but anyone can speak out of the silence) and wrote pamphlets against slavery. He spoke against slavery in local meetings but also took numerous journeys in his lifetime of traveling ministry. Especially in his forays south to Delaware, Maryland, and Virginia, he met unfriendly opposition, people who wanted to argue in favor of slavery, even in Quaker meetings (but, significantly, no one seems to have offered any violence against him). Refusing to argue, Woolman stated his case simply and plainly, but not without some subtlety again: He cited the slaves' natural right to freedom and appealed to the Golden Rule, but he also pointed out the debasement of slaves and the corrupting moral effects of slavery on masters, their progeny, and society as a whole.

The wider implications of a society based on exploitation, cruelty, injustice, and luxury were always there in Woolman's thinking, and in his later preaching and his writing he explored those implications. As a reformer, he started with children, practicing and advocating an exemplary nonpunitive raising and education of children, both male and female, in an age that excluded girls and heavily applied the rod. He worked for the just treatment of Indians, once making a wilderness journey deep into hostile Indian territory to speak with them. He developed an inclusive respect for life, reaching out to all races and religions and condemning cruelty to animals. With clear implications for capitalism, he preached a simple lifestyle, fair treatment for workers, and the fair sharing of the world's resources (later the Fabian Society hailed him as a precursor of socialism).

For a humble tailor and farmer, Woolman left a large imprint on American history and on the world. He might even be called the conscience of America. He and other abolitionists influenced the gradual passage of laws against slavery, especially in the Northern states. As Slaughter records, "it became mandatory in 1776 for all Quakers living under the authority of Philadelphia Yearly Meeting to release their slaves," and "[t]he Pennsylvania Abolition Act of 1780 was the first adopted by a legislative body anywhere in the world." In addition, Woolman influenced education, especially in Quaker schools that remain the best in the land. Woolman's imprint can also be seen on such movements as the humane treatment of animals, vegetarianism, nonviolence, and drinking of fair-trade coffee (although he probably would not imbibe). Finally, his *Journal* remains a source of spiritual inspiration for readers everywhere.

Woolman's personality was sometimes hard to take and seemed to become more extreme as he grew older. Always a sympathetic writer and interpreter, Slaughter refers to the older Woolman's "hyperdedication." For example, Woolman had a concern about approving a traveling minute (letter of travel) to England for Elizabeth Smith because her furniture indicated some impurity. On his trip to England, he insisted on sleeping in steerage, where the sailors' foul language shocked him. He rushed from the dock to London Meeting, where the English Quakers found him dirty and uncouth. His appearance created a sensation as he made his progress through England, walking from one end to another and saving souls despite his failing health. He died of smallpox in York and is buried there.

Harold Branam

Review Sources

Booklist 105, no. 1 (September 1, 2008): 13.
Christian Century 125, no. 18 (September 9, 2008): 42-44.
Kirkus Reviews 76, no. 13 (July 1, 2008): 693.
The New Yorker 84, no. 32 (October 13, 2008): 145.
Publishers Weekly 255, no. 22 (June 2, 2008): 36.

BEHIND MY EYES

Author: Li-Young Lee (1957-   )
Publisher: W. W. Norton (New York). 106 pp. $24.95
Type of work: Poetry

A profound and haunting collection that touches on isolation, love, loss, and spiritual growth

Li-Young Lee was born in Jakarta, Indonesia, to parents of Chinese heritage. Before leaving China in 1949 after the Communists took control, his father had served as Mao Zedong's personal physician. Life in Indonesia was extremely difficult for the Lee family. Because of Sukarno's oppressive regime, the family suffered at the hands of the authorities and were forced to escape from the country. After living for short periods of time in Hong Kong, Macau, and Japan, the family finally settled in the United States in 1964. In each of his volumes of poetry, Lee has tapped into the experiences of exile, loss, and strength of family in order to add weight to his poetry. Lee published his first book of poetry, *Rose*, in 1986. Since then, he has published two highly regarded poetry volumes and a memoir. *Behind My Eyes* is his fourth collection of poetry and a worthy addition to his oeuvre. Since each collection is a labor of love, there have been significant gaps of time between each book of poetry. The first was published in 1986, the second, *The City in Which I Love You*, was published four years later in 1990, and the third, *Book of My Nights*, was not published until 2001. Since each of Lee's volumes were highly praised, his fourth collection was eagerly awaited. Over the years, he has gained a rather large readership. It is rare for a book of poetry to sell in the many thousands, but Lee's third volume sold more than ten thousand copies. In addition to his reputation as a fine poet, he published a powerful memoir, *The Winged Seed: A Remembrance*, in 1995. The memoir touches on what life was like for the Lee family in Indonesia, the years they spent in one place after another, and the struggles they had in adjusting to life in a small town in Pennsylvania. The family endured every hardship with love and perseverance. The Before Columbus Foundation honored this extraordinary book with an American Book Award.

Just as Lee's poetry, his memoir is rooted in the past. In addition to his own personal past, he has inherited his family's past. The past has so many metaphysical and magical layers. For anyone, the past can be a burden that stifles a person's ability to move forward. For Lee, it was necessary for him to expose what lives in memory, what festers in the past. He knew that he had to use the tools of the poet in order to become the master of his collective past. Over the years, he has learned that it is a never-ending process. As soon as one layer is exposed, it is discovered that there is so much more that needs to be faced.

Lee's father casts a huge shadow on everything around him. Larger-than-life, he

Li-Young Lee is the highly acclaimed author of four books of poetry and one nonfiction book. He also has been the recipient of several literary awards, including the Whiting Writer's Award, the Lannan Literary Award, and an American Book Award.

was a physician in China, a political prisoner in Indonesia, an evangelical minister in Hong Kong, and—eventually—a minister in a Pennsylvania Presbyterian church. The struggle to survive as an outcast, refugee Chinese immigrant was always paramount. There was no way to escape oneself. The poet son has learned this, realizing that it is best to confront his identity. In most of what Lee has written, he revisits the bonds that hold a family together, the love that helps members of a family to survive against terrible trials, and the way that memory connects people to the past and to one another. Through close observation of his father, Lee struck a universal chord in his first volume of poetry. The struggles of his father become the struggles of every father who attempts to hold his family together against the powers of tyranny. For his second collection, Lee turned the spotlight onto himself, onto his own identity as a Chinese American. Lee is concerned with how the individual fits into the whole, into the world around him, and into the world of his ancestors. While the past runs through all of Lee's volumes, he turned inward more deeply in his 2001 collection. This introspection led the poet to a heightened sense of self. Like a restless spirit, Lee looks into the face of mortality. In *Behind My Eyes*, his fourth collection, the poet expands on the themes that have been grandly illuminated in his previous volumes. Exile, sacrifice, mortality, loyalty, and the power of the past pervade the new collection with a stunning audacity. The reader is carried along by words that radiate compassion, concern, and an almost colloquial purity.

With a total of thirty-nine poems, *Behind My Eyes* is divided into three sections. The richness of the collection can be found in the poet's way of writing about the refugee experience, the experience of not belonging. At a young age, Lee discovered that it was necessary to appear as if you fit in with those in a new country. The immigrant always is under suspicion, viewed by those around him as someone who will upset the balance of power and how the social fabric is held together. An immigrant family must negotiate for a place in society. In the first section of *Behind My Eyes*, Lee writes words of advice for all refugees in the poem "Self-help for Fellow Refugees." He enumerates the rules of the road, offering words of wisdom and of caution. He opens the poem, "If your name suggests a country where bells/ might have been used for entertainment," then it is necessary for the refugee "to dress in plain clothes/ when you arrive in the United States,/ and try not to talk too loud." For someone attempting to settle in the United States, it is a difficult gauntlet to run, especially if you come from a different and strange culture. Lee is able to win over the reader to his extraordinary family history by employing concise and straightforward images. There is a disarming simplicity found in the language of his poetry. He has stated that he was influenced in his poetry by classical Chinese poetry and by the King James Version of the Bible. Classical Chinese poetry is noted for using descriptions of the natural world as expressions of human emotions. As a poet, Lee has learned how to be a close observer of the environment around him and how to set the appropriate mood for the reader. He takes great care in revealing the "sacred" in everyday experiences. For this reason, he has been favorably compared to the great nineteenth century American poet Walt Whitman. Lee has said that his poetry and the world which he inhabits are one and the same. The qualities that he has utilized throughout his life in order to make sense of the world are the very same qualities that he utilizes to construct his poetry. Lee envisions that everyone will, at one time or another, come face to face with some kind of "spiritual" revelation. This revelation is a building block in the poetic process. The poet believes that all art can lead one to wisdom. He writes in order to communicate with something or someone greater than himself. For Lee, this creative process is never-ending. He is consumed by both poetry and by life. The poem "Seven Happy Endings" revolves around giving a proper name to the unification between himself and his wife. The poem opens, "Love, after talking all night,/ where are we? Where did we begin?" For him, there must be a name that he can give to "we," "us," and "this." Some of the ideas he proposes are: "Shadows on the garden wall./ A man rowing alone out to sea./ Seven happy endings." His wife, though, seems to be perfectly happy with where they are, with "two rooms, and a door to divide them." She also is content with the "Borrowed music from an upstairs room./ And bells from down the street/ to urge our salty hearts." Lee has promised seven endings, but he is unsure of what they will be. He understands that he knows "nothing about endings." Beginnings are what he understands. His relationship with his wife "always feels like beginning." This is more than merely the two of them; it is the "beginning of reality itself." Toward the end of *Behind My Eyes*, Lee includes a poem that is a tender portrait of his relationship with his wife. In "Virtues of a Boring Husband," the poet admits that, "Whenever I talk, my wife falls asleep./ So, now, when she can't sleep, I talk./ It's like magic." His talking calms her down, makes her feel safe. For the poet, his wife plays the role of muse and sounding board. At one point in the poem, Lee speaks of what the sages have said about "moving up a ladder of love." If he is remembering correctly what the sages "have said," then love of another starts first with love for that person as "object," followed by as "presence," and then as "essence," and finally as "disclosure of the divine." As he continues to ponder these ideas out loud, it is his wife who surrenders to sleep. He realizes that it is time to stop talking, and so he kisses "her forehead . . . before leaving the bed and closing/ the door behind" him. For this volume, Lee has stated that he wanted to delve deeper into issues that always have prodded him. He desired to have in-depth arguments with God. For him, it took seven years to grow sufficiently as a poet and as a person in order to write *Behind My Eyes*. While he felt that confusion surrounded *Book of My Nights*, in the new collection he has found more clarity of purpose. Whether he is speaking about the immigrant experience or about close personal relationships, Lee still sees himself as the outsider, as someone who remains tied to the past. As a poet, it is his nature to want to use language in order to explain and to comprehend more coherently. He also realizes that even language can become a barrier to growth and to revelation. With *Behind My Eyes*, Lee has confronted the incongruities of life, and he has discovered that opposites can coexist. The attentive reader can immerse himself in these dualities presented by the poet and feel both challenged and comforted.

Jeffry Jensen

Review Sources

Booklist 104, no. 8 (December 15, 2007): 18.
Harvard Review, June, 2008, p. 219.
International Examiner 35 (April 16, 2008): 11.
Publishers Weekly 254, no. 46 (November 19, 2007): 38.
World Literature Today 82, no. 3 (May/June, 2008): 8.

THE BIN LADENS
An Arabian Family in the American Century

Author: Steve Coll (1958-   )
Publisher: Penguin Press (New York). Illustrated.
   671 pp. $35.00
Type of work: Biography, current affairs, history
Time: c. 1900 to the early twenty-first century
Locale: The United States, Sudan, England, Pakistan,
   Afghanistan, and the Middle East, especially Saudi
   Arabia

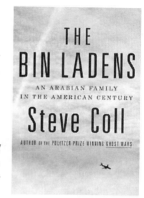

*Coll illuminates the life of Osama Bin Laden by setting
it against the rise to unimaginable wealth of his family,
builders to the Saudi royal family at a time of unprecedented development*

Principal personages:
> MOHAMMAD BIN LADEN (c. 1908-1967), founder of the Bin Laden
>   family and its business empire
> SALEM BIN LADEN (1944 or 1945-1988), his eldest son and successor
> BAKR BIN LADEN (1945 or 1946-   ), brother and successor of Salem
> OSAMA BIN LADEN (1957 or 1958-   ), son of Mohammad, half
>   brother of Salem and Bakr, jihadist, and organizer of 9/11 attacks on
>   the United States
> ABDULAZIZ,
> SAUD,
> FAISAL,
> KHALID,
> FAHD, and
> ABDULLAH, successive kings of Saudi Arabia

One of the most extraordinary stories of the last century is the establishment of the Kingdom of Saudi Arabia and its transformation in the course of a single generation from poverty and obscurity to unsurpassed wealth and influence. In *The Bin Ladens*, Steve Coll recounts the story and its familiar actors: Abdulaziz Bin Saud, who set out from Kuwait one day in 1902 with a few ragtag followers to reconquer the little town of Riyadh, formerly part of his family's possessions, and who within a quarter of a century went on to take the Hejaz in the west and the holy cities of Mecca and Medina; the Englishman Harry St. John Bridger Philby, Arabia's greatest explorer, personal friend of King Abdulaziz, and an advocate of American development of the oil fields; the self-indulgent King Saud, who inherited from his father a society reeling in an effort to accommodate the technological and consumerist fruits of that development with the demands of Wahhabism, a particularly austere form of Islam; the devout King Faisal, another son of Abdulaziz, who first used oil as a political weapon against

Steve Coll worked for twenty years at The Washington Post, *where he won a Pulitzer Prize in 1990 for explanatory journalism. He is the author of six books, including* Ghost Wars: The Secret History of the CIA, Afghanistan, and Bin Laden, from the Soviet Invasion to September 10, 2001 *(2004), which won him a second Pulitzer Prize.*

the West; and his three, to date, successors, Khalid, Fahd, and Abdullah.

However, in addition to the House of Saud, another family, from even more modest beginnings, found its fortunes unrecognizably changed over the first half of the twentieth century. Around 1900, Awadh Bin Laden decided to leave his village in present-day Yemen to avoid threats generated by the death of a borrowed ox. He died young, but his sons Mohammad and Abdullah soon found themselves doing well in Jeddah, on what would become the Saudi Red Sea coast. Eventually Mohammad would forge a close relationship with the Saudi royal family and establish a role as the king's chief builder, and this at a time when oil revenues were pouring into dynasty-consolidating, prestige-enhancing construction projects in Mecca and Medina, not to mention into the creation of the kingdom's first real roads and into the building of numerous royal palaces. If all this meant keeping a constant wary eye on the whims of spoiled princes and waiting months or longer to be paid, it also meant stupendous and increasing wealth: The most notorious of Mohammad Bin Laden's grandchildren, one of twenty-five brothers and twenty-nine sisters, would inherit about eighteen million dollars in 1988 as his share of the family pile when Salem, Mohammad's eldest son and successor, was killed in a plane crash, as his father had been.

Notwithstanding his business savvy, Mohammad Bin Laden was practically illiterate and ignorant of the non-Arab world. It was Salem who began bringing the Bin Ladens into contact with the West, especially the United States. Salem was an engaging and charismatic figure who "believed in his Learjet and his MU-2 and his jeans and guitar and harmonica," as a friend put it. Secular and Westernized, he represented the company's interests well in Europe and in the United States during the boom years of the 1970's; and it was he who encouraged his brothers and even his sisters to pursue graduate education in the United States. More than a quarter of the fifty-four did so.

One who did not was Osama. He was the single offspring of Mohammad and a Syrian girl who was about fifteen when he was born and who was divorced by her husband within three years. Shy and obedient as a boy, he would be radicalized by a teacher at his elite high school in Jeddah. Despite his later claims of a long-standing hatred of Americans as enemies of Islam, at this stage of Osama's life there was little exceptional about him beyond his piety. He was "perfectly integrated" into the family, according to a sister-in-law, playing soccer, working for the family companies, and buying expensive cars with his allowance, even, in typical teenage style, totaling one of them.

The greatest strength of Coll's book is that it portrays Osama not as a diabolical figure of unique evil or as a paragon of Islamist virtue but as the comprehensible product of his time and place. Just as his later role in Al Qaeda would be molded by knowledge and techniques acquired in his family's companies, so did his earliest contributions to the Islamist cause flow naturally from the life he led.

He began as a young man who tried to live a strict Muslim life within Saudi society. When a Saudi official wanted to circumvent Pakistani involvement in the channeling of funds and arms to the Afghans fighting the Soviet occupation of their country, it was suggested that prominent mujaheddin be invited on the pilgrimages to Mecca and Medina so they could be wooed privately. As Coll rhetorically asks, "who better to help manage such invitations, and to participate in the ensuing charitable and religious festivities, than Osama Bin Laden, a scion of the family that played such an influential role in the holy cities?" Coll further observes, "His volunteerism remained inseparable from his family's identity and its business strategy." Osama would later base himself in Peshawar, a city close to the Pakistan-Afghanistan border. There he worked on media operations and education, as if he were producing glossy Bin Laden brochures that promoted the accomplishments of his family's businesses. His elder brother Salem flew in, too, and filmed orphans created by the war, thus appealing to the orthodox Muslim obligation to succor such unfortunates.

Soon Osama wanted a more active role, and he asked Salem for portable antiaircraft missiles. Stung by the social and intellectual condescension of some of his Muslim Brotherhood associates (the widow of one described him as "not a very educated man [and] easy to persuade"), Osama began to talk of diversity and equality and to spread his money around to rival groups. This egalitarianism was spawned in part by the management styles of Mohammad and Salem. As a Bin Laden, Osama had also learned about administration and the handling of money. In addition, he was interested in what Coll calls "the technologies of global integration": The Bin Ladens had always possessed the latest gadgets. Many Islamists could preach the ideology of fundamentalist jihad. Only Osama could fuse seventh century rhetoric with twentieth century innovations.

He showed himself to be human and hypocritical in other ways, too. When Kuwait temporarily disappeared from the world's map in 1990 (when Saddam Hussein attempted to annex it to Iraq), many Saudis panicked, fearing the same fate for their country. Osama deposited $450,000 in a Swiss bank account as a safety measure and thus began earning $2,500 a month in interest. Later, he would condemn "usury" and the way in which it allegedly enabled "the Jews" to control the economy of the United States, and he would see the presence of coalition "infidel" forces in Saudi Arabia as an outrage upon Islam. At the time, however, he seemed to have no problem with the "outstanding support," in the words of no less an Unbeliever than U.S. Army General Norman Schwarzkopf (who was in charge of the coalition forces in the Gulf War), that Bin Laden Telecommunications afforded U.S. troops or with the handsome profits such support brought.

In time, Osama began to have problems with the Saudi establishment, which disapproved of some of his jihadist activities. Osama left for Sudan, whence he would be ejected due to U.S. pressure. He moved on to Afghanistan, a considerably rougher environment, and his hatred for the United States deepened. "Zionists" and "Crusaders" wanted to take the oil that had been deposited in the birthplace of Islam by God in order to further the triumph of the true faith. The drunken and whoring Saudi princes who had rejected Osama collaborated with them.

Stripped of much of his wealth by the events of the previous five years, Osama went back to marketing and fundraising for Al Qaeda, which he had helped to found. He saw the power of global satellite television networks, gave interviews to CNN and ABC, and recognized before most what Al-Jazeera, an Arabic-language channel based in Qatar, could do. By now the U.S. Central Intelligence Agency (CIA) was listening in on calls from his satellite telephone and getting a sense of Al Qaeda's global presence. Nevertheless, a lack of specificity in intelligence gleanings did not prevent the bombings of U.S. embassies in East Africa. As all the world knows, the same applies to the terrorist attacks of 9/11, organized from remote Afghanistan by a technologically savvy Bin Laden family member whose father and half-brother had both died in plane crashes.

While Osama was using his satellite telephone to direct attacks on the United States, some of his relatives were hoping to make yet more money by investing in that same technology in Washington. The fraught relationship—noted for its compound of admiration, envy, resentment, and hatred—that many in the Third World have with the United States is well reflected in Coll's book, as is the mixture of greed and contempt with which the West has historically responded to Saudi wealth and ostentation. The inextricable melding of cultures, including the global mobility of which Osama had taken such cruel advantage, is even more on display.

The last section of *The Bin Ladens* deals with efforts at damage control made by leading members of a family which now had an unfortunate name; it narrates, too, the story of the flight organized to get Bin Laden family members domiciled in the United States out of the country. Some of the younger passengers looked and sounded more American than Arab; one had just acquired a fake identification card to get into bars and clubs, a piece of laminated plastic he did not foresee using much in Saudi Arabia. Another daughter—who apparently elected to stay, spoke no Arabic, and did not possess a Saudi passport—gave an interview to Barbara Walters. She wanted to become a popular singer and appealed to Americans not to "judge" her "because my values are just like yours."

Coll's thoroughly researched and cleverly written book fascinates. He can turn the occasional phrase: His last, memorable simile describing Osama is to be found on the book's final page. Osama, still "exploiting the channels and the ethos of global integration," is likened to "a Barbary pirate with a marketing degree."

M. D. Allen

Review Sources

Booklist 104, no. 15 (April 1, 2008): 4.
The Daily Telegraph, April 27, 2008, p. 42.
Kirkus Reviews 76, no. 6 (March 15, 2008): 281.

Library Journal 133, no. 8 (May 1, 2008): 84.
Los Angeles Times, April 1, 2008, p. E1.
The New York Review of Books 51, no. 9 (May 27, 2004): 19-22.
The New York Times Book Review, May 25, 2008, p. 11.
The Observer, May 11, 2008, p. 22.
Publishers Weekly 255, no. 13 (March 31, 2008): 54.
The Times Literary Supplement, August 8, 2008, p. 25.
The Washington Post, March 30, 2008, p. T3.

THE BISHOP'S DAUGHTER
A Memoir

Author: Honor Moore (1945-   )
Publisher: W. W. Norton (New York). 365 pp. $25.95
Type of work: Memoir
Time: 1919-2003
Locale: New York City

Moore explores her complex relationship with her father, the revered Episcopal bishop of New York, Paul Moore, Jr., and the impact that his hidden homosexual life had on his priesthood and his family

Principal personages:
> BISHOP PAUL MOORE, JR., a bishop of the
> Episcopal Church
> JENNY MOORE, his wife
> HONOR MOORE, his daughter

Honor Moore first delved into her family history when she published the well-received *The White Blackbird* in 1996, the story of her mercurial maternal grandmother, painter Margarett Sargent. In *The Bishop's Daughter*, she ranges closer to home as she probes the private and public life of her famous father, Bishop Paul Moore, Jr. In recounting her often difficult relationship with him, she comes to terms with a distant, sometimes cruel parent, who was a beloved and respected church leader but who also harbored a secret so painful that it indelibly scarred his relationships with those who loved him most.

In her "Prologue," Moore opens with an image that haunts the book's pages from beginning to end. It is Easter morning in the Cathedral of St. John the Divine in New York City. The choir has finished singing, when three knocks sound in the silence. Then

> the massive doors swing open, an ethereal shaft of sunlight floods the dark, the roar of
> the city breaks the gigantic quiet, and there at the far end of the aisle, in a blaze of morning light, stands the tall figure of a man. My flesh-and-blood father, the bishop.

The contrast between the phrases "my flesh-and-blood father" and "the bishop" captures the tension between the human and the holy that characterized Paul Moore throughout his life. Cloaked in his rich vestments and surrounded by glowing light, the bishop seems godlike and inapproachable. Yet as Honor Moore draws on her own reminiscences, as well as on letters, diaries, and interviews with family and friends, she divests her father of his episcopal accoutrements, demythologizing him in order to discover the man's true self and the reasons for their often contentious relationship. As she does so, it becomes clear that his bishop's crook and miter are not the only things that set Paul Moore apart.

In "Father," the first section of her book, Moore offers an overview of the future bishop's family pedigree and education. Grandson of William Moore, one of the founders of the Bankers Trust Co. and contemporary of such notables as Andrew Carnegie and Henry Clay Frick, Paul Moore was born to a life of wealth and privilege. His family had residences in New York City, New Jersey, Florida, and Prides Crossing, Massachusetts, where he met his first wife and the mother of his nine children, the beautiful socialite Jenny McKean. From an early age, he was sensitive about his family's favored status. He once dove to the floor of a chauffeured limousine as it drove through a blighted neighborhood because he was ashamed to be seen riding in luxury while others were living hand to mouth. His pang of conscience would blossom into full-blown social activism early in his ministry.

While attending the exclusive St. Paul's School, an Episcopal-run boarding school in New Hampshire, Paul underwent a conversion. After his graduation from Yale, he entered the Marine Corps in 1941 and survived a gunshot wound that just missed his heart. His narrow escape from death further cemented his religious sensibilities, and he came to believe that his life was spared for a higher purpose.

After he was ordained to the priesthood in 1949, Reverend Moore became the rector of a parish in Jersey City, New Jersey. His experience in the inner city gave birth to the social activism that would be the hallmark of his ministry. When he was named Dean of Christ Church Cathedral located in conservative Indianapolis, Indiana, he continued to speak out in favor of liberal causes. In 1964, after he was appointed Suffragan Bishop of Washington, D.C., he marched for civil rights with Dr. Martin Luther King, Jr., in Selma, Alabama; protested the Vietnam War; and berated presidents and other government officials for their lack of concern for the poor. In the last sermon he preached before his death in 2003, he strongly criticized President George W. Bush for initiating the war in Iraq.

Moore's brief biography of her father lays the foundation for part two of her book, titled "Daughter." With her declaration, "And so I have come into the story," the genre changes from biography to memoir. She writes movingly and with obvious pain about her struggle to understand why her father was often distant, aloof, and sometimes indifferent to his wife and family. Honor recalls a time when Paul, then a student at General Theological Seminary in New York, brought her to a service of evensong:

> Once after supper, my father swept me up into his black seminarian's cape . . . we climbed the stairs to the seminary and stepped along the grassy path to the chapel. I could already hear it, something like the rushing of the wind, the coming of a storm. We were late, and as we slipped into the pew in the candlelit church full of men, I understood that the rushing sound was singing. . . . I was scared and so I leaned against my father . . . but he didn't look down at me or put his big hand on my head. . . . Now he belonged to something else, this big and strange sound, so deep and loud it made me shake. . . . After that night, I looked at my father with a new curiosity. . . . He was in touch with something that couldn't be seen but was also real. . . . Across the street in the dark, inside the red tower, in the honey light of the candles, was a landscape like a dream, a place to which my father belonged and from which my mother and I were excluded.

◇

*Honor Moore is the author of poetry
collections* Red Shoes *(2005),* Darling
(2001), and Memoir *(1988). She is also
the author of the biography* The White
Blackbird: A Life of the Painter
Margarett Sargent by Her
Granddaughter *(1996), which was
named a* New York Times *Notable
Book. She lives in New York City.*

◇

The passage is both poignant and ironic. Moore's description echoes the dramatic scene at St. John the Divine where the bishop appeared at the door in his regal vestments. The ecclesiastical trappings in which her father felt at home heightens the aura of "otherness" that often surrounds those who enter the priesthood. Her assessment that he seemed "in touch" with something unseen enhances the mythology that frequently envelops the clergy. Moreover, the fact that the seminary was a male fraternity further separated Honor from her father and his vocation. Up until 1975, when the ordination of women was sanctioned by the Episcopal Church, women were prohibited from becoming priests or deacons. Honor's first contact with Paul's ecclesiastical life should have solidified the father-daughter bond, but it only increased the distance between them. Finally, the juxtaposition of this excerpt with the revelation in the next paragraph that Paul had his first full-fledged affair with a married male instructor at the seminary only intensifies his "otherness." The fact that he had a wife and child did little to lessen the influence of his hidden conflict and only served to separate him psychologically and emotionally from his family.

While Paul was periodically surrendering to his "addiction," as he later termed his homosexuality, Honor was exploring her own sexuality. She is open about her love affairs with men, her abortion, her fifteen-year period of loving women, and her return to dating men. She dealt with her sexual confusion by participating in years of therapy, not knowing that her father was bisexual. Jenny had told Honor that she and Paul were having problems in their marriage, and Paul confirmed it. Honor, however, assumed that her parents' marriage was a conventional Christian union between two heterosexual people.

In "Revelations," part three of the book, Honor relates a conversation with one of her mother's friends who told her that Jenny had guessed that Paul had had gay lovers. Brenda, his second wife whom he married after Jenny's death, discovered it was true. Paul's desire for men was very much at odds with church policy on homosexuality at the time he was serving as a priest and later as a bishop. Honor notes, however, that her father believed that "sexuality and religious feeling came from the same place in the psyche"—a heretical idea in the era Paul answered his call to the priesthood. While he was an exemplary priest, he did not fully accept himself as a gay man.

As both father and daughter struggled with their sexuality, Honor tried to help her father accept his gender orientation. In an effort to close the ever-widening emotional gap between them, Honor invited her father to join her in therapy sessions. At first he refused, but then he assented. Their common therapy treatments did not produce the intimacy that both the bishop and his daughter had hoped. Paul remained a remote figure to the end of his life. On one of Honor's visits during Paul's final illness, she reached out to him, but violently he drew back. "I love you," he said, an expression of terror and distaste on his face, "but not . . . so . . . close." He tried to recover himself. "I mean I love you, but . . . ." I had been helping him finish his sentences, and so I helped him complete this one " . . . not that much."

"Yes," he said, holding himself apart, "not that much."

Closure came for Honor after her father's death when, out of the blue, she received a telephone call from a complete stranger. In a chapter titled "Andrew Verver," Honor recounts the conversation she had with the man who claimed to have been Paul's "sexual life" for the previous thirty years. The bishop's daughter drew solace from the fact that her father had enjoyed emotional fulfillment, not just sexual pleasure, with Verver. The chapter caused a firestorm of controversy when it was excerpted in *The New Yorker*, and admirers of the bishop—as well as members of his own family— accused his daughter of sullying his memory. Yet Honor's sensitivity and generosity of spirit are evident when she recounts the story of the pilgrimage she and Verver made to her father's grave.

Some readers may view Bishop Moore as a hypocrite because of his double life. Honor suggests, however, that because homosexuality was an anathema during the era in which he came of age, Paul had no choice but to keep his sexual orientation a secret. Doing so was necessary in order to fulfill his primary passion, which was to serve God. From the 1950's to the 1970's, the church was far from ready to wrestle with the question of whether to ordain gay clergy—until Bishop Moore pushed the issue to the forefront when he ordained a lesbian to the priesthood in 1977. His action could be viewed as an expiation for his own reluctance to acknowledge his homosexuality and as a willingness to create a path for gay clergy that had never been available to him. One wonders how he would react now that the Episcopal Church nears schism over the consecration of Gene Robinson, who was made bishop of New Hampshire shortly after Paul's death in 2003.

Throughout *The Bishop's Daughter*, Honor treats Paul with forgiveness, respect, and ultimately love. Her compassionate portrait of her father is in stark contrast to the memoir of Frank Schaeffer, another scion of a prominent Christian, who wrote *Crazy for God* (2007), a sharp-edged, tell-all story about his well-known parents, evangelicals Francis and Edith Schaeffer. Moore's beautifully written memoir is a wonderful tribute to the quest for redemption and love she and her father shared, and it serves as a poignant reminder that grace often reveals itself amid the struggles and pain that afflict the lives of flawed human beings.

Pegge Bochynski

Review Sources

Booklist 104, no. 16 (April 15, 2008): 8.
Elle 23, no. 10 (June, 2008): 118.
Kirkus Reviews 76, no. 4 (February 15, 2008): 185.
Lambda Book Report 16, nos. 1/2 (Spring/Summer, 2008): 12.
Library Journal 133, no. 8 (May 1, 2008): 66.
Ms. 18, no. 2 (Spring, 2008): 75.
The Nation 286, no. 25 (June 30, 2008): 46.
The New York Times Book Review, May 11, 2008, p. 57.
Newsweek 151, no. 19 (May 12, 2008): 55.
Publishers Weekly 255, no. 9 (March 3, 2008): 38.

THE BLACK HOLE WAR
My Battle with Stephen Hawking to Keep the World Safe for Quantum Mechanics

Author: Leonard Susskind (1940-   )
Publisher: Little, Brown (New York). 470 pp. $27.99
Type of work: Science
Time: 1981-2008

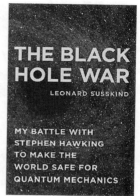

A partly historical, partly autobiographical account of a recent controversy in theoretical physics by one of the physicists involved

Principal personages

NIELS BOHR, Danish theoretical physicist and Nobel laureate, one of the central figures in the development of quantum mechanics

ALBERT EINSTEIN, German-born American physicist best known for his work on relativity theory but also one of the key contributors to early quantum theory

RICHARD FEYNMAN, American physicist and author, Nobel laureate for his contributions to quantum theory

STEPHEN HAWKING, current occupant of Isaac Newton's chair at Cambridge University and one of the principal contributors to the quantum theory of black holes

JOHN POLKINGHORNE, British physicist turned Anglican priest, one of the principal proponents of the anthropic principle

LEONARD SUSSKIND, the author, professor of physics at Stanford University, one of the principal contributors to the theory of black holes

GERARD 'T HOOFT, Dutch theoretical physicist, Nobel laureate for his contributions to the quantum theory of elementary particles and one of Susskind's allies in the black hole war

Modern physics abounds in concepts that capture the imagination. Perhaps no concept has had greater impact on the popular imagination than that of the black hole, a concentration of mass so great that even light cannot escape its gravitational attraction. Black holes can be understood in terms of Albert Einstein's general theory of relativity. The quantum theory of black holes is generally attributed to Stephen Hawking, a British physicist who realized that a black hole could actually evaporate, becoming smaller and emitting elementary particles created from the vacuum as it does so. *The Black Hole War* of the title is a dispute among physicists over the content of black holes, that is, whether the identity of the particles that made up a black hole becomes forever lost to science.

Susskind's book provides a description of the dispute, character sketches of the

◇

Leonard Susskind has been the Felix
Bloch Professor of Theoretical Physics
at Stanford University since 2000. He
received his Ph.D. degree from Cornell
University in 1965, and he has taught
at Yeshiva University and the
University of Tel Aviv. He is a member
of the National Academy of Sciences
and has written several books on
modern cosmology.

◇

disputants, an introduction to the more eso-teric concepts, and anecdotes from scientific conferences and academic culture generally, interspersed in a way that keeps the reader en-tertained. There is Susskind himself, who de-spite his august academic accomplishments—he holds an endowed chair at Stanford—finds a great deal of humor in physics and its devel-opment. There is Hawking, who as Lucasian Professor of Mathematics holds the chair once occupied by Isaac Newton and has been battling Lou Gehrig's disease since graduate school. Hawking now lectures from a wheel-chair using a voice synthesizer; in earlier times he used human translators. Despite his physical limitations, Hawking is regarded as a great showman who can hold an audi-ence's rapt attention. There is Gerard 't Hooft, who early in his career was able to solve some of the key problems of the so-called standard model of elementary particle physics and who is regarded by Susskind as one of the cleverest people in physics. Going back in time there is Albert Einstein, whose equations of general relativity pro-vide the theoretical framework for the big bang cosmology and who rejected the quantum theory as incomplete, and Neils Bohr, mentor to a generation of quantum physicists, who defended it successfully against many of Einstein's counter exam-ples.

Susskind provides qualitative explanations for many modern physics concepts, some of which are part of the average physicist's intellectual toolkit and some of which are familiar only to researchers in the esoteric realm of black holes and strange particles. As he describes it, the human brain, which has evolved to understand the physics of everyday life—for example, how to hit a target with a rock—has to un-dergo a certain amount of rewiring to deal with events outside routine experience. The need for rewiring became apparent when it was realized that light traveled at great but finite speed. Further rewiring is needed to deal with very large and very small num-bers, distances, and time intervals and spaces of different dimensions. Physical theo-ries are nowadays most naturally formulated mathematically, and to communicate them to the layman writers such as Susskind make extensive use of mental pictures and analogies. The analogies will be more helpful to some readers than others.

Many readers will be familiar with the Heisenberg Uncertainty Principle, which states that the position and momentum (mass times velocity) of a particle cannot be si-multaneously known with perfect precision. An important consequence of this is the realization that at an atomic level all matter is in constant motion. Heisenberg and Bohr considered position and momentum to be complementary observables. One could measure the position of a particle in one type of experiment at the cost of giving up information about its momentum, or measure its momentum in another, giving up information about its position. Bohr elevated the notion of complementarity to a gen-eral principle, noting that properties often come in complementary pairs, for which being precise about one implies being imprecise about the other. There is a form of uncertainty principle that treats time and energy as complementary variables. This implies that while energy is conserved over any significant time interval, the principle of energy conservation can be violated for short times, and on the shortest time scales there can be major fluctuations in physical variables. The picture that emerges is not an easy one for human brains to grasp.

The notion of a black hole actually predates relativity. All that is necessary is to have enough matter fall within a small enough volume so that the escape velocity from its surface, located at the Schwarzschild radius, equals the speed of light. In relativity theory, distances and time intervals can vary with the position of the observer. An observer being pulled into a black hole would perceive nothing unusual about the passage of time. A second observer would see the first frozen in time at the Schwarzschild radius.

The history of physics over the past two centuries has been marked by the unification of theories for different phenomena into ever more general theories. This began in the early nineteenth century as a theory of electromagnetism revealed that electricity and magnetism were aspects of the same physical force and that light was an electromagnetic wave, which led to the theory of relativity. The development of quantum mechanics and quantum field theory in the twentieth century provided a coherent description of electromagnetic and nuclear phenomena culminating in the so-called standard model. The unfinished business of fundamental physics is reconciling quantum mechanics with the theory of gravitation.

According to Susskind, the black hole war began in 1981 at a small scientific meeting sponsored by Werner Erhard, the founder of the est Training movement. At this meeting Hawking asserted that information about the particles falling into a black hole would be irretrievably lost. This was inconsistent with the conservation laws known to be true outside of black holes and, since black holes could evaporate, would mean an additional source of entropy and a need to discard trustworthy principles of physics. Susskind and 't Hooft immediately realized the problem, which would take about twenty years to resolve and lead to a number of new concepts in physics. Among these are black hole complementarity, the holographic universe, and extensions of string theory.

Black hole complementarity refers to the different realities that govern a particle falling into a black hole and an observer watching one fall into the hole. The first process is a smooth falling with nothing exceptional about it. The second is of infinite duration—the particle seems frozen at the Schwarzschild radius.

Even stranger is the holographic principle, which claims that the full structure of the universe is contained in a two-dimensional surface, in much the same way that a hologram allows the construction of a three-dimensional image. The hologram's information is contained in a two-dimensional array. By similar reasoning, the information needed to describe the particles that had fallen into a black hole is contained just outside the Schwarzschild radius, that is, for an observer outside the black hole, and available for release in the Hawking radiation released while the hole evaporates. Since information, at a fundamental level, is related to entropy, this is really a statement about the entropy of a black hole, important for extending the second law of thermodynamics, the law-of-entropy increase, to a universe with black holes in it.

To make the holographic principle plausible, Susskind enters into a presentation of string theory. This theory remains controversial within physics: Providing a unified approach to gravitation and the other forces is appealing in its universality but offers very little that can be tested by experiment. In string theory, all particles are treated as one-dimensional strings vibrating in a multidimensional space. The common three dimensions of ordinary space are inadequate. Required are nine spatial dimensions, six of which are of finite extent. To grasp this type of space, a major amount of brain rewiring is necessary. Susskind goes further, to introduce the modern theory of D-branes, which will require even more "rewiring" of the reader's brain.

Throughout his exposition, Susskind provides interesting sidelights on the personalities in physics and on academic culture. He describes his encounters with Richard Feynman, iconoclast, master showman, and genius, first as a young physics professor in 1972. The reader finds Hawking in his wheelchair, racing down a hill in San Francisco at breakneck speed, to the astonishment of his able-bodied friends. The reader learns that at one of the colleges of Cambridge University, only full professors are permitted to walk on the grass; all lower ranks must keep to the walkways.

Susskind is a frequent writer and speaker on science and religion and was intrigued by the juxtaposition of religious symbolism and scientific cosmology found on the Cambridge University campus. He confesses to a mild case of "cathedralitis," in which the stained glass and the vaulted archways of the Cambridge colleges inspire a sort of religious feeling even in the nonbeliever. The modern Cambridge faculty includes outright atheists as well as many committed to traditional religion. Susskind wonders why religious feeling has persisted, when it conveys no evolutionary advantage Particularly interesting is John Polkinghorne, a Ph.D. physicist based at Cambridge who entered the Anglican priesthood later in life. Polkinghorne is one of the major proponents of the anthropic principle, the claim that, had the fundamental constants of nature, the mass of the electron, or the constant in Newton's law of gravitational force been even slightly different, the world as we know it, with life based on the chemistry of carbon compounds, could not possibly exist. Whether this principle, along with string theory and D-branes, will endure as physics progresses remains to be seen.

Donald R. Franceschetti

Review Sources

Discover 29, no. 7 (July, 2008): 73.
Library Journal 133, no. 11 (June 15, 2008): 89.
Los Angeles Times Book Review, July 13, 2008, p. R2.
Nature 454 (July 31, 2008): 579-580.
New Scientist 199 (July 5, 2008): 46.
The New York Times Book Review, August 24, 2008, p. 16.
Publishers Weekly 255, no. 20 (May 19, 2008): 48.
Science News 174, no. 9 (October 25, 2008): 29.
Sky & Telescope 117, no. 2 (December, 2009): 43.

THE BOAT

Author: Nam Le (1978-   )
Publisher: Alfred A. Knopf (New York). 272 pp. $22.95
Type of work: Short fiction
Time: 1945 to 2005
Locale: Worldwide

Le's first book offers seven short stories that cover the globe and feature an amazingly varied cast of central characters; his plots include assassinations in Colombia, a failed family reunion in New York City, religious festivals in Iran, and escape from Communist Vietnam

Principal characters:
    NAM LE, a character named after the author,
      struggling with writer's block
    JUAN PABLO "RON" MERENDEZ, a teenage assassin in Colombia
    HENRY LUFF, a middle-aged New York painter who tries to meet his
      long-estranged daughter
    JAMIE, an Australian teenager who faces a vicious bully
    MAYAKO, a Japanese schoolgirl who survives the bombing of Hiroshima
    SARAH MIDDLETON, an American lawyer visiting her college friend in
      Tehran
    MAI, a sixteen-year-old Vietnamese refugee cast on the open sea

The most outstanding feature of the Vietnamese Australian writer Nam Le's first book, *The Boat*, is the remarkable variety of the seven short stories in the collection. Only the first and the last story deal with Vietnam. The others cover a wide range of locales, taking the reader to Colombia, New York City, Australia, Japan, and Iran. They span six decades from the end of World War II to the early twenty-first century. Each story tells a fresh tale, and Le masterfully presents central characters who have to meet an existential challenge.

"Love and Honor and Pity and Pride and Compassion and Sacrifice" introduces Le's readers to his convictions and self-understanding as a writer. Cleverly mixing the autobiographical and the fictitious, the central character is named Nam Le like the author himself. The character Le is given many of the author's characteristics, but the author adds strong fictional deviations. By doing so, Le challenges the reader not to fall into the trap of reading his fiction as a mere exploration of his personal experience.

Like his author from 2004 to 2005, Le is a Vietnamese Australian ex-lawyer who has become a fellow at the famous Iowa Writers' Workshop that has nurtured many contemporary literary talents. As Le is facing a final deadline to write a story, he is visited by his estranged father from Australia. Now Le tries any trick to overcome his writer's block, and he uses an old typewriter instead of a computer to stop himself from endlessly revising. While thinking, he remembers a conversation with a fellow aspiring writer. It is through this imaginary conversation that author Le offers a strong view of his beliefs as a writer.

A friend offers Le a surefire shortcut to solve his problem: "just write a story about Vietnam." That fits with Le's observation of the contemporary American literary market. As an instructor tells him, "ethnic literature's hot" and "visiting literary agents" admonish young writers to write only from their own "*background* and *life experience*." Against

∽
Nam Le worked as a lawyer in Australia before receiving a fellowship from the Iowa Writers' Workshop in 2004. His short stories won for Le writer's fellowships and the Michener-Copernicus Society of America Award in 2007, and "Cartagena" earned him the Pushcart Prize XXXII that same year. In 2008, Le was fiction editor of the Harvard Review.
∽

this, Le's friend quotes the words of William Faulkner, which give the story its title. This list that starts with "Love and Honor" suggests that literature should be about what truly matters in human experience. As a parting shot, his friend tells Le that he admires him for his struggle against an easy way out: "You could *totally* exploit the Vietnamese thing. But *instead*, you choose to write about lesbian vampires and Colombian assassins, and Hiroshima orphans—and New York painters with hemorrhoids."

The Boat features stories on all those topics, with the exception of the lesbian vampires, indicating Le's fondness to mix fact with fiction.

As Le yields to the temptation to write an "ETHNIC STORY" to make his deadline, he chooses as its subject his father's survival of the infamous 1968 My Lai massacre of American troops in Vietnam. In reality, author Le's father grew up in a different location, in Rach Gia, south of My Lai, and has no connections to that atrocity.

In the story, Le is poetically punished for abandoning his quest for true literary art as his father burns the typewritten pages of that story in the gasoline drum of a homeless man they had befriended earlier. The reader will not find this story among author Le's fiction.

True to Le's belief in the necessity to expand the horizon of his fiction, "Cartagena," which won the 2007 Pushcart Prize, takes the reader into the world of teenage Colombian assassins. Violent social and dire economic circumstances, as well as a vicious civil war and the international cocaine trade, have turned the children's lives into premature hell. Juan Pablo Merendez, called "Ron" for his childhood feat of drinking Ron de Medellin tequila without vomiting, slithers into a criminal life. It began once he and his friend Hernando were kidnapped by a corrupt policeman and a pedophile Colombian businessman.

After Hernando killed both their captors with the policeman's gun, Ron decided to throw in his lot with the assassination squads of underground figure El Padre, himself a victim of Colombia's cruel war against radical Communist insurgents. Now Ron kills for money that allows him to buy a safe house in the barrio for his mother, who lost her husband to right-wing militias—Le is careful to show that murder is committed on both sides of the Colombian political divide.

Eventually ordered to kill Hernando, who works to get street kids out of gangs, Ron refuses and is called to meet El Padre. Characteristically for Le's central characters, Ron is pushed to the limit of endurance by his author. Le stops Ron's story just short of its likely conclusion, but he does not leave much doubt about the eventual dark outcome.

In "Meeting Elise," fifty-something New York painter Henry Luff desperately tries to meet with his estranged daughter, Elise. She is a famous cellist about to be married to her British manager. Henry has not seen his daughter since her Russian mother took her away as a toddler after Henry started an affair with his young model, Olivia. Told from a convincing first-person point of view, Henry is a character whose body seems to give out when his hemorrhoids are diagnosed as likely indicators of colon cancer. His mental collapse in the face of Elise's ultimate rejection is reminiscent of Nobel Prize winner Saul Bellow's character of Wilhelm Adler in his 1956 novel *Seize the Day*. "Meeting Elise" shows impressively how Le can create pathetic characters that evoke a reader's pity for their demoralizing situation.

"Halflead Bay" presents a moving coming-of-age story in which Jamie, a good-natured high school kid in a backwater, run-down Australian seashore town, has to face Dory Townsend, a vicious bully, rapist, and murderer. Jamie's winning football goal has pushed his school into the final and suddenly has given him a certain clout at school and the dubious attention of the popular girl Allison Fischer, Dory's girlfriend.

As Jamie struggles with family problems—his mother is dying of multiple sclerosis—he is haunted by the idea of incurring Dory's wrath for accepting Allison's obvious invitation. He remembers how Dory viciously beat up a previous rival and, with his sycophant buddy Lester, raped and killed a Chinese girl, "the young woman's body . . . found in the swale—within shouting distance of where Dory lived with his uncle." The police let the teenagers go for lack of direct evidence and underlying institutional racism.

After Jamie sleeps with Allison, he is challenged to a fight by Dory. Moved by the appeal of Jamie's father, who brings into his office his wheelchair-bound mother, and concerned about Jamie's availability for the football final, the principal effectively cancels the fight. Yet Jamie feels cheated and challenges Dory at his shack. Allison is there and betrays Jamie by goading on Dory to beat up Jamie before his father comes up and leads him away. The story strikes a fine balance between Jamie's need to prove himself and his realization that his father genuinely cares about him.

From its narrative structure, "Hiroshima" is a story about the irony of fate. Not being granted one's dearest wish may actually save one's life because of a cruel twist of circumstances. The story's narrator, Mayako, is a third grader evacuated from Hiroshima at the end of World War II in the Pacific. She wishes nothing more than to be reunited with her parents and big sister, who continue to live in the city. On August 6, 1945, Mayako feels faint heat on her cheeks from the flash of the distant atom bomb, which signals the deaths of her family and her survival.

What makes Le's "Hiroshima" particularly powerful is his authentic rendition of the mind-set of Mayako. She has totally internalized imperial Japanese propaganda of the period. By telling the story completely from her point of view, showing her belief in honor and sacrifice without the slightest trace of doubt, Le creates a masterful tale that moves his readers to great compassion for his young protagonist.

"Tehran Calling" features thirty-something lawyer Sarah Middleton, who, after breaking up with her lawyer colleague Paul, decides to visit her Iranian college friend Parvin during the Shiite's Ashura festival in Tehran. The story closely follows Sarah as she enters the alien city for the first time.

Once Sarah meets Parvin at the home of her privileged parents, she encounters the cultural fissure between official religious doctrine and private transgressions. Parvin leads a party of reformists, and Sarah learns about the tragedies in her friend's life, such as the death of her brother in the Iran-Iraq war of the 1980's. Determined to challenge the authorities with a play about a thirteen-year-old girl killed by religious radicals, Parvin disappears and her fiancé Mahmoud goes with Sarah to find her. When Sarah sleeps with Mahmoud after their close call with the militias, while Parvin is still unaccounted for, there is a sense of multiple betrayals that underlines quite a few of Le's stories.

Only the final story of Le's book returns to the topic of Vietnam. "The Boat" tells of the harrowing experience of sixteen-year-old Mai. Her family has placed Mai on a boat full of refugees trying to escape the hardships of Communist Vietnam in the late 1970's. A storm wreaks havoc with the boat, and the refugees find themselves without engine power and rapidly dwindling resources. Mai befriends Quyen, mother of the six-year-old boy Truong. The boy shares the same name of one of the author's brothers, yet another instance in which Le mixes the autobiographical and the fictional. Truong attracts Mai's attention because he sings a forlorn Vietnamese folk song, reminding her of her mother.

As the ship's captain, the saintly Anh Phuoc, tries to steer the boat toward a friendly coast with the help of an emergency sail, people start dying. Like a Bodhisattva who could enter Nirvana but chooses to stay in this world to guide others to Buddhist fulfillment, Phuoc has made the passage to freedom already, but he chooses to return to Vietnam to rescue others.

Indicative of the narrative doubling in "The Boat," first Mai falls seriously ill but recovers. Then it is Truong's turn, and the boy dies on the day that land is finally in sight. By contrast, the author's real brother survived such an ordeal.

Le's *The Boat* met with enthusiastic critical reception in the United States. Michiko Kakutani, the influential critic of *The New York Times*, praised his work for its portrayal of characters facing extreme life circumstances. A day after this favorable review, the paper published a rave interview of Le. With a sense for irony, he met the journalist at the same New York restaurant where Henry waits in vain to encounter his daughter Elise in "Meeting Elise." Critics overwhelmingly agree that Le has succeeded in offering an extraordinary first collection of short stories.

R. C. Lutz

Review Sources

Booklist 104, no. 17 (May 1, 2008): 69.
Entertainment Weekly, May 16, 2008, p. 70.
Esquire 149, no. 6 (June, 2008): 44.
Kirkus Reviews 76, no. 7 (April 1, 2008): 325.
Library Journal 133, no. 8 (May 1, 2008): 62.
The New York Review of Books 55, no. 18 (November 20, 2008): 38-40.
The New York Times Book Review, June 8, 2008, p. 8.
Publishers Weekly 255, no. 3 (March 31, 2008): 37.
The Times Literary Supplement, October 10, 2008, p. 21.
The Washington Post, July 16, 2008, p. C8.

BOOKS
A Memoir

Author: Larry McMurtry (1936-　　)
Publisher: Simon & Schuster (New York). 259 pp.
　$24.00
Type of work: Memoir

A semiautobiographical account of the author's life as a bookman, providing glimpses into the arcane and complex trade of bookseller and highlighting interesting books, characters, and personages he has known

Principal personage:
　　LARRY MCMURTRY, author and bookseller

A bookman is a person who lives for, by, and with books. Not simply a bookseller, a bookman (or bookperson) is someone for whom books are a governing metaphor, providing not only financial but also social and intellectual support. It would seem that with the advent of online bookselling, the physical bookstore, particularly the secondhand and antiquarian bookstore, may be a thing of the past, but in this memoir Larry McMurtry, author of *Lonesome Dove* (1985) and *Terms of Endearment* (1975), among many others, in a ramble through his life as a bookman, lovingly and somewhat dryly illuminates his love of books and how his life has been shaped by them and the people who buy and sell them.

McMurtry has had a dual career: novelist/essayist and bookman. For many years he has operated Booked Up, first in Washington, D.C., and more recently in his hometown Archer City, Texas (the prototype for the fictional Thalia in McMurtry's 1966 novel *The Last Picture Show*). This Booked Up is a massive bibliographic enterprise, sprawling over four separate locations (including a former automobile showroom) in the small north-central Texas town.

Books: A Memoir is as much a memoir of books as it is of McMurtry, and it begins with a description of a box of nineteen books, adolescent literature given to McMurtry as a child by an older relative. McMurtry writes that the books "changed my life." These books are the genesis of both McMurtry's intellectual life and the memoir itself, launching the book on its seriatim evocation of important books and bookpeople that have influenced McMurtry's life.

McMurtry's first book, from the box of nineteen, is Sergeant Silk, *The Prairie Scout* (1929). Few people (except book lovers) can remember the first book that they ever read. It is significant that McMurtry can, and he chronicles how this early collection set him on his diverse reading and acquisition journey.

McMurtry's journey is not without its stumbles. He tells of books that he sold for a relatively small amount of money that soon after realized a much higher price. "*Les*

Larry McMurtry won the Pulitzer Prize for his novel Lonesome Dove *(1985) and was the screenwriter, with Diana Ossana, of the 2005 film version of E. Annie Proulx's story "Brokeback Mountain." Several of his books have been made into films, including* Horseman, Pass By *(1961, as* Hud*),* The Last Picture Show *(1966), and* Terms of Endearment *(1975). McMurtry has written more than twenty novels, several screenplays, and collections of essays. He operates a multilocation bookstore, Booked Up, in Archer City, Texas.*

Jeux de la poupée, the famous tortured-doll book by the Belgian surrealist Hans Bellmer," was sold by McMurtry for $45, then sold by another for $120, and later was on sale for $5,000. Another time, a bookstore McMurtry managed acquires valuable historical letters that are likely stolen.

The writer regales the reader with stories of the bookpeople he has known through the years: Dorman David (the acquirer of the shady letters), "who seemed to simply attract good things" (but was a poor businessperson and eventually left the country to avoid bankruptcy); David's mother (and McMurtry's early employer), Grace, a charming woman who had nineteen telephones in her home; Gershon Legman, mysterious scholar of erotica who hid his library of books, in a French Templar monastery, from McMurtry. While the personalities are not always eccentric or offbeat, McMurtry shows them respect.

Perhaps some of the best stories involve the bookshops, dozens of which McMurtry mentions in passing: Lowdermilk's in Washington, D.C., the auction of whose books started the original institution of McMurtry's D.C. store; an unnamed bookshop whose proprietor slept in the store; another bookstore run by "a nice retired CIA man." The stores are clearly characters in their own right, places that live and evolve with the acquisition and sale of libraries, stocks of other bookstores waning with the passage of time, the death of the booksellers, and the advent of online bookselling. McMurtry portrays the bookstores as organic, evolving entities. In many ways these moments in the memoir—in which McMurtry notes the passing of a long-lived or memorable bookstore or bookseller—become an elegy for a way of work and life now lost. These anecdotes are augmented by ones about the people who own and work in the stores and the varied customers who enter, with their diverse requests and reasons for seeking a particular book.

The stories—small, intimate portraits of transactions with like-minded bookpeople—are perhaps not significant in themselves but in aggregate are quite telling. It is in the compilation that the memoir gains its force, the accretion of one story after another and one book after another. By the middle of the book the reader begins to share McMurtry's quiet excitement over a good find, a good deal on a book, an interesting collector or bookseller. It is a quiet enthusiasm, but nonetheless a seductive one.

Even so, this memoir does not follow a traditional linear structure, though the book does (generally) begin with McMurtry's childhood and end with a list of the bookstores McMurtry dealt with that are now shadows of their former selves or gone altogether. This is an easy, but not typical, book to read. The chapters are quite short (109 chapters in a book less than 260 pages long), making the memoir much more a series of vignettes than a continuous narrative. This might be a problem for a reader expecting extended commentary on a particular book or character. (As McMurtry writes, "Here I am thirty-four chapters into a book that I hope will interest the general or common reader—and yet why should these readers be interested in the fact that in 1958 or so I paid Ted Brown $7.50 for a nice copy of *The Anatomy of Melancholy?*")

Books: A Memoir is essentially a ramble, a saunter, a serendipitous walk through McMurtry's long experience with books. For example, the sixth chapter—less than two pages long—starts with a discussion of how McMurtry's childhood isolation on a ranch shaped his reading, then mentions the Republic Pictures serials (with footnotes on books about them), and ends with a reflection on the persistence of the Yellow Peril fears of the early twentieth century. In addition, in chapter 5 the reader finds out why it is necessary to discover that McMurtry took Katherine Drew's history class at Rice University (because, as he notes, McMurtry was helped in learning history by having read the *World Book* encyclopedia as a child).

As a result, the book is quite informal, with a slightly desultory and laconic style, as if the chapters were preliminary notes for a more ambitious project or perhaps for a long essay rather than for a book-length study. Some chapters could be transcripts for a speech. To judge the book on this element alone, however, would not be completely fair. Indeed, this reads like a meandering walk through a large and diverse bookstore, where one finds by surprise books on one topic shelved with books on completely different topics (The Web site for McMurtry's bookstore asserts that the books are arranged "whimsically"). This memoir, then, provides an effective metaphor for McMurtry's life, engaging for readers who understand books not only as repositories of stories and information but also as mileposts of an individual's intellectual progress and of a culture's social and moral development. While this is no *Education of Henry Adams* (1918) in scope, it can certainly be said to be an "education of Larry McMurtry" and the beginning of an education for a booklover as well.

Bob Whipple

Review Sources

Booklist 104, nos. 19/20 (June 1, 2008): 28.
The Christian Science Monitor, July 8, 2008, p. 13.
Kirkus Reviews 76, no. 10 (May 15, 2008): 58.
Library Journal 133, no. 13 (August 15, 2008): 84.
The New York Review of Books 55, no. 13 (August 14, 2008): 54-56.
The New York Times Book Review, September 14, 2008, p. 31.
Publishers Weekly 255, no. 21 (May 26, 2008): 54.

THE BRASS VERDICT

Author: Michael Connelly (1957-   )
Publisher: Little, Brown (New York). 422 pp. $26.99
Type of work: Novel
Time: The present
Locale: The Los Angeles area

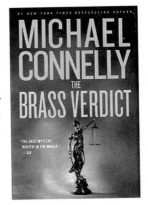

Connelly's two sleuths, defense attorney Michael Haller and police detective Harry Bosch, share the spotlight in this novel about the murder of a Hollywood mogul's wife, her lover, and the film producer's lawyer

Principal characters:
> MICHAEL HALLER, a defense attorney,
> formerly a Los Angeles public defender
> HARRY (HIERONYMOUS) BOSCH, a Los
> Angeles Police Department detective
> WALTER ELLIOT, Hollywood film producer, on trial for murdering his
> wife and her lover
> NINA ALBRECHT, Elliot's secretary and lover
> MARY TOWNES HOLDER, the chief judge and administrator of the Los
> Angeles Superior Court system
> DENNIS (CISCO) WOJCICHOWSKI, a freelance investigator and Haller's
> trusted legman

A distinguishing trait of Michael Connelly's novels—starting with *The Black Echo* (1992) and continuing to *The Overlook* (2007)—is the deliberate manner with which he incrementally develops the character of his primary detective, so that Hieronymous Bosch is by the thirteenth book a more fully realized persona than is the norm for the mystery genre. Details of his checkered career with the Los Angeles Police Department, of his failed marriages and subsequent liaisons, of his difficult relationship with his daughter, of his efforts to resolve questions about his past, and of his passion for jazz loom large, albeit tangentially related to plot. In *The Lincoln Lawyer* (2005), Connelly introduced a new sleuth, defense attorney Michael Haller, who uses a Lincoln Town Car as his office and shares with Bosch an uneven career path, rocky relationships with women, and troubled parenting. Readers presumably will learn more about him in subsequent books. In *The Brass Verdict*, Haller's second appearance, Connelly pits Bosch against Haller, a detective supporting the prosecution versus an attorney for the defense. Presenting them as adversaries adds texture to the narrative and makes ironic the eventual revelation that they are half-brothers, sons of the late J. Michael Haller, a famous criminal defense lawyer.

Whereas the Bosch novels are police procedurals, the Haller books are primarily legal thrillers or procedurals, though written in the same gritty, realistic style. Almost a third of *The Brass Verdict* takes place in court, and the novel recalls Erle Stanley Gardner's formulaic Perry Mason books, which also portray a defense attorney in battles of wit and will who occasionally twists the law in behalf of clients. Haller, who has been disciplined by the bar for questionable behavior, believes "a trial is a contest of lies" and offers this mantra at the beginning of the novel: "Cops lie. Lawyers lie. Witnesses lie. The victims lie." Later he adds: "Clients lie. Even jurors lie." In sum, a courtroom lawyer cannot be concerned only with innocence, guilt, or justice but often must resort to connivance and manipulation, which reinforces Haller's cynical belief that he lives in a corrupt milieu. In the Bosch novels, wayward cops and other rogue law enforcers are exposed; in *The Brass Verdict*, corruption in a court system is Connelly's focus, and he follows his standard narrative pattern of an apparently simple case unfolding into complexity as Haller pursues

∿

Michael Connelly, a native of Florida, has worked as a newspaper crime reporter. The Black Echo *(1992) received an Edgar Award for the best first novel of the year, and he also has received the Grand Prix Award (France) and Anthony, Macavity, and Shamus prizes. In 2003-2004 he was president of the Mystery Writers of America.*

∿

new leads. A present crime has its origin in an earlier one, past events provide clues to present motives and events, and exposure and unraveling threaten reputations, positions, and lives.

The Brass Verdict (the title refers to a killing that comes down to simple street justice) starts with a reflective prologue about Haller as public defender beating attorney Jerry Vincent in a trial that ends the latter's prosecutorial career. Fifteen years later, Vincent is a successful defense attorney whose current clients include Hollywood film producer Walter Elliot, who is charged with murdering his wife and her lover. While preparing his case, Vincent is killed, and Haller inherits his former rival's practice, a timely windfall because Haller had not worked for two years while recovering from a gunshot wound (suffered at the end of *The Lincoln Lawyer*) and addiction to painkillers that required rehabilitation.

While familiarizing himself with the complexities of the high-profile and lucrative Elliot case and dealing with other Vincent clients, Haller is distracted by death threats that murder-homicide detective Bosch investigates. The Elliot case is Connelly's main plot, and though Vincent's murder at first seems unrelated, its connection is apparent when the Federal Bureau of Investigation becomes involved. Beyond these plots is one involving another former Vincent client, Eli Wyms, a man who is apprehended during a shooting spree. A recurring Connelly device is to enrich his novels with seemingly irrelevant characters and incidents whose significance slowly emerges. The Wyms case is an example. Wondering why Vincent would take it pro bono and expend so much effort on it, Haller realizes that hapless Wyms's troubles somehow may provide the "magic bullet," key evidence Haller will spring upon the court at a crucial moment to clinch his victory.

Elliot, who twelve years earlier had "traded in his wife for a newer model," suspected she was having an affair with their German interior decorator and was concerned about her threat to divorce him. He says he discovered the pair's bodies in his home and called 911, but because gunshot residue is on his hands and clothes, and he had motive and opportunity, the police arrest him. His position is tenuous (though no weapon has been found), but he is unconcerned about the possibility of a conviction and dismissive of Haller's requests for cooperation. Frustrated, Haller says: "There's something I don't know about this case and you are holding back on it with me . . . . You are too confident . . . . It's like ya know you are going to walk." Much later Elliot tells Haller a story of his Florida past, including indebtedness to the mob, whom he says killed his wife so she would not get half his fortune. Haller's skepticism increases, and when he threatens to quit the case, he describes Elliot's reaction: "I saw his face grow tight with checked anger. In that moment, I knew he could be a killer, or at least someone who could order it done."

Albeit frustrated by an uncooperative client, Haller is a skilled courtroom advocate, deftly tailoring his querying of witnesses to lead the prosecution astray, such as when he wants to shift the opposing attorney's attention from something. While preparing for his days in court, Haller also continues to review Vincent's financial records and concludes that he transferred a large portion of Elliot's advance to someone as a bribe and was killed because of it. Pressed, Elliot tells Haller that the trial is fixed, but with the understanding there would be no delays or continuances. When Vincent decided to delay the trial, he was murdered before filing a motion. Reviewing the possibilities, Haller realizes "that there was only one aspect that would change if the trial were delayed and rescheduled . . . the jury pool changes week to week." Elliot tells Haller that Vincent was offered a chance to salt the jury, to empanel someone who would support the defense during deliberations and stand fast for acquittal, but the trial would have to remain on track to assure that the plan would work. Haller assumes that Vincent decided to ask for a continuance because he came across exculpatory evidence and thus did not need a fix. He already had the magic bullet.

Haller, rusty from two years' absence, has to juggle two demanding problems: getting his client acquitted and resolving the bribery matter. Central to both, apparently, is juror number seven, and Haller asks his private investigator Cisco to shadow this person and learn everything about him. In the event, the legman gets what his boss needs: A legitimate potential juror's name and perhaps his summons were hijacked, and a ringer took his place. Connelly thus introduces another plot to his multiple narrative, further increasing the pressure on Haller, who is being stalked by a potential assassin, thinks the trial has been fixed by parties unknown, and has an uncooperative client who may be complicit in three murders. Nevertheless, he says, "I felt like a guy flipping a three-hundred-pound sled in midair. It might not be a sport but it was dangerous as hell and it did what I hadn't been able to do in more than a year's time. It shook off the rust and put the charge back in my blood." So inspired, he is ready for the defense phase of the trial. Before the session begins, however, the judge calls

Haller and the prosecutor into his chambers and shows them an anonymous letter: "Judge Stanton, you should know that juror number seven is not who you think he is and not who he says he is. Check Lockheed and check his prints. He's got an arrest record." Juror number seven, indeed a ringer, goes missing, but the judge decides to resume the trial with an alternate. When Haller informs him, "Elliot stiffened and looked like somebody had just pressed a letter opener two inches into his back . . . . I looked at the pleading look on my client's face and realized he'd never had any faith in his own defense. He had been counting solely on the sleeping juror."

Haller's first defense witness, a freelance videographer who responds to crime scene reports on police scanners, shows his video of Elliot's arrest, focusing on the patrol car and Elliot in handcuffs. The second witness is the driver of the car that took crazed gunman Wyms to jail and confirms that his vehicle later transported Elliot. Haller is now ready to call his star witness, a forensics expert whose testimony is that the gunshot residue on Elliot's hands and clothing was inconsistent with that which results from firing a weapon but rather was transferred by contact. In other words, Elliot was contaminated by residue in the vehicle that transported him. On the cusp of this success, Haller learns from Cisco that his contacts in Florida report that Elliot's tale of being in thrall to the mob is a lie. Confronted, Elliot admits he cribbed his story from a rejected film script in order to light a fire under Haller, to "bring your best game" and be "goddamn relentless." He then describes how he, with Nina Albrecht's help, committed the double murder, taking care to wear gloves and to dispose of the gun, but never thinking of residue transference. When Haller asks him if he killed Vincent, he replies, "No, I didn't. But it was a lucky break because I ended up with a better lawyer."

In a Connelly novel, prior to a plethora of rapidly moving events signaling the approaching conclusion, the detective usually is lured into a life-threatening trap. Indeed, Haller is ambushed at night by the phony juror (David McSweeney), but Bosch and FBI agents arrive at the crucial moment. To cap the evening, Bosch tells Haller that his client Elliot and Albrecht, his secretary and lover, were dead, probably killed by juror number seven, and that the judge would discharge the jury and end the trial. After that formality, Haller goes to Judge Holder's chambers, tells her, "I know that you are for sale and that you tried to have me killed," and presents his reconstruction of the events, including her sending McSweeney to kill Elliot and then him. She protests, but since McSweeney has sung, the judge and her lackeys are indicted for conspiracy to commit murder and corruption in plots spanning many years. Finally, Haller admits to Bosch that he sent the anonymous letter and thus "started this whole thing tumbling," because he wanted McSweeney off the jury so he could "then win the case fair and square," but did not expect the judge to consult with colleagues, including Holder, about the letter. Connelly spins yet another twist to the convoluted plot when Bosch tells Haller that McSweeney had killed only Vincent; the family of Mitzi Elliot's murdered lover exacted their revenge by shooting Elliot and Albrecht and immediately returning to Germany. This unexpected Connelly fillip, which shocks Haller, is gratuitous and unnecessary, but regular readers have come to expect such last-minute surprises.

Connelly's novels, heavily promoted by his publisher and supported by his extensive tours, are best sellers worldwide because they are compellingly readable, even if he is not a skilled prose stylist. The first-person narrative voice of his sleuth always is flat and unchanging, and everyone else sounds the same, unlike the characters of Elmore Leonard, a master of realistic dialogue in whose novels everyone has a distinctive voice. However, Connelly's complex plots invariably are page turners, sometimes with contrived denouements, but always with unexpected conclusions. Important, too, are Bosch and Haller, whose professional acumen trumps their flaws and who basically are likable men with whom the reader empathizes and looks forward to meeting again in a later novel.

Gerald H. Strauss

Review Sources

Booklist 104, no. 22 (August 1, 2008): 5.
Entertainment Weekly, October 17, 2008, p. 18.
Library Journal 133, no. 14 (September 1, 2008): 114.
The New York Times, October 13, 2008, p. 1.
The New York Times Book Review, October 19, 2008, p. 30.
Publishers Weekly 255, no. 33 (August 18, 2008): 38.
The Wall Street Journal 252, no. 98 (October 24, 2008): A17.

BREATH

Author: Tim Winton (1960-   )
Publisher: Farrar, Straus and Giroux (New York).
  218 pp. $23.00
Type of work: Novel
Time: The late 1960's and early 1970's
Locale: Sawyer, a small mill town near Angelus, on the
  western coast of Australia

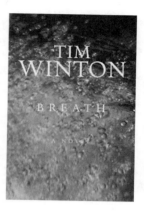

A coming-of-age story about a young man who learns about life and death from a guru surfer and his American wife

Principal characters:
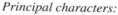
  BRUCE PIKE ("PIKELET"), adolescent boy
    who later becomes a paramedic
  IVAN LOON ("LOONIE"), his reckless companion during adolescence
  BILLY SANDERSON ("SANDO"), a mid-thirties ex-surfing champion
  EVA SANDERSON, Sando's wife, a twenty-five-year-old American skiing
    champion
  QUEENIE COOKSON, a girl with whom Pikelet had a relationship in high
    school

Although many American readers may not be familiar with the fiction of Tim Winton, he is one of Australia's most popular writers. His novel *Cloudstreet* (1991) topped the list of favorite books compiled by several thousand Australian radio listeners in 2002 and also by several hundred members of the Australian Society of Authors. His novel *Dirt Music* (2001) was third and fourth on the two lists, respectively.

After publishing a well-received collection of short stories, *The Turning* (2004), Winton returns to the novel format. *Breath* is a traditional bildungsroman about the coming of age of a young man in a small town on the western coast of Australia in the early 1970's. It begins with a brief account of the middle-aged protagonist Bruce Pike making an emergency call as a paramedic in an Australian city. Later, after Pike awakens from a dream of being underwater and seeing himself swimming down to rescue himself, he plays his didjeridu (an Australian wind instrument) and begins the story of his youth in Sawyer, a small mill town a few miles from the sea on the western coast of Australia.

Pike is a solitary child with parents older than those of his friends; the only thing he excels at is swimming. He is eleven when he meets Ivan Loon, nicknamed Loonie, a twelve-year-old, who tricks people into thinking he is drowning in the river by holding his breath for a long time under water. On a dare, Pike, nicknamed Pikelet (little fish), proves he can hold his breath for a long time, also. Thus begins the central metaphor that gives the book its title and unifies it thematically.

Loonie is an urchin, usually on his own, and given to taking chances, something

∼

Tim Winton is one of Australia's best-known writers. His novels The Riders *(1994) and* Dirt Music *(2001) were short-listed for the Booker Prize. His novels* Shallows *(1984) and* Cloudstreet *(1991) won the Miles Franklin Award.*

∼

that the more timid Pikelet yearns to emulate. The two boys fulfill their desire for risk one day when they bicycle to the ocean and watch a group of surfers. Although Pike says he could not have expressed it when he was a boy, he realizes now that what so fascinated him about surfing was seeing men do something beautiful, something pointless and elegant, that he had not seen before in the ordinary men, such as his father, in his hometown. The two boys become obsessed with surfing, chopping firewood to earn enough money to buy used surfboards and learning the sport by watching a group of surfers. They are just on the cusp of adolescence when they meet Billy Sanderson, nicknamed Sando, a surf bum who lets them leave their boards at his house on the beach.

Winton's most explicit statement of the novel's unifying theme occurs when he shifts narrative perspective back to the adult Pike blowing on his didji, saying he has been thinking about the enigma of respiration as long as he can remember. He notes how funny it is that you never really think much about breathing, until it is all you ever think about. He remembers the birth of his two daughters and the moment after they are suctioned and draw their first breaths. He thinks about the rude shock of respiration, which in a moment or two becomes automatic, that is, until your first asthma attack or the first time you encounter a stranger trying to draw breath; then you can no longer take breathing for granted. When the novel shifts back to the primary time frame of Pike's adolescence, he and Loonie practice holding their breath until they are so good at it that Pike thinks this is what sets them apart from everyone else.

Pike's relationship with Loonie is a combination of admiration and fear. Whereas Loonie hurls himself at the world like a madman, Pikelet cautiously holds back; Loonie fascinates Pikelet, but also exhausts him, making him glad sometimes to get back to the routine of school after their weekend trips to the beach, admitting that he likes the privacy of books. At the beginning of summer vacation, the two boys discover a box of magazines under Sando's house filled with pictures and stories about his legendary surfing competitions. During the summer, Sando teaches them about surfing and shows them the riskiest places to surf, encouraging them to even more hero-worship, while Eva, Sando's young American wife, seems only to tolerate them and scorn their idolatry of her husband.

Related to the theme of breath in the book is the theme of taking risks, facing danger, something that Loonie embraces manically, but from which Pikelet holds back. In an interview, Winton has said that he intended *Breath* to be about how young people struggle to escape the ordinary, how they try to find a place for themselves by doing what others fear to do. However, Pike often wonders if their risk taking is nothing more than a rebellion against the monotony of drawing breath. *Breath* is also about, Winton has said, how the sea can combine both dramatic wonder and soothing calm. Sando's house is filled with books by Jack London, Joseph Conrad, and Herman Melville.

The relationship between Pikelet and Loonie shifts as Sando first favors one and then the other. When Loonie is injured and cannot surf for a time, Sando goes surfing alone with Pikelet, making Loonie jealous. When Pikelet, recklessly encouraged by Sando, refuses to take a treacherous wave, he begins to wonder if he is indeed only ordinary. When Pikelet gets pneumonia, Sando takes Loonie to Indonesia to search for more dangerous waves. While they are gone, Pikelet, although he has a relationship with Queenie Cookson, a girl at his school, becomes sexually involved with Sando's wife Eva, who seduces the boy in order to compete with her husband for his attention. Eva was once a famous skiing champion, until she made a bad landing; she now has a limp. While Sando goes out to face danger, she stays home alone, smoking pot and unable to take her own risks with death. She tells Pikelet that she misses being afraid. Winton's risk-taking theme takes on a dangerous erotic element when Eva gets Pikelet to participate in her sexual thrill seeking with the use of a cellophane bag over her head so that she comes close to suffocation at the height of sexual pleasure. Winton's twin themes of breath and death merge emphatically here. Pikelet, however, always the cautious one, only pretends to choke Eva, putting his fingers under the plastic bag to break the seal and blowing breath into her face while shouting at her.

When Sando returns, Eva is pregnant and he assumes the baby is his. Loonie does not return; he is no doubt off to follow his own demons, chasing even more danger.

Pikelet's transformation into an adult—with the death of his father, with his marriage to a university teacher, with the birth of his two daughters, with his decision to come full circle from someone who teased death by holding his breath to a paramedic who often breathes life into others—takes place rather hurriedly in the last dozen pages of the novel. Pike later finds out that Billy Sanderson has become an investment guru and a motivational speaker. He reads a newspaper story about the death of Eva, who has been found hanging on a bathroom door of a hotel in Oregon with a belt around her neck. Later, after his divorce, he finds out that Loonie has been killed in a barroom shooting in Rosarito, Mexico. The novel ends with Pike in his late forties, visiting the town of Sawyer, taking his board down to the ocean, and enjoying for a few moments a sense of grace, of dancing on the waves. However, his final understanding is that there was something careless about Eva that he mistook for courage in the same way that he misread Sando's vanity for wisdom. He now thinks that thriving on risk is a perverse effort to deal with what everyone is terrified of: that whatever life they are living is the only life they will have and that it will soon be over.

Readers usually expect a coming-of-age story such as this one to come early in a writer's life. Winton's decision to write it midway through his career is probably due more to the thematic design he conceived for the novel than it is to personal experience, although he did indeed grow up in a small town on Australia's western coast. This is not a rough-edged realistic account of the trials and adventures faced by a young boy as he tries to find a place for himself. Rather, this is a highly formalized, tightly structured literary novel that has the symbolic structure of a novella. It is not like Charles Dickens's *Great Expectations* (1861); it is more like Herman Melville's *Billy Budd* (1924). Pikelet and Loonie are Jekyll and Hyde doubles, the mild side versus the wild side. Sando is a two-dimensional ex-hippie who reads Carlos Castenada,

a self-styled wannabe epic hero, a mentor who tries to mold the lives of his young aco-
lytes in his own image. Eva is the wounded woman who seduces the young protégé
out of jealousy of his devotion to the bigger-than-life hero. What holds the novel together, other than the traditional plot structure of the initiation of a young man, is the
thematic device suggested by the title—that breathing, the most essential human activity, is also the most unconscious and taken-for-granted ordinary activity. Consequently, to be able to manipulate breathing—by holding one's breath, by putting a
plastic bag over one's head to come as close to death as possible—is a way to make
the ordinary extraordinary.

Winton makes surfing the medium by which the young men defy death in this
novel because it carries with it a certain mystic aura. While dangerous in its defiance
of nature, it is also delicate and beautiful, a human way to triumph over the chaotic
and uncontrollable sea, to do something purely for its aesthetic form and its dangerous
challenge. Winton presents these elements in a tight thematic pattern in which breath
and breathing—from sleep apnea to erotic self-asphyxia—are described in a lyrical
style that often exceeds his narrator's linguistic ability, even if Pike does love books.
Although Winton's control of his material is unobtrusive enough that one could read
this novel as a simple coming-of-age story, to do so would be to overlook all the work
he has put into making it a lyrical bit of narrative poetry.

Charles E. May

Review Sources

The Economist 387 (April 26, 2008): 108.
Kirkus Reviews 76, no. 7 (April 1, 2008): 329.
Library Journal 133, no. 7 (April 15, 2008): 78-79.
Los Angeles Times, June 1, 2008, p. R2.
The New York Review of Books 55, no. 13 (August 14, 2008): 28-29.
The New York Times Book Review, June 8, 2008, p. 17.
The New Yorker 84, no. 20 (July 7, 2008): 95.
Outside 33, no. 7 (July, 2008): 34.
Publishers Weekly 244, no. 14 (April 7, 2008): 40.
The Spectator 307 (May 3, 2008): 36-37.

BUT DIDN'T WE HAVE FUN?
An Informal History of Baseball's Pioneer Era, 1843-1870

Author: Peter Morris (1962-   )
Publisher: Ivan R. Dee (Chicago). 286 pp. $27.50
Type of work: History
Time: 1843-1870
Locale: The United States

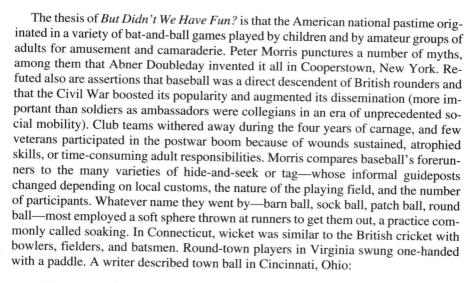

A comprehensive social history of baseball's formative age when modern rules were codified and fraternal clubs such as New York's Knickerbockers and Cincinnati's Red Stockings began to employ professionals

Principal personages:
DANIEL ADAMS, a founder of the
    Knickerbockers
JIM CREIGHTON, pitching sensation who
    died at age twenty-one
FRANK PIDGEON, a founder of Brooklyn's Eckford Club
HARRY WRIGHT, captain of the Cincinnati Red Stockings

The thesis of *But Didn't We Have Fun?* is that the American national pastime originated in a variety of bat-and-ball games played by children and by amateur groups of adults for amusement and camaraderie. Peter Morris punctures a number of myths, among them that Abner Doubleday invented it all in Cooperstown, New York. Refuted also are assertions that baseball was a direct descendent of British rounders and that the Civil War boosted its popularity and augmented its dissemination (more important than soldiers as ambassadors were collegians in an era of unprecedented social mobility). Club teams withered away during the four years of carnage, and few veterans participated in the postwar boom because of wounds sustained, atrophied skills, or time-consuming adult responsibilities. Morris compares baseball's forerunners to the many varieties of hide-and-seek or tag—whose informal guideposts changed depending on local customs, the nature of the playing field, and the number of participants. Whatever name they went by—barn ball, sock ball, patch ball, round ball—most employed a soft sphere thrown at runners to get them out, a practice commonly called soaking. In Connecticut, wicket was similar to the British cricket with bowlers, fielders, and batsmen. Round-town players in Virginia swung one-handed with a paddle. A writer described town ball in Cincinnati, Ohio:

> There were no basemen to whom the ball was thrown, but the sphere was hurled directly at the base-runner. As the excitement of the game intensified the ball began to be made harder and heavier to aid the throwing. This led to an unusual number of accidents, resulting from the players being hit by a too solid ball. It was this dangerous outgrowth of town-ball playing which first suggested to some Yankee mind (whom nobody knows) to put basemen on the bases and let the ball be thrown to them instead of at the runner.

Fielders did not wear gloves, leading to telltale finger deformities. When four-foot stakes were used, runners ran around them in order to avoid injuries. This practice of not touching the bases continued even after flat stones and bags filled with sand or sawdust replaced the stakes. Sometimes two runs were credited if a batsman circled the bases and then made it safely to first again. Before pitchers became dominant, high scoring games of a hundred runs or more were not unusual.

In 1845 members of New York's Knickerbocker Club drew up twenty rules, many dealing with matters of etiquette and sportsmanship. The umpire's role was two-fold—to settle arguments pertaining to the rules and to record for posterity what happened. Often a local dignitary ensconced in an easy chair under an umbrella, he rarely injected himself in disputes on the field. Better positioned were the players themselves, who were expected to be fair and honorable. The infield was diamond-shaped, set at forty-two paces from first to third and home to second (in the 1850's bases were designated to be placed ninety feet apart). Among the innovative rules were the abolition of soaking (or throwing at runners) and making two-strike foul balls do-overs rather than in play or strike three. A batter was out if a fielder caught the ball in the air or on first bounce. Though not set in stone, the number of players was customarily nine. In the infield were three basemen plus a shortstop, whose main function initially was to retrieve throws from outfielders. Widespread acceptance of these rules outside New York proceeded slowly. Following their 1856 publication in *Porter's Spirit of the Times*, they gradually won wider acceptance. In 1858 Daniel Adams formed the National Association of Base Ball Players (NABBP), which adopted the Knickerbocker rules. The elimination of soaking allowed for a harder ball that traveled farther and made the game more exciting. As William A. Cochran wrote, the faculty at Wisconsin's Beloit College

was in heavy sympathy with the boys, and cheered them with their presence as well as by their voices. The grave, sedate, dignified President was an habitué of the ball ground, and it is reported that he would become so enthused at times that he would rise in his carriage and wave his silk hat, in a very dignified manner, to cheer the boys.

Sister sororities and other female spectators brought out the best in handsome New York shortstop Bernard Hanigan. He was so popular with "the belles of the village," one wag remembered, that the Union Club of Morrisania attracted "a more numerous bevy of pretty girls at their matches" than any of their rivals. The lively, rubbery balls necessitated larger fields. Evicted from various Manhattan sites, the Knickerbockers discovered the aptly named Elysian Fields across the Hudson in Hoboken, New Jersey. In 1969 Boston aldermen banned baseball on the Commons, but a pro-ballplayer slate of candidates won eight of twelve contests in the ensuing election. Baseball returned to the Commons.

Social clubs were commonly organized by occupation: milkmen, bartenders, firemen, attorneys, shipbuilders, government workers, and even clergymen. The sober photographs that have survived from that era only hint at the fun and esprit de corps that belonging to a team engendered. Baseball was often just one of the club's recreational activities (cricket and harness racing were also popular). Rosters generally were open to all willing members. Exhibitions pitted bachelors against married men, newcomers against old timers, corpulent "whales" against "shrimps," and so on. The Knickerbockers donned distinctive team uniforms of white flannel shirts, blue pantaloons, and straw hats, and the custom spread (one photograph unearthed by Morris even shows a team name, Union Club, displayed on bats). A ceremonial coin toss determined who batted first. In contrast to red cricket spheres, balls were white (a symbol of purity), at least at the outset of a contest. A ball might last an entire game, or until somebody knocked its stuffing out. At first there was no standard size or regulation for the material used. Some had a bullet in the middle, others a sturgeon's eye. A Boston player recalled:

Peter Morris is the author of Baseball Fever: Early Baseball in Michigan *(2003),* A Game of Inches: The Stories Behind the Innovations That Shaped Baseball *(published in two volumes in 2006,* The Game on the Field *and* The Game Behind the Scenes*), and* Level Playing Field: How the Groundskeeping Murphy Brothers Shaped Baseball *(2007). He is a former national and international Scrabble champion.*

> It was not difficult to procure an old rubber shoe for the foundation of a ball. Many a dear old grandma or auntie of today will remember having stockings and mittens being begged of them, which were knit at home by hand, to be unraveled for ball stock. When leather was not to be had, a cheap and easy way to cover a ball was with twine in a lock stitch, called quilting.

Etiquette dictated that onlookers cheer good plays for both sides and only hiss at demonstrations of poor sportsmanship. Processions to the field featured the singing of club songs. Rivals, victors and vanquished, gave three cheers for opponents at game's end. At the customary post-game banquet, the defeated team's captain presented the ball (or a clean replica) with names, score, and date duly recorded. Barnstorming tours by the Excelsiors of Brooklyn (1859-1860) and the Washington's National Club (1866-1867) spread these ceremonies. A player on a Kalamazoo, Michigan, team recalled:

> When we went to an outside town to play we paid our own expenses. There was no admission fee charged. I remember the first game we played with Jackson. We played for the supper and we also paid for the supper. But it was a good one, I tell you. They had to play hard to win and they deserved a good meal.

Inevitably, with civic pride at stake during the proliferating intercity competition, regional challenges, and tournaments (some taking place at county or state fairs), the competitive drive threatened cherished customs. Bunting, once not considered a sporting method of reaching base, became more common. So did intentionally trapping the ball to turn, in modern parlance, a double play. Lamentably, the honor system crumbled. Increasingly, umpires were called upon to render judgment calls. Some batsmen waited interminably for a good pitch, necessitating rules for called strikes and eventually balls. The NABBP discontinued the one-bounce rule, deeming it to be a vestige of child's play. Aggressive social organizations lured "stars" with job offers or emoluments under the table even when, as in the case of Patsy Dockney, they had a reputation for carousing and public drunkenness. In 1858 promoters of a contest featuring all-stars from New York and Brooklyn charged admission. The following year, Jim Creighton, whose underhand motion made him the nation's first formidable pitcher, jumped to the Excelsiors. By 1868 the proliferating practice of "revolving" (switching teams) undermined club allegiance. Philadelphia's Keystone Club lost several mainstays after veteran Fergy Malone joined the cross-town Athletics, a team that defeated a Pottsville nine 107-2 (Jimmy Foran made all three outs in the initial inning, the first two in the second, then quit in humiliation). It became impractical for those with legitimate jobs to play multiple games a week or go on tour. In St. Louis, the Union and Empire clubs strove to remain nonprofessional, but they were no match for visiting squads until they upgraded their roster with semi-pros. In Cincinnati, six thousand fans watched the Buckeyes square off against the Red Stockings, and rumors abounded that gamblers had enticed a few players into throwing the game. In 1869, bowing to the inevitable, the NABBP permitted payment to team members. That year Harry Wright's Red Stockings toured extensively and enjoyed an undefeated season. By the following spring, the team had disbanded, a casualty of budget tightening, alleged boorishness (one player entered a tavern in uniform), and unexpected setbacks from rivals who outbid them for talented "revolvers." Reacting against the trend toward professionalism, organizations staged "muffin" games where the score took a back seat to food, spirits, silliness, and general merriment. Morris labeled them a parody of the excesses besetting the game and a reminder to Americans that baseball was meant to be fun. Though the amateur tradition came to encompass industrial leagues, school curricula, and church teams, the "muffin" tradition survived in "donkey ball," where players sat atop four-legged animals, and, more important, in pickup games all around the world.

Morris uses a plethora of primary source quotes. The best capture charmingly the flavor of a bygone era. Smoky Joe Wood, for instance, recalls playing for his hometown of Ness City, Kansas.

> The ballgame between two rival towns was a big event then, with parades before the game and everything. The smaller the town, the more important their ballclub was. A team that beat a bigger town would practically be handed the keys to the city. For players who lost a game by making an error in the ninth inning, the best thing to do was hit the road, because the town would never let them forget it.

James B. Lane

Review Sources

Kirkus Reviews 76, no. 4 (February 15, 2008): 186.
Library Journal 133, no. 2 (February 1, 2008): 77.
The New York Times Book Review, April 6, 2008, p. 6.
Publishers Weekly 254, no. 43 (October 29, 2007): 38.
The Washington Post Book World, April 6, 2006, p. BW16.

CALLED OUT OF DARKNESS
A Spiritual Confession

Author: Anne Rice (1941-   )
Publisher: Alfred A. Knopf (New York). 245 pp. $24.00
Type of work: Memoir, religion
Time: 1941-2008
Locale: New Orleans, Dallas, and San Francisco

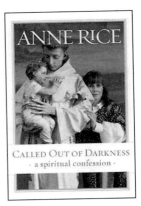

Rice traces her journey from Catholic believer to athe-ist to committed Christian in this account of spiritual and literary transformation

In October, 2004, Anne Rice shocked her legions of loyal readers by announcing that she would never again pen the American gothic novels that had catapulted her to the top of best-seller lists. Proclaiming that she had re-newed her commitment to Jesus Christ and returned to the Catholic faith of her child-hood, she insisted that she would write "only for the Lord."

At the time of her announcement, she had published twenty books that had dealt with the supernatural, beginning with *Interview with the Vampire*, which appeared in 1976. The main character, Lestat de Lioncourt, a French nobleman who became a vampire in the eighteenth century, rivaled Bram Stoker's Count Dracula in fame, and to the delight of Rice's adoring fans, he appeared in subsequent books of the Vampire Chronicles series. In addition to writing about vampires, witches, mummies, and other beings of the occult, Rice wrote adult and erotic fiction under the pseudonyms Anne Rampling and A. N. Roquelaure. She is one of the most popular authors in mod-ern history, and more than one hundred million copies of her novels have been sold. Several of her books have been adapted for film, television, and the stage and have also inspired musical compositions by various artists.

In spite of warnings that she was committing career suicide, Rice kept her promise to confine her writing to Christian-themed books. In 2005, she published *Christ the Lord: Out of Egypt*, the first in a trilogy of novels based on the life of Jesus. *Christ the Lord: The Road to Cana*, the second in the series, appeared in 2008. Well received by critics, the books were lauded for vivid, well-researched, and reverent portrayals of Jesus.

While hardcore fans of Rice's vampire stories were dismayed by the new direction that her writing had taken, spiritually inclined readers were intrigued. Both groups, however, asked the same question. How could a renowned writer of best-selling gothic novels renounce the genre that made her career and become a committed Christian who writes only for God? Rice attempts to answer this question in *Called Out of Darkness: A Spiritual Confession*. Reflecting on her life and work, Rice chron-icles her Catholic upbringing, a thirty-eight-year detour through atheism, and a return to her Catholic faith at age fifty-seven in 1998.

Rice lays the foundation of her account by offering a lengthy retrospective of the ways in which her Catholic faith suffused her childhood. Born into a devout Irish Catholic family in New Orleans, Louisiana, she grew up in an all-white neighborhood. Her neighbors and extended family were all Catholics. Her father went to seminary briefly but left and eventually became a postal worker. She had two aunts who were nuns. Her mother, who became an alcoholic after Rice's grandmother's death, made sure her two daughters and son were grounded in Catholicism.

Steeped in the trappings and practices of her faith, Rice was a faithful churchgoer until the age of seventeen. She describes in detail the churches where she worshiped and the feast days that were so much a part of church life. However, it is the pageantry of the mass that most captivated her:

> Daily mass was extremely interesting because the priest wore vestments of watered taffeta with thick embroidery, and even the altar boy wore a lovely white lace-trimmed surplice over his black robe. The priest said the Mass in Latin, facing away from us, and moved back and forth across the altar as he consulted an enormous book. The altar boy rang small golden bells at the moment of the Consecration when the priest spoke in Latin the words of our Lord from the last Supper, "This is my body . . . This is my blood." . . . Our feelings were those of immense gratitude and wonder. We believed in this miracle as we believed that streetcars passed our house, or that rain fell in great soft glimmering sheets in the afternoons.

Her evocative descriptions open a window on the brand of Catholicism practiced in the 1940's and 1950's that may seem foreign to young contemporary Catholics of the early twenty-first century, who have been raised in the wake of the sweeping changes of Vatican II. The Latin mass, rich vestments, and ornate churches reflected an almost magical world where the authority of priests and nuns was trusted and unquestioned. In fact, Rice notes that not even a whisper of scandal touched the religious of her day, and any allegations of priests engaging in pedophilia or other misbehavior were unheard of. Rice's memories of this early period of her life exude the rosy glow of nostalgia and reflect a world that is sheltered from everything by the comforting yet dominant influence of Mother Church.

Anne Rice is the best-selling author of twenty-eight books, including Interview with the Vampire *(1976),* The Queen of the Damned *(1988),* Memnoch the Devil *(1995),* Blackwood Farm *(2002),* Blood Canticle *(2003),* Christ the Lord: Out of Egypt *(2005), and* Christ the Lord: The Road to Cana *(2008). A native of New Orleans, Louisiana, she resides in Rancho Mirage, California.*

Rice notes that one reason the church had such a strong hold on her young imagination was because "[i]ntermingled with my religious experiences at this time were preliterate aesthetic experiences which left a lasting mark." Her mother and father encouraged their children to appreciate and participate in the arts. Their mother often took Anne and her sister, Alice, who also became a noted writer, to museums and the theater. Rice accompanied her father, also a writer, to the library. Oddly for a future author, words did not hold as much appeal for the young Rice as did artwork and images. Reading was difficult for her, and she claims that "[w]hen I went to school and began to read, I lost an immense world of image, color, and intricate connections." Her aversion to reading continued until she attended Texas Women's University in Denton, Texas. There she was no longer constrained by the banned-books policy of the Roman Catholic Church. Instead, works by Søren Kierkegaard, Martin Heidegger, Jean-Paul Sartre, Albert Camus, and Immanuel Kant beckoned her from the library shelves.

Her intellectual and psychological awakening, however, did not stop at the library door. She notes, "It was the modern world—wanting to know the great incidents and heroes and heroines of the world . . . that caused me to leave the church." Other reasons contributed to her eroding faith—her mother's death from alcoholism, her father's remarriage to a woman who was a Baptist, her family's removal from the insulated life of the Catholic community in New Orleans to the unfamiliar secular environment of Texas, her awakening sexuality, and the fact that she was "growing up." She acknowledges that, little by little, her faith began to "crack apart," yet there was a defining moment when she abandoned belief. During a conversation with a priest, he insisted that because of her strong Catholic upbringing she could never turn her back on the church. His comment struck a raw nerve and, as she tells it, she "was no longer a Catholic when I left the room." She did not return to the church for thirty-eight years.

Although Rice makes plain why she left the church, it is less clear why she reembraced faith after such a long absence. The fact that she and her husband returned to New Orleans to live in 1988 may have had a psychological and spiritual influence. Members of her family and the Catholic community in which she had spent her childhood were still there, but the church of the 1980's and 1990's was not the same institution she had left nearly four decades before. She observes that the Catholic attitude toward marriage was more relaxed and that separations and divorces were more accepted, Catholic couples were no longer having so many children, and views on sex were no longer as rigid. The ceremonies of the church changed as well, and Rice remarks that she "mourned" the passing of the Latin mass.

Although Rice approved of many of these changes, they also caught her off guard. Her comments about returning to New Orleans and finding the Catholic Church transformed may surprise readers. She maintains that she knew nothing of the changes precipitated by Vatican II—an odd claim since even atheists would have been aware of the extensive media reports of the council held between 1962 and 1965. She was also largely unaware of the social upheaval of the 1960's and 1970's. Again her attitude is surprising because at the time she was living with her husband on Haight Street in San Francisco in the middle of a hippie enclave. By her own admission, she writes that she "drifted through the contemporary world, blind as usual to what was happening politically and religiously." One wonders how she could have been so detached from current events in such a turbulent time.

As disconnected as she was from the occurrences that were shaping society, she was growing more deeply connected to God. Lacking conscious awareness of the process of her reconversion, she drifted unknowingly toward faith. While an atheist, she began to collect religious artifacts and, when visiting other countries, was drawn toward churches and cathedrals. When she and Stan traveled to Jerusalem, the land where Christ had walked captivated her, and later she began obsessively to read books about Jesus. A trip to Rio de Janeiro, Brazil, was the fulfillment of a long-held dream where she saw the "great statue of Jesus Christ with his arms outstretched." Echoing Flannery O'Connor, she describes herself as "Christ haunted" during these years of searching. Finally, on December 7, 1998, she surrendered to God.

Perhaps the most exuberant and passionate chapter of Rice's "confession" is the one that she opens with the question "What happens with faith returns?" Her profound love for God is apparent when she proclaims joyously that:

> I didn't care about the framing of the doctrine. I cared about Him. And He was calling me back through His Presence on the altar. He might have used the falling rain to call me back; He might have used the music of Vivaldi. He might have used the statue of Christ and Francis that was on my desk. But, no, He used the doctrine of the Real Presence.

Her years of doubts and searching were over, and Rice began to disentangle herself from her literary legacy of vampires and witches in order to dedicate her talents completely to God. It seems that the priest who told her that she would never really leave the church behind was right after all. Thirty-eight years of unbelief could not erase the imprint the strong faith of her childhood had left on her heart and soul.

In the introduction to her spiritual memoir, Rice notes that "I want to tell as simply as I can—and nothing with me as a writer is ever really simple—the story of how I made my decision of the heart." Although she lacks the scholarly precision of a Kathleen Norris or the grittiness of an Anne Lamott, Rice does tell her story with beautiful simplicity and engaging honesty. With the exception of her curious tendency to gloss over life-changing events, such as the death of her daughter, Michele, at age six, and the death of her beloved husband, she offers a transparent account of her spiritual journey. Interested readers should be satisfied with Rice's answer to the question "Why did you reconvert to Christianity?"—and find much inspiration as well.

Pegge Bochynski

Review Sources

America 199, no. 18 (December 1, 2008): 34-35.
Booklist 104, no. 22 (August 1, 2008): 2.
Elle 24, no. 2 (October, 2008): 316.
Kirkus Reviews, 76, no. 15 (August 1, 2008): 78.
Publishers Weekly 255, no. 37 (September 15, 2008): 62.
Vanity Fair, no. 578 (October, 2008): 164.

CAPITOL MEN
The Epic Story of Reconstruction Through the Lives of
the First Black Congressmen

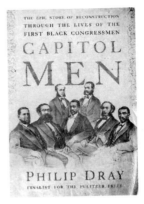

Author: Philip Dray (1959-   )
Publisher: Houghton Mifflin (Boston). 463 pp. $30.00
Type of work: History
Time: 1865-1877
Locale: Washington, D.C.; the post-Civil War Southern
   states; Kansas

*A study of the Reconstruction of the American South
with emphasis on the contributions of black congressmen
and other black officials*

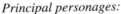

Principal personages:
   BLANCHE K. BRUCE, Mississippi senator
   RICHARD (DADDY) CAIN, South Carolina
      clergyman and congressman
   FREDERICK DOUGLASS, former slave and champion of black
      congressmen
   ROBERT BROWN ELLIOTT, lawyer and South Carolina congressman
   PINCKNEY BENTON STEWART PINCHBACK, Louisiana senator and acting
      governor
   JOSEPH H. RAINEY, South Carolina congressman
   HIRAM RHODES REVELS, Mississippi senator
   ROBERT SMALLS, South Carolina congressman
   GEORGE H. WHITE, North Carolina congressman, the last black member
      from Reconstruction
   ULYSSES S. GRANT, president of the United States through much of
      Reconstruction

   Philip Dray begins *Capitol Men*, his study of Reconstruction, with an adventure in
the harbor of Charleston, South Carolina. It occurred one year after a more famous incident that happened nearby: the surrender of Fort Sumter to Southern secessionist
forces. The mulatto pilot of a Confederate transfer ship, the *Planter*, stole the vessel
and delivered his own family and a small group of runaways and slave crewmen to the
Onward, a Union ship blockading the harbor. This daring accomplishment was a
demonstration—one of many in Dray's book—of the courage, initiative, and re-
sourcefulness often displayed by slaves that generations of slavemasters had not been
able to acknowledge. The leader of this group was Robert Smalls, the son of a slave
woman who lived at Beaufort on one of the Sea Islands off the South Carolina coast
and a white man who was either her white master or a Charleston merchant.
   Union naval forces had attacked the Sea Islands the preceding November, but the
Confederates had not tried to defend them, and plantation owners quickly vacated,
leaving behind their homes and their slaves. During the spring of 1862, when Smalls

performed his naval theft, Northern abolitionists, sensing a gold opportunity to demonstrate that slaves could be their own masters,
descended on the islands, and a new era began
for these people. The Port Royal experiment,
as it was called, was not an easy adjustment,
but it raised the question of possibilities for
further confiscation of land formerly owned
by whites. These possibilities turned out to be
minimal.

*Philip Dray won the Robert F. Kennedy
Book Award and the Southern Book
Critics Circle Award for* At the Hands
of Persons Unknown: The Lynching of
Black America *(2003). The book was
also a finalist for the Pulitzer Prize.*

Even observers sympathetic to African Americans wondered whether former
slaves, free after the war, had the capacity to function as the citizens they became by
virtue of Article 14 of the Constitution in 1868. To the surprise of many, and to the
horror of many white Southerners, the new citizens showed that, given the chance,
they could. Consequently, the promises of Article 14 and Article 15, passed two years
later, were successfully undermined, and black Americans generally, and in the South
particularly, had to face another century of cursorily limited citizenship.

In this book, Dray shows the accomplishments of black men who, in the process of
serving the Union, unleashed a retaliation by the South and the resignation of the
North to that retaliation. He explains why, despite the efforts of black Americans and
those of their supporters, Reconstruction failed. Plantation owners, committed to
their ingrained notion of the basic inferiority of blacks, had no desire to see their former slaves become their congressmen. In states with large black populations, whites
began to learn, if not to admit, that blacks were far abler than their former masters supposed. The whites also feared retaliation in states with proportionately large black
populations such as South Carolina, Louisiana, and Mississippi, although credible evidence of such a desire or goal is lacking. The movement was sabotaged in the South,
federal support declined, and blacks saw their hopes dashed. From 1901, when Robert
H. White, who had long outlasted the other black congressmen, finished his term, until 1973, when Andrew Young and Barbara Jordan took office, no African American
held a seat in Congress.

Dray's contribution to the study of Reconstruction focuses on the achievements of
black legislators, but for the most part he has organized his material topically. To assess several of these men, the reader must dip into the various chapters. Two early
chapters, however, are named for two of the most colorful of the "capitol men,"
"Daddy" Cain of South Carolina and P. B. S. Pinchback of Louisiana. Cain, a free-
born man originally from Virginia, pursued the goal of devising a mechanism by
which blacks might obtain land in South Carolina; the measure of his qualified success, however, is found only in the book's final chapter.

Pinchback, another Virginian and the child of a slave woman and her white master,
pops up in Dray's book several times as Louisiana state senator, lieutenant governor
(and, for a few weeks, acting governor), appointed U.S. senator, and elected member
of the House of Representatives. During the Civil War, the light-colored Pinchback,
who could pass for white, was a steward on a Mississippi River steamboat. He saw no

future opportunity there, abandoned ship for military service in the Union Army in New Orleans, met equally discouraging results there, ran for the Louisiana state senate, apparently lost to a white opponent, charged election fraud, and was awarded the seat by the state commission on elections. Then he managed to participate in a gunfight with another mulatto on Canal Street in New Orleans and was arrested, although he and his opponent were soon freed. Despite the turbulence of his personal life, Pinchback demonstrated a talent for promoting civil rights. He argued successfully for a bill that fined any steamboat master or hotel manager who refused accommodations because of a person's race. The bill passed—but it was not enforced.

While Mississippi strove to regain admission to the Union, its considerable black population was able to secure one senatorial seat for a black man. That man was Hiram Rhodes Revels, from a free black family in North Carolina. Educated for the ministry in the North, he served as a missionary in Kansas and as a chaplain to a black Civil War regiment in Maryland. As a consequence of his enlistment in the Freedmen's Bureau, he found himself in Mississippi, the state legislature's choice to hold the same seat in the United States Senate which Jefferson Davis had abandoned in 1861 to become president of the Confederacy. In his maiden speech Revels opposed the readmission of Georgia, where, two years earlier, whites had impelled the removal of thirty-two elected black state legislators from office. This speech helped to generate an outcry that resulted in the reinstitution of a federal military governor in Georgia and the subsequent reinstatement of the blacks. A few months later Georgia was back in the Union.

Revels favored a conciliatory approach toward former secessionist officials. He spoke in favor of amnesty for these men as a gesture toward the racial harmony for which he held high hopes. Believing Mississippi to be "well reconstructed," he thereby gained favor with whites in the North who shared—or hoped to share—his optimism, but he displeased many blacks who tended to support disenfranchisement of these officials.

Like Cain, Robert Brown Elliott showed no trace of white ancestry. Even Henry Ward Beecher, a famous preacher with an abolitionist background and brother of *Uncle Tom's Cabin* (1852) author Harriet Beecher Stowe, saw danger in a strong influence of "unmixed Africans." When Elliott came to Congress from South Carolina in 1871, he presented a puzzle. His origins were unclear, but he could speak French and Spanish and quote the classics. Here was a decidedly black man with a keen mind and oratorical ability which could not be attributed to miscegenation. He leaped capably into the struggle for the Ku Klux Klan Act, opposed by some Northern representatives who considered that the states should maintain themselves against the racial outrages of the Klan. Elliot could argue tactfully in the legislature, but he knew how to fight for his rights. He resisted—and sometimes won—when refused service by railroad, hotel, and restaurant managers at a time when even the long-famous Frederick Douglass often had to endure their slights.

Elliott and another black South Carolina congressman, Joseph Rainey, were called on to defend residents of Hamburg, a small black village where an ugly racial incident began on the hundredth anniversary of the nation's independence, July 4, 1876, when white officials confronted a black militia group attempting to parade during the celebration. The death of a white rifle club member from the nearby city of Augusta set off a barrage of killing of blacks and mutilation of their bodies. Rainey made a powerful speech in Congress to the effect that blacks were becoming "vassals and slaves again."

He was very nearly correct. The inauguration of President Rutherford B. Hayes after his much-disputed victory over Samuel Tilden in the centennial year election of 1876 is often regarded as a marker of the end of Reconstruction. Along with the Republican Hayes, the nation received a tide of new Democrats in the House of Representatives. In withdrawing federal troops from the South, Hayes was acknowledging the changing mood of the nation. Even some of the black legislators were conceding that the Southern white reaction against Reconstruction was reaching a point too dangerous to blacks to justify continuing an expensive and discouragingly futile effort.

Black leaders often expressed sharply contrasting opinions on what was good for members of their race. Some thought that as white Southern resistance to Reconstruction swelled and as the reluctance of the federal government to support it increased, hope for future prosperity might lay in the west. Kansas became the favorite destination in the period from 1878 to 1880. The weather was more moderate, the land was well watered and yet clear of swamps, and a network of roads and railroads was growing. Rainey and Douglass saw merit in what became known as the Exoduster Movement, but Senator Blanche K. Bruce of Mississippi thought otherwise. Bruce, a mulatto native of Virginia who had been educated alongside his white half-brother and later had lived in Missouri, Kansas, and Ohio before settling in Mississippi, considered that blacks were by nature "unmigratory." Not only were they better suited to the South, a mass movement out of the South would threaten the livelihood of those who remained. Bruce also led a congressional inquiry into the harassment of a black cadet at West Point. The case traveled to the West Point supervisor, the commander of the Army, and finally to President Hayes, but the cadet, Johnson Whittaker, was judged a liar and a coward and thrown out of the institution. The best efforts of black legislators often ended in such discouraging ways.

One challenge on which Rainey and Bruce worked together was an attempt to save the constituents of a failed enterprise, the Freedman's Saving and Trust Company, formed to encourage savings among former slaves who were now wage earners. The bank prospered for a few years but made some risky loans and was devastated by the financial panic that struck in 1873. Continuing efforts by the two legislators and by Douglass, who had enthusiastically backed the idea of the bank from the beginning, got nowhere.

Dray's book ends, as it began, with Smalls. A story still told in Beaufort, South Carolina, relates that after the war Smalls took in the wife of his former master, poor and disoriented. She apparently did not know that the Civil War and slavery had ended and that her former slave had served in Congress and had met with President Abraham Lincoln. Reportedly, she stayed with him until her death.

Robert P. Ellis

Review Sources

Kirkus Reviews 76, no. 15 (August 1, 2008): 116.
Library Journal 133, no. 12 (July 1, 2008): 92-93.
The Nation 287, no. 14 (November 3, 2008): 30-33.
The New York Times Book Review, September 28, 2008, p. 20.
The New Yorker 84, no. 32 (October 13, 2008): 145.
Publishers Weekly 255, no. 24 (June 16, 2008): 40.
The Washington Post Book World, September 21, 2008, p. BW04.

CHRONICLES OF MY LIFE
An American in the Heart of Japan

Author: Donald Keene (1922-   )
Publisher: Columbia University Press (New York).
  208 pp. $27.95
Type of work: Autobiography
Time: 1930-2006
Locale: Japan, New York City, Cambridge, Massachusetts

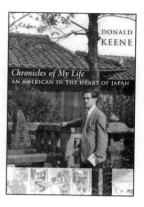

An autobiography concentrating primarily on Keene's early interest in the Orient, his specialization in Japanese, his role as a translator in World War II, his education at Columbia, Harvard, and Cambridge, his association with Japanese writers and playwrights, as well as his discussion of some of the many books he published

Principal personages:

DONALD KEENE, the author, an expert in Japanese life and literature
ABE KŌBŌ, close friend of Keene, a major novelist and playwright
ARTHUR WALEY, translator of Murasaki Shikibu's *The Tale of Genji* (c. 1004) and the person who inspired Keene's work
SERGE ELISSÉEFF, Harvard professor who became Keene's model of how not to teach
TSUNODA RYŪSAKA, Keene's first teacher in Japanese classes at Columbia and reader for his master's and Ph.D.
NAGAI MICHIO, Keene's closest friend in Japan
MISHIMA YUKIO, Keene's friend, who was a celebrated Japanese writer and reactionary activist who committed suicide
LEE, Columbia classmate who interested Keene in Chinese characters, which were the basis for his study of Japanese
JACK KERR, Columbia classmate with whom Keene studied Japanese during a summer in North Carolina

Donald Keene's autobiography, which contains some material already covered in his earlier memoir, *On Familiar Terms* (1994), is essentially the story of how a young American boy became infatuated with the Orient and eventually became a noted scholar who wrote books, translated the work of outstanding Japanese writers, and anthologized the major works of Japanese literature. This is not a coming-of-age story in the usual sense; it is about the making of a scholar. Keene reveals little about his childhood, which he sees as unremarkable. The family had financial problems; his parents quarreled much of the time (they were divorced when Keene was fifteen); and he was an "outsider," an unathletic, unpopular boy whose hobby was collecting stamps and whose only friends were other stamp-collecting "nerds." The highlight of his youth was a trip he took when he was nine to Europe with his father. In Paris he attended an

~

The Shincho Professor of Japanese Literature and University Professor Emeritus at Columbia University, Donald Keene has written more than thirty books, among them Emperor of Japan: Meiji and His World *(2005), an anthology of Japanese literature, and the definitive multivolume history of Japanese literature. He has also served as guest editor of* Asahi *and has lectured at many institutions, including Harvard and Cambridge universities.*

~

international exhibition, where he visited the Indo-Chinese pavilion and had his first experience with foreign food: being served a fish with its head still attached. He also fell in love with the French language and eventually became fluent in it.

Throughout his public school education, he was the best student in his class and skipped two grades without difficulty. Being smaller and younger than his classmates, he compensated for his lack of athletic ability by excelling in literary studies: He edited the high school magazine, for which he wrote several stories, and he wrote the school plays. Thanks to the assistance of Miss Tannenbaum, his English teacher, he won a Pulitzer Scholarship to Columbia University, which he entered when he was just sixteen, two years younger than his classmates. His Columbia experience shaped the rest of his life. Acting on Miss Tannenbaum's advice, he studied Greek and Latin and took a course in the humanities. His teacher was Mark Van Doren, whose teaching strategy he eventually adopted as a model. Fortuitously, in Van Doren's class, he was seated alphabetically next to a Chinese American named Lee, who whetted his interest in Oriental languages by teaching him Chinese characters. He and Lee ate lunch together every day, and Keene also took a lesson once a week with him. By this time, World War II had begun, and Keene, a pacifist, describes himself as torn between his hatred of war and of the Nazis. At a bookstore, he saw Arthur Waley's translation of the Japanese work *The Tale of Genji*, which he purchased for forty-nine cents. He said of the book that it became "a refuge from all I hated in the world around me." Despite his dislike of the militaristic Japanese, he responded favorably to an invitation from Jack Kerr, and he, Kerr, and Paul Baum spent a summer studying Japanese with Inomata Tadashi. Keene's knowledge of Chinese characters helped him learn Japanese. On Kerr's recommendation, he took a class in Japanese thought from Tsunoda Ryūsaka, who later helped him with his graduate degrees. He was at first the only one in the class, but two other students, one of whom was Baum, enrolled later.

Keene's studies at Columbia were interrupted by the bombing of Pearl Harbor. Ryūsaka was briefly interned as a suspected spy, but he was soon released. Lee went into hiding for a while because he feared violent retaliation because of his ancestry. Keene applied and was accepted to the Navy Japanese Language School at the University of California at Berkeley, where he studied for eleven months before graduating (as valedictorian) and beginning his duties in the Pacific, first at Pearl Harbor, where he translated captured Japanese documents, and then in the Aleutian Islands, where the Americans were retaking islands held by the Japanese. He then went to Hawaii, where he continued his study of Japanese, and he spent the rest of the war on Okinawa.

After the war Keene was sent not to Japan, but to China, where he interviewed and read the diaries of Japanese prisoners held in China. Upset by the rampant corruption in China, especially with the conduct of the war crimes investigation, he asked to be transferred. Although he was supposed to return to Hawaii, he went to Japan, where he attempted to find the families of the Japanese prisoners he had met in China. He finally returned to Hawaii, then moved to the United States, where he resumed his studies at Columbia under Ryūsaka. Keene wrote his master's thesis on Honda Toshiaki and his dissertation on Chikamatsu Monzaemon's *Kokusenya kassen* (pr. 1715; *The Battles of Coxinga*, 1951), both of which he had studied with Ryūsaka.

In six months Keene became fluent in Chinese, and in 1947 he decided to switch to Harvard University to continue his study of Japanese, to which he felt more "temperamentally suited." Unfortunately, Serge Elisséeff, the professor Kene left Columbia to study under, proved to be a disappointment, not only in what Japanese he knew but also in the way he lectured, reading from notes. His teaching style became the model of what not to do. Keene wanted to "pass on my enthusiasm, my love for Japanese literature, not to relay facts that could easily be found in books." So when he received a Henry Fellowship to Cambridge University, he gladly accepted and finished his degree there, after taking some time off to visit Italy, where his only draft of his dissertation was stolen, and he had to rewrite it. While at Cambridge, Keene taught a course in Japanese conversation and met Bertrand Russell, E. M. Forster, and Arthur Waley, whom he tried to emulate. In his spare time Keene visited London, where he indulged his passion for opera. He especially loved *Norma* (1831), with Maria Callas in the title role, and he acknowledged that of all drama opera was his favorite.

He then returned to Columbia, where every year he was able to spend his summer vacations visiting Japan, immersing himself in Japanese culture. He translated Japanese poetry (one of his translations is included as well as his comments on the problems of translation); published essays on bunraku and nō, two types of drama; studied singing in Japanese; acted in kyōgen (comic drama); began his history of Japanese literature; and wrote for the journal *Asahi* (for which he eventually became a guest editor).

During the 1960's he also developed friendships with many Japanese writers, including Michio Ngai, Kōbō Abe, and Yukio Mishima. For the next twenty years Keene continued publishing books, winning prizes (the Kikuchi Prize) and honors (a Doctor of Letters degree from Cambridge in 1991), and becoming embroiled in the awarding of international literary prizes, notably the Formentor and the Nobel Prize. After his retirement at age seventy in 1992, he received the PEN/Ralph Manheim Medal for Translation and continued writing books, among them the highly acclaimed biography of Emperor Meiji, greatest of the Japanese monarchs.

In addition to his discussion of his travels, his writings, and his friendships, Keene includes interesting anecdotes, among them his meetings with Yoko Ono and Greta Garbo. Among the most fascinating episodes are the political machinations involved in the selection of the recipients of prestigious literary awards and his travels in Indonesia and Cambodia. Interspersed throughout the book are Keene's opinions about French opera (a real passion), Japanese architecture (he explains how the design of a room reflects Japanese cultural traditions), the growing acceptance of Japanese writing into world literature, and the role of bicycles at Cambridge. Lightening the text, which can hardly be described as self-deprecating, are the humorous, whimsical drawings of Akira Yamaguchi and one photograph, among all the staged photos of literary giants, of a young Keene performing the role of Tarō Kaja in the traditional comic drama *Chidori* (plovers or gulls) in 1956.

In its focus on his academic life as a Japanese scholar and his emotional, physical, and cultural movement from the United States to Japan ("The center of my world has moved to Japan"), Keene's autobiography omits his personal life, except for a brief mention of his father, who was included perhaps because he took Keene with him on a lengthy trip, which whetted his interest in travel and other cultures. He mentions several male friends, but there does not seem to be much "depth" in their relationships, which consist mainly of academic discussions and a great deal of drinking. When one relationship seems to be moving in an intimate direction, Keene seems skittish, and the relationship remains at the cordial level. He does mention Russell asking him if he had had a love affair and adding that he would not be shocked if he had not, but Keene does not include his answer. In fact, "relationships" may not be the right term to describe his dealings with people. Reflections, not emotions, are the "stuff" of this memoir. (Ironically, the hero of Keene's treasured *The Tale of Genji* is a man who does have emotions and seems the opposite of Keene.) The book is interesting to academicians, but there is too little of the "human" element to engage the general reader.

Thomas L. Erskine

Review Sources

Kirkus Reviews 76, no. 3 (February 1, 2008): 133.
The Times Literary Supplement, May 9, 2008, p. 26.

THE COLLECTED PROSE OF ROBERT FROST

Author: Robert Frost (1874-1963)
Edited by Mark Richardson
Publisher: The Belknap Press of Harvard University
  Press (Cambridge, Mass.). 378 pp. $39.95
Type of work: Essays, short fiction

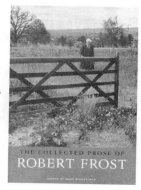

An intriguing assortment of prose pieces from one of America's most honored twentieth century poets

Robert Frost is foremost a renowned American poet, and *The Collected Prose of Robert Frost* should whet the interest of those who wish to read what he said about writing poetry. This volume also will be of interest to those who desire to be exposed to everything the poet wrote. The editor, Mark Richardson, must be commended for his diligence in completing this project. Over time, major poets such as Frost are often taken for granted, dismissed after their work has been squeezed dry of all fresh meaning. It can take new collections of the poet's work or new critical material to jar the public's perception of what the poet truly accomplished.

Many readers recognize Frost as an award-winning poet who wrote about rural themes while employing common speech patterns. His vast popularity can be linked to his use of traditional poetic forms and his approachable subject matter. While his poetry may seem simple, it is never simplistic. For a more complete understanding of his approach to poetry, it is advisable to read the relevant essays, letters, notes, and lectures Richardson has compiled.

Through hard work and persistence, Richardson has established himself as an expert on everything related to Frost. He coedited with Richard Poirier the 1995 collection *Robert Frost: Collected Poems, Prose, and Plays* and wrote the 1997 critical study *The Ordeal of Robert Frost: The Poet and His Poetics.* Many of the prose pieces included in the 1995 collection also are included in *The Collected Prose of Robert Frost.* While there is some overlap with previous volumes of Frost's prose, this is the first critical edition of his collected prose. It is organized in chronological order, beginning with Frost's high school prose of 1891 and 1892 and ending with statements that he made in 1963. Richardson begins the collection with an informative "Introduction." He is quick to point out that Frost was always reluctant to publish his prose, both editors and publishers finding the poet "peculiarly uncooperative" whenever approached on the subject. Richardson also notes that, even after Frost's death, very little of his prose was collected, and that was in *Selected Prose of Robert Frost* (1966), *Robert Frost: Poetry and Prose* (1972), and *Robert Frost on Writing* (1973). While Richardson applauds the publishing of these volumes, he is critical of them for not including a large selection of Frost's prose and for the texts being "marred by occasional inaccuracies."

Robert Frost is considered a giant of twentieth century American poetry. He published several award-winning volumes, including New Hampshire *(1923),* Collected Poems *(1930), A* Further Range *(1936), and* A Witness Tree *(1942). Frost is the only American poet to have won the Pulitzer Prize in poetry four times. Although he made his reputation as a poet, Frost also wrote essays, notes, letters, prefaces, and lectures.*

Richardson had a chance to correct some of these problems in the 1995 collection he coedited with Poirier. For this volume, he took it upon himself to add supplemental material, producing a more complete picture of how Frost wrote. In addition to reprinting "all of the prose Frost is known to have prepared for print," Richardson has provided "extensive and detailed notes on Frost's habits of composition, on important textual issues, and on related matters." The editor has made this collection invaluable by adding these detailed notes and by making it possible for "the reader to consult in one place all information presented in connection with a given item," as well as providing "a kind of loosely consequential narrative of Frost's total career as a writer of prose." With this much attention to detail, the collection can, therefore, be of use to both the general reader and the scholar. It is obvious that the editor wholeheartedly believes that a poet of Frost's stature deserves to have his other writings published and analyzed. While the value of the high school editorials and the stories Frost wrote for poultry magazines may be questioned, there are a number of remarkable essays that clearly enunciate Frost's opinions on the art of poetry. It is obvious after reading some of the essays and looking at Richardson's corresponding notes that Frost could express himself well about how he wrote his poems. It is not always the case that a first-rank poet can explain his art and his way of crafting a poem. This allows for a greater understanding of the poet under discussion and can be helpful to a poet in the construction of his or her own work.

In addition to this collection, there have been several other vital books recently published that concern Frost. In 2001, *The Robert Frost Encyclopedia* (edited by Nancy Lewis Tuten and John Zubizarreta) was published. Deirdre Fagan's *Critical Companion to Robert Frost: A Literary Reference to His Life and Work* was published in 2007, as was Peter J. Stanlis's *Robert Frost: The Poet as Philosopher. The Notebooks of Robert Frost*, edited by Robert Faggen, was published in 2006. Faggen is also the author of *The Cambridge Introduction to Robert Frost* (2008) and the editor of *The Cambridge Companion to Robert Frost* (2001). With all this attention being focused on Frost, it is hoped that a more balanced appreciation of his literary accomplishments will be forthcoming. It is not unusual for a major author to go in and out of favor over time, and it seems that with so many books now revisiting Frost that he will gain from the fresh exposure. Although Frost has remained a widely read poet, he has been a misunderstood one. With the publication of *The Collected Prose of Robert Frost* and the other books previously mentioned, this misunderstanding should be greatly reduced. Through the reading of his extraordinary essays and his notebooks, the reader should come away with a far richer assessment of Frost's creative process. He was an endlessly curious and complex person, and, as with most thoughtful writers, he could hold contradictory opinions about various topics. Frost has been praised for his ability to paint vibrant portraits of rural New England life in his poems, but the poems do not end there. Although born in San Francisco, California, he grew up in New England. It was the New England milieu that he became so adept at capturing in his poetry. While attending high school in Lawrence, Massachusetts, Frost wrote some of his earliest editorials. In the December, 1891, editorial "Physical Culture," he speaks of the need to have a "good mind" as well as a "sound body." In his already finely developed sense of observation, he speaks about standing on a street corner and watching men and women hustle past. Frost surmises that someone would see that "scarcely one in ten is erect and well built." The commentator concludes that it is a good idea to make use of the gymnasium, especially the new Young Men's Christian Association (YMCA) gymnasium that was to be built in Lawrence.

While the early editorials and short stories are youthful curiosities, Frost truly shines as a critical thinker in his essays and lectures. He did not write much in the way of criticism, but the few times he did are worth digesting. Since he did not have a high opinion of literary criticism, it is remarkable that any critical essays exist at all. Frost was suspicious of anyone who claimed to be an authority on a poem. For the poet, it is the reader who should be the ultimate critic of a particular poem. As he stated in his brilliant essay "Education by Poetry: A Meditative Monologue" (1931), "Poetry provides the one permissible way of saying one thing and meaning another. People say 'Why don't you say what you mean?' We never do that, do we, being all of us too much poets. We like to talk in parables and in hints and in indirections—whether from difference or some other instinct." While the sciences or history may instruct, poetry exists to provide something closer to enjoyment or possibly even wisdom. Always apprehensive of academic criticism, Frost found that not much originality came from the education process. He hoped that students would be taught to think and not merely to repeat what they had been told. For him, school and poetry do not mix. In his 1925 "Introduction to *The Arts Anthology: Dartmouth Verse 1925*," Frost concludes, "We are here getting a long way with poetry, considering all there is against it in school and college. The poet, as everyone knows, must strike his individual note sometime between the ages of fifteen and twenty-five. He may hold it a long time, or a short time, but it is then he must strike or never. School and college have been conducted with the almost express purpose of keeping him busy with something else till the danger of his ever creating anything is past." These are harsh words, and it is no wonder that Frost never finished his studies at Dartmouth or Harvard University. He learned to be protective of his own poetry and of poetry in general. Poetry should not become the victim of how a student is taught to read a poem in school. The true appreciation of a poem comes through the spontaneous act of immersion into the poem by the reader.

In his 1951 "Poetry and School," Frost emphatically states that "poems are not meant to be read in a course any more than they are to be made a study of." For all of his misgivings about what goes on in schools and colleges, Frost was forced to serve as a lecturer in order to earn a living. He could not support his family merely on his earnings as a poet. While he certainly was grateful to academia for lending support to poetry, he also felt that academia could suffocate the poet. Throughout his essays, lectures, and prefaces, Frost wrestles with how the poet and the educational system can best coexist. Toward the end of his life, he had become the face of American poetry, a public figure whose words and actions held national weight. Richardson has done a national service by gathering these fascinating, mischievous, mundane, ornery, and important prose works by one of America's greatest modern poets.

Jeffry Jensen

Review Sources

Library Journal 133, no. 2 (February 1, 2008): 69-70.
London Review of Books 30, no. 21 (November 6, 2008): 29-30.
The New York Review of Books 55, no. 19 (December 4, 2008): 48-50.
Publishers Weekly 254, no. 42 (October 22, 2007): 46.
The Times, May 15, 2008, p. 7.

THE COMFORTS OF A MUDDY SATURDAY

Author: Alexander McCall Smith (1948-   )
Publisher: Pantheon Books (New York). 240 pp. $23.95
Type of work: Novel
Time: The early twenty-first century
Locale: Edinburgh, Scotland

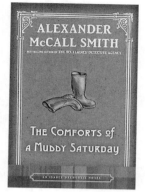

Scottish philosopher Isabel Dalhousie seeks to save the reputation of an Edinburgh physician as she worries about her own relationship with her lover Jamie

Principal characters:

ISABEL DALHOUSIE, a wealthy Edinburgh divorcé in her early forties and editor of *The Review of Applied Ethics* who analyzes the ethics of the most mundane aspects of life

JAMIE FRASER, a professional musician in his late twenties and father of Isabel's child

CHARLIE, the sixteen-month-old son of Isabel and Jamie

JOHN LIAMAR, Isabel's former husband, who has left scars on her psyche

GRACE, Isabel's long-time housekeeper who has assumed the role of Charlie's nurse

CAT, owner of a delicatessen in Edinburgh and Isabel's unmarried niece whose long history of unsuccessful relationships includes one with Jamie

CHRISTOPHER DOVE, Isabel's professional nemesis, who recently attempted to wrest the editorship of *The Review of Applied Ethics* from Isabel

NICK SMART, an American composer, who competes with Isabel for Jamie's time and affection

MARCUS MONCRIEFF, an Edinburgh physician embroiled in a pharmaceutical research scandal

STELLA MONCRIEFF, Marcus's wife, who is determined to clear her husband's name at all cost

NORRIE BROWN, Marcus Moncrieff's nephew and medical colleague

EDDIE, an odd and enigmatic employee in Cat's delicatessen

BROTHER FOX, a wild inhabitant of Isabel's garden, who attracts the attention and affection of Isabel and her family

The Comforts of a Muddy Saturday is the fifth book in McCall's Isabel Dalhousie Novel series, a collection of light mysteries centered around the daily life of a wealthy Scottish philosopher. Isabel enjoys a successful professional life as the owner and editor of *The Review of Applied Ethics*. She is engaged in all aspects of the intellectual and cultural life of her native Edinburgh. An avid collector of art, especially by Scottish artists, she frequents art galleries and attends concerts, especially those in which

~

The creator of the popular No. 1 Ladies' Detective Agency series, Alexander McCall Smith is a retired professor of medical law at the University of Edinburgh. Born in what is now Zimbabwe, he has lived in Edinburgh, Scotland, for most of his life, and he has authored a wide variety of legal books, children's literature, and adult fiction.

~

her lover Jamie performs as bassoonist. Her inherited wealth has provided her with considerable financial security as well as the means to sponsor a variety of philanthropic activities.

McCall draws his readers into the mind of his main character via a constant stream of introspective reflections and self-analysis. As a philosopher, Isabel sees issues of motivation, guilt, innocence, and chance in all the aspects of her personal world. Her philosophical training encourages her to examine the motives and ethical implications of even the most everyday matters. A dinner invitation at the beginning of the novel, for example, leads Isabel, wrongly it turns out, to suspect that her hosts only invited her so they could meet Jamie, who is considerably younger than she is. The submission of an article to Isabel's journal by Christopher Dove, a scholar who had once tried to replace her as editor, generates an elaborate analysis of ethical motivation. Isabel thinks through Dove's possible reasons for submitting the article and agonizes about her moral obligations to accept the article for publication.

Isabel also worries about the personal choices of her niece Cat, who has had a long succession of men in her life and seems unable to form a long-term commitment. Isabel is concerned that her relationship with Jamie, one of Cat's former boyfriends, as well as the birth of Charlie may result in a permanent rift between herself and her niece. Much to Isabel's relief, by the end of the novel, Cat is becoming reconciled to Isabel's happy life and demonstrates some affection toward her young cousin.

The birth of Isabel's son Charlie and his growing demands upon her time and emotions have challenged the philosopher to examine her maternal responsibilities in the context of her wider professional and social interests. While she loves her son, Isabel the philosopher reflects almost daily on the choices she makes in balancing Charlie's needs and her other obligations and in working quality time with Charlie into her other activities.

Most importantly, she mulls over every nuance of her relationship with Jamie and worries that their age difference will inevitably lead to a break-up. She is especially concerned that the responsibilities of their relationship and especially of fatherhood will lead Jamie to resent his loss of freedom. Jamie, on the other hand, seems quite content with his situation. He loves Isabel and enjoys his role as a new father.

Isabel's feelings of insecurity lead her to take an instant dislike to Nick Smart, a pretentious American composer whom she meets at one of Jamie's concerts. She is suspicious of Nick's motivations and jealous of every minute Jamie spends with him. Eventually she learns, much to her relief, that Jamie's interest in Nick is little more than professional, but not before she has been awkwardly ungracious to Nick. She has unfairly suspected the composer of persuading Jamie to seek an exciting career opportunity in New York, while in fact Nick kindly has been helping Jamie work on a musical composition for Isabel.

Isabel's wide circle of friends and acquaintances appear again and again in the Isabel Dalhousie Novel series. This installment is no exception. In *The Comforts of a Muddy Saturday*, Grace, Isabel's strong-minded housekeeper, now cares for Charlie with an attitude more maternal than servile. Her role is relatively minor compared to those in previous novels. Here the housekeeper serves as little more than a background source of concern and tension for Isabel, who strives to ensure that Grace does not monopolize the young Charlie and allows primary care to fall to his parents. Repeatedly Isabel and even Jamie must politely remind Grace of their parental rights in order to spend time with their own son.

More prominent in the plot of *The Comforts of a Muddy Saturday* is Eddie, the emotionally disturbed employee in Cat's delicatessen, with whom Isabel interacts closely as she tends the shop while her niece vacations in Sri Lanka. Mild conflicts emerge as Eddie struggles to understand Isabel's generosity toward customers and even beggars. Isabel is fond of Eddie but curious about his past and his personal life. She invites Eddie home to dinner, where the sight of Isabel's art collection further challenges the lower-class Eddie. After dinner Jamie asks Eddie to demonstrate his recently acquired skill in hypnotism on him, but Eddie accidently hypnotizes Isabel instead. In the process he uncovers in her a lingering and embarrassing affection for her ex-husband John Liamar. The conscious Isabel argues that she no longer loves Liamar, but this episode, combined with Jamie's understanding reaction to it, reminds the rational philosopher about the powers of the irrational and helps her to feel more secure in Jamie's love.

Isabel's wealthy lifestyle becomes more than an awkward topic of conversation with Eddie. When he asks Isabel for 500 pounds, she assumes he needs the money because of a drug or girlfriend problem and readily gives it to him. When she learns that he really wanted the money to pay for surgery for his father, Isabel is disappointed in Eddie's "lie" and expects both an apology and a return of the money as the morally correct course. Isabel's generous and well-intentioned efforts to help Eddie are, in the end, unsuccessful, and her unfair reading of Eddie's motivation and her response to their misunderstanding create an awkwardness that is not resolved in *The Comforts of a Muddy Saturday*.

Isabel's tendency to involve herself in the problems of acquaintances such as Eddie and even strangers is, in fact, a major focus of the Isabel Dalhousie Novel series. Jamie discourages such "intermeddling" or interference in other people's lives, but Isabel's compulsion to engage in such activity drives the "mystery" plots of McCall Smith's novels. The first book in this series, *The Sunday Philosophy Club* (2004), for example, centers around Isabel's "investigation" into the suspicious death of a young man. *The Careful Use of Compliments* (2007) deals with an apparent painting forgery. In *The Comforts of a Muddy Saturday*, Smith, a retired professor of medical law, weaves into the plot his own professional interest in medicine, and especially bioethics, as his protagonist finds herself examining the questionable circumstances surrounding the testing of a medical drug that has left two people dead and destroyed the career of Marcus Moncrieff, a reputable Edinburgh research physician.

Isabel becomes involved in this pharmaceutical scandal at the request of Moncrieff's wife, Stella. Initially Isabel accepts the "facts" of the case as described by both husband and wife and comes to suspect Moncreiff's nephew, Norrie Brown, and, subsequently, the pharmaceutical company itself of framing Moncreiff. Once again, Isabel misreads people's motivations, as she assumes that Marcus's nephew is harboring a grudge against his uncle and interprets the warnings of David McLean, a lawyer for the pharmaceutical company, as veiled threats. In the end, Isabel learns that her basic assumptions about personal motivation in this case are groundless, even as she offers Marcus a way forward for his professional life.

As Isabel is thus challenged by failure and disappointment in *The Comforts of a Muddy Saturday*, she demonstrates resilience and a philosophical positivism that enable her to move beyond her frustrations, especially in her dealings with Eddie and the Moncrieffs. Not only does her relationship with Cat become somewhat more positive after her niece's return from Sri Lanka but also Isabel is reassured of Jamie's loyalty and affection as she watches him interact lovingly with their son and as she sorts out her misunderstandings regarding Nick.

These episodes in Isabel's life conclude, as the title suggests, in the comforts of a muddy Saturday at home, where Isabel and Jamie spend some quiet time with their son in the garden. Isabel feels a sense of personal security and satisfaction watching Charlie play in the grass, while his father works in the garden (and muddies his feet). This peaceful domestic scene is observed not only by Isabel but by a wild fox who lives in her garden and whom she and Jamie endearingly call "Brother Fox."

Like Grace and Cat, Brother Fox is a regular character in the Isabel Dalhousie series. He considers Isabel's garden his territory. At the end of *The Right Attitude to Rain* (2006), for example, Brother Fox enjoyed some culinary delicacies Cat had left as a peace offering for her aunt. In *The Comforts of a Muddy Saturday*, Brother Fox digs up flower bulbs that Jamie must replant in the last scene of the novel. Grace complains about the damage the fox does, worries that the fox might somehow harm Charlie, and wants to call an exterminator. Isabel does not share her housekeeper's concerns. She and Jamie enjoy rather than resent these intrusions by Brother Fox into their lives and feel a special bond with the creature. Jamie, in fact, surprises Isabel with an expensive painting of a fox that becomes a special demonstration of his love for her. He also buys for Charlie a stuffed toy fox with which the real Brother Fox makes yet another mark on their lives at the end of *The Comforts of a Muddy Saturday*.

Thomas J. Sienkewicz

Review Sources

Booklist 104, no. 22 (August 1, 2008): 5.
Christianity Today 52, no. 11 (November, 2008): 74.
Kirkus Reviews 76, no. 15 (August 1, 2008): 3.
Publishers Weekly 255, no. 30 (July 28, 2008): 50.

THE COMMONER

Author: John Burnham Schwartz (1965-   )
Publisher: Nan A. Talese/Doubleday (New York).
    351 pp. $24.95
Type of work: Novel
Time: 1934-2003
Locale: Tokyo and Karuizawa, Japan

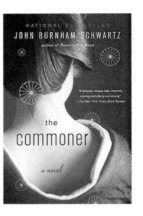

A commoner who finds that by marrying a prince she has lost her freedom and her identity later helps another woman to escape from the same fate

Principal characters:
>HARUKO ENDO, a commoner, a princess after her marriage and later empress of Japan
>SHIGE, her husband, the crown prince of Japan and the emperor after his father's death
>YASUHITO ("YASU") or PRINCE TSUYO, their son, later the crown prince and Keiko's husband
>KUMIKO, his younger sister and a princess until her marriage to a commoner
>THE EMPEROR, Shige's father and a scholarly, unworldly man
>THE EMPRESS, Shige's mother and Haruko's bitter enemy
>MRS. OSHIMA, Haruko's chief lady-in-waiting and the empress's spokesperson
>TSUNEYASU ENDO, Haruko's father and the owner of a sake brewery
>MRS. ENDO, his wife and Haruko's mother
>MIKO KURODA, Haruko's best friend since school days and a longtime resident of the United States
>KEIKO MORI, the daughter of a diplomat and Yasu's wife
>REIKO, the daughter of Keiko and Yasu

As the title suggests, John Burnham Schwartz's *The Commoner* is set in a society where there are sharp distinctions between ordinary people and those of noble or royal ancestry. Though the novel is part an indictment of social stratification based on birth, its primary theme is the conflict between ancient customs and new ideas.

The Commoner is narrated in the first person by Haruko Endo, the title character. Haruko is the only child of Tsuneyasu Endo, a prosperous Japanese businessman, and his wife, a conventional homemaker. Haruko begins her story with a description of an idyllic childhood. From the time of her birth in 1934, Haruko is petted and protected, not only because she is her parents' only child but also because only a young woman with an unspotted reputation can expect to make a suitable marriage. The walled garden where she spends so much of her time symbolizes her existence: She is kept in a beautiful, safe place, where she can do whatever she likes. Haruko has no desire to escape, nor is she interested in what is going on beyond the wall. An economic depression passes almost without her noticing it. When the war comes, Haruko is aware of food shortages, and when her family is evacuated from Tokyo, she knows that they are fleeing from the bombings. However, her father's business survives, and two years after the end of the war, the Endos move back to Tokyo and settle down in their new house, which is much like the one that had been destroyed. Though she cannot ignore the devastation all around her, Haruko is soon preoccupied with her schoolwork at the Sacred Heart Convent School.

John Burnham Schwartz is the author of three previous novels, Bicycle Days *(1989),* Reservation Road *(1998), and* Claire Marvel *(2002). His books have been translated into more than fifteen languages. Schwartz has also written for* The New Yorker, The New York Times Book Review, The Boston Globe, Vogue, *and* Newsday.

She later muses that it was there, under the strict rule of the nuns, that she acquired the habit of silence and the capacity for self-control that later became so important to her. Her best friend, Miko Kuroda, is less submissive. Unfortunately, after they graduate, Miko's father, a diplomat, takes his family with him to his post in Washington, D.C., and Miko enrolls in an American college. Later she marries an American. Thus Haruko loses her only confidante.

Meanwhile, the Endos have begun to spend their summers in Karuizawa, a picturesque country village. There Haruko catches her first glimpse of Shige, the crown prince of Japan. Though after the war Shige's father, the emperor, has declared himself to be a human being instead of a god, his people still hold him in awe and even repeat farfetched stories about his miraculous powers. They extend the same attitude toward his heir.

By the time she is a senior at Sacred Heart University, Haruko is attracting suitors, but she insists that she is not interested in marriage. She would rather be a teacher, she tells her father, like many of her ancestors; he blasts that dream by pointing out that all of those she mentioned were men. It is clear that her only option is to become a wife and mother. However, though her parents bring one promising young man after another to meet their daughter, Haruko does not like any of them. Her parents are puzzled by her attitude, but they are not tyrants; they do not intend to force their only child into marriage with a man she does not like. Meanwhile, Haruko is perfectly happy, especially when she is perfecting her considerable skill at tennis.

Ironically, it is a game of tennis that brings Haruko into contact with a young man who does appeal to her. Because he is the crown prince of Japan, she assumes that they will never be more than acquaintances. However, he seems to like the fact that, to the horror of onlookers, she does not let him win the game. Shige is obviously attracted to Haruko. As the months pass, he manages to see her frequently; meanwhile, he rejects one after another of the young women suggested to him by the committee entrusted with choosing his consort. Finally, the prince's tutor, Dr. Takeshi Watanabe, comes to Endo on Shige's behalf, requesting Haruko's hand in marriage. He is amazed when her father refuses the offer and begs that she be eliminated from consideration. Endo's reasoning is that because Haruko is a commoner, she would never be accepted at court, and that as a result her life would be miserable. He proves to be right.

Although Endo promptly sends his daughter to Europe, hoping to end the matter, Shige is determined to make Haruko his wife. After her return, since the presence of the press has made casual encounters impossible, Shige pursues his courtship by phone. Impressed by his intelligence, his sensitivity, and above all his assurance that he accepts change and even welcomes it, at least in moderation, Haruko finally accepts his proposal. The next seven chapters of this first section of the novel describe the preparations for the wedding, the ceremony itself, and the couple's ride through the city afterward.

Though *The Commoner* is divided into four parts, the first part of the novel is by far the longest, constituting half of the book. It may seem odd that in a novel whose subject is the marriage of a commoner to a prince, so much time is spent on what would seem to be the least glamorous part of the heroine's life. However, in order to show how she is stifled by her marriage, the author must first establish who Haruko is. Later, her malevolent mother-in-law will suggest that Haruko is a disrespectful, ill-mannered young woman without respect for tradition; however, in these early pages it is made clear that Haruko is not a rebel like her friend Miko Kuroda. Haruko accepts the authority of her parents and her teachers, and like them she is in awe of the Emperor. If she is independent-minded enough to trounce the crown prince in a tennis match, she intends no disrespect toward him; the fact that early in their relationship she sees him as a human being, not a prince, is one reason Shige is so strongly attracted to her.

However, even before the wedding there are hints that the two young people will not be permitted to live in peace. Endo's impression of the court is only too accurate. It is ruled by people who not only adhere to centuries-old traditions but also use them as the basis of their own power. If Haruko persuades Shige to suggest a change, the prince is reminded that this is how it has "always" been done, and even if it is pointed out that the supposed tradition is a fairly new development, the imperial staffers are deaf to argument. With Shige's help, Haruko might have been able to deal with such matters, but she has two personal enemies at court who resent the fact that she is a commoner and are determined to break her spirit. One of them is the empress; the other is Mrs. Oshima, who was appointed by the empress to be Haruko's chief lady-in-waiting. Mrs. Oshima is the empress's spy and her mouthpiece; she hears every word Haruko speaks and observes every move she makes, reports to the empress, then repeats the empress's criticisms to Haruko. Since it would be disrespectful to disagree with the empress, even at second hand, Haruko is helpless. She cannot turn to Shige, for she soon learns how much he is intimidated by his mother.

When on their wedding night the newlyweds are given instructions on how to produce a boy, Haruko begins to suspect that, though Shige loves her, the rest of the court and, indeed, the Japanese people value her only as the future mother of an heir to the throne. After she does produce a son, Yasuhito, or "Yasu," as he is nicknamed, she assumes that, having fulfilled her function, she will be left in peace. However, when Haruko is still breastfeeding him, the empress has him weaned and taken away from his mother, insisting that Haruko must return to her scheduled appearances. Haruko has learned to be silent, and now she finds that she cannot speak at all. When she is sent home for a rest, her father tells her she must honor her commitment, and her voice comes back. In time she gives birth to a daughter, Kumiko.

In the last two sections of the novel, the author proceeds to the next generation. Though among commoners, women now have new opportunities, the women at court are as trapped by adherence to old customs as those of Haruko's generation. The only answer, it seems, is for a princess to marry a commoner, give up her title, and learn to cook. Earlier in the novel, it was mentioned that Shige's sister had done just that and was living happily as an ordinary, upper-class woman. In the 1980's, Kumiko makes the same choice, and as a result she has a much more satisfying life than her mother.

With the death of his father in 1989, Shige becomes emperor, and Yasu takes his father's place as crown prince. He knows that his primary duty is to marry and produce a male heir so that the dynasty can continue. When Haruko asks "Why?," she is accused of irreverence. In any case, like his father, Yasu falls in love with a commoner, Keiko Mori. However, Keiko has her mind set on a diplomatic career. She gives in only after Haruko, now the Empress, pleads with her and promises her protection. Though, unlike her own mother-in-law, Haruko is kind to Keiko, Haruko finds that she cannot smooth Keiko's way at court, where women are still supposed to remain silent, or defend her inability to produce a son. When Haruko sees her daughter-in-law falling into despair, she contacts her old friend Miko, and through her efforts Keiko and her little daughter Reiko escape into anonymity and freedom.

The Commoner is a book built on contrasts: the difference between commoners and royalty, between women and men, between self-expression and self-control, between change and custom. What makes the book so thought-provoking is that Schwartz takes pains to understand a point of view with which he clearly disagrees; though he may agree with Haruko's question, he admits that if a dynasty is indeed to continue, there must be an heir. Critics praise *The Commoner* for its compelling narrative structure and for its subtle characterization. It is also described as an important novel because it shows a society in change that is also, in many respects, not changing at all. Though the emperor of Japan may have been forced to admit that he is not a god, Schwartz suggests that there are still many commoners who do not believe him.

Rosemary M. Canfield Reisman

Review Sources

Book World 38 (February 10, 2008): 11.
Booklist 104, no. 8 (December 15, 2007): 23.
The Christian Science Monitor, January 22, 2008, p. 13.
Kirkus Reviews 75, no. 21 (November 1, 2007): 1125-1126.
Library Journal 132, no. 19 (November 15, 2007): 51-52.
The New York Times Book Review 157 (February 24, 2008): 27.

The New Yorker 84, no. 2 (February 25, 2008): 74.
People 69, no. 3 (January 28, 2008): 58.
Publishers Weekly 254, no. 42 (October 22, 2007): 33.
USA Today, January 31, 2008, p. 5D.
The Wall Street Journal 251, no. 21 (January 26, 2008): W8.

CONCEIVING PARENTHOOD
American Protestantism and the Spirit of Reproduction

Author: Amy Laura Hall (1968-   )
Publisher: Wm. B. Eerdmans (Grand Rapids, Mich.).
  452 pp. $32.00
Type of work: History, religion

An exploration of Protestant—especially Methodist—popular church literature in the twentieth century, showing significant capitulations to such anti-Christian trends as eugenics, the corporate control of motherhood, and the campaign to present nuclear power as benign and inevitable

In 1905, German scholar Max Weber published *The Protestant Ethic and the Spirit of Capitalism*, a foundational text in the development of the discipline of sociology. Weber argued that Western capitalist economies gain their unique character and remarkable dynamism not—as Karl Marx had held—from changes in class structure but from the "worldly asceticism" of its religious makers. Weber believed that Martin Luther and John Calvin had destroyed the deep emotional securities found in Catholicism; in their place arose uncertainty about "election" (predestination). However, anxiety about salvation could, Weber argued, be allayed by work. Additionally, Protestants were to avoid ostentation and the accumulation of goods. When this ethic of self-denial combined with the "work ethic," the result was the regime of saving, investing, and calculating that are the prerequisites of capitalism. As her title—*Conceiving Parenthood*—indicates, Amy Laura Hall seeks to interpret American Protestantism along Weberian lines, but with a special focus on norms of family life that have evolved since Methodism's fervent early days on the American frontier. A pro-life feminist, she teaches theological ethics at the Divinity School at Duke University. Significant to her account is the fact that Hall is the mother of two daughters, one of whom is adopted.

Her general thesis is that American Protestants have too readily fulfilled Weber's characterizations, forsaking their best theological impulses in doing so. They have indeed been controlling and "mercantilist" when they should have been extravagantly generous and celebratory. They have been narrowly calculating in too many phases of life, identifying success with wealth and status rather than with solidarity and service. Worst of all, they have allowed themselves to be manipulated by capitalist culture into thinking that their children must be perfect or, at least, earn perfection in a Darwinian struggle for prominence.

Against this broad trend, Hall places the example of Methodism when it was "filled with new wine," heedless of institutional and familial correctness. Born in England in the first half of the eighteenth century, Methodism "embraced the holy work of open-air stump preaching, coal-mine conversions, women preachers . . . and wor-

Amy Laura Hall teaches theological ethics at Duke University. As a member of the Bioethics Task Force of the United Methodist Church, Hall has addressed the World Council of Churches in Geneva and academic audiences in Zurich, Cambridge, Edinburgh, and Oxford about her work on reproductive ethics. Her book Kierkegaard and the Treachery of Love *was published in 2002.*

ship that mixed shopkeepers, factory workers, and Oxford-trained dons in ways that seemed ill conceived to many in power." Hall particularly admires the example of Jonathan Kozol, whose emphasis on the permanent worth and blessedness of all children pushes his readers to extend their imagination beyond the family, embracing as their own the children of the poor and rejected. That this Jewish revolutionary pedagogue should be a hero of Hall's book is an irony that her theology—focused on God's surprising grace—can easily encompass.

Hall advances her case by treating four topics that at first appear to be unrelated. Indeed, one of the book's achievements is the demonstration of their thoroughgoing connection. They are the campaign to make American homes "hygienic"; the corporate takeover of childrearing and homemaking through the marketing of "expert information" and related products such as infant formula; the conscription of church elites into the American eugenics movement, whose "poisonous messages echo still"; and the complacent reception by Protestants of the propaganda effort to make Hiroshima seem necessary and nuclear power an unambiguously good thing. In recent decades, failure to resist the darker temptations of genetic manipulation builds on the same tendency.

Hall argues these far-reaching theses by adopting the strategies of both the popular culture studies movement and postmodernist discourse analysis. She examines such mass-market periodicals as *Parents, Ladies' Home Journal, Better Homes and Gardens,* and *McCall's* because their readership was "markedly Anglo-Saxon, mainline Protestant." She pays especially close attention to *Together,* a Methodist magazine designed to compete with these secular publications. In addition to commenting on particular articles and editorials in these magazines, Hall does "close readings" of photographs, illustrations, and, especially, advertisements. Indeed, of the 135 figures that enliven the book, the majority are advertisements. This research strategy makes for lively viewing and reading, but it also limits the book in significant ways because the relation among advertising, public opinion, and core attitudes is exceedingly complex. The fact that many expensive advertising campaigns do not actually succeed is only one facet of this complexity.

In chapter 1, "Holy Hygiene: *Parents'*, Protestantism, and the Germ-Free Home," Hall vividly illustrates the commercial and cultural impact of the late-nineteenth century discovery of pathogens and effective antisepsis. Drawing on the work of social historian Rima Apple, she traces the rise of "scientific motherhood," a movement to reform old-fashioned homemaking practices through the use of electrical appliances, sterilization, and disinfection, the new teachings of home economics and pediatrics, and—ominously—eugenics. Hall's overarching claim is that while the new research labs, institutes, university courses, medical expertise, and mass-marketed products seemed "value-free" attempts to improve public health, they actually promoted a lethal hidden agenda. Hence, advertisements for Lysol, Maltine, Gold Dust Twins soap, and evaporated milk were not just about the benefits of cleanliness; they also positioned women and mothers in oppressive social frameworks.

By purchasing these products, they would not only be cleansing their homes and children more effectively, they would also be advancing the cause of "the race." For "scientific motherhood" came of age during the first flourishing of theories of "racial hygiene" in the United States, and it incorporated many of its themes: the necessity of keeping "favored" races separate from "failed" races; the superiority of "Nordic" peoples; the inherent primitiveness and filth of black Africans; and the threat posed by immigrants from central and southern Europe. (Readers who associate such ideas only with the National Socialists will be surprised to learn about the American Eugenics Society, some of whose founders published books that inspired German race theory.)

Hall also detects in her sources strongly sexist and classist messages. Thus, Lysol's claims about the advantages of douching stressed both contraception and the need for women to remain sexually appealing to their husbands. At the same time, the woman who used Lysol and similar products would be allying herself with an educated elite. If this meant confinement in a sterile home and an obsession with germs, at least women could feel that they were "progressive." As Hall puts it, "For my reading of 'the germ-free home,' the aspiration to craft families of providential promise teetered on the knife edge of maternal self-loathing, whereby a woman's own body became a site of potentially hidden menace." Viewed theologically, the submerged rhetoric of the hygiene craze invited Christians to separate themselves out from the germ-ridden "other." Hall insists that followers of Jesus—especially Methodists whose entire history has been one of evangelizing the ordinary and the outcast—violate their central calling by such drawing apart. In other words, providing safe and clean environments only for one's own children is simply heretical.

Chapter 2, titled "The Corporate Breast: 'Scientific Motherhood' During the Century of Progress," moves Hall's critique closer to the present. The title derives from the official name of the 1933 Chicago World's Fair: "A Century of Progress: 1833-1933." Relying especially on Christina Cogdell's book *Eugenic Design: Streamlining America in the 1930's* (2004), Hall explores advertisements placed in medical journals and popular family magazines by such companies as Nestlé, Gerber, Johnson & Johnson, Scott, and Enfamil. She finds two intersecting trends: the persistence of themes rooted in the "science" of evolutionary progress and an appropriation of the language of "natural" by the makers of distinctly less-than-natural child-care products. The ultimate aim of these commercial campaigns was, believes Hall, the transformation of the meaning of "natural" and "ordinary." "Normal" everyday life, to meet these implicit standards, had to become enhanced by a vast panoply of toys, nutritional supplements, sexually rejuvenated moms, and evenings filled with televised entertainment. What especially interests Hall about the Chicago World's Fair is the way "primitive," backward, and unprogressive people were displayed. Thus, juxtaposed to the World of Tomorrow were the Midget Village, the Old Plantation, and Ripley's Odditorium. Freaks of nature were not merely present as lures to the curious, she argues. They were living lessons in the importance of genetic purity, Anglo-Saxon excellence, and the dangers posed by Negroes.

Conceiving Parenthood's third chapter, "To Form a More Perfect Union: Mainline Protestants and the American Eugenics Movement," traces the impact of race-purification ideas on prominent clergy and laity in the early decades of the last century. Hall's argument is made possible by such recent works as Matthew Frye Jacobson's *Whiteness of a Different Color: European Immigrants and the Alchemy of Race* (1998); Wendy Kline's *Building a Better Race: Gender, Sexuality, and Eugenics from the Turn of the Century to the Baby Boom* (2001); and Edwin Black's *War Against the Weak: Eugenics and America's Campaign to Create a Master Race* (2003). What Hall brilliantly adds is information about Protestants' enthusiasm for the American Eugenics Association, birth control, sociological studies of "cacogenic" rural families, and intelligence testing.

She details the disturbing fact that, under the sway of eugenic ideas, the church began to question its own work of caring for the poor. Christian charity, it was argued, was "dysgenic," as it perpetuated unfit lives. Indeed, some theologians began to argue that salvation's first phase was realized in the protection of a healthy biological heritage, coded language for racial "cleansing." In doing so, they effectively biologized the meaning of "grace," making it synonymous with mental and physical fitness.

Hall believes these anti-Christian patterns of thought persist into the present. Protestant Christians, she states, are "eager to forge a promising future for their families . . . by way of technologies, neighborhoods, and schools of distinction, leaving behind those who do not measure up and cannot keep up in a competitive, streamlined market culture." In her final substantive chapter, "For Domestic Security: The Atomic Age and the Genomic Revolution," she presses these claims with even more force. Still working historically, she first reviews the early postwar political and commercial effort to present atomic energy as promising an abundant, safe future for Americans. Just as the small, upwardly mobile "nuclear family" was becoming normative, the atom became "domesticated" in the form of power plants. Americans were inundated by advertisements that connected such power to a limitless future of consumption. This campaign served to block out the memories of the horrors of what happened in Japan and anesthetize citizens to the sufferings posed by above-ground nuclear testing.

As a dominant cultural symbol, the "peaceful atom" gave way, claims Hall, to the double helix. Thus, the remainder of the book explores the implications of the Human Genome Project, genetic screening, and the role of large pharmaceutical companies in persuading the public to purchase its products. Hall fears that Christian ethics and lay opinion will focus narrowly on particular biotechnological issues at the expense of basic public health concerns. Worse, though, is the temptation to trace individual defects to genetic inheritance. Such a perspective, she argues, rests on the assumption that defects and deficits are fixable—if not now, then in some more controllable genetic future. This notion runs counter to essential Christian orientations, which subsume the family under the wider notions of "God's people." Membership in the body of Christ is open to all and proceeds by means of adoption. Because adoption is incompatible with ideas of racial and genetic purity, it becomes Hall's central closing metaphor. Christians do not in fact recognize "unfitness"; adopting children—and new members—is their "natural" way. Thus, the present task is to present stories of resistance to the cultural dominance of Darwinism. In practical terms, asserts Hall, "resistance involves eschewing the various means by which I am to distinguish my own daughters from children who seem vaguely 'backward,' from those who are considered 'at risk,' from neighborhoods that seem forsaken by God, and from schools deemed by quantified percentages to be subpar."

Hall's contribution is a substantial one, especially to Christian parents trying to withstand the ethos of individualistic competition and success-through-achievement. That much of her evidence comes from advertising—well displayed throughout the volume—makes the book very engaging. Hall's dedication to Methodism, whose shortcomings she persistently documents, is refreshing at a time when "mainline" denominations are declining.

Nevertheless, *Conceiving Parenthood* could have been a better book. Hall's editors failed to eliminate both academic jargon and authorial process-talk. Clarity of argumentation is compromised by ungainly chapters into which too much material is packed. One is never quite sure about the audience Hall wants to address. While apparently a theological critique of a submerged but powerful current in American history, the book keeps moving toward feminist-postmodernist cultural commentary. For example, "The Corporate Breast" is nearly ninety pages long, yet it contains almost no references to the church or to theology. This drift in focus—coupled with Hall's reluctance to indicate at regular intervals how her main argument is developing—diminishes the book's power. The problem is best exemplified by the fact that while the Weber thesis is invoked in the title and referenced in the introduction, she actually does nothing with this crucial intellectual connection. One might therefore predict that particular sections of the book will be carefully studied, with relatively few readers actually making it through to the end.

Leslie E. Gerber

Review Sources

Christianity Today 52, no. 7 (July, 2008): 55.
Publishers Weekly 254, no. 51 (December 24, 2007): 48.

CONCRETE REVERIES
Consciousness and the City

Author: Mark Kingwell (1963-   )
Publisher: Viking (New York). 292 pp. $24.99
Type of work: History
Time: The twenty-first century
Locale: New York, Shanghai, Tokyo, Toronto, and other
cities around the globe

*The questions that Kingwell asks in this cultural essay
on the transnational global city—New York, Shanghai, Tokyo, Toronto—are "How do cities shape people?" and
"How do people shape cities?"*

Concrete Reveries begins with a meditation on concrete, the gray, malleable stuff that turns hard when set and
is one of the principal building blocks of modern cities. Mark Kingwell describes the
texture as having a tough muscularity and thinks of the iron rebar inside as its skeleton. The rain marks chiaroscuro patterns on its micro-pitted surface. For him, a concrete wall seems to weep in the rain as the water runs down the surface, appearing like
mascara on a crying face. Although he finds concrete beautiful, especially in the rain,
Kingwell points out that it is a material that people love to hate in preference to natural
building products such as wood or finished stone. He admits concrete has been abused
as a building material, constructing, for example, Soviet-style apartment blocks, face-
less structures such as parking lots, and the soulless academic boxes that have become
synonymous with the modern university. In the defense of concrete, however, Kingwell observes that although any material becomes the sum of its treatments, it does
not need to be so.

  Concrete is not just basic to the structures of the urban moment: It is also central to
the perceptions of the city, especially in creating the idea of the contemporary, alienated metropolitan imagination, the concrete jungle that permeates the modern artistic
sensibility. "Concrete is also expressive and rewarding, a human material for all its
toughness. It is capable of making a complex statement, exciting a nuanced reaction,"
Kingwell writes, and he notes that at one time concrete was lauded as a revolutionary
building material, as avant-garde as glass. In spite of its solidity and seeming intracta-
bility, concrete is nevertheless a plastic material, as architect Frank Lloyd Wright observed, one seeking form by an elemental alchemy of the stuff of the earth—sand,
rocks, and so on. It is an argument designed to counter the natural materials critics.
This back-and-forth debate—between concrete's perceived negative aspects and its
qualities made positive under Kingwell's creative gaze—forms a tension that typifies
the intellectual structure of the book. It is one of the purposes of his study to encourage his readers to learn to observe textures, and by extension the city, as surfaces writ
large in new and different ways, expanding his readers' experience of the urban space.

Kingwell posits that the transnational global city is the most significant machine ever produced by humans. Every major urban center is a testament to a human desire to master nature in the drive for order, cleanliness, and beauty that is the center of the civilizing project, according to Sigmund Freud. As Kingwell notes: We are cities and cities are us. "And yet, we fail," he writes, "again and again, to understand them correctly. Almost all of our models of metaphors for thinking about cities are inadequate . . . ." Cities are not biological, but they exhibit organic features: They experience growth, disease, and decline. They are more than architecture, violence, or commerce, although all three are part of the city's character. Kingwell quotes the urbanist Kevin Lynch, who identifies five ways of attempting a unifying model for the city: "an organism, an economic engine, a communications network, a system of linked decisions, and an arena of conflict." All are helpful ways to envision the city, but none is adequate to sum up the breadth of the ways to experience it.

∼
Mark Kingwell is a professor of philosophy at the University of Toronto and Senior Fellow of Massey College. He is a contributor to Harper's Magazine, *and he frequently appears on radio and television. He teaches and writes about cultural issues, design, and architecture.*
∼

Cities are not just systems, markets, or arenas but, as Kingwell describes them, collisions of natural conditions, material forces, and human desire. They are tangles of vectors and imponderables. First and foremost, though, cities are places, areas of significance, physical staging grounds. "Places are environments, sites of action, horizons of concern." With these evocative observations, Kingwell begins a philosophical and physical investigation into what he describes as the built environment, especially the late-model form of cities. *Concrete Reveries* directs its readers to work from the outside in when thinking about the city, moving from the physical object to the philosophical contemplation of it, moving from architecture to consciousness. Kingwell intends his readers to achieve a renewed appreciation for the complexity of their conscious lives and their being in place and, more practically, a sense of urgency for their engagement in the creation of new democratic cities. Every city is, in a sense, a city of the imagination, an unrealized project. The book is not a blueprint, Kingwell writes, but rather a series of incomplete sketches for thinking and arguing about what places, namely cities, mean to humans.

Kingwell begins his exploration of urban space in New York City, the place he calls the capital of the twentieth century, in the way that Walter Benjamin, the German cultural critic, labeled Paris the capital of the nineteenth century. Just as Benjamin excavated in his extraordinary *Arcades Project* (1989) the urban environment of Paris as the birthplace of modernity, so, too, does Kingwell plumb the depths, sift the sediment, and troll the streets of the cities he explores. Like the flâneur, that walker in the city made famous by the nineteenth century French poet Charles Baudelaire who has no particular object or even destination for his walk around the city, Kingwell lets his thoughts and imagination be guided by the structure of the streets, the buildings flanking them, and the crowds mingling on the sidewalks.

The flâneur is the observer who meditates over each event, moment of contact, and striking visual, allowing these to direct his mind, if not his feet. The seemingly random meanderings of the walker belie the coherence of the thoughts engendered by the observations on that walk. Like those urban explorers before him, Kingwell comments on his surroundings to draw broader lessons from them, and in his case he quickens the pace. He cites the jaywalker as the new urban pedestrian, one who moves at a faster speed, with perhaps more purpose, creating a dynamic to refashion not only the idea of the city but also his observations on the new environment of the twentieth, now twenty-first, century metropolis.

As a philosopher, Kingwell cites his intellectual sources—from the ancients, such as Plato, to the moderns, such as Jacques Derrida—in reshaping his view of the topology of ideas surrounding the urban experience. His text is evocatively and generously illustrated by a wide variety of visual images, and his narrative is punctuated by references to other such popular commentators on the urban scene as Lewis Mumford and Jane Jacobs. Saul Bellow, Henry Miller, Sylvia Plath, Tom Wolfe, Woody Allen, and Walt Whitman are quoted or referenced along with a list of other urban artists who add to the cultural and intellectual mosaic of the book. There is so much going on here that it is impossible to adequately summarize the book's content.

The fun of reading *Concrete Reveries* is found in the various ways Kingwell combines ideas, generates new ones, and re-forms the reader's concepts of the city, of how it works, and of how it influences perceptions. One of this multiexperiential narrative's strengths is following the multiple paths Kingwell's mind takes and enjoying the means by which he arrives at his conclusions. It is instructive to watch Kingwell play with his references, bounce ideas off the architecture that has become so banal a part of the urbanized-world landscape, and challenge his readers to engender some thoughts of their own.

Concrete Reveries is a philosophical meditation, dense at times, occasioned by the experience of the city. Urban space offers a multiform site for the exercise of human desire and the exploration of the self. Kingwell describes the streets as a fluid site for interaction. With their thirst for stimulation, humans can best realize it in the ever-changing kaleidoscope of otherness and spectacle that makes up the thoroughfares of the city. The interaction between the individual and the street-level urban environment can foster "new forms of selfhood, new subject positions and nodes of identity, by way of our being outside ourselves: the dance of movement on the streets, the kinesthesis of walking, the artwork of self-presentation." The rationalization of the city—with its linearity, its laws, and its rules—gives way to appropriating the city scene as a democratic play, undermining the potential restrictions of the concrete reality of the urban environment. Thus, in its restrained chaos and its organized fluidity, the city can, if approached in the right way, aid the individual citizen in his or her personal development.

Kingwell concludes: "The self, conscious of itself as embodied consciousness, crossing and recrossing the thresholds of the city, creating new ones, is a kind of alien body within the civic order. This imaginary self leaves traces of its swift meander behind, in the form of interactions and encounters. It constantly charts its possibilities. In search of wonder, it opens its gaze to the existence of the others, moving here and there, and shifts the brusque call of authority into a warmer message of shared vulnerability and desire, a shared second-person space."

Kingwell has written a challenging, thoroughly original, and rewarding book that plots the impact the transnational modern global city has made on the consciousness of the contemporary human psyche. His opening reverie on concrete points to the direction, from the solid to the intellectual, that his peregrination through the urban landscape will take and demonstrates the impact that a freewheeling meditation on the physical can have on consciousness. He accompanies his text with a comprehensive bibliographic essay that contains sources for further reading and a listing of the origins of the references throughout the book. It is also fully indexed.

As demanding as *Concrete Reveries* can be and as tricky as Kingwell's prose sometimes is, making the effort to stay with him on his journey ultimately does pay off. Readers will come away with a better understanding of the urban landscape and with an increased appreciation of how an informed and critical eye can expand knowledge of the city and of its inhabitants.

Charles L. P. Silet

Review Sources

Booklist 104, no. 22 (August 1, 2008): 12-14.
Library Journal 133, no. 13 (August 15, 2008): 88.
Publishers Weekly 255, no. 21 (May 26, 2008): 48.
The Wall Street Journal 252, no. 39 (August 15, 2008): W3.
The Wilson Quarterly 32, no. 4 (Autumn, 2008): 99.

THE CRAFTSMAN

Author: Richard Sennett (1943-   )
Publisher: Yale University Press (New Haven, Conn.).
    326 pp. $27.50
Type of work: Sociology, psychology, technology, ethics
Time: Medieval times through early twenty-first century

Sennett envisions a material culture in which human be-ings—through better understanding the process of making things—can skillfully craft their own places in the world

People tend to have strong opinions about material culture, and what is viewed as advancement by one may be another's anathema. The continuum ranges from those who experience acquisition (and thus ever-increasing production) as their birthright and those who may not possess as much or gain it as easily but who are nonetheless aspiring and acquiring to those who do not participate appreciably or successfully in the material culture as well as the iconoclasts who are consciously choosing to forgo it. Despite differing practices and perspectives, the culture of materialism seems likely here to stay. As it becomes irrefutable that materialism is endangering the ecology of the planet, long-term ramifications and ethics are increasingly being emphasized. People are asking what is good and what is enough and what is good enough. People are also asking about work. What is work for, and what does it mean to do work well?

Richard Sennett addresses such issues in *The Craftsman.* He investigates—among other things—the history of craftsmanship; how work is (or could better be) organized; distinctions between job and career; the correlation between disciplined work and a settled mind; and the interconnectedness of work and play. Sennett values the sense of craftsmanship that was exemplified in earlier times and documents its diminishment. He argues, however, that its essence is still present in the technological world, evidenced by such examples as open-source computer software, particularly Linux, which Sennett refers to as a public craft. Refuting polarizing viewpoints, Sennett asserts that material culture matters. To that end, this first volume of Sennett's planned trilogy lays the foundation by investigating craftsmanship as "an enduring, basic human impulse, the desire to do a job well for its own sake." He explains that the second volume will explore the creation of rituals to deal with aggression, while the third will focus on making sustainable environments. Sennett says that all three books consider the dangers of material culture and look at technique as a cultural issue, yet each book is intended to be independent.

Sennett traces the fear of material civilization back to the Greek myth of Pandora. The story is that Zeus ordered Hephaestus (god of craftsmanship, bringer of civilization) to create Pandora (goddess of invention), who was sent to earth as a punishment for Prometheus's wrongdoing. Pandora, possessed of talents, was also given a box (or jar, terminologies differ; Sennett sometimes refers to Pandora's casket), which she was told not to open. Pandora disobeyed, and thus she released all the ills of humanity. Sennett cites the modern secular interpretation of this myth, in which the evils in Pandora's casket are no longer seen as put there by angry gods but are somehow intrinsically the fault of humankind.

◇

Richard Sennett is professor of sociology at New York University and the London School of Economics. The recipient of numerous honors, he was awarded the Hegel Prize in 2006. His most recent books include The Culture of the New Capitalism *(2006) and* Respect in a World of Inequality *(2003). Sennett is also a classically trained musician.*

◇

Sennett believes that "experts in fear of their own expertise" create new technologies almost in a detached way and then turn them over to the general public without a framework of how their work should be used. He references instances in wartime (obviously, the atomic bomb) as well as in peacetime (the ecological crisis, for example, for which Sennett believes "technology may be an unreliable ally in regaining control"). Sennett disagrees, however, with people who idealize the simpler ways of the past as well as those who eschew technological trends for the future. He unfolds his disagreement with influential political theorist Hannah Arendt and well-known German philosopher Martin Heidegger, among others, explaining that "fear of Pandora creates a rational climate of dread," and dread can cause paralysis. Sennett sees technology as a risk, for sure, but certainly not as the enemy.

A student of Arendt almost half a century before, Sennett says that he was inspired by her ideas, but, even then, he felt they were not sufficient to deal with materialism and the technology inside Pandora's casket. He argues that the division between *Animal laborens* (humanity as beasts of burden who ask "how," where work is seen as a never-ending necessity) and *Homo faber* (people asking "why," producing a life in common) is false because it "slights the practical man or woman at work." In order to deal with the issues of Pandora's casket, Sennett calls for what he terms a more vigorous cultural materialism, including a fuller general understanding of how people produce things. Rather than present the public—after the fact—with what has already been produced, Sennett says that engagement with materialism must start earlier. *The Craftsman* is his attempt to jump-start the conversation, and this intellectually and emotionally stimulating expedition is likely to do just that—although it may not completely satisfy readers looking for reductive reassurance. Sennett's approach to materialism is to ask "what the process of making concrete things reveals to us about ourselves," and in doing so, he advocates for the blending of doing and thinking.

Western civilization, where a rather wide chasm exists between working with the hand and working with the head, typically has trouble with such balance. Sennett delves into craftsmanship historically as a means to examine both current practices and what craftsmanship has the potential to mean. Along the way, he clears up misconceptions even as he expands the concept of craft from skilled manual labor to include the doctor, the artist, the parent, even the role of citizen of the world. All of these improve, he says, when they are practiced as skilled craft. Sennett explains that good craftsmanship involves "a dialogue between concrete practices and thinking," evolving into "sustaining habits," in turn establishing "a rhythm between problem solving and problem finding."

The Craftsman is organized into three sections of several chapters each, focusing in turn on the craftsman, the craft, and craftsmanship. Sennett moves easily through the centuries, suggesting that "developments in high technology reflect an ancient model for craftsmanship, but the reality on the ground is that people who aspire to be good craftsmen are depressed, ignored, or misunderstood by social institutions."

Sennett considers in detail the master-apprentice relationship—including, among other things, an investigation of medieval workshops (using guilds of goldsmiths as a detailed example), the workshop of Antonio Stradivari (generally considered the most significant luthier of all time), and institutions such as modern hospitals and laboratories.

Discussion of *The Encyclopedia, or Dictionary of Arts and Crafts* (published in thirty-five volumes between 1751 and 1772) is particularly thought-provoking. Edited mainly by Denis Diderot, it described in words and pictures how to do practical things in fields ranging from agriculture to military science to masonry. Sennett says that this book put work with the hands on par with mental work, such that "the craftsman stood out as the emblem of Enlightenment." Shortly afterward, the Industrial Age created a turning point in human society. In Adam Smith's *The Wealth of Nations* (1776), considered the first modern work of economics, it was asserted that machines would destroy the Enlightenment. Sennett chooses instead to advance the counter position held by Diderot and others, explaining that its true implications may only be becoming clear centuries later. Sennett formulates Diderot's position as follows:

> The enlightened way to use a machine is to judge its powers, fashion its uses, in light of our own limits rather than the machine's potential. We should not compete against the machine. A machine, like any model, ought to propose rather than command, and humankind should certainly walk away from command to imitate perfection. Against the claim of perfection we can assert our own individuality, which gives distinctive character to the work we do.

Sennett advances the view that doing things perfectly is not the same as doing them well, and technological progress is not improvement unless it also enlightens people about themselves.

In the section on craft, Sennett explains that all skills—even abstract ones—begin in the body, and that in order to gain technical understanding, the imagination must be involved. In one perceptive and hilarious chapter, he uses three recipes for cooking chicken to illustrate the power of tacit knowledge as well as the distinction between expressive and denotative instruction. Sennett's extended discussion of resistance and ambiguity is also especially insightful, explaining how working with material challenges can foster understanding of the resistances and unclear boundaries that exist between people. "In labor as in love," Sennett says, "progress occurs in fits and starts."

The third section considers motivation and talent for quality-driven work. Arguing that motivation is more important than talent, Sennett agrees with the Enlightenment view that nearly everyone can become a good craftsman (he says he uses this term throughout as inclusive of men and woman). Asserting that craftsmanship is often thwarted rather than encouraged in many modern organizations, he distinguishes between social and antisocial expertise, highlighting the ill effects of the latter. He also explains how the gradual accrual of knowledge and skills creates "a sustaining narrative" in a person's life, which a well-crafted organization would want to support and encourage. In his conclusion, Sennett traces the growth of American pragmatism, of which he is a proponent, and clearly reiterates the book's central argument: "the craft of making physical things provides insights into the techniques of experience that can shape our dealings with others." It is interesting to consider that in a world full of problems, between and among individuals and nations, the key to understanding and mutual progress may have been in people's hands all along.

The Craftsman has been generally well received by critics, who cite Sennett's brilliant mind and command of wide-ranging material. A few have questioned the book's historical sense, and many have expressed surprise that a work on craftsmanship would itself contain so many typographical errors. For the most part, however, such things do not diminish the book's significance. Many reviewers have commented on Sennett's writing style. Rather than expound in a straightforward fashion, he embarks on an erudite, multifaceted quest full of references and examples, with subject matter, continents, and centuries juxtaposed to create "ah-ha" moments for the reader. Sennett sometimes introduces an idea, then leaves it—only to pick up the thread later and expect readers to be right with him on the cusp of his thought. While some readers may be frustrated by what seem to be digressions, others will likely be engrossed and invigorated.

Ultimately, *The Craftsman* is an intellectual journey rather than a means to an end. On one level, readers are asked to follow the artifacts of Sennett's investigation, with all the idiosyncratic twists of a personal essay. Readers are also expected to have basic background knowledge; Sennett says he includes context for his references only where he feels it will be needed. Sennett is a polymath, so whether he will be on target with any individual reader is an open question. On a deeper level, however, readers are being encouraged to chart their own course, to create a wholeness of knowledge for themselves from the parts provided. Rather than simply offer information, this book is likely to stimulate expansion on the level of consciousness, essential for readers in order to make the imaginative leap for which Sennett argues—to understand the value of experience itself as a craft.

Jean C. Fulton

Review Sources

American Scholar 77, no. 2 (Spring, 2008): 128-131.
The Guardian (London), February 9, 2008, p. 6.
New Statesman 137 (February 11, 2008): 58-59.
The New York Review of Books 55, no. 16 (October 23, 2008): 28-30.
The New York Sun, April 23, 2008, p. 14.
The New York Times Book Review, April 6, 2008, p. 20.
The Observer (London), February 17, 2008, p. 25.
The Sunday Times (London), February 10, 2008, p. 44.
The Wall Street Journal 271, no. 72 (March 27, 2008): D7.

CREDIT AND BLAME

Author: Charles Tilly (1929-2008)
Publisher: Princeton University Press (Princeton, N.J.).
   183 pp. $24.95
Type of work: Sociology, philosophy

This study of giving and receiving credit and blame places an emphasis on the relationship between those who assign and receive credit and those who assign and receive blame, essentially defining such relationships as ultimately seeking justice in human relationships

Principal personages:
   GEORGE WASHINGTON, first president of the United States
   ABRAHAM LINCOLN, sixteenth president of the United States
   WARREN G. HARDING, twenty-ninth president of the United States
   RICHARD MILHOUS NIXON, thirty-seventh president of the United States
   BILL CLINTON, forty-second president of the United States
   JEFF and MICHAEL DERDERIAN, brothers who owned The Station, a nightclub in West Warwick, Rhode Island
   DANIEL BIECHELE, manager of the rock band Great White
   FYODOR DOSTOEVSKI, Russian realistic novelist

   Shortly after Charles Tilly's death on April 29, 2008, Lee C. Bollinger, president of Columbia University, where Tilly had held the Joseph I. Buttenwieser Professorship in the Social Sciences, noted that Tilly "could write, interpret, and explain virtually anything to curious minds." Bollinger went on to say that during Tilly's fifty-year academic career, he had published more than six hundred articles and fifty-one books and monographs. *Credit and Blame*, released around the time of Tilly's death, amply demonstrates the breadth and depth of his thinking and writing. His two books that immediately preceded *Credit and Blame*—*Why?*, published in 2006, and *Democracy*, published in 2007—bear a relationship to Tilly's final publication. *Why?* seeks to understand explanations that are used to get to the roots of human actions and reactions. As Tilly pondered such questions, he began to focus on people's acceptance of credit and assignment of blame as they affect human relationships.
   In *Why?*, Tilly categorizes explanations into four classifications that he calls dereliction, deviance, distinction, and good fortune. He points out that if one misses an appointment, an explanation might be that one is having a "senior moment." This explanation is generally sufficient if one is explaining such a dereliction to family members or close friends. It is not appropriate, though, if one is attempting to explain a missed appointment for an important job interview. Considerations relating to blame, inher-

~

During a teaching career spanning fifty years, Charles Tilly published studies in a daunting array of topics, most sociologically oriented. Following a distinguished academic career at the University of Michigan in Ann Arbor, Tilly became a professor of social sciences at Columbia University. He is also known for his books on French culture, including Strikes in France, 1830-1968 *(1974), with Edward Shorter, and* The Contentious French *(1986).*

~

ent in this earlier study, led Tilly to a deeper probing of how people deal with blame in various contexts.

In *Democracy*, Tilly focuses on how people often misinterpret what democracy is. As in *Credit and Blame*, he probes deeply into misunderstandings of many principles and conventions that people have grown so accustomed to that they fail to arrive at a critical understanding of those principles and conventions.

Tilly's explanation of the two major terms he considers in his work, credit and blame, is useful. He cites the Oxford English Dictionary, the most comprehensive etymological dictionary of the English language, for the origins of these terms. Credit is derived from the Latin word *credere*, which means to trust or to believe. Historically, its participial form, *creditum*, refers to something entrusted to another person, including a loan. Tilly is accurate in contending that where there is credit there also exists a human relationship between those receiving and those giving credit.

Blame is derived from the Latin *blasphemare*, which means to revile or blaspheme. Implicit in this term is, as in the other term upon which Tilly is focusing, a human relationship between one who blames and one who receives blame. He emphasizes that both of the terms he is exploring generally involve human relationships, a point he reiterates throughout his book.

In discussing the trials relating to a Rhode Island nightclub fire in which more than one hundred people died, Tilly relates how, during the sentencing of the Derderian brothers, who owned the nightclub, and a band manager, Daniel Biechele, who ignited the fireworks that spawned the deadly conflagration, victims and those related to victims swarmed into the courtroom to place blame and demand justice for their losses.

Throughout *Credit and Blame*, Tilly demonstrates how those who ascribe blame are ultimately seeking what, in their eyes, constitutes justice. In most cases, an eye-for-an-eye retribution is sought by an injured public that is predictably disappointed at what might be considered light sentences. Tilly points out, however, that "judges try to keep decisions on the unemotional tracks of existing codes. They steer discussion away from popular justice toward what a 'reasonable person' would do in the circumstances." In *Democracy*, Tilly provides similar cogent examples of how the masses misinterpret situations in which they have vested interests.

In essence, Tilly assesses how emotion often thwarts reason in instances where credit is given or blame is ascribed. He cautions that blame is not necessarily credit turned upside down, although, in some situations, such may be the case. He concludes that blame may be a distortion of credit rather than the opposite of it.

In discussing the differences between credit and blame, he contends that "credit calls up a justification that associates giver and receiver in the same moral milieu, while blame separates two moral settings from each other." This is perhaps the most cogent distinction Tilly makes between the two entities of his topic.

In some instances, credit may quickly become blame. Tilly cites the death in office of President Warren G. Harding in 1923. At the time, many Americans viewed Harding's death as an irreparable loss. More mourners lined the route of his funeral train than at any time since the train carrying Abraham Lincoln's body made its way from Washington to Illinois.

Soon, however, the credit the public ascribed to Harding diminished as tales of his cronyism and his adultery in the White House circulated. Credit turned to blame, and Harding's reputation was damaged beyond repair.

Lincoln, on the other hand, did not enjoy universal credit immediately following his assassination. It took a strenuous effort to convince a wary public of Lincoln's greatness and to acknowledge his contributions to the public good.

In cases in which moral dilemmas are posed, credit may be ascribed to a person for a given act and blame may be ascribed to another person for the same act. Such is particularly true of many political figures. Lincoln is credited with putting an end to slavery and with advancing significantly the cause of human rights in the United States, acts for which his subsequent public image was burnished through the years.

Certainly in Lincoln's day, he was credited for both these advances. At that time, however, much of the South and some pockets of discontent in the North regarded the Civil War as an intolerable act of Northern aggression and placed the blame for the destructive war on Lincoln.

Tilly provides a list on page 133 of *Credit and Blame* of "Scholars' Ranking of U.S. Presidents, 2000." Only three of the presidents—George Washington, Lincoln, and Franklin Roosevelt—were ranked as great. Tilly notes that all three served during wartime and that, in all three cases, the United States won the war during which they served.

He goes on further to note that three of the presidents the scholars ranked as failures—Franklin Pierce, James Buchanan, and Andrew Johnson—served in peacetime but that considerations of war were fundamental in the ranking of all three. Pierce and Buchanan were deemed failures for not striving more vigorously to prevent the Civil War, and Andrew Johnson was considered a failure for mismanaging Reconstruction following the Civil War. The scholars involved in this survey were fundamentally concerned with matters of credit and blame as they assessed the contributions of every president from Washington to Bill Clinton.

It is interesting that these scholars ranked Clinton as average, placing him in the same list as such lackluster presidents as Chester Arthur, Calvin Coolidge, and John Quincy Adams. Although he could be credited with effective foreign and economic policies, he obviously evoked rancor and blame because of his unfortunate dalliance with Monica Lewinsky, a peccadillo that was generally thought to besmirch the dignity of his office.

An even more flagrant case of this sort was the two-term presidency of Richard M. Nixon that produced an admirable foreign policy. Nixon deserved considerable credit for bringing about an accord between his nation and China, a monumental diplomatic undertaking. Nevertheless, the presidential scholars placed Nixon on their list of below-average presidents.

Nixon was tainted by the unpopular Vietnam War that raged during his terms of office. His presidency was, in the eyes of many, connected with political corruption that led eventually to the resignation of Vice President Spiro Agnew for tax evasion in 1973. Many people were convinced that Agnew's crimes were more numerous than those of which he was found guilty. The crowning blow for Nixon, however, was the Watergate scandal for which he was eventually forced to accept the blame, resulting in his resignation from the presidency under the threat of an impeachment trial, which he was almost certain to have lost.

Tilly delves into the past to consider questions of credit and blame in some venerable texts, including Fyodor Dostoevski's *Prestupleniye i nakazaniye* (1866; *Crime and Punishment*, 1886), whose very title reminds one of Tilly's. Tilly explores the mind and motives of the novel's murderous protagonist, Rodion Romanovich Raskolnikov, in the light of the credit-blame dichotomy at the heart of his study.

Raskolnikov, finally captured, tried, and exiled to Siberia for his crime, is followed there by the prostitute Sonya, who loves Raskolnikov and ultimately redeems him, making him realize that in the end people must take responsibility for their actions, good or bad. Having reached this understanding, he now acknowledges that his redemption lies in working to earn credit and in accepting the blame for his misdeeds. Tilly contends that crediting and blaming are essentially social acts and that, in human relationships, responsibility consistently trumps luck or happenstance.

In his discussion of war monuments, Tilly finds concordant examples of credit and blame. Such monuments commemorate events for which the winning side (usually the side erecting the monuments) claims credit. There is in most such situations, however, a losing side, so the very act of erecting a monument casts a shadow of blame.

Tilly cites as his examples the Hermann Monument in Germany, begun in 1838 by Ernst von Bandel, a German sculptor. The monument commemorates Armin (mistranslated as Hermann in later years), who, early in the first century of the common era, defeated three Roman legions led by Publius Quinctilius Varus in the Teutoburg Forest. Armin came to represent German resistance to the French forces that had conquered much of Germany during the Napoleonic Wars.

The rub was that von Bandel's sculpture was not completed until 1875, some thirty-seven years after it was begun. By that time, as Tilly recounts, "Prussia had trounced France in the Franco-Prussian War of 1870-1871, Napoleon III's Second Empire had collapsed, Prussia had taken Alsace and much of Lorraine from France as spoils of war, and Germany had united under Prussian leadership." In other words, in the thirty-eight years that had elapsed, the purpose of the sculpture lost its relevance.

Tilly's book is not for the weak of heart. It perhaps undertakes to provide too much detail about its quite narrow subject. As Tilly jumps from example to example, some readers will predictably become confused by the broad span the text is covering.

R. Baird Shuman

Review Sources

The New York Times Book Review 255, no. 14 (August 17, 2008): 10.
Publishers Weekly 255, no. 14 (April 7, 2008): 56.

THE CROWD SOUNDS HAPPY
A Story of Love, Madness, and Baseball

Author: Nicholas Dawidoff (1962-   )
Publisher: Pantheon Books (New York). 288 pp. $24.95
Type of work: Autobiography
Time: 1965-2004
Locale: Washington, D.C., New Haven, Boston, and New York

Dawidoff's autobiographical coverage of his attempt, through an identification with the Red Sox and with literary characters, to cope with his absentee father

Principal personages:
    NICHOLAS DAWIDOFF, the author
    SALLY DAWIDOFF, his sister
    HEIDI DAWIDOFF, his long-suffering mother
    DONALD DAWIDOFF, his father, who suffers with mental problems
    ALEXANDER GERSCHENKRON, his grandfather, a Harvard professor
        and Red Sox fan
    ANNETTE HAMBURGER, his high school and college friend

Nicholas Dawidoff's *The Crowd Sounds Happy: A Story of Love, Madness, and Baseball* is autobiographical, and it focuses on Dawidoff's attempts to come to terms with his absentee father, who is slowly descending into madness. In December, 2000, Dawidoff wrote an article for *The New Yorker* about his relationship with his father, and this book amplifies on that material, placing it in a broader context. The book begins as it ends, with his father. His mother, Heidi, is leaving Donald and Washington, D.C., with her children, three-year-old Nicholas and Sally, the baby. They move to New Haven, Connecticut, where Heidi finds work as a teacher, supporting her family by herself since Donald is not paying alimony or child support. Although his parents are divorced, Nicholas and his sister make monthly visits to their father in New York, where he moved after losing his job. In the course of the book, it is revealed that Donald, who graduated from Harvard and Yale Law School and who was an excellent lacrosse player, had mental problems in school and while he was employed first in New York and then in Washington. Donald's story is about a promising young man whose fortunes declined because of his mental illness. As a child, Nicholas was aware of a problem, but his mother shielded him from a full knowledge of his father's condition.

In order to stay solvent and sane, Heidi exercises rigid control of her children and her life. Her scrimping and saving and her insistence on doing the right thing (such as returning extra change from a cashier) result in her children being "good," but it also ostracizes them from other children. Because Heidi will not allow a television set in the house, Nicky and Sally are cultural outsiders among the neighborhood children.

Timid and athletically inept, Nicky is always the last one picked in the neighborhood and school kickball games.

The only competition he excels at is reading, and he defeats Binder, his academic rival, by reading more books, but the victory is tainted. Wanting to look good before Miss Swainback, his teacher, Nicky lies to her about reading Sir James Barrie's play *Peter Pan* (pr. 1904). For the guilt-ridden Nicky, his "transgression" cannot be redeemed by his actually reading *Peter Pan*. He must suffer, just as he has paid for asking a friend about where his sister is and finding out that she had been

~

Nicholas Dawidoff's previous books include The Fly Swatter *(2002), which was a finalist for the Pulitizer Prize;* In the Country of Country *(1998), which is about country music; and* Baseball: A Literary Anthology *(2002), which he edited. He has received Guggenheim, Civitella Ramieri, and Berlin Prize fellowships, and he is now the Anschutz Distinguished fellow at Princeton University.*

~

killed earlier. Nicky's imagination, the product of a morbidly sensitive nature, dwells on the dead girl and leaves him feeling vulnerable. His only escape from the real world is in books, and his favorites are the Hardy boys novels, Willa Cather's *My Ántonia* (1918), and baseball stories. Reading about the Hardys' independence, Cather's Midwest, and athletic success enables him to cope with his kickball failures, his dependence on his mother, and the bleak urban landscape that is New Haven.

His visits to see his father are frightening and confusing. On one trip, his father abandons Nicky, and only by racing can he catch up with his father and avoid being lost. Nicky's trips to Croton, New York, where his Aunt Susi and Uncle Tony live, do bring him some welcome relief because his mother seems calmer around her sister. Tony and Susi are a "real" couple, and Susi loves the New York Mets and Tom Seaver. In the same way, Nicky's New Hampshire summers with his mother's father, a Harvard professor, are relaxing and enjoyable because the two listen to the Red Sox games on the radio. As they listen, his grandfather makes the game seem like a fairy tale with the Boston Red Sox as "knights-errant" and the New York Yankees as "horrible Gilgameshian obstacles to glory." Dawidoff mentions two athletic outings with his father: the Mets game they attend goes to extra innings, and Nicky discovers that his father does not even like baseball; the other, a football game between Columbia and Harvard, makes his father aware that he cannot go back to his athletic past. Finally, Nicky realizes that the children's visits are attempts "to make my father seem like a normal dad."

A year after the Mets outing, Heidi takes Nicky, whose obsession with baseball now includes baseball cards, to Cooperstown, New York, to visit the Baseball Hall of Fame. What should have been a wonderful experience soon becomes a nightmare when he sees that most of the visitors are fathers and sons who share their love for the game. He blames his loss to another boy in a game of baseball trivia to his lack of a real father, with whom he could have talked baseball. Despite the unpleasant visits, he continues to make the trek to his father in New York. Nicky comes to fear the city, which he portrays with hellish imagery, and he feels vulnerable. He does not want to go to New York, but he knows if he does not go, "I would be without any father at all."

Filling in for his father are a series of surrogate dads, such as Mr. Sullivan, the family's upstairs neighbor. As Nicky and Mr. Sullivan watch Hank Aaron break Babe Ruth's career home run record, the sensitive Nicky sympathizes with Al Downing, who gave up the home run. Mr. Sullivan empathizes with Nicky, who senses that "somebody who was not your father could briefly feel like one, might even want that as much as you did, and that it might be okay to reveal yourself a little." When he later sees Mr. Sullivan drunk, Nicky is disillusioned and realizes that he wants more from his neighbor, from his baseball coach, and from his Uncle Tony, but that when he "touches their limits, the disappointment was outsized. I wasn't theirs."

Nicky's life is beset by fear, guilt, and humiliation. The disappearance and death of Jennifer Noon, a classmate, at the hands of a "strange man" terrifies him and makes him think of his "strange" father. When he finds a two-year supply of *Penthouse* magazines at the curb, he brings them home, but he immediately gives them to his mother because he knows that he is doing something he should not. Another incident demonstrating his sexual naiveté occurs when he sees a couple crawling out from under a front porch: "Then it occurred to me that where they had just come from was a place I knew nothing about." One of Nicky's main concerns is his delay in reaching puberty. His teammates even call him "Pubie," a takeoff on the Hubert "Hubie" Green of professional golfing, but the nickname is only one of the many his classmates heap on him. Because he is unwilling to fight or even to defend himself, he becomes the victim of both verbal and physical abuse.

Because of his grandfather's influence, Nicky switches his allegiance from the Mets to the Red Sox, and he begins listening to their games on the new Realistic Chronomatic 9 clock radio. Just listening to the game becomes high drama as announcer Ned Martin describes the action and the ballplayers. To aid his heroes, Nicky indulges in a lot of superstitious behavior, such as being kind to his mother and Sally and making promises to God if He will produce a Red Sox victory. The 1978 season receives a great deal of attention in the book. The Red Sox start strong, fade as summer ends, stage a comeback, and are tied with the hated Yankees at the end of the season, necessitating a playoff game, which they lose when Red Sox star Carl Yastrzemski strikes out. When the Sox fail, Nicky says that he "was back on my own without them." In a way, the "inadequacy of the Red Sox exactly matched my own."

Nicky's favorite Red Sox player is Ted Williams, whose story, told in his book *My Turn at Bat* (1969), "felt like mine." Nicky and Williams have a lot in common: divorced parents, troubled boyhood, refuge in baseball, attempting to share friends' dads, awkward with girls, feeling that nobody likes them, envying a friend's closeness to his father, highly motivated but insecure. As he reads and rereads Williams's autobiography, Nicky feels that Williams is "there for me" and even fantasizes that he and Williams could take in a couple Westerns and have some milk shakes together, activities that Williams says he enjoys when he is feeling low.

Breaking Away (1979), a film about a young man who dreams of success as a bicyclist, also provides ties to Nicky's situation since the main character, Dave Stoller, also is estranged from his father. The film concerns a reconciliation between father and son, but it also involves class, the fraternity boys, and the "townies." Nicky's "class" is ambiguous: Although he attends a prestigious private school, thanks to a scholarship, he is not really an upper-class youngster. He feels that "I didn't quite belong anywhere."

When he turns eighteen, however, things change: He is bigger, more popular, and even assertive. When he stops the physical abuse by attacking a larger classmate, the other students notice that Nicky "fought back." He becomes friends with Annette Hamburger and even enjoys, despite the wound inflicted by the girl's braces, his first real kiss. When his mother asserts, "The good stories are about struggle," he understands that the expression relates to his own life. After high school, Nicky attends Harvard, just as his father did, and he becomes increasingly concerned that he may become like his father—after Harvard, he goes to New York, and the situation worsens. He says, "Father's Day was for me like Valentine's Day for the brokenhearted."

At Thanksgiving dinner in 1991, Nicky decides not to see his father any more. Eight years later his father dies, and when Nicky delivers the eulogy, he understands that his father had expressed his love for his son by avoiding him. The Red Sox do finally win the World Series, but his account of the playoffs and series in 2004 lacks the intensity and detail he gives to the team when they fail. Near the end of the book, Nicky says, "Now that they were winners, I saw that happiness cannot exist without sadness," a statement that mirrors his boyhood observation that the sweetness of the pomegranate is hidden within its bitter husk. Though the book ends on a positive note, the overall tone of the book is bittersweet, reflecting the ambiguities of life. Even the title is uncertain: In *The Crowd Sounds Happy*, "sounds" suggests "seems."

Thomas L. Erskine

Review Sources

Booklist 104, no. 17 (May 1, 2008): 64.
Library Journal 133, no. 2 (February 1, 2008): 77.
Publishers Weekly 255, no. 13 (March 31, 2008): 49-50.
The San Diego Union-Tribune, March 30, 2008, p. E4.
The Washington Post, May 6, 2008, p. CO7.

DANGEROUS LAUGHTER
Thirteen Stories

Author: Steven Millhauser (1943-   )
Publisher: Alfred A. Knopf (New York). 244 pp. $24.00
Type of work: Short fiction

Millhauser's eclectic collection of short fiction, ranging from accounts of towers built to heaven to stories about uncontrollable laughter

Principal characters:
ELAINE COLEMAN, a young woman who goes missing in "The Disappearance of Elaine Coleman"
DAVID, the protagonist and narrator of "The Room in the Attic"
WOLF, a rebellious young intellectual in "The Room in the Attic"
ISABEL, Wolf's mysterious sister in "The Room in the Attic"
THE MASTER, a maker of exquisite miniatures in "In the Reign of Harad IV"

Steven Millhauser is an inexhaustibly creative writer whose stories reflect a broad range of interests and a remarkable ability to shift perspective and thus examine the commonplace from a completely uncommon vantage. In *Dangerous Laughter: Thirteen Stories*, his influences vary from American writers such as Edgar Allan Poe (as shown in "The Room in the Attic") and John Barth (in "The Disappearance of Elaine Coleman") to early postmodernists such as Argentine short story writer Jorge Luis Borges (shown by "In the Reign of Harad IV") and Italian fabulist Italo Calvino (as demonstrated in "The Tower"). The writer's focus moves from the intensely personal to the philosophically inquisitive and to abstracted ruminations on principles. In the way that some books are considered to be "novels of ideas," Millhauser (like Borges and Calvino) can be considered a short story writer of ideas. His eclectic and diverse stories demonstrate that Millhauser seems to see things differently than most and to notice things the rest of the world typically overlooks.

Dangerous Laughter is introduced by the story "Cat 'n' Mouse," which serves as an appropriate preamble to Millhauser's postmodern sensibility. The story chronicles the eternal and continuous struggle between a cartoon mouse and his animated feline adversary, reminiscent of the Hanna-Barbera animation studio's long-running and popular *Tom and Jerry* cartoons. Millhauser's approach in rendering these characters into literary fiction could have easily been ironic. Instead, even as cat and mouse plot cruel mischief against each other (as in the *Tom and Jerry* cartoons, the cat is typically the aggressor, finding again and again to his chagrin that the mouse is a step ahead of him, so that the cat's own designs return to haunt him—the trick cigar explodes in the cat's mouth; the birthday cake with dynamite for a candle blows up the cat; the sudden blizzard brought on flash-freezes the cat instead of the mouse)—they each eventually realize that he is defined by the other. In effect, the struggle of each creature against his nemesis is the only reason either animated character has for existence.

~

Steven Millhauser entered the Ph.D. program in English at Brown but never completed the degree. He introduced his creative and postmodern style of fiction with Edwin Mullhouse: The Life and Death of an American Writer, 1943-1954 *(1972). His literary reputation was solidified when his novel* Martin Dressler: The Tale of an American Dreamer *(1996) won the Pulitzer Prize.* Dangerous Laughter *is his seventh collection of short fiction.*

~

Dangerous Laughter is organized according to shared thematic motifs. Part one is titled "Vanishing Acts," and it groups together personal stories of loss, dissolution, and disappearance. The second section is titled "Impossible Architectures," and it groups together stories that deal in distant ways with impersonal and improbable artifices—a tower breaking into heaven; a dome that covers first a house, then a city, a nation, a continent, and eventually a world; a mirror town built adjacent to a real town, the first municipality's twin in every particular save the double's nonexistent citizenry; and models of houses, furniture, and implements built at an almost invisible microscopic level. The last section is called "Heretical Histories," and it offers stories that range from considerations of alternate ways to view the purpose and usefulness of history to a first-person account by a member of Thomas Edison's laboratory, a tale about the magical, artistic excellence of a photographer and painter whose works seem to come to life, and a brief dissertation of fantastical and imaginary fashion trends.

Despite the four groupings (including the introductory story, listed as "Opening Cartoon") used to organize the contents of *Dangerous Laughter*, the stories can, in a broader sense, be separated into two categories: works driven almost entirely by ideas and works driven by character (even if still extraordinarily rich with ideas). Like the books of Calvino about fictional, fantastical cities and what their cultures might be like, such as *Le città invisibili* (1972; *Invisible Cities*, 1974), many of Millhauser's stories tend to ask "what if?" questions in pursuit of a philosophical answer. Particularly the stories listed in the "Impossible Architectures" sequence fall into the former category, although stories from "Vanishing Acts" and "Heretical Histories" do as well. Stories such as "The Tower," "The Dome," "Here at the Historical Society," and "A Change in Fashion" contain no plot, more or less no dialogue, and no actual characters to speak of; the reader does not become engaged in a protagonist's particular dilemma or ambitions. "The Tower," for example, is loosely based on the biblical Tower of Babel; in this version of the tale, the builders of the tower—after generations and generations, the act of construction so long in its fulfillment that the tower has its own culture, residents, and systems—actually do succeed in reaching heaven, at which point they have no idea what to do. In "The Dome," the idea of sealing off the external world around a house and a neighborhood eventually spreads to encapsulate continents and one day the world; the story is an extended rumination on our human need to filter the world and experience it secondhand rather than face to face. Primarily, these stories best function as allegories. Man is meant to always be striving (in this case, building a tower to heaven); should humans ever achieve a presumably unattainable goal, they would be lost. "The Dome" seems to be in some ways about the constant human struggle between security, on the one hand, and life, on the other.

Although these stories are interesting as "tales" in the classical sense of the word (which argues that the point of a story is to prove a point, as in cautionary tales, fables, and parables), they are less successful as modern short stories, in which typically the focus is more on character and less on scenario. The best of the "idea" stories in *Dangerous Laughter* fall more into the Borges than the Calvino camp in that they, while still driven by ideas, also anchor those ideas with plot and character. "In the Reign of Harad IV" is not successful because it deals with the creation of microscopic models as an idea, but rather because it is also focused on the ambition and need of the Master miniature maker in his quest to perfect his craft. "A Precursor of the Cinema" tells of a painter who creates visual effects that seem almost lifelike in terms of effects of motion and movement; like "In the Reign of Harad IV," "A Precursor of the Cinema" depicts an artist who (literally in this case) disappears into his art.

Similarly, the best stories in the collection taken as a whole are equally as creative as "The Dome" and "A Change in Fashion," but the intricate, sometimes surreal plots and skewed perspectives are united with character and theme in a way that accomplishes more than the cerebral machinations of the former stories. "The Wizard of West Orange" is set in Edison's workshop in 1889 and composed in diary fashion by one of Edison's less important employees. Even as Edison and his crew strive to perfect motion pictures, the narrator of "The Wizard of West Orange" becomes obsessed with the work performed on the "haptograph," a device that perfectly mimics touch. To the narrator, the haptograph seems a bridge to a new eon in human development. "Mimicry," he records in his diary. "Splendor of the haptograph. Not just the replication of familiar tactile sensations, but capacity to explore new combinations—pressures, touches, never experienced before. Adventures of feeling. Who can say what new sensations will be awakened, what unknown desires? Unexplored realms of the tangible. The frontiers of touch."

The titular story, "Dangerous Laughter," tells of a youthful fad that moves through a group of teens. The teenagers gather in parties and laugh spontaneously, for no particular reason, until reason and caution are lost behind the laughter. One girl, Clara Schuler, emerges from her shy cocoon under the aegis of the laughter fad and refuses to let go of the craze when the other teens move on to weeping parties. Slowly, Clara loses her sense of self and eventually falls into a fit of laughter from which she cannot recover. Similarly, the title character of "The Disappearance of Elaine Coleman" seemingly suffers not from an abduction or random act of violence but rather from a retreat from the world, leaving behind her community (as voiced by the unnamed narrator in the story) who struggles to reconstruct her identity.

Perhaps the most effective story in the collection is "The Room in the Attic." David is a high school athlete who has always been the kind of teenager he is expected to be; he has a girlfriend, a few knock-around friends, and a more or less normal life. His senior year is changed when a new, ferociously intelligent boy called Wolf transfers into David's class. As Wolf and David become friends, Wolf brings him home to meet his sister Isabel. To visit Isabel, however, David must enter a pitch-black room and never turn on a light or open a curtain. The story is reminiscent in some ways of Poe's "The Fall of the House of Usher," with its strange twins Roderick and Madeline, and also calls to mind another pair of legends. In some versions of "The Beauty and the Beast," the woman hostage does not see her captor face to face until they have come to care for each other. Additionally, in one variant of the legend of the love between the Roman god of love Cupid and Psyche, Cupid visits Psyche but only in the dark; he cannot consort with her once she knows his identity.

David is soon obsessed with Isabel and spends every afternoon with her. He is at first convinced that he must see her, but at some deeper level he realizes that he is as much infatuated with the idea of her and what she represents in terms of mystery as he is infatuated with her physical form. David says,

> Sometimes, I had the sense that Isabel was revealing herself to me slowly, like a gradually materializing phantom, according to a plan that eluded me. If I waited patiently, it would all become clear, as if things were moving toward some larger revelation.

As his relationship with Isabel progresses toward its inevitable conclusion, David is forced to realize what countless young people before him have: When one eats from the tree of knowledge, then one must leave the lands of innocence and safety behind, along with one's youthful naïveté.

Millhauser is an intensely creative short-story writer, with a vast imagination and an ability to direct it in many different channels. His craft is at its peak when his nimbly creative intellect keeps pace with his ability to empathize and create realistic characters that reflect human virtues and foibles.

Scott Yarbrough

Review Sources

Booklist 104, no. 7 (December 1, 2007): 4.
Kirkus Reviews 76, no. 1 (January 1, 2008): 10.
Library Journal 133, no. 3 (February 15, 2008): 99.
O, The Oprah Magazine 9, no. 3 (March, 2008): 178.
Publishers Weekly 254, no. 50 (December 17, 2007): 33.
Review of Contemporary Fiction 28, no. 2 (Summer, 2008): 161-162.

THE DARK SIDE
The Inside Story of How the War on Terror Turned into a
War on American Ideals

Author: Jane Mayer (1955-   )
Publisher: Doubleday (New York). 392 pp. $32.00
Type of work: History, current affairs
Time: 2001 to the present
Locale: The United States and the Middle East

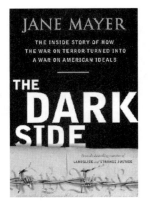

An account of the events and personages of the United States' interrogation policies of the "war on terror" in the aftermath of September 11, 2001

Principal personages:
GEORGE W. BUSH, president of the United
    States
RICHARD CHENEY, vice president of the
    United States
DAVID ADDINGTON, legal counsel to the vice president
JOHN ASHCROFT, United States Attorney General
JACK GOLDSMITH, head of the Justice Department's Office of Legal
    Counsel
ALBERTO GONZALES, United States Attorney General
COLIN POWELL, Secretary of State, 2001-2005
CONDOLEEZZA RICE, Secretary of State, 2005-2009
DONALD RUMSFELD, Secretary of Defense
GEORGE TENET, Central Intelligence Agency (CIA) director
JOHN YOO, lawyer in the Office of Legal Counsel

Jane Mayer's *The Dark Side* is a masterful account of the U.S. government's "war on terror" interrogation program that followed al-Qaeda's attacks of September 11, 2001. It relates the capture and seizing of suspects from the Middle East and elsewhere, their incarceration at Guantanamo, Abu Ghraib, and other sites, and the methods employed by American officials to gain information in order to prevent another 9/11. It is a story of fools and knaves and a few heroes and constitutes one of the darkest chapters in history of the abuse of rights that are guaranteed by the U.S. Constitution, the Geneva Conventions, and decades of tradition. This is history with a point of view: Mayer is not an admirer of the Bush administration's use of extreme interrogation techniques.

On the Sunday after the attack on New York City's Twin Towers and on the Pentagon in Washington, D.C., Vice President Dick Cheney, appearing on the television program *Meet the Press*, stated that "[w]e'll have to work sort of the dark side . . . . And, uh, so it's going to be vital for us to use any means at our disposal." Over the years that followed, extreme measures—including water boarding, sleep deprivation, sexual intimidation, and other physical and psychological methods—were employed to break down detainees in order to obtain supposedly crucial information regarding past and future terrorist activities.

Like other state governors who ascended to the presidency, George W. Bush had little experience and perhaps little knowledge of foreign affairs. Conversely, Cheney had an agenda, the result of long political experience. He had been chief of staff in the Gerald Ford administration, had served in the Congress, and had been Secretary of Defense in the administration of George H. W. Bush. Cheney became convinced that the executive

Jane Mayer, granddaughter of the eminent Civil War historian Alan Nevins, graduated from Yale University and did graduate work at Oxford University. As a journalist, she has written for The Wall Street Journal, The New Yorker, *and* The New York Review of Books. The Dark Side *was a finalist for the 2008 National Book Award for nonfiction.*

branch had lost its legitimate governmental authority as the result of the Watergate affair in the early 1970's. He sought to regain for the presidency what he considered its rightful power.

If Cheney was somewhat the éminence grise of the administration's response to the events of 9/11, the point man was David Addington, Cheney's legal counsel. Addington had served in the Ronald Reagan administration and was responsible for many of the "signing statements" that Reagan and George W. Bush used to modify and dilute the intent of congressional laws. However, Cheney and Addington were not alone in advocating suspect actions. After 9/11, elements in the Central Intelligence Agency (CIA) argued the necessity to execute suspected terrorists out of hand as well as to conduct espionage within the United States, which by law it was forbidden to do. Whether the origin was the CIA, Cheney and Addison, or other sources, as one individual put it, the gloves were off when it came to ferreting out dangers to the United States. As Mayer points out, both Abraham Lincoln's suspension of habeas corpus and Franklin Roosevelt's internment of Japanese Americans went further than did the Bush administration in threatening civil liberties. The difference was that Bush and his advisers claimed that the president had the legal right to do whatever he believed necessary. A crucial figure on giving legal justification for such wide-ranging presidential powers was John Yoo, a deputy chief in the Office of Legal Counsel in the Justice Department. In a series of legal memos, Yoo claimed that the requirements of national security trumped all other constitutional or legal restrictions placed upon a president, a legal interpretation that most constitutional scholars deplored. Never had a vice president's office been more powerful in American history, and in most matters Cheney or Addington had the last word with Bush before any major presidential decisions. Other relevant departments, such as the State Department, and persons, such as Secretary of State Colin Powell and National Security Adviser Condoleezza Rice, were simply bypassed or ignored.

Cheney, Addington, and Yoo, and most of the other like-minded advocates of unlimited presidential power in times of national crisis, had no direct experience with counterterrorism, with military service, with the Muslim world. In the immediate aftermath of 9/11, neither the CIA nor the Federal Bureau of Investigation (FBI) had more than a handful of Arabic speakers. Mayer notes that the administration's worldview was similar to that of the popular television show *24*, in which the protagonist Jack Bauer frequently resorts to torture to obtain information to make the world safe for American democracy. However, the real world is not *24*, and torture, however defined, does not necessarily lead to actionable information.

The Dark Side is about what was done with those captured on a foreign battlefield or seized in some other circumstance. Mayer does not make the claim, but, war being war, some of the captured were probably killed, perhaps intentionally. To people such as Addington, the prisoners had greater value being kept alive because of the information that they supposedly had regarding future terrorist actions. There was perhaps some justification for this in the weeks and months immediately following the events of September 11, 2001, but as the years dragged on, the secrets that terrorist suspects might have held became irrelevant and out of date. In addition, most of those seized were relatively low-level figures, the foot soldiers, whose knowledge of the plans of Osama bin Laden and others was extremely limited or was nonexistent in the first place.

Nevertheless, hundreds were captured, and the issues became where to house them and how to elicit from them the supposed crucial information. Guantanamo had the advantage of being controlled by the United States under a 1903 agreement with the Cuban government, but it was not American territory, and thus the inmates, or "illegal enemy combatants," would be isolated from constitutional guarantees and could be tried by military commissions, another decision by the Cheney cohorts that Bush signed on to with no other input. In the interim, to get information from the inmates, various extreme techniques were employed. Bush and others in the administration denied that torture was used, but the term "torture" was very narrowly defined. In August, 2002, Yoo wrote an in-house memo describing torture as only that which led to "organ failure, impairment of bodily function, or even death." Anything short of those was deemed acceptable.

Guantanamo prison camp, established in January, 2002, was not the only facility that housed captives. "Rendition" was often elsewhere, and the CIA in particular had numerous black sites or facilities in "friendly" nations around the world, including some in Eastern Europe and in the Middle East. Most renditions remained hidden from the public, but a CIA nightmare occurred in Italy when thirteen or more CIA officials were discovered staying in first-class hotels and running up credit card charges of $145,000 in one rendition escapade. At the black sites, extreme measures were used before they were possibly transferred to Guantanamo. As has been pointed out, even by lawyers within the administration, the employment of many of those techniques, whether or not they met the legal standard of what might be torture, would largely prevent later legal trials of such suspects because of the methods used to gain information.

Even in the cases of such high-level figures as al-Qaeda logistics chief Abu Zubayda and Khalid Sheikh Mohammed, the information gleaned through water boarding and other problematic techniques was often suspect. Mohammed was definitely connected to the planning for 9/11, but what he told the inquisitors was often intentionally misleading, irrelevant, and of little use. Sometimes what resulted from extreme measures was patently untrue, as in the case of one suspect whose confinement in Egypt's notorious facilities gained a "confession" that Iraq's Saddam Hussein and al-Qaeda were cooperating in terrorist activities and that Iraq had weapons of mass destruction, information that played a role in the decision to invade Iraq in 2003 in spite of doubts within the CIA that the confession was reliable. With Zubayda, Mayer argues that the FBI got more information using more humane methods than did the CIA using harsher techniques. Others, more knowledgeable about interrogation techniques than policy makers in the White House, were doubtful that extreme techniques would succeed, and they claimed that prisoners, if treated humanely, often were willing to talk, perhaps even to brag, about their aims and accomplishments.

There were heroes such as Jack Goldsmith, a conservative lawyer and head of the Justice Department's Office of Legal Counsel (OLC) beginning in the summer of 2003. After taking over the OLC, he argued that there was no justification in the law for Yoo's claims that in wartime the president's power was absolute in the treatment of wartime captives. Goldsmith was also troubled by the government's decision to bypass the court set up by the Foreign Intelligence Surveillance Act regarding domestic spying, and he opposed the renewal of the Terrorist Surveillance Program. Ultimately, pressures led to his resignation, but not before he had withdrawn the blanket endorsement given to the CIA to use extreme measures. However, little changed after his departure: The new OLC head authorized whatever the administration deemed necessary. In the Congress, few took up the issue of torture, possibly fearing to appear to be soft on terrorism. One who did was Senator John McCain, who himself had been a victim of torture while a prisoner during the Vietnam War. In 2005, McCain introduced an amendment to a Defense Department bill prohibiting the military from using methods not authorized in the *Army Field Manual*. Cheney lobbied Congress against it and Bush threatened to veto it, but it passed anyway. However, Bush, with Addington's input, added a "signing statement," stating that the law would be enforced only in a manner consistent with his role as commander in chief, and a secret memo from the post-Goldsmith OLC claimed that in any event none of the CIA's methods constituted torture.

It is impossible to gauge the extent of the use of extreme measures. The CIA claims it was minimal, but the victims have claimed otherwise. Until 2005, the CIA kept extensive tapes of the interrogations, but they were destroyed, probably to prevent provable examples of torture. The destruction of such evidence could be considered to be a criminal act, but at the time of the writing of *The Dark Side* no one had been indicted for that action or for any other violations of U.S. laws or international treaties. Although the administration denied using torture, it justified extreme measures by the results obtained, claiming that the United States did not suffer another 9/11 attack. Whether this was because crucial information had been gained through extreme measures is impossible to prove because the Bush administration has refused to give specific information about any attacks that were foiled.

Because administration figures have refused, for obvious reasons, to discuss interrogation practices toward "illegal enemy combatants," it can be argued that Mayer largely presents only one side. Nevertheless, as it stands, *The Dark Side* is a damning indictment of the Bush administration's interrogation policies.

Eugene Larson

Review Sources

The Economist 388, no. 8591 (August 2, 2008): 86-87.
Library Journal 133, no. 18 (November 1, 2008): 116.
The New York Times, July 22, 2008, p. 19.
The New York Times Book Review, August 10, 2008, p. 4.
Policy Review, no. 151 (October/November, 2008): 80-85.
Time 172, no. 4 (July 28, 2008): 18.
The Times Literary Supplement, October 31, 2008, p. 10.

DAVID MAMET
A Life in the Theatre

Author: Ira Nadel (1955-   )
Publisher: Palgrave Macmillan (New York). 278 pp.
  $26.95
Type of work: Literary biography
Time: 1947 to the present
Locale: Chicago, New York, and Los Angeles

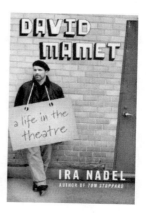

The first full-length biography of a prominent contemporary American dramatist, who is also the writer of screenplays, novels, essays, and children's books

Principal personages:
  DAVID MAMET, author of nearly three
    dozen plays and more than two dozen
    screenplays
  BERNARD (BERNIE) and LENORE (LEE) MAMET, the playwright's parents
  LINDSAY CROUSE, actress and Mamet's first wife
  REBECCA PIDGEON, actress and Mamet's second wife
  SANFORD MEISNER, influential acting teacher and Mamet's mentor
  GREGORY MOSHER, longtime director and producer of numerous Mamet
    plays
  WILLIAM H. MACY, one of the group of actors often associated with
    Mamet's plays

The subtitle *A Life in the Theatre* that Ira Nadel has selected for his biography of David Mamet, replicating the title of his subject's 1977 play, signals that readers should not expect an expansive, full-blown narrative covering events from the dramatist's birth to the present. Rather, Nadel focuses almost exclusively on Mamet's prolific output as a writer, largely for stage and screen. One reason for this strategy may be, as Nadel notes, that Mamet tends to be circumspect, "maintaining a wall around himself," preferring to be defined by what he does instead of who he is. Another may be—surprisingly so for an academic scholar—that Nadel chose not to research the available archival material containing Mamet's 175 journals from over a thirty-five-year period, relying instead on secondary sources. Nor is there evidence that he saw need to speak with Mamet directly, though he does quote from interviews by others with the dramatist. Eschewing any interest in psychologizing his subject or delving into his personal relationships, Nadel lays claim only to what is, for a contemporary biographer, the modest aim of "telling . . . 'WHAT HAPPENS NEXT,'" though admittedly this is Mamet's chief intent as well. The result is a workmanlike rendition of mostly already-known facts, accompanied by extensive plot summaries.

What emerges is a portrait of a bifurcated individual: a Midwesterner born-and-bred in Chicago, yet at home in and lauded on the world's stages; someone who is street-

~

Ira Nadel is professor of English at the University of British Columbia, Vancouver, where he is a Distinguished University Scholar and Fellow of Canada's Royal Society. Previously, he has written critical biographies of James Joyce, Ezra Pound, Leonard Cohen, and Tom Stoppard.

~

savvy and suspicious of appearing overly intellectual, yet touted as the theatrical heir of Samuel Beckett and Harold Pinter; a critic of capitalism and consumerism, yet a ready participant in the Hollywood system. The first several chapters, about a quarter of the book, chronicle Mamet's birth in 1947 on Chicago's South Side to Bernard and Lenore Mamet, a labor lawyer and a teacher, respectively, who were descendants of Polish Russian Jews; his early years going to films, taking piano lessons, and listening to stories told by his maternal grandfather; his stints on radio and television; his nonstellar record at a progressive school; and his voracious reading of works by Willa Cather and Theodore Dreiser at the Chicago Public Library. After his parents' fractious marriage ended in divorce, Bernard remarried three days later, fathering two more sons; Lenore, too, married again, to another Bernie, who turned out to be physically abusive to Mamet's sister. The young Mamet was first introduced to theatergoing at Hull House and later at Second City. One of the side stories Nadel sketches is the rather remarkable position of Chicago as an incubator for writers and actors, second only to New York (and of Mamet's part in that development), with its myriad of storefront and regional playhouses, including the Organic, the Ivanhoe, the Royal Court, the Goodman, and Steppenwolf.

Mamet's attendance at Goddard College—focused on experiential learning that allowed him to write a play for his senior thesis—began his love affair with the geography and hardworking craftsmen of Vermont. Eventually, he would buy a home, build a writing cabin in the woods in Cabot, and use it as the setting for a novel, *The Village* (1994), and a screenplay, *State and Main* (2000), as well as a collection of essays, *The Cabin* (1992), and a travelogue, *South of the Northeast Kingdom* (2002). While a student, Mamet learned about the theater of Bertolt Brecht, worked backstage Off-Broadway, and began to study acting—which he would teach when he returned to Goddard as a faculty member in the early 1970's after a period of depression and psychoanalysis, about which Nadel provides no illuminating details. It was at Goddard, too, that Mamet started to assemble a coterie of actors (beginning with William H. Macy, but later including such Mamet regulars as Mike Nussbaum, Joe Montegna, Felicity Huffman, and Ricky Jay) who would work with him at the St. Nicholas Theater in Chicago and at the Atlantic in New York.

Mamet's return to his hometown and the launching of his playwriting career with *Sexual Perversity in Chicago* (1974) began his long association with Gregory Mosher, artistic director of the Goodman Theater, with whom he collaborated on an adaptation of what he considered the greatest American novel, Richard Wright's *Native Son* (1978). After this point, the biographical material becomes sketchier, mostly a spine to support the plot summaries and to draw some connections between the outer life—playing poker in a junk shop, sailing on an ore boat, working in a North Side real estate office—and the art: the award-winning *American Buffalo* (1975),

Lakeboat (1982), and the Pulitzer Prize-winning play *Glengarry Glen Ross* (1984). Mention is made of his marriages to two actresses, first Lindsay Crouse and then Rebecca Pidgeon, who converts to Judaism for Mamet, and the births of his children; his moves from the Chelsea section of Manhattan to Boston, to Vermont, and finally to Los Angeles; his study of the Hebrew language and two visits to Israel; and his popularity in Great Britain and the increasing number of honors he receives, including a festival devoted to him at the Goodman. Through it all, Nadel is often annoyingly repetitive, as when, for instance, he twice quotes within a few pages Mamet's credo about constructing a scene, the basic element of stagecraft: "'Who wants what from whom? What happens if they don't get it? Why now?'"

The later chapters of Nadel's study proceed as much by topic as by chronology, with several recurrent motifs: the differences between working in theater and in film; the Hobbesian nature of business in America; the ubiquity of the confidence game in human interactions; the connection between language and power; machoism and the masculine ethos; and a renewed interest in Judaism. Sometimes these focal points coalesce around a body of work produced during a certain chronological period in Mamet's career and so receive coherent development; but mostly the reader needs to pull them together from disparate mentions. For long stretches, Mamet is simultaneously producing fiction and nonfiction prose, dramas, and a string of films that he either writes and/or directs—such as *The Verdict* (1982), through *The House of Games* (1987), to *The Winslow Boy* (1999). In writing for the theater, Mamet subscribes to an Aristotelian emphasis on characters in conflict and a Beckettian minimalism that leaves out things once deemed essential by the audience. Actors in his plays must build their characters from doing rather than thinking—a technique he learned from his teacher, Sanford Meisner, at the Neighborhood Playhouse during his formative years. The film medium, unlike theater, allows three opportunities to get things right—in the writing, in the shooting, and in the editing processes, but the greatest of these is the last. Mamet takes his cue from Russian director Sergei Eisenstein—to whom he pays visual homage in the steps sequence in *The Untouchables* (1987)—by affirming that cinema art resides in the juxtaposition of cuts to create meaning. Despite Mamet's extensive work in films (and recently television), he will excoriate producers as hustlers in such plays as *Speed-the-Plow* (1988) and even critique his own pact with Tinseltown as a sacrifice of artistry in such satiric works as his adaptation of *Faustus* (2004).

Filmmaking comes in for the same moral indignation at Mamet's hands as other forms of business in America: unfettered capitalism with its ruthless competition and its unchecked individualism becomes predatory in nature (something Mamet's favorite sociologist, Thorstein Veblen, warned against), warping values and destroying lives. A business ethic that sanctions, even demands, the commodification of all values, so that everything is measured in terms of material gain and loss, destroys the bonds of connection between human beings in *American Buffalo*, leaving the hardwon restoration of community just the slimmest of possibilities. There may be a modicum of camaraderie in the guise of honor among thieves in *Glengarry Glen Ross* as the real estate salesmen band together against the unseen owner-managers, but the base amorality of bilking their clients is still the order of the day. There is a long tradition in American literature of the confidence man, and Nadel stresses Mamet's place in that tradition, noting the recurrence of the con in works such as his film *Heist* (2001), not only as a means of individual survival but also as a way of deceiving the other. It is related to the bluff in poker, one of those pastimes such as hunting that lend an aura of machismo and misogyny to the mostly male inhabitants of Mamet's world. The spare language of that world, sometimes called "Mametspeak," is full of bravado and profanity that reflects an absence of affective response, a deliberate attempt to camouflage rather than reveal emotional emptiness. One pattern that Nadel hints at but that he well might have emphasized more thoroughly is the presence of homosocial bonding and the atmosphere of homoeroticism that pervades several of Mamet's works, such as *The Cryptogram* (1985) and *The Edge* (1997). It appears not only in a 2006 episode of the television series *The Unit*, with a soldier's love letter addressed not to a wife but to a gay comrade, but also, as Nadel discusses in the most sustained literary analysis in this volume, in Mamet's play *Edmond* (1982), a hellish fable about urban emptiness and violence, where the title character ultimately finds surcease from an existential angst in a homosexual relationship with his black cellmate.

What has increasingly filled Mamet's own life is a renewed commitment to the practice of Judaism, reflected in several works in various genres: the play *The Disappearance of the Jews* (1983), the film *Homicide* (1991), the novel *The Old Religion* (1997), and the essay collection *The Wicked Son* (2006). Although there was little evidence of the Jewish religion in the nonobservant home where Mamet grew up, he was secretly bar mitzvahed. To Mamet's mind, ill-advised attempts at assimilation feed a sense of paranoia and lead to feelings of self-loathing; so he focuses not only on anti-Semitism but also on a sense of victimization that is self-imposed, counteracting these with an aggressive defense of Israel and an admonition to those Jews who know little about their faith. While Nadel displays a ready familiarity with the Mamet canon, his book is unlikely to satisfy either those readers who are seeking a definitive biography or those desiring a work of solid literary criticism. Although certainly a step up from the standard showbiz biography, this effort neither probes Mamet the man deeply enough nor offers much in the way of a compelling interpretation of the work produced by Mamet the writer, or of his place among his peers. So while Nadel's claim that Mamet resides "at the pinnacle of contemporary American drama" may be justified, here it remains unconvincingly demonstrated.

Thomas P. Adler

Review Sources

American Theatre 25, no. 9 (November, 2008): 80-81.
Kirkus Reviews 75, no. 22 (November 15, 2007): 1192.
Library Journal 132, no. 20 (December 15, 2007): 120.
Los Angeles Times, February 21, 2008, p. E11.
The New York Times Book Review, February 24, 2008, p. 11.

DAY

Author: A. L. Kennedy (1965-   )
Publisher: Alfred A. Knopf (New York). 274 pp. $24.00
Type of work: Novel
Time: 1939-1949
Locale: England and Germany

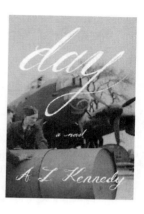

A former Royal Air Force sergeant looks back on his life in order to see a way, if any, ahead

> *Principal characters:*
> ALFRED F. DAY, Royal Air Force turret
>   gunner, prisoner of war, and film extra
> JOYCE ANTROBUS, his lover
> STRUAN MACALLUM PLUCKROSE, Royal Air
>   Force navigator
> VASYL, a film extra interned at camp for displaced persons
> IVOR SANDS, owner of a London bookstore
> THE GOOD GERMAN, former German soldier, now a film extra and
>   resident of England

A. L. Kennedy is finally receiving the kind of recognition she has long deserved—deserved, in fact, ever since the publication of her first book, *Night Geometry and the Garscadden Trains* (1990). This is not to suggest that Kennedy has been toiling away in obscurity for the past two decades. *Night Geometry and the Garscadden Trains* was well received, and Kennedy has been selected for two of *Granta* magazine's three Best of Young British Novelists issues (1993 and 2003). Nonetheless, although her first two novels—*Looking for the Possible Dance* (1993) and *So I Am Glad* (1995)—have been much discussed, they have been overshadowed by fellow Scot Janice Galloway's debut, *The Trick Is to Keep Breathing* (1989). The trick for writers who cultivated their own patch of Scotland, in those times before Irvine Welsh's popular novel *Trainspotting* (1993), was to get noticed at all outside the United Kingdom, especially in the United States. The American edition of *So I Am Glad* did not appear until 2000, one year after *Original Bliss*, a novella published in the United Kingdom in 1997 as part of a collection of Kennedy's short fiction. Therein lies another hurdle that Kennedy had to get over. She is, like Lorrie Moore in the United States, a master short-story teller who alternates between collections and novel. Her work in the one form (where her brilliance shines most intensely) has worked against her achieving greater fame in what Pascale Casanova calls "the world republic of letters," where, because literary size does unfortunately still matter, the novel rules. Admittedly, Kennedy's two most recent novels (also her longest)—*Everything You Need* (2002) and *Paradise* (2004)—have received mixed reviews. With the publication of *Day*, however, mere respect has turned into nearly universal acclaim. The novel has already won the Costa Prize (formerly the Whitbread) in Britain, the Saltire Award in Scot-

~

Alison Louise Kennedy was born in Dundee, Scotland, and studied English and drama at Warwick University. She has written four collections of short fiction, five novels, two works of nonfiction. and a screenplay, and she frequently contributes to a number of British newspapers.

~

land, and major prizes in Austria and Germany, and Kennedy has been selected for a Literary Award (worth $150,000) from the Lannan Foundation in the United States. Will all the attention cause the prolific and demanding but decidedly low-key author to give up her budding career as a stand-up comedian? Probably not.

Day succeeds so well in large part because Kennedy brings the psychological, atmospheric, and stylistic intensity of her short fiction to bear on a long narrative that develops in chronologically knotted bursts rather than progressing linearly. The novel begins in 1949 on a film set in Germany, where Alfred F. Day plays a prisoner of war (POW). It is a part he knows well, having spent time in a real POW camp after his Lancaster bomber was shot down in July, 1944, during a raid on Hamburg. From this moment, the twenty-five-year-old Day (and the two-hundred-and-eighty-page *Day*) travels back over the previous decade: to his time in the POW camp, to his Royal Air Force (RAF) training and nearly thirty missions as a turret gunner, to his wartime love affair with an officer's wife he meets while on leave in London, and, more fleetingly, to his long-suffering mother and abusive father in a small town in Staffordshire in England's West Midlands. Recounting *Day* in this fashion makes the novel seem much more orderly and readerly than it actually is, for what Kennedy has written is really a stream-of-consciousness, day-in-the-life novel, such as James Joyce's monumental *Ulysses* (1922) and Virginia Woolf's more circumscribed *Mrs. Dalloway* (1925). Woolf and Joyce wrote just as film—the medium Orson Welles described as "a ribbon of dream"—began to influence fiction writers. Kennedy, who already has one film to her credit—*Stella Does Tricks* (1994), adapted from one of her short stories—combines a number of cinematic techniques, such as cross-cutting and lap dissolves, with the free association and free indirect discourse of the dreamlike novel's second-person narration. She does so both to rewrite history from Day's highly personal perspective and to rescue the written word from the shock and awe of visual media's spectacularizing of history. (*Day* may be set during and just after World War II, but it was written and presumably is meant to be read in the context of the disastrous U.S. attack on Iraq and its prolonged aftermath.)

The depth of Kennedy's research—conducted at the Imperial War Museum in London and at the Lincolnshire Aviation Centre—is evident throughout the novel, but the historical facts are never pedantically presented merely to edify the reader, and they never detract from Kennedy's famously opaque style. The novel's authenticity strangely but effectively combines with an intertextuality that provides a literary frame of reference and bits of comic relief and that tells the reader far less about the autodidact Day than it does about the postmodern Kennedy. Randall Jarrell's sardonic poem "The Death of the Ball Turret Gunner" comes quickly to mind, as does Michael Powell and Emeric Pressburger's *A Matter of Life and Death* (1946) and *The*

Life and Death of Colonel Blimp (1943), about which Kennedy wrote a short study for the British Film Institute's film classics series in 1997; Muriel Spark's *The Girls of Slender Means* (1963), another novel about Britons dealing with war's aftermath; David Lean's *Brief Encounter* (1945); and Kurt Vonnegut's *Slaughterhouse-Five* (1969). *Day* also alludes to more recent writers who have sought to revitalize the war novel: Pat Barker's *Regeneration* trilogy (1990-1995) and Sarah Waters's *Night Watch* (2006), which, like Martin Amis's *Time's Arrow* (1991), tells its story backward. *Day* also includes jokey references to the films *The Longest Day* (1962)—at five feet, four inches, Alfred Day is "usefully short"—*Alfie* (1966), and, via Joyce's husband's surname, Antrobus, to the first of the "Carry On" films, *Carry on Sergeant* (1958), cowritten by John Antrobus. However, Kennedy's novel includes another form of intertextuality. As one reviewer noted, or rather complained, *Day* is a compendium of clichés from war novels and war films: "bands of brothers, courage under fire, doomed love triangles, postwar guilt." However, instead of succumbing to the clichés, in the fashion of *Pearl Harbor* (2001), or simply parodying them, postmodern style, *Day* makes them humanly and aesthetically real.

For all of its narrative brilliance, *Day* is a novel made in the image of its protagonist and his time; it is a study in repression in an era of rationing. In the local dialect, which he tries mightily to escape, "day" means "don't," and "don't" is pretty much what Day does and has been taught to do by his domineering father and his schoolteachers. In this novel of small, confining spaces (home, town, gun turret, POW camp) and of loss, Day is at war not only with the enemy but also with himself. Far more than an enemy that, as part of a bomber crew, he never actually sees until he is captured, he hates his father and especially himself, sometimes for the choices he has made but most often for those he has not. When his mother dies, Day chooses to fly with his mates rather than return early for the funeral, but a preoccupied Day fails to stave off a fighter attack in which his closest crewmate, the upper-class, part-Scottish Pluckrose, is killed. Guilt-ridden, Day comes to believe that his mother did not die in a freak accident but was murdered by his father. The "soft" Day attacks his father in the dark and from behind, but even in this act of filial revenge, Day becomes a passive spectator when his father falls in the canal and slowly drowns while calling out for help. In his love affair with Joyce, the sexually inexperienced Day is the passive partner.

Day is far too passive and self-effacing to tell his story directly, in the first person. He narrates from within the Perspex bubble of his metaphorical gun turret, and it is the sheer ordinariness of his observations that have led some reviewers to wish that Kennedy had developed the novel's secondary characters more: the crew; fellow loner Ivor Sands, who owns the bookshop where Day works, whose mother also died during the war; the Good German Day meets on the film set who returned to his native Hamburg after the war to find his city destroyed and his family dead, except for an aunt gone mad; and especially Vasyl, one of the many displaced persons (DPs) working as film extras: "someone you heard about: rumours of bad history and a knife." Vasyl claims to be a Ukrainian who had been forced to fight on the German side, but he later admits that he is Latvian and that when the Germans arrived in his town, their mere presence unleashed a bestial savagery that Vasyl and others directed at their Jewish neighbors. Vasyl and his story trouble Day so much that he tries to expose Vasyl as a criminal in order to prevent his immigrating to England. No less disturbed by Vasyl's lengthy account of his murder of a classmate, readers also understand—as at some level Day undoubtedly does—that Vasyl's brutal act is not altogether different from the part Day played in the firebombing of "Hamburg on the Magic Night."

Day's death wish is evident long before he sees Hamburg burning; it is evident in his choosing to play the most vulnerable part (to use film language), that of turret gunner. In choosing to return to Germany as an extra in a film set in a POW camp, Day in effect chooses to return to his past in order to relive it, with his narration taking the form of his life flashing (albeit slowly, over several days) before his eyes. He is a man drowning in his own failings, and his narrative seems at times a long suicide note. As the film wraps up, two extras, fellow Brits, offer Day a new life (a new day): fake papers that will give him a new identity and the chance to make a new life for himself amid the chaos of postwar Europe. Day refuses, returns to London and to Joyce, whom he has not seen in six years. "Where have you been?" she asks. The answer is the novel that bears Day's name.

At the beginning of her book *On Bullfighting* (2001), Kennedy explains that just as she contemplated ending her life, she heard someone singing "her least favourite folk song in all the world," a "piece of pseudo-Celtic pap" entitled "Mhairi's Wedding," and she ended up writing *On Bullfighting* instead. *Day* is like that: an Emily Dickinson-like letter to the world that never—or rarely—wrote to Day, or rather a suicide note as well as a delaying action as Day looks back over his past and considers whether to have a future.

Day opens with a funny bit about Day growing a moustache. "An untrained observer might think he was idling, at a loose end in the countryside, but this was not the case. In fact, he was concentrating, thinking his way through every bristle, making sure they would align and be all right." Only at novel's end, when he returns to Joyce, do we realize how he had been planning this all along, growing the moustache to cover the scar that resulted from his capture, because Day wanted very much to be the man she wanted. His odyssey over, Day comes home, no longer Homer, to a Penelope encumbered with a husband psychologically damaged from the war. If things do not end quite happily ever after, they certainly end better than they might: somewhere between Ernest Hemingway's *The Sun Also Rises* (1926) and Powell and Pressburger's *A Matter of Life and Death*. Because the Luger he takes from Vasyl at the beginning of the novel does not go off, Chekhov style, Day gets to love another day, but that, as they say, is another story.

Robert Morace

Review Sources

The Economist 386 (January 26, 2008): 81-82.
Kirkus Reviews 75, no. 20 (October 15, 2007): 1070.
Los Angeles Times, January 27, 2008, p. R7.
New Statesman 136 (April 23, 2007): 67.
New York 41, no. 2 (January 14, 2008): 64-65.
The New York Review of Books 55, no. 7 (May 1, 2008): 44-47.
The New York Sun, January 9, 2008, p. 11.
The New York Times Book Review, January 20, 2008, p. 14.
Publishers Weekly 254, no. 42 (October 22, 2007): 34.
The San Diego Union-Tribune, January 13, 2008, p. E4.
The Seattle Times, January 20, 2008, p. J7.
The Spectator 305 (November 17, 2007): 48.
The Times Literary Supplement, April 20, 2007, p. 19.

THE DAY FREEDOM DIED
The Colfax Massacre, the Supreme Court,
and the Betrayal of Reconstruction

Author: Charles Lane (1961-   )
Publisher: Henry Holt (New York). 326 pp. $27.00
Type of work: History
Time: 1873-1876
Locale: Grant Parish and other places in Louisiana

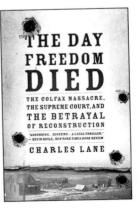

A compelling and scholarly account of the brutal kill-
ings of more than sixty African Americans, the criminal
convictions of three white supremacists, and the overturn-
ing of their convictions by the U.S. Supreme Court

Principal personages:
> JAMES R. BECKWITH, U.S. Attorney in New
>   Orleans who prosecuted the case
> CHRISTOPHER COLUMBUS NASH, ex-
>   Confederate officer who led the attack on the courthouse
> WILLIAM J. CRUIKSHANK, large landowner who was convicted of murder
> WILLIAM B. WOODS, federal circuit judge who was later named to the
>   Supreme Court
> JOSEPH BRADLEY, pro-Southern Justice of the Supreme Court
> WILLIAM SMITH CALHOUN, white Republican who was the largest
>   landowner in Colfax

Journalist Charles Lane's book *The Day Freedom Died* focuses on the Colfax
Massacre of 1873 and its consequences, providing an insightful window into Louisiana society during the turbulent age of Reconstruction. In telling the story, Lane begins with a perceptive analysis of the political and social conditions in the South following the Civil War. He presents a gripping description of the gruesome attack on
the Colfax courthouse, resulting in the deaths of between sixty-two and eighty-one
African Americans (or Freedmen)—the single most deadly race-based episode during the period. He then examines the two federal trials in which three of the participants were found guilty of civil rights violations. Finally, he describes and analyzes
the landmark U.S. Supreme Court decision, *Cruikshank v. United States* (1876),
which overturned the convictions and made it much more difficult for the federal government to protect the rights of the Southern Freedmen.

The Colfax Massacre occurred when Louisiana's Reconstruction regime was still
upheld by federal troops and supported by a coalition of Freedmen, carpetbaggers
(Northerners in the South), and scalawags (local white Republicans). Lane emphasizes that the majority of white Southerners believed that continuing military occupation was unjust, and they were bitterly indignant at Republican policies aimed at im-
posing a degree of racial equality. Angry whites called for the establishment of so-

called redeemer governments, which included two main goals: first, restoration of the local Democratic Party to power, and, second, establishment of public policies based on white supremacy. In the wake of the Civil War, the Ku Klux Klan and other extremist groups conducted a reign of terror and intimidation in numerous areas of the South. Lane points out, for instance, that Louisiana was the scene of more than a thousand political murders between April and November of 1868. Although the two Enforcement Acts of 1870 and 1871 weakened the Ku Klux Klan to some extent, white racists continued to use violence to promote the cause of "redemption."

~

Charles Lane, a former editor for Newsweek *and* The New Republic, *has worked as a journalist in several countries, and he has published articles in* Foreign Affairs *and other prestigious reviews. Before taking a six-month leave to write about the Colfax massacre, he covered the Supreme Court for* The Washington Post.

~

White supremacists were extremely active in Louisiana's Red River valley, including the small parish of Grant, which the Republican state government had organized in honor of President Ulysses S. Grant in 1869. The parish had a population of about 2,400 African Americans and 2,200 whites. Its capital was Colfax (named after Grant's vice president, Schuyler Colfax), a hamlet located in the middle of a large estate owned by William Calhoun, a liberal defender of Freedmen's rights and the Republican Party. Since the Civil War's end, a considerable amount of violence, usually related to race, had occurred in the parish. When elections were held, almost all Freedmen voted for Republicans, while most whites supported the Democratic Party. In 1872 the Democrats joined with dissident Republicans to form an electoral coalition of so-called Fusionists. In the bitterly contested election of that year, registered voters in the parish consisted of 776 African Americans and 630 whites. After the votes were counted, the Fusionists claimed victory, which, according to Lane, was "almost certainly" based on the fabrication of returns and the intimidation of black voters. On January 18, 1873, Republican Governor William Kellogg accused the Fusionists of fraud and named the entire Republican slate as victors.

The Fusionists in Grant Parish, however, refused to accept the governor's edict, and they continued to occupy the Colfax courthouse. In reaction, two white Republican leaders, Robert Register and Daniel Shaw, surreptitiously entered the courthouse during the night of March 25. The next day, the new Republican officials took control of the building. To maintain control, about three hundred men, women, and children, mostly Freedmen, stayed in and around the courthouse. Among whites in the parish, rumors spread that revolutionary blacks were preparing to exterminate all the white people.

The Fusionists were determined to retake the building, using whatever force might be necessary. Christopher Columbus Nash, a veteran Confederate officer who had been the Fusionist candidate for sheriff, was the group's leader. Calling for help from white supremacists in neighboring parishes, Nash soon had a force of about 165 militiamen, of whom about half were former Confederate soldiers. All of the men were armed with good-quality firearms. They also possessed a small but usable cannon from the war. In contrast, only about half of the Freedmen had firearms, mostly old shotguns and hunting weapons of poor quality. Expecting that an invasion was imminent, the Freedmen dug a shallow, makeshift trench around the courthouse. They also used old steam pipes in a futile attempt to improvise crude cannons.

On April 13, Easter Sunday, Nash announced to the militia that it was time to march on Colfax. He advised that "anyone who was afraid to die for the cause" should step out of line, and about twenty-five men did so, leaving a force of some 140 men. Arriving at the courthouse about noon, Nash promised the occupiers they would not be harmed if they stacked their weapons and withdrew in peace. The women, the children, and the few white occupiers agreed to leave. About 150 African American men refused to capitulate. The shooting soon began. After a few hours, the militia used the cannon. Then they forced a Freedman to set the building on fire, causing about sixty occupiers to flee in panic, and Nash's men pursued them on horseback, killing as many as possible. Eventually, the remaining Freedmen displayed a white flag, and they were allowed to surrender. Although there is some dispute about what happened next, survivors testified that a large number of the unarmed prisoners were slaughtered while pleading for their lives. Prominent planter William J. Cruikshank was later identified as having shot at least two prisoners. Three of the white attackers had been killed, although the nature of the bullets suggested that they had died from friendly fire. For the next few days, the streets of Colfax were littered with dead bodies. Most of the Louisiana newspapers reported that rebellious Freedmen had provoked the confrontation. The Northern press, in contrast, tended to blame the white attackers for the bloodshed.

In Lane's view, the real hero is the U.S. Attorney in New Orleans, James Roswell Beckwith. As soon as Beckwith learned of the atrocities in Colfax, he was determined to investigate the event and prosecute as many of the guilty as possible. His power to bring charges in federal court was based on Section 6 of the Enforcement Act of 1870, which applied to private individuals and criminalized conspiracies to deny citizens' constitutional rights. Two deputy U.S. marshals traveled to Colfax to investigate the murders and to collect evidence.

On May 8, Beckwith convened a grand jury, mostly composed of men of color, and he succeeded in getting indictments against ninety-seven defendants. To undertake the dangerous job of arresting these persons, U.S. marshal Theodore DeKlyne sailed from New Orleans to Colfax with two dozen mounted state police and a few U.S. infantrymen. However, most of the indicted men, including Nash, learned about DeKlyne's mission and went into hiding. After twenty-two days in Grant Parish, DeKlyne and his men were able to find and capture seven of the men, including Cruikshank.

On February 25, 1874, the first of two federal trials began, with nine defendants charged with first-degree murder. Beckwith sought the death penalty. He called fifty witnesses, including more than three dozen Freedmen and a few white liberals from Grant Parish, most notably the large landholder William Smith Calhoun. Led by conservative attorney Robert Marr, the defense called seventy-nine witnesses. On March 16, following vigorous speeches and questioning of witnesses, the jury acquitted one defendant and was unable to agree about the culpability of the others. Federal Judge William Woods had no choice but to declare a mistrial. The second trial, which had eight defendants, lasted from May 20 to June 10. This time, Beckwith called eighty-nine witnesses, and Marr called ninety-nine witnesses. Although none of the defendants was declared guilty of murder, Cruikshank and two others were found guilty of violating the constitutional rights of citizens. The three men were sentenced to ten years in prison and fines of five thousand dollars. A majority of Southern whites were infuriated with the outcome. The *New Orleans Bulletin* declared that it proved "that Southern white men have no rights that Republican officials are bound to respect."

On June 27, however, Justice Joseph Bradley of the U.S. Supreme Court, who was riding circuit in the Deep South, overturned the convictions and ordered the three men released on bail. Bradley based his ruling on two points. First, Bradley wrote that the indictments had not specifically charged that the defendants had been racially motivated to violate citizens' civil rights. Second, building on the recent precedent of a group of lawsuits known as the Slaughterhouse Cases, Bradley wrote that the Fourteenth Amendment was applicable only to state governments, and that Congress had no power to legislate punishment for criminal actions by private individuals—a power reserved to the states in the Tenth Amendment. The ruling meant that the defendants could only be prosecuted in state courts, where it was unlikely that whites would be punished for crimes against blacks.

Lane writes that Bradley's decision "had a swift, bloody impact on Grant Parish." On July 25, white supremacists gathered in Colfax to honor the defendants by holding a large barbecue. One group of extremists rode through the black quarters randomly firing pistols, and then six miles from town, they murdered two Freedmen, Frank Foster and Jim Cox. None of those who witnessed the crimes dared to testify against the killers. Although the new sheriff had knowledge about the persons responsible, he was incapable of arresting them. In other parts of Louisiana and the South, a new organization, called the White League, was spreading a wave of violence.

On March 27, 1876, the U.S. Supreme Court finally issued its decision, *Cruikshank v. United States*, in which all the justices basically endorsed Bradley's earlier conclusions. Under the *Cruikshank* precedent, federal prosecutors would only be able to bring cases under the Enforcement Act when whites attacked blacks specifically because of their race and with the intent to violate a small number of constitutional rights relating to federal as opposed to state citizenship. Under the decision, federal prosecutors would rarely be able to prosecute crimes against the Freedmen, no matter how egregious. Lane persuasively argues that the failure to punish the perpetrators of the Colfax slaughter and the narrow interpretation of federal authority in *Cruikshank* were important "milestones" on the tragic road toward the establishment of "Jim Crow," the rigid system of white supremacy and segregation that would continue until the civil rights revolution of the 1950's and 1960's.

Lane's book focuses on an important topic that has received relatively little attention in standard historical accounts of the period. Eric Foner's *Reconstruction: America's Unfinished Revolution* (1988), for instance, devotes less than a page to the event. In addition to Lane's book, another interesting volume, Leanna Keith's *The Colfax*

Massacre: The Untold Story of Black Power, White Terror, and Death of Reconstruction (2008), has been published. The two books take similar perspectives on issues of civil rights, and both have their strengths. Keith has written a compelling and fast-moving narration that concentrates on the massacre, the participants, and local lore. Some general readers interested primarily in the dramatic aspects of the incident itself might prefer to read her book. Lane's book, however, is also readable, and it provides much more detail and analysis about the criminal trials and the Supreme Court's decision. Lane has unquestionably made a valuable contribution to the study of race relations during the Reconstruction era.

Thomas Tandy Lewis

Review Sources

Booklist 104, no. 11 (February 1, 2008): 18.
Hill 15, no. 43 (April 18, 2008): 20.
Kirkus Reviews 75, no. 24 (December 15, 2007): 1280.
Library Journal 133, no. 5 (March 15, 2008): 79-80.
The New York Times Book Review, May 18, 2008, p. 24.
Publishers Weekly 255, no. 1 (January 17, 2008): 49.

DEATH WITH INTERRUPTIONS

Author: José Saramago (1922-   )
First published: As intermitências da morte: Romance,
2005, in Portugal
Translated from the Portuguese by Margaret Jull Costa
Publisher: Harcourt Books. 238 pp. $24.00
Type of work: Novel
Time: The future
Locale: Unspecified country the size of Portugal

Saramago offers a fictional exploration of what life would be like in a country where people suddenly stopped dying; from this simple premise, the story touches a great many aspects of modern society, suggesting that a world without death would not be as perfect as might be supposed

Principal characters:
THE QUEEN MOTHER, very elderly and near death at the end of the old year
THE DIRECTOR GENERAL, the head of the national television authority
THE GRAMMARIAN, a stuffy expert on proper usage
THE CELLIST, a middle-aged member of a symphony orchestra
GOVERNMENT OFFICIALS, peasants, and other nameless citizens
DEATH (also called DEATH), a young woman carrying a scythe

When awarded the Nobel Prize in Literature in 1998, the Portuguese novelist José Saramago was praised as the creator of "parables sustained by imagination, compassion, and irony," which afford fresh insights into the complexities of human life. His latest novel is true to the form that he has made his own. Like many of his best fictions, it asks the question "What would happen if?"

Saramago's 1987 novel *Jangada de pedra* (*The Stone Raft*, 1995) asks "What would happen if the Iberian peninsula broke away from the European continent and floated in the Atlantic? What would change politically or economically?" His 1989 novel *História do cerco de Lisboa* (*The History of the Siege of Lisbon*, 1996) asks "What would happen if a proofreader inserted the word 'not' into a work of history?" In what may be his best-known parable, the 1995 novel *Ensaio sobre a cegueira* (*Blindness*, 1997), Saramago imagines what would happen if almost everyone in a city suddenly went blind. The story was made into a feature film in 2008.

Death with Interruptions (published in England as *Death at Intervals*) asks the question "What would happen if people suddenly stopped dying, no matter how injured, ill, or elderly they might be?" Like *Blindness*, it has an essayistic quality, providing a "panoramic view" of the country rather than details about specific lives. The narrator, who occasionally identifies himself as such, neither names the characters nor describes them, but simply accounts the events of a half-year as the unnamed

A former journalist, José Saramago has published more than two dozen books of fiction, poetry, and essays over the last sixty years. He won the Nobel Prize in Literature in 1998. Thirteen of his earlier novels have been translated into English.

country descends into chaos. Many lie on their deathbeds in a state of suspended animation, the country's queen mother among them. Hospitals become impossibly overcrowded. Gravediggers must go abroad to find work. Members of the mafia find new work and indeed perform a public service as they spirit the comatose out of the country. The military plans a coup. Churchgoers pray for the return of death.

Seven months into the crisis, another crisis occurs when the state television authority receives a letter from death, saying that normal activities will resume at midnight that night. Everyone who would have died in the first half of the year will die now—more than sixty thousand in a country of ten million. In the future, anyone who had not been on the point of death will be given a week's written notice before the fatal hour. The return of death is a boon for funeral directors and other idle workers and eases the crisis in old-age homes.

As life returns to normal, attention shifts to death. People study the strange letter, written on violet-colored paper. Grammarians and graphologists replace the philosophers in public speculations. All the signs—the irregular letters, "the chaotic syntax, the complete lack of very necessary parentheses, the obsessive elimination of paragraphs, the random use of commas," and much more—suggest the author is a young woman. It seems incredible, but as new sightings are reported at the foot of a bed or the scene of an accident, there is confirmation. Death is more than a feminine noun, in Portuguese and the other Romance languages; death is also very human.

The rest of the novel tells death's story, as she dashes off letters to the dying and tries to have a life of sorts, attending concerts and shopping for clothes. She has the snits and crushes one would expect of an inexperienced young woman. She is not at all the terrifying abstraction that the pundits have imagined. She is not even the supreme power; she is more like an intern or a representative. All too human, she even has something in common with the story's narrator.

Everything the grammarian denounced in the public letter—the syntax, the comma faults, especially "the intentional and almost diabolical abolition of the capital letter"—can also be found in the novel. Not only titles of office but names of classical deities and famous people such as the cellist's beloved Johann Sebastian Bach are left uncapitalized. Question marks and quotation marks are also omitted. In the absence of standard editing conventions, a reader must either slow down and engage with the text or skip over large chunks of the story (at least there are paragraph and chapter breaks). Coming halfway through the story, the grammarian's remarks apply inescapably to the narrator as well and to the author who created him. The remarks give the novel a quality that critics call self-reflexive, a reference to the story's own fictional quality and to the creation of this fiction.

Earlier in the story the narrator apologizes to readers for the "overhasty judgment" that placed the emphasis on prominent public figures rather than ordinary people. The focus then shifts to the people of the countryside and the experience of living in a country where no one dies. However, only when death is identified and particularized do other characters emerge with any sort of individuality. Even so, only death has a name, and she prefers the lowercase "death." There is a fable here, the moral of which seems to be that death makes us who and what we are, that only humans have the awareness they will die. Saramago, an outspoken atheist, hints in this direction when he chooses as the epigram for this book a quote from the philosopher Ludwig Wittgenstein, which suggests that anyone who thinks deeply about death is likely to think new thoughts, with new words and images.

Death with Interruptions is, then, Saramago's own meditation on death, along with a social commentary. As an atheist, he can easily imagine how church officials would squirm at the loss of a major selling point. How could they talk about resurrection and last judgment? Then again, as a communist, he can just as easily imagine how insurance executives would cringe and struggle to find new ways to market policies and persuade policy holders to keep up their payments.

Throughout the novel, Saramago plays with storytelling conventions and, in doing so, draws the reader into his project. The narration switches from third-person accounts to first-person comments about the narrator's intentions and from ostensibly reliable descriptions to clearly unreliable predictions. Then, once death has entered the story, the point of view shifts twice to the second person, and the reader is asked to think and see as death would. The effect is to break down the life-and-death opposition, so that death is just another dead person, though one experiencing some things "for the first time in her life."

When death becomes a character in a story and speaks to other characters, there are many opportunities for dramatic irony. The words she speaks have one meaning for her and the reader, but quite another for a character like the first cellist in a symphony orchestra. Emerging as a principal character in the story—the person who never receives his summoning letter because the postal service repeatedly returns it to sender—the cellist has the impression that he never quite gets death's drift when she appears in person. He is likened to a reader who cannot quite understand a line of poetry.

Paradoxically, when death ceases to be the enemy of mankind and God and becomes a character in a story, a new kind of myth-making begins. Atropos, eldest of the three Fates in Greek mythology and the one that cuts the thread of life with her famous shears, becomes the *Acherontia atropos* (or death's head moth), so called because its thorax has a marking that looks like a human skull. A photograph of this rare species appears on the dust jacket. The moth has a mythological name, the Acheron being one of the four rivers of the classical underworld, but the moth is part of the natural order. Death, too, is part of nature. This does not make it benign; death is, after all, the world's most dangerous "serial killer."

In the complete absence of personal names for characters—perhaps the only innovation that Saramago's readers will not have encountered in earlier novels—names from myth and legend loom large. The references to literary characters outside the novel both elevate the role of ordinary humans and deflate the mystique of death and dying. References to Achilles, whose wrath is the stated subject of Homer's *Iliad* (750 B.C.E.), lead to comparison of the modern city to ancient Troy. A passing reference to the sea goddess Amphitrite, in a description of a musical performance, gives a sense of the sublime and transcendental to the artistry of a composer such as Bach. Meanwhile, however, a reference to Count Dracula and the horrors of Transylvania appears in a statement that death is less scary than the popular imagination makes it out to be.

Margaret Jull Costa, who has translated some two dozen novels from Spanish and Portuguese, won the Weidenfeld Translation Prize for her translation of Saramago's *Todos os nomes* (1997; *All the Names*, 1999). Costa has faithfully preserved the idiosyncrasies of Saramago's prose, which she has compared to that of the innovative Irish novelist James Joyce. She even follows such innovations as "maphia" for "mafia," this one to indicate a new kind of state-sponsored racketeering. Nevertheless, when the Portuguese idioms would be lost in translation, she has appropriate English ones to substitute, perhaps more appropriate for British readers than for Americans but still right for the characters and situations.

The first reviews of Costa's translation have praised her graceful rendering of Saramago's broad social satire and his clever interplay of absurd and profound ideas. Some have found the novel "frustratingly tricky to plow through" (*The Washington Post*) and "unfocused" when compared to Saramago's earlier work (*The New York Times*), while others have praised the language as "deadly serious in its mythic élan" (*Guardian Review*) and as entirely appropriate to the author's "thought experiment" (*New Statesman*). One review has compared the strange wandering sentences to a chorus of mixed, sometimes discordant voices talking about recent events (*The New Yorker*). The consensus seems to be that the novel demands a close reading and will reward anyone who makes the effort.

Searching for a precedent, some reviewers have compared Saramago's novel to the 1934 film *Death Takes a Holiday*. There is similarity, to be sure, notably the possibility that a mortal can fall in love with death and death can reciprocate. However, there is a striking difference. The film leaves no question why Frederic March's character wants a vacation in the land of the living and why he wants to pose as a mere mortal, albeit of the dashingly handsome sort. The novel never explains why death stops working at the end of the old year or why she later picks up where she left off. Like the Prodigal Son and other good parables, *Death with Interruptions* raises more questions than it answers.

Thomas Willard

Review Sources

Kirkus Reviews 76, no. 16 (August 15, 2008): 17.
Library Journal 133, no. 14 (September 1, 2008): 122.
The New York Times, November 12, 2008, p. 6.
The New York Times Book Review, October 26, 2008, p. 19.
The New Yorker 84, no. 34 (October 27, 2008): 88-91.
Publishers Weekly 255, no. 29 (July 21, 2008): 136.
The Washington Post, October 5, 2008, p. N6.

DELUSION
A Novel of Suspense

Author: Peter Abrahams (1947-   )
Publisher: William Morrow (New York). 297 pp. $24.95
Type of work: Novel
Locale: Belle Ville, Louisiana, and Little Parrot Cay, Caribbean

A woman and her family struggle with the repercussions of a testimony that put an innocent man behind bars for murder when that man is set free

Principal characters:
NELL JARREAU, a forty-something woman whose testimony against Alvin DuPree put him in jail for murder
ALVIN DUPREE, also known as Pirate, the man wrongly convicted of murder who served twenty years of prison sentence
CLAY JARREAU, police officer who put DuPree behind bars, now Nell's husband
NORAH JARREAU, daughter of Nell Jarreau and adopted daughter of Clay Jarreau
JOHNNY BLANTON, the young man whose murder was the cause for DuPree's imprisonment
DUKE BASTIEN, Clay Jarreau's best friend who runs a construction business
KIRK BASTIEN, the brother of Duke Bastien, the mayor of Belle Ville, a partner in Bastien's construction business
LEE ANN BONNER, a reporter who wants to write DuPree's story
JOE DON YELLER, Norah Jarreau's boyfriend

As its title clearly indicates, Peter Abrahams's twentieth novel explores the idea of a life lived as a delusion. It was well received by critics and acclaimed as being a model of the suspense genre that goes beyond formula work. In this novel, almost every character holds a belief that undermines and shatters identity, status, and relationships. Focused equally on Nell Jarreau and Alvin DuPree (Pirate), the book uses a limited omniscient point of view that gives readers glimpses into such personality motivators as innocence, naiveté, and barely suppressed anger. The confused maze of DuPree's mind, in particular, provides a fascinating look at what these qualities mean when one is distanced from trauma by a delusion about what really happened.

The use of irony builds suspense in the novel as the characters reveal aspects of their personalities that uphold their delusional versions of life. DuPree has spent twenty years in prison. During that time he has been both the victim and the perpetrator of violence, but at the beginning of the novel, just before he is released as the result of the emergence of new evidence, he has finally found peace. He has associated himself with the biblical character of Job, internalizing the message of hope found in that book of the Bible. He is sure his favorite verses— "And the Lord turned the captivity of Job, when he prayed for his friends: also the Lord gave Job twice as much as he had before"— are prophetic when his innocence is proven. Despite his assurances to himself that it is the biblical message that provides peace, his sense of tranquillity is more often physically mani-

~

Peter Abrahams has written numerous suspense novels for adults, and he has recently entered the young adult market. His honors include an Edgar Award nomination for best novel for Lights Out *(1994) and the Agatha Award for Best Children's/Young Adult novel for* Down the Rabbit Hole *(2005).*

~

fested in the act of stroking the silky tassel of the ribbon that marks his place in the Bible. That delusion of peace deserts DuPree, however, when he is sent back into society. Once out of jail, he struggles to understand the varied people and situations he confronts: a reporter, Lee Ann Bonner, who wants to write a prize-winning book about his imprisonment; his thoughts of vengeance against the woman who sent him to prison; the idea that a guilty person has remained free while he was jailed; and his criminal tendencies. He centers his peace on two things: the book of Job and a homemade weapon that he hides in the empty space that is left behind after he lost an eye in prison. During the first days of his freedom, he finds that society is still brutally classist, and he turns to the familiarity of violence when he cannot interact in more acceptable ways.

Nell provides a complete contrast to DuPree. He was an uneducated criminal delinquent when Johnny Blanton was murdered, and Nell was Johnny's educated middle-class girlfriend. DuPree had already dabbled in the dark side of criminal behavior, and Nell had never been confronted with evil. The fact that Nell has been sheltered from most aspects of life, even from the repercussions of the violence that she witnessed as her boyfriend was murdered, foreshadows her inability to see past the façade of her life. As a result, when DuPree is freed from jail and her testimony is questioned, Nell's whole life is destabilized. Among other issues, she is forced to confront her daughter's anxious concerns about whether Blanton's murder was covered up by Clay Jarreau, the man to whom Nell has been married for almost twenty years and who has filled the role of Norah's father. Norah even invokes William Shakespeare's *Hamlet* (1601) through a reference to the king's ghostly warning that his death was contrived by his brother Claudius and his widow Gertrude. As Nell's life unravels, readers are confronted with the question of what reality is and whether their versions of their lives are valid or deceptive.

The use of literary reference is not a new technique for Abrahams. DuPree's reliance on Job and Norah's invocation of *Hamlet* can be seen as echoes of his style in earlier works. For example, Abrahams's 1994 novel *Lights Out* revolves around the main character's obsession with Samuel Taylor Coleridge's long poem *The Rime of the Ancient Mariner* (1798). More recently, his Echo Falls series for young adults brings in references to Sherlock Holmes as a central character building tool.

The characterization also confronts the issue of innate evil as DuPree fights against his instincts to lash out at those he perceives as dangerous to him. He considers hurting Lee Ann, Nell, and Norah as they talk to him about the crime, but since all three women have positive motives in seeking him out, he is able to maintain his peace. When he is found next to Lee Ann's dead body, he is once again perceived as evil. As the novel draws to a close and the true culprit is discovered, DuPree does attack an innocent bystander, losing his peace and his salvation.

Abrahams invokes a sense of realism as he confronts a variety of societal problems while his characters career out of control. A hurricane, Bernardine, has swept through Belle Ville, leaving carnage and disrupting lives. As the physical damage to the city has been mainly confined to the Lower Side, racial tension becomes a dark undertone to the story's outcome. Repairs in this area of the city are neglected until the mayor is forced to look past the delusion that everything is being cleaned up in an appropriate way. Racial problems become more of a focus when the evidence that should have exonerated DuPree twenty years earlier has been found in the locker of a dead African American police officer who served as Clay Jarreau's partner when Blanton was murdered. Doubt rises about whether this officer's death, as he was saving a child after the hurricane, was accidental, causing an inquiry into whether he was murdered for the evidence he held. This man's years of exemplary public service are challenged merely because of his race.

Beyond racial tension, political intrigue becomes a possible motivation in the murder. Kirk Bastien has been elected to the office of mayor, despite some troubling issues. He is a partner in a construction company that stands to profit mightily from the hurricane damage and that stood to profit twenty years earlier by the death of a brilliant geology graduate student who had questioned the safety factor of a major project. The reference to the damage caused by Katrina is obvious as the characters struggle to beat back the repercussions of nature's fury. Nell is forced to face the reality that neither her husband nor her life is perfect every time the wind blows across town, and she complains about the stench left over from Bernardine.

Another theme that the novel attacks is the validity of eyewitness testimony. As Nell remembers Blanton's murder, she struggles with her identification of DuPree as the murderer. Striving to understand how she might have accused the wrong man, she seeks out the help of a hypnotist and of a professor who is an expert on the issue of eyewitness testimony. Learning that police officers can mislead witnesses with subtle gestures, she questions Clay's pursuit of DuPree as the killer and starts to suspect her husband is the murderer. As the plot unravels, the strong belief in the legal system is undermined as delusional.

Mystery-suspense novels are often plot driven, and this work is no different. The complications of the characters' lives move the mystery forward, and subtle foreshadowing leads to a questioning of who is guilty and who is innocent. DuPree's innocence is only superficial. Through the use of inner monologue, DuPree's motives are revealed. Readers learn that he is plagued by the desire to harm those who attempt to accept him, and the ultimate irony occurs when Nell finds him next to the dead body of Lee Ann, so that he is accused of yet another murder he did not commit. His situation is a classic case of being in the wrong place at the wrong time. His violent nature takes over his actions as the novel draws to a close, and he figures out who the real killer is but too late to save his soul. Nell's innocence in the murders seems to be clear, yet her unwillingness to face the delusion of her marriage and her life becomes the basis for a plot twist that reveals the truly guilty. Clay has lived for twenty years with the knowledge of who the real killer is, yet he covers up the truth, and an innocent man serves jail time while the murderer goes free. As the novel progresses, Abrahams provides so many possible killers and motives that readers may be surprised to discover the identity of the murderer and the motive. Some readers, however, may figure out the murderer before the plot's revelation.

In this book, Abrahams creates a multilayered work that challenges our perception of life. Though the characters are a bit one-dimensional, the plot spirals them into an abyss of doubt that questions what motivates action and whether innocence is real or perceived. If it is real, who is at fault when something goes wrong? If it is perceived, how many lives are affected and how are delusions revealed? Abrahams's skillful use of irony manipulates readers' expectations of what the foreshadowing means. The delusion is more than just an issue of the characters' understanding of their lives and of their belief systems. It forces readers to question what delusions they may have about their lives and their belief systems.

Theresa L. Stowell

Review Sources

Booklist 104, no. 11 (February 1, 2008): 5.
Globe & Mail, April 26, 2008, p. D12.
Kirkus Reviews 76, no. 4 (February 15, 2008): 159.
Library Journal 133, no. 7 (April 15, 2008): 70.
Publishers Weekly 255, no. 7 (February 18, 2008): 136.

DE NIRO'S GAME

Author: Rawi Hage (1964-   )
First published: 2006, in Canada
Publisher: HarperPerennial (New York). 320 pp. $14.00
Type of work: Novel
Time: 1982
Locale: Beirut and Paris

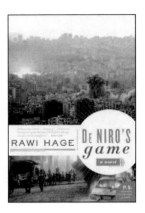

Best friends since childhood, two young men come of age in Beirut during the Lebanese civil war; only one escapes as brutality, criminality, and betrayal bring their relationship to a tragic end

Principal characters:
> BASSAM, a young man coming of age in
>   Beirut during the civil war
> GEORGE, nicknamed De Niro, Bassam's best friend
> NABILA, George's aunt
> RANA, Bassam's girlfriend
> LAURENT and NICOLE AOUDEH, a wealthy couple befriended by George
> RAMBO, Bassam's torturer
> RHEA MANI, George's half-sister, living in Paris
> ROLAND and MOSHE, Mossad agents based in Paris

The title of this novel, *De Niro's Game*, refers not only to the character of George, who is nicknamed De Niro after the American actor, but also to the suicidal Russian roulette that Robert De Niro's character is forced to play in Michael Cimino's 1978 film about the Vietnam War, *The Deer Hunter*. The title does not, however, simply refer to the game of Russian Roulette that will finish the story of George and Bassam. It also describes the situation of young men in a world in which survival seems to be increasingly an inexplicable matter of chance and in which the value of life is treated with a careless disregard. Additionally, it is a world in which violence is perceived as virtually the only effective solution to any problem, and although on one level the reckless young men are convinced of their invincibility, their irresponsible conduct—in a world without hope or options—takes on a suicidal ideation.

The narrative explores the friendship of two Lebanese young men within this context. Bassam and George come of age in Beirut during the Lebanese civil war. The militias that have taken over the city are little more than powerful criminal gangs; the city, besieged by bombs and bullets, has become not only a war zone but also an amoral, lawless space that easily accommodates theft and violence. As a result, the young men growing up in this place and time find they are becoming socialized into criminality.

Bassam is drawn into this world through the offices of his friend George, who in-

vites him to steal a bit of cash from the ca-
sino run by the powerful Christian militia that
governs their section of town. George pulls
Bassam in deeper by tricking him into a job
smuggling liquor and drugs. While Bassam is
in a state of panic and determined to escape
Beirut and the underworld in which he has become enmeshed, his friend George feels neither helpless nor powerless. He rises in the
ruthless world of the militia but, at the same
time, loses his moral compass, callously be-
traying a friend and eventually taking part in
the Phalangist massacre of Palestinian women

*Born in Beirut, Lebanon, Rawi Hage
lived through nine years of the
Lebanese civil war and immigrated to
Canada in 1992. He is a writer, a
visual artist, and a curator, and he
resides in Montreal. De Niro's Game
won the 2008 McAuslan First Book
Prize, the 2006 Paragraphe Hugh
MacLennan Prize for Fiction, and the
2008 IMPAC Dublin Literary Award.*

and children at the refugee camps of Sabra and Shatilla. George's corruption is also
indicated by his strange sexual involvement with a wealthy young couple, Laurent
and Nicole Aoudeh; he ends by addicting Nicole to drugs and is responsible for the
murder of her husband.

Unlike George, Bassam is not drawn to the world of power and criminality. Having lost both his father and more recently his mother when a bomb hits their apartment, he is looking to get out. However, although Bassam's path gradually diverges
significantly from George's, there is also considerable intermingling, almost twin-
ning, of the two. Bassam has a brief love affair with George's attractive aunt, Nabila;
in turn, George steals Bassam's girlfriend, Rana. More and more, Bassam appears to
be not George's friend but his rival and then his dupe. For instance, Bassam is stuck
taking the blame for George's crimes, such as the murder of Laurent, and is as a result
cruelly tortured by a thuggish soldier named Rambo. Bassam's position becomes
even more untenable after he vengefully murders his torturer and after he passes information from his communist uncle to a contact in Beirut. This favor leads to the
death of Al-Rayess, the highest commander of the Christian Lebanese forces.

The web of violence and intrigue into which Bassam has been drawn is troubling,
but even more disturbing is Bassam's struggle with the disintegration of his personality. This breakdown is indicated by the narrative style, which on the one hand is edgy
and hard-boiled and on the other hand is poetic and strangely healing, as if the madness into which he is descending contains also the seeds of his recovery. While beset
with a flow of dreams and fantasies that take him both out of himself and deeper into
himself, Bassam's harsh side finds validation in the famous Albert Camus novel
L'Étranger (1942; *The Stranger*, 1943). When Bassam escapes to Paris after the death
of George, the concierge at his hotel gives him the Camus novel, which offers Bassam
an existential context in which to understand why he has adopted an empty, alienated
perspective that not only makes it difficult for him to assign value but affords him little or no sense of personal agency.

It is in this mood that Bassam acquaints himself with the wife and daughter of
George, whose address Nabila had given him. A sexual encounter with George's half-
sister leads him to stalk a man he considers his rival, although what Bassam thought

was a personal matter is a political one. Bassam learns that Rhea's friend Roland, as well as her friend Moshe, are in reality Mossad agents, who backed Al-Rayess against the Muslims. Furthermore, Bassam discovers that the Mossad recruited George as one of their agents. Since Roland and Moshe are certain Bassam can lead them to the missing George, once again Bassam is ensnared in political intrigue related to the volatile political situation in Lebanon. Although Rhea seems only concerned about George as a half-brother, and about Bassam as his friend and her lover, Bassam realizes that even in Paris, and even in his personal life, the political situation in Lebanon—connected as it is to global politics—is inescapable.

Roland and Moshe are correct that it is Bassam who knows the whereabouts of George. He confesses to Rhea that George had been sent to bring him back to headquarters to be tortured and killed for the murder of Laurent. Bassam goes on to tell Rhea that George, in a moment of consideration for his childhood friend, gave him a chance to end it all immediately by handing him his revolver and suggesting that he play "De Niro's game" of Russian roulette. When Bassam's spin of the cylinder comes up empty, George unexpectedly takes a turn himself, as if giving Bassam yet another chance. Unlike Bassam, George is unlucky; he puts a bullet through his brain.

It is at this point that Bassam escapes, only to wander the streets of Paris still armed with a revolver and still psychologically trapped in the pattern of brutality and criminality created by the warlords. Realizing that it is likely he will be persecuted as an Arab in France, unable to imagine that he will ever find a place for himself in French society, and hounded by Roland and Moshe, Bassam returns to his early fantasy of finding sanctuary in Rome. The first chapter in this novel is, in fact, titled "Rome," speaking to Bassam's desperate dream of escaping the war-torn city of Beirut. At novel's end he returns to the possibility that this is the way out of his terrible situation, even going so far as to buy a ticket to the Eternal City. Whether Bassam will ever actually get to Rome is left open; in some ways, he is simply back to square one. By the end of this novel, however, Bassam has descended from petty thuggery into more serious complicity with evil; there is no doubt that there is blood on his hands—that he is a good example of Sartre's famous phrase concerning the "mains sales" or "dirty hands" that come to anyone drawn, however unwillingly, into the modern world of power politics.

While Bassam has approached the zone of madness and evil, he has never fallen into his friend George's abyss of torture, terror, crime, and treachery. In the end, however, Bassam is utterly alone. The tragic end of his relationship with George, his escape from Beirut, and his anticipated second escape from Paris have left him in a condition of rootless alienation. It is clear that the context of a brutal civil war and an unraveling society have shaped the character of Bassam as he struggles to come into his manhood; like other young men of his generation, he has become ruthless, nihilistic, and utterly alone. Although George's Aunt Nabila described these young men as not unlike the abandoned dogs that now ran wild through the city of Beirut, Bassam is a more complex figure. He does not want to degenerate into the treacherous, amoral George, and his inner life demonstrates that he is working to understand the situation into which he has been thrown and, in so doing, transcend it. Of special interest in this regard is the way in which Bassam is constantly imagining other historical eras, as layers beneath the present one; he imagines he is a soldier in Napoleon's army, or that he is being persecuted by the Gestapo. He imagines Beirut when it was an ancient Roman city, and the historical affiliation of Lebanon and Rome, in fact, adds resonance to Bassam's fixation on finding sanctuary in Rome, which had in the time of the Roman Empire exercised sovereignty over the territory that later became Lebanon. While Bassam's confused, dreamlike inner life may seem at times unwholesome and miasmatic, his fantasies and ruminations possess a kind of wisdom that allows him to see himself through the difficulties of coming of age during an age of crisis. His obsession with Rome, for instance, which at first appears irrational, actually expresses an aspiration to have a place in a more universal society, one not sundered by sectarian interests, as has happened in Bassam's home country of Lebanon.

While Bassam may strain toward an ancient Roman universality, this narrative is a mélange of cultural ingredients: There are Arabic poetic elements to Bassam's inner life, and the narrative also indicates a political perspective associated with the Arabic peoples of the Middle East. Furthermore, though Hage is not a Frenchman, he deploys French philosophy quite effectively, and he uses one of the great French novels of the twentieth century as an explanatory model for his own predicament.

Although English is not his first language, Hage has chosen to write this and subsequent fiction in English, one of the two languages that inform the culture of Montreal, where he now lives. The global reach of this novel and the way it addresses a political situation of international interest and implication are impressive. Nevertheless, its greatest achievement is in the psychological acuity with which Hage renders the intense and complicated inner life of a troubled boy caught between good and evil, madness and sanity, life and death. A mosaic of cultural influences and filled with incident to the point that the narrative could be described as a thriller, the novel is enriched by the vitality of Hage's language and his astute reading of character.

Margaret Boe Birns

Review Sources

Booklist 103, no. 18 (May 15, 2007): 19.
Books in Canada, December, 2006, pp. 5-7.
International Fiction Review, January, 2007, p. 196.
Journal of Third World Studies 25, no. 1 (Spring, 2008): 293-297.
Kirkus Reviews 75, no. 12 (June 15, 2007): 573.
Library Journal 132, no. 12 (July 1, 2007): 77.
Los Angeles Times, February 24, 2008, p. R5.
Maclean's 119, no. 22 (May 29, 2006): 40-41.
Publishers Weekly 254, no. 16 (April 16, 2007): 26.
The Village Voice 52, no. 33 (August 15, 2007): 54.
The Washington Post, June 24, 2008, p. C8.

DESIGN IN THE AGE OF DARWIN
From William Morris to Frank Lloyd Wright

Author: Stephen F. Eisenman (1956-   )

Publisher: Mary and Leigh Block Museum of Art, Northwestern University (Evanston, Ill.). 141 pp. $36.95

Type of work: Essays, fine arts, history of science

Time: 1859-1910

Locale: England and the United States

A book of essays and photographs of objects that explores the interaction of design and the concepts of evolution in nineteenth century England and the United States

Principal personages:

CHARLES DARWIN, British naturalist and author of *On the Origin of Species by Means of Natural Selection* (1859)

WILLIAM MORRIS, British designer and author

CHRISTOPHER DRESSER, British botanist and industrial designer

C. R. ASHBEE, British craftsman and socialist

C. F. A. VOYSEY, British architect and designer

LOUIS SULLIVAN, American architect

FRANK LLOYD WRIGHT, American architect and designer

Design and evolution were topics of great significance during the nineteenth century, and *Design in the Age of Darwin* examines the interactions between evolutionary theories and design after the publication of Charles Darwin's *On the Origin of Species by Means of Natural Selection* in 1859. Although debates about natural history had many nuances, the main division between "intelligent design" and Darwin's view of evolution shared an emphasis on the importance of the way plants and animals were designed and adapted to function within their environments. A key difference was in the agency of design. "Intelligent design," especially as articulated by the Reverend William Paley in *Natural Theology* (1802), argued that such "intelligent design" in nature is ultimately the work of the Creator, God. Darwin, in contrast, saw design as evidence for the struggle for survival, and he proposed that evolution occurred by incorporating the most functional and adaptive designs to meet the challenges of survival.

Design in the Age of Darwin originated in an exhibition held at the Mary and Leigh Block Museum of Art at Northwestern University. Stephen F. Eisenman, professor of art history at Northwestern University, conceived and curated the exhibit whose purpose was to explore how British and American architects and designers responded to the challenges presented by Darwin's theory of evolution. The book accompanies this exhibition. Through five essays, the book explains and probes many facets of this time when "the theory and practice of design were closely tied to the theory of evolution." Sixty-nine color plates of some of the objects and designs in the exhibition along with additional illustrations allow the reader to view the visual evidence.

One starting point in approaching this topic is the third essay in this volume, "Designing Evolution: Darwin's Illustrations," by Jacob W. Lewis. Darwin wrote a number of books on natural history, and many were studies that

~

Stephen F. Eisenman is a professor of art history at Northwestern University. He is the author of several books and catalogues on nineteenth century art, including Nineteenth Century Art: A Critical History *(2007).*

~

demonstrated the kind of detailed evidence on which Darwin drew from close examination of natural phenomena to present his theory of evolution in *On the Origin of Species*. In addition, toward the end of his life, Darwin grappled with the implications of evolution for the human species in *The Descent of Man* (1871) and *The Expression of Emotions in Man and Animals* (1872). Thus, Darwin faced some major design issues himself. First, he needed to find ways to bridge the gap between the close visual observation of the naturalist and the abstract theories that this detailed visual evidence engendered. Second, his theory of evolution and natural selection was "a glacially slow process" over time. Darwin had to devise ways to capture, in effect, a time-lapse process within the confines of the concrete physical and visual presence of a book. To an extent, the designers and architects whose works are presented in this book confronted the same fundamental design challenges.

Lewis's essay discusses Darwin's eclectic approach to providing illustrations for his books. *On the Origin of the Species* had only one illustration, a schematic diagram that Darwin devised to represent a tree of life showing the stages of evolution of various species from extinct ancestors. In other books, Darwin often selected wood engravings from previously published sources, some of which were too abstract and archetypal to capture the sense of change and adaptation so essential to his evolutionary theory. For *The Expression of Emotions in Man and Animals*, Darwin used some photographic images. However, at this early stage in the development of photography, these staged and altered images fail to illustrate the spontaneity of emotional expressions. While Lewis concludes that Darwin "adapted well" to these visual problems, the evidence in this essay points to a struggle with the limitations of visual presentation of Darwin's theory of evolution.

In contrast to Darwin, who was using design to illustrate a single theory of evolution, designers and architects drew on multiple sources and concepts to create their works. Eisenman's introductory essay, "Design in the Age of Darwin: From William Morris to Frank Lloyd Wright," provides an overview of how these issues varied with the individual designers who are represented in the exhibit. After discussions of the principal division in the evolutionary debate between "intelligent design" and Darwin's evolution by natural selection as well as the basic design issues concerning form and function, method of manufacture, and historical evolution of design, Eisenman turns to the centerpiece of the essay by contrasting the approaches of William Morris and Christopher Dresser.

When Morris was designing ornamental patterns based on plant forms, he echoed the Darwinian view of the particular and the mutable in organisms within their environmental context. At the same time, Morris rejected the linearity of evolutionary development when he evoked the return to earlier stages of civilization, especially the Middle Ages, which, for Morris, celebrated the communal socialism in which hand craftsmanship was valued.

Dresser, on the other hand, was a formalist. He saw within each plant an ideal archetype, and his plant illustrations and designs emphasized this abstracted archetypal form. His book *Unity in Variety*, published in 1859 just months after the appearance of *On the Origin of the Species*, aligned his design philosophy with "intelligent design" since he attributed this underlying unity of natural forms to "one intelligence," that is, God. However, because his designs were based on "models, prototypes, templates, and infinite repeatability" and so well suited to mechanical reproduction, in the realm of industrial manufacture, Dresser verged into Darwinian ideas about fitness of designs for their purpose.

The case of these two designers, Morris and Dresser, demonstrates how they selected, adapted, and blended Darwin's ideas about evolution with other aesthetic, social, and political currents of thought. This process continued in England with the British designers C. R. Ashbee and C. F. A. Voysey. In the United States, the architects Louis Sullivan and Frank Lloyd Wright were heirs to the impact of evolutionism on design. Eisenman's essay concludes with a coda on how Darwinian ideas were reshaped by these designers and architects as they moved toward a modernist style at the beginning of the twentieth century. In addition, three of the essays discuss specific aspects of the work of these designers.

Zirwat Chowdhury, in his essay "C. F. A. Voysey: An Aesthetic of Independence and Interdependence," writes about how Voysey integrated the functionalist design approaches of Morris as well as those of John Ruskin with the formalist designs of Dresser. Voysey was an architect who also designed decorative art. His wallpaper designs seem more aligned with the typological versions of natural forms that Dresser advocated. However, the designs incorporate some of the sense of interdependence of forms, the kind of "contingencies" that Morris and Ruskin espoused. In production, Voysey also distanced himself from the communal situation favored by Morris and emphasized adaptation to modern manufacturing methods and fitness for purpose that were closer to Dresser's ideals.

Angelina Lucento's essay, "Evolution and Homogenic Love in C. R. Ashbee's Guild of Handicraft," takes the reader into another realm of Darwin's impact, social Darwinism, especially as articulated by Herbert Spencer. Although Ashbee rejected the "survival-of-the-fittest" aspect of social Darwinism, he was drawn to the idea of humanity striving toward perfection. Ashbee, under the influence of the scholar Edward Carpenter (who, in turn, drew on the work of the French writer Jean-Baptiste Lamarck), was attracted to the idea that homogenic love was the force driving humanity to perfection. Ashbee eventually formed a Guild of Handicraft in which Ashbee followed some of the ideals of Morris in the communal production of useful handcrafts, especially tableware, that reflected Ashbee's design philosophy that forms should be "true to both the patterns of nature and the materials from which they had been created." In Ashbee's efforts, the mixture of strains from differing aspects of evolutionary thought grafted to a social system based on a homogenic theory of sexuality demonstrates the complexity of influences on design in the wake of Darwin.

These intellectual, scientific, social, and aesthetic currents also animated American culture. Two architects, Sullivan and Wright, who worked around the turn of the twentieth century in the Chicago area are highlighted in this exhibit and book. The essay by David van Zanten, "Louis Sullivan, Herbert Spencer, and the Medium of Architecture," is devoted to these architects. He focuses on Sullivan's drawings to demonstrate the architect's "organicist, evolutionary" approach not only to architectural ornament but also to ground plans that developed from the inside out. Both Sullivan and Wright designed their buildings to be part of and responsive to their environmental surroundings. Both architects, however, blended these organic, evolutionary elements with stylized abstraction as well as machine production reminiscent of Dresser's designs.

The book and exhibit call attention to the way architecture and design developed during the age of Darwin. However, the book is problematic in several ways. First, except for the essay on illustrating Darwin's books, Darwin and his writings, especially the influential *On the Origin of the Species*, remain elusive. There is little evidence that these designers and architects read Darwin directly. While it is apparent that ideas about evolution articulated by Darwin and others were key elements in the directions that architecture and design took, a discussion of how Darwin's writing on evolution circulated and gained a wider audience could have bridged the gap between Darwin's work, on the one hand, and the drawings and decorative arts that are so handsomely illustrated and discussed in the book.

A second problem is a lack of integration and focus of the material presented. There are so many currents and crosscurrents and so many intersections and divergences in the ways that designers responded and reacted to ideas about evolution and embodied these concepts in their designs. Darwin's theory of evolution took many forms when applied to social and political arenas. The growth of industry and technological progress allied itself with many aspects of evolutionary thinking. Because designers and architects were closely connected to both social organization and methods of production, the ancillary lines that emerged from the challenges of Darwin's views of evolution are also key to understanding the way design was practiced.

The five essays in the book are too discrete and specialized to guide the reader through the tangled web of the interplay and the intersection of so many ideas and theories. Despite Eisenman's good introductory essay, which endeavors to bring these multiple strands together, too many loose ends remain dangling. In effect, there is not enough unity in the variety.

Examining the interaction between design and the myriad forms of evolutionary thinking that Darwin's book *On the Origin of Species* stimulated is an important intellectual project, and this book provides a good starting point for continuing exploration of these issues and ideas.

Karen Gould

Review Sources

The Daily Northwestern, July 10, 2008, http://media.www.dailynorthwestern.com.
North by Northwestern, May 18, 2008, http://www.northbynorthwestern.com.
Time Out Chicago 169 (May 22-28, 2008).

THE DEVIL GETS HIS DUE
The Uncollected Essays of Leslie Fiedler

Author: Leslie Fiedler (1917-2003)
Edited and with an introduction by Samuele F. S. Pardini
Publisher: Counterpoint (Berkeley, Calif.). 315 pp.
$26.00
Type of work: Literary criticism

This sampling of Fiedler's criticism shows how he anticipated recent trends in literary analysis and studies of popular culture

A provocative and influential literary critic, Leslie Fiedler established his reputation as a maverick when he published his essay "Come Back to the Raft Ag'in, Huck Honey!" in *Partisan Review* in 1948. This essay proposed that the relationship between Huck and Jim not only has homoerotic overtones but also serves as a literary archetype found in other American classics, such as Herman Melville's *Moby Dick* (1851) and James Fenimore Cooper's *The Deerslayer* (1841). The critical establishment was not pleased with this hint of sex and miscegenation in American classic novels about male bonding, but the scandal made Fiedler famous. By the time he developed his ideas further in his 1960 book *Love and Death in the American Novel*, Fiedler had established himself as one of the best literary analysts of his generation.

After his heyday in the 1960's and 1970's, his star dimmed, in part because of scholarly interest in the French theorists of the 1980's, but Fiedler kept publishing books and articles in journals and magazines such as *Esquire*. His showman's side expressed itself when he appeared on talk shows such as *Today* and *The Merv Griffin Show*, and he even portrayed a Gypsy caravan driver in a full-length feature film that was never released. Since Fiedler's death in 2003, his work has not received much valedictory attention, so Samuele F. S. Pardini sought to redress that by assembling Fiedler's uncollected essays into *The Devil Gets His Due*. In his introduction to the volume, Pardini finds that "literary criticism is in crisis," mostly because of a general lack of appreciation for or knowledge of major American critics and the heritage they represent. He hopes that this sampling of essays will find a younger audience who may not know how much Fiedler influenced contemporary criticism, especially in relation to popular culture.

Pardini assembled the essays thematically, moving from an early section that explained Fiedler's critical agenda to other sections devoted to Mark Twain's writings, American literary criticism, pop modernism, writers of the 1950's and 1960's, and cultural studies. As Pardini points out, the book "covers almost sixty years of critical work," but his effort to get readers to look at Fiedler's writings thematically can make the essays hard to place in historical context. For instance, Fiedler be-

~

Leslie Fiedler was a prolific critic who often wrote about American literature and popular culture in terms of psychology and mythology. His most influential work was Love and Death in the American Novel *(1960). In 1998 Fiedler received a Lifetime Achievement Award from the National Book Critics Circle.*

~

gins his essay entitled "The Ordeal of Criticism" in mid-conversation with other writers, and one has to hunt through the acknowledgments page to find that it came from *Commentary* in 1949. Similarly, when Fiedler blasts the "totalitarian" nature of political correctness in his discussion of "The Canon and the Classroom: A Caveat," his insights make sense in terms of his essay's publication in 1992, but not at all in terms of the essays of the 1950's that immediately preceded it in the collection.

Aside from these abrupt historical shifts, one can still tell that Fiedler did much to redefine criticism in terms of style and of content. In his early essay "Toward an Amateur Criticism," Fiedler advocated "the language of conversation—the voice of the dilettante at home" in opposition to jargon-laden criticism, finding that "the ideal form for critical discourse is the irresponsible, non-commercial book review." One can see how his critical strategies anticipated controversy when Fiedler declares that "the critic's unforgivable sin is to be dull." Fiedler also struggled against the predominant focus on high modernist literature in the 1940's and 1950's, especially the works of William Butler Yeats, T. S. Eliot, James Joyce, Henry James, and Herman Melville. Instead, he liked to celebrate what he called "good bad" writers, such as Harriet Beecher Stowe and James Fenimore Cooper. While critics working within the modernist tradition might champion style, allusion, and the internal architecture of classic works such as James Joyce's *Ulysses* (1922), Fiedler prefers the "mythopoeic power of the author" and his or her ability to stir up the "collective unconscious, the evocation of closely shared nightmares of race and sex." Sometimes Fiedler takes this tendency to democratize aesthetic taste to an extreme. For instance, at one point he claims that television "represents the fulfillment of all to which the popular arts have aspired from the start," but otherwise his openness to other writers and other forms of storytelling greatly widened the possibilities for critical discourse.

At times, Fiedler attempted to turn the standard critical reception of a famous author on its head. For instance, in his essay "Ezra Pound: The Poet as Parodist," Fiedler explores Pound's uneasy relationship with the American poetic tradition, especially when he tried to reject the influence of Henry Wadsworth Longfellow or Walt Whitman. Pound rebelled against Whitman's celebration of democracy, but he found himself obliged to adapt Whitman's voice for his own ends in his collection entitled *Lustra* (1916). Ultimately, Pound tried out various voices with mixed success, so Fiedler designates Pound's magnum opus the *Cantos* (1917; complete edition, 1948) as a "mock epic" in which is heard "Nobody talking in garbled and half-understood tongues . . . about Nothing at all," not the highest praise for the culmination of Pound's life work. Fiedler has nice things to say about William Faulkner and Robert Penn Warren, but in both cases he highlights the populist side of their writings. Instead of discussing one of the more canonical novels, Fiedler spends much of "Pop

Goes the Faulkner" meditating on how Faulkner's scandalous and pornographic *Sanctuary* (1931) may be "the essence, the very center of his achievement," having more in common with Dashiell Hammett than with James Joyce.

From the beginning, Fiedler tended to focus on an author's violations of the ethical conventions of his day. In doing so, according to Fiedler, the author may then uncover the deeper psychological forces at work underneath society's polite veneer. In Freudian terms, Fiedler clearly prefers the id to the superego. He finds that the artist is against "everything in ourselves that responds to . . . law and order appeal." Where other critics might like to draw clear lines between high and low Art, or accepted and unacceptable material, Fiedler clearly likes to mix things up, upset other people's categories, especially when it comes to race and sex. This tendency explains the title of his essay "Giving the Devil His Due." The author has the right to acknowledge "our deepest ambivalence toward violence, toward sex, toward our parents, toward our mates, toward our children, toward our secret selves, toward the daylight deities we are proud to boast we honor alone." So it should come as no surprise that Fiedler celebrates Ken Kesey's *One Flew over the Cuckoo's Nest* (1962), in spite of admitting to the misogyny of the novel. He takes pleasure in dissecting the convoluted history of censorship and praise in relation to Twain's 1884 masterpiece in "*Huckleberry Finn*: The Book We Love to Hate," and he even wrote a short essay on a little-known piece of pornography written by Twain in *1601* (published anonymously in 1880). Fiedler made it his critical technique to look for archetypes in revolt against received morality.

Given his interest in ambivalent works of literature, Fiedler also wondered about both public and academic acceptance of various writers. Aside from his aggravation with critics inflating the importance of the high modernists, he also questioned in "Looking Back After Fifty Years" why John Steinbeck's *The Grapes of Wrath* (1939) could be considered a classic in spite of its acknowledged "didacticism, sentimentality, stereotyping, and melodrama." Fiedler finds much to decry in the novel, but he says it succeeds with readers because of the "archetypal resonance" that it shares with Margaret Mitchell's *Gone with the Wind* (1939) and with such characters as Hamlet, Falstaff, Odysseus, Tarzan, and Sherlock Holmes. Given his critical lens that tries to acknowledge the reasons for popular appeal, Fiedler has no trouble writing about Kurt Vonnegut, who managed to attain pop classic status with mixing of genres, especially science fiction. When it comes to James Branch Cabell, Fiedler notes how his critical reputation has completely disappeared, but his novels, such as *Jurgen* (1919), may still find a new audience as fantasy novels for adolescents. Given Fiedler's tendency to write in broad strokes without much in the way of specific evidence, one wonders how well some of these authors would hold up under a closer stylistic analysis, but then again Fiedler is interested more in the myths that they convey than in the details.

Especially toward the latter third of the collection of essays, Pardini shows how Fiedler mixed in creative nonfiction and cultural studies with his literary analysis. One gets the sense that Fiedler would have liked to figure out a way for his criticism to cross over into artistry, so his notes on a canto of Dante's *Inferno*, from *La divina commedia* (c. 1320; *The Divine Comedy*, 1802), are written in end-stopped lines with rhyme directly opposite Dante's verse on the page. In "Giving the Devil His Due," Fiedler claimed that "literature is what I know about, literature is what I am interested in, literature is what I am committed to," yet given the way his criticism tended to dissolve the hierarchy of literature, films, and television, it makes sense that Fiedler would increasingly write about films. He had already found that Cooper's largest influence was inspiring the Western, so when he turned to Vietnam, he focused on films such as *Apocalypse Now* (1979), *The Deer Hunter* (1978), and the Rambo series as well as the works of Ernest Hemingway and Joseph Conrad to explore myths and countermyths in reaction to the war. One might wonder about including Rambo in this study, but Fiedler makes a good point about how the film series conveys the basic American countermyth, in which "the value of fighting for God and Country is not questioned and combat heroism is glorified." Pardini includes in this collection both this essay, "Mythicizing the Unspeakable," and "Who Really Died in Vietnam? The Cost in Human Lives" perhaps as a way for the reader to consider correlations between the class differences of those who fight and those who stay home to protest.

Even though Fiedler's rebellious stance may seem quaint by today's standards, since his ability to shock has diminished with time, one can still find his influence in a broad range of critics and popular-culture scholars. Every time someone discusses the myth of the hero in the film *Star Wars* (1977), that person owes something to Fiedler. Marcus Greil, a major rock-and-roll critic, acknowledges Fiedler's influence in *Mystery Train* (1975), his study of the mythical aspects of rock and roll. Fiedler was the first critic to use the word "postmodern" in relation to literature, and he ushered in an era when the predominant academic interest was in race, gender, class, and queer theory, although he ironically complains in "The Canon and the Classroom: A Caveat" about the way political correctness has caused English professors to exclude dead white authors, such as Nathaniel Hawthorne, Melville, and Hemingway, from their class reading lists. Perhaps the major heir to Fiedler's fiefdom is Camille Paglia, the writer of *Sexual Personae: Art and Decadence from Nefertiti to Emily Dickinson* (1990). Like Fiedler, Paglia prefers to challenge the critical orthodoxy, and she revels in popular culture, cheerfully free-associating Lord Byron and Elvis Presley or Emily Dickinson and sadomasochistic bondage. So it makes sense that Paglia wrote on the book jacket of an edition of *Love and Death in the American Novel* (1960) that "Fiedler created an American intellectual style that was truncated by the invasion of faddish French theory in the '70's and '80's. Let's turn back to Fiedler and begin again." This collection of Fiedler's essays can help awaken readers to a wide-ranging critical heritage about which little is known.

Roy C. Flannagan

Review Source

Los Angeles Times, May 4, 2008, p. 8.

DIARY OF A BAD YEAR

Author: J. M. Coetzee (1940-   )
Publisher: Viking Press (New York). 229 pp. $24.95
Type of work: Novel
Time: 2007
Locale: An undisclosed city in Australia

This novel fuses three narratives into one, describing the writing process and examining relationships among neighbors, coworkers, lovers, and generations. Coetzee takes advantage of the physical paper by placing each story on the same page and separating it by a single line

Principal characters:
SEÑOR J C, the aging protagonist who hires Anya to transcribe his writings
ANYA, Señor C's seductive young neighbor and secretary
ALAN, Anya's jealous and money-obsessed boyfriend
MRS. SAUNDERS, Anya and Señor C's nosy neighbor

With *Diary of a Bad Year*, J. M. Coetzee cleverly examines the ways in which people relate to one another, their immediate community, and the international community, by weaving together three separate tales to form an experimental and intellectual novel. Each of the three stories appears on the same page separated by a line, working together harmoniously throughout the novel. The reader is free to read each story all the way through in its entirety, read them one after another within each chapter, or read all three at once. While each narrative can stand on its own, reading the three together provides each additional background, depth, and substance.

The novel's protagonist, J C, or Señor C, is a somewhat autobiographical representation of Coetzee. Both men were born and raised in South Africa, both taught in the United States, both reside in Australia, both are established authors and educators, and both have coincidentally written a book called *Waiting for the Barbarians* (1980). The similarities end there, however. Coetzee is well groomed, healthy, and a noted vegetarian, while Señor C suffers from Parkinson's disease, has poor teeth, wears smelly and fraying sweaters, and eats meat regularly. Older than Coetzee, Señor C reflects upon his position in his later solitary life, lamenting

In public life the role I play nowadays is that of distinguished figure (distinguished for what no one can quite recall), the kind of notable figure who is taken out of storage and dusted off to say a few words at a cultural event (the opening of a new hall in the art gallery; the prize-giving at an eisteddfod) and then put back in the cupboard.

Alone and of retirement age, Señor C has given up writing novels. He does, however, eagerly accept an invitation to partake in a writing effort in which six writers from around the world will share their opinions on democracy, pedophilia, origins of the state, Guantanamo Bay, and many other topics. "The book itself is the brainchild of a publisher in Germany. Its title will be *Strong Opinions*. The plan is for six contributors from various countries to say their say on any subjects they choose, the more contentious the better, six eminent writers pronounce on what is wrong with today's world. " Señor C jumps at the opportunity to collect and to compose his thoughts on politics and society and share them with others. Obsessed with world politics and international relations, he sees this writing opportunity as the perfect platform to express his views and the perfect time to do so since he finds it

> Interesting that at the moment in history when neo-liberalism proclaims that, politics having at last been subsumed under economics, the old categories of Left and Right have become obsolete, people all over the world who had been content to think of themselves as "moderate"—that is, as opposed to the excesses of both Left and Right—should be deciding that in an age of Right triumphalism the idea of the Left is too precious to abandon.

Señor C's essays for "Strong Opinions" form the first of the three narratives that create the novel. These writings consist of heady viewpoints expressing Señor C's, and one can only assume Coetzee's, opinions on the state of the world. Señor C discusses the origin of the state and how those ideals have evolved into the modern state, concluding that

> The modern state appeals to morality, to religion, and to natural law as the ideological foundation of its existence. At the same time it is prepared to infringe any or all of these in the interest of self-preservation.

The essays offer a harsh critique of the George W. Bush administration, questioning its motives and operations while accepting its power by acknowledging that

> We may thus legitimately speak of an administration which, while legal in the sense of being legally elected, is illegal or anti-legal in the sense of operating beyond the bounds of the law, evading the law, and resisting the rule of law.

Señor C places under equal scrutiny Great Britain, Australia, and other democracies that have supported the United States, claiming, "Democracy does not allow for politics outside the democratic system. In this sense, democracy is totalitarian." He is relentless in his accusations against Bush, as he examines and explores the origin, effects, and purpose of the War on Terror, accusing the administration of ignoring international and domestic laws and adopting a new Machiavellian position that holds "infringing the moral law is justified when it is necessary." He expounds upon the administration's misrepresentation and fabrication of facts by suggesting, "By nature politics is uncongenial to the truth, they say, or at least to the practice of telling the truth under all circumstances."

Señor C's quiet and secluded lifestyle is turned upside down while doing laundry in his apartment's basement. A young Filipina neighbor, Anya, enters wearing a skimpy red shift, and Señor C describes her "black black hair, shapely bones. A certain golden glow to her skin, *lambent* might be the word." Aware of her beauty and youth, Anya goes out of her way to move seductively and to act flirtatiously while participating in mindless small talk with Señor C. He is instantly taken by her and realizes

> As I watched her an ache, a metaphysical ache, crept over me that I did nothing to stem. And in an intuitive way she knew about it, knew that in the old man in the plastic chair in the corner there was something personal going on, something to do with age and regret and the tears of things.

Upon finding out that she is currently unemployed, Señor C hires her to transcribe his scribbled notes at three times the going rate. Anya reawakens within Señor C youthful feelings, allowing Coetzee the opportunity to explore society's relationship with age, class, and gender. Upon Anya's entrance, the reader is introduced to the second voice of the three-part harmony, that of J C's relationship to Anya.

As Anya's relationship with Señor C intensifies, the final part of the harmony emerges. Anya's voice allows the reader a glimpse into her thoughts and feelings as well as an external look at Señor C. In her initial introduction, Anya comes across as somewhat self-absorbed, constantly reveling in the power she has over men and the ways in which she uses her feminine charms against them. She toys with Señor C, admitting,

> As I pass him, carrying the laundry basket, I make sure to waggle my behind, my delicious behind, sheathed in tight denim. If I were a man I would not be able to keep my eyes off me.

However, as she begins typing Señor C's essays, she engages in discussions of the work with the author, and though she is not as articulate, she defends her beliefs and encourages Señor C to write on lighter, more entertaining topics. Although the dialogue comes across almost as a monologue because of the division in narratives, Anya's discussions and debates over Señor C's writings offer a fresh and lighthearted perspective to otherwise dense topics. Anya's narrative also introduces the reader to Alan, Anya's boyfriend. As she becomes more enthralled with the writings and the person behind them, Alan becomes increasingly jealous and suspicious of the old man's motives, accusing him of possessing a senile lust for her. Having grown fond of Señor C, Anya defends him by trying to convince Alan that the writer "wants to cuddle me on his knee. He wants to be my grandfather, not my paramour."

J. M. Coetzee was born in Cape Town, South Africa, and became an Australian citizen in 2006. He won the Booker Prize for Life and Times of Michael K *(1983) and for* Disgrace *(1999), and he received the Nobel Prize in Literature in 2003.*

A forty-year-old financial analyst who is concerned entirely with accumulating money and wealth, Alan too begins reading Señor C's essays, pointing out their faults to Anya at every opportunity. At times Alan's voice dominates Anya's section of the novel, as he opines, criticizes, and argues against the old man's views. His jealousy turns into an obsession, and he secretly plants spyware on the writer's computer through a disc Anya unknowingly installed to upload her work. Through the spyware, Alan is able to track everything Señor C does, and the boyfriend finds the writer's bank account, which contains three million dollars. He devises a plan to move the money into an offshore bank account, live off the interest, and return the original sum without Señor C ever being the wiser. Alan feels an entitlement and an obligation to make the money work for him,

> as though the old man were a Spanish galleon going down on the high seas with a hold full of gold from the Indies, that would be lost forever if he, Alan, didn't dive in and save it.

Anya discovers Alan's plans, and she struggles to put a stop to them and possibly their relationship. She proves her depth when she prevents Alan's plan from coming to fruition and chastises him for his ill behavior toward her elderly friend.

Divided into two parts, the second section of *Diary of a Bad Year*, entitled "Second Diary," reveals a softer side of the characters than the first section, "Strong Opinions." In "Second Diary," Anya has left Alan and has returned home to live with her mother. She keeps in contact with Señor C through letters, and she also checks up on him through a secret correspondence with their neighbor, Mrs. Saunders. Señor C takes Anya's advice and begins writing about lighter topics, such as cricket, personal dreams, views on love, and birds congregating in the park across from his apartment. This turnabout within the characters changes the reader's relationship and opinions of them and provides them with an additional layer of complexity.

Coetzee challenges the reader in *Diary of a Bad Year* by taking advantage of the physical page and allowing the reader to choose how he or she will consume the individual parts to develop the complete story. The essays are cerebral yet accessible, consisting of subject matter that is both thought provoking and timely. The two personal narratives are displays of human interaction that cross social and generational boundaries, offering an emotional respite from the academics of the first section. Coetzee delivers a unique reading experience, as the reader is transformed from a passive voyeur into an active participant that determines what course the novel will take.

Sara Vidar

Review Sources

America 199, no. 5 (September 1, 2008): 24-26.
The Atlantic Monthly 301, no. 2 (March, 2008): 104.
Booklist 104, no. 3 (October 1, 2007): 5.
Esquire 149, no. 1 (January, 2008): 19.
Harper's Magazine 316 (January, 2008): 83-84.
Kirkus Reviews 75, no. 20 (October 15, 2007): 1065-1066.
London Review of Books 29, no. 19 (October 4, 2007): 5-7.
The Nation 286, no. 7 (February 25, 2008): 29-34.
New York 41, no. 3 (January 21, 2008): 94.
The New York Review of Books 55, no. 1 (January 17, 2008): 23-25.
The New Yorker 83, no. 41 (December, 24, 2007): 140-143.
O, The Oprah Magazine 9, no. 1 (January, 2008): 143.
Publishers Weekly 254, no. 37 (September 17, 2007): 31.
The Spectator 304 (September 8, 2007): 43.
The Times Literary Supplement, August 24, 2007, pp. 3-7.

DICTATION
A Quartet

Author: Cynthia Ozick (1928-   )
Publisher: Houghton Mifflin (Boston). 179 pp. $24.00
Type of work: Short fiction
Time: The early 1900's; the late twentieth century; the
    1930's; and the 1940's
Locale: London, New York City, and Fascist Italy

*Four long stories link several themes characteristic of
the author's work in both her fiction and her literary criticism*

    Principal characters:
        JOSEPH CONRAD, a Polish-born novelist
        HENRY JAMES, an American novelist living
          in England
        LILIAN HOLLOWES, Conrad's secretary
        THEODORA BOSANQUIT, James's secretary
        MATT SORLEY, an aging Jewish actor
        FRANCES, his wife, who composes crossword puzzles
        TED SILKOWICZ, a young theater director
        ELI MILLER, an elderly actor from the bygone Yiddish theater
        FRANK CASTLE, a devout Catholic attending a theological conference
        VIVIANA TERESA ACCENO, a peasant chambermaid
        PERCY NIGHTINGALE, a conference participant
        PHYLLIS, the narrator, a college student
        SIMON GREENFELD, a relative of Phyllis
        ESSIE, Simon's wife

In *Dictation: A Quartet*, Cynthia Ozick presents four long stories, three of them previously published: "Dictation," "Actors," "At Fumicaro," and "What Happened to the Baby?" An admirer of Henry James's work in her early years, Ozick later freed herself from his influence. The title story, "Dictation," is an exuberantly witty exercise in imagination in which James, his spoken words mimicking his elaborately constructed prose, discusses literary matters with the young Joseph Conrad, the apprentice novelist. James and Conrad were acquainted—that much is history. The rest of the story is the author's invention.

Conrad, visiting the master in his country home, learns that James, his hands crippled by years of gripping his pen, has hired an amanuensis to type his dictated words on a newfangled invention, the Remington. Conrad worries: Might the intervention of the typist and her machine break the sacred relationship between the brain and the pen?

Nine years later, after Conrad has achieved success, he meets James again in London. However, Conrad's hands have been crippled by gout; he, too, has hired a secretary with a Remington. Conrad and James debate weighty literary questions, such as whether a writer's fiction reveals the dark secrets of his inner self, as Conrad believes, or masks his true identity, as James believes. The comedy turns on the ironic irrelevance of this debate when the two amanuenses, portrayed under their real names, take matters into their own hands and conspire to interfere with the texts of their employers.

Theodora Bosanquit, James's secretary, is a schemer who sets out to seduce Lilian Hollowes, Conrad's shy, awkward secretary who is secretly in love with her employer. Conrad has hoped to prevent a meeting between the two women, fearing that his secrets would be revealed. Nevertheless, Theodora outmaneuvers him and introduces herself to Lilian, taking her to tea and ferreting out personal details of her life.

Having failed to seduce her, Theodora plays upon Lilian's secret worship of her employer and her jealousy of Conrad's wife.

Cynthia Ozick is an acclaimed novelist, short-story writer, and essayist. Among her awards are the National Book Critics Award, four O. Henry first prizes for the short story, a National Endowment for the Arts fellowship, and a Guggenheim fellowship. She has been a finalist for the Pulitzer Prize and the Man Booker International Prize.

Lilian agrees, albeit reluctantly, to Theodora's plot. The scheme is intriguing: Is it possible for each typist to copy a passage from her employer's text and have the other insert it into her writer's manuscript without being detected? Certainly, says Theodora; the artistic ego, believing in its own genius, will assume that the substituted passage is of his own brilliant invention. The two supposedly altered stories are James's "The Jolly Corner" and Conrad's "The Secret Sharer."

Ozick revels in linguistic play and, with an unerring gift for dialogue, mimics James's pretentious diction and Conrad's passionate outpourings. She even hints at a liaison between Theodora and a young Virginia Woolf, identified only as Ginny. Should anyone detect anachronisms, Ozick assures readers, in an impish footnote, that this is, after all, just fiction.

Perhaps this is a diabolical instance of feminist revenge against the great men who treat their secretaries as inferiors. Certainly the story poses an intriguing literary puzzle: If the amanuenses, mere employees in the service of genius, succeed in their scheme, who can claim ownership of a literary text?

In "Actors," Matt Sorley, the stage name of Mose Sadacca, is nearly sixty, an unemployed actor who prides himself on the wit and subtlety of his work. He pretends to attend auditions, rejecting the "geezer" roles that he is offered, and he disdains his occasional stereotyped roles in television series. Frances, his long-suffering wife, resents having to support them both by creating crossword puzzles. Her arcane vocabulary is the source of much of the humor in the story.

To the rescue comes Ted Silkowicz, a trendy young director who offers Sorley a role he cannot refuse: the lead in an updated version of William Shakespeare's *King Lear* (1608), a revival of the bygone Yiddish melodrama. There is one condition; Sorley must agree to meet with the deceased playwright's father, Eli Miller, a retired actor living in a Jewish home for the elderly. This visit, with Frances along for support, is a masterpiece of comic misunderstanding. Is Miller hovering over the edge of sanity or uttering artistic truth about the greatness of Yiddish theater?

After first dismissing the play as "The Lear of Ellis Island," Sorley begins to inhabit the role. Abandoning all subtlety, he howls and gestures in an excess of melodramatic emotion. The success of the play will depend upon the audience's willingness to accept as tragedy the unfamiliar style from the past.

On opening night, Sorley, believing that an unannounced guest in the audience is a director whom he hates, delivers an over-the-top performance in the first act. The second act is interrupted by the guest, Miller, who has escaped from the institution and thunders down the center aisle in outrage against the travesty of a performance: "Liars, thieves, corruption! In the mother tongue, with sincerity, not from a charlatan like this!" The audience loves it and roars with laughter, sending Sorley into the wings in defeat and humiliation. Well schooled in theatrical tradition, Ozick poses the question: Does artistic truth lie with the trendy young director, the old Yiddish actor, or Sorley, who struggles vainly to maintain his own integrity against the incongruities of competing theatrical visions?

In "At Fumicaro," Frank Castle has anticipated with pleasure his invitation to a conference for Roman Catholic intellectuals who will debate the role of the Church in the world. Three dozen men will meet daily for Mass and for discussion of current church issues at the Villa Garibaldi on Lake Como. Frank, unmarried at the age of thirty-five, has practiced celibacy for six months, preparing for a transport of religious enlightenment.

His spiritual aspirations are abruptly interrupted by his lust for Viviana, a pregnant teenage chambermaid he first encounters as she is vomiting into the toilet in the bathroom she is supposed to be cleaning. Instantly—and incongruously—smitten with love, Frank promises to marry her and take her home to New York.

Frank alternates visions of lust with moments of common sense (these perhaps more believable than his unbridled passion) during which he fears that Viviana is exploiting him and intends to steal his money. Viviana, however, has the peasant instinct for survival, and she is wise in the ways of men. She understands the fate that awaits her as the mother of an out-of-wedlock child in Italy's conservative society.

Viviana's promiscuous mother Caterina refuses to believe the truth: Her daughter has been impregnated in an unwilling encounter with one of her own lovers. She is baffled by Frank's willingness to marry Viviana, but she happily supports the marriage that will rescue her daughter from her predicament. Percy Nightingale, a cynical latecomer to the conference, offers another point of view, denouncing Frank as a fool for planning to elope with a chambermaid. The conference quickly degenerates into chaos, with the pretentious intellectuals falling asleep over the debris of their food.

Viviana is deeply religious, with a primitive faith that impels her to worship an ancient stone figure that Frank knows is a pagan artifact. Her superstitions become even more evident when she falls down in prayer before museum figures of the Virgin and Christ Child. Frank foresees the embarrassment that she will cause him in the pretentiously sophisticated world of his New York peers. Still, consumed by lust and his Catholic sense of guilt, he marries her, envisioning himself as the rescuer of his young bride. She will be both his penance and his salvation. Although "At Fumicaro" has received mixed reviews, it is an example of the author's fascination with the comic possibilities of opposing forces, here the superstitious peasant and the self-torturing intellectual who find each other in an incongruous match.

"What Happened to the Baby?" is a dark satire on the consequences of lying and deception, narrated by Phyllis, a college student at New York University. Phyllis, whose parents have moved to Arizona, resents her mother's request to take care of "Uncle" Simon, her mother's cousin. Phyllis recalls unpleasant childhood experiences at Uncle Simon's meetings. Simon has invented GNU, an artificial language designed to replace Esperanto. Phyllis's mother, despite her husband's protests, believes in Simon's genius and donates money to his cause. She blames Simon's wife Essie for the mysterious death of their baby years ago. At Simon's meetings, Essie, with theatrical ardor, entertains the audience by performing chants and poems in GNU. However, these gatherings, initially successful, always end in chaos, with shrieking and ridicule bordering on violence.

Improbability and deception follow relentlessly as the narrative turns to Phyllis's college years. Simon and Essie have divorced; he lives in a filthy apartment with a refrigerator full of rotting food. He has a new set of followers, led by Phyllis's roommate Annette, who is collecting money for the cause but pocketing it. Phyllis spends the money sent by her mother for Simon on herself and lies to her mother, telling her that Simon's language has gained acceptance. In the meantime, Phyllis's mother has become a wealthy entrepreneur by selling fake Native American artifacts in her gift shop in Arizona.

Edging toward death, Simon evokes Phyllis's pity. She supports him with the money her mother now sends for Phyllis. Hoping that Simon and Essie will reconcile in their old age, Phyllis visits Essie in their old apartment where she, too, lives in squalor. Here the comedy takes a darker turn as Phyllis learns the story of the baby's death.

Pregnant by another man, Essie had tricked Simon into marrying her. One day, as a cruel joke, she told him that he was not the baby's father. The events of the narrative mount in improbability. The young couple had rented a summer cottage in the Catskills where Simon, a habitual philanderer, fell in love with their neighbor Bella, a devotee of Esperanto. Baby Retta died one night when Essie, who was caring for Bella's baby son, put both children into the same crib. When the boy became ill during the night, Essie sent Simon for the doctor. Instead, he spent the night with Bella. When the doctor arrived in the morning, the boy had recovered, but Baby Retta, apparently smothered, was dead.

Consumed with guilt, Simon rebelled against Esperanto with the mad scheme to create his own language. Essie blamed Simon for the baby's death and wreaked her revenge by pretending to encourage his followers, then inviting the Esperantists to disrupt his meetings and humiliate him. The trips abroad to research language were a lie; Simon and Essie spent their summers in the Catskills, where Simon mourned at Retta's grave.

The final words of the story echo the tirade of Miller in "Actors," suggesting a motif that links the four stories in this collection. Essie's words slide seamlessly into the thoughts of Phyllis to become the perception of the author herself: "Lie, illusion, deception. . . was that it truly, the universal language we all speak?"

The collected stories, dating over a period of twenty-five years, represent constant themes in Ozick's work: the witty playfulness of language, the juxtaposition of opposites, and unexpected plot reversals. Her stories are a darkly satiric view of the all-too-human weakness for self-deception and lying and the consequences that follow, her characters getting what they deserve. Critics have described Ozick's fiction variously as fantasy, farce, allegory, or tragicomedy. Her work is highly regarded for its intellectual complexity and mastery of the nuances of language.

Marjorie Podolsky

Review Sources

Booklist 104, no. 11 (February 1, 2008): 5.
The Christian Science Monitor, May 6, 2008, p. 16.
Commentary 126, no. 2 (September, 2008): 68-72.
Kirkus Reviews 76, no. 3 (February 1, 2008): 111-112.
Library Journal 133, no. 5 (March 15, 2008): 66-67.
Los Angeles Times, April 27, 2008, p. R4.
The New York Times Book Review, April 20, 2008, p. 11.
Publishers Weekly 255, no. 2 (January 14, 2008): 37.
The Washington Post, April 13, 2008, p. T10.

DID LINCOLN OWN SLAVES?
And Other Frequently Asked Questions About Abraham Lincoln

Author: Gerald J. Prokopowicz (1958-   )
Publisher: Pantheon Books (New York). Illustrated.
   352 pp. $24.95
Type of work: Biography
Time: 1809-1865
Locale: The United States

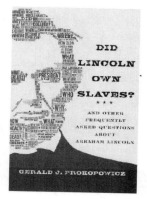

Informal but nonetheless authoritative study of President Lincoln written in the form of question-and-answer discussions by a noted scholar

Principal personage:
   ABRAHAM LINCOLN (1809-1865), sixteenth
   president of the United States

On April 14, 1876, on the eleventh anniversary of President Abraham Lincoln's assassination, Frederick Douglass eulogized the sixteenth president at the dedication of the Freedmen's Memorial in Washington, D.C. Claiming there was little need to speak at length about Lincoln's life because that "ground has been fully occupied and completely covered," Douglass went on to say,

> The whole field of fact and fancy has been gleaned and garnered. Any man can say things that are true of Abraham Lincoln, but no man can say anything that is new of Abraham Lincoln. His personal traits and public acts are better known to the American people than are those of any other man of his age. He was a mystery to no man who saw him and heard him.

Douglass was certainly correct in saying that Lincoln was better known to most Americans than any other person of his time. Was he, however, correct in arguing that nothing new remained to be said of the man? That is almost certainly not the case if Gerald R. Prokopowicz's *Did Lincoln Own Slaves? And Other Frequently Asked Questions About Abraham Lincoln* is an accurate reflection of the state of Lincoln studies.

The most frequently asked question about Abraham Lincoln may not be whether he owned slaves but whether the world really needs yet another book about him. Exact figures are impossible to find, but it is clear that more has been written about the sixteenth president of the United States than about any other American—or almost anyone else, for that matter. Despite Douglass's skepticism about the possibility of saying anything new on the subject, more than fifteen thousand books have been published about Lincoln since his assassination in 1865. That number averages to more than one hundred entirely new Lincoln books a year, and that rate was certainly increasing during the bicentennial year of Lincoln's 1809 birth. An Amazon.com search of books about Lincoln published during 2008—the year before the bicenten-

Gerald J. Prokopowicz earned a doctorate in history at Harvard, studying under Lincoln biographer David Herbert Donald. He served as historical director of the Lincoln Museum in Fort Wayne, Indiana, and is chair of East Carolina University's history department. Among his publications are The Reform Era and Eastern U.S. Development, 1815-1850 *(1998) and* All for the Regiment: The Army of the Ohio, 1861–1862 *(2000). He is a member of the Abraham Lincoln Bicentennial Commission Board of Advisors.*

nial—yielded 427 new titles, a figure more than double the combined totals for new books that year about Presidents Ronald Reagan, George H. W. Bush, Bill Clinton, and George W. Bush.

At a conservative estimate, fifteen thousand Lincoln books must contain at least three million pages, with more than one billion words. Such staggering numbers again beg the question: With so much already published about Lincoln, what can possibly remain to be learned about the man that is not already known? What questions about him can there be that have not already been answered?

In his brief introduction to *Did Lincoln Own Slaves?*, Prokopowicz addresses these issues immediately. He begins by citing a remark attributed to the Russian novelist Leo Tolstoy: "Historians are like deaf people who go on answering questions no one has asked them." After pointing out that professional historians have a duty to ask innovative questions that others may have not yet posed, he steps back to consider, "But who are we to say that whatever questions the public may already be asking about history are not the 'right' ones?" Similar questions might be asked of all scholarly fields in the arts and social sciences. After all, whom should scholarship serve?

Prokopowicz answers that question implicitly by explaining that the purpose of his book is to answer questions about Lincoln that are asked by members of the public, not by scholars. In this, he succeeds brilliantly. Always fascinating and often witty, his book is such a pleasure to read that one wonders why its question-and-answer format is not used more frequently by scholars. Moreover, subject matter has a great deal to do with the book's strengths. It should be safe to say few questions are frequently asked about Millard Fillmore, Franklin Pierce, or James Buchanan, Lincoln's immediate predecessors in the presidency. Lincoln stands out because he succeeded in the face of the most difficult challenges faced by any president in U.S. history. In addition, as Prokopowicz's book demonstrates repeatedly, Lincoln was also an endlessly fascinating human who continues to be full of surprises. There are reasons that thousands of books have been written about him.

Although Prokopowicz is himself a distinguished scholar, he is also peculiarly well placed to know what questions members of the public actually ask about Abraham Lincoln. For nine years, he was resident historian at the Lincoln Museum in Fort Wayne, Indiana, where he talked with visitors on an almost daily basis. The words "frequently asked" in his book's title are clearly more than mere hyperbole. At the same time, those words might be read as a warning flag. Readers approaching a book titled *Did Lincoln Own Slaves? And Other Frequently Asked Questions About Abraham Lincoln* might expect it to be a collection of trivia. The book however, is anything but that. In roughly 250 pages of its main text, it poses more than 325 questions that are arranged in roughly the same chronological sequence as events in Lincoln's life. These questions are grouped within twelve chapters, each of which concludes with a brief discussion of further readings. Prokopowicz supplements these references with nearly thirty pages of detailed endnotes. The book also contains a substantial bibliography and an excellent index.

Prokopowicz's discussions of each question range in length from a few words ("What was Lincoln's middle name?" "He didn't have one.") to many pages. One of his longest discussions answers a question about "how Lincoln failed at everything he tried . . . until one day he was elected president." Prokopowicz uses more than seven pages to analyze each of Lincoln's alleged failures, while arguing that his "successes far outweighed his setbacks." He concludes by suggesting that the notion that Lincoln had experienced mostly failures has grown out of the public's need for reassurance that their own failings need not bar them from ultimate success. Prokopowicz is at his best in his chapter on the Civil War (1861-1865), which is another of his areas of expertise. His chapter on Lincoln as the "Emancipator" is also very strong. Although Prokopowicz is clearly a devoted admirer of Lincoln, he does not blink in dealing with questions about Lincoln's motives for abolishing slavery and his not-always-admirable attitude toward African Americans.

When read from cover to cover, the questions and answers in this book add up to an exceptionally readable narrative biography that feels like a warm fireside chat with an expert who answers every question thoughtfully and respectfully, never making his interrogators feel ignorant or foolish. If Prokopowicz's classroom teaching techniques reflect his approach in this book, then he must be a popular professor.

Prokopowicz stresses that his book is "not meant to substitute for a full-length scholarly biography" and suggests that anyone who has read at least a half-dozen books on Lincoln is unlikely to find anything new in his book. Here he may be overly modest. It is probably true that readers already well familiar with Lincoln's life will find little historical information with which they are not already familiar in Prokopowicz's book. However, they may find other things of at least equal value: new ways of looking at Lincoln and a better understanding of how the modern American public views the man. Despite the ocean of books already published about Lincoln and the interest in him taken by the public, it is clear a substantial gap exists between what many people believe to be true about Lincoln and what is really known about him. Prokopowicz's book helps close that gap, and it should encourage other biographers and historians to make their own work accessible to wider audiences.

A book such as *Did Lincoln Own Slaves?* has a singular advantage over standard biographies in being freer to address issues that most biographers would regard as unnecessary distractions. An interesting example appears in the book's third question, which immediately follows "When and where was Lincoln born?" and "Is the cabin still there?" After explaining that no authentic version of Lincoln's birthplace cabin still exists, Prokopowicz answers the third question: "Haven't I seen the cabin somewhere else?" The surprising answer is "You probably have." As Prokopowicz explains, not only are all "birthplace cabins" replicas, most are copies of the cabin at the

National Park Service's Lincoln memorial near his actual Kentucky birthplace, and that cabin itself is a partly fanciful replica. It is not surprising that people get confused about Lincoln.

Of the many questions Prokopowicz heard over the years, some

> were stimulating, provocative, or perceptive. Some were funny or weird. Some were based on legends, myths, or half-remembered history lessons. Many were asked out of a desire to learn, while others revealed the speaker's prejudice or ignorance.

The descriptive terms that Prokopowicz uses accurately reflect the mix of questions in his book. Some questions are, indeed, funny, weird, or ignorant. One wonders whether someone really asked Prokopowicz this: "About the original Lincoln birthplace cabin—is it true that Lincoln helped his father build it with his own hands?" It is certainly one of the weirdest questions that Prokopowicz raises, but he simply dismisses it out of hand and moves on to questions about Lincoln's ancestry. In a much later section, he offers a thoughtful reply to another seemingly foolish question about whether Lincoln could dunk a basketball. While pointing out that the game of basketball was not invented until 1891, Prokopowicz suggests that the six-foot-four Lincoln might have been able to dunk a ball and devotes a half-page to discussing Lincoln's known athletic skills, which were impressive.

Another example of a thoughtful reply to an ignorant question is Prokopowicz's response to: "Are there any recordings of Lincoln's voice?" Instead of merely dismissing the question after explaining that no practical technology for recording existed during Lincoln's time, he discusses what is known about the sound of Lincoln's voice. Moreover, he makes the subject even more interesting by comparing what is known about how Lincoln sounded to how actors Henry Fonda and Raymond Massey spoke when they played Lincoln in films that are still frequently shown on television.

In addition to oddball queries, speculative questions appear. The chapter on Lincoln as a politician ends with two such questions: "If he were alive today, what party would Lincoln belong to?" and "If Lincoln were running for office today, could he get elected?" Answers to such questions can naturally be only informed guesswork, but Prokopowicz treats both questions seriously by examining the nature of Lincoln's political views in the context of his time and allowing readers to try to place Lincoln within a modern-day context.

Did Lincoln Own Slaves? does such a fine job of connecting past and present, it seems a shame that Prokopowicz did not finish the book a year or two later, so he could have brought Barack Obama into the discussion. Some people see Obama's rise to the U.S. presidency as beginning the third "chapter" in the evolution of American freedom at which Lincoln's presidency formed the center. In this view, the first chapter began with the Declaration of Independence that set the United States on the path to a democratic and egalitarian society. The second chapter began with the culmination of the Civil War, which settled the question of preserving the national union and abolishing the institution of slavery, which Lincoln regarded as a stain on the nation's democratic principles. The third chapter thus begins in 2009, with the election of an

African American to the highest office in the land—an event that many see as a belated fulfillment of the promise of freedom offered by emancipation.

Many comparisons have been made between Lincoln and Obama. Both were Illinois state legislators who rose to the presidency with comparatively little experience in Washington politics but with growing national reputations as exceptional orators. Both entered their presidencies during times of extraordinary national crises, and both began their presidencies by appointing to their cabinets some of their most powerful political rivals. While such comparisons may well be the subjects of countless future questions about future presidents, however, what is most obviously—and unavoidably—missing from *Did Lincoln Own Slaves?* is a discussion of what Lincoln himself might have thought about the possibility of a black president.

R. Kent Rasmussen

Review Sources

America's Civil War 21, no. 1 (March, 2008): 63-64.
Publishers Weekly 254, no. 46 (November 19, 2007): 52.
Time 171, no. 6 (February 11, 2008): 84.

THE DRAINING LAKE

Author: Arnaldur Indriðason (1961-   )
First published: Kleifarvatn, 2004 in Iceland
Translated from the Icelandic by Bernard Scudder
Publisher: Thomas Dunne Books, St. Martin's Press
   (New York). 312 pp. $24.95
Type of work: Novel
Time: 2004
Locale: Lake Kleifarvatn and Reykjavik, Iceland; Leip-
   zig, Germany

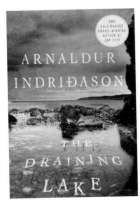

*This Nordic crime fiction deftly solves the mystery at its
center and also reveals the inner turmoil of its characters*

   Principal characters:
      SUNNA, a hydrologist who discovers the
         skeleton in Lake Kleifarvatn
      ERLENDUR SVEINSSON, a detective obsessed with missing persons
      ELINBORG, the partner of Erlendur who writes cookbooks
      SIGURDUR ÓLI, the partner of Elinborg, he and his wife have no children
      MARION BRIEM, the former boss of Erlendur who is dying of lung cancer
         and is partially paralyzed
      ILONA, Tómas's love, a Hungarian student opposed to the Communist
         regime
      TÓMAS, socialist Icelandic student, lover of Ilona
      LOTHAR WEISER, East German Communist, recruiter of students, double
         agent
      EMIL, Tómas's friend and betrayer, also known as Leopold

The Draining Lake is many different books in one: a murder mystery, a crime
novel, an espionage novel, a missing-persons novel, a psychological novel about
loneliness, a mythic novel, and a character study of its central figure, Erlendur
Sveinsson. Arnaldur Indriðason skillfully interweaves these elements into a complex
and fascinating novel. Events and characters on one story path lead the reader into another and then back to the central story, which is the murder mystery. Arnaldur (the
first name is used according to Icelandic custom) succeeds in juxtaposing the intrigue
of the various story threads in such a way that they remain separate and could stand
alone as a self-sustaining story.
   The structure of the novel is given texture by the use of repeated images and situations in the various stories. Tómas, the Leipzig student, observes a couple who walk
hand in hand every evening; at the end of the novel, Sunna and her new companion
walk off hand in hand. Tómas lives in the memories of Ilona; Leopold's girlfriend
lives in the memories of her life with him; and Erlendur's thoughts constantly return
to his brother, who has died tragically.
   The setting of the novel is Iceland, but it plays a greater role than merely providing

a location. The country and its traditions, its myths, its mysteries, and its physical attributes of climate, terrain, and weather set the tone of the work. The climate is harsh, with its cold, its damp, and its long dark season. Similarly, life is harsh, with its obstacles, its disappointments, its dangers, and its failures. Iceland is reflected in Erlendur's life and in his cold temperament. He is estranged from his children and rarely socializes. He lives alone in an apartment with only the bare essentials, except for one luxury: a large collection of books that provides him an escape from the dreariness of reality.

After working as a journalist and film reviewer, Arnaldur Indriðason published his first crime fiction novel, Synir dufstens (sons of dust), in 1997. This was the first book in his popular Detective Erlendur series. He received the Glass Key Award for Nordic crime fiction in 2002 and in 2003 and the CWA Gold Dagger Award for best crime novel in 2005.

Traditionally, Iceland's people had a close connection to the land, but many who lived in the country have moved to the cities to earn a living, and their lives are colored by a sense of displacement. The majority of Arnaldur's characters suffer from a sense of not belonging and are ill at ease in their lives. Life in Iceland is precarious because of its natural phenomena; Erlendur is haunted by the loss of his younger brother in an avalanche. Iceland's cold, snow, and darkness provide an atmosphere of immobility and sameness. Arnaldur exploits this concept to create irony and tension in his novel. Nothing ever happens in Iceland, an opinion constantly repeated by the foreign envoys encountered by Erlendur and his colleagues, and yet people disappear, lakes mysteriously drain, and the dead bodies of murder victims appear.

The novel begins with Sunna, a hydrologist, discovering a skeleton in the mud of Lake Kleifarvatn, which has been mysteriously draining since a recent earthquake. The Reykjavik police are called in to conduct an investigation, and the team of detectives working on the case includes Erlendur, who is obsessed with missing-persons cases; Elinborg, a female detective who has written a cookbook; and Sigurdur Óli, a no-nonsense detective. The skull shows evidence of a severe blow to the head and is attached to a radio transmitter bearing Russian words. There are, however, no clues to the identity of the murder victim. Once it is determined that the skeleton is the remains of a body put into the lake sometime around 1970, the detectives begin reopening unsolved cases of persons reported missing about that time.

One of these cases is a man who left a black Ford Falcon at the train station and the woman he was to marry outside the dairy shop where she worked. Erlendur is particularly drawn to this case, and he discovers that the abandoned woman is still waiting for her missing lover. In pursuing the renewed investigation, Erlendur finds that there was no record of the man's identity at the time of his disappearance. From his interviews with the woman, Erlendur does, however, find out that the man, known as Leopold, sold farm machinery made in East Germany and that on the day of his disappearance he had an appointment to meet a prospective client, Haraldur, at his farm.

Further investigation results in Erlendur locating the black Ford Falcon, with its missing hubcap. As a result of Erlendur's tenacity, Haraldur eventually tells him that

Leopold was at the farm and that Haraldur's mentally challenged brother stole the hubcap, which Haraldur buried along with a wallet that had fallen out of Leopold's pocket. Erlendur digs up the items; the hubcap belongs to the Falcon and the wallet reveals the name of the man whose skeleton had been found in the lake. All of this leads Erlendur to the Icelandic students and finally to Tomás. Before the police arrive, Tomás writes a letter containing the details of how and why he killed Emil and then shoots himself.

Arnaldur's introduction of his second story line is veiled in mystery. The discovery of the skeleton receives considerable attention from the media, including lengthy coverage on television. In chapter 3, an unidentified man watching the coverage begins to reminisce about his days as a young socialist studying in Leipzig, East Germany. He also ponders what will happen in regard to the person found in the lake, but he reassures himself that it happened a long time ago and that there was no one to care about the murdered man whose skeleton had been found.

This is the beginning of the story of the Soviet activities in Iceland during the Cold War and of the Icelandic students recruited and sent to study at the university in Leipzig. It is a story of naïve faith in a political system, of disappointment, of disillusionment, and of loss. In telling the story of the Leipzig students, Arnaldur gives his narrative an almost poetic quality, with his descriptions of objects, places, and sensory stimulants. As the mysterious man who was watching the news remembers, he once again smells the aromas of Leipzig, he sees again the desolation brought about by World War II, and in contrast he relives the wholesome bountiful Christmas feast that the Icelandic students shared as a result of gifts from home.

Eventually, Arnaldur gives a name to this man who watches and remembers: Tomás, who is one of several Icelandic students studying in Leipzig, all ardent socialists who believe the socialist system is the path to improving people's lives. His friend from school in Iceland, Emil, is a student there, as are Hannes, Rut, Karl, and Hrafnhildur. Life at the university is different from their lives at home in Iceland. There are food shortages, and they live in a dilapidated villa where rats run rampant. With the exception of Rut, who does not return to Leipzig after Christmas vacation, they manage to deal with the physical hardships and look forward to the day when socialism will have eradicated such difficulties. However, there are other differences besides a harsher lifestyle; there is the system of surveillance and personal spying that most of them find unjust and wrong.

Hannes is the first to be deeply disillusioned by socialism as practiced in Communist East Germany. Emil accepts the Communist Party line and becomes more hardline as he refuses to consider the system might be less than the panacea he believes it to be. Tomás fails to understand the Soviet system and how it is modifying not only the tenets of socialism but also the relationships between comrades and friends. During this time Tomás meets and falls in love with Ilona, a Hungarian student. Tomás's naïveté proves disastrous for both Hannes and Ilona. Trusting in friendship, Tomás tells Lothar Weiser, an East German who has befriended the students from Iceland and who is his own mentor, about Hannes's disillusionment with the political system. Shortly thereafter, Hannes is expelled from the university and sent back to Iceland. His plans for a career as an engineer are destroyed.

Ilona, who has witnessed the use of Soviet military force in Hungary, is a dissident among the students; she participates in secret meetings and is working against the party. Although Tomás realizes that he should not have trusted Lothar, he still believes in the friendship and loyalty between the Icelanders and shares this information with his friend Emil. Soon, Ilona is arrested and disappears. Tomás refuses to believe that she will not be released and come back to him. He seeks out Lothar, and he asks Emil for help. Eventually, he understands that she will never come back to him, but out of habit he keeps searching for her. Finally, he is asked to leave East Germany. He returns to Iceland; he never marries but lives in solitude remembering and searching for answers as to why Ilona was arrested.

Arnaldur permeates his novel with the theme of loneliness as he delves into the personal lives of his characters. At the beginning of the novel, Sunna the hydrologist is out walking alone when she discovers the skeleton. Since her divorce, she has found no one with whom to share her life. Erlendur's former boss, Marion Briem, who never married and never had children, lives alone. Suffering from lung cancer and partially paralyzed, she is confined to her chair and spends her days watching John Wayne Westerns. Leopold's girlfriend lives a lonely life, waiting for a man who will never return. Tomás lives in solitude with his letters and his memories. The man who keeps calling Sigurdur Óli lives an empty life, continually blaming himself for his wife's death. The lives of Sigurdur Óli and Bergthorá are colored by the sense of loneliness experienced by the childless couple who desperately desire a child.

The portrayal of Erlendur's personal life adds significantly to the novel and its themes of disappearance and loneliness. The detective is obsessed with cases involving missing persons, since his life is filled with the voids left by missing persons. Erlendur is repeatedly drawn back to the place where his younger brother was lost in an avalanche. Erlendur's family is among the missing, for he has been divorced for a long time and also estranged from his children, Eva Lind and Sindri. Even Valgedur, with whom he has become romantically involved, seems to be missing far more than she is present in his life.

The Draining Lake, the sixth book in Arnaldur's Erlendur series, is an important addition to the genre of Nordic crime fiction. This genre has gained popularity and stature with each of his books.

Shawncey Webb

Review Sources

Booklist 104, no. 22 (August 1, 2008): 42.
Kirkus Reviews 76, no. 15 (August 1, 2008): 23.
Library Journal 133, no. 14 (September 1, 2008): 103.
New Statesman 136 (July 30, 2007): 60.
Publishers Weekly 255, no. 29 (July 21, 2008): 140-141.
The Wall Street Journal 252, no. 105 (November 1, 2008): W13.

ETERNAL ENEMIES

Author: Adam Zagajewski (1945-   )
Translated from the Polish by Clare Cavanagh
Publisher: Farrar, Straus and Giroux (New York).
116 pp. $24.00
Type of work: Poetry

The enemies named in Zagajewski's title are love and time, enemies which the poet reconciles in this meditative collection of poems that moves the reader through many places and people he has loved

The title of Adam Zagajewski's latest volume of poetry, *Eternal Enemies*, comes from his poem "Epithalamium," a poem to celebrate a wedding, in which he notes that despite the difficulties of sharing one's life with another, it is only in marriage that love joins with time to let partners see each other "in their enigmatic, complex essence,/ unfolding slowly and certainly, like a new settlement. . . ." Many reviewers have noted Zagajewski's concern with time in earlier volumes. Because the poet's life has been a witness to political upheavals, and since political upheaval often results in exile, as it did for Zagajewski, it is not surprising that in these poems time is inextricably bound with place. "The sovereign of clocks and shadows," the poet says, referring to how time has intervened between a loved place and the young man, now considerably older, who once loved it

Indeed, the collection's first poem, "Star," recounts a return to a lost home, and its second poem, "En Route," in its fourteen short stanzas is a sort of travelogue from Belgium to Mont Blanc to Sicily. Other poems name streets in the poet's home cities of Lvov and Krakow; Rome and Syracuse are settings for some poems; the United States (where Zagajewski spends part of each year teaching) is the setting for others. Some of these are intended to evoke a sense of the place described. In "En Route," for example, the great Greek temple at Segesta, Sicily, is called "a wild animal/ open to the sky," suggesting its isolated location as well as its lack of a roof. In "Stagliano," Zagajewski compares the memorial statues of professors, lawyers, children, and even dogs in the famous Genovese cemetery to the fossilized remains of Pompeii, another place where tourists may meet the past. Ironically, Zagajewski notes in "Syracuse" that tourists run the risk of being "imprisoned in our travels." The poet's Polish homeland frequently informs these poems. (That Zagajewski writes in Polish is a measure of how deeply he claims his national heritage.) In "Evening, Stary Sacz," he describes nightfall in the modern town that has emerged from ancient roots. The time of day is marked with the usual tea kettles and television sets, but it also harbors the memory of angels that once inhabited its skies, though now they have been replaced by a policeman on a motorcycle. Even the knife that slices bread for the evening meal seems to recall episodes in the town's more violent past.

Zagajewski is skilled at using details such as the tea kettle and bread knife to evoke both place and emotion, a fact the reader experiences frequently in these poems. Often the mood is melancholic, characteristic of the East European voice. In "Rainbow," for example, he looks at Long Street and Karmelicka Street in Krakow, the ancient university city where the poet himself was educated. The streets are filled with "drunks with blue faces," with used bookshops, and with "rain, rats, and gar-

~

Adam Zagajewski was born in Lvov, Poland, and educated at Jagiellonian University in Krakow. He left Poland for Paris in 1982. His books include Mysticism for Beginners *(1997) and* Without End: New and Selected Poems *(2002). He lives in Krakow, Paris, and Chicago.*

~

bage." It is a city where childhood "evaporated/ like a puddle gleaming with a rainbow of gasoline." Even the university appears to its long-departed alumnus as a clumsy seducer of naïve youth. In "Camogli," a brief sketch of an Italian fishing village in November, the details of houses, cats, fishing nets, and pensioners seem innocuous, but behind them the sea's relentless waves suggest a past in which lofty goals have been lost like youth and dreams. In "Bogliasco: The Church Square," the sea seems to wash the minor events of the day into "oblivion."

The cities and towns of Zagajewski's native Poland are logical places for him to confront his personal past as well as the past of his nation. Similarly, the cities of Sicily, with their rich legacy of Greece lying alongside their modern stones, invite the poet to examine the relationship between past and present. Zagajewski, however, is often more concerned with art and artists than with the simple artifacts of history. For some poems, artists are the subject matter; for others they appear as allusions. Many will be familiar to English readers of poetry. "Brodsky," for example, offers a brief biography of Joseph Brodsky, the Russian poet, who, exiled in the United States, became the U.S. poet laureate in 1991. It must surely please Zagajewski to know that Brodsky taught himself Polish in order to translate his favorite poet, the Pole Czesław Miłosz. Zagajewski offers a sketch of Brodsky's life but is most interested in his "Favorite topic: time/ versus thought . . . ." Zagajewski reminds the reader that "irony and pain" characterize Brodsky's voice and concludes by noting a modest tenderness that offsets Brodsky's perfections. Still other poems deal with the late eighteenth century English poet William Blake and with Karl Marx, the nineteenth century political philosopher of communism, and his life in London.

Other of Zagajewski's subjects, such as Polish futurist writer Aleksander Wat or avant-garde writer-director Tadeusz Kantor, will be more familiar to readers with some knowledge of Polish literary history. The ease with which the Internet identifies the unfamiliar (and sometimes reminds the researcher of American parochialism) means that such names offer no real stumbling block to the poems. In any case, Zagajewski makes the significance of the artists clear enough. In "The Power Cinema," a poem dedicated to Polish actor Wojciech Pszoniak, Zagajewski recalls the seductive charm of films in his youth. In "Tadeusz Kantor," he pictures Kantor in Krakow, where the writer-director was connected with the Academy of Fine Arts, and recalls how as a young man he dismissed the senior artist as irrelevant and flawed.

Later, when he saw Kantor's much-praised play *Umarła klasa* (pr. 1975; *The Dead Class*, 1979), he recognized the man's genius. As an adult, "I saw how time/ works on us . . . ." and understood Kantor's achievement in the play's themes concerning life's mysteries: "what wars are, seen or unseen, just or not,/ what it means to be a Jew, a German, or/ a Pole, or maybe just human . . . ."

It should be no surprise that Zagajewski addresses the poetry of Miłosz, one of the best known of contemporary Polish poets. Here his topic is the achievement of Miłosz's work and the significance of poetry itself. Zagajewski praises the great sweep of Miłosz's poetic stances: "poems written by a rich man, knowing all,/ and by a beggar, homeless,/ an emigrant, alone. . . ." Miłosz's work can momentarily show that life is "rounder,/ fuller, prouder, unashamed . . . ." That poetry is an art that can lift the reader out of the limits of self is one of this volume's central themes, joining many of its disparate locations and human subjects. In "Our World," dedicated to the contemporary German novelist W. C. Sebald, for instance, Zagajewski considers the voice of a writer he never knew and the power of the dead man's art to evoke his particular vision of the world. In "Poetry Searches for Radiance," the poem's title encapsulates his premise: " . . . poetry is the kingly road/ that leads us farthest." Significantly, the middle stanza of the poem describes a moment when a waiter in a Chinese restaurant mysteriously begins to weep. Poetry's search for kingly radiance is not limited to life's grandest moments but defines brief glimpses into worlds difficult to understand. This is the power that gives the reader access to Erinna of Telos, who died at the age of nineteen somewhere around 350 B.C.E, leaving only a few hexameters as well as to the ancient people who painted on cave walls and to painters from every era and to the old man—evidently Zagajewski's father—who sits in an apartment in the charmless city of Gliwice, recalling the past in both its beauties (kisses, gooseberries) and its horrors (the bombs of World War II, the political terrors of 1968). That past is not lost, because it is fixed in art.

The last poem in the volume is the longest, "Antennas in the Rain." It is composed of seven pages of one- and two-line stanzas, not necessarily closely related. Many of them draw their images from poems earlier in the volume. One references an earlier poem about the liturgy of the Orthodox church. Plato reappears, and dolphins and a number of painters claim images. Vermeer appears, for example, represented by his picture of a woman who knits in front of a dark doorway. Many of the stanzas carry the vividness and allusiveness of haiku: "May evening: antennas in the rain." That seems to be the intention of these lines, to catch threads of image and ideas much as an antenna might. One line mocks the academic fondness for categories; the professor counts six types of longing (while the poet hints that there may be many more). One line describes the sign that identifies an air-conditioned bus and also notes its destination—a day trip to Auschwitz. One offers a fragment of an American country-western song, a few present brief pictures of Krakow and Lvov. Some lines are bits of conversation; some seem mockingly addressed to the poet: "Oh, so you're the specialist in high style?" In the Washington, D.C., Holocaust museum, the poet recognizes "my childhood, my wagons, my rust." A salesgirl tells the speaker that she comes from Vietnamese boat people. A few lines later he notes that boat people are "the only nation free of nationalism." His father is quoted again, saying that he spends all of his days remembering. One line is a note to himself: "Pay the phone and gas, return the books, write Claire."

The effect of this montage is to summarize much of what Zagajewski has said throughout this volume. The artist must speak "from within the moments" that the antennas capture. The artist puts the reader in touch with the ordinary objects that create the texture of life. If poetry is "joy hiding despair," under that despair it offers "more joy," which evidently rises from the world the writer forces readers to see anew. From this the reader may understand the poem's last four contradictory injunctions. "Speak from within" has long been a theme of art. "It is not about poetry" implies that, despite Zagajewski's many poems in which the topic has appeared to be poetry, the real subject is how to be alive. "Don't speak, listen" calls the artist to give attention to the world he lives in. The last—"Don't listen"—suggests that at some point the heart can do the work.

Ann D. Garbett

Review Sources

Booklist 104, no. 14 (March 15, 2008): 17.
The Nation 286, no. 25 (June 30, 2008): 38-42.
Publishers Weekly 258, no. 3 (January 21, 2008): 154.
World Literature Today 82, no. 2 (March/April, 2008): 8.

EVERYTHING IS CINEMA
The Working Life of Jean-Luc Godard

Author: Richard Brody (1958-   )
Publisher: Metropolitan Books (New York). 701 pp.
   $40.00
Type of work: Biography
Time: 1930 to the present

A biography of the French film director that places particular emphasis on how life and art are commingled in the methods he has used to produce one of the most distinctive bodies of work in contemporary cinema

The career of Jean-Luc Godard has been a fascinating, tempestuous, and often controversial journey that featured engagements with charged social and political issues as well as an idiosyncratic approach to the process of filmmaking. His first feature film, *À bout de souffle* (1960), better known by its English title, *Breathless*, appeared at a seminal point in the history of the nouvelle vague, or New Wave, a movement that revolutionized the French cinema and continues to be influential throughout the world. His flirtation with Maoism and the radical left, dramatized in *La Chinoise* (1967), alienated him from the film industry's traditional sources of funding as well as from many fans of his previous films. His return to less overtly politicized filmmaking in 1979 inaugurated a series of unusual projects, in particular the six-hour documentary *Histoire du cinéma* (1989-1998), that have sharply divided both critical opinion and the reactions of theater audiences. There is no question that Godard, whether praised or scorned, has created a body of work that must be taken into account in any history of world cinema.

In *Everything Is Cinema: The Working Life of Jean-Luc Godard*, Richard Brody provides an account of his subject's life and films, focusing particularly on the complex relationship between the two. It is Brody's hypothesis that Godard typically, and perhaps to some extent obsessively, used his life experiences as the source of the thematic content of his films, with the latter being best understood as a kind of self-analysis in progress that reveals what their director feels and thinks.

This overt linkage between life events and what has been produced as art is an obvious temptation to a biographer, not least because one would be surprised if there were no relationship whatsoever between the experiences of the creator and what has subsequently been created. The dangers of such a potentially reductive approach, however, in which it is assumed that experience is automatically transformed into artistic content, must also be acknowledged, not least because this leaves little room for an individual's imagination and technical craft to operate. As a result, although *Everything Is Cinema* is in many respects a valuable contribution to the history of contemporary filmmaking, it does at times make facile and problematic as-

sumptions about the one-to-one correspondence between Godard's life and his films.

Brody begins his narrative of Godard's career with a brief consideration of his family
background and childhood. Born into a prosperous upper-middle-class milieu in 1930, the
young Godard was just old enough to experi-
ence France's crushing defeat by Germany at the beginning of World War II, after
which a collaborationist regime at Vichy was established that attracted the support of
several members of his family. This early fascination with political power and its expression through violence—as a child Godard rooted for the success of the German
army and marked its advances with pins on a map—prefigures his adult attraction to
left-wing militancy, interestingly reversing the conventional arc from youthful rebellion to adult conformity. It is also indicative of the intimate and often surprising details of his background, long familiar to French readers of his as yet untranslated autobiographical writings, that Brody has now made available to English-language
enthusiasts of Godard and his work.

Richard Brody is a film critic, an editor at The New Yorker, *and an independent filmmaker.* Everything Is Cinema *is his first book.*

After the war, Godard enrolled in a school of engineering in Paris, but in a pattern
that would be repeated several times before he finally committed to the cinema as a
career, he soon found himself spending more time watching films than studying for
his courses. Several subsequent encounters with formal education suffered the same
fate, and by the mid-1950's he had become one of a group of young filmmakers-to-be,
including François Truffaut, Jacques Rivette, and Eric Rohmer, all of whom would go
on to have distinguished careers as directors. This nouvelle vague or New Wave of
filmmakers, as it was soon christened by the Parisian media, was steeped in the aesthetic of postwar American films, and utilized improvised scripts and a kinetic visual
style—both necessitated by the need to keep production costs low—in films that
seemed fresh and innovative compared to the quest for formal perfection characteristic of classic French cinema.

Here as elsewhere, Brody provides evocative descriptions of this milieu and of the
conception and realization of Godard's feature films. For this alone *Everything Is
Cinema* constitutes an essential addition to the study of its subject. It is in the author's
interpretation of the personal significance of *Breathless*, however, that his hypothesis
concerning the relationship between Godard's life and cinematic productions begins
to seem somewhat forced. Brody asserts, for example, that the difficulty the film's
protagonist, a petty crook on the run from the police, has in obtaining help from his
friends mirrors Godard's problems in financing the film. However, this is unsup-
ported by any corroboration from Godard or from those who knew him at the time,
and it also ignores the salient fact that the criminal's abandonment by his associates
and even a lover—the femme fatale who features in *Breathless*, as elsewhere—is a
standard plot device in crime films. The same can be said of Brody's claim that both
Godard and the film's protagonist are preoccupied with the problems young men have
in achieving adulthood, which is similarly ungrounded in any supporting evidence,
and is likewise a staple element of coming-of-age narratives in any film genre.

Breathless remains, in any event, a critical and commercial success that has lost none of its freshness over the years, and yet, unlike the all-too-common contemporary practice of producing a string of derivative sequels, Godard did not follow it up with the equivalent of *Breathless II*. His next two films were completely different and suffered completely different fates: *Le Petit Soldat* (1963), an attack on France's repression of the Algerian revolt, was banned by the French authorities until the end of hostilities, and when it was finally released, it seemed badly dated. *Une Femme est une femme* (1961), filmed later but released earlier, is a strange amalgam of musical comedy and deliberately intrusive effects that undercut the viewer's expectations about narrative cohesion, and it severely disappointed most of those who saw it.

Although both films, as well as much of Godard's subsequent work, have been ignored by those who expect the cinema to provide smoothly pleasing entertainment, it is clear from the book's extensive and detailed accounts of their genesis and production that Godard was in search of something largely antithetical to the conventionally well-made film. With regard to actors, for example, Godard has consistently asked that they forget their formal training and react in spontaneous, unplanned ways to the situations in which he puts them; this has led to accusations that he does not know what he is doing, which is in one sense true—he frequently has no specific outcome in mind—but is in another sense misleading, since it is precisely the unanticipated and potentially breakthrough performance that he seeks and often obtains. His scripts, similarly, usually materialize only on the day when they are to be enacted, and even then they may be changed or sometimes abandoned, thus adding cameramen and other technicians to the list of those who have found working with Godard a form of hell on earth. *Everything Is Cinema* provides day-by-day, and sometimes shot-by-shot, descriptions of how this works out on the sets of Godard's films, and thus it will be of particular interest to those who like to go behind the scenes of what is typically experienced only in finished form.

In the late 1960's, Godard was strongly affected by the political protests of the students and workers who wished to revolutionize French society, with his film *La Chinoise* taking a strongly pro-revolutionary stance and once again provoking state repression and societal disapproval. Where *Le Petit Soldat* had attacked government policy from a reformist point of view, *La Chinoise* came down firmly on the side of the Maoist left, and it did so in such a strident, uncompromising manner that Godard found himself cut off from most of his friends and business associates.

For the next decade his film projects seemed largely determined by whatever others were willing to offer him. Although he did manage to obtain various commissions from French, British, and Italian television, the material he submitted was so self-indulgent and unconventional that it was found unsuitable for broadcast. His films fared little better: *Le Vent d'est* (1969) offered directions as to how militants could buy weapons and make bombs, ensuring that it would not be released in France, and *Vladimir et Rosa* (1970), a sympathetic depiction of American radicals, suffered the same fate. In *Tout va bien* (1972), however, the casting of Jane Fonda and Yves Montand, both bewildered by Godard's nontraditional directing style but willing to stick it out because of their ideological sympathies with his politics, resulted in a film that presented a French factory worker's strike in 1968 with a relatively evenhanded and narratively engrossing treatment of the issues involved. Brody follows the twists and turns of Godard's fortunes during this period closely and revealingly, although the biographer's tendency to identify what happens in the films with what happens in his subject's life continues, and is unpersuasive because of the reductiveness of his approach and the lack of supporting evidence for his assertions.

At the end of the decade, Godard experienced a dramatic shift in critical and commercial acceptance with *Sauve qui peut* (1980), in which a focus on the dynamics of sexual relationships replaced previous concerns with revolutionary politics. Brody, as usual, asserts that the film reflects Godard's own difficulties with those close to him, and, as usual, this is not convincingly argued. Whatever Godard's personal problems, however, *Sauve qui peut* was received as a return to cinematic excellence, and it also coincided with the election of a Socialist government committed to state support of French culture. As a result, his applications for financing new films were quickly approved, and he benefited from several commissions from the state-controlled French television network.

Godard responded with a wide range of productions, some of them (most notably the *Histoire du cinema* documentary) completions of projects on which he had previously been working, and others that continued his involvement with controversial political and social issues: *Hail Mary* (1984), a depiction of the sexuality of Jesus Christ's mother, earned it instant condemnation from Pope John Paul II; *Germany Nine Zero* (1991) attacked American foreign policy and argued that France should look to Russia as a model; *Notre Musique* (2004), with its pro-Palestinian stance, was denounced by Jewish groups. These films, while in no danger of breaking box-office records, have attracted a substantial portion of the audience for cutting-edge cinema, and so they have restored Godard to the directorial eminence that he forfeited during the years between 1967 and 1979.

This unusual and complicated story is lucidly recounted in *Everything Is Cinema*, which fully justifies its subtitle's claim to describe *The Working Life of Jean-Luc Godard*. Although Brody's notions about the correspondence between his subject's life and the plot developments of his films need to be taken with several grains of salt, this is otherwise an important addition to understanding the career of one of the world's foremost film directors.

Paul Stuewe

Review Sources

Art in America 96, no. 9 (October, 2008): 42.
Film Comment 44, no. 3 (May/June, 2008): 79.
Harper's Magazine 317 (October, 2008): 88-94.
Kirkus Reviews 76, no. 5 (March 1, 2008): 226-227.
Library Journal 133, no. 5 (March 15, 2008): 73.

New Statesman 137 (July 7, 2008): 55-56.
The New York Times Book Review, July 13, 2008, p. 12.
Publishers Weekly 255, no. 6 (February 11, 2008): 57.
Sight & Sound 18, no. 8 (August, 2008): 92.

EXPERIMENTS IN ETHICS

Author: Kwame Anthony Appiah (1954-   )
Publisher: Harvard University Press (Cambridge, Mass.).
   274 pp. $22.95
Type of work: Ethics, philosophy

The author looks at traditional theories of ethics and their contemporary relevance through the lens of empirical research in the social sciences

In 1973 the noted psychiatrist Karl Menninger asked in his book the question *Whatever Became of Sin?* In a new century, the questions posed to moral philosophy by work in the social sciences have not gone away. Kwame Anthony Appiah, a philosopher, takes another look at competing conclusions drawn about human behavior in philosophy and in modern experimental science. He brings together data from other sciences to form a vision of what makes the good human life. An interesting pursuit for a philosopher, the book is put forth as an experiment of sorts.

Appiah asks pertinent questions. Are the traditional ahistorical categories and methodologies of ethics moot in an age of science? Have the conclusions of experimental science overridden the conclusions of philosophy? Empirical studies either have called into question existing terms and categories of ethics or they have reinforced them. The author assumes a teleology to human existence, taking up Aristotle's belief that ethics has to do with the ultimate aim or end of human life.

The book begins with a chapter that considers the history of ethical theory, noting the wide interests beyond philosophy that some past philosophical giants pursued. It is not totally new to examine ethics from the existential perspectives of history or of real life. Nevertheless, in many periods of history, considerations of moral philosophy were lifted out of the more mundane and messy world of real life. An ahistorical perspective tends to postulate unchanging universal conclusions about right and wrong; historical reality is deemed unrelated to moral conclusions. Questions of the connection between the "is" of reality and the "ought" of morality are often framed as a chasm between the irrelevant findings of empirical science and the "unnatural" world of philosophy. Over centuries bridges between the two have either been built with enthusiasm or blown up with vigor and intent.

The author asks further questions: Do individuals set the standards for their own ultimacy, for their own sense of happiness? Is happiness merely a warm and fuzzy feeling deep within individuals that has no referent elsewhere? Siding more with moralists who believe in some universal components to moral judgments, Appiah debunks the theory that individual relativism is a sufficient criterion for human contentment. A person is not happy just because he or she has a subjective experience of same.

*Born in London and raised in Ghana,
Kwame Anthony Appiah is the
Laurence S. Rockefeller University
Professor of Philosophy at Princeton
University, where he directs the Center
for Human Values. He has written* The
Ethics of Identity *(2004) and*
Cosmopolitanism: Ethics in a World of
Strangers *(2006) as well as three
detective novels.*

Chapter 2 considers "The Case Against Character." Recent times have seen a turn to so-called virtue ethics, which holds that a virtuous person will perform virtuous acts. This conclusion makes the central task of ethics the development of character in the individual person. Moral focus is not so much what the person does as who the person is. The assumption is that, if one is a person of virtue, "good" actions will follow. Further, a virtuous person will have a good life, as virtues are in themselves worth having. On the contrary, contemporary studies by social psychologists find that people do not seem to possess any sort of unified "virtue" package. Real-life decisions may pose choices among or between values. All values cannot be actualized in every concrete situation. Perhaps the only way to save a spy from discovery and execution (value: protecting human life) is to lie to the evil authorities (disvalue: dishonesty in speech).

Likewise, researchers suggest that behavior is driven by nonmoral contextual elements rather than by the character of the agent. Not virtue but circumstances are the determinants of moral action. Helping a passerby with change, for example, is more apt to occur if the helper is brought into a good mood by the smell of croissants from the bakery in front of which he stands.

The author does not want to jettison completely the notion of virtue, although he takes a much more nuanced view than either the virtue ethicists or the antivirtue ethicists. While virtue ethics concentrates on an inward model of self-development, Appiah would place more emphasis on social contexts that favor good action. If a situation does not force choices among competing values, a person can more easily choose one good without compromising another. Creating contexts that do not pose the moral agent the hard choice between or among values is desirable. Culture plays a part in doing this.

In the end, the conclusion is that human flourishing, eudaimonia, comes from doing what is right rather than being virtuous. Flourishing is not simply a matter of getting what one wants. Virtue and happiness are connected, and human flourishing is more apt to occur in situations that do not compromise the person's values.

In the next chapter, the author makes "The Case Against Intuition." He tackles what he dubs the "intuition problem." Affirming that moral behavior is a matter of intuition has its difficulties. On examination one finds people—even philosophers—differ as to what conclusions they intuit about morality. There is a suspicion, says Appiah, "that our common sense may be littered with perishable and parochial prejudice," cultural and personal biases that color what behaviors are considered moral. In an age of slavery, for example, it would be difficult to view keeping human beings in bondage as morally wrong. Living in the home of the Artful Dodger of Charles Dickens's *Oliver Twist* (1839) might make it difficult to view stealing as an immoral act.

Sometimes the way questions are framed changes how individuals think about them. Sometimes how individuals feel in a given circumstance can alter their behavior. Appiah concludes that feelings, emotions, biological realities—all of which contribute to "intuition"—must be supplemented by normative demands. While a situation may color how people come to moral choice, the author asserts that moral behavior is more than the sum of the situational parts.

Perhaps a more adequate answer to what comprises a good ethical system is found in examining the chapter "The Varieties of Moral Experience." The premise, well illustrated, is that for human beings culture and nature cannot be separated. Each person is born into a certain language and into a set of cultural mores that externalize "nature" in a concrete fashion. Stabilization of genetically inscribed behavioral dispositions (nature) occurs culturally. The force of any contemporary values environment—being a Muslim is good; being a Democrat is bad; women are superior to men—will shape what is seen at a particular historical time byte as "good." Without a particular language of behavior (which culture provides), human beings do not conceive of moral possibilities. On the other hand, one can demonstrate that certain values seem to transcend culture. All people seem to have a sense of compassion, fairness, purity, and other values that are not culturally specific. What is culturally specific, though, is how these values, which appear to be hard-wired in human nature, are expressed in the here and now. Language is particular to culture. Language holds norms and values. Stories demonstrate values as perceived in a particular culture. Bottom line: Persons bent on shaping their lives ethically are bound within the cultural, institutional, and linguistic reality of their time.

The final chapter summarizes the major arguments of the author. He examines the claims of individual relativism, which sees happiness as a matter of satisfying one's personally felt desires. Standards for happiness are not the product of individual whim but rather are supported by objective criteria. This idea floats through the whole book and is not unique here. Values are objective, even when one is faced in the concrete with choices among values that can be realized in the here and now. When a person must break a promise to have dinner with a friend in the face of another competing value judged more urgent, it is not that the person does not recognize the value of keeping his word to a friend. Regret at not realizing a value is not the same as moral blame. Still, which values rise to the surface in making a choice may be dictated to some extent by one's place in history or in the particular culture.

The author tackles the difficult debate about the place of nature in the moral equation. Among philosophers, much debunking of the connection between what "is" and what "ought" to be has occurred. Appiah takes a middle-road approach, as he rejects both a sanitary autonomous ethics, which sees moral conclusions completely divorced from human existential reality, and a total reliance on science to come to moral conclusions. He quotes British philosopher Gilbert Ryle, who notes that " physicists may one day have found the answer to all physical questions, but not all questions are physical questions."

Human beings hold values, and they hold many in common. Nevertheless, morality is not simply a matter of people voting as to which values will be held collectively. Morality is not a democratic process. A show of hands does not dictate the hegemony of certain values nor how they are to be applied in moral decision making. As the author says, "Normative theories, if they are sensible, do not offer algorithms for action." Even wonderful cases, often designed to teach method in ethics (the author speaks of "quandary ethics"), are abstract realities. They cannot with certitude predict the best moral judgment in a real moral dilemma. As Appiah notes, with characteristic humor, such "scenarios, relentlessly abstract, [are] rendered with all the sfumato of an Etch-a-Sketch drawing." While the author does use many excellent and classic moral cases in his treatment, even the reader discovers that discomfort accompanies the choices that are presented. Perhaps it is the reader's intuition that affirms the author's premise: There is no real answer for a moral dilemma that is itself not real.

The author does examine the intersecting elements between traditional philosophical ethics and modern social research, but he does not consider the stages of moral development considered by psychologist Lawrence Kohlberg or the feminist studies of Carol Gilligan. Such considerations may have thrown additional light on differences of similar cohorts with different individual reactions to scenarios. This addition would have added another chapter to the book, however.

This book is a rigorous read. Those who venture in should be cautioned that the author assumes an understanding of standard philosophical moral method. A novice in philosophical ethics will have a hard plow through the text. The author assumes at least a passing knowledge of various approaches to ethics as he makes his case for an integrated moral landscape. This is a provocative book, questioning assumptions about the efficacy of various moral theories and doing so with reasonable arguments. Nevertheless, its ideas are fresh and comprehensive. This makes the book well worth the plod. It should have a place in the secondary bibliography of a fundamental morals course as well as in graduate studies.

Dolores L. Christie

Review Sources

Booklist 104, no. 7 (December 1, 2007): 6.
Library Journal 132, no. 18 (November 1, 2007): 70.
Nature 453 (May 29, 2008): 593-594.
The New York Times Book Review, February 3, 2008, p. 22.

THE EYE OF THE LEOPARD

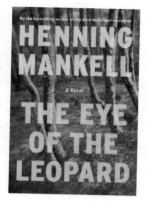

Author: Henning Mankell (1948-   )
First published: Leopardens Öga, 1990, in Sweden
Translated from the Swedish by Steven T. Murray
Publisher: The New Press (New York). 315 pp. $26.95
Type of work: Novel
Time: 1956 to 1988
Locale: Sweden and Zambia

Shifting between Africa and Sweden, this novel explores the interplay between destiny and choice

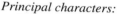

Principal characters:
> HANS OLOFSON, a Swedish man who owns
>   a farm in Zambia
> JUDITH FILLINGTON, the woman from
>   whom he takes over the farm
> LUKA, his servant
> STURE, his boyhood friend
> JANINE, "the Noseless One," a young woman disfigured by a botched
>   surgery
> PETER MOTOMBWANE, a journalist
> LARS HÅKANSSON, a corrupt Swedish aid official
> JOYCE LUFUMA, a woman on the farm, and her four daughters

Henning Mankell is best known for the series of novels featuring police detective Kurt Wallander, with cumulative sales of more than twenty-five million copies worldwide. Thanks to the success of this series, other books by Mankell have been widely translated, some of them written after Wallander had become a familiar name, others written earlier. Many of these books are set in Africa or move between Europe and Africa as Mankell himself has done, dividing his time between his native Sweden and Maputo, Mozambique, where since 1985 he has directed a theater company.

In *Kennedys Hjärna* (*Kennedy's Brain*, 2007), for example, first published in 2005, a Swedish archaeologist, Louise Cantor, returns home from a dig to find her son Henrik—a young man, her only child—dead in his bed, apparently the victim of a drug overdose. Convinced that something more lies behind his death, she begins to investigate. The trail leads to an AIDS "mission" in Mozambique, one of a number of such villages in several African countries, presided over by a mysterious American philanthropist, Christian Holloway, who proves to be an egomaniacal villain of James Bondian proportions. The "missions" have hidden laboratories where new AIDS drugs are tried out, both on people who are already ill and on healthy people who have been lured there by promises of being lifted out of poverty.

As this summary may suggest, Mankell doesn't shy away from melodrama. Indeed,

Henning Mankell is a theater director and a playwright as well as a novelist, dividing his time between Africa and Sweden, his homeland. His books featuring police inspector Kurt Wallander have been adapted for television and film in Sweden and have been translated into many languages.

a straight plot summary of *Kennedy's Brain* would sound utterly over the top. But there is more to Mankell than melodrama. His fiction is not only moralistic—as a good deal of melodrama is—but also didactic. Lessons are imparted in dialogue and in the protagonists' reflections. *Kennedy's Brain* is animated by a fierce anger against the citizens of the "developed" world, who are charged with responsibility for Africa's woes, whether by active collusion or culpable ignorance and naïveté. Cantor (and hence the reader) gets a tutorial in the realities of African life—as Mankell sees them—from a young African woman. At the same time, Mankell's fiction has an imaginative richness that the typical thriller lacks. He is a master of compelling images and striking scenes that linger in the memory, and he excels at conveying the darting movement of thought.

All these qualities are apparent in *The Eye of the Leopard*, which was published in Sweden in 1990, a year before the first Wallander book, but which is only now appearing in English. *The Eye of the Leopard* shifts between a farm in the back country of Zambia, where the Swedish protagonist, Hans Olofson, has been living for eighteen years, and Sweden, where he was born and raised. The narrative shifts repeatedly in time as well, from the present (near the end of the 1980's) to scenes from Olofson's boyhood and young manhood in Sweden and then again to episodes from his African sojourn, beginning with his arrival in September, 1969.

The stage is set for this fluid movement in time by a prologue of sorts, in which Olofson tosses and turns in the grip of malarial fever. The novel can thus be read as a feverish act of recollection and reckoning, half voluntary, half involuntary. This fluidity is underscored in the prologue by shifts in point of view, from third person to first person and back again.

His memory first takes him back to 1956, when he was twelve years old. He has awakened in the night—just as he awakens so many years later, on his farm in Africa—disturbed by the sound of his father, obsessively scrubbing the floor in the kitchen. The boy's mother left her husband and son long before. The father works hard, drinks too much, mutters to himself, falls into rages now and then. The boy's mind wanders:

The darkness of night is a split personality, both friend and foe. From the blackness he can haul up nightmares and inconceivable horrors. The spasms of the roof beams in the hard frost are transformed into fingers that reach out for him. But the darkness can also be a friend, a time in which to weave thoughts about what will come, what people call the future.

The man wrestling with fever in Africa, insects crawling in the sweat on his face—these things the twelve-year-old boy curled up in bed in the cold Swedish night remembers. In turn, the boy remembers an earlier moment, playing with some kids in the ruins of a factory where bricks were made. Separated from the others, he experienced for the first time the sharp taste of self-awareness:

> For as long as he had not established his own identity, he was just *somebody* among all the others, he had possessed a timeless immortality, the privilege of childhood, the most profound manifestation of childishness. At the very moment that the unfamiliar question of why he was who he was crept into his head, he became a definite person and thus mortal.

One burden of the novel is to explore the mystery of identity—why we are who we are and not someone else—and the interplay of destiny (character is destiny) and choice.

Olofson's memories of growing up in Sweden, alternating with African scenes, center on his friendship with Sture, a boy from a higher social class, and their relationship with a young woman in her twenties, Janine, who was terribly disfigured in a botched operation when she was seventeen years old. The Noseless One is an outsider, living alone, her only community provided by a church that Mankell mocks for its rigid piety. At first, Olofson and Sture cruelly make fun of Janine, as many do, but then they are ashamed of themselves, reproached by her kindness and long-suffering nature. They become friends, entering her private world, where she listens to old jazz records and plays along on her trombone. Sometimes she puts a bulbous red clown's nose over the place where her nose should be, and she teaches the boys to dance.

The idyll does not last. But Janine's inchoate dream to go to Africa—not to convert anyone, Mankell makes clear, but simply to do good and help others in a place where her particular disfigurement wouldn't stand out so much, where many are terribly disfigured by injury and disease—plants a seed in Olofson's mind.

Janine doesn't fulfill her desire to go to Africa. She drowns, a suicide. Olofson betrays her—and in doing so betrays himself. In 1962, the year of the Cuban missile crisis, with the superpowers seemingly on the brink of war, Janine stages a quixotic crusade, standing on a corner in the little town with a handmade sign that reads: "No to the atom bomb. Only one earth." She is an embarrassment to the townspeople and the subject of ridicule. To avoid contamination, Olofson joins in the ridicule. Later he visits her covertly, but the damage has been done.

After a restless few years he finds himself on a plane to Lusaka, in Zimbabwe. He visits the back-country mission that inspired Janine, then ends up working for a woman who runs a farm by herself, her husband having gone mad. When she can no longer stand the stress of the job, she arranges with Olofson to take over the farm. He keeps saying he won't stay, but he does.

Most readers will wonder why he stays, given the unrelenting grimness of Mankell's account. The white farmers are generally portrayed as irredeemably racist, some of them monsters of cruelty. A suave Swedish aid worker, Lars Håkansson, turns out to be a poster boy for corruption; one of his sidelines is taking pornographic photos of young African women and selling them to collectors in Germany. All of Africa's problems are attributed to the evils of colonialism.

Against this Mankell poses images of an idealized, essentialized Africa. His images are not prettified—on the contrary—but they are idealized nonetheless. Olofson's friend, the journalist Peter Motombwane, turns out to be part of a rebel movement, the "leopard movement," that is killing white farmers to restore the land to the people and destabilize the corrupt government. Olofson is forced to kill his friend in self-defense. He concludes that Motombwane's methods were wrong—"he chose the wrong weapon at the wrong time"—but he sees him as a kindred spirit: "Peter Motombwane, he thinks. Peter, Janine, and me." These are the people who understand the world "in order to change it," in contrast to the corrupt bureaucrats "who understand the world in order to exploit it." Given that code, Olofson feels no remorse after he serves as Håkansson's jury, judge, and executioner.

It is clear that Mankell loves Africa. His depiction of the widow Joyce Lufuma and her four daughters as the hope for "the future of Africa" is moving and heartfelt. But that love depends in part on notions of an unchanging African essence that don't seem to correspond to the actual lives of Africans in all of their particularity. For example, as a devoutly secular European intellectual, Mankell is repelled by the notion of religious conversion—a theme that comes up explicitly in the novel on several occasions. But in Africa—where, in fact, both Christianity and Islam have long histories—there will soon be more Christians than on any other continent. Mankell would seem to be in a position of instructing Africans about how to be authentically African. There are a number of different ways in which to understand the world in order to change it, some of them compatible with one another, some not.

As a footnote, it should be added that a character named Lars Håkansson turns up in *Kennedy's Brain* as well. He, too, is a corrupt Swedish official—in this case, an adviser to the Ministry of Health in Mozambique—and a thoroughly nasty piece of work, like his namesake in *The Eye of the Leopard.* Perhaps this is a private joke or a curse of Mankell. If so, it would be in character, for along with his moral intensity comes a trickster's spirit.

John Wilson

Review Sources

Booklist 104, no. 14 (March 15, 2008): 26.
Entertainment Weekly, April 18, 2008, p. 67.
Kirkus Reviews 76, no. 8 (April 15, 2008): 386.
Library Journal 133, no. 9 (May 15, 2008): 91.
Publishers Weekly 255, no. 10 (March 10, 2008): 57.
The Spectator 307 (May 31, 2008): 43-44.

FAULT LINES

Author: Nancy Huston (1953-   )
First published: Lignes de faille, 2006, in France
Translated from the French by Nancy Huston
Publisher: Grove Press, Black Cat (New York). 320 pp.
  $14.00
Type of work: Novel
Time: 2004, 1984, 1964, and 1944
Locale: California, Montreal, New York, Israel, and Germany

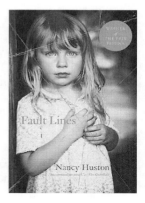

Psychological trauma is engendered and replicated within a single family over four generations as a consequence of a Nazi project that uprooted children from homelands occupied by the Germans during World War II

Principal characters:
> ERRA, also known as KRISTINA, an uprooted Ukrainian girl adopted by a
>   German family
> GRETA, Kristina's sister
> JANEK, an angry Polish boy adopted by the same family
> SADIE, a resentful, illegitimate Canadian daughter of Erra
> ARON, Sadie's failed playwright husband
> RANDALL, Sadie's confused and neglected American son
> SOL, Randall's emotionally disturbed son
> TESS, Sol's indulgent and overprotective mother

Fault Lines, divided into four parts, has four narrators, each of whom is six years old at the time of the telling. Spanning four generations, the story begins in 2004 but rewinds through successive narrators, each of whom is the parent of the child in the previous section. While each segment is set in an historical era marked by war and political upheaval, there is just one gradually disclosed family secret rooted in Nazi Germany. This explains not only the family history but also the many political-historical situations that shaped the characters of the wounded and wounding family members whose fault lines reach into the twenty-first century.

The first six-year-old is Solomon, nicknamed Sol, who is worshipped by his mother as a little god-king. His resulting narcissism requires the reader eventually to view the creepy Sol as a victim of an emotional illness that may be the consequence of the way his mother has chosen to raise him. His mother's Christian evangelism and the self-esteem movement have had an influential role in creating the arrogant but weak and anorexic Sol. His psychological development is also depicted within the context of the foreign policy of the U.S. government with regard to the war in Iraq, which both of his parents unquestioningly support. In fact, Sol's father Randall works for the military effort by exploring ways to create an army of warrior-robots.

~

Nancy Huston was born in Canada, was brought up in Germany and the United States, and as a young adult emigrated to France. She has won awards for many of her novels, including Fault Lines, *which won the Prix Femina in 2006. She lives in Paris with her husband, the philosopher Tzvetan Todorov, and her two children.*

~

While his doting mother has deluded herself into believing that her child rearing is an enlightened one that has produced in Sol a paragon of virtue and innocence, the boy's inner life is warped and sadistic. As a consequence of the excessive sanitizing of his life, Sol is driven to seek out the evil hidden and undisclosed by his mother, and his ability to access this evil through an unsupervised Internet connection allows him to live a double life. His discovery of the torture of Muslim prisoners by American soldiers at Abu Ghraib, for instance, creates in Sol a fascination with brutality and with sexualized brutality, and he gravitates to Web sites that show pornography or violence or, ideally, both. Although Sol seems to be an evil little creature, at the same time the reader understands that his upbringing may be a very subtle form of abuse. His eating disorder, his manipulative and exploitive relationship to his mother, and the falsity of the self she has insisted on constructing for him all suggest that the fault line Sol represents in the family may end not in the success of which he feels he has been assured but in a cataclysmic earthquake. This bad seed, however, is not only connected to the cultural and political dynamics of the United States. Huston uses the phrase "fault line" to suggest that Sol must be understood in relationship not to the present but to the fissures that go back to Sol's grandmother and great-grandmother, with their roots in Europe. Sol's unsightly brown birthmark, for instance, is a genetic heritage from his grandmother Erra; even when Sol's mother attempts to have it surgically removed, it remains as an ugly scar that indicates the continuing presence of the past. Sol's ties to the past are further emphasized when his grandmother Sadie insists that the entire family revisit the German village in which Sol's great grandmother was raised. Sol's visit to Germany is the first of the unsettling geographic dislocations that the reader comes to understand as a recurring family pattern.

This theme of uprooting is further explored in the next chapter, which takes place in 1984 and which features Randall, Sol's father, as a six-year-old. Randall's controlling and perfectionist mother, Sadie, obsessed with her family roots in Germany, ruthlessly relocates her son and his acquiescent father to Haifa, Israel, in order to research the Nazi Lebensborn (Fountain of Life) project that bred blond, blue-eyed boys and girls or took blond, blue-eyed children from various conquered territories and recycled them into German families. Huston relocates Sadie's family at the time of the civil war in Lebanon, and even more specifically the massacres at the Palestinian refugee camps at Sabra and Shatilla. The zealous Sadie, who has converted to Judaism, defends Israel's role in these massacres against her dissenting Jewish husband; the resolution of this conflict, however, as far as Randall is concerned, is saved for his little Palestinian friend Nouzha. Randall is sure Nouzha has put a vengeful curse on his family as a result of the massacre, resulting in the tragic crippling of his mother in what appeared to have been an unrelated accident.

The third narrative voice is that of six-year-old Sadie in 1964; the political context is the shadow of the Cuban Missile Crisis. Since her mother is preoccupied with pursuing a singing career, Sadie's Montreal grandparents are raising her. While Sadie's charming and playful mother attempts to rescue Sadie from her harsh grandparents, the appearance of Janek, a long-lost figure from the old country, changes everything. Always feeling the outsider, Sadie begins to view herself as even more an interloper when her mother marries Janek, changes her name to Erra, relocates to the United States, and seeks world renown as a musical artist. The depressive Janek, whom Sadie does not like, is an eventual suicide, further causing her to question her mother's choices in life.

As with Randall and Sol, Sadie has inherited her mother's birthmark. Though her mother Erra's same birthmark is the source of artistic power, this imperfection also indicates the disruptive relationship between mother and child that marked Erra's childhood. Erra's story, told when she is a six-year-old living in Germany, is set in 1944. At this time, she knows herself as a German child named Kristina. An older boy named Janek, whom the family adopts to replace the son they lost in the war, tells Kristina something she had suspected earlier as a result of the hurtful words from her sister Greta during an argument over a doll. Janek tells her that she, too, was kidnapped and adopted by a German family, as he was. Janek, who appeared a minor aspect of the earlier narrative, becomes a crucial component of the final chapter. It is the angry Janek who makes irreparable the estrangement from her family, begun with Erra's rivalry with her sister, and encourages her to break from them completely. The break with this mother is a consequence of Kristina's realization that her adoptive mother had participated in the Lebensborn project that led her to take Kristina as her own child. However, even without this devastating realization, it is clear from the beginning that Kristina's mother, not altogether consciously, privileged her biological daughter over her adoptive one; this is especially suggested by Greta's receiving a beautiful doll one Christmas that is clearly superior to the gift given Kristina.

After the war, Kristina is told that she is Ukrainian, but that her family is dead; she is adopted by another Ukrainian family that has relocated to Canada. She also dedicates herself to a musical based on singing wordless songs. Her need to do this moves beyond simple ambition, since it becomes a way to indicate the trauma of having been deprived of her mother tongue and of having been subjected to the abandonment, not only by her German caregiver, but also by her dim and traumatic memories of neglect in the orphan asylum in which she was placed when she was taken from her birthmother. Singing with no language becomes for Erra a way to express what it means to have no mother. Erra's petite stature also suggests that her loss at the age of six of the woman she thought was her mother has kept her a permanent child whose singing, however joyful, is destined on one level to voice this loss. Erra returns to Germany, and the last impression the reader has is of her as the six-year-old she once was, still quarrelling with her sister Greta over the possession of the desirable Christmas doll. Her new name, Erra, also points to the circumstances of her wounding childhood, since her adoptive name is not connected to her Ukrainian roots but is taken from an ancient Near Eastern god of war and pestilence.

An intriguing aspect of this novel is the way in which Kristina-Erra's victimization in Nazi Germany, which has never been consciously available to Sol or his parents, nevertheless haunts the latest generation based in California. The German society's decision to start the clock at zero after the war has in reality not left the past behind. Randall has traveled far away temporally and spatially from the suffering caused his grandmother by the eugenic policies of the Nazis, but his family is scarred nevertheless, although in an unexpected way. The twenty-first century sees Randall involved in the creation of a robotic army that his mother Sadie describes bitterly as the achievement of the perfect Nazi military machine; his son Sol at times appears to be a little Hitler-in-the-making.

Additionally, the tragedy of Erra's childhood has inaugurated a pattern of selfish or self-absorbed mothering in tandem with a pattern of weak and despairing fathers. Huston's point is that the dysfunctions of the family can be understood as a consequence of the destruction of Erra's original identity, nationality, religion, and language. The fault lines created by this psychological catastrophe are made more dire by the suppression of the truth in the cause of making a complete break with the past. That Huston sets her saga during times of war and terror adds a political dimension to all that has gone badly for this family since World War II. It is not only the family but also the world that seems somehow to have gone wrong.

This carefully planned and beautifully executed novel is a tour de force, as Huston uses the voices of six-year-olds to narrate a personal story, which opens up to larger historical contexts. Interestingly, her depiction of each child's perceptions includes as much sophistication as naïveté, so that each child seems to know a great deal and yet have a great deal more to learn. Huston effectively deploys dramatic irony in a way that affords the reader an understanding of the family's complex and tragic destiny that is never quite given to the novel's confused children. Huston has created a type of mystery-thriller in this novel about suffering passed through many generations. The reader is engaged with the narrative as a witness to the events portrayed, as a fascinated detective seeking clues embedded in history, and a psychoanalyst investigating the mysteries of the soul.

Margaret Boe Birns

Review Sources

Booklist 104, no. 22 (August 1, 2008): 36.
The Guardian, March 15, 2008, p. 17.
Kirkus Reviews 76, no. 16 (August 15, 2008): 45.
Library Journal 133, no. 12 (July 1, 2008): 61.
The New York Times Book Review, November 2, 2008, p. 7.
Publishers Weekly 255, no. 22 (June 2, 2008): 25.
The Times Literary Supplement, March 7, 2008, p. 21.

FIDELITY

Author: Grace Paley (1922-2007)
Publisher: Farrar, Straus and Giroux (New York). 83 pp.
$20.00
Type of work: Poetry

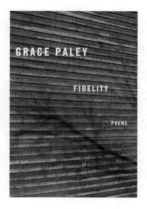

In plainspoken but often witty poetic style, Paley comments on growing old, loss of family and friends, her own illness and death, feminism, war and peace, and hope for the future

Grace Paley, who died of breast cancer in 2007, is perhaps best known for her short stories, which were originally published in leading magazines and eventually in book form in 1959, 1974, and 1985. In 1994 her book *The Collected Stories* was a finalist for both the Pulitzer Prize and the National Book Award. However, Paley began her career by writing poetry, from her teenage years into her mid-thirties, switched over in the 1980's to publishing mostly poetry, and rounded out her career with the posthumous poetry collection *Fidelity*. Although her early poetry was apparently derivative, reflecting in part her study with W. H. Auden, her efforts in poetry might have helped her develop the distinctive voice and dialogue for which her stories are famous. She was noted for reading her stories aloud as she composed them and later when she taught classes.

Poetry seems the more natural genre for Paley. Her stories tend toward open form; they have been criticized as being plotless, emphasizing, instead, character and voice. Poetry allows Paley more freedom of form: She writes in loose free verse, leaving some poems untitled and dispensing with conventional punctuation by indicating pauses with lineation and spacing. Poetry also allows the distinctive voice to be hers unambiguously. For a woman who has something to say, why bother with fictional pretense or dramatic personas? In poetry, she could speak more personally and directly, with more bardic authority, although the autobiographical element was never far away, even in her stories. The title *Fidelity* seems to be a poetic continuation of her main character in the stories, Faith (a thinly veiled substitution for Grace).

Much has also been made of Paley's New Yorker, Jewish background. Her parents, Isaac and Manya Goodside (originally Gutseit), were Jewish socialists from the Ukraine who, persecuted by the czar, immigrated to New York City, where their daughter Grace was born, raised, attended college without taking a degree, and at age nineteen married film cameraman Jess Paley. However, other influences are also important in Paley's career. After having two children, Paley and her husband divorced, which might explain the feminist influence on her work. Nevertheless, feminist influence did not keep her from getting married again in 1972 to Robert Nichols, a landscape architect and writer. In 1988 they moved to Thetford, Vermont. This more varied background comes out in *Fidelity*.

~

Grace Paley was an antiwar activist, a
distinguished short-story writer, and a
poet. Her Collected Stories *(1994) was*
a finalist for the National Book Award
and the Pulitzer Prize. Fidelity *was*
published posthumously.

~

Another notable influence in *Fidelity* is the philosophy of the Quakers (Religious Society of Friends), especially the Quakers' peace testimony. Paley was working with the American Friends Service Committee for peace when she met her second husband. During the Vietnam War, she was an antiwar activist and joined a peace journey to Hanoi. After the war, Paley continued working for peace and nuclear nonproliferation, getting arrested several times. In interviews Paley worried about the dangerous world she was leaving to her children and grandchildren (to whom *Fidelity* is dedicated). Several poems in *Fidelity* express Paley's antiwar sentiments, especially "Fathers," "Thank God there is no god," and "To the Vermont Arts Council on Its Fortieth Birthday."

Other Quaker attitudes and beliefs reflected in the poems are the liberal interpretation of belief in God ("Thank God there is no god"), belief in the just sharing of the world's resources ("An Occasional Speech at the Interfaith Thanksgiving Gathering"), natural acceptance of dying, feminism, and a liberal attitude toward sexual orientation. "Sisters," for instance, opens with the flat statement "My friends are dying/ well we're old it's natural . . . ." Nevertheless, the friends live on in memory: "I have not taken their names out of/ conversation gossip political argument/ my telephone book or card index . . . ." (A couple of the friends mentioned are "Claiborne," probably Sybil Claiborne, an antiwar activist and writer, and "Deming," probably Barbara Deming, a prominent Quaker activist and writer.) She remembers "their seriousness as artists workers/ their excitement as political actors . . . vigiling fasting praying in or out/ of jail . . . ." In the poem's strong conclusion, which might sum up the book's theme, she remembers

> their fidelity to the idea that
> it is possible with only a little extra anguish
> to live in this world   at an absolute minimum
> loving brainy sexual energetic redeemed

Most of the poems in the collection apply this upbeat ideal to common experiences such as growing old, often mentioned. The book begins with a barrage of references to old age. "Proverbs" offers the injunction that "a person should be in love most of/ the time this is the last proverb/ and may be learned by all the organs/ capable of bodily response." "Anti-love Poem" gives the opposite advice: "turn away that's all you can/ do old as you are to save yourself from love." "On Occasion" memorializes senior moments: "I forget the names of my friends/ and the names of the flowers in/

my garden." A later untitled poem describes a whole congregation of debilitated old-timers in a nursing home scene as seen through the perspective of a little girl.

Paley applies her upbeat ideal to growing old by using humor, laughing about her own senior moments and balancing the nursing-home scene with the fresh perspective of the little girl, who finds the Dantesque scene "interesting." A couple of short untitled poems also mention the freedom to be oneself, uninhibited by rules and conventions, that comes with old age. However ambiguous and lonely, this freedom is in some ways the climax of one's life. "Windows" is about how, for those who keep their minds and senses active, fresh perceptions are possible even in old age: Paley looks out her window and is excited by the suddenly new way she sees Smarts Mountain across the river. She also reacts in Wordsworthian fashion to a drive through Vermont: "my heart leaps up when I behold/ almost any valley or village in/ the embrace of US eighty-nine/ from White River to Lake Champlain."

Other poems deal with the experiences of illness and pain that often accompany growing old. One untitled poem recites the litany of ills suffered by Paley and her women friends—lungs ruined by a smoking husband, Parkinson's disease, double pneumonia, the need for walkers, inability to type. Nevertheless, Paley addresses illness and pain with typical humor: "my own/ illness was headlined in the Times for/ some reason I was proud . . . ." She writes about tumors on her spine and head being "extraordinarily competitive," even though she religiously ate "organic and colorful fruits and/ vegetables" and drank a daily glass of red wine "as suggested by *The New York Times*." Paley also notes that "I have experienced the amputation/ of my left breast," but "still after extreme surgeries/ many of us in the pharmaceutical/ west are able to live well . . . ." She and her surviving "sisters" also find comfort and consolation in each other, which is perhaps how one can understand the "love poem" to her friend Mabel, a "useful person one of the/ five or six in this world," who has "done more good than any of us do-/ gooders even when impeded by/ George's brains girls gardens . . . ."

Death is a release from illness and pain, as Paley remembers from her parents and grandmother who "were in great pain at leaving/ and were furiously saying goodbye." The main complaint Paley has about death is that it takes away family members, friends, and spouses. Otherwise, she is "a little ashamed/ to have written this [untitled] poem full/ of complaints against mortality which/ biological fact I have been constructed for . . . ." The same human biology that results in death also makes new life possible—children and grandchildren. This natural paradox is symbolized by dying and decaying trees out of which new growth comes in two poems ("Education" and "This Hill") at the end of the collection.

Paley sees hope for the future in the newer generations. "Fathers" celebrates the observation that "Fathers are/ more fathering/ these days they have/ accomplished this by/ being more mothering," which Paley attributes to "women's lib" and which is "exciting for an old woman." "Birth of a Child" celebrates the hope that "was always there" in contrast to the cringing world's need for "creating hope": "why/ be so grandiose/ just do something/ now and then." "Detour" celebrates the ability of children and grandchildren to get around the "detritus" and even "heaviest/ sorrows" of the older generation: "luckily their/ children have imperiously/ called offering their lives a/ detour thank god they've all/ gotten away."

A few of the poems comment on the process of creating poetry itself. Writing a poem relieves pressure: " . . . something/ which has pressed upon my breath beyond bearing/ will appear in words take shape and singing/ let me go on with my life." "Their Honest Purpose Mocked," which begins with diaries and notebooks and ends with children whose legs are blown off by land mines, seems to acknowledge that a completed poem exists within and is perhaps modified by the full context of the world it can never capture. Some such realization seems to inform "I Went Out Walking": "My poems had gotten so heavy/ I went out walking . . . ," whereupon Paley meets "another poet . . . his backpack/ already fat with poems and/ a pen in his teeth." In "Night Morning" productivity for Paley does not come so easily: "To translate a poem/ from thinking/ into English/ takes all night/ night nights and days . . . also the newest English/ argues with its old/ singing ancestry . . . ." Similarly, in "The Irish Poet," a creative writing class breathes "a long communal sigh" at "the early abysmal drafts/ of great poets" while "the Irish poet/ smacks his head and sighs his own sigh . . . ."

It is not surprising that, inspired by such models as Wordsworth and the Quakers, Paley has a plainspoken poetic style. The simplicity of her style, however, is somewhat deceptive: It does not prevent her from expressing some complex concepts, such as the tenuous nature of meaning, or from coining some colorful phrases, such as "the tele-/ phonic electronic digital nowadays," "the pharmaceutical/ west," and "curious bombs like bouquets called/ cluster . . . ." A number of poems are built around conceits. Paley's plain-spoken style is also enriched by her sense of humor, with its reversals, paradoxes, understatements, and self-deprecation: She includes herself among "do-gooders" who have "big mouths" (thereby anticipating and disarming her critics).

In addition to plain style and humor, an outspoken social and political consciousness distinguishes Paley's poetry. Besides examples of this consciousness already noted, other poems attack the rich, such as "The Hard-Hearted Rich," "An Occasional Speech at the Interfaith Thanksgiving Gathering," and "It Doesn't Matter If." The collection's title poem, "Fidelity," expresses and explains this consciousness: Paley cannot allow herself to get immersed too much in "the dense improbable/ life" of characters in a book because "how could I desert that other whole life/ those others in their city basements . . . ." Paley's poetry is clearly an extension of her activism.

Other poets, especially young graduates of creative writing programs, who too often write obscurely and have little to say (which might be why they write obscurely), could learn much from Paley's work. There is nothing wrong with writing poetry clearly, using humor, and expressing a social and political consciousness. If more poets wrote like Paley, perhaps contemporary American poetry would not be such an obscure, minor enterprise.

Harold Branam

Review Sources

Booklist 104, no. 13 (March 1, 2008): 43-44.
Library Journal 133, no 3 (February 15, 2008): 108.
The New York Times Book Review, April 6, 2008, p. 5.
Publishers Weekly 255, no 3 (January 21, 2008): 156.

FINE JUST THE WAY IT IS
Wyoming Stories 3

Author: E. Annie Proulx (1935-   )
Publisher: Scribner (New York). 221 pp. $25.00
Type of work: Short fiction
Time: Approximately 500 B.C.E. to the early twenty-first century
Locale: Wyoming and Hell

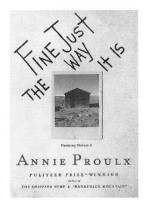

Proulx's third collection of Wyoming-based fiction adds to her impressive repertoire, with more stories from an author who knows the hardscrabble West

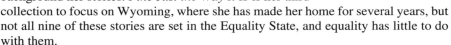

E. Annie Proulx is a national treasure, writing with intelligence, razor-sharp wit, and impeccable research to background her stories. *Fine Just the Way It Is* is her third collection to focus on Wyoming, where she has made her home for several years, but not all nine of these stories are set in the Equality State, and equality has little to do with them.

The two that take place in Hell are fun, and "I've Always Loved This Place" is even better if one is familiar with Dante's epic, *La divina commedia* (c. 1320; *The Divine Comedy*, 1802), especially the first canto, the *Inferno*. In this version, the Devil, hoofs, horns, and all, suspects that a looming religious war on Earth may cause Hell to become too crowded and decides to upgrade. He plans to add more landscaping, as well as a tenth circle for tobacco lobbyists and corporate executives. Grumpy old Charon, who ferries him over Acheron, the river of woe, argues that his crossing is "fine just the way it is." The Devil is inspired by the wreckage of New Orleans after Hurricane Katrina, and on the marshy bank of the Styx he muses, "I've always loved this place," but he cannot resist adding crocodiles. He also manages to find ideal accommodations for the Tour de France cyclists, for they have earned their place in his domain.

Likewise, "Swamp Mischief" is a satire, the author's revenge on a whole group of people, as the Devil predicts which new guests, such as shoe designer Manolo Blahnik, will arrive in Hell (dentists and highway engineers are already there), where e-mail is mostly spam and computers are programmed to crash five times a minute. Reading that a disgruntled earthly ornithologist is offering to sell his soul for a pterodactyl, the Devil proceeds to construct a few from the resident English sparrows and fit them with sharks' teeth, in order to seal the bargain. Obviously, Proulx had a good time writing these.

Irony is almost a constant in Proulx's work. Occasionally it is muted, as in "Family Man," a contemporary story that takes place at the Mellowhorn Retirement Home, where old-timer Ray Forkenbrock tapes his memories for his granddaughter Beth. Now eighty-four, he grew up in the silence of the big plains and remembers with regret an elderly horse catcher who died in the rain. Ray was mounted on horseback and still feels guilty that he did not offer the man his horse. After a host of seemingly unrelated anecdotes and an encounter with a woman from his past who disappears as suddenly as she arrived, Ray finally reveals a family secret that he has carefully guarded all these years. However, Beth does not understand, and his grief and shame are meaningless to her.

E. Annie Proulx has published eight books, including The Shipping News *(1993), which won the National Book Award for Fiction, the Pulitzer Prize, and the* Irish Times *International Fiction Prize, and* Close Range: Wyoming Stories *(1999), containing the O. Henry Prize-winning story* "Brokeback Mountain."

A harsher irony appears in "The Great Divide," which chronicles a young family's tough times during the Great Depression and war years. In 1920, Hi Alcorn and his pregnant wife Helen journey to their new Colorado homestead site, part of a growing development called Great Divide. The glow of marriage has not yet faded, and they have great plans to improve the land, but fate does not allow it. By the following year, crop prices are down, leading Hi to try bootlegging whiskey to bring in some money, but instead he is jailed. Each time the couple get their lives in order, something else goes wrong. Ten years later they are living in Wyoming with four children, and Hi is out of work again. Helen's sister and her husband Fenk Fipps arrive with a job offer: Hi can help Fenk trap wild horses for animal feed. Unfortunately, Fenk is cruel to the animals, and Hi quits to work in the coal mines. A few years later, Fenk again offers Hi a similar job catching horses. Accidentally kicked by his own horse, Hi finds himself with a broken leg that will usher in far more serious consequences.

One of the more unusual stories is "Deep-Blood-Greasy-Bowl," inspired by a 2,500-year-old firepit and the traces of a Native American civilization discovered in 2004 when Proulx was building her house. She imagines how life might have been during this period: an early fall, the leaves beginning to turn, the shaman chanting as a hunting party seeks bison for winter food. The tribe's treasure is a powerful gray stone bowl that will hold the blood of the slaughtered animals. At every summer's end, the hunters camp near a cliff, yet for several years no bison have come. However, this year one man has dreamed of the herd's arrival, and the shaman plays his flute to lure bison into a trap as the others hide. The hunters will corral the animals and head them over the cliff, using no horses, bows, or arrows—their weapons only knives, spears, and cunning. No animals are allowed to escape; otherwise they might pass the knowledge of the treacherous cliff to other herds.

"Them Old Cowboy Songs," one of the best of this collection, is Proulx's tribute to those forgotten pioneers who left no record behind. Archie Laverty's parents, Irish immigrants, die suddenly when the boy is seven, and he is taken in by the Widow Peck. After she goes to "the land of no breakfast forever" in a grass fire, leaving him one hundred dollars, Archie works as a ranch hand for her stingy son, Bunk Peck. In 1885, young Archie marries even younger Rose Mealor, homesteads with the widow's gift, and builds a cabin, singing all the while. The couple's love is idyllic, but the work is hard until Bunk lays off his cowboys for the winter and curly-haired

Archie must find a job elsewhere. He rides off toward Cheyenne, and the pregnant Rose, who up until now "seemed unaware that she lived in a time when love killed women," is suddenly made aware that they are "two separate people, and that because he was a man he could leave any time he wanted, and because she was a woman she could not." Proulx's awareness of the inequity of women in the early West is evident here, and love is clearly not the answer.

Archie finds another job, but the new rancher will not hire married men, so he pretends to be single. He cannot contact Rose or even acknowledge her existence, but he did leave a note in a neighbor's cabin asking him to look in on her. The neighbor, however, has already gone to New Mexico. In July, Rose, who cannot be more than fifteen, gives agonizing birth alone to a stillborn child. There is no happy ending here, and the traces of the two lovers quickly vanish from the earth.

A contemporary version of one woman's life on the range is shown in "Tits-Up in a Ditch," in which a hapless rancher describes how he found his milk cow flat on her back, dead in a muddy ditch. Here Proulx addresses the general disregard for women and the devaluation of their roles on the ranch and in life. Sons are idolized; daughters are ignored. This fact is discovered by Dakotah Lister, abandoned by her unmarried mother and raised by indifferent grandparents, Bonita and Verl. Arthritic Verl aches and complains, while Bonita in effect runs the ranch.

Verl's opposite is wealthy Wyatt Match, with a university education and radical Eastern ideas. Match, who wants to get into politics, has to become an archconservative in order to be elected to the state legislature. Married to a resourceful fifth-generation ranchwoman, he later divorces her to marry a new young wife from California, while his former wife and her brother continue to manage his ranch. Match criticizes Verl ("a trash rancher"); Verl, whose idea of "the pioneer spirit of freedom" is not wearing a seat belt, informs his wife that they do not need any outsider telling them what to do, especially one from California, because "Wyomin is fine just the way it is."

The child Dakotah seeks affection from her grandparents but does not get it; instead, she is expected to do chores, which she hates. She is a misfit in school as well. In high school she is attracted to feckless Sash Hicks, dropping out before graduation to marry him and become a waitress at Big Bob's. At about the time she and Sash decide to divorce (he is going into the Army), she is fired because of her pregnancy. When her son is born and named after his great-grandfather, both Bonita and Verl melt.

Bonita urges Dakotah to join the Army as well, in order to get training and an education while they care for her son. She is ultimately assigned to the Military Police, but in "Eye-rack" her Humvee is hit by a roadside bomb and she loses her right arm. After she is sent to Walter Reed Hospital to recuperate, Bonita shakily informs her that Baby Verl fell out of Big Verl's truck and was killed. Sash Hicks is also in Walter Reed, brain-damaged and gravely wounded. His parents have been unable to find out details about their son's condition because they cannot afford to go see him, but when they learn of the seriousness of his wounds, they do not want to. Dakotah discovers that she is still Sash's legal wife, and as she is trapped by society's expectations, her world slides away.

Proulx crafts her stories meticulously: A giant sagebrush grows in the Red Desert and strange things happen; after an argument with her lover, a woman embarks on a ten-day wilderness hike alone, a hike they had planned to take together. It may be tempting to read the stories straight through, but it is better to savor them slowly, one at a time, to enjoy the subtleties characteristic of her work. Notable are her remarkable vocabulary and her wonderful ear for accents, skills she has demonstrated in all of her books. She is very good at burying apparently innocuous information that results in a gut-punching twist at the end.

A few critics have speculated that Proulx may be disenchanted with Wyoming, and a British reviewer condemns her choice of silly names, missing the exaggerated frontier humor that is the whole point. (Even minor characters take on a life of their own; her improbably named Fenk Fipps and Wacky Lipe somehow seem exactly right.) Cutting through the sentimentality, Proulx continues to cast a cold eye on the legendary West.

Joanne McCarthy

Review Sources

Booklist 104, no. 17 (May 1, 2008): 5-6.
Kirkus Reviews 76, no. 10 (May 15, 2008): 15.
Library Journal 133, no. 11 (June 15, 2000): 64.
The New York Review of Books 55, no. 16 (October 23, 2008): 41-45.
The New York Times Book Review, September 7, 2008, p. 7.
Outside 33, no. 10 (October, 2008): 38.
People 70, no. 11 (September 15, 2008): 67.
Publishers Weekly 255, no. 21 (May 26, 1008): 35.
The Times Literary Supplement, September 12, 2008, pp. 19-20.
Virginia Quarterly Review 84, no. 4 (Fall, 2008): 266-267.

FIRE TO FIRE
New and Selected Poems

Author: Mark Doty (1953-   )
Publisher: HarperCollins (New York). 326 pp. $22.95
Type of work: Poetry

This collection combines twenty-three new poems and a selection of Doty's best poems from seven previous volumes

Mark Doty's poems in *Fire to Fire*, winner of the National Book Award, are about the large issues of life: human mortality, the transitory beauty of nature, the transformative influence of human aspiration, and the power to realize that aspiration. A self-described poet of the sublime, he has cultivated a style combining plain-spokenness with the elevated diction that often characterizes the sublime.

That Doty has a "democratic" sense of the sublime—validating the struggle of all creatures toward something larger than themselves—accounts in part for the great popularity of his work. He shows ordinary people confronting what he has called "the raw fact of our inadequacy in the face of the world," but reaching out to become allied with forces vastly superior to human nature. This inclusive notion of sublimity is consistent through the eight volumes of poetry represented in this collection. The poem from which this book takes its name—"Fire to Fire," first appearing in *School of the Arts* (2005)—includes these lines: "If I were a sunflower I would be/ the branching kind,/ my many faces held out/ in all directions . . . "

The new poems are contained in the first section of the book, titled "Theories and Apparitions," which was published in Britain as a stand-alone volume. The first poem of that section, "Pipistrelle"—named for the most common of Britain's fourteen bat species—illustrates Doty's proclivity for appreciating diverse perspectives without exalting one above another. This habit even diminishes any sense of rivalry with other poets, as he describes himself and a friend writing in two different veins (the friend's "lyrics" and Doty's "tale") about their sighting of the small creature, which could be counted as one of the "apparitions" in the title of this section. The opening lines belong to the friend: "His music, Charles writes,/ makes us avoidable," meaning that the bat's sonar keeps it from bumping into objects. Doty, in contrast, calls the bat an "emissary of evening," An emissary would not avoid but would seek out those for whom a message is intended. Doty decides that this encounter "is my personal visitation," and the thought humbles him: ". . . I with no music/ to my name save what I can coax/ into a line, no sense of pitch,/ heard the night's own one-sided conversation." This is Doty's poem, so he continues "filling in the tale." Reflecting upon bats, he realizes that "Only some people can hear their frequencies," and he is one of them. Just so, not everyone can hear all the nuances of a poem. Then comes a passage that reveals

Doty's distinguishing intellectual modesty: "Is it because I am an American I think the bat came/ especially to address me, who have the particular gift/ of hearing him? If he sang to us, but only I/ heard him, does that mean he sang to me?"

In "Pipistrelle," as in much of his work, Doty uses an everyday experience to enter by small steps into deep questioning and meditation. Soon, however, he becomes concerned that he may be reading too much into the experience, inspiring though it may be. Does his poem, he wonders, tend to "worry my little aerial friend/ with a freight not precisely his?/ Does the poem reside in experience/ or in self-consciousness/ about experience?" In the

Mark Doty is the author of several books of poems, including School of the Arts *(2005),* Source *(2002), and* My Alexandria *(1993). His memoir about love and loss,* Dog Years, *was a* New York Times *best seller in 2007. Among Doty's honors are the National Book Critics Circle Award, the* Los Angeles Times *Book Prize, a Whiting Writers Award, and two Lambda Literary Awards. In 1993 he became the first American poet to receive the T. S. Eliot Prize in Great Britain.*

midst of such fervent questioning, the natural setting in which he and Charles saw the bat exerts a calming effect, and in the end he is left with what appears to be a simple contrast between self-conscious art and the natural phenomenon that inspired it: "Listen to my poem, says Charles./ A word in your ear, says the night." Doty's preference between the two seems pretty clear; yet he leaves the contrasting viewpoint intact, undiminished in force. Elsewhere he has written, "It's a very large and capacious house, American poetry. I have no desire for everyone to work in the same way."

In keeping with this philosophy, Doty has chosen a simple, straightforward form—generally, unrhymed stanzas from two to four lines long, each with three to four beats. One can barely detect any craft in his work, so skillfully does he make the difficult look simple. His work represents a return to formalism, not form for its own sake, but as an avenue to depth of thought and feeling. Despite his seeming artlessness, he is not the heir to the spontaneous Beats; indeed, Doty says that while he respects spontaneity, his own poetic practice is "quite the opposite." Thus, he does not fully subscribe to Jack Kerouac's theory of "spontaneous bop prosody" or Allen Ginsburg's "first thought best thought," but he believes in "sitting" with the poem as long as one can endure any attendant pain. Developing writers, he says, often stop too soon, believing they have finished a piece, but actually they are just avoiding emotional discomfort. He is wary of finishing a poem too quickly so that it presents only "what is familiar, the stories we already know, what we expect to hear from ourselves." Doty observes, "The longer we can stay submerged in not knowing what we're doing, the more we're going to discover in the process of writing." He adds that his poem "In the Airport Marshes" required two years for completion. That poem concludes with the line, "How do you reckon your little music?" The poem is partly about creating poetry, about finding the words to convey to the listener the meaning an experience has for the speaker.

Doty's preference for the deliberate and well-considered goes beyond stylistic consideration. This is clear from the distinction he makes between "theories" and "apparitions" in the section of new poems. Like the little bat, many other "apparitions" in this section tend to be animals that can evoke an aesthetic response by purely mechanical, unconscious means. The pipistrelle cannot know that to a human being—at least to a poet—its cries sound "somewhere between merriment and weeping." In a poem explicitly titled "Apparition," a peacock ("oracular pear," Doty calls it) spreads "the archaic poem of his tail" into " . . . an arc of nervous gleams,/ a hundred shining animals/ symmetrically peering/ from the dim/ primeval woods . . . " Two other poems also titled "Apparition" are about human subjects, but these poems, too, deal with mechanical actions and rote responses. In "Apparition (Favorite Poem)," a boy reciting from Percy Bysshe Shelley's famous poem is seen

> repeating a crucial instruction
> that must be delivered, word for word,
> as he has learned it:
>
> *My name is Ozymandias, King of Kings,*
> *Look on my Works, ye Mighty, and despair.*

The "theories" in this section's title are poems that begin with simple anecdotes or comments and develop into meditations on large issues. Doty's titles include "theories" of narrative, of the soul, and, he says, "five theories of beauty, which I keep returning to because I never seem to get it right." The poet takes a deceptively casual approach, often humorous, and leads the reader into the subject. His "Theory of the Sublime" recounts a "happening" art project in which Doty simply clapped his hands for thirty-seven minutes while an artist records him on videotape. With no other direction than this, the poet finds himself "reaching for some sort of rhythm to perform" and slowly discovers a natural pattern of the body in which " . . . the pulse becomes firmer more persistent,/ Life of a tree unfurling, green burl spreading out/ Its swath of selfhood, an actuality . . . " After his initial sense of inadequacy, he ponders, while clapping, the creation of the sublime in nature and art, such as Barcelona's massive Templo Expiatorio de la Sagrada Família church, begun by Antoni Gaudí in 1882 and still under construction in the twenty-first century. At the end of the clapping session, the artist stops recording and indicates with approval that "something has happened here." Indeed, the poet has achieved a distance from the ordinary that has allowed him to perceive both the greatness of sublime art and his own smallness. Elsewhere Doty has noted that physically large works of art, which inspire a sense of awe, have been made by human beings—sometimes several generations of them—moving over large areas of canvas or stone to create their work. He feels it even more paradoxical that this realization could have been brought about by "something as ephemeral as 37 minutes of clapping."

Much of the sublime art that so inspires him is Christian art. Implicitly or explicitly, many of Doty's poems ponder Christian themes. Doty once told an interviewer that while growing up he had Protestant Christian ideas drummed into him, especially that of life's transitory nature and what he calls "a built-in obsession with mortality."

While he believes that much of his influence was negative, his poetic explorations seek to bring out what is fresh and alive in Christian faith. The poem "Citizens," about the commonplace outrage of nearly being hit by a truck in Manhattan, addresses the Christian theme of forgiveness, as well as the Zen concept of letting anger go. The truck driver grins as Doty shouts indignantly, *"what are you doing, act like a citizen."* Later, Doty wonders what kind of "citizen" he must be to have stayed angry so long. He recalls the story of a Zen monk who carried an elderly woman across the river, only to be asked by a fellow monk, *"How could you touch her when you vowed not to"* traffic with women. "And the first monk says, *I put her down/ on the other side of the river./ Why are you still carrying her?"* In time, Doty realizes he is angry because the truck driver "Made me erasable,/ A slip of a self, subject to. How'd I get emptied . . . question." The poet concludes

> I don't care. If he's one of those people miserable for lack
> Of what is found in poetry, fine.
> ***
> When did I ever set anything down?

Poets set all their thoughts down on paper.

The best example of a Christian theme made fresh and alive is "Messiah (Christmas Portions)," originally published in *Sweet Machine* (1989) and included in *Fire to Fire* as one of Doty's finest poems. "Messiah" describes a choir of ordinary people coming together under "the Methodist roof" to sing George Frideric Handel's famous oratorio. They are "blacks and whites," a

> cloudbank of familiar angels:
> that neighbor who
>
> fights operatically with her girlfriend, for one,
> and the friendly bearded clerk
>   from the post office,
>   —tenor trapped
> in the body of a baritone? Altos
> from the A&P, soprano
> from the T-shirt shop . . .
>
> ***
>
> Silence in the hall,
> anticipatory, as if we're all
> about to open a gift we're not sure
>   we'll like;
>
>   how could they
> compete with sunset's burnished
> oratorio? Thoughts which vanish,
> when the violins begin.

> Who'd have thought
> They'd be so good? . . .
>
> This music
> demonstrates what it claims;
> glory shall be revealed.

Near the end of the poem is the central message of the experience:

> Aren't we enlarged
> by the scale of what we're able
> to desire? Everything,
>   the choir insists,
>   might flame;
> inside these trappings
> burns another, brighter life,
>   quickened, now,
>
>   by song . . . .
>   Still time.
>   Still time to change.

It is significant that it is common people whose actions lead the way to these perceptions. The poet acknowledges the doubt that such people as the woman who "fights operatically" can deliver something this great, but the success of their concerted effort reveals a truly Christian message in the best sense.

The "Christmas Portions" of the poem's title refers to the parts of Handel's *Messiah* (1742) that are generally sung at Christmas: Part I (The Birth) and the "Hallelujah" chorus. In addition, Doty may also mean by "Portions" that through their own desire for and pursuit of the sublime, these ordinary singers have secured their true portion in life.

People sing *Messiah* from a desire to be uplifted. Doty writes poems for much the same reason. A poem is the outcome of a sometimes arduous process of thought and feeling, a process of digging ever deeper for the truth. Writing poems can be a discipline that can shape the lives of poet and reader for the better.

Thomas Rankin

Review Sources

The Advocate, April 8, 2008, p. 59.
Booklist 104, no. 14 (March 15, 2008): 16.
Lambda Book Report 16, nos. 1/2 (Spring/Summer, 2008): 18-19.
Library Journal 133, no. 6 (April 1, 2008): 86.
Publishers Weekly 255, no. 8 (February 25, 2008): 53.

FLYING HIGH
Remembering Barry Goldwater

Author: William F. Buckley, Jr. (1925-2008)
Publisher: Basic Books (New York). 208 pp. $25.95
Type of work: Memoir, history
Time: 1964
Locale: San Francisco, the site of the 1964 GOP convention; Connecticut, at Buckley's residence and at *National Review* headquarters; and "All over the place and accordingly *Flying High*," including a journey from Christchurch, New Zealand, to the Antarctic

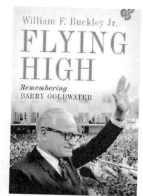

Buckley's posthumously published book describes the "grand time" that he and Goldwater had leading the counterrevolution against the orthodoxies of the Left and against those Republicans the two conservative stalwarts perceived as accommodating those orthodoxies

Principal personages:
> WILLIAM F. BUCKLEY, JR., the author
> BARRY GOLDWATER, the 1964 presidential candidate and Arizona senator who is Buckley's subject
> GENERAL DWIGHT EISENHOWER, two-term U.S. president, 1952-1960
> LYNDON B. JOHNSON, politician who defeated Goldwater for the presidency
> JOHN F. KENNEDY, assassinated U.S. president, 1960-1963
> RICHARD M. NIXON, U.S. president, who resigned in 1974
> RONALD REAGAN, two-term Republican president, 1981-1989, who ended the Cold War
> BRENT BOZELL, the author's brother-in-law, ghostwriter of Goldwater's *Conscience of a Conservative*, and *National Review* editor
> MARVIN LIEBMAN, father figure of the young right-wing Republicans, close personal and professional friend of the Buckleys
> WILLIAM A. RUSHER, publisher of the *National Review*
> GEORGE WILL, writer, fellow conservative, and long-time friend of the author

Political pundit and prize-winning playwright George Packer declared in a May, 2008, essay in *The New Yorker* titled "The Fall of Conservatism" that the philosophical roots of the party that nominated Republican John McCain are "older and deeper" than Ronald Reagan and the end of the Cold War. "They extended back to William F. Buckley, Jr.'s mission statement, in the inaugural issue of the *National Review*, in 1955, that the new magazine 'stands athwart history, yelling Stop'; and to Barry Goldwater's seminal book, *The Conscience of a Conservative* (1960), in which he wrote, 'I have little interest in streamlining government or in making it more efficient,

William F. Buckley, Jr., was the author of more than fifty works of fiction and nonfiction. He was the founder (in 1955) and former editor-in-chief of National Review *and the former host of the television show* Firing Line. *He was awarded the Presidential Medal of Freedom in 1991.*

for I mean to reduce its size. I do not undertake to promote welfare, for I propose to extend freedom. My aim is not to pass laws, but to repeal them. It is not to inaugurate new programs, but to cancel old ones.'" Among the perhaps unintentional services of Buckley's spare volume, *Flying High*, is to remind readers that Goldwater did not write a word of *The Conscience of a Conservative* and probably did not read the manuscript prior to publication. This reader was put in mind of Yogi Berra's response to former pitcher-turned-Houston columnist Larry Dierker's inquiry to Berra about how his first book was doing: "I don't know. I haven't read it yet." Buckley's brother-in-law, *National Review* editor Brent Bozell, ghostwrote the book.

Buckley refers to his being snubbed by Goldwater's advisers as a speaker at the 1964 convention as an instance of sequestration, a word with which in its political context this reviewer was unfamiliar. The year after Goldwater lost to Lyndon B. Johnson, Buckley enacted a riposte sequestration when he mounted a futile third-party bid for the mayoralty of New York City but declined to announce Goldwater's endorsement.

That the prevailing winds of party politics could not alter the affection each felt for the other is reflected in an aside revealed by Buckley five pages from the end of *Flying High*. Shortly after thanking Goldwater for the endorsement and explaining why he was not using it, Buckley received a phone call. The senator, en route to New York, invited him "and anyone else you'd like" to join him for lunch. The collective response of Buckley's associates is "What is he up to?" The reply is "He was being a nice guy." Goldwater is remembered today mainly as Reagan's unsuccessful forerunner, but Buckley shows that there was much more to the man. In *Flying High*, he reveals the pilot, the "child of the Grand Canyon," the nonconformist who, to assess the John Birch Society, showed up incognito at a Palm Beach John Birch bash wearing denim jeans, a cowboy hat, and boots. Perhaps Buckley quotes Goldwater's exaggeration—"Every other person in Phoenix is a member"—as a reminder to Buckley that the "problem" would not be unfamiliar to an Arizona senator. Asked how Buckley had acquitted himself performing a harpsichord concerto in Phoenix, Goldwater quipped: "Wonderfully. Absolutely first rate. Of course this is the first time I ever went to a concert."

Flying High is pitched as a memoir, but the "pitch" is far from perfect. Buckley enlists the memoirist's favorite ally: invented dialogue. When Walter Jenkins, an L.B.J. aide, is revealed to be a homosexual, Goldwater forbids his staff to exploit the disclosure. "Don't you understand, Barry, this election is about morality in government," someone is supposed to have said. To which Goldwater is supposed to have shot back, "Jenkins has a wife and six children. Leave him alone." A deft paraphrase would have been less suspect. The book, though "factually reliable," is not, Buckley acknowledges, "strictly factual, in that conversations are reported as having taken place word for word." *Flying High* demonstrates the facility of a man who adopted eccentric scenarios to capture the essence of a conservative mien. Buckley tempered the elitism of *God and Man at Yale* (1951), his first book, and even, during Goldwater's ascent to the nomination, masterminded the Republican Party's compromises on civil rights legislation. While never letting down his guard as a conservative who detested vulgarity, Buckley knew what many Ivy League mandarins forget: that is, that the vulgus is often right and the nobiles often wrong. Who else, in the midst of his rashness to run for mayor of New York, could sum up his whole effort when, replying to a questioner who asked what he would do if he won, tellingly countered: "Demand a recount"?

In *Miles Gone By* (2004), Buckley's previous book—one that purports to be his autobiography but that consists of recycled material from his oeuvre—Buckley already covered his role in Goldwater's campaign. Readers may have appreciated a fuller account, however, of the origin of these famous words from his acceptance speech: "I would remind you that extremism in the defense of liberty is no vice. Let me remind you also that moderation in the pursuit of justice is no virtue." Buckley claims General Dwight Eisenhower agreed to the inclusion of the word "extremism" when Goldwater reminded the wartime commander his leadership of the Allied forces across the English Channel in 1944 could only be described as an extreme position against Adolf Hitler. However, earlier Buckley acknowledged putting words in Ike's mouth that were never uttered.

In his review of his long-time antagonist's last book, former *Nation* editor-publisher Victor S. Navasky concludes that, "through no fault of his own [Buckley] was absent at the creation [of the Goldwater candidacy]." While acknowledging that Goldwater might well have been unaware of all the sequestrations, Navasky also remembers that in Goldwater's autobiography, which the Arizona senator is assumed to have written and to have read, Goldwater reported that the leader of his brain trust "had passed the word down that the candidate should distance himself personally and professionally from the *National Review* people." In a three-page coda, Buckley, an exacting stylist whose choice of mot was usually juste, not once but twice in his book's final words applies to his hero the adjective "unique," whose essential meaning is "the only one." Could such a one pay higher tribute?

Richard Hauer Costa

Review Sources

Booklist 104, no. 15 (April 1, 2008): 4.
Kirkus Reviews 76, no. 6 (March 15, 2008): 279-280.
Library Journal 133, no. 8 (May 1, 2008): 86.
National Review 60, no. 11 (June 16, 2008): 48-49.
The New York Times Book Review, May 25, 2008, p. 8.
Publishers Weekly 255, no. 11 (March 17, 2008): 59-60.
The Wall Street Journal 251, no. 103 (May 2, 2008): A13.

THE FOREVER WAR

Author: Dexter Filkins (1961-   )
Publisher: Alfred A. Knopf (New York). 368 pp. $25.00
Type of work: Current events, history, memoir
Time: 1998-2006
Locale: Afghanistan, New York City, and Iraq

Prizewinning New York Times *correspondent Filkins presents a compelling and brilliantly written account of his experiences reporting on the wars in Afghanistan and Iraq*

Dexter Filkins in *The Forever War* provides his readers with a vivid, emotionally searing, and intensely personal description of his experiences covering the wars in Afghanistan and Iraq. In doing so, he continues a distinguished reportorial tradition pioneered by American war correspondents in the interwar years of the 1920's and 1930's. One of the first and most influential of these was Vincent Sheean's *Personal History* (1935). In this book, Sheean gave a highly subjective account of his experiences covering conflicts that ranged from Morocco to China to Palestine. Sheean was a product of the literary modernism that was ushered in by the moral disaster of the Great War. He was a member of the lost generation, unmoored from Victorian moral absolutes and from confidence in progress. He identified his own confusion at the mad, bloody rush of events in the 1920's with the situation of the Western democracies, paralyzed by recent and bitter memories of trench warfare and morally helpless in the face of emergent totalitarianisms. Sheean's record of personalized history culminated in an epiphany at the Acropolis in Athens, when he embraced a vaguely collectivist vision of life born of conversations with a Communist revolutionary. Sheean's response to his experiences was unexceptional for an engaged intellectual with leftist leanings during the "Red Decade." More significant was the pattern his best-selling memoir set for the literarily ambitious newsmen who came after him. Reports from Europe and Asia in the 1930's, during World War II, the Korea War, and the Vietnam War, were every bit as personal as history. The reporter was not a detached observer; he was an active participant, sharing in the danger, excitement, camaraderie, and horror. He was constantly attuned to the effects of his experiences on his psyche and his evolving perceptions about authority.

There were variations on this theme. Michael Herr, writing about the Vietnam War in *Dispatches* (1977), was deeply influenced by the New Journalism of the 1960's, and he developed a powerful, highly literary style of writing that captured detail with almost hallucinogenic clarity. Herr's prose shaped a generation of reportorial memoirs. Thematically, however, he and his heirs followed the path laid down by Sheean.

Filkins echoes Sheean and Herr on every page of *The Forever War*. Even though he is describing a Near Eastern and Islamic world alien to the experience of most

Dexter Filkins is a journalist who has reported for the Los Angeles Times *and* The New York Times. *He won the 2004 George Polk Award for War Reporting. After leaving Iraq, he was a fellow at the Carr Center for Human Rights Policy at Harvard University.*

Americans, the reader nonetheless is in familiar territory. When Filkins writes about Muslim warlords and American generals attempting to impose order on chaotic madness in Afghanistan and Iraq, the reader is comfortably ensconced in the modernist theater of the absurd bequeathed by twentieth century literature and philosophy. It in no way denigrates Filkins's reporting to say that the reader has been here before. Through Filkins's eyes the reader sees what the reader expects to see. Not until a reader encounters a journalistic memoir with a radically different perspective on war, on authority, and on the meaning of human life will there be evidence of a new, emergent literature of the twenty-first century.

Filkins's *The Forever War* is not a conventional narrative about the wars in Afghanistan and Iraq. It is an impressionistic account, conveying a mood rather than a reasoned assessment of the Bush administration's war on terror. Ultimately, it is a meditation on war and the "other." As such it draws on that mainspring of modernist reportage, a correspondent's journey into a Joseph Conrad heart of darkness. What Sheean found in the Rif War and the first bloodlettings between Muslims and Jews in the Holy Land, and what Herr encountered amid the firefights in Vietnam, Filkins discovers in the streets of Kabul and Baghdad. He sees combat in the company of the U.S. Marines in places such as Falluja in Iraq. This is conventional warfare, grim, relentless, and bloody urban battle. It is nerve-wracking and awful, but something akin to what other men saw in Normandy and Hue. More telling is the unconventional warfare, the undifferentiated bloodshed launched by the Taliban in Afghanistan and especially by al-Qaeda in Iraq. Filkins observes that terror is the root of the overly familiar word terrorism. He lived for years with the slaughter of men, women, and children, who died horribly only so that their deaths would horrify others. Filkins also lived with the knowledge that he was a target, that at the whim of seemingly omnipresent killers he could be taken, tortured, and ritually butchered for the edification of zealots surfing the Internet. Like his predecessors, Filkins is acutely conscious of the psychological toll he suffers from his daily exposure to human carnage. At the end, he grew numb to the death around him. He lost the self-defense instincts that had helped him survive in the past.

Filkins brilliantly traces his mental and moral trajectory with a series of vignettes describing his attempts to keep up with his running in Baghdad. Here his personal story intentionally merges with the history of the Iraq conflict and the descent of Baghdad into chaos. Filkins liked to run along the Tigris River near the offices of *The New York Times*. At first this is easily done, and he is accompanied on his runs by friendly children. Over time, security measures increasingly constrict his route, the growing claustrophobia of his running mirroring the deterioration of the country and his inner trauma.

The great strength of Filkins's book lies in his eye for detail and an ability to capture general truths through a telling anecdote. Filkins reported from Afghanistan before 9/11 and the advent of the Americans. He covered the desultory war between the Taliban and the Northern Alliance, which was the only organized indigenous force opposing their rule. He describes with some irony the evanescence of political alliances in this seemingly endless civil war, meeting the same men serving on one side and then on the other. He also frequently encountered the dark, sharp side of Taliban repression.

Filkins was present when Taliban justice was publically dispensed in a soccer field. He watched as a pickpocket lost his hand and a young man accused of murder was shot to death. He also noticed the growing presence of Arabs in the country, as Osama bin Laden with his men and money became increasingly important to the Taliban regime. One day he stood in line in the Kabul airport next to a group of Arab women, speaking with Saudi accents. The women were covered by burkas, but they wore expensive and stylish designer shoes. The women were complaining about their husbands, whose fantasies about holy war kept them confined to what they called a "cursed place."

Filkins was in New York on 9/11, and he rushed to the site of the World Trade Center, arriving not long after the Twin Towers collapsed. He found himself amid scenes of horror and destruction that reminded him of the Third World. Filkins wandered into One Liberty Plaza, across the street from a mound of debris being sifted through by firefighters with dogs. He entered an abandoned Brooks Brothers store and spent the night there, wrapped in an oversized sweater. His work abroad had followed him home.

The title of Filkins's book, *The Forever War*, evokes comparisons with Joe Haldeman's classic science fiction novel of the same name, published in 1974. Haldeman's novel was a dark meditation on the Vietnam War, positing a future war in space, which, like the conflict in Southeast Asia, seemed to bring pointless destruction without end. It would be easy to assume, given this title, that Filkins is trying to make a political statement, condemning the American invasions of Afghanistan and Iraq. The Iraq War, in particular, became widely unpopular at home, as many world leaders denounced what was called American unilateralism, and the evening news nightly regaled viewers with the bloody results of car-bombings and improvised explosive devices (IEDs). As the years dragged by, the once-triumphant American military seemed mired in a Near Eastern quagmire from which there was nothing to be gained or to be won. Filkins, in fact, ends his account in 2006, just before the surge strategy of General David Petraeus dramatically changed conditions on the ground in Iraq. Despite this, Filkins's book is not a political tract. While there is little within its pages to warm the heart of a Pentagon official, it is not a sustained attack on the American war effort. Filkins does find plenty to criticize, from arrogance and cultural insensitivity on the part of American officials,to the traditional American overreliance on technology. However, he is not blind to the ruthless brutality of al-Qaeda and the Iraqi insurgents. He ruefully acknowledges that one reason he and other reporters remained alive was because the terror masters wanted him to continue sending bad news home. Filkins also makes a point of exploring the grim remains of the regime the

Americans overthrew. Saddam Hussein ruled by terrorizing the Iraqi people. Filkins visited one of Saddam's torture chambers, a chilling amalgam of the medieval and the modern, stone cells with chains, and sinister operating rooms with refrigerated aluminum morgue trays for the bodies. People attempting to recover the remains of loved ones murdered by Saddam's security forces often had to pay for the bullets used to murder them. Filkins believes that much of the brutality that haunted Iraq after the American liberation was rooted in the social and psychic dislocation produced by decades of depraved tyranny.

Instead of politics, Filkins charts the vagaries of the human soul under stress, his own and others. While aware of the larger forces at work in the history that he covered, he is chiefly concerned with the individual, with the personal. The genre in which he writes demands introspection; Filkins's real gift, one that makes *The Forever War* a truly outstanding work, is his capacity to empathize with the Afghans, Iraqis, and Americans he encounters. Again and again, readers are presented with unforgettable evocations of people caught up on all levels of an intractable war. Filkins met many leaders, among them Ahmad Shah Massoud, the charismatic leader of the Northern Alliance in Afghanistan, murdered by al-Qaeda just days before 9/11; Colonel Nathan Sassaman, an aggressive American commander in Iraq; and Ahmad Chalabi, the enigmatic Shiite politician who played a key role in encouraging the American government to overthrow Saddam. The portraits he paints of these different men are subtle and nuanced, when it would be easy to fall into caricature. However, Filkins's heart belongs to the other ranks, the ordinary men and women living with the consequences of their leaders' decisions. He writes movingly of the Afghan and Iraqi interpreters who saved his life on more than one occasion, risking their own in an uneasy attempt to find an accommodation between East and West in a war zone. At the moral center of the book is an incident that occurred when Filkins and photographer Ashley Gilbertson were embedded with the Marines during the second battle of Falluja in November, 2004. After heavy fighting that saw nearly a quarter of the company that they were with become casualties, Filkins and Gilbertson had seen few dead insurgents. Gilbertson needed a photograph of a dead insurgent for his newspaper. He and Filkins asked their companions if they could backtrack and photograph a corpse that had been found at the top of a minaret. The Marines agreed and protectively took the lead up the tower. As they neared the top of the stairway, the Marine in front was shot and killed. The Americans suddenly found themselves in an ambush. They fought their way out, but Lance Corporal William L. Miller had died for a picture. Feeling guilty for being the occasion of their son's death, Filkins visited Miller's parents twice. Instead of attacking him, they thanked him for letting them know how their son died. The book ends with Filkins waving to them on the ramp to an interstate. It is a final note of grace in a compelling personal history.

Daniel P. Murphy

Review Sources

Booklist 104, no. 22 (August 1, 2008): 28.
Commentary 126 (October, 2008): 42-45.
Kirkus Reviews 76, no. 14 (July 15, 2008): 61.
The Nation 287, no. 14 (November 3, 2008): 25-30.
The National Interest, no. 97 (September/October, 2008): 87-96.
National Review 60, no. 21 (November 17, 2008): 55-56.
The New York Times, September 12, 2008, p. 34.
The New York Times Book Review, September 14, 2008, p. 1.
Publishers Weekly 255, no. 26 (June 30, 2008): 15.
Washington Monthly 40, no. 9 (August-October, 2008): 40-42.

FOUNDING FAITH
Providence, Politics, and the Birth of Religious Freedom in America

Author: Steven Waldman (1962-   )
Publisher: Random House (New York). 304 pp. $26.00
Type of work: History, religion
Time: 1776-1823
Locale: Connecticut, Georgia, Maryland, Massachusetts, New Hampshire, New York, North Carolina, Pennsylvania, Rhode Island, South Carolina, and Virginia

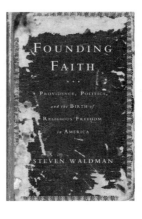

An examination of the Founding Fathers' relationship to their faiths and the growth of religious tolerance in the United States

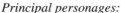

Principal personages:
GEORGE WASHINGTON, commander of the
    Continental Army during the American
    Revolution and first president of the United States
BENJAMIN FRANKLIN, publisher, inventor, ambassador to France, and
    delegate to the Constitutional Convention
JOHN ADAMS, second president of the United States
THOMAS JEFFERSON, author of the Declaration of Independence and third
    president of the United States
JAMES MADISON, the moving force behind the Constitutional Convention
    and fourth president of the United States

One of the most informative accounts of early American life comes from Peter Kalm, a Swedish naturalist passing through the northern colonies in the late 1740's. Upon reaching Albany, in the colony of New York, he was struck by the friction between the townspeople and the British, whose garrison was substantive proof of their imperial rule. The inhabitants, whose dress and speech among the troops reflected British tastes, remained fiercely loyal to their Dutch roots. Although the colony had belonged to the British crown for more than fifty years, the citizens of Albany were only nominal subjects of the king: They hated the British—whom they regarded as an occupying force—and preferred to speak among themselves the language of their Dutch ancestors. That would seem to reinforce the notion of rebellion in its embryonic state, a people who would revolt against their perceived oppressors in less than thirty years; however, Kalm also noted that they had equal contempt for their colonial neighbors, that "Albanians" had no difficulty in bartering for silver that bore the names of their murdered New England neighbors. This small observation about America's colonial past underscores some salient features of the American character—a keen distrust of a distant central authority and a fierce determination to retain one's belief system. To phrase it in more basic terms, one of the difficulties that faced the post-Revolution leadership was the tension between the national government and the centrifugal effect of thirteen culturally distinct colonies.

Never was this more evident than in the issue of religion, the subject of Steven Waldman's *Founding Faith: Providence, Politics, and the Birth of Religious Freedom in America*. The book largely focuses upon the treatment of the issue at the Constitutional Convention of 1787 through the early nineteenth century. The structure of Waldman's book is solid and workmanlike. He prefaces his discussion of religion in the early republic with brief profiles of the men who set the pattern for religious tolerance in the new nation, the Founding Fathers. Like a good playwright, Waldman provides a brief synopsis of each of the main characters, which functions as a kind of dramatis personae for his restaging of one of history's key moments. While some may question the necessity of reprising such well-known careers, this approach is central to Waldman's goal of correcting what he perceives to be current misconceptions regarding the religious views of the Founders. While evangelists often paint the Founders as extremely religious in order to advance their own agenda of employing government to promote faith, advocates of separation of church and state tend to claim that these leaders were

Formerly a correspondent for Newsweek *and an editor of* U.S. News & World Report, *Steven Waldman currently edits the largest Web site devoted to spirituality and faith,* Beliefnet.com. *His writings include a book about the legislative process that resulted in AmeriCorps,* The Bill *(1995), and numerous articles in* National Review, Slate, The Atlantic Monthly, The New York Times, The Washington Post, *and* Washington Monthly.

Deists—people who felt that God created the universe but did not intervene in human affairs. This is probably the least satisfying segment of a book that makes a profoundly original contribution to the subject of religious tolerance. It is due, in part, to the fact that a précis of any aspect of a person's life cannot fully capture the nuances and subtle shifts of that most intimate of subjects, one's belief system. These men led public lives, and as such even their most private correspondence would certainly have been written with a good deal of restraint. Thus, while it is instructive to learn that George Washington believed that God protected him from injury during battle, this is a common conceit among soldiers in all wars. Perhaps more telling was the fact that this Anglican "never kneeled" in church and "did not generally take communion." These significant omissions suggest a pro forma acceptance of a public necessity rather than an affirmation of faith.

The book's discussion of the Founders' personal beliefs is even more problematic when it deals with Benjamin Franklin. Waldman is on solid ground when describing Franklin's seismic shift away from the harsh Calvinism of his native Boston, a Protestant sect that affirmed that those who will be saved on the Day of Judgment have already been chosen by God. Good works count for nothing. As anyone who is familiar with the inventor's life knows, much of Franklin's later career was devoted to those very acts so haughtily dismissed by his Puritan forebears. Waldman is also accurate in his conclusion that Franklin's "true faith was religious pluralism," but what eludes the author is the essentially utilitarian nature of Franklin's character. The subject of religion receives scant attention in Franklin's autobiography. While Waldman acknowledges the fact that Franklin tinkered with formal religion in order to shape it more to his liking, he seems to miss the ironic nature of the autobiography toward religion. When Franklin grows irritated by what he perceives to be the inefficiency of formal religion, his attempts to fashion one of his own come across as parody. Of the Founding Fathers profiled in Waldman's book, it is Thomas Jefferson who appears to have made the most determined attempts to retain the essence of the teachings of Jesus—whom he did not consider divine—in the form of selected passages as moral precepts. The common thread that emerges from Waldman's well-researched synopses is a belief that formal religion is necessary insofar as it contributes to the public good.

With the formal conclusion of hostilities between Britain and its former American colonies in 1783, the Founders were compelled to grapple with the problem of religion in the new nation. As delegates assembled in Philadelphia for the Constitutional Convention of 1787, they confronted the dilemma of how to foster religion—which they held necessary for promoting virtue—and what role the government would play in that. While most Americans today tend to accept the notion of a distinct separation between the state and the beliefs of the governed, Waldman's text demonstrates just how revolutionary this concept was in the late eighteenth century. Even in the Age of Reason, religion was tightly regulated by the state, with monarchs such as Britain's George III as the titular leader of the church. The problem was exacerbated by the fact that the thirteen colonies' distinct regional differences were reflected in their differing religious preferences. In Southern states such as Virginia, the Anglican faith was dominant; a Northern neighbor, Massachusetts, trumpeted Congregationalism. If for no other reason, Waldman's book is to be praised for the skill with which he dispels the myth that Americans always supported religious freedom. Quakers, Baptists, Catholics, and Jews were openly harassed with the endorsement of the legal system. As *Founding Faith* makes clear, the new nation was not without an alternative model. As the leader of the Continental Army during the American Revolution, Washington had to create an effective fighting force despite the regional differences of its members. By quelling anti-Catholic sentiments within the army's ranks, he sought to win more adherents to the cause. Tolerance of this particular sect was practiced not only to retain those already in the army and to win recruits from Canada but also to gain material support from France. Acceptance of other sects within the ranks such as Unitarians, Lutherans, and Calvinists was also part of a concerted plan to lure Hessian mercenaries from the British army.

While that most inspiring affirmation of freedom—the Declaration of Independence—speaks eloquently of the need for liberty, it makes no mention of religious freedom. This is not surprising, given the fact that this was more of a mission statement than a legal document. It was in drafting the Constitution, the actual blueprint for governing the nation, that the Founders were compelled to address the role of religion in the new nation. Waldman's crisp text carefully follows the evolving treatment of the issue throughout the convention. Although a ban on laws regarding religion failed to pass, a prohibition of religious tests for public office did. He convincingly argues that this was a radical move for its time, inasmuch as eleven states did require such tests. Whatever path the new government would eventually take, Waldman emphasizes the framers' concerted efforts to avoid promoting particular faiths. Waldman's impressive research allows him to stand on firm ground as he contrasts what he contends are oversimplifications by today's conservative and liberal elements with their counterparts at the convention. The Constitution has always been something of an ideological battleground, with various factions arguing their points of view from both the written text as well as what they claim was implied by the Founders. However, unlike their modern counterparts, evangelists in 1787 wanted a separation of church and state in order to prevent persecution.

To anyone who has not read the Constitution in its entirety, it may come as something as a shock to learn that the document makes no mention of God. While the Declaration of Independence contends that the people are "endowed" with rights "by their creator," the Constitution focuses on the notion of power coming from the people. If the Founders were as religious as the book asserts, why did they create this deistic void? Modern conservatives focus on what they contend is implied by the Constitution, homing in on traditional religious values. Liberals, on the other hand, hold that this deistic absence proves that the Founders saw no role for religion in the new nation.

Waldman walks a middle ground between these extremes on the ideological spectrum: While the Founders held that religion was important, they believed that the best way to promote religion was for the federal government to maintain a hands-off approach. As the book repeatedly states, the language of the Constitution is deliberately vague because it was the product of a series of compromises. Even the Bill of Rights, which was instituted in order to win passage of the Constitution, only prohibits Congress from passing legislation that would establish an official religion or limit the freedom of religion. Incredibly, the Founders were concerned only with the role of religion and its relationship with the national government. They reasoned that if the federal government kept aloof, religion would flourish on its own, and history has validated that stance. The individual states were free to act on their own in this regard, with the result that "official" state-supported religions did not end until 1833, and strict separation of religion and government at all levels did not occur until the passage of the 14th Amendment after the Civil War. *Founding Faith: Providence, Politics, and the Birth of Religious Freedom in America* proves that the separation of church and state is a concept that evolved over time, an eloquent testament to the wisdom of the nation's Founders.

Cliff Prewencki

Review Sources

The American Spectator 41, no. 10 (December, 2008-January, 2009): 91-94.
Kirkus Reviews 76, no. 2 (January 15, 2008): 85.
Library Journal 133, no. 3 (February 15, 2008): 110.
The Nation 286, no. 22 (June 9, 2008): 42-48.
The New York Times Book Review, April 13, 2008, p. 22.
Newsweek 151, no. 11 (March 17, 2008): 63.
Publishers Weekly 255, no. 4 (January 28, 2008): 59.

FRANCO AND HITLER
Spain, Germany, and World War II

Author: Stanley G. Payne (1934-   )
Publisher: Yale University Press (New Haven, Conn.).
   328 pp. $30.00
Type of work: History

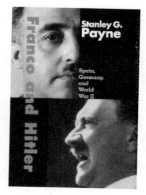

Payne, an authority on European fascism and the history of modern Spain, debunks conventional wisdom about Spanish neutrality during World War II, documenting Francisco Franco's admiration for Adolf Hitler, Spain's alliance with the Third Reich, and its ambivalence toward Jews facing Nazi annihilation

Principal personages:
   GENERAL FRANCISCO FRANCO (1892-1975),
      the dictator of Spain
   ADOLF HITLER (1889-1945), chancellor of Nazi Germany

Stanley G. Payne's study of Spain during World War II belongs to the myth-busting genre of historical writing. The first myth it dispels, ironically, involves the book's title, *Franco and Hitler*, which is misleading insofar as it implies a close personal relationship between General Francisco Franco, the Spanish dictator, and Adolf Hitler, the chancellor of Nazi Germany. Payne's subtitle, *Spain, Germany, and World War II*, more accurately identifies his book's contents.

Franco and Hitler met only once. Their encounter took place on October 23, 1940, at Hendaye, a town on the Spanish border in southwestern Nazi-occupied France. Payne calls that meeting "perhaps the most mythified event" of Franco's lengthy political career. This myth held that Franco kept Hitler waiting, outtalked him, and frustrated the führer by keeping Spain out of World War II and preserving Spanish neutrality. In fact, Franco's tardy arrival resulted not from political calculation but from the decrepit Spanish railroad's inability to get him there on time. Franco did talk at length, but what he said scarcely indicated neutrality. Franco thanked Hitler for all that Nazi Germany had done to support Spain, and he also affirmed Spain's intention to be Germany's military partner. In the autumn of 1940, Hitler wanted such cooperation from Spain, hoping that it would facilitate the conquest of Gibraltar and help to block the British while Nazi Germany prepared to invade the Soviet Union. Franco, however, was cautious, for he wanted to ensure terms of engagement with Nazi Germany that would best serve Spain's interests, including its territorial ambitions in North Africa and the economic and military aid that Spain sorely needed.

Hitler left Hendaye thinking he had what he wanted at the time, a Spanish pledge to join Nazi Germany's war effort. As World War II progressed and eventually turned against the Third Reich, Hitler would reconsider the desirability of direct Spanish

Stanley G. Payne is Hilldale-Jaume Vicens Vives Professor of History Emeritus at the University of Wisconsin-Madison, where he began teaching in 1968. He is the author of more than fifteen books that focus on modern Spanish history and fascism, as well as many articles and book chapters on those topics.

military efforts because Franco's ill-equipped forces required more German support than their combat was worth. Meanwhile, Franco left Hendaye uneasy about Hitler's inattention to the Spanish concerns that remained foremost on Franco's mind. The result was a German-Spanish wartime relationship that remained in flux, maintained not by Franco and Hitler directly, apart from periodic correspondence between them, but primarily by the interaction and intrigue among their diplomatic surrogates. Though in flux, Spain's support for and dependence upon Nazi Germany did not amount to Spanish neutrality, at least not until Nazi Germany's complete defeat was undeniable.

Payne makes his case with a detailed analysis that begins with the dismantling of other myths, some of them surrounding the Spanish Civil War (1936-1939), which enabled Franco to approach the heights of his long-lasting power. In particular, Payne resists the oversimplification that this struggle pitted democracy against fascism. With the proclamation of the Second Spanish Republic in April, 1931, a democratic breakthrough did take place in Spain, but Payne argues that the regime failed to meet rising economic expectations. Soon increasingly nondemocratic factions on the left and right vied for control. A right-wing military revolt in the summer of 1936 led, in Payne's words, to "an intense civil war of the most violent and atrocious kind." Supported by Joseph Stalin (1879-1953) and the Soviet Union, as well as by American and European volunteers in the left-wing International Brigades, the Republican forces battled the insurgent Nacionales (Nationalists) who, with help from Hitler and Benito Mussolini (1883-1945), the Italian fascist leader, announced victory on April 1, 1939. Nationalist control of Spain included bloodthirsty repression, which, according to Payne, resulted in 28,000 to 30,000 executions.

Notable for his valor and leadership during earlier colonial combat in Morocco, Franco had loyally served the Second Republic until 1936 when its leftist leaders deposed him as chief of the general staff. Still the Spanish military's most prominent officer, Franco was the obvious choice when the nationalist junta sought the military leadership required for successful advances against Republican strongholds. Franco had early contact with the rebel leadership but was not at first in the junta's vanguard. By the civil war's end, however, he would enjoy more power than any previous Spanish ruler, directing Spain's destiny for forty years. Spain went through varied phases during those decades, but Payne criticizes the allegation that changing circumstances showed Franco's lack of persistent convictions. Spanish nationalism and imperialism, authoritarian rule, Catholic hegemony, social conservatism, anticommunism, and economic strategies that favored Spanish corporate interests—these dominant ingredients emerged early and remained late in Franco's worldview.

Even before the civil war ended, Franco had become the caudillo, the closest Spanish equivalent to führer or duce, as Hitler and Mussolini, respectively, were called. The caudillo's version of fascism, accompanied by the chant of "Franco, Franco, Franco," tilted him toward the Axis powers, Germany and Italy, although it never embraced Hitler's anti-Semitic racism and was more resolutely Catholic than Mussolini's regime. By the time that World War II began, with Nazi Germany's invasion of Poland on September 1, 1939, Spanish law "permanently entrusted" governing power to Franco. "In formal juridical terms," Payne asserts, the Spanish state, while allowing "a limited semi-pluralism," had become "the most thoroughgoing personal dictatorship in Europe." Franco's state political party was the Falange Española Tradicionalista (FET), the broad rightist coalition he forged, that included but was not controlled by the most extreme Spanish fascists. Franco benefited from their support as well as from FET's loyalty, but he remained wary of partisan initiatives when they conflicted with what the caudillo determined was best for Spain. Nevertheless, Payne contends, Franco and the FET shared the basic conviction that Spain should be closely linked to Nazi Germany.

Meanwhile, in the early autumn of 1939, Mussolini strongly supported Hitler but was not yet ready to enter the European war that the führer had started. Therefore, Mussolini created a concept, nonbelligerence, to identify Italy's status. This idea differed from neutrality in at least two ways. First, nonbelligerence had no standing in international law. Second, as Payne points out, "nonbelligerence was not in any way a form of neutrality, but rather a repudiation of neutrality in favor of a special status of pre-belligerency." Seizing Mussolini's idea, Spain officially embraced nonbelligerence, not neutrality, on June 12, 1940, clearly signaling its intention to side actively with the Axis powers and Nazi Germany in particular. Only the tides of war—coupled with economic and military weakness, Franco's insistence that Spain's commitment of troops would have to be well repaid, and pressure from Great Britain and the United States—kept most Spanish troops on the sidelines during World War II. Spain's primary contributions to Hitler's war effort consisted of supplying natural resources—especially much-needed tungsten—in support of the German navy and providing a safe haven for Nazi intelligence gathering. In at least one significant way, however, the Spanish military fought fiercely on Hitler's side.

On June 22, 1941, Hitler broke his nonaggression agreement with Stalin and invaded the Soviet Union. The Spanish government, which tended to identify "its own battle in the Civil War with the military initiatives of Germany," Payne says, responded enthusiastically. Hitler's advance seemed sure to destroy the Soviet Union and communist ideology itself, thus completing a process whose first blows had been struck in the period 1936-1939 by the Nationalist victory against Soviet-backed communism. Franco himself hailed the German invasion, although he was less enamored when pro-German pressure mounted to send Spanish troops to support Hitler on the new eastern front. The caudillo, however, did not stop the formation of a volunteer unit, which, taking its name from the color of the Falangists' uniform shirt, came to be known as the Blue Division.

According to Payne, Franco and other leaders in his regime "interpreted the intervention of the Blue Division as Spain's contribution to a broader conflict, the European resistance to Soviet communism, a common European enterprise of which the Spanish Civil War marked an earlier high point." In any case, the Blue Division, its members totaling about forty-five thousand, fought for Hitler in the war's most lethal campaigns. The division's casualties included as many as 4,900 dead and 8,700 wounded. Hitler's evaluation of the Spaniards' performance was so favorable, Payne reports, that "he had a special medal created to award its members, something that he did for no other foreign unit." Although the division was formally disbanded in October, 1943, as the war turned increasingly against Nazi Germany, more than two thousand of its members still stood with their German comrades. "The Blue Division," Payne summarizes, "marked the height of Spanish collaboration in the German war effort."

As some members of the Blue Division returned to Spain, they brought disturbing reports about German mass murder of Jews. Spanish diplomats, especially those in the Berlin embassy, became increasingly aware that Nazi Germany had pronounced a death sentence on Europe's Jews. Contrary to favorable reports that have circulated about the Franco regime's benevolent policies toward European Jewry during World War II, Payne contends that "a fair conclusion would be that Spanish policy discriminated against Jews less than did that of most European countries, but there was no plan to especially favor or assist them, except with regard to Sephardim [formerly Spanish Jews] who could claim citizenship rights." As noted, Franco's Spain was not racially anti-Semitic, but anti-Semitism was by no means absent. Spain's wartime policy was to be stingy with entrance visas for Jewish refugees but more generous with transit papers, which would enable Jews to pass through the country. Some claims hold that as many as seventy thousand Jewish refugees found safety in Spain, at least temporarily. Payne's research finds that figure exaggerated; a number between twenty thousand and thirty-five thousand is more likely.

The diplomat Angel Sanz Briz, assisted by an Italian named Giorgio Perlasca, stands out as the greatest Spanish rescuer of Jews during the Holocaust. In 1980 Yad Vashem, the Israeli Holocaust memorial, honored him as one of the "Righteous among the Nations." Stationed in Budapest during the autumn and winter of 1944-1945, Sanz Briz, writes Payne, "managed to protect about 2,300 Jews in Hungary, while issuing transit visas to between five hundred and twelve hundred others who were able to escape abroad." Payne adds that Sanz Briz "might have accomplished even more had he received greater assistance from Madrid." Payne minces no words in summing up his demythologizing of the Franco regime's Jewish policies during World War II: "There was no concern for Jews in general, save in the final phase in Budapest. . . . Spanish policy was so dilatory and sometimes contradictory as to border on indifference."

By May, 1944, Spain no longer tilted toward Nazi Germany. Instead, Franco's Spain sought to gain favor with the Allies. During the decades of the Cold War between the Soviet Union and the West that ensued after 1945, Franco's anticommunist regime enjoyed a considerable amount of that favor, but in Payne's judgment, "the 1940's were to a large extent a lost decade for Spain." Payne's book appropriately drives final nails into that coffin by demonstrating that the "neutrality" of Spain during World War II must go down in history as a myth that has been justly debunked.

John K. Roth

Review Sources

Journal of Military History 72, no. 4 (October, 2008): 1320-1322.
World War II 23, no. 2 (June/July, 2008): 75-76.

A FREEWHEELIN' TIME
A Memoir of Greenwich Village in the Sixties

Author: Suze Rotolo (1943-   )
Publisher: Broadway Books (New York). 371 pp. $22.95
Type of work: Memoir
Time: Primarily 1961-1966
Locale: Primarily Greenwich Village, New York City;
    also Italy, Cuba, and England

A touching memoir of Greenwich Village during the 1960's through the eyes of Bob Dylan's girlfriend at the time

Principal personages:
> SUZE ROTOLO, a young activist and artist
> who became involved with Bob Dylan
> during the early 1960's
> CARLA ROTOLO, her older sister
> GIOACHINO PIETRO "PETE" ROTOLO, her father, who was a labor
> organizer
> MARY PEZZATI ROTOLO, her mother
> WOODY GUTHRIE, a legendary American singer-songwriter
> BOB DYLAN, a talented singer-songwriter who would change the face of
> popular music
> DAVE VAN RONK, a well-respected folk singer and close friend of
> Rotolo and Dylan

In a relaxed, conversational writing style, Suze Rotolo, in *A Freewheelin' Time*, reminisces about her place in the history of the turbulent 1960's and her part in the Bob Dylan saga. The vibrant Rotolo was Dylan's girlfriend after his move to New York City. Born in the borough of Queens, New York City, in 1943, she was the daughter of radical parents, and she became famous for being pictured with Dylan on the cover of his groundbreaking 1963 album, *The Freewheelin' Bob Dylan*. Some of Dylan's early landmark songs are found on this album, including "Blowin' in the Wind," "A Hard Rain's A-Gonna Fall," and "Masters of War." Rotolo was surprised to find that the photograph of them as a couple was ultimately used for the cover.

Their relationship began as two people who inspired each other. Unfortunately, Dylan became a larger-than-life figure, impossible to deal with. Rotolo had "trouble talking or reminiscing about the 1960's" because of Dylan, stating that he was "an elephant in the room of my life." When they first met, she was seventeen and Dylan was twenty. He had come to New York to work on his music and to meet the legendary American singer-songwriter Woody Guthrie. While this memoir is most certainly the story of Rotolo and Dylan, it is also a love story about place and time. Greenwich Village of the early 1960's was where creative people from all over found their way and where artists, poets, and musicians would meet and share ideas. It was in this mix that Rotolo and Dylan lived.

Over the years, Suze Rotolo has been active in many social causes, including the Civil Rights movement during the 1960's. She is an artist and teacher who makes her home in New York City with her family. A Freewheelin' Time is her first book.

Over the years, the legend of Dylan has grown, supported by increasing numbers of books, articles, and films. Scholars, journalists, and those who were there have tried to give the public an accurate picture of Dylan—who he was, who he is, and who he wanted to be. Rotolo remained silent for many decades about the early 1960's and her relationship with Dylan because, as a private person, she did not want to get into a literary shouting match with others about where reality ends and fantasy begins. In *A Freewheelin' Time*, she tells her side of the story, on her terms. This is not a tell-all, with bombshell moments that will leave the reader gasping. For the most part, it is a respectful sojourn down memory lane, with no bitterness or vindictiveness.

Rotolo states early in the memoir: "Secrets remain. Their traces go deep, and with all due respect I keep them with my own. The only claim I make for writing this memoir of that time is that it may not be factual, but it is true." For some readers this disclaimer may not be enough. Certainly some who thirst for Dylan souvenirs will not be satisfied with her "truth." In that regard, Rotolo may find herself in a no-win situation. She must have decided that this memoir was not for the fanatical fans or even the archaeologists of all things Dylanesque. The story told, as she emphatically states, "is mine."

In their years together, Dylan and Rotolo believed that they could be a force for change. While both were "sensitive" souls, Dylan also was "tough and focused" and possessed a "healthy ego." As Rotolo recounts, these qualities helped to make him a successful artist. Upon arrival at Greenwich Village, Dylan entered the folk music scene, and Rotolo first saw him perform at Gerde's Folk City. At this Village venue, Dylan played harmonica with several musicians, worked in a duo with fellow folksinger Mark Spoelstra, and performed solo. During this period, the young Dylan was in the process of establishing his identity as an artist, as a "rambling troubadour, in the Guthrie mode." While numerous books and articles have been written about the Village and about Dylan, this memoir is unique for its female voice. A few women close to Dylan have written about their relationship with him. Joan Baez, who has written two autobiographies, did not dwell on her relationship with Dylan in either one. It is possible to recommend several books that delve into the evolution of Dylan, including Robert Shelton's *No Direction Home: The Life and Music of Bob Dylan* (1986), Tim Riley's *Hard Rain: A Dylan Commentary* (1992), Clinton Heylin's *Bob Dylan: Behind the Shades* (1991) and *Bob Dylan: A Life in Stolen Moments—Day by Day, 1941-1995* (1996), Howard Sournes's *Down the Highway: The Life of Bob Dylan* (2001), Robert Santelli's *The Bob Dylan Scrapbook, 1956-1966* (2005), and Dylan's own memoir, *Chronicles* (2004). With so much already available about Dylan for public consumption, a reader may approach with some trepidation anything new published about the early 1960's and about the singer. Since Rotolo has remained silent about those heady days, her memoir does provide a fresh perspective from a person who can fill in some of the colors on a portrait of a man who became an iconic figure in music.

While the reader may open this memoir in order to learn more about Dylan, it is the story of a young girl from Queens who struggles to find her identity that holds most of the fascination in the book. In a real sense, the main character of the story is New York City's Greenwich Village, a magnet that drew those who had dreams of changing the world and changing themselves and where they could be exposed to "the cross-fertilization of different styles." While Rotolo was referring to Gerde's in that statement, to a large degree it applies to the whole Village scene. It was not only music that was expanding but also art, social causes, political issues, and cultural concerns. It was literally a "freewheelin' time" when change seemed to be in the water.

In addition to the music figures, Rotolo introduces the reader to an assortment of fascinating characters, including club owners, friends, and relatives. She was considered a "red-diaper" baby since her parents were members of the American Communist Party. Her father, Gioachino Pietro "Pete" Rotolo, came to the United States from Sicily in 1914 at the age of two. Although a talented artist, he was unable to support his family as a painter, so he became a factory worker and eventually a union organizer. In this family milieu, Rotolo learned to be socially aware. Both of her parents had been "radicalized" by the anti-immigrant attitude that they first witnessed during the 1920's. Growing up in Queens during the 1950's, Rotolo felt like an outcast, and she took refuge in literature. Tragically, her father died in 1958. His sudden death was extremely upsetting, and she describes the shock as "a trauma" that created "a freeze frame." The death of her father became her "yardstick" by which all tragedies would be measured. She graduated from high school in 1960. Most of the children who would be considered "red-diaper" babies were "raised on Woody Guthrie, Leadbelly, and Pete Seeger." Raised in an environment that considered social activism an essential ingredient of a person's consciousness, Rotolo grew up "working class, bohemian, and schooled by my Marxist parents in equality for all." She writes with tenderness about how devastated her mother was by the death of her husband. By the age of forty-seven, she had been widowed twice and "survived breast cancer." The reader senses the heartbreak and perseverance of the Italian immigrant family.

Making the most of what America had to offer was not always easy, and it was necessary for Rotolo to work several odd jobs. At the same time, she was involved with the Civil Rights movement. It was in this environment that she first met Dylan in July, 1961. She describes him as looking "oddly old-time" and "charming in a scraggly way." There was something about him that reminded her of "Harpo Marx, impish and approachable." However, she observed "something about him that broadcast an intensity that was not to be taken lightly." For the next four years, these two would become well acquainted, with Rotolo finding him "funny, engaging, intense, and he was persistent." For the author, "[t]hese words completely describe who he was throughout the time we were together; only the order of the words would shift depending on mood or circumstance."

According to Rotolo, she and Dylan had much in common, "including a mutual need for a comfortable place away from the chaos of life." Each provided a "safe haven" for the other. Nevertheless, the author also learned about how "evasive and secretive" Dylan could be, even with her. They began living together in the Village after Rotolo turned eighteen. Although he was a master storyteller, he was also a great weaver of myths, and over time his vagueness and his unwillingness to tell the truth about himself grated on Rotolo and created a divide between them. She was hurt that he had not even told her that his birth name was Robert Allen Zimmerman. When she accidentally viewed his draft card, that truth was revealed. While it was a struggle, she remained loyal to Dylan and his attempt to re-create himself. His persistence soon paid off, and he became a leading folksinger on the frothy music scene that included such performers as Dave Van Ronk, Ramblin' Jack Elliott, Odetta, Judy Collins, José Feliciano, and many more.

There was much bubbling on many creative fronts in the Village, and Rotolo uses a light hand to introduce the reader to her world. She does not overanalyze it, saying that there "were so many talented people who practiced their art form and sharpened their skills" during this amazing point of time. Some of these "talented people" made a name for themselves, while others "burned out and lost their way." Dylan finally transformed himself into the mythical figure that he so yearned to be. Along the way, some had to step out of the shadows of this myth, and in *A Freewheelin' Time*, Rotolo shows how she charted a different course.

Jeffry Jensen

Review Sources

Booklist 104, no. 16 (April 15, 2008): 16.
Interview 38, no. 3 (April, 2008): 92.
Library Journal 133, no. 6 (April 1, 2008): 85-86.
Los Angeles Times, May 15, 2008, p. E10.
The New York Times Book Review, September 7, 2008, p. 16.
The Observer, September 21, 2008, p. 26.
People 69, no. 19 (May 19, 2008): 60.
Publishers Weekly 255, no. 6 (February 11, 2008): 57.

FRIENDS OF LIBERTY
Thomas Jefferson, Tadeuscz Kościuszko, and Agrippa Hull—
A Tale of Three Patriots, Two Revolutions, and a Tragic Betrayal
of Freedom in the New Nation

Authors: Gary B. Nash (1933-   ) and Graham Russell
    Gao Hodges (1946-   )
Publisher: Basic Books (New York). 328 pp. $26.00
Type of work: History, biography
Time: The late eighteenth and early nineteenth centuries
Locale: The American colonies and the United States

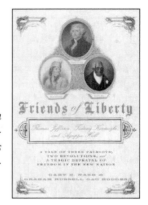

*The authors examine Kościuszko's relationships with
Jefferson and Hull, focusing on their ideas and actions regarding slavery in the early American republic, with Hull's
life providing a fascinating example of the black experience in those years*

Principal personages:
THOMAS JEFFERSON (1743-1846), president
    of the United States, 1801-1809
TADEUSCZ KOŚCIUSZKO (1746-1817), Revolutionary War officer, Polish
    patriot
AGRIPPA HULL (1759-1848), African American Revolutionary War
    soldier who served as Kościuszko's orderly

In their book *Friends of Liberty*, Gary Nash and Graham Russell Gao Hodges use
the life experience of three men to illuminate the thorny issues of slavery and race relations in the early years of the American Republic. Thomas Jefferson is familiar to
all. Tadeuscz (Thaddeus) Kościuszko is likely to be recognized only by those of Polish descent, although his bravery and devotion to freedom in the American Revolution and the 1794 Polish insurrection deserve to be celebrated. Few have heard of
Agrippa Hull, whose life history has only recently been discovered and has proved
important enough to be included, along with presidents and millionaires, in the magisterial twenty-four-volume *American National Biography* (1999). Hull is not really
part of a triumvirate; he was Kościuszko's orderly during the war, and there is no evidence he ever spoke to Jefferson. However, his biography will prove fascinating to
readers for what it reveals about African American life in rural Massachusetts during
Revolutionary and early America.

Hull, who claimed he was the son of an African prince, was born in Northampton,
Massachusetts, March 7, 1759, to free African American parents who were members
of the Congregational Church, having been admitted when theologian Jonathan Edwards was minister. Although Massachusetts did not specifically approve recruiting
African Americans until April, 1778, Hull volunteered on May 1, 1777, when word
spread that the British army, led by General John Burgoyne, was moving south from

Quebec. He was assigned as orderly to Colonel John Patterson, leader of the Berkshire County regiment, and later commanding general at Saratoga. Hull was present at Burgoyne's surrender at Saratoga, a scene he proudly described to the youth of Stockbridge for the rest of his life.

Kościuszko, a younger son of not very prosperous minor Polish nobility who lived off the labor of their serfs, turned to the military for a career. After graduating from the Royal Military Academy, he was sent to France in 1768 to study military engineering. Strongly influenced by Jean-Jacques Rousseau, Kościuszko openly criticized serfdom and slavery, and he became a deist. A failed love affair led to his departure from Poland in 1775.

∼

Gary B. Nash is professor emeritus of history at the University of California, Los Angeles, and the author of two dozen books dealing with early American history and the history of African Americans. He was president of the Organization of American Historians in 1994-1995. Graham Russell Gao Hodges is George Dorland Langdon, Jr., Professor of History at Colgate University and author of Root and Branch: African Americans in New York and East Jersey, 1613-1863 *(1999).*

∼

The following year Kościuszko decided to join the American Revolution, and in October he received a colonel's commission as an engineering officer charged with building fortifications. Nash and Hodges would like to date Kościuszko's friendship with Jefferson to 1776, but the best they can assert is that the two might have met while Kościuszko was in Philadelphia, although there is no record of any encounter until much later.

The authors note that Jefferson, despite being a substantial slave owner, strongly supported antislavery positions in his Declaration of Independence and in his draft constitution for Virginia, which banned further importation of slaves, which he expected would cause the institution to wither. When serving on a committee to revise the laws of Virginia, Jefferson tried and failed to include a provision freeing at age twenty-one all slaves born after passage of the law. As the book progresses, the authors contrast Jefferson's early statements with his failure to free his own slaves.

During the Saratoga campaign, Hull met Kościuszko, the military engineer responsible for building the defenses at Bemis Hill that stopped Burgoyne. When Patterson and Kościuszko were charged with fortifying and defending West Point, Hull went with them. After serving as Patterson's orderly for two years, he switched to Kościuszko in May, 1779, for the next fifty months. A favorite Hull anecdote concerned the time at West Point when Kościuszko returned unexpectedly to find Hull dressed in the colonel's uniform, leading a lively party of enlisted men; to Hull's relief, Kościuszko was amused and joined the festivities. When Kościuszko went south to serve with American forces there, Hull accompanied him. His experiences as a surgeon's assistant after the 1781 Battle of Eutaw Springs provided Hull with grisly anecdotes of holding down wounded soldiers while doctors operated without benefit of anesthesia.

Hull was mustered out of service at West Point on July 23, 1783, his treasured honorable discharge signed by George Washington. Hull worked odd jobs and served as occasional butler for Theodore Sedgwick. Lawyer Sedgwick successfully defended an African American woman against attempts by her former owner to claim her services, asserting that she had been freed by the newly enacted Massachusetts constitution, which effectively ended slavery in the state. Hull and his new wife moved with Sedgwick to Stockbridge, Massachusetts, where Hull bought a half-acre of land in 1784. He continued to acquire land, and by 1792 he owned about eleven acres, sufficient to meet the property requirement for voting in Massachusetts. Exactly how Hull managed to save the funds for the purchases at a time when many white veterans were unable to afford buying land is unclear.

Memoirs of Stockbridge residents and visitors such as Francis Parkman describe Hull as a respected citizen of the town. His wartime anecdotes made him a favorite of young boys; no wedding was complete without the presence of the African American patriarch. Hull slowly increased his property holdings. He was always first among black families on Stockbridge's assessment rolls, ranking above one-third of white property owners. When Hull died on May 21, 1848, he left his wife and children a home lot and house, twenty-eight acres of land, and personal property worth $167.50.

In 1783 Congress promised Kościuszko a five-hundred-acre tract in the Northwest Territory and agreed to reimburse his back pay of $12,280, with interest, when it had money. Kościuszko returned to Poland in September, 1784, for the next four years acting as a small Polish landlord, living off the labor of his serfs. When reform movements stimulated by the American and French revolutions shook Poland, Kościuszko was called to service in 1789 and commissioned a major general. His delaying actions when the Russian army invaded Poland in 1792 made Kościuszko a national hero, even though he could not prevent the Russians from occupying the country. After failing to interest French revolutionaries in helping Poland, Kościuszko returned to his country in March, 1794, calling for an insurrection against the occupiers and assuming the role of army commander-in-chief. In April Kościuszko's forces defeated a numerically and technically superior Russian army near Kraków, but the combined Russian and Prussian forces were too much for Kościuszko, whose army lost to them in June. He was badly wounded, captured, and confined to a St. Peterburg prison. Polish historians note that Kościuszko's May 7, 1794, proclamation partially abolishing serfdom and granting civil liberties to peasants was the first time in Polish history that peasants were officially regarded as part of the nation, a status previously reserved for nobility.

After Czar Paul succeeded Catherine the Great in 1796, he freed Kościuszko, granting him an estate with fifteen hundred peasants attached to the land. Despite his detestation of serfdom, Kościuszko could not refuse the gift without insulting the czar. He placed his sisters in charge of land and serfs and departed for the United States, arriving in Philadelphia to a hero's welcome on August 17, 1797. Kościuszko slowly recovered from his wounds, which had festered during his imprisonment. Congress issued him a land warrant for five hundred acres in Ohio and awarded him back pay for service during the Revolutionary War that, with interest, amounted to $18,912.

Kościuszko and Vice President Thomas Jefferson were united by their favorable view of the French Revolution. When Kościuszko wanted to return secretly to Europe to try to convince the French to help free Poland, Jefferson arranged for him to get an American passport under a false name. Jefferson helped Kościuszko draft a will regarding the money he planned to leave in the United States and agreed to act as executor of the will, which directed him to use funds remaining at Kościuszko's death to free as many slaves, either his own or those of other owners, as the money would cover, to educate them and to establish the freemen on their own land. The main thrust of Nash and Hodges's book (which is the substance of the subtitle's claim of a "tragic betrayal") is their condemnation of Jefferson for failing to carry out Kościuszko's intentions.

Readers need to turn to volume two of Miecislaus Haiman's biography of Kościuszko to discover how scrupulously Jefferson and his private banker, who invested the money in bank shares and Treasury bonds, carried out their fiduciary duties. The approximately twelve thousand dollars Kościuszko left in their care regularly produced about a thousand dollars a year in interest, which a Baltimore merchant agreed to transmit without charge. This money was Kościuszko's main support during the rest of his life, successfully reaching him in Europe despite the disruptions of the Napoleonic Wars and the War of 1812. At his death, the carefully invested fund had increased to $17,099.

Jefferson declined to act as executor under the will, claiming he was too old to undertake the complexities of the task. Nash and Hodges are contemptuous of his excuses, and they seem particularly incensed that seventy-four-year-old Jefferson devoted his remaining energies to pursuing his cherished idea of founding a university for Virginia rather than enforce Kościuszko's will. This well-written, informative book is disfigured by the authors' frequent attempts to denigrate Jefferson's motives. They note that when the Haitian rebellion against France occurred, Jefferson's duty as secretary of state was to maintain favorable relations with France, but then the authors criticize him for not praising the rebellious slaves. When Congress failed to act on a petition to revoke the 1793 Fugitive Slave Act, they gratuitously suggest Jefferson may not have regretted Congress's inaction, even though they present no evidence to support their assertion, since Jefferson never mentioned the petition, either publicly or privately. When Jefferson did not comment on South Carolina's 1803 attempt to reopen the slave trade, the authors accuse him of tacit support of slavery.

Nash and Hodges reject the excuse that freeing slaves was too difficult for Jefferson to undertake, citing one of Jefferson's Randolph cousins who did free his slaves in his will. Their account of what happened supports Jefferson more than the authors'. The widow did her best to carry out her husband's wishes, but debts and mortgages forced sale of most slaves. She managed to free only five bondsmen. After discovering that freeing slaves, educating them, and settling them on land in Virginia violated the laws of the state, the executor appointed to replace Jefferson tried to use the funds to support a school for free blacks in Maryland, but this, too, was blocked.

The final complication was a claim by the children of Kościuszko's two sisters that they were entitled to all of his assets by the provisions of Kościuszko's April 2, 1817, will, leaving his Polish property to them, with instructions to finally free his serfs. The issue was fought through the federal courts for three decades before being decided in 1852 by the Supreme Court of the United States. Although the court recognized that Kościuszko intended to have his American estate used to benefit African Americans, it ruled that the provisions of his European will legally voided the one Jefferson held; therefore Kościuszko's nieces were entitled to his American estate, by then worth nearly fifty thousand dollars.

This was indeed a tragic outcome for Kościuszko's good intentions, but it was certainly not one Jefferson intended, and it could only be called a betrayal by imputing the worst motives to Jefferson.

Milton Berman

Review Sources

Booklist 104, no. 13 (March 1, 2008): 45.
The Boston Globe, April 8, 2008, p. E4.
Entertainment Weekly, March 28, 2008, p. 69.
Kirkus Reviews 76, no. 2 (January 15, 2008): 80.
The New York Review of Books 55, no. 11 (June 26, 2008): 46-48.
Publishers Weekly 255, no. 2 (January 14, 2008): 47.

THE FRUIT HUNTERS
A Story of Nature, Adventure, Commerce, and Obsession

Author: Adam Leith Gollner (1976-   )
Publisher: Scribner (New York). 280 pp. $25.00
Type of work: Natural history, travel

Gollner travels around the world in search of exotic fruits largely unknown in North America, and explores the scientific, historical and sociological origins of fruits and of humans' obsession with them

At the center of Adam Leith Gollner's *The Fruit Hunters: A Story of Nature, Adventure, Commerce, and Obsession* lies a strange truth: although there are tens of thousands of edible and delicious fruits growing around the world, the relatively wealthy and sophisticated grocery shopper in North America typically returns again and again to the same twenty or thirty. Worldwide, according to the United Nations, the most widely consumed fruits are bananas and plantains, apples, citrus fruits, grapes, and mangoes—foods that, save perhaps for the mangoes, would not alarm the most incurious and conservative eater. What of more exotic fare? People in the developed world eat mountains of strawberries, but what about the "crackleberry, whimberry, bababerry, bearberry, salmonberry, raccoon berry, rockberry, honeyberry, nannyberry, white snowberry and berryberry"? As a self-avowed fruit obsessive, Gollner attempts in this book to describe his pursuit of the world's tastiest and most legendary fruits, and of the men— they are mostly men—who grow, smuggle, trade, graft, sell, and market them.

Like Walt Whitman's poetry, *The Fruit Hunters* is full of lists, bits of trivia, short anecdotes, and an earthy fascination with sex. There is no central narrative arc. Instead, the book reads like an accumulation of facts and ideas acquired here and there, at this time and that, with subtle repeated threads that might signal authorial control or something more fascinating: the slightly untamable mind of the true fruit obsessive. To bring some order to this material salad, Gollner has organized the volume into four sections—"Nature," "Adventure," "Commerce," and "Obsession"—though each section borrows freely from the others. The result is a cheerful, energetic account.

"Nature" introduces, among countless other things, two fruits that will stand in this book as emblems for what Gollner's readers are missing: the mangosteen and the durian. Gollner finds his first mangosteen, "known as the queen of fruits in Southeast Asia," in the Chinatown section of Montreal, and it quickly becomes one of his favorites. As he will do throughout the book, he struggles to describe its taste: "I could say that it tastes like minty raspberry-apricot sorbet, but the only way to truly know a mangosteen is to try one." Although mangosteens are commonly available in Chinese markets in Canada, Gollner learns only after he has brought an assortment of Chinatown fruits as a gift for a friend in New York that they are illegal in the United States.

〜
*Adam Leith Gollner has written about
food for* The New York Times, Orion,
Gourmet, *and* Bon Appetit. *An
accomplished musician, he is a member
of a Canada-based synth punk trio. He
lives in Montreal and Los Angeles.
Gollner won the McAuslan First Book
Prize from the Quebec Writers'
Federation for* The Fruit Hunters.
〜

As Gollner and the reader will learn, several fruits are illegal to import; many of the laws have to do with transporting pests but many others have only political and commercial origins, and smuggling fruit is big business.

The durian is introduced in "Nature," but its full story is not told until the second section, "Adventure." Although its flesh is sweet and delicious, the fruit emits a strong odor that "has been compared to rotting fish, stale vomit, unwashed socks, old jockstraps, low-tide seaweed," and other equally appealing things. The smell is so strong that when Gollner and a friend hosted a durian-tasting party in a New York apartment building, other tenants evacuated and called the gas company. No wonder durians are banned in many public spaces throughout Asia. In the most extended narrative in the book, Gollner travels to Borneo to sample the twenty-seven species of durian that grow there, and he finds a fruit-lover's paradise, with an assortment of obsessed fruit hunters, including the botanist Voon Boon Hoe. The author discovers that trekking through the jungle to find fruit is less effective than visiting a village market at the edge of the jungle; at one visit to a market in Kuching, he eats "dukus, rambutans, soursops, mangosteens, and durians." Gollner next travels to Bangkok on his way to the islands in southern Thailand where he meets a group of raw foodists—people who consume only raw fruit and raw meats—living idyllically in bungalows on the beach on the island of Koh Phangan. Next he visits a community of fruitarians, who eat only fruit, and digresses to offer a survey of the history, religious symbolism, nutrition, and botany of fruit.

Gollner's next quest is for the legendary "lady fruit," whose shell looks remarkably like the female anatomy and which is said to be the "fruit from which women originate." Researching in Montreal, Gollner learns that the fruit is actually named the coco-de-mer, that it is endangered, and that it grows only in the Seychelles. His journey to the valley where the coco-de-mer palms grow, his furtive attempts to taste the protected fruit, and his guilty smuggling of one of the fruits past the customs agents back in Canada make for one the liveliest and most entertaining parts of the book.

The section on "Commerce" focuses on the people who discover, grow, manipulate, modify, ship, and market the fruits that are available commercially. Gollner tells the story of the Ichang gooseberry from New Zealand, which did not sell well in North America until it was renamed the kiwi. He introduces Gary Snyder, inventor of the grapple, an apple that tastes like a grape, and Myra Gordon, executive director of the wholesale fruit market at Hunts Point, New York. He explains why most fruit at the grocery store tastes like cardboard: because it is picked unripe, shipped long distances, waxed, gassed, and manhandled.

The last section, "Obsession," describes people who have rejected overprocessed cardboard grocery-store fruit in favor of fresh, locally grown diverse varieties—the fruit hunters. After discussing pesticides and legal wrangling, Gollner ends his book on an exuberant note with stories about groups such as the Seed Savers and Renewing America's Food Traditions and people such as Stephen Wood, whose Poverty Lane Orchard in New Hampshire produces heritage apples, and Hugh Daubeny, who has bred new fruit varieties including the Tulameen raspberry. Gollner's message in this section is clear: It is not necessarily ancient fruit that he values, but delicious fruit, and not one fruit but the wide, awe-inspiring variety.

The Fruit Hunters resembles Susan Orlean's *The Orchid Thief: A True Story of Beauty and Obsession* (1998) and Eric Hansen's *Orchid Fever: A Horticultural Tale of Love, Lust, and Lunacy* (2000). All three feature strong narrative voices, plucky narrators traveling to out-of-the-way locations in pursuit of exotic plants, and a cast of quirky, obsessed characters, interwoven with passages of history and natural history. Where Orlean presents John Laroche and his pursuit of the elusive ghost orchid, and Hansen describes orchid smuggler Henry Azadehdel, Gollner tells the tale of his dog-ged attempts to interview David Karp, also known as the Fruit Detective. Karp appears and reappears through the book, often unable to honor the author's request for an interview but able to suggest another interesting fruit fancier with another unusual fruit. Whether due to their own personalities or to Gollner's struggles to capture them, the oddball characters in *The Fruit Hunters* are never quite as vibrantly humorous as those Orlean and Hansen describe. When, after more than two hundred pages of wish-ing, Gollner finally obtains his interview in chapter 14, Karp seems more interested in his ego than in talking about fruit, and Gollner spends much of the chapter describing a dinner party during which no interview occurs. In the end, the book devotes less than four full pages to the day Gollner spends with Karp at home and in the field, and the eccentric Fruit Detective never leaps off the page in full-blown wackiness the way Laroche and Azadehdel do.

At times, scenes that might have been intriguingly weird turn into near-misses be-cause Gollner chooses not to develop them further. In chapter 15, the author and his friend Liane visit the Children of Light, a dwindling group of "immortals" who live in the California desert eating only fruit and waiting for the apocalypse. Again, the book gives only a few pages to these fascinating people, and the few quotations from Elder Philip and Elect Star make one long for more. Gollner reports that "the Children of Light write their own kindergarten-like hymns," but although he and Liane join in the singing he does not quote any lyrics. When, on the way home from the compound, the couple notice "an enormous fire . . . raging near the compound," they do not turn back to investigate or to help because they are "too freaked out." Instead, Gollner keeps driving, although he calls on his cell phone to make sure everyone is safe.

The Fruit Hunters, intentionally or not, becomes part of a dialogue with several other food books published around the same time: Michael Pollan's *The Omnivore's Dilemma: A Natural History of Four Meals* (2006) and *In Defense of Food: An Eater's Manifesto* (2008), Bill McKibben's *Deep Economy: The Wealth of Commu-nities and the Durable Future* (2007), and Barbara Kingsolver's *Animal, Vegetable, Miracle: A Year of Food Life* (2007) come immediately to mind. Gollner seems glee-fully unconcerned about the social and environmental costs of transporting fruit thou-sands of miles or of traveling thousands of miles to taste exotic fruits, making the implicit argument that the chance to taste these fruits is worth any price. While *The Fruit Hunters* might have made a reasoned argument that fruit tourism is harmless or even a force for good, it instead sidesteps the issue almost entirely. Gollner makes a nod to eating seasonally and locally, noting "the importance of cultivating a relationship with someone working in a quality fruit store, ideally someone who sources local fruits." Nevertheless, many of the fruits he eats—only at their peak—are imported from Spain, China, South America, or other distant lands. One wonders whether McKibben would throw up his hands in surrender at his first taste of mangosteen, or whether he would insist that for the common good some individual pleasures must be forsaken.

Gollner does take up the issues of genetic modification, crop diversity, pesticide and fertilizer use, and migrant workers in a chapter titled "Mass Production: The Geopolitics of Sweetness." Here, he demonstrates his strength as a reporter to succinctly present complex stories, as he describes a late-night act of ecoterrorism at a strawberry farm, the history of the modern banana, and the Bhopal chemical disaster in clear, sure prose.

The Fruit Hunters is Gollner's first book, and it is sadly marked by infelicities of style that one might have expected experienced editors to smooth over. The author alternates between a clipped newspaper style and sentences such as: "Penultimate ripeness, when the finicky ethers reach organoleptic gold, when acids and sugars reach the ague of their imbroglio, is fleeting." Misuse of the word "penultimate" aside, Gollner is faced with a difficult challenge in trying to capture exotic tastes in exotic words, and often his descriptions, such as this one, are merely bewildering. The text contains enough dangling modifiers ("Known as the queen of fruits in Southeast Asia, its hard, purplish and ocher shell . . . "; "Arriving at the interrogation booth, the customs agent glances at my form . . . ") and misspellings ("Witchita"; "Beaurocracy") to weaken the authority Gollner establishes with his thorough and wide-ranging research.

Still, it is an exciting first book. Gollner has shown an inquisitiveness and a willingness to get out of the library and into the rainforest in search of information, and his young and enthusiastic voice will serve him—and his readers—very well, whatever his next project should be.

Cynthia A. Bily

Review Sources

Booklist 104, no. 15 (April 1, 2008): 15.
Entertainment Weekly, May 30, 2008, p. 91.
Kirkus Reviews 76, no. 6 (March 15, 2008): 284-285.
The Gazette (Montreal), May 31, 2008, p. I3.
The New York Times Book Review, June 1, 2008, p. L10.
Publishers Weekly 255, no. 7 (February 18, 2008): 143.

GERARD MANLEY HOPKINS
A Life

Author: Paul Mariani (1940-   )
Publisher: Viking (New York). 496 pp. $32.95
Type of work: Literary biography
Time: 1844-1889
Locale: England and Dublin, Ireland

Mariani's critical biography examines the literary and religious commitments that led Hopkins to his extraordinary poetics and to his insistence on the efficacy of God's love

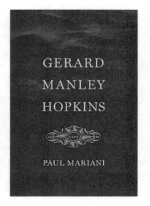

Principal personages:
GERARD MANLEY HOPKINS, poet-priest whose nineteenth century works of innovative and devout poetry have greatly influenced modern poets
ROBERT BRIDGES, lifelong friend and confidant of Hopkins who saw to the posthumous publication of his poetry
JOHN HENRY NEWMAN, leader of a movement to reinstate Roman Catholic beliefs in Anglican worship who later converted to Catholicism and attained the rank of Cardinal
IGNATIUS LOYOLA, founder of the Society of Jesus (Jesuit) order and author of *Religious Exercises* (1522-1524)

In a review of Robert Bernard Martin's *Gerard Manley Hopkins: A Very Private Life* (1991), Paul Mariani—a practicing Catholic and a poet himself—called for a biography that would uncover Hopkins's true inspiration for writing "some of the most powerful poetry of the last two centuries": his love of God. Such a biography would "take into account Hopkins's mature life . . . the entire twenty years Hopkins spent as a Jesuit" and reveal a man "shaped by his intense indwelling," that is, his inner quest to remain faithful to Christ.

In *Gerard Manley Hopkins: A Life*, Mariani has now written that biography. His text begins with Hopkins's youthful conversion to Catholicism, assesses the consequences of his decision to leave the Anglican fold, and goes on to cover his years as a Jesuit priest. Within this framework, Mariani describes the origins of Hopkins's groundbreaking poetry, with its unique rhythms and unparalleled intensity. His work offers Hopkins scholars and readers, who have long relied on Mariani's *Commentary on the Complete Poems of Gerard Manley Hopkins* (1970), a full version of the poet-priest's adult life.

The Hopkins biography is constructed in four sections. The first, "We Are So Grafted on His Wood: 1844-1868," quotes the last line of "Barnfloor and Winepress," a poem celebrating the great Eucharistic sacrifice made by Christ. As Mariani interprets

～
Paul Mariani is an award-winning poet and biographer who has written the lives of poets William Carlos Williams, John Berryman, Robert Lowell, and Hart Crane. He is a professor of English at Boston College.
～

the line, it describes the strength of Hopkins's early commitment to Christianity: "He has seen something, he confesses, has seen into the magnificent mystery of God's love for him and for millions of others like and unlike himself." In the same manner, Mariani's chapter titles stress Hopkins's religious convictions.

The first two chapters, "In the Breaking of the Bread: Horsham & Home, 1866, and the Early Years" and "The Dense and Driven Passion: Oxford & Hampstead, 1866," substantiate the vital importance of Hopkins's conversion. After several years of intense soul-searching, the youth became a Catholic while still a student at Oxford University. His philosophical studies and the influences of professors, tutors, and colleagues led him to believe that the Anglicans had failed to follow the true teachings of Christ. Anglican theorists considered the Eucharistic ceremony to be symbolic rather than a manifestation of God's actual presence, a position that Hopkins strongly rejected. Without an acknowledgement of God-incarnate in the bread and wine, any observance of Christianity inevitably lacked logical depth and spiritual enlightenment.

After his conversion, Hopkins graduated from Oxford with highest honors, receiving two "firsts" in his field, Classical Greats; however, as a Roman Catholic, he was given no preferential recognition or even acceptance by his countrymen. Animosity between Anglicans and Catholics, originating during the fifteenth century reign of King Henry VIII, continued to relegate English Catholics to the fringes of mainstream society. In these circumstances, Hopkins's family believed that their oldest son had made a grave mistake and found further cause for grief in his decision to become a Jesuit. Hopkins's Catholicism disqualified him from partaking of Anglican sacraments with his family, and in a heartbreaking letter his mother asked if he were truly lost to her. After the influential John Henry Newman received Hopkins into the Catholic faith in 1866, the young convert expressed feelings of peace and joy, emotions that encouraged him to study theology and enter the priesthood.

In consenting to God's call to priesthood, Hopkins gave up personal control of his future in hopes of experiencing a vigorous and joyful spiritual life. He believed that his acceptance of the Jesuit vows of poverty, chastity, and obedience would create an opportunity to strengthen his indifference to worldly concerns, a principal goal of the order. Church leaders would now determine where he would live and what he would do, freeing him to focus on his inner struggle to emulate the life of Christ. With this priority in mind, he burned his finished poems and set aside all plans to write more, although his journals reflect an ongoing philosophical quest to formulate satisfactory views on the nature of reality and the role of language in human perception. These core interests grew as the years passed and emerged when he returned to writing poetry.

Part II of Mariani's biography, "Walls, Altar and Hour and Night: 1868-1877," follows Hopkins as he studies theology and performs the duties of a priest in training. As a novice, and periodically thereafter, he participated in the spiritual exercises prescribed by Society of Jesus founder Ignatius Loyola, who envisioned a corps of religious militants performing apostolic, missionary work. Loyola compared spiritual exercises—ones including frequent silent retreats filled with meditation and prayer—to physical exercises, activities designed to incorporate the entire being.

Hopkins contemplated such topics as God's creation, sin, the life of Christ, correct attitudes toward worldly possessions, humility, the Crucifixion, the Resurrection, and Godly love. He viewed redemption and salvation as the only worthy goals in life. As Mariani explains, Hopkins's devotion required "kenosis," an act of self-emptying, and the omission of personal concerns in order to emulate Christ on the cross. On the other hand, Hopkins refused to compromise his cherished belief that words held inspirational meaning that could be understood through reason and contemplation.

After two years as a novice and his first set of vows in the priesthood, Hopkins was sent to the college of Stonyhurst as a scholastic to continue his academic training. There, in 1872, he discovered the work of John Duns Scotus, a medieval Franciscan who asserted that God's constant renewal of the world could be seen in each human, tree, flower, and so on. This philosophy supported Hopkins's Platonic views on the individuation of things, often poignantly expressed as delight in God's presence in the beauty of art and nature. The poet referred to this presence as "instress," existence as opposed to nonexistence, a quality of "Being" that could inspire if only humans would look beyond the mundane aspects of life. The poem "God's Grandeur," written in 1877, depicts the "dearest freshness deep down things" and describes the "Holy Ghost over the bent/ World broods with warm breast and with ah! bright wings." The forms assumed by instress provided "inscape," a contour somewhat similar to a landscape that Hopkins used to shape his poems.

After nearly a decade had passed, Hopkins took up writing poetry again in the winter of 1875 when the rector of St. Beuno's seminary suggested that he compose a tribute to five nuns who had recently died in a shipwreck. Prior to their deaths, they had been ejected from Germany under the provisions of the anti-Catholic Falck laws. Unfortunately, the editor of the foremost Jesuit publication rejected "The Wreck of the Deutschland," and Hopkins's poetic talent remained practically irrelevant to his career as a priest. An 1877 failure to win approval for a fourth and final year of theology study meant that he would never attain "Professed" standing and would instead be relegated to the lower rank of "Spiritual Coadjutor," one unqualified for advancement.

In spite of Hopkins's intellectual brilliance and great popularity with other students, his propensity for argument and his "somewhat obstinate love of Scotist doctrine" had been evaluated as out of step with current Jesuit theology. Hopkins's predisposition to go his own way in spite of well-meaning advice caused Jesuit superiors to doubt his usefulness to the order. His poor health and lack of aptitude for administration may also have persuaded them to end his seminary training. Even so, Hopkins composed several outstanding sonnets, including "The Windhover" and "Pied Beauty," during this period.

In parts III and IV, "In Harness: 1877-1884" and "Dublin: 1884-1889," Mariani chronicles Hopkins's inner struggle and describes his frequent bouts of physical exhaustion as he cycles through the church calendar with its numerous Biblical ceremonies, maintains his devotional exercises, and works at ministering, preaching, and teaching. Although Hopkins's sense of duty compelled diligence, he could not seem to fit in and was often moved with little warning. Eventually he received a seemingly prestigious teaching appointment as Fellow of University College in Dublin. However, the school proved to be small and dilapidated. In addition, the Irish campaign for home rule increased the intolerance, religious and otherwise, directed at Hopkins as an Englishman and former Anglican. The great poverty and suffering of Dubliners added to Hopkins's emotional burden and increased his longing to serve elsewhere.

Hopkins soon faltered under the heavy workload he had been assigned, and he suffered a further decline in physical and mental health. His despair led him to write sonnets of deep desolation, although readers familiar with Ignatian spirituality cite an overall pattern of trial and redemption in the poems. Mariani, who attended a thirty-day Jesuit retreat before writing the biography in order to heighten his awareness of Hopkins's situation, depicts the poet-priest's psychological state in his last years with compassion and insight.

Almost all of Hopkins's poetry remained unpublished at the time of his death in 1889 because editors invariably viewed them as odd and unappealing. His preference for "sprung rhythm" (scanning by accents rather than syllables) and other curious techniques troubled them. Hopkins believed that rhythm was generally misunderstood in his day, and he worked tirelessly to reconstitute the language in his poems, drawing on Welsh, Shakespearean, and even Anglo-Saxon influences. He recommended reading the poems aloud to show the speech patterns and nursery rhythms that he believed replicated the instress of God's ongoing re-creation of the world. Even his life-long friend Robert Bridges (who would later become poet laureate) repeatedly expressed frustration with Hopkins's strange style. Nevertheless, Bridges collected Hopkins's poems and saw to their publication in 1918, almost thirty years after their author's death. Since then several of Hopkins's poems have been cited as being among the best in the English language, and his collected works have greatly influenced later poets such as John Berryman and Hart Crane.

Throughout his biography, Mariani details his critical analysis of Hopkins's poetry and affirms his respect for Hopkins's accomplishments as a priest using a day-to-day, month-to-month construct. He deftly weaves together quotations from Hopkins's journals, sermons, poetry, and correspondence, supplementing and extending passages with paraphrases that frequently echo Hopkins's own style. Early drafts of poems and journal entries present Hopkins's sources of inspiration, and Mariani connects those life experiences to later poems by placing quotations from finished works nearby. These interpolations tend to break up the chronology of the narrative, and while some readers may find these movements back and forth in time distracting, the result is a work of dynamic intensity. *Gerard Manley Hopkins: A Life* concludes with comprehensive documentation and a selected bibliography.

Margaret A. Koger

Review Sources

America 199, no. 16 (November 17, 2008): 22-24.
Booklist 105, no. 4 (October 15, 2008): 12.
Kirkus Reviews 76, no. 16 (August 15, 2008): 64.
Library Journal 133, no. 16 (October 1, 2008): 70.
Publishers Weekly 255, no. 37 (September 15, 2008): 56.
The Washington Post Book World, November 2, 2008, p. BW10.

THE GHOST IN LOVE

Author: Jonathan Carroll (1949-   )
Publisher: Farrar, Straus and Giroux (New York).
   308 pp. $25.00
Type of work: Novel
Time: The present day
Locale: A quiet city, somewhere on the East Coast

When Benjamin Gould refuses to die at his appointed time, he takes control of his own destiny with all of its idiosyncrasies

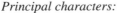

Principal characters:
> BENJAMIN GOULD, a young man who
>   chooses his own destiny
> GERMAN LANDIS, his former girlfriend who
>   gets pulled into Ben's insanity
> PILOT, Ben's late girlfriend reincarnated and brought back into his life
> LING, the part of Ben that is a ghost and is in love with German
> STANLEY, the Angel of Death
> STEWART PARRISH, the worst part of Ben personified and sent to stop his
>   self-discovery
> DANIELLE VOYLES, a young woman who has also missed her appointed
>   time to die

   A talking dog, a lesbian ghost, the angel of death, and a host of personified character traits are just a handful of the quirky characters in Jonathan Carroll's surreal fantasy novel *The Ghost in Love*. This is Carroll's sixteenth fantasy novel in a career that began with the publication of *The Land of Laughs* (2001). As in many of his other works, there is a connection to a fantasy world and to an exploration of the consequences of human actions.

   The story starts with the ghost preparing a gourmet meal for the woman she loves. Looking on and conversing with the ghost while she cooks is the dog. In a flashback, readers find out that Ling, the first of Ben Gould's personified emotions readers meet, appears when Ben, on the way home from the animal shelter where he has chosen a pet for his new girlfriend, slips on the ice and hits his head. At the moment when Ben should have died, Pilot, his new dog, sees a ghost appear across the street. Ling is that ghost. She has been told by the Angel of Death that there has been a computer glitch in heaven, and she has been assigned to watch over Ben since he did not die at his appointed time and heaven is not sure what will happen to him as a result. This begins the questioning of fate and of who is ultimately in control of human destiny: individual humans or a higher power. At the point when Ben chooses to survive, he embarks on a journey of self-discovery that will lead him to understand who he, German, and even Pilot really are.

Ling is the part of Ben that is a ghost. According to the novel, it is the ghost's job to take care of unfinished business. The nature of Ben's unfinished business becomes confused as the novel progresses. At the beginning of the novel, when German arrives to pick up Pilot for her weekend of custody, it would seem that Ben's purpose is to understand why he has lost the love of his life. Though Ling is part of his unconscious, she does not really comprehend how he was stupid enough to have destroyed the relationship. German also deals with the issue, and throughout the novel all three mourn the loss of the relationship.

~

Jonathan Carroll has written fourteen novels, including The Wooden Sea, *a* 2001 New York Times *Notable Book. A former English teacher, Carroll now writes full time at his home in Vienna, Austria. The impact of Carroll's writing has been compared to that of C. S. Lewis.*

~

In trying to understand what has happened to set his life spinning out of control, Ben goes on a journey of self-discovery. This quest begins with his near death experience, and it continues as Ben realizes he is sharing the experiences of Danielle Voyles, a young woman who has also survived an accident that should have left her dead. An inability to understand why he is able to see what Danielle sees, to taste what she eats, and to read her thoughts scares Ben into bizarre behaviors that eventually drive German away. In trying to win German back, Ben decides to share with her what is happening to him. He takes her to Danielle's apartment, where it is revealed that though Ben can see Danielle, she cannot see him. He is invisible to Danielle. Thinking that Ben and Danielle are putting on an act, German angrily flees the scene. As the story progresses, German and Danielle connect in a strange way, and Danielle becomes one of Ben's guides on his journey. No quest is complete without a nemesis, and Ben's foil is Stewart Parrish. Stewart first appears in a pizza parlor where Ben and German are having dinner. At the table next to the couple sit the angel of death and Ling the ghost in human form. Parrish wanders into the restaurant in the guise of a homeless bum. In a series of confusing events, Stewart eventually stabs the angel of death, almost killing him. Stewart does not appear again for several chapters. When he does reappear, it is at a point in Ben's past where Ben and Ling have gone in search of security.

During this trip back in time, Ben realizes his childhood love, Gina Kyte, was a shrill, bossy little girl rather than the sweet child he remembered. Remembering the reality of that young friendship shows Ben that he has built his life around an illusion. This discovery spurs an aggressive mission to stop Ben from learning more about himself, and Stewart appears in Ben's past to stop his evolution. As the novel moves back to the present, Ben learns more about himself and begins to evaluate his personality. By the end of the novel, Ben has discovered that though he is ultimately in control of his destiny and of his life, some aspects of his own personality do not want him to be the boss of his future.

In one of the final chapters, Ben, German, and Pilot struggle with his worst character traits come to life. He is unable to win this fight on his own, so German takes control of her own destiny and calls up the parts of her own personality that love Ben in order to protect him. The mishmash of resulting characters causes a public ruckus that is both confusing and humorous. The novel concludes with the beginning of the journey of the rest of Ben's life, which strangely enough commences with a food fight in a grocery store.

In the journey motif, Carroll offers the novel's strongest thematic issue: what happens to a person after death. The novel challenges traditional views of heaven, fate, and reincarnation. Heaven, in Carroll's world, is not functioning correctly, so therefore God is not infallible. For example, when Ling is informed that she needs to watch over Ben because of the computer virus in heaven, she does. However, since she really has very little power over him, and he does not even recognize that he has a ghost to guard him, this relationship is useless at best until he starts to realize that he is different from most people. Later on in the novel, Ling is told that her computer virus was a lie, a definite contradiction to the infallibility of God; instead, Ben, like a number of other people around the world, has just taken control of his own fate by refusing to die. In doing so, Ben undermines the idea that a person's life is predestined and that there is a specific time to live and to die. Further confusing the issues of fate and destiny, Ben is able to travel through time in such a way that he could have changed his future. Throughout the novel, Ben has the ability to personify both his best and his worst personality traits in walking, talking, functioning beings, which also complicates identity in relation to the idea of a predestined personal narrative. Finally, Carroll confronts reincarnation with Pilot, Ben's dog. Once Pilot is able to communicate with Ben, he reveals that he is the reincarnation of Ben's former girlfriend, a girl who died when she fell off the motor scooter that Ben was driving when he lived in Italy. Contrary to expectation, as Pilot is threatened to be reincarnated again as a human, Ben is horrified. Humanity is, to him, a step down from canine life. Carroll's ability to treat these complicated and serious issues with humor and irony stimulates more questions than concerns, encouraging readers to consider their own beliefs about life.

Irony is a constant source of humor and of challenge in the novel. The death experiences that Ben and Danielle reject are one example. Ben should have died while taking home his first major gift to German. This should have been the start of the best relationship he would ever have. Instead, his relationship begins its decline, and his refusal to die leads to the temporary death of his romance. Danielle also refuses to die, but when she discovers that she can choose to live in the place where she was happiest, she essentially decides to live in the past, literally. She withdraws from life to remain in a moment in her past, and she only returns to life to help Ben save himself. When that has been accomplished, she disappears into that simple moment in her past. The humorous personification of Ben's and German's emotions and their subsequent battle in very public venues is another instance of irony in the novel. Just at the point when Ben thinks there may be some hope for his romance, an army of his worst personality traits attacks. He finds out that every negative thing he had ever thought had come to life and was willing to fight to stay alive. Anger, frustration, violence, and hatred were just a few of the emotions who appeared in human form to thwart Ben's dawning comprehension that he controls his own destiny. The irony continues as German is able to bring to life all the aspects of Ben that she loves to help thwart the attack. Ironically, the conclusion is that Ben, Danielle, and German can choose their own fates, but in charting their own destinies, they affect everyone around them. Parts of Ben want to harm German, while German can call up the elements of his personality that she loves to save both of them. For Danielle, her choice to retreat to that past moment of happiness affects the other people in her apartment building, allowing them to live eternally in their moments of ultimate joy.

Ultimately, Carroll is posing a question: What would happen if humans had to take responsibility for their own emotions, behaviors, and destinies? If Ben can accept that he is accountable for his life rather than some outside force, then other people who have refused to die will also have to be accountable for their own actions. This might start an uproar in members of the human race who too often want to blame someone else for their foibles and faults.

Although it is often eclipsed in the shadow of Carroll's fantasy of a changed world, the love story should not be ignored. Ben is in love with German, and she loves him. Ling's mad obsession with German is a reflection of the depth of Ben's feelings. The choice of a female ghost to represent the strongest part of Ben's love for German is one that challenges the gender of that emotion. The reconciliation between the lovers offers a sense of hope. Danielle's love story is more involved. Danielle learns self-love when she picnics with twenty-nine versions of herself and finds that moment in her life when a simple dinner with a boy was her happiest moment. Choosing to remain in that moment of innocent love is Danielle's way of defying eternity. She will not have to make decisions or even to live. She can choose as her fate to remain in one moment of her past.

Theresa L. Stowell

Review Sources

Booklist 104, no. 21 (July 1, 2008): 6.
Kirkus Reviews 76, no. 16 (August 15, 2008): 43.
Library Journal 133, no. 14 (September 1, 2008): 114.
Publishers Weekly 255, no. 31 (August 4, 2008): 41-43.

THE GIVEN DAY

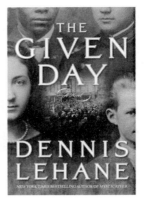

Author: Dennis Lehane (1951-   )
Publisher: William Morrow (New York). 704 pp. $27.95
Type of work: Novel
Time: 1919
Locale: Boston

Lehane's eighth novel and first foray into historical fiction is an epic-length saga of political and social unrest in 1919 Boston, a city plagued by influenza, reeling from the implications of World War I, terrorized by anarchist bombings, and bracing for an impending police strike

Principal characters:
> AIDEN "DANNY" COUGHLIN, a Boston
> police officer
> CAPTAIN THOMAS COUGHLIN, Danny's father and a high-ranking police
> officer
> CONNOR COUGHLIN, Danny's brother and assistant district attorney
> JOE COUGHLIN, Danny's youngest brother
> ELLEN COUGHLIN, Danny's mother
> LIEUTENANT EDDIE MCKENNA, Danny's godfather and a powerful
> Boston police officer
> STEVE COYLE, a Boston police officer and Danny's partner
> MARK DENTON, a police officer and union organizer
> NORA O'SHEA, a servant in the Coughlin household
> LUTHER LAURENCE, an African American athlete who becomes a
> servant in the Coughlin household
> LILA WATERS LAURENCE, Luther's wife
> ISAIAH GIDDREAUX, a leader in the National Association for the
> Advancement of Colored People (NAACP)
> YVETTE GIDDREAUX, Isaiah's wife and a leader in the NAACP
> DEACON SKINNER BROCIOUS, a criminal from Tulsa
> SMOKE, a Tulsa criminal who is hunting Luther
> FREDERICO ABRUZZE, an Italian immigrant and Danny's neighbor
> TESSA ABRUZZE, Frederico's daughter
> BABE RUTH, a famous baseball player
> JOHN HOOVER, a lawyer for the Department of Justice, later known as
> J. Edgar Hoover

Dennis Lehane began his successful writing career by producing a series of award-winning detective novels (most notably 1998's *Gone, Baby, Gone*) featuring Patrick Kenzie and Angela Gennaro. He expanded his craft with the publication of *Mystic River* (2001) and *Shutter Island* (2003), two tightly wound and deftly plotted suspense thrillers. Now, with the publication of *The Given Day*, Lehane has demonstrated that his talent as a writer extends well beyond that of genre fiction. In an epic-length, exhaustively researched novel, Lehane offers readers a close view of Boston in the chaotic, disturbing year of 1919.

The Given Day opens with a prologue, set in Ohio in September, 1918. The World Series between the Boston Red Sox and the Chicago Cubs is going on, and the teams are traveling by train from Boston to Chicago when mechanical problems cause an unexpected delay. On the train is the famous (and famously drunk) Babe Ruth. The players, waiting for the train to be repaired, come upon a group of African American baseball players, and a game ensues. Everyone is in good humor until the African American team begins to win and several dubious calls go the way of the white team. Ultimately, the black team walks off the field before a confrontation erupts; Babe goes back to the train feeling ashamed and angry.

The prologue serves three purposes: First, it demonstrates that this will be a book about justice and injustice, power and servitude,

Dennis Lehane is the author of eight novels, including Gone, Baby, Gone *(1998),* Mystic River *(2001), and* Shutter Island *(2003). Lehane has also written for the critically acclaimed HBO drama* The Wire. *A native of Boston, he and his wife have homes in Boston and on the Gulf Coast of Florida.*

and moral integrity and moral bankruptcy. Second, it introduces early one of the secondary themes of the book, the relationship between the races. Third, the prologue introduces one of the two protagonists of the novel, Luther Laurence, a munitions worker in Ohio and an outstanding athlete. However, the waning of the war in Europe means that the demand for ammunition is slowing, and white men returning from the war will be taking the jobs. When Luther is dismissed, he and his pregnant fiancé Lila move to Oklahoma, where they marry and Luther begins both legal and illegal work. As a result of his illicit activities, he ends up taking part in the murder of Deacon Skinner Brocious, a notorious Tulsa gangster. Consequently, he must hurriedly leave Tulsa and his beloved Lila. He soon finds himself in Boston, where he takes a job as a servant in the home of Captain Thomas Coughlin, a powerful police officer.

Coughlin has three sons: Danny, a Boston policeman; Connor, a lawyer and the Suffolk County assistant district attorney; and Joe, the youngest of the family, still living at home with his mother and father. Danny, the major character in the novel, is headstrong, rebellious, and confident; he both loves and dislikes his father, respects him and disdains him. Much to his family's dismay, he has chosen to live in an Italian neighborhood in a small apartment rather than continue to live in his father's home. At the same time, however, Danny is not without ambition. His wants to make his father proud, and he wants to advance in the police force. The question around which the novel pivots, however, is an old one: to what degree do the ends justify the means? For Danny, this means coming to terms with his ambition, with his understanding of right and wrong, and with his sense of justice and injustice.

Also in residence in the Coughlin household is Nora O'Shea, a young immigrant woman that Thomas found on the side of the road one cold winter evening and brought home to be nursed to health. Although she is a servant in the Coughlin home, she is very much a part of the family and the source of romantic competition between Danny and Connor, a competition that ultimately leads to anger and threatens the stability of the Coughlin family.

A frequent visitor to the Coughlin home is Lieutenant Eddie McKenna, Danny's godfather and another powerful Boston police officer. After Danny narrowly survives an anarchist bombing of a police station, he is persuaded by his father and McKenna to report back to them on police union meetings and eventually to infiltrate dissident groups in the city as an undercover agent.

As a result of this work, Danny slowly changes his ideas and values. When his partner Steve becomes ill, Danny sees how little value is placed on an ordinary policeman's life. Disabled by disease and unable to resume work, Steve has no means of support and slides into alcoholism. In addition, Danny sees firsthand that the common beat cop is being asked to work longer hours for less pay and in terrible conditions. Increasingly, Danny finds himself in sympathy with the union and ultimately becomes a leader in the movement. His involvement with the union (as well as his love for Nora) finally causes him to break with his family.

At the same time that Danny is working as an undercover policeman, Luther becomes acquainted with Isaiah and Yvette Giddreaux, the founders of the Boston chapter of the NAACP. Luther works for them, restoring the building that houses the organization. What he most wants, however, is to be reunited with Lila and to see their baby. His troubles continue to haunt him as the Deacon's henchmen track him to Boston and threaten his life.

Even worse than the gangsters from Tulsa, however, is McKenna. McKenna traces Luther's past and uses it to force him to betray the Giddreauxs. Lehane's portrait of McKenna is terrifying; rarely does one find a villain in a novel who is both vicious and nuanced. McKenna is a racist, a sadist, and a Machiavellian manipulator. It is a mark of Danny's growing maturity when he and Luther, working together, take down McKenna.

A more complicated portrait, however, is that of Thomas Coughlin, perhaps the strongest rendition of any character in the novel. Coughlin is representative of a successful member of an immigrant community, one who has clawed his way into the middle class. He has done so by acting according to his own code of conduct, one that includes graft and corruption as a police officer. Unlike McKenna, however, Thomas is not a cruel or cowardly man. He does not single out those weaker than himself and torture them for his own pleasure. Rather, he is a man who places the welfare of his family before all else. Although he holds his beliefs strongly, he is unable to permanently reject any member of his family for going against his wishes. He emerges from the events of the 1919 police strike a changed man, one who knows that the only thing worth living for is love.

Lehane makes use of the notable events of the time period to provide not only the setting but also the plot for his novel. Early in the novel, Lehane recalls the terrible influenza pandemic of 1918-1919. Boston was one of the hardest hit cities, and Lehane's description of poor people suffering and dying is potent. In addition, by 1919, World War I was ending, and American soldiers were coming home. The United States was on the brink of profound political, moral, and philosophical change, a transition that Lehane successfully exploits.

Further, Boston in 1919, along with other major cities in the United States, experienced a rash of terrorist bombings by anarchists bent on disrupting the social fabric of the country. The fear of anarchists and "Bolsheviks" drove some citizens to xenophobic hatred of non-English-speaking immigrants. It would be easy to dismiss this as wrong-headed stereotyping; Lehane, however, in his creation of Frederico and Tessa Abruzze, demonstrates how complicated the situation was. He places the two directly in Danny's path. On the one hand, Frederico and Tessa appear to be well-meaning and good-hearted immigrants struggling with the prejudice against immigrants. Danny finds himself in sympathy with the pair and begins an affair with Tessa, who he thinks is Frederico's daughter. Only later does he discover that the two are anarchists who want to kill him. Lehane thus sets up a situation that is counter to expectation in the attempt to show all sides of the time period.

Perhaps the least successful segments of *The Given Day* are the Ruth interludes. Although the opening prologue is effective, the recurring cameo appearances by the Babe serve to interrupt, not to propel, the story lines. Rather than focusing the action, these segments tend to distract the reader. In addition, it is possible that Lehane has taken on more than one novel can effectively handle—placing either Danny or Luther at the scene of every major historical event in 1919 requires the manipulation of the plot nearly to the breaking point.

That said, ultimately the strength of the characters and the masterful handling of the setting thrust *The Given Day* to a shattering climax during the Boston police strike of 1919. Lehane's exposition of the reasons for the strike, his depiction of the betrayal suffered by the men organizing the union, and his narration of the utter lawlessness of the days when the police would not walk the streets anchor the novel. At once a gripping narrative and a realistic historical glimpse into the past, *The Given Day* is a book to savor.

Diane Andrews Henningfeld

Review Sources

American Libraries 39, no. 8 (September, 2008): 69.
Booklist 104, no. 22 (August 1, 2008): 5.
The Boston Globe, September 21, 2008, p. K4.
The Boston Herald, September 24, 2008, p. 16.
The Christian Science Monitor, September 30, 2008, p. 25.
Entertainment Weekly, September 26, 2008, p. 96.
Kirkus Reviews 76, no. 13 (July 1, 2008): 662.

Library Journal 133, no. 13 (August 15, 2008): 69.
Los Angeles Times, September 22, 2008, p. E1.
The New York Times, September 18, 2008, p. E1.
Publishers Weekly 255, no. 27 (July 7, 2008): 37.
USA Today, September 23, 2008, p. 4D.
The Washington Post Book World, September 21, 2008, p. BW15.

GOD AND RACE IN AMERICAN POLITICS
A Short History

Author: Mark A. Noll (1946-   )
Publisher: Princeton University Press (Princeton, N.J.).
209 pp. $22.95
Type of work: History, religion
Time: The 1770's to 2007
Locale: The United States

A relatively short survey of the interconnections among race, religion, and politics in the history of the United States

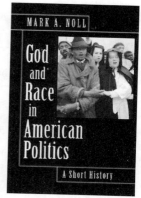

God and Race in American Politics is a revised and expanded version of the Stafford Little Lectures, which Mark Noll delivered at Princeton University in 2006. He begins his book by announcing a broad two-pronged thesis: "Together, race and religion make up, not only the nation's deepest and most enduring moral problem, but also its broadest and most enduring political influence." In actuality, Noll proposes an additional thesis, which is clearly stated: "The history of American race, religion, and politics from Nat Turner to George W. Bush is a narrative in which contradictions, antimonies, and paradoxes abound." Despite this broad reference to "race," however, Noll's book is almost entirely devoted to the historical relationships between African Americans and European Americans, and it contains almost no material about Native Americans, Hispanics, and Asians. A serious scholar, Noll has been teaching, writing, and thinking about the topics of the book for many years, and he is obviously very familiar with the large literature—both original and secondary sources—devoted to the field. Both scholars and curious readers will find that his seventeen pages of endnotes provide an excellent guide to the best books and articles that deal with aspects of the interconnections among religion, race, and politics in U.S. history.

The year 2008 was an auspicious time for the appearance of Noll's book. In addition to Barack Obama's election as the nation's first African American president, questions of race and religion were often center stage during both the primaries and the general election. All of the major candidates firmly identified with some faith-based tradition. Obama's twenty-year membership in an Afrocentric church led by Jeremiah Wright, Jr., an outspoken minister committed to black liberation theology, shocked and confused many voters, especially some white conservatives. Obama's selection of Senator Joseph Biden as his running mate was widely interpreted as an attempt to attract the support of moderate Catholics. On the Republican side, Senator John McCain received a great deal of criticism for his initial acceptance of John Hagee, a fundamentalist minister who made statements highly offensive to Catholics and Jewish voters. Finally, McCain's selection of Sarah Palin, who had ties to

~

A professor of history at Notre Dame University, Mark A. Noll is an evangelical Christian scholar committed to a liberal version of the social Gospel. His previous works include The Scandal of the Evangelical Mind *(1995),* America's God: From Jonathan Edwards to Abraham Lincoln *(2002), and* The Civil War as a Theological Crisis *(2006).*

~

fundamentalist and Pentecostal churches, was highly praised by religious conservatives and ridiculed by secular progressives.

Certainly there have been many other times in American history when combinations of religious and racial concerns have had great political significance. By the time of the Missouri Compromise of 1820, American churches were taking fundamentally different positions over the issue of slavery, usually depending on their geographical location. The growing slavery controversy always overlapped in political matters, such as federalism and Manifest Destiny. From Abraham Lincoln's election in 1860 until the end of Southern Reconstruction in 1877, the churches in the North and the South disagreed about whether the federal government should support the rights and interests of the former slaves. Following the 1880's, however, when a conservative Supreme Court supported the right of states to practice Jim Crow segregation, most religious leaders and politicians in the North tended to ignore the existence of white racism, whereas those in the South either endorsed or implicitly accepted the status quo in race relations. From the presidential election of 1948, when the Democratic Party endorsed a civil rights platform, until the achievements of the Great Society in the 1960's, arguments both for and against civil rights legislation were often based on religious morality, and this has also been true concerning more recent issues, such as court-ordered busing and affirmative action programs.

Noll might have given greater weight to the sociological distinction between churches and sects. Whereas the former have often emphasized engagement in secular politics, the latter have been much more likely to focus almost exclusively on individual salvation and nonsecular concerns. Because of his own bias as well as the book's theme, Noll tends to focus on politically active churches. It is true that those groups that claim to avoid political engagement tend to indirectly reinforce the cultural and legal status quo, just as Martin Luther King, Jr., declared in his "Letter from Birmingham City Jail" (1963). Historically, it has been relatively rare for religious groups to support viewpoints that are highly unpopular in the areas where they live. Reflecting his support for liberal activism, Noll emphasizes the social Gospel tradition to an extent that is disproportionate to its historical influence. He might have included more material about the politically engaged churches that have often promoted conservative, reactionary, and sometimes intolerant policies, a tradition that goes back to the Puritans' support for the massacres of Indians and the execution of Quakers.

Emphasizing the central importance of the Bible before and during the Civil War, especially among Protestants, Noll correctly observes that both opponents and defenders of slavery "deployed the Scriptures to defend their own convictions and skewer the convictions of their opponents." As a liberal Christian, no doubt, he would have liked to endorse abolitionist Theodore Weld's *The Bible Against Slavery* (1837), but as an honest scholar, he is forced to admit that both Old and New Testaments "either took the existence of slavery for granted or made no obvious moves to eliminate it." He endorses the position of Congregationalist minister Leonard Bacon, who wrote: "the evidence that there were both slaves and masters of slaves in the churches funded and directed by the apostles cannot be got rid of without resorting to methods of interpretation that will get rid of everything." The best the abolitionists could do was to point to passages that indirectly condemned slavery by implication, particularly Jesus's so-called Golden Rule: Do unto other people what you would want them to do unto you.

Although debates about slavery and racism have often overlapped, Noll correctly observes that they are different issues. While admitting that the Bible never directly condemns the practice of slavery, he asserts that "the Bible is much clearer in its teachings against racism than it is about its permission of slavery." This assertion, however, is highly questionable. The Bible never makes a distinction between race and ethnicity, and one of the principal themes of the Old Testament (or Jewish Scripture) is that the Israelites are Yahweh's Chosen People—a separate race based on their parentage and common ancestry. In chapter 25 of Leviticus, Yahweh is quoted as authorizing the Israelites to make slaves of non-Israelites (not members of their own race), and in chapter 7 of Deuteronomy, the Israelites' deity is quoted as commanding the total destructions of the Canaanites. In the New Testament, St. Paul and other writers occasionally assert that all humans are created by the same deity, but one looks in vain for any condemnations of racial prejudice and discrimination outside the realm of the Christian church. These early Christians were sectarians who expressed little interest in governmental policies of any kind.

Noll correctly emphasizes that following the Civil War, the various regions of the country became more firmly committed in their electoral allegiances. Of special interest is his quantitative comparison among various regions, highlighting the differences between New England politics and the eleven states of former Confederacy. In New England from 1880 to 1916, for instance, Republicans won 83 percent of state contests for president, whereas in the Confederate states, Democrats prevailed in 100 percent of the presidential elections. From 1920 to 1984, even with the popularity of New Deal programs, Republicans won 60 percent of the New England contests, but their victories decreased to only 38 percent of the elections between 1980 and 2004. In the Confederate states, in contrast, Democrats won 93 percent of the presidential elections from 1920 to 1948; they won only 56 percent of the elections from 1952 to 1976; and this further declined to only 12 percent from 1980 to 2004. Although Noll acknowledges that many factors account for these regional differences, he cogently argues that "race and religion were nevertheless of first importance."

Noll also provides an excellent analysis of the Civil Rights movement. While recognizing that cultural changes and nonreligious factors were significant, he persuasively argues that African American churches "provided the indispensable foundation" for the accomplishments of the movement. Observing that the African American experience resulted in a theological voice that "differed markedly from other varieties of American religion," he emphasizes the importance of black prophetic theology, as epitomized in the sermons of preachers such as Martin Luther King, Jr. Utilizing the historical research of John Chappell, Noll argues that most white churches—mainline Protestant, evangelical, and Roman Catholic—either accepted or actively promoted the movement. Although many opponents of the movement were motivated by "deep religious beliefs," these beliefs were rejected by the majority of denominations, even conservative ministers such as W. A. Criswell of Dallas. In contrast to Chappell, however, Noll acknowledges the survival and continuing influence of anti-civil rights sentiments.

Emphasizing the "moral complexity" of the nation's history, Noll persuasively declares that religion in American history has been the source of both good and evil; that "reliance on the Bible has produced spectacular liberation alongside spectacular oppression." He is not entirely correct, however, when he writes that the "racist practices" of the Jim Crow system "have never influenced spiritual or social developments anywhere else in the world." The existence and example of Jim Crow, for instance, provided some encouragement to the Dutch Reformed ministers and others who supported the establishment of apartheid in South Africa following World War II.

One major problem with Noll's book is his idiosyncratic treatment of Calvinism, which he vaguely describes as the "direct and activistic application of religious principles to public problems." While it is true that the Puritans and other Calvinists have often been involved in political and secular matters, their emphasis has been on otherworldly beliefs and practices. Calvinism has usually been defined in terms of the five points (or TULIP): total depravity, unconditional predestination, limited atonement, irresistible grace, and the preservation of the elect. Contrary to Noll's assertion that the Calvinist paradigm has been the dominant approach to American Christianity, most churches, especially since the Great Awakening of the early eighteenth century, have accepted an eclectic version of Arminianism, which assumes the human capacity to make indeterminate choices. This has been true of almost all African American churches, as well as the majority of white denominations, including Methodists, Disciples/Churches of Christ, Pentecostals, Mennonites, Catholics, Cumberland Presbyterians, Quakers, and many others.

Another problem with the book is Noll's tendency to make excessive generalizations about the characteristics of different periods in American religious history. After the Civil War, for instance, he writes that the Bible no longer functioned as the preeminent moral authority in the country, but that the exalted place of Scripture "was replaced by heightened commitments to a national civil religion and to the authority of scientific expertise." Certainly Noll can point to leading intellectuals who replaced beliefs in the Bible with Darwinism and scientific advancements, but it is doubtful that such a transformation took place among the majority of the population. After making extreme observations, Noll usually admits that there are qualifications. He writes, for instance, that from the 1880's until 1945, "religion exerted only a sporadic influence on national politics," and then in the next paragraph he acknowledges that "religion did surface episodically in the intervening years as a political force." This is followed by a listing of religiously inspired movements—such as the temperance crusade, the fundamentalist-modernist controversy, and the growth of the Catholic Church as a national power—which appear to refute the initial generalization.

The last chapter of the book, "Theological Conclusion," is highly personal and unusual. His most controversial assertion is that the Christian doctrine of the Incarnation is relevant to the secular and political realm: "God offers in the work of his Son, Jesus Christ, and in the power of his Holy Spirit, the transforming prospect of redemption . . . . [T]he manifestation of God in Jesus Christ . . . offers the hint . . . for how the commingling of contradictions, antinomies, and paradoxes can occur in other spheres of life." It is unlikely that many readers will find this mystical perspective to be meaningful. Those who are secular humanists will simple chuckle and view the whole idea of the Incarnation as nonsensical, whereas the vast majority of pious Christians who believe in the truth of the doctrine will consider it to be applicable only to their individual salvation—not a message about how to reform a secular society.

Thomas Tandy Lewis

Review Sources

The Chronicle of Higher Education 55, no. 6 (October 3, 2008): B18-19.
The Humanist 68, no. 6 (November/December, 2008): 44-45.

GOVERNESS
The Lives and Times of the Real Jane Eyres

Author: Ruth Brandon (1943-   )
Publisher: Walker (New York). Illustrated. 303 pp.
  $25.99 (simultaneously published in Great Britain as
  *Other People's Daughters: The Life and Times of the
  Governess*)
Type of work: History, sociology
Time: From the 1780's to 1979
Locale: Principally England but also Italy, Vienna, Russia, Canada, and Siam, Thailand

*Brandon gives an account, based on the lives of six
women, of the demographic, economic, and social forces
that led to the rise and fall of the governess, who thrived in
England from the beginning of the nineteenth century into
the twentieth century*

> *Principal personages:*
> AGNES PORTER, longtime governess to the family of the earl of Ilchester
> MARY WOLLSTONECRAFT, author of *A Vindication of the Rights of
>   Woman* (1792)
> CLAIRE CLAIRMONT, mistress of the English poet Lord Byron and
>   mother of their daughter Allegra
> NELLY WEETON, a Lancashire woman and governess
> ANNA LEONOWENS, author and governess to the wives and children of
>   the king of Siam
> ANNA JAMESON, author

For most educated Americans, the word "governess" will recall certain English novels read at school or in college: Charlotte Brontë's *Jane Eyre* (1847) or her sister Anne's *Agnes Grey* (1847) or perhaps William Makepeace Thackeray's *Vanity Fair* (1847-1848). The word may recall also mild puzzlement at the thousand indefinable distinctions of the English class system as represented in these and other novels. In *Governess*, Ruth Brandon quotes a passage from Louisa May Alcott's *Little Women* (1868-1869) in which Meg is patronized by a visiting Englishwoman when Meg says that she is a governess. The Englishwoman talks of "most respectable and worthy young women [who] are employed by the nobility, because, being the daughters of gentlemen, they are both well-bred and accomplished."

If all governesses had been so employed, then their lot would have been happier, as Brandon makes clear. Aristocrats had large houses, in which a handsome room or two could be allocated to the young lady who taught their children, thus providing all involved with privacy and dignity. Socially secure, members of the nobility did not need to maintain a prickly emotional distance from the governess or to regularly insult her to make a point. They did not fear that their own daughters might have to ply the dreaded trade if Papa's business went under, as a good many Papas' businesses did.

∼

Ruth Brandon began her career as a producer for the British Broadcasting Corporation. She lives in London and has written ten nonfiction books. Her book Caravaggio's Angel, *a mystery that combines art and French history, was also published in 2008.*

∼

The trade was dreaded. It was known to involve long hours, little pay, the awkwardness of living in someone else's house, and banishment to a social limbo. Governesses were neither mistress nor maid but members of some indeterminate class, paid at the rate of servants but possessed of the tastes and desires of those who employed them, whose intellectual and moral superiors they sometimes were. Young ladies who became governesses were advised to forget about marriage for the duration; and those who indulged in love affairs with their employers (or their employers' sons) rarely moved up in that longed-for social and financial haven. To top the thing off not so nicely, most governesses would find it difficult to get work after the age of forty or so. The bourgeoisie preferred to hire cheerful young women whose spirit had not yet been broken by toil and by exclusion.

Governess is a series of half a dozen biographical sketches, preceded by a general account of the origins and nature of the institution and followed by an occasionally name-clotted chapter narrating the advances in women's education that made it obsolete. The first of the six women, Agnes Porter, who spent her working life as governess to the family of the earl of Ilchester, was perhaps the most fortunate. However, even she, affectionately devoted to her charges, found her position untenable when the widowed earl remarried. Governess and new countess did not get along. Eventually, Agnes was able to serve a second generation of the Ilchester family, a post she held until her retirement, when one of the earl's daughters married and started having children of her own. Despite its tensions, her relationship with the family was longstanding and based on mutual affection and respect.

The next two chapters are the longest, forming together about two-fifths of the book. They deal principally with famous women not usually thought of as governesses. The charismatic and intelligent Mary Wollstonecraft, later to be the author of the feminist tract *A Vindication of the Rights of Woman*, went as governess to Ireland, to the family of Lord and Lady Kingsborough. She stayed there less than a year due, apparently, to a slightly fraught relationship with the lady and never worked in that capacity again. Her sisters were not so fortunate. Eliza and Everina lacked both the talent and the pizzazz of Wollstonecraft. For them, there could be no employment but as a governess or as a teacher in a school. The tenor of their lives is best caught by a quotation from a report to the effect that by mid-century governesses and female general servants made up "by far the largest classes of insane women in asylums."

If Wollstonecraft took one of the few avenues open to women by becoming an author, then Claire Clairmont took another: She became a groupie, throwing herself at Lord Byron, moving back in with the Percy Bysshe Shelleys (she was stepsister to Mary Godwin, Shelley's wife), because Byron would not allow her to follow him abroad. After that, she taught English to the daughters of an Italian family in Florence until that arrangement became unworkable. Isolated and cruelly denied access to Allegra, her daughter by Byron, Clairmont began living in obscurity the fifty-seven years of life that remained to her. She worked as a governess for twenty of them and recorded poignantly her sufferings: "What a life! Has Hell any thing worse to offer?"

Clairmont's letters survive because of the glittering people she knew. Nelly Weeton's survive by chance: A local historian found copies in a junk shop in the distinctly unglittering Lancashire town of Wigan. They record the sort of thwarted provincial life that must have been lived by millions of women, especially that majority denied anything more than a rudimentary education. Weeton "burned" to learn languages, math, and geography, but she was restricted to sewing, teaching, and housework. Her time as a governess, voluntarily undertaken to avoid crushing loneliness, was happy enough until her first employer took to drink. The chronic bad temper of the lady of the house ended her next position. To become a mother, and to avoid more loneliness and the persecution of her family, Weeton married a brutal man who thus became the owner of her hard-won investments and savings. The marriage was wretchedly unhappy until she signed a deed of separation that imposed punitive conditions, including limited access to her daughter.

Brandon has somewhat oddly made what she calls a "small and random selection of women," and certainly the life of Anna Leonowens is in stark contrast to that of poor Weeton. Between 1862 and 1867, Leonowens lived in Bangkok, serving as governess to the wives and children of the king of Siam. (*The King and I*, the 1951 Broadway musical by Richard Rodgers and Oscar Hammerstein II, which inspired the 1956 smash-hit film with Deborah Kerr and Yul Brynner, was based on information from her two volumes of memoirs.) That much is true, but further research has shown that some of the claims Leonowens made about her life are meretricious. Her father was a sergeant, not a captain, and her mother was probably half Indian. She fooled no one in British expatriate society, and she was not received. Leonowens wielded some genuine power at the king's court, however, acting as his amanuensis and giving advice about foreign relations in the capacity of the superior English lady she was not. She made the king's heir pro-British at a time when Britain and France were jockeying for power in Southeast Asia. Despite a genuine contribution to Britain's imperial role, she found success in her subsequent spinoff career as a lecturer primarily in the United States, which was ignorant of subtle British class gradations.

Anna Jameson, too, grew up in a classless limbo. Her father was an artist and thus permitted, within limits, certain unconventionalities while still being allowed into the drawing rooms of the socially established. There was no money, however, when Jameson reached the age of sixteen, and she spent many of the next fifteen years as governess, in which role she traveled with one family through France, Switzerland, and Italy. At the age of thirty-one, she contracted a passionless, on her side, marriage with Robert Jameson, a lawyer. When his career took him to Dominica, then Canada, Jameson declined to live with him. Her husband, effectively deprived of a wife, yet paid her three hundred pounds a year, enabling her to live as a writer: Here, at least, is one woman whose ambitions were helped by an unequal marriage. She produced essays with titles such as "Woman's 'Mission' and Woman's Position" and responded to the Governesses' Benevolent Institution's first report with "On the Relative Social Position of Mothers and Governesses."

It will be perceived that Brandon has posed a problem, and her book, intelligent and entertaining as it is, does not entirely solve it. She claims that the letters and journals governesses certainly wrote have not tended to survive: Individual governesses may be mentioned in the memoirs of the prominent or successful but, of no note socially and poor, their own writings have mostly vanished. (One reviewer, Kathryn Hughes, writing in *The Guardian* of London, regrets that Brandon has not sought new sources in archives available now on searchable databases. Such sources, she says, must surely exist.) Furthermore the writings that have survived do not always make agreeable reading. Those epistles of Eliza and Everina Wollstonecraft and those extracts from the journals of Weeton fail to lift the heart. It is, therefore, the slightly paradoxical case that readers of a book that justifiably insists on the stultifying hopeless frustration of the average governess's life spend a good part of their time reading about an ambitious, confident, and talented woman who acquired a reputation as an author (Wollstonecraft); a woman who knew, and slept with, Byron (and probably Shelley) and who, wretched as she sometimes was, even in the less dramatic times of her life, traveled in Italy, Austria, and Russia (Clairmont); a woman who lived in Siam and tutored the family of its king (Leonowens); and a woman who was effectively financially independent (Jameson). That these women suffered is not denied, but many a pallid provincial governess would have savored their experiences and their lives, notwithstanding the miseries, failures, and agonies. Late Victorian English novelist George Gissing's *The Odd Women* (1893)—"odd" in the sense of "superfluous"—tells of the Maddens, impoverished but genteel sisters who form part of the demographic discussed in Brandon's book, middle-class women who are unable to find suitable husbands and who lack fathers or brothers in whose houses they can live. The occupations available to them without loss of caste can be counted on the fingers of one hand. They look for means of living without breaking into their capital and lament, among other things, that "the (governess's) place at Plymouth" involves "[f]ive children and not a penny of salary. It was a shameless proposal." *The Odd Women* is a grainy, realistic, quotidian portrait of the plight of tens of thousands of women.

Brandon's book has been generally very well received. Some reviewers, including *The Scotsman*'s Lesley McDowell, regret that the experience of the typical governess is absent. On the other hand, Martin Rubin writes in *The Washington Times* that *Governess* is "fairly sizzling with fascination," Frances Wilson in *The Daily Telegraph* celebrates a "beautifully told, effortlessly thoughtful study," and Sally Vickers in *The Independent* finds "[t]he accounts of these women's lives . . . riveting, and the conclusions of this excellent book thoughtful and beautifully expressed."

M. D. Allen

Review Sources

The Daily Telegraph, April 20, 2008, p. 43.
The Guardian, March 22, 2008, p. 8.
Kirkus Reviews 76, no. 7 (April 1, 2008): 338.
Library Journal 133, no. 7 (April 15, 2008): 95.
London Review of Books 30, no. 14 (July 17, 2008): 32-33.
The New York Times, May 25, 2008, p. 6.
The New York Times Book Review, May 25, 2008, p. 6.
The New Yorker 84, no. 15 (May 26, 2008): 77.
Publishers Weekly 255, no. 9 (March 3, 2008): 39-40.
The Spectator 306 (March 15, 2008): 48-50.
The Wall Street Journal 251, no. 104 (May 3, 2008): W8.

GUSTAV MAHLER
A New Life Cut Short (1907-1911)

Author: Henry-Louis de La Grange (1924-   )
First published: Gustav Mahler: Le génie foudroyé,
    1907-1911, 1984, in France
Updated, enriched, and translated from the French by
    Henry-Louis de La Grange
Publisher: Oxford University Press (New York). Illus-
    trated. 1,758 pp. $140.00
Type of work: Biography, music
Time: 1907-1911
Locale: The Northeastern United States, especially New
    York City, and Europe, especially Austria

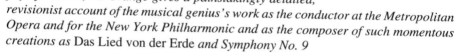

In this culminating volume of his monumental biogra-
phy of Mahler, La Grange gives a painstakingly detailed,
revisionist account of the musical genius's work as the conductor at the Metropolitan
Opera and for the New York Philharmonic and as the composer of such momentous
creations as Das Lied von der Erde *and Symphony No. 9*

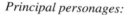

Principal personages:
> GUSTAV MAHLER (1860-1911), Austrian-Jewish composer and
> conductor whose tenure at the Vienna State Opera (1897-1907) was
> particularly significant
> ALMA MARIA (SCHINDLER) MAHLER (1879-1964), Mahler's wife from
> 1902 to 1911; later married architect Walter Gropius, then writer
> Franz Werfel

During his life Gustav Mahler engendered ardent adulation as well as ruthless criticism, and this was especially true of what has been the most unsatisfactorily understood period of his career, the "American years," when his conducting centered on the
Metropolitan Opera and New York Philharmonic orchestras. By making use of a massive amount of new material, including previously unknown letters and other documents, as well as such untapped secondary sources as the reviews of all of Mahler's
concerts, Henry-Louis de La Grange in *Gustav Mahler* has deepened knowledge on
this important phase of what the author calls in the subtitle *A New Life Cut Short,* during which Mahler had his greatest triumphs as a conductor and composed some of his
most significant works. La Grange also corrects numerous errors, distortions, misin-
terpretations, and myths that have accumulated about these final years, for example,
that the problems Mahler encountered in the United States precipitated his final illness and death.

La Grange discovered his life's mission in 1945, when he was enraptured by a performance of Mahler's Symphony No. 9 conducted by Bruno Walter at Carnegie Hall.
For more than fifty years, he has devoted a substantial amount of his time and energy to

The son of a French baron and American heiress, Henry-Louis de La Grange was educated in the United States (at Yale) and in Paris (with Nadia Boulanger). Independently wealthy, he pursued a career as a musicologist. His work on Mahler has been honored with several awards in England, Austria, and France.

collecting as much data as possible to illuminate Mahler's life and accomplishments. The author's research, which has become more extensive and erudite over the years, has complicated his published books, especially in English. For example, Doubleday brought out an English version of *Mahler* in the United States in 1973, but in 1979 La Grange published a much expanded and updated French version of the first volume that now covered the years 1860 to 1897 (whereas the American edition had covered 1860 to early 1902, when Mahler became engaged to Alma Schindler). In 1984 La Grange decided that, instead of giving his English readers an abridged second volume of his ever-enlarging Mahler biography, he owed them a complete version. This new English edition, which would be structured in four volumes, began to be published in 1995 by Oxford University Press with the second volume, *Gustav Mahler: Vienna, the Years of Challenge, 1897-1904*. This was followed in 1999 by the third volume, *Gustav Mahler: Vienna, Triumph and Disillusion, 1904-1907*. Even though these volumes dealt with shorter periods of time, their lengths became greater, a trend that has continued with the fourth volume. In the second volume, La Grange covered seven years of Mahler's life in about 125 pages per year; in the third, he needed 250 pages per year; and in the fourth, he used about five hundred pages per year. The English versions were much longer than the French ones because La Grange added new material. This fourth volume does not represent the completion of his Mahler biography, because he has revised, expanded, and updated the French version of the first volume. He has promised that the new English edition of Volume 1 will be published within a few years, thus bringing to a conclusion one of the most magnificent biographies of a composer ever written.

As a biographer, La Grange believes in taking a scientific approach, insisting that valid interpretations must be based on well-established facts. Behind his Mahler project is his comprehensively detailed chronology, for which he has gathered relevant information for almost every day of Mahler's life. Furthermore, realizing that these facts have to be understood in context, in this fourth volume, he provides readers with insightful descriptions of the New York social and musical milieu in the early twentieth century. His capsule histories of the Metropolitan Opera (the Met) and the New York Philharmonic deepen awareness of the complex relationship between Mahler and the city's moneyed aristocracy and its musical community. As in his earlier positions in Europe, Mahler forged his artistic success in the New World amid fierce rivalries among theaters, orchestras, and music critics. One of the reasons the Met hired Mahler was to help it surpass the successes of Oscar Hammerstein's Manhattan Opera House. La Grange is particularly interested in such music critics as Richard Aldrich of *The New York Times* and Henry Krehbiel of the *New York Tribune*, and he devotes substantial space to extended excerpts from reviews of these and other critics about

Mahler's work as a conductor and a composer, bringing out their perceptiveness as well as their prejudices, including doses of anti-Europeanism and anti-Semitism. As a conductor, Mahler was caricatured as tyrannical rather than democratic, and as a composer he witnessed his works being criticized as derivative, long-winded, tasteless, and trite.

The first biography of Mahler appeared in his lifetime, and many others have been published in the ensuing hundred years. La Grange, familiar with these accounts, emphasizes throughout his fourth volume how his interpretations markedly differ from those of the past. In the traditional view, Mahler's tragic American years continued the misfortunes of his earlier life. As a child and adolescent, Mahler experienced the deaths of seven of his brothers, and as a young adult he had to confront the deaths of his parents and one of his sisters as well as the suicide of his brother Otto. Furthermore, his later years as director of the Vienna Court Opera were unhappy, and in 1907 he had to cope with the death of his four-year-old daughter and the diagnosis of his heart disease. Nevertheless, La Grange stresses that the evidence overwhelmingly shows that Mahler was not a death-haunted, despairing man during his American years. With grace and courage, he overcame his European catastrophes, and, since his heart problems turned out to have been exaggerated, he was actually in good health and high spirits during most of his career as an American conductor. La Grange is especially severe on those analysts, mainly European, who claim that the money-grubbing and materialistic culture in the United States contributed to the demise of the profoundly idealistic and mystical Mahler. The letters of Gustav and Alma Mahler, as well as many other documents, create a contrary picture. Mahler was energized by the opportunity to develop the Met and New York Philharmonic orchestras into world-class ensembles. Despite being busier than he had been in Europe, he rarely missed a performance, and many of his concerts were popular successes, much to the chagrin of hostile critics.

This new volume profits from recently discovered letters between Alma Mahler and her lover Walter Gropius, then a young architect. La Grange, who knew and interviewed Alma, is well aware that she deleted, doctored, even falsified information about her life with Gustav in her memoirs, but, based on much new data, he is able to create a fascinating account of what he calls "the tragic summer of 1910," when Mahler learned of the love affair between Gropius and his wife. Alma insensitively blamed her adultery on her husband, who neglected her in favor of his work. Emotionally devastated, Mahler later consulted with the psychoanalyst Sigmund Freud, but with no knowledge of the Gropius affair and a poor grasp of Alma's narcissism, Freud, after a single four-hour session, diagnosed Mahler as suffering from a "mother fixation," predicting that he would fail as a musician if his neuroses were ever cured. La Grange refutes Freud's analysis by showing that, while under great duress, Mahler still completed sketches for Symphony No. 10 and also managed to persuade Alma to remain with him.

A further testimony to the strength of Mahler's spirit was his dedication to the complex preparations for the premiere of his Symphony No. 8, sometimes called the *Symphony of a Thousand*, because of the large number of performers it requires. In fact, at the Munich premiere on September 12, 1910, Mahler conducted an orchestra of 170, a chorus of 850 with eight soloists and an organ, which totaled well more than a thousand, before an audience of 3,200, which included, besides members of the Bavarian court, such celebrities as writer Thomas Mann, composer Richard Strauss, and conductor Leopold Stokowski (who would later conduct the American premiere). The performance of this symphony, which was structured around a hymn to the Holy Spirit and the last scene of Johann Wolfgang von Goethe's *Faust* (1808), was the colossal triumph of Mahler's career, though many Munich and Viennese critics remained unimpressed.

During Mahler's 1910-1911 concert season in New York, he became ill, but La Grange, unlike many analysts, does not attribute this to Mahler's personal tragedies in Europe and the United States, but to a bacterial infection, endocarditis, which was then incurable. La Grange blames Alma and like-minded writers for creating the ridiculous "legend" that Mahler died of a broken heart. Mahler himself recognized that his "dear little beasts" were killing him. Records show that Mahler had planned to return to New York for the next season, but, as the disease spread from his heart to his lungs, he returned to Austria, where he died and was buried. The obituaries, which La Grange analyzes, reflected the divided opinions that had characterized Mahler's musical life in Europe and America.

La Grange approaches Mahler's music in two ways, biographically, throughout the 1,277 pages of the book's principal section, and musically, through meticulous analyses of *Das Lied von der Erde*, Symphony No. 9, and the unfinished Symphony No. 10, in three (of the thirty-three) appendices that make up one-fourth of the book's length. His interpretations of these late works, all of which premiered after Mahler's death, stress the composer's love of life rather than his despair over death. *Das Lied von der Erde* passionately celebrates the beauties of nature and humanity while blending two of the composer's great loves, the symphony and song. La Grange attacks such interpreters as conductor Leonard Bernstein who see Symphony No. 9 as the composer's farewell to life. For example, Bernstein's interpretation of the syncopated motif in the symphony's opening as a representation of Mahler's heart arrhythmia makes no sense, since Mahler's heart was in good shape when he composed the symphony and cardiologists have told La Grange that such a rhythm would be impossible for a human heart. Finally, La Grange sees Symphony No. 10 as a masterpiece that never reached fulfillment, with its themes that illustrate Mahler's undying faith in music, humanity, and such transcendental values as love.

In a written work of such immensity, inevitable flaws do occur, including avoidable repetitions of facts and ideas. There are some factual as well as typographical errors, including a paragraph that ends mid-sentence on page 832 only to be repeated on page 833. Some readers may be bothered by the numerous digressions that interrupt the narrative flow, but others may find these interesting. For example, La Grange devotes much space to a discussion of Mahler's religious views. Although raised in a secularized Jewish family, Mahler was later baptized, married, and buried as a Roman Catholic, though La Grange thinks that Mahler's spirituality is best described as an undogmatic blend of Christianity, Buddhism, and other philosophical and theological beliefs. These and other digressions, as well as the main text and all the supplements, reveal La Grange's deep devotion to discovering the genuine truth of a musician he deeply admires. Since enthusiasm is often contagious, his dedicated labors may now inspire not only Mahlerians but also others, new to the worlds of music Mahler created, to explore their wonders, which, through many concerts and recordings, keep his spirit alive.

Robert J. Paradowski

Review Sources

The Evening Standard, March 5, 2008, Section A, p. 42.
Harper's Magazine 317 (July, 2008): 88-94.
The New York Sun, April 17, 2008, Arts and Letters, p. 16.
Prospect, no. 146 (May, 2008): 80.
The Times Literary Supplement, August 1, 2008, pp. 3-5.

THE HAKAWATI

Author: Rabih Alameddine (1959-   )
Publisher: Houghton Mifflin (Boston). 361 pp. $26.00
Type of work: Novel
Time: The late twentieth century to 2003
Locale: Beirut and Urfa, Lebanon; Los Angeles; Cairo
   and Alexandria, Egypt; Samarkand, in Central Asia;
   the Underworld

*Upon his return home to Lebanon, the narrator is in-
spired to recount stories from his family history and to re-
tell ancient Arabic tales that are an integral part of his heritage*

Principal characters:
   OSAMA AL-KHARRAT, the narrator, a computer programmer
   LINA AL-KHARRAT, his sister, a businesswoman
   FARID AL-KHARRAT, their father, a car dealer
   LAYLA KHOURY AL-KHARRAT, Farid's beautiful, strong-willed wife
   JIHAD AL-KHARRAT, Farid's younger brother, a storyteller
   ISMAIL AL-KHARRAT, formerly ISMAIL GUIRGOSSIAN, Farid's father, a
      hakawati
   FATIMA FAROUK, Osama's best friend and a high-spirited, independent
      woman
   SALWA, Lina's daughter
   FATIMA, a slave girl and the heroine of one of the Arabic tales
   AFREET-JEHANNAM, a jinn and Fatima's lover
   BAYBARS (MAHMOUD), the youngest son of the king of Samarkand and
      the hero of another Arabic tale
   OTHMAN, a former brigand and Baybars's devoted second-in-command
   LAYLA, his wife and fellow-warrior

The opening paragraph of Rabih Alameddine's *The Hakawati* ends with the words
"Let me tell you a story." Thus the narrator and, implicitly, the author state the book's
purpose. To the Lebanese, a "hakawati" is a highly skilled storyteller, such as Ismail
al-Kharrat, the narrator's paternal grandfather, to whom the title specifically refers.
However, though they might not have Ismail's spellbinding powers, many of the
other characters in the novel also like telling stories. Moreover, Osama al-Kharrat,
who as the narrator has collected and retold all of the stories in the book, might well be
considered a twenty-first century hakawati. His purpose, and thus the purpose of the
author, is not only to tell stories but also, in the words used in the introductory paragraph, to take readers "on a journey beyond imagining."

The hakawati tradition also explains the novel's seemingly random structure. Sto-
rytellers are not bound by the demands of reason or even by a disciplined imagina-

tion. They wander where their fancy takes them. Thus, though the primary setting of *The Hakawati* is Beirut, Lebanon, the book begins in an unspecified place, where a nameless emir is deeply troubled because his wife has not been able to give him a son. Fatima, their slave, offers to travel to Alexandria, consult a healer who lives there, and return with a remedy. The emir and his wife are delighted, and Fatima leaves with their good wishes.

Rabih Alameddine's earlier novels were Koolaids: The Art of War *(1998) and* I, The Divine: A Novel in First Chapters *(2001). His collection* The Perv: Stories *appeared in 1999. In 2002, he received a Guggenheim Foundation fellowship.*

With this subplot underway, Osama introduces himself. He has just returned to Beirut after twenty-six years in the United States, where, after completing his schooling, he made his home in Los Angeles, working as a computer programmer. With Fatima Farouk, his best friend since childhood, Osama heads for the hospital to see his father Farid. Though presumably Osama has come home to spend the feast of Eid al-Adha with his family, in fact he has been informed that though his father has been ill before, this time he is not expected to survive. Before the two arrive at the hospital, however, the narrator returns to the story of the legendary Fatima. He describes how she persuades a band of brigands to kill each other, leaving her with two traveling companions: the stable boy Jawad and the one remaining brigand, Khayal, who transfers his loyalties to her in part to save his life and in part because he is in love with the boy. Leaving the three asleep in the desert, the narrator moves to Farid's hospital room, where Osama and his sister Lina al-Kharrat are sitting with their father.

As the novel proceeds, Osama's memories of his earlier years and of the stories his grandfather Ismail told him are interrupted periodically for accounts of the adventures of Fatima. Her triumphant return to the emir's court prompts the introduction of a second major subplot. When his wife asks the emir for a story of heroic deeds, he begins his account of the legendary hero Baybars. At that point in the story, the author moves back and forth among the three major narrative lines. In the hands of a less gifted writer, this approach would lead only to confusion, but Alameddine seems to sense instinctively just how long he can leave a narrative in progress before his readers forget the details of the plot.

Osama's story is by far the most complex of the three. Inevitably, his return to Beirut prompts him to recall his early years, when his father was building up an automotive empire. He also remembers his father's younger brother Jihad, who was a mainstay in the business until his untimely death. Though Uncle Jihad insisted that car dealers such as him were the new hakawati, in fact, unlike Farid, Jihad appreciated his father's skill and was himself a spellbinding storyteller. When Osama's grandfather, Ismail, decided that it was time for his ten-year-old grandson to see a professional hakawati in action, it was Jihad who accompanied Ismail, Osama, and Lina to the seedy café where what turned out to be an inferior performance took place.

Some of Osama's most treasured memories involve his mother, Layla, originally Layla Khoury. As a child, he particularly liked hearing the story of his parents' courtship. Long before he was introduced to her, Farid had decided that he had to make her his wife. When she became engaged to another man, Farid was crushed. However, Jihad encouraged him by pointing out that in stories, an angel always appeared to aid the hero. Farid's angel turned out to be Jihad. At their first meeting, Layla and Jihad discovered that they had the same attitude toward life and literature; in other words, they were soulmates. It did not take long for Layla to see her fiancé through Jihad's eyes, and as soon as she did, the engagement was over. Though as a gay man, Jihad could not become Layla's husband or even her lover, she knew that he would always be her best friend. Convinced that the ideal husband for Layla was Farid, who was already desperately in love with her, Jihad promptly took charge of his brother's courtship. While Layla was checking up on Farid's character and his prospects, Jihad informed his brother about her likes and dislikes, emphasizing her particular passion, poetry. It was the hakawati Ismail, however, who ensured Layla's capitulation; he identified the one poet whose lines, recited by Farid, made it impossible for Layla to refuse her suitor.

One of the ways that Alameddine links his narratives is by repeating the names and the characteristics of major characters. For example, Layla is one of the most admired people in the al-Kharrat family, not only for her sensitivity but also for her strength of character. By insisting that before she married him, Farid must become financially successful and provide her with a fine house, Layla motivated Farid to work hard and make a success of his business. It is true that, as Osama discovered when his father came to Los Angeles to visit him, Farid did not succeed as well in fulfilling Layla's third condition, marital fidelity.

In her independent spirit, Osama's mother resembles another Layla, the one who appears in the story of the great warrior Baybars. When his right-hand man, Othman, decides that he cannot be happy without a wife, Baybars suggests that his friend turn the matter over to his mother. She chooses a beautiful young woman whom she encounters at the shrine of the Lady Zainab, where she is praying. Not until they are married does Othman discover that though she is a sister of the high judge of Giza, Layla is not a virgin but a runaway and a branded "dove," or prostitute. When he expresses his disappointment, Layla makes it clear that it does not matter that she is not the answer to his prayers, for he was selected by the Lady Zainab to be the answer to hers. Layla prayed for a friend, an adventurer, a companion, and a man who could make her laugh. If he does not make an effort to please her, she points out, she will make Othman the most miserable of men; if he does, he will have a wonderful marriage. Othman capitulates, and Layla reveals herself to be a fearless fighter and a brilliant strategist, who is invaluable both to her husband and to Baybars.

Another example of linked names and personalities is that of the two Fatimas. Fatima the slave girl stoically endures having her hand chopped off by the terrible jinn Afreet-Jehannam and proceeds to seduce him. When the jinn is captured by the magician King Kade, Fatima finds King Kade, turns him into a woman, lets her attendant imps eat him, and then brings her lover back to life by performing sexual acts on him. Though Fatima is often cruel, she does prove herself to be a faithful lover and a devoted mother.

Osama's friend Fatima Farouk is another of Alameddine's strong-minded women. Though she has become wealthy by marrying one rich man after another, Fatima has insisted on maintaining her independence; for instance, when she is at her home in Rome, she will not allow her current spouse to visit her. Nevertheless, though no one would accuse Fatima of marital fidelity, like the other Fatima she is devoted to those she loves. At the end of *The Hakawati*, there are just four people at Farid's deathbed: Osama, Lina, Salwa, and Osama's faithful friend Fatima.

Unlike Fatima Farouk, Osama's sister Lina has become successful not by using men but by avoiding them. As a young, rebellious girl, Lina fell in love with a radical militiaman. When her family learned that she was pregnant, they insisted on a wedding. Osama came home to attend it, and everyone tried to pretend that it was a love match. However, though the bridegroom appeared for the ceremony, he left immediately afterward, and he took no further interest in his wife or in his daughter Salwa. That disillusionment was enough; Lina had nothing more to do with men. She began working at the car dealership, and when the death of Jihad left her father too dispirited to manage the business, Lina took over. She was rewarded with success in business and with success as a mother, and even while she is grieving over the loss of her father, she can look forward to the imminent birth of a grandchild.

Though love and marriage are important in *The Hakawati*, Alameddine also looks at relationships between parents and children. The story of Baybars begins with him being adopted as a boy by Sitt Latifah and ends with Baybars's reunion with his biological father, the king of Samarkand. Like the biblical Joseph, Mahmoud, who later became known as Baybars, was sold into slavery by his envious brothers, and, like Joseph, he later had a brilliant career. Osama's grandfather Ismail was the son of an English doctor, Simon Twining, and his Armenian servant Lucine Guirgossian. Like the biblical Ishmael, the boy was despised by his father's wife, who finally drove him away. When he took the surname al-Kharrat, which is literally translated as "the fibster," Ismail not only rejected his mother's name and thus his past history but also claimed his new identity as a hakawati.

At the end of the novel, Osama is easing his father's passing by telling him stories. It is a suitable conclusion for a book that demonstrates, both in its substance and in its style, how art enriches and transforms life. "Listen," the word with which *The Hakawati* begins and ends, is an admonition that should be taken seriously, for Alameddine's novel is a work that will richly reward everyone who reads it.

Rosemary M. Canfield Reisman

Review Sources

Booklist 104, no. 14 (March 15, 2008): 27.
Kirkus Reviews 76, no. 3 (February 1, 2008): 103-104.
Lambda Book Report 16, no. 3 (Fall, 2008): 25.
Library Journal 133, no. 4 (March 1, 2008): 73.
The New York Times Book Review, May 18, 2008, p. 8.
Publishers Weekly 255, no. 8 (February 25, 2008): 48.
The San Francisco Chronicle, April 20, 2008, p. M1.
The Times Literary Supplement, July 11, 2008, p. 21.
The Wall Street Journal 251, no. 98 (April 26, 2008): W1-W7.

HAPPY TRAILS TO YOU

Author: Julie Hecht

Publisher: Simon & Schuster (New York). 209 pp. $24.00

Type of work: Short fiction

Time: The late 1990's to 2004

Locale: Nantucket

The female narrator, a professional photographer putting together a collection of her work, tries to cope with the modern world and the unwelcome changes coming to Nantucket Island

Julie Hecht's collection of seven short stories under the ironic title *Happy Trails to You* takes us into the consciousness of a representative contemporary type: the deeply dissatisfied, slightly neurotic, politically liberal (and politically correct) professional woman who finds contemporary American life to be bewildering, frightening, and alienating. The volume's title, which is also the title of the last story in the collection, evokes a very different United States, the optimistic 1950's, when Roy Rogers and Dale Evans, one of the country's happily married chirpy television couples, could rescue those in distress without so much as smudging their Western costumes. Each episode ended with the sappy song, "Happy trails to you, until we meet again. . . . Keep smiling until then."

These are hardly stories in a traditional sense. There is never a plot, and seldom is there even a narrative line. Rather, the stories tend to record the narrator's quirky, sometimes sad, sometimes humorous responses to the people and the world around her. One would not call the method stream of consciousness, at least not in the sense of James Joyce or Virginia Woolf. The reader is privy to the narrator's interior monologue, and she is a kind of contemporary female Hamlet, continually soliloquizing on the fact that "the time is out of joint."

The title of the first story, "Over There," evokes another song, this one from World War I. The world the narrator enters when she visits her elderly, hard-of-hearing neighbor at Christmastime is nearly as foreign as the one British troops encountered in the trenches in 1914. As a nondrinking vegan and non-Christian, she is surrounded by heavy-drinking, ham-eating revelers who find her as exotic as she finds them offensive. Her attempt at a gift is some slices of over-baked cranberry bread. Oddly, considering the circumstances, she finds herself wishing she had a family. A second visit finds the old woman alone with her decrepit dog and overweight cat, but the narrator is equally out of place, constantly wanting to point out the need for recycling or the dangers of global warming. As she is about to leave, the sight of the old woman eating dinner evokes memories of her father, living out his last years alone.

The reader may find it difficult at this stage to know how to take the narrator.

In the late 1970's, two of Julie Hecht's stories were published in Harper's Magazine, *and the second won the O. Henry Prize. Later her fiction appeared in* The New Yorker. *In 1997, her short stories were collected in a well-received book,* Do the Windows Open? *She won a Guggenheim Fellowship in 1998. Her other books include* Was This Man a Genius? Talks with Andy Kaufman *(2001) and the novel* The Unprofessionals *(2003).*

Should the reader sympathize with her loneliness and rigorous habits, values, and attitudes, or is she a pathetic figure, substituting political correctness, recycling, and vegetarianism for family, friends, and a significant inner life? In the following six stories, the reader will likely develop a complicated relationship with this pained, struggling woman.

"Being and Nothingness" finds the narrator spending far too much time watching news programs and fretting over President Bill Clinton and the Monica Lewinsky affair. Her concerns are partly political, partly personal, and partly for the state of the country. Her reference points are Ralph Waldo Emerson and Henry Thoreau, who represent for her closeness to nature, integrity, and, one suspects, a simpler world, where one could ignore the newspapers of the day and focus on building an inner life, This is something the narrator struggles to do, but she cannot because of the media, her absent psychiatrist, and the general gloom in the country. "Thoreau would have the mind feed upon the works of nature, and not trouble itself about the news," she says. At the instigation of her yoga teacher, she visits the Nantucket Atheneum Library, where Emerson and Thoreau once spoke. It provides some relief: "Every thought which passes through the mind helps to wear and tear it," she quotes, and then she adds, "I had picked up some of the vibes."

What is reflected here, among other things, is a cluttered mind, driven anxious by information overload, a distaste for conservative Republicans, and perhaps (as noted above) the absence of support from husband, friends, or professionals. Tiny acts of kindness, like a gift of a small tin box, are rare events in an otherwise indifferent world.

"A Little Present on This Dark November Day" takes place during the summer before and the few days after the George W. Bush-John Kerry election of 2004. As before, there is only the most slender of narrative lines, with a series of characters and incidents connected only by chronology and place. One focus is the handsome actor-waiter, whom she helps to find a natural cure for his sore throat. Another is the diner-restaurant where he works and where Kerry had previously eaten a meal, a subject of extended conversation between the narrator and the restaurant's chefs. At the other end of the political spectrum are her encounters in another restaurant with conservative Republicans. The day after the reelection of "the Alfred E. Neuman president," the narrator can barely get out of bed, so deep is her disappointment, but she musters enough energy to help the Polish gardener plant bulbs for next spring. A week later, the bookstore manager gives her some miniature prints of medicinal plants in a little brown bag marked "A little present on the dark November day." She will frame and hang it with other keepsakes.

This is a wistful, tragicomic tale, capturing accurately the hope and the disappointment experienced by some during the 2004 campaign and election. The narrator has mellowed since the Clinton-Lewinsky affair. She seems less neurotic and obsessive, though her vegetarian and homeopathic principles remain alive and well. The bulb planting and the little present from the bookstore owner offer a glimmer of hope and friendship after a bitter election.

There are lighter moments, too, in "Thank You for the Mittens," in which the narrator drives to a friend's house to leave a gift as thanks for the wool mittens the friend knitted for the narrator. As luck would have it, the narrator is allergic to wool. Mention of allergies takes the narrator back to her childhood, the discovery of her allergies to wool and sulfa drugs, the ridicule she endured because of the hats her mother knitted for her. Hoping to leave her gift on the porch and then go for a walk, the narrator is instead invited in for a visit. While she is there, the family's dog eats an entire chocolate cake, a delightfully absurd episode that causes a great deal of hand-wringing, some online research, and a call to the vet. The dog will be all right. Other trivial domestic matters arise, and one not so trivial: her observations of the family's alcoholic teenage son. Layered above domestic trivia are larger personal and political concerns, neatly combined in a single sentence: "I felt I had to send [presents] to anyone who had helped me in any way in our new cruel and tough society." It is a sentence that might stand as a theme of the book: the need for small acts of kindness in a society the narrator perceives as hostile and cruel, both to people and to the environment. In a final irony, however, the narrator leaves without saying thanks for the mittens.

"Get Money" begins with an easy errand: obtaining cash for the Jamaican house maid who needs it to fly home. It develops along the way into a meditation on immigrant workers, the filth and germs clinging to money, the narrator's outrage when the Jamaican warms soup containing meat in her microwave, the high real estate prices and overdevelopment of Nantucket, and cultural differences between the Jamaican maid and herself. The title has a double meaning. It refers in part to the comic way in which the narrator attempts to withdraw money from the ATM machine, with one foot holding open the door so there is air in the cubicle, an arm stretched out to reach the keys, using the card to punch the keys, since they are laden with germs. The other meaning relates to inflated real estate prices and the fact that neither the maid nor the narrator will ever have enough to purchase a home on Nantucket.

> And now the past decades of peace and quiet in Nantucket were gone. Building, hammering, nail guns shooting, chain saws, jackhammers, power mowers, motorcycles, trucks, and boombox cars were among the sounds replacing birds singing.

The generation gap and menstrual cramps are the primary subjects of "Cramps Bark." The narrator encounters two young women in their early thirties and is continually distressed by what they do not know about the recent past. For a member of the generation that coined "Don't trust anyone over thirty," this constant reminder of her age and of the resulting cultural gap between her and Jayne (the pretty woman she nicknames Brigitte Bardot) and Olive (who works in the bookstore and the diner-restaurant) is depressing and debilitating. With Jayne, the difference expresses itself in clothing styles and pop culture references; with Olive, the issue is menstrual cramps and their remedies. The narrator is constantly having to repeat information that Olive seems incapable of retaining, such as the efficacy of raspberry leaf tea with cramp bark.

> Then I decided to give up. I was worn out explaining botanical remedies and the history of everything. I saw the future—myself old and resigned, worn down by the world changes, the way I'd seen people even older than those in my parents' generation grow weary and sigh, shake their heads, and refuse to explain anymore.

In the background, as nearly always, is the lack of healthy food and cooking at the diner-restaurant. Melancholy, humor, and realism merge in this examination of the generations.

In "Happy Trails to You" we meet the narrator in childhood and her family. It also contains the funniest line in the book: Reflecting on her childhood understanding of the Pledge of Allegiance, she says: "I understood the word 'Witchitstans,' a republic of witches in control of America. Just the way it is now." Not surprisingly, the narrator reveals a sad and lonely childhood and adolescence, then abruptly shifts to "the dreaded phone call" from her agent, requesting that she do an interview. After initial resistance, she agrees to talk to the eager young journalist on the phone, and she even finds it an agreeable experience. The interviewer is a Texan even less health-conscious than any of the other characters in the book, and he is a gay man in a fundamentalist family. Worse, he found himself involved in a scheme to make money by buying old houses and moving them to new locations. His story unfolds as a comedy of errors from a bad home repair film. As their conversations continue, new topics arise: politics, Richard Rodgers and Oscar Hammerstein's musicals, her parents' love of songs from these musicals, and their spontaneous singing of them.

> I wondered how I'd gone from that beautiful morning in childhood to this kind of middle-of-night morning, listening to those jokes about those song titles this way.
> How did it happen? If I thought about it for the rest of my life, and researched it as history. . . I might understand the whole story.
> The best would be to live it all over, from the beginning. This time I could do it right.

So ends this collection of funny/sad, hopeful/pessimistic, resigned/angry, self-righteous/self-deprecating stories. They are not for those looking for solutions to complex problems, happy endings, or optimistic outlooks. These are stories for adults who have lived long enough to be disillusioned, who are trying to cling to principles and ideals, and who find age not creeping up but flying by on "time's winged chariot." Hecht sees contemporary life for what it is, or at least how it appears to one with a conscience and memory. It is not a pretty picture, but in her hands it is insightful, thought-provoking, and challenging. One cannot help but wonder whether the election of Barack Obama will cheer up her everywoman narrator. It would be nice to think so.

Dean Baldwin

Review Sources

Booklist 104, no. 15 (April 1, 2008): 25.
Kirkus Reviews 76, no. 6 (March 15, 2008): 262.
Library Journal 133, no. 9 (May 15, 2008): 97.
Publishers Weekly 255, no. 10 (March 10, 2008): 58.
The Virginia Quarterly Review 84, no. 4 (Fall, 2008): 267.

HAVANA GOLD

Author: Leonardo Padura (1955-   )
First published: Vientos de Cuaresma, 2001, in Spain
Translated from the Spanish by Peter Bush
Publisher: Bitter Lemon Press (London). 286 pp. $14.95
Type of work: Novel
Time: Spring, 1989
Locale: Havana, Cuba

In Padura's second novel in his Havana Quartet featuring Lieutenant Conde, the policeman must find the rapist and murderer of a teacher in the high school that Conde had attended years earlier

Principal characters:
> MARIO CONDE, also known as "the Count,"
> a Havana police lieutenant in charge of investigating the murder of Lisette Delgado
> LISETTE DELGADO, a twenty-four-year-old high school chemistry teacher who was beaten, raped, and then strangled to death with a towel
> SKINNY CARLOS, Conde's longtime friend, wheelchair-bound due to a war injury
> KARINA, a beautiful but elusive redhead, age twenty-eight, whom Conde meets and immediately loves, despite knowing almost nothing about her except that she plays the saxophone
> MAJOR ANTONIO RANGEL, Conde's superior who constantly watches Conde and presses him to get the case solved

Havana Gold, first published in Spanish as *Vientos de Cuaresma* (the winds of Lent), opens on a windy Ash Wednesday in the spring of 1989. Lieutenant Mario Conde is not an ordinary police officer, and neither is his beat. He lives and works in a poor area of the crowded city of Havana in an era when Cuba is undergoing drastic changes due to the withdrawal of Russian support. What makes Conde different from others in his police unit is his introspection and his sensitivity to events and people. He is a reader, and he has learned not to lend his novels because they are seldom returned. He is also a would-be fiction writer, though this is more a dream than a reality. He is a heavy drinker when he can get something alcoholic, but he does not drink alone. Coffee is even more difficult to get, but about that and about much of his situation, he has learned to accept the conditions over which he has no control. What he cannot accept is that a murderer in his own district could avoid being brought to justice.

The case he must deal with becomes more personal to Conde because the victim was a young teacher at Pre-University High School, Conde's alma mater, and his investigation stirs nostalgia and a keen awareness of the differences there since he had been a student. The teacher, Lisette Delgado, was apparently well liked by and friendly with her students. Yet she was found dead in her apartment, a victim of both rape and murder, not necessarily by the same person; evidence suggests that at least two men raped her. Marijuana is found in the apartment, and drugs become a major issue: where they come from, who benefits, the effect of usage on the individual, the social repercussions, the connections with the police.

Leonardo Padura is possibly Cuba's most successful writer on the international scene, best known for his contribution to the detective fiction genre in the Havana Quartet, four novels set in 1989 featuring Police Lieutenant Mario Conde. Padura is a two-time winner of Spain's Dashiell Hammett Prize for Best Literary Crime Novel. He is also a journalist, essayist, and scriptwriter.

The police are not portrayed in a favorable light. Rather than finding support and fellowship with the other police as is often true in police procedural novels, the police around Conde are generally more hindrance than help. Major Antonio Rangel, Conde's immediate superior, is typical of the others in the department. He is jealous because he knows Conde is better at solving cases than he could ever be. He keeps a tight rein on Conde and pressures him to solve the murder quickly, but without exposing any police corruption. Conde must essentially solve the case alone and might even solve it faster without the nuisance of the others.

Conde investigates and learns more about the murder victim, and it appears that Delgado was not the model teacher she was presumed to be. She fraternized with her students outside the classroom, and the marijuana trail begun in her apartment leads to the revelation that she participated in drugs and in sex with a variety of men, including perhaps ex-students and students, a Mexican boyfriend, and the headmaster at her school. Evidence indicates that she had sex with two men shortly before she was strangled, at least one of whom raped her. The suspects keep increasing rather than being easily eliminated.

Conde's visit to Pre-Uni school is full of emotion and nostalgia. The school building, like so many of the buildings in the barrio and the rest of Havana, shows years of neglect. What Conde sees in the behavior of the students, including their seeming lack of respect for teachers and learning, brings him wistful memories of his seemingly more innocent schooldays and the fun and companionship he shared with his close friends during those years.

This nostalgia for the past that no longer exists either for him or for the city is a theme that runs throughout the novel. It is stronger than ordinary for an adult looking back to his youth, because the present is so noticeably more impoverished and circumscribed than the past he can remember. It is hard for Conde to accept the finality of the economic woes and political restrictions that he has witnessed. He has learned to adjust, but he cannot pretend that he does not know that things could be better; he has known them to be better.

The depressing changes in Cuba that Conde has witnessed add to his tendency to philosophize about life and his personal situation, just as the lack of collegial coworkers in the police department contributes to his tendency to be a loner. He has no immediate family. His only friend is Carlos, called Skinny, who was thin as a boy but now weighs nearly three hundred pounds. As a result of being shot in warfare in Angola, he is confined to a wheelchair. Skinny has his mother Josefina to care for him and cook for him, but no other friends than Conde. Skinny likes baseball and listens to it on radio or watches it on television when possible. Although Conde benefits by seeing an old friend and eating Josefina's cooking, he and Skinny cannot do anything together except talk and drink, and it sometimes seems more an obligation than a pleasure for Conde to visit.

When Conde has to work long hours, he feels guilty for not seeing Skinny; and he feels even more guilty when he neglects his old friend because he has suddenly become enamored of a woman he has met by chance. Conde's feelings of romance and his lust are triggered almost immediately when he comes across a woman alongside the road standing by a car with a flat tire. Conde, who cannot afford a car and rides a bus, stops to help her, although it takes him a long time to figure out how to change a tire. She introduces herself as Karina. He notices everything he can about her body; he is hooked. She is enigmatic, and he spends hours waiting for her to call or to answer the phone, and he desperately wishes to be with her more. She is a jazz fan and plays a saxophone, giving Conde fantasies, such as a naked Karina playing the sax for him. Sometimes his visions are more than met: There is one especially vivid and graphic scene of their being together.

This longing for sex, love, and connections sometimes draws Conde away from his work, as well as from his visits to Skinny. Although Conde is a tough guy, he is also vulnerable and lonely. His only long-term faithful companions are a sometimes ignored friend in a wheelchair and, perhaps appropriately enough, a fighting fish in a fishbowl in Conde's apartment.

Leonardo Padura writes serious fiction, and the criminal plot is only one aspect of the novel. In addition, Padura has contributed to the detective fiction genre the presentation of a homeland familiar to him but not until much later to readers in other countries. The atmosphere of the city of Havana in 1989 pervades the novel.

The writing and publication history of the Conde novels have added interest and contributed to the impact Padura's works have made internationally. Padura has said in interviews that *Havana Gold* holds a very special place in his heart because it was written about the worst times in Cuba following the collapse of the Soviet Union. Among other things, there was a severe shortage of paper and virtually no publishing available. He was able to enter this novel for the Cuba Union of Writers prize, and because it won it was published. It was the first of his novels to be released in his country.

Havana Gold is the second book in the series, but the novels have not been published in English in the original order, so that the translations do not follow the chronological order of events in Conde's police career. It made it impossible for readers to follow the sequence as intended, and even now that all four books have been translated, confusion remains. *Havana Gold* is often called the fourth book because that was the order of publication in English. In the original Spanish, however, *Havana Gold* was first published in 1994, but it did not appear in English until 2008, the last of the four in the quartet.

The original order in Spanish is *Pasado perfecto* (1991; *Havana Blue*, 2006), *Vientos de Cuaresma* (1994; *Havana Gold*, 2008), *Máscaras* (1997; *Havana Red*, 2005), and *Paisaje de otoño* (1998; *Havana Black*, 2006). The release of the English translations over the years 2005 to 2008 started with *Havana Red* and concluded with *Havana Gold*. To further complicate things, although the series is referred to as a quartet, there is a fifth Conde novel, *Adiós, Hemingway* (2001; English translation, 2005), in which Conde has changed the focus of his career. This fifth book was the first translated into English.

The unusual publication history of the five books, both inside and outside Cuba, with the translations in several languages appearing well over a decade after original publication, calls attention to the courage and tenacity implicit in Padura's decision to write about his native country in an era that presented numerous challenges and difficulties. By writing this series he was joining writers in other times and places who chose to tell the truth as they see it despite the prevailing oppression and censorship of authorities. Padura's protagonist, Lieutenant Conde, has likewise learned to work within difficult and often depressing confines; he does not openly confront the official system, nor does he whine about it, but his protest against the system that forms the backdrop of his life is always implicit.

The publication record also signals that there have been changes in Cuba in the fourteen years since *Havana Gold* was first published. The fact that Padura and other artists have been able to distribute their work outside of Cuba has improved conditions for them and the way Cuba is perceived in other countries. Reading *Havana Gold* in English carries with it the poignant recognition that Lieutenant Conde's story of feeling isolated and cut off from the world, which reflected the situation of Havana in 1989, has reached beyond those confines, even if Conde, with his author, remains in his homeland.

Lois A. Marchino

Review Sources

Booklist 104, nos. 19/20 (June 1, 2008): 50.
Publishers Weekly 255, no. 19 (May 12, 2008): 39-40.
The Times Literary Supplement, June 20, 2008, p. 21.

THE HEMINGSES OF MONTICELLO
An American Family

Author: Annette Gordon-Reed
Publisher: W. W. Norton (New York). Illustrated.
  798 pp. $35.00
Type of work: Biography
Time: 1735-1835
Locale: Albermarle County, Virginia; Paris; and Washington, D.C.

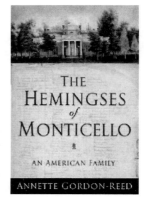

A landmark work of history and biography, reconstructing not only the history of an African American family born into slavery but also the emotional life of the slaveholder, Thomas Jefferson, who presided over so much of the family's destiny

Principal personages:
> THOMAS JEFFERSON, third president of the United States and a
>   slaveholder
> SALLY HEMINGS, Thomas Jefferson's slave and concubine
> ELIZABETH HEMINGS, Sally's mother
> JAMES HEMINGS, Sally's brother
> JAMES MADISON HEMINGS, Sally's son
> MARTHA WAYLES JEFFERSON, Thomas Jefferson's wife
> MARTHA JEFFERSON RANDOLPH, Thomas Jefferson's daughter

It would be difficult to exaggerate the importance of the groundbreaking *The Hemingses of Monticello*, winner of the National Book Award for nonfiction. As Annette Gordon-Reed points out in her meticulously researched narrative, many others have inquired into the emotional and private life of Thomas Jefferson, especially the historian Fawn Brodie in *Thomas Jefferson: An Intimate History* (1974). Brodie's controversial work was praised and attacked because it was highly speculative. On the one hand, certain critics admired her effort to reconstruct Jefferson's affairs with Sally Hemings and Maria Cosway, even when evidence was absent. However, to make her point, Brodie had to resort to a kind of psychohistory that many professional historians disparaged. Gordon-Reed made great advances on Brodie's approach in *Thomas Jefferson and Sally Hemings: An American Controversy* (1997), but she did not argue then that there was conclusive evidence linking the two in a sexual liaison. Instead, she pointed out how previous historians (some of them racist) had discounted the stories about Hemings's importance in Jefferson's life and denied that he could have possibly mated with a slave. Jefferson was sanctified, and Hemings was disparaged.

Gordon-Reed's first book on Jefferson and Hemings received respectful reviews because of her impeccable scholarship and handling of Jefferson historiography.

The subsequent availability of DNA evidence that made it virtually certain that Jefferson had fathered children by Hemings shifted the ground, so much so that historians such as Joseph Ellis could no longer doubt Jefferson's relationship with Hemings and his role as the father of her children.

Annette Gordon-Reed is a professor of law at New York Law School and a professor of history at Rutgers University. She is the author of Thomas Jefferson and Sally Hemings: An American Controversy *(1997). She is a graduate of Dartmouth College and Harvard Law School. She lives with her family in New York City.*

In *The Hemingses of Monticello*, Gordon-Reed goes much further than her previous book in fully imagining the world in which Jefferson interacted with his slaves. This was an environment in which the Jefferson and Wayles families were intertwined with the marriage of Jefferson to Martha Wayles and with his inheritance of his wife's property and slaves, including several of the Hemingses. Sally Hemings, the daughter of slave master John Wayles and thus the half sister of Jefferson's wife Martha, grew up in the privileged atmosphere of house slaves treated with special care by Jefferson himself.

The author avoids the kind of speculative language that weakens the narratives of Brodie and others. Largely absent from Gordon-Reed's account are such suppositional words and phrases as "must have been," "probably," and "perhaps." Rather than forcing speculation about Jefferson's motivations, she carefully charts his stays at Monticello, Paris, and Washington, D.C., noting when Hemings became part of his household, when the births of her children occurred, the instances of special treatment that the Hemings family received from Jefferson, and the commentary Jefferson's actions provoked among his neighbors, family, political allies, and enemies. Consequently, a dense historical context is constructed that reveals how integral slavery was to Jefferson's physical and mental well-being.

Absolutely crucial to Gordon-Reed's argument is Jefferson's eight-year residence in Paris. Here he cohabited with his slaves, Sally Hemings and her brother James, even arranging for James to be trained as a superlative French chef. While tracing Jefferson's behavior, Gordon-Reed also relies on the testimony of Sally's son, James Madison Hemings, who provides the most direct evidence of his mother's relationship with Jefferson. Earlier historians and biographers had accused Madison (the name he preferred) of fabricating and exaggerating his connection to the Jefferson family. Similarly, the oral tradition linking the Jeffersons and the Hemingess received little respect from Jefferson scholars. Gordon-Reed demonstrates, however, that Jefferson often remained in daily contact with the Hemings family, taking considerable pride in the accomplishments of Sally's sons.

That Jefferson did not explicitly acknowledge the existence of his African American family should not be surprising, Gordon-Reed explains. Any avowed sexual link to Sally would be used—as indeed it was—by his political enemies to attack Jefferson's integrity. John Quincy Adams wrote satirical verse about Jefferson's affair with Hemings, and Jefferson knew it, Gordon-Reed points out. Indeed, contemporary newspapers were full of gossip about the "dusky Sally" that Jefferson kept as a "concubine," the term normally used for black women who were the mistresses of slave masters, a not uncommon fact of life in the antebellum South.

Most telling in Gordon-Reed's account is her use of inference, a linking together of discrete data that become, in her narrative, a startling revelation of how many of those close to Jefferson collaborated in concealing the fact of his miscegenation (the term then in use to describe the coupling of blacks and whites). In her Amazon.com interview, Gordon-Reed commented on the crucial role inference plays in her book:

> It's a combination of what people said about their lives, inferences from the actions they took, and a consideration of the context in which they were living. Some people have problems with the use of "inferences." I don't, so long as they are reasonable. In fact, I would trust the reasonable inferences from a person's repeated behavior through the years over what they say any day, because people can say anything. I do believe that actions often speak louder than words. Contrary to popular belief, there are lots of actions on the part of Jefferson and Hemings that "speak" about the basic nature of their relationship.

A case in point is Abigail Adams, who became a close friend of Jefferson during her husband's John's stay in Paris as an American diplomat. Jefferson's nine-year-old daughter Polly was supposed to arrive in London (where the Adamses were then residing) accompanied by an older chaperone. Instead, her guardians in Virginia sent her in the company of Sally Hemings, then only in her early teens (somewhere between fourteen and sixteen). Abigail Adams's letters to Jefferson are full of complaints about Sally. The young slave was not a fit companion for Polly, wrote Adams with considerable vehemence, although with no specific examples of Sally's inadequacy. Sally was indeed young for the role assigned her, but Gordon-Reed points out that she would hardly have been chosen to accompany Polly on a long ocean voyage if Sally had been deemed inadequate to care for Thomas Jefferson's child.

Jefferson's behavior at this point also requires considerable pondering. Gordon-Reed points out that he had often been criticized for excessive concern for his family when the affairs of public life demanded his full attention. He was so devoted to his wife that he promised her on his deathbed not to remarry—a promise that he kept. By all accounts, he was a doting father. Nevertheless, he did not hasten to London to take charge of his daughter, and she, in turn, was distressed that she would have to travel on to Paris and meet him there.

Gordon-Reed notes an array of factors involved in interpreting the attitudes of Adams and Jefferson. Given eighteenth century manners and decorum, Adams could not say what was perhaps on her mind: that including the young slave girl in the middle-aged Jefferson's Paris household might be an act of impropriety, for it was well known that male slaveholders often treated their female "property" as concubines. By the same token, Jefferson—contrary to his usual behavior as a devoted father, one who had importuned his friends in Virginia for more than two years to make the proper arrangements to send his daughter to him—seemed to act out of character by not rushing to Polly in London.

Historians who have not wanted to countenance any sort of untoward behavior on

Jefferson's part have been reluctant to speculate on his motives, Gordon-Reed notes. So she turns to Connor Cruise O'Brien, who she admits is hostile to Jefferson, to suggest, as O'Brien does, that Jefferson did not want to appear in London in the guise of a slaveholder. To do so would not only have embarrassed the Adamses, it would also have done damage to his own image. It was one thing to know Jefferson owned slaves; it would be quite another to actually see him take charge of Sally Hemings.

Gordon-Reed demonstrates why previous accounts of this episode in the Jefferson-Hemings saga demands more thought. Like a lawyer working with circumstantial evidence, Gordon-Reed has fashioned a narrative explanation founded on deep reading in eighteenth century sources and an exhaustive interpretation of secondary sources and of Jefferson's interaction with his white and black families. Her method of working is much like a historiographical novel—William Faulkner's *Absalom, Absalom!* (1936) comes to mind—in which different versions of the past are subjected to multiple points of view in an overriding and authoritative narrative structure.

Much of the value of Gordon-Reed's book, then, is not only her fresh and comprehensive reading of Jefferson the man, the politician, and the slaveholder but also of the slaves that he could not bear to part with or parted with on his terms—usually after they repaid his support by a stipulated term of service. Thus Sally's brother, James, won his freedom, but only after years of exercising his skills as a chef trained in Paris at Jefferson's expense.

The ultimate mystery of *The Hemingses of Monticello*, however, is Sally herself, who never left a record of exactly what Jefferson meant to her. The closest readers can come to her is through her son, Madison, whose account now becomes more significant given the full historical context that Gordon-Reed is able to assemble

The tone of Gordon-Reed's book is compassionate and empathetic. She is not, in other words, judgmental. She is profoundly aware of historical context and the mixed motivations of individuals. She does not make Sally a heroine or Jefferson a villain. In an amazon.com interview she aptly sums up her nuanced and tolerant view of Jefferson, his world, and ours:

> Jefferson was contradictory, but we are, too. Who does not have intellectual beliefs that he or she is not emotionally or constitutionally capable of living by? I find it more than a little disingenuous to act as if this were something that set Jefferson apart from all mankind. It's always easier to spot others' hypocrisies while missing our own. He dealt with the conflict between recognizing the evils of slavery, to some degree, by fashioning himself as a "benevolent" slave holder and taking refuge in the notion that "progress" would one day bring about the end of slavery. It wouldn't happen in his time, but it would happen. That is not a satisfactory response to many today, but there it is.

Gordon-Reed's words are embodied in a book that is a model for the way history should be reconstructed.

Carl Rollyson

Review Sources

Booklist 104, no. 22 (August 1, 2008): 31.
Essence 39, no. 5 (September, 2008): 96.
Library Journal 133, no. 13 (August 15, 2008): 96.
The New Republic 239, no. 7 (October 22, 2008): 35-39.
The New York Review of Books 55, no. 15 (October 9, 2008): 15-17.
The New York Times Book Review, October 5, 2008, p. 17.
The New Yorker 84, no. 29 (September 22, 2008): 86-91.
Newsweek 152, no. 15 (October 13, 2008): 51.
Publishers Weekly 255, no. 28 (July 14, 2008): 57.
The Wall Street Journal 252, no. 68 (September 19, 2008): W2.

HIS ILLEGAL SELF

Author: Peter Carey (1943-   )
Publisher: Alfred A. Knopf (New York). 288 pp. $24.95
Type of work: Novel
Time: 1972
Locale: New York City; Queensland, Australia

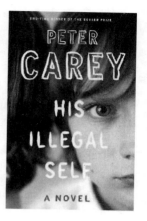

The story of a young boy taken from his privileged New York City life to a life among 1960's rebels and hippies on the run from American and Australian authorities

> *Principal characters:*
> CHE SELKIRK, a precocious, protected seven-year-old son of unmarried 1960's radicals, who lives with his grandmother in New York, until being taken by Anna Xenos to Australia
> SUSAN SELKIRK, his fugitive mother
> DAVID RUBBO, his fugitive father
> PHOEBE SELKIRK, his wealthy maternal grandmother
> ANNA XENOS, also known as DIAL, a young Radcliffe graduate about to take a faculty position at Vassar when she is asked to bring Che to his mother
> CAMERON, Che's sixteen-year-old neighbor and babysitter
> TREVOR DOBBS, an Australian hippie
> JEAN RABITEAU, also known as RABBITOH, an Australian hippie
> PHIL WARRINER, an Australian lawyer

In Peter Carey's novel *His Illegal Self*, seven-year-old Che Selkirk has been living with his grandmother since he was two, because his politically radical mother was charged with a bank robbery and has been fleeing the Federal Bureau of Investigation (FBI) ever since. To shield him from knowledge of his outlaw parents, Grandmother Selkirk keeps the boy in her isolated home on Kenoza Lake in upstate New York, only occasionally staying at her Upper East Side apartment. There, one day, a tall blond woman named Dial steps off the elevator, and Che mistakenly believes her to be his mother. He willingly accompanies her and his grandmother on a brief shopping trip to Bloomingdale's, after which Che is to meet secretly with his mother and then be returned to his grandmother. Things, however, go terribly wrong. The arranged meeting in New York is changed to Philadelphia, then canceled when Che's mother is killed planting a bomb. In a panic, Dial essentially kidnaps the boy, taking him to Seattle, where he fleetingly sees his father, then finally to Australia, where the rest of the novel takes place and where Che and Dial endure physical, emotional, and relational trials that change their lives profoundly.

Carey's thirteenth novel, like those before it, ventures into experimental territory, though with characters less strange, idiosyncratic, and fantastic than appear in many

~

Peter Carey was born in Australia and lives in New York City, where he directs the writing program at Hunter College. He has twice received the Booker Prize for fiction.

~

of his previous ones. The method, however, bears the Carey trademark—rapid cutting between scenes, flashbacks, an occasional flash forward, and above all the highly original style and voice. Somewhat more conventional, too, is the form of the novel, which at times verges on the picaresque, at other times on the "foundling" genre as exemplified, for instance, by Henry Fielding's *Joseph Andrews* (1742). There are echoes, too, of Charles Dickens's *Oliver Twist* (1837-1938).

Carey's free-indirect point of view vacillates between the two main characters, Che and Dial, and out of the often-conflicting viewpoints of this pair comes much of the novel's emotion and appeal. Seven-year-old Che presents problems for Carey, because the boy cannot seem too wise for his years, especially because he has led an extraordinarily sheltered life, deprived even of television for fear he might see news reports and photographs of his "most wanted" parents. His tenuous connections to the outside world are provided by Cameron, the sixteen-year-old neighbor expelled from Groton who supplies Che with bits of information about his infamous parents, including a *Life* magazine photograph of his absent father, which Che carries along with other scraps as talismans of a family that might have been. It is Cameron who predicts, "They will come for you, man. They'll break you out of here." Then, too, there is Che's starchy and willful grandmother, who secludes him at Kenoza Lake and in her posh apartment, ensuring that the emotionally starved boy will bond immediately with Dial, who seems the fulfillment of Cameron's prophecy.

So nicknamed because "she said dialectic had been invented by Zeno," Dial comes from a solidly working-class background. Her father, a real revolutionary for Greece in 1945, employed her nights and weekends in his South Boston sausage factory while she attended Harvard. With her five feet, ten inches in height, good looks, and hippie clothes, she was "an SDS goddess" (although one who lacked commitment to the movement), and she was headed for an academic life. Her meeting with Che proves fateful, however, as his enthusiastic embrace and instant bonding fill an unrealized need.

> He looked at her adoringly, little glances, smiles. She thought how glorious it was to be loved, she, Dial, who was not loved by anyone. She felt herself just absorb this little boy, his small damp hand dissolving in her own.

It is a short while after this tender moment, however, that life suddenly becomes surreal for Dial and Che. Exploiting Che's sketchy understanding of places and events, Carey sends the pair to Philadelphia, then Oakland, then Seattle, then (paid off by the movement) to Australia. Carey's technique is designed to answer a reader's obvious question, "Why doesn't she simply return Che to his grandmother and go on with her planned academic life?" Panic might be one answer, fear of arrest another, since she has obviously if unwittingly "kidnapped" the boy. For Dial, who has time in airplanes and motels to consider her situation, her move to Australia seems more than a little improbable.

Improbable or not, Australia is the setting for the rest of the novel and the struggle Dial and Che face to survive while dodging the authorities and overcoming their naïveté. Considering that this is 1972 and considering the collective paranoia that was abroad at the time, it is not unlikely that Dial and Che would find themselves in a hippie community in Queensland, drawing strength from one another and from an odd mix of inept escapees from capitalism. Chief among these is Trevor Dobbs, who with his friend Rabbitoh picks up Dial and Che as they head north from Brisbane into the teeth of a hurricane. During the next few days, the tension between Che and Dial intensifies. She is preoccupied with finding a safe haven, away from the authorities who would surely jail her for kidnapping. Che, however, is focused on finding his father, returning home, and staying in motels, where he and Dial can live safely and comfortably, as they did briefly in Oakland. The movement, however, has trapped Dial, first by involving her in the planned meeting with Che's mother, then by spiriting her and Che out of the country with a wad of American money that Dial cannot convert in Australia without arousing suspicion. In a move that infuriates Che and seems crazy even to Dial, she purchases a pair of run-down cabins on the edge of the Australian rain forest near a hippie commune. Her position now perfectly echoes her surname: "Her name was Anna Xenos. Xenos means displaced person, stranger . . . ."

However improbable some readers might find aspects of Carey's plot, the physical and emotional geography of the novel is rendered with vivid intensity. Part of the emotional tug of war occurs between Che and Dial, as he begins to realize that she is not, as he first assumed, his mother. For her part, Dial is torn between the pain of telling and the lie of pretending, increasingly pressured by Che's curiosity and suspicion, and sometimes hurt by his persistent longing for the father who has never had time for or interest in him. Their best moments occur when she reads to him from Jack London's *The Call of the Wild* (1903) and Mark Twain's *Adventures of Huckleberry Finn* (1884); their worst moments occur when they quarrel. Not surprisingly, Trevor becomes the father substitute, putting the boy to work hauling sledges of seaweed to mulch his garden and rewarding him with stories of his life as an orphan being physically and sexually abused by priests. Tension among them rises as both Che and Trevor pump Dial for answers. Is Che an orphan? Where is his father?

Moments like these lead to questions of identity. Dial knows she does not belong in Australia with this ragtag bunch of hippies; she is a scholar, an academic. Che is even more confused, longing to know his parents, loving and not loving Dial, hating where he lives, yet maturing every day as the hardships of life in the bush take him far beyond his cozy, sheltered life in the United States. When the crisis comes and he confronts Dial about his parents and why she brought him here, he runs from the truth.

As the third part of the novel's emotional triangle, Trevor is both a comforting and a threatening presence. Having entrusted her money to him (Trevor hides it with his "stash"), Dial is bound to him without being able fully to trust him. His own paranoia and furtiveness, engendered first by his life in the orphanage and then by the official suspicion that surrounded all who sought an "alternate lifestyle," intensifies the reader's uneasiness for Dial and Che. In the end, they have no choice but to trust Trevor's experience and instincts, but he exists as a menace waiting to pounce until the novel's swift, unexpected conclusion.

The personal conflicts and identity struggles occur against the surreal background of radical politics in the Nixon era and the lush Australian coastal rain forest. These are territories Carey knows well, having himself spent time in the late 1970's in just such a community north of Brisbane. The main point of contention between Dial and her neighbors is the cat she and Che picked up, which offends by killing birds. As a symptom of the petty quarreling endemic to communes, this device works well. Natural, harmless in itself, it offends Dial's neighbors by doing what it cannot help but do. In a touching scene, Dial tenderly breaks the cat's neck and tearfully buries it. However, the hippies, for all of their pettiness and paranoia, rally to her side when Che disappears and is feared lost or drowned. Their fear is not unfounded. As the novel nears its close, it comes to resemble a thriller, as those hunting for Che and his abductor come closer and closer to their settlement, and the police raid, wantonly smashing doors and furniture. Lawyer Phil Warriner's trip to the United States to arrange Che's return ends in frustration.

Readers will differ over whether Carey's ending is satisfying. What is less in dispute is the novel's energy, both narrative and stylistic. Its swift, jagged narrative builds in a series of emotional and situational climaxes; the characters deepen and grow. Carey's earlier novels focused on social and political problems, but with the exception of calling into question the radical politics of the 1960's and 1970's, and the geographical and political ignorance of Americans such as Dial, this is a novel about people and their elemental struggles with their emotions, relationships, and identities. Constantly shifting in a free-indirect point of view, Carey explores his main characters' emotional lives and psychological needs, juxtaposing adult and child viewpoints and needs without favoring either. Che often sees more clearly than Dial, yet she is the adult who understands more broadly. Tensions between them are less often resolved than simply suspended like particles in a supersaturated solution.

Carey's style is swift and direct, with the intensity of William Faulkner's, without the long sentences and polysyllabic vocabulary. His descriptions, whether of dingy hotels or the Australian rain forest, ring with colorful authenticity. He has a gift for precise and sometimes quirky metaphors and similes: "Grandma's wrist was pale and smooth as a founder's belly"; "The conversation continued like water dribbling from a hose."

However one approaches this novel, it will bear, perhaps even demand, rereading. Those already familiar with Carey's fiction will no doubt be fascinated by this latest experiment; those unfamiliar with his work may find this novel an inviting entrance to his verbal world. As a vivid re-creation of a moment in U.S. political and social history, it will appeal both to those who lived through those times and to those who want to experience them. There are no heroes here, though there are villains—the self-righteous and self-centered revolutionaries and their enemies, the violent and vindictive police. Dial and Che are the unwitting victims of both groups, who turn a simple act of kindness into a life-shattering experience.

Dean Baldwin

Review Sources

Booklist 104, no. 6 (November 15, 2007): 5.
Kirkus Reviews 75, no. 21 (November 1, 2007): 1116.
Library Journal 133, no. 1 (January 1, 2008): 80.
London Review of Books 30, no. 5 (March 6, 2008): 16.
New York 41, no. 6 (February 18, 2008): 61-62.
The New York Review of Books 55, no. 4 (March 20, 2008): 12-14.
The New York Times, February 5, 2008, p. 1.
The New York Times Book Review, February 10, 2008, p. 14.
People 69, no. 7 (February 25, 2008): 54.
Publishers Weekly 254, no. 40 (October 8, 2007): 34.
Review of Contemporary Fiction 28, no. 1 (Spring, 2008): 183-184.
The Spectator 306 (February 16, 2008): 55-56.
Time 171, no. 7 (February 18, 2008): 60.
The Times Literary Supplement, February 15, 2008, pp. 23-24.
World Literature Today 82, no. 5 (September/October, 2008): 65-68.

A HISTORY OF HISTORIES
Epics, Chronicles, Romances, and Inquiries from Herodotus and Thucydides to the Twentieth Century

Author: John Burrow (1935-   )
Publisher: Alfred A. Knopf (New York). 517 pp. $35.00
Type of work: History

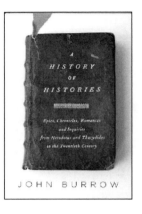

A history of the writing of history, from the first Greek historians to the major trends in history writing of the late twentieth century

The word "history" means both the remembered past and the process of telling the past. The second sense indicates that what is known of the world before the present always comes from someone's telling, and the different ways in which people have told about the world have been shaped by their understandings, goals, and preoccupations. The recorded past is presented in particular human voices, so that reading history is the double act of hearing the tellers and hearing what they are telling us. John Burrow, in *A History of Histories*, describes the variety of the voices.

Burrow begins with what he considers the first recognizable voices of historians, those of Herodotus and Thucydides. Before Herodotus (born between 450 and 430 B.C.E.), there had been recordings of events, notably by the Egyptians, but no reflections on events or interpretations of them. Herodotus, inspired by the rise of the Persian empire and its invasion of Greece, wrote the work known as *Historiai Herodotou* (c. 424 B.C.E.; *The History*, 1709) in order to memorialize the great human achievements of the struggle between the Greeks and the Persians. This would be the motivation of most of the ancient histories in Burrow's recounting and even a number of the more modern ones. It was certainly a motivation for the writings of the successor of Herodotus, Thucydides, who investigated the events of the Peloponnesian War, when the Greeks proceeded to fight among themselves in the years following their defeat of the invading Persians. Both Herodotus and Thucydides, wishing to create memorials, wrote epic narratives, creating one of the forms of history that would pass through the centuries.

Following a generally chronological approach, Burrow moves from the two Greek founders to histories of the Greeks in Asia, as mercenaries of the Persians and then as invaders. In reaching the historians of Alexander's campaigns, there appears a curious chronological quirk of historical writing. While Herodotus, Thucydides, and Xenophon (author of the epic of the adventures of Greek mercenaries in Persia) were writing about events that had occurred in their own lifetimes and in which they were involved, Alexander's historians wrote centuries after the Macedonian conquests. Should a chronological telling place the historian according to the historian's lifetime or the time of the historical narrative? Grouping all of the "ancients" together, Burrow

uses the latter strategy for the Alexander historians Arrian and Curtius Rufus, but waits
until the Enlightenment to deal with Edward
Gibbon's Roman history.

Following the Greeks with the Romans,
Burrow considers the major historians of Rome.
Consistent with the expansion of this new empire and its inclusiveness, several of the historians were not acutally Roman. Polybius, for
example, was Greek. Josephus, who wrote on
the Jewish revolt, was a Jewish Pharisee. The
Roman historians also looked at peoples who
were new to historical consideration, as when

*John Burrow received his B.A. in 1957
and his Ph.D. in 1961 from Cambridge
University, and he became a Professor
of European Thought at Oxford.
Burrow is a Fellow of the British
Academy and an Emeritus Fellow of
Balliol College, Oxford. In 2008, he
was the Bennett Boskey Distinguished
Vistiing Professor in History at
Williams College in Massachussetts.*

Tacitus provided observations on the Germans. The Roman historians, especially
Tacitus and Livy, would also provide models for future historians, down to the modern period.

Because of the chronological approach, Burrow's *A History of Histories* is also,
necessarily, a history of the world (or at least the Western world), requiring divisions
into epochs and periods. Burrow's epochs are fairly traditional. He moves from the
ancient world to that of Christendom, which presented a new, forward-moving
scheme of history derived from theology. The Bible gave a new theme to historians,
the idea of the people of God. It also gave them a new subject, the church. With the
general decline in literacy, though, early Christian historical writers, such as Gregory
of Tours, tended to lose their analytical capacities and fall into chronicling. The English historian Bede, as Burrow presents him, played a unique role, telling the story
both of the English church and of the English people, preparing the way for the revival
of secular history.

Secular history returned through the writing of annals and chronicles of the deeds
of the knights. Burrow derives the sophisticated historical works of the Italian humanists Giovanni Villani, Niccolò Machiavelli, and Francesco Guicciardini from civic
chronicles written during the late Middle Ages. He also discusses the interest of these
humanist writers in the ancient Romans, suggesting that history continually looks
back at models for rendering the past as well as at the past itself.

In taking up modern history, in which the past becomes something to be studied
rather than remembered, Burrow renders a service to all readers and writers of history
by defending the early modern antiquarians. Regarded in their own day as mere collectors and frequently looked down upon even today, the antiquarians, especially of
England, not only assembled and preserved valuable historical sources but also kept
alive local history as attention turned to national and political subjects. Burrow gives
a pivotal position and an entire chapter to Edward Hyde, earl of Clarendon (1609-
1674), whose *The History of the Rebellion and Civil Wars in England* (1702) provided the foundation for all future histories of the English Civil War. Readers may
question whether Clarendon should really receive roughly the same amount of space
as Herodotus, but one could argue this issue, given the role of the civil war in shaping

England and the importance of England for later world history. Following Clarendon, the study of the past reached an intellectual and artistic high point with the works of David Hume, William Robertson, and Gibbon. The discussion of Gibbon is particularly interesting, as Burrow details both the influence of ancient writers, such as Tacitus, and of contemporaries on this major shaper of modern thought.

As the Persian and Peloponnesian wars had been the critical events calling for the attention of the ancient Greeks, the revolutions in England and France became points of concentration for modern historians, especially the English and the French. Thomas Babington (Lord) Macaulay read his own Whig politics into the English Civil War, presenting it as leading the way to growing parliamentary democracy. Views of the French Revolution were more contentious, since its meaning was still a political issue in the nineteenth century and may well continue to be a political issue. In a unique declamatory style, Thomas Carlyle presented the French Revolution as the violent drama of growing realities casting off the dead forms of the past. Jules Michelet and Hippolyte Taine, two of the most important French historians of the nineteenth century, offered different versions of the revolution as a popular uprising. For Michelet, the revolutionary masses were "the people," often acting in unfortunate ways, but acting in concert and in the name of the emerging new nation. For Taine, those same masses were "the mob," anarchic and uncontrolled. The contrast between the two French scholars demonstrates that in modern times history is often separated from ideology only with difficulty, if at all.

One of the ideological themes that appeared in the nineteenth century was that of history as the story of freedom. Burrow give two examples of this trend. In the *Constitutional History* (1874-1878) of William Stubbs, the traditional political actors of the past, the rulers, began to recede into the background and history became the story of the emergence of constitutional institutions. The Swiss Jacob Burckhardt, in his interpretation of the Italian Renaissance, identified the rise of autonomous individuals as a characteristic of the rise of modernity.

In a sudden move to the United States, Burrow brings together two historians from different origins and eras. Bernal Díaz, who lived in the sixteenth century, was one of the companions of Hernán Cortés in the conquest of Mexico. Díaz wrote an account of the adventure that is still interesting today. William Hickling Prescott was one of the first major historians in the United States, and he is best known for his 1843 classic *The Conquest of Mexico*. The justification for presenting these two historians in the same chapter is clearly that Díaz was Prescott's major source. However, earlier in the book, more than one hundred pages separated Edward Gibbon from his sources in the ancient world. A consistent chronological progression is difficult to maintain when the subjects are always looking across the centuries. From Prescott, Burrow moves to major historians in the United States concerned with their own country, Francis Parkman's history of the American West and Henry Adams's account of the growth of the United States as a nation.

Germany, not seen since the entry on Tacitus, reenters Burrow's account in the nineteenth century. The German historians of this time were leaders in the professionalization of history, and they helped to determine the character of history as an academic discipline rather than as the concern of philosophic gentlemen or politicians out of office. Leopold von Ranke was especially important for creating a professional consensus about what history should be, as much through his personal connections with other historians as through his thinking and writing.

Burrow presents twentieth century history as movements in diverse directions. The "Whig history" of Macaulay and Stubbs—the presentation of history as a steady movement toward democratic institutions—came under criticism. Professionalization raised the question of whether history was an art or a science. The Annales school in France drew attention to the underlying structures of history and to cultural interpretations as a subject of history. Marxism arose as a grand narrative for some. Anthropological approaches became more common. The idea of world history became more common, even if most academic historians still tend to be highly specialized in time and place.

A History of Histories is an intriguing and erudite work, but one that does have its limits and eccentricities. Some readers may feel that it should properly be called "A History of Western Histories." While he does not pretend to extend his consideration beyond European and North American historians, readers might consider how Burrow's personal view of historical writing has been informed and directed by his European outlook. Nowhere in these pages will one find a mention of the ancient Chinese historian Sima Qian (c. 145-86 B.C.E.), who wrote a massive work on two thousand years of Chinese history and laid the groundwork for all succeeding Chinese history writing. There is also no mention of the medieval North African Muslim philosopher and historian Ibn Khaldun (1332-1406), who left behind a history of the world that has influenced modern Western as well as non-Western historians. Burrow leaves the impression that history moved geographically as well as temporally, beginning in Greece, spreading for a few centuries throughout the Roman Empire, then taking up residence mainly in England and France, taking a brief tour of northern Italy during the Renaissance, and popping up in the United States and Germany during the nineteenth century.

Carl L. Bankston III

Review Sources

Booklist 104, no. 16 (April 15, 2008): 22.
The Evening Standard, December 3, 2007, p. 39.
The New Republic 238, no. 10 (June 11, 2008): 37-41.
The New Yorker 84 (March 24, 2008): 79.
Policy Review, no. 150 (August/September, 2008): 106-111.
The Times Literary Supplement, February 15, 2008, p. 14.
The Wall Street Journal 251, no. 92 (April 19, 2008): W9.
The Washington Times, March 9, 2008, p. B06.

HITLER'S PRIVATE LIBRARY
The Books That Shaped His Life

Author: Timothy W. Ryback (1954-   )
Publisher: Alfred A. Knopf (New York). 278 pp. $25.95
Type of work: History
Time: 1915-1945
Locale: Germany

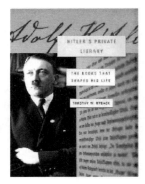

Of the sixteen thousand books owned by Adolf Hitler, some twelve hundred reside in the Library of Congress, and another eighty at Brown University; Ryback analyzes the books that defined and directed the development of Hitler's major attitudes and beliefs

Since World War II, countless biographies and analyses of German chancellor Adolf Hitler have appeared in print. From Nazi sociology to his personal sociopathy, all elements of Hitler's life, including every word spoken or written by and about him, have been painstakingly scrutinized, elucidating the mind of the man whose psychopathology led to the death of more than fifty million people.

One aspect of Hitler's life, however, has been little examined: his obsession with books. "I can never remember Adolf without books. Books were his world," recalled an associate. Hitler explained, "I take what I need from books." Following German-Jewish art critic and philosopher Walter Benjamin's belief that books reveal and preserve their owner, Timothy W. Ryback examined some of the twelve hundred Library of Congress volumes, plus some of the eighty housed at Brown University, to draw insightful and incisive conclusions about their owner, Hitler.

Building on two prior studies, *The Hitler Library: A Bibliography* (2001) by Philipp Gassert and Daniel Mattern and *Führer olvas* (2000; *Hitler's Library*, 2003) by Ambrus Miskolczy, Ryback's *Hitler's Private Library: The Books That Shaped His Life* compellingly studies the provocative notion that Hitler (little known as a bibliophile) acquired and reinforced his most pernicious theories from books.

From weapons manuals and historical biographies to classic great fiction; from adventure novels and religion to the occult; from seething anti-Semitic tracts and political history to art and architecture—literally from militarism to mendacity—Hitler's eclectic literary tastes lay bare his mind and his morality, and even more revealing are the marginalia he penned in his books. Analyzing effectively in chronological order and blending seamlessly the personal and the historical, Ryback expertly traces, through the 1920's, 1930's, and 1940's, the evolution of Hitler's psyche from genesis to genocide.

Critic Max Osborn's *Berlin* (1909) was bought in 1915 by twenty-six-year-old World War I message runner Hitler, who, despite his rejection by the Royal Academy of Arts in Vienna, considered himself an artist. Osborn's book was important because it celebrated two of Hitler's lifelong obsessions: Prussian elements in Berlin's archi-

tecture and German ruler Frederick the Great's
eighteenth century military successes, both of
which inspired Hitler's promise to make Berlin the world's capital.

~

*Cofounder and codirector of the
Institute of Historical Justice and
Reconciliation, Timothy W. Ryback is
the author of* The Last Survivor:
Legacies of Dachau *(1999) and
numerous articles on the Holocaust.*

~

After reading poet Anton Drexler's book-
let *Mein politisches Erwachen* (1923; my political awakening), Hitler concluded, "I saw
my own development come to life before my
eyes." Although he did not consider himself
an anti-Semite in his youth, Hitler became fixated on Drexler's thesis that Jews
owned 80 percent of German money, thereby controlling the economy. In 1919,
Drexler introduced Hitler to politician Dietrich Eckart, who ultimately became Hitler's mentor. A newspaper reported that Eckart's anti-Semitism was so virulent that
for his lunch he could well eat "a half dozen Jews along with his sauerkraut." Eckart
and Hitler soon became intellectual partners in hate, relishing Eckart's writing such
chilling absurdities as that the death of "six million men" and "tens of thousands of
children" during the Crusades was the fault of the satanic Jews. Eckart also produced
a highly regarded adaptation of Norwegian playwright Henrik Ibsen's play *Peer Gynt*
(pr. 1867), a book he gave to Hitler in 1921. In the plot, Peer Gynt's overweening ambition for global conquest causes mass destruction, and after it, he achieves ultimate
absolution. Hitler obviously identified with the play's protagonist.

Clearly, the most significant way to be preserved by one's books is to write one. In
the Hitler collection at the Library of Congress are a dozen or so copies of Hitler's famous manifesto *Mein Kampf* as well as the books that are its intellectual antecedents,
such as American industrialist Henry Ford's *The International Jew* (1921), an anti-
Semitic treatise that excoriates Jewish plans to rule the world. Hitler described Ford
as "my inspiration." Originally titled *A Four and a Half Year Battle Against Lies, Stu-
pidity, and Cowardice*, Hitler's magnum opus was composed during his brief time in
Landsberg prison. With its poor spelling, grammar, and punctuation, it was published
in 1925 with the shorter title *Mein Kampf* (*My Struggle*, 1933). One scathing review
called it "Hitler's end"; another said the book casts "doubts about the mental stability
of the writer"; and a third humorously renamed it "*Sein Krampf* (*It Is Cramp*)." Still,
Hitler followed this first autobiographical volume with a political tract in which he
horrifyingly states that "the Hebrew corrupters of the people [should have been] held
under poison gas," as German soldiers were in World War I.

To filmmaker Leni Riefenstahl, director of the notorious 1935 Nazi epic *Triumph
des Willens* (*Triumph of the Will*), Hitler explained that he had never had a formal education, so, "Every night I read one or two books, even when I go to bed very late." Indeed in the 1930's, concurrent with his rise to political power, Hitler's collection and
consumption of books became even more voracious. Although he loved books, giving
a book to Hitler as a gift could be risky, as was learned by Henriette von Schirach (the
wife of Hitler's youth leader) when she gave Hitler a history of his Austrian birthplace
(inscribed "To our beloved Führer in celebration") and was thereby welcomed into
Hitler's inner circle. Although he had known her since she was nine and called her

"my sunshine," she was later banished when she mentioned her fear that Dutch Jewish women were being dragged off to concentration camps. "You are sentimental," Hitler screamed at her. "You have to learn to hate. What have Jewish women in Holland got to do with you?"

Hitler's attitudes were strongly shaped by the writings of nineteenth century German philosopher Johann Gottlieb Fichte, who described an imminent "Volkskrieg, a people's war," and proclaimed that Germans and their language were superior to all others in Europe. Furthermore, Fichte's solution to the "Jewish question" was to decapitate all Jews simultaneously and place on their shoulders new heads, devoid of all Jewish ideas. Similarly, Professor Hans F. K. Günther's *Rassenkunde des deutschen Volkes* (1923; racial typology of the German people) celebrates Aryan racial purity and superiority. Hitler's growing contempt for Jews is revealed in his marginalia on a 1934 reprint of scholar Paul de Lagarde's *Deutsche Schriften* (1878-1881; German essays), a collection of nineteenth century anti-Semitic writings arguing that Jews must be kept separate because of their inferiority and toxicity. Hitler underscored a passage that announced that Germany is solely for those who "feel German [and] who think German," implicitly not Jews, and boldly highlighted the assertion, "Each and every irksome Jew is a serious affront to the authenticity and veracity of our German identity."

Ryback includes two intriguing chapters on Hitler's strange and strained relationship with the Catholic Church. Racial separatist Alfred Rosenberg wrote *Der Mythus des 20. Jahrhunderts* (1932; *The Myth of the Twentieth Century*, 1982), contradicting Catholic teachings by advocating polygamy as well as the bizarre notion that St. Peter was really "a Jewish agent . . . enslaving the peoples of Europe." The Vatican threatened to excommunicate those who read Rosenberg's eight hundred-page book; ironically, Hitler, officially a Roman Catholic, owned two copies. By contrast, Bishop Alois Hudal's tract *Die Grundlagen des Nationalsozialismus* (1937; foundations of National Socialism) attempted to soften the rough edges of Nazism and to align it with Catholicism, since both concepts "shared a common belief in blind obedience to authority," the infallibility of their leader, and long-standing contempt for the Jews. Munich Archbishop Michael Faulhader, a moderate Church official, refused to provide names of Jews baptized into Catholicism, since the Nazis insisted that, despite baptism, a Jew remained a Jew. Ironically, Hitler wrote in *Mein Kampf* that he had long desired to become an abbot and told his sister that "the good Lord holds a protective hand over me."

Just before Germany's invasion of Poland in 1939, Hitler assured his generals that in war, "the victor will not be asked afterward whether he told the truth or not . . . it is not right that matters, but victory." By 1940, about half of Hitler's library contained books about historical militarism and military vehicles. He was also, however, comforted by popular novelist Karl May's adventure stories of the American West, since May's hero used incredible craftiness and skill to destroy his enemies. Dr. Hugo Roch's insight into a great strategist and thinker, Alfred von Schlieffen, in *Schlieffen* (1926), provided advice on military matters that Hitler followed, such as conquering Belgium and Holland first, then going east to conquer Russia, thereby avoiding a war on two fronts. A German edition of *Amerika in den strijd der kontinenten* (1943; America in the battle of the continents) by Sven Hedin, a Swedish explorer whom Hitler admired, was another powerful influence. Hedin completed three American book tours preaching in lectures that Hitler had tried to stop the war many times, that U.S. president Franklin D. Roosevelt had caused World War II, and that America would lose the war.

While the Allies attacked German positions in Africa, Hitler clung to Hedin's thesis that Germany would be victorious, calling Roosevelt, "a puppet of the Jews." By 1945, with Hitler's Thousand Year Reich collapsing around him, he took great comfort from a 2,100-page tome, the 1858 biography of Frederick the Great written by English essayist Thomas Carlyle. Carlyle hated the Irish, blacks, and Jews, and the parallels between Hitler and Frederick are striking. Carlyle wrote that Frederick said, "I devour my books," to prevent insanity. When news of Roosevelt's sudden death reached Hitler, he gleefully hoped that, like Frederick, his own last-minute salvation was imminent. When this failed, Hitler dictated his last will and testament in which he continued to assert, as had Hedin, that he did not want or cause the war in 1939, and that the war was caused solely by the "propaganda of International Jewry."

In analyzing the range of authors and topics in Hitler's library—from William Shakespeare and Miguel de Cervantes to military history, anti-Semitic rants, religion, and adventure stories—Ryback cogently demonstrates that Hitler's obsession with reading and books reveals his intellectual and moral development. While many people read inductively, opening their minds to great writers' ideas, Hitler wrote in *Mein Kampf* that he read mostly deductively, desiring to have his prejudices confirmed, since for him reading was equivalent to "collecting 'stones' to fill a 'mosaic' of preconceived notions." He boldly asserted that blind obedience must take precedence over free thought, expression, and will. Even if a leader is wrong, he said, "following a bad decision will achieve the final goal better than personal freedom."

The final goal—genocide and mass destruction—was clearly advocated in *Mein Kampf* and the books Hitler consumed. Reading was such a "deadly serious business," reported one colleague, that the sign on Hitler's study said "ABSOLUTE SILENCE." Certainly Hitler has left behind deadly, absolute silence.

"Books have their fates," wrote critic Walter Benjamin, as do the readers and owners of books. Ironically, Hitler's first book—Max Osborn's *Berlin*—escaped the Nazi book burnings of 1933, solely because this book, by a Jewish author, was in Hitler's possession. Indeed, many of the books not in Hitler's private library suffered a public fate that presaged a more tragic one, which had been chillingly forecast by German-Jewish poet Heinrich Heine more than a century before: "Wherever they burn books, they will also, in the end, burn human beings."

Howard A. Kerner

Review Sources

Booklist 105, no. 2 (September 15, 2008): 16.
Christianity Today 52, no. 11 (November, 2008): 74.
The Economist 389 (October 4, 2008): 90.
Kirkus Reviews 76, no. 16 (August 15, 2008): 87.
Library Journal 133, no. 17 (October 15, 2008): 70.
The New Republic 239, no. 11 (December 24, 2008): 32-35.
The New York Sun, September 24, 2008, p. 11.
Publishers Weekly 255, no. 33 (August 18, 2008): 56.
The Seattle Times, October 16, 2008, p. 16.
The Washington Post Book World, October 26, 2008, p. BW10.

HOME

Author: Marilynne Robinson (1943-   )
Publisher: Farrar, Straus and Giroux (New York).
   325 pp. $25.00
Type of work: Novel
Time: 1956
Locale: Gilead, a fictional small town in Iowa

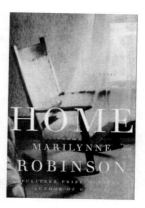

This companion to Robinson's novel Gilead *recounts the Boughton family's struggle for reconciliation and healing amid disappointed hope and irretrievable loss*

Principal characters:
> GLORY BOUGHTON, the youngest of eight Boughton children, a thirty-eight-year-old high school English teacher, who comes home to care for her dying father
> JACK BOUGHTON, forty-three, one of Glory's four brothers, the family's prodigal son, who returns to Gilead after a twenty-year absence
> ROBERT BOUGHTON, the widower father of Glory and Jack, a retired Presbyterian minister
> JOHN AMES, Robert's closest friend, a fellow Protestant clergyman in Gilead

"This life on earth is strange business," thinks Glory Boughton as she prepares supper for her frail father, Reverend Robert Boughton, and her brother, Jack. Their father rejoices that they have come back to Gilead, the 1950's Iowa town created by Marilynne Robinson in her novel *Home*. Boughton needs his daughter's care, but the circumstances of Glory's homecoming are fraught with regret deeper than the realization that her father is dying. A long, ill-fated love affair and an abandoned teaching career make her wonder what has become of her life.

"Home to stay!" is how Reverend Boughton greets Glory, but "her heart sank" as she heard those words, which open the novel, for failure and loss haunt her return to Gilead. Times were better before she left home for good, but in 1956, the year in which *Home* is set, coming home makes her say, "I hate this town . . . because it reminds me of when I was happy."

"There's no place like home," goes an old song, but Glory's question—"What does it mean to come home?"—leaves little room for nostalgia. That question applies to Jack, the family's prodigal son, more than to Glory, for without explanation he returns after a twenty-year absence, unbroken even by his mother's funeral. If his story ends more darkly than Jesus's parable of the prodigal son in the New Testament's Gospel according to Luke (15:11-32), which this novel recalls, the Boughton relationships, uncovered layer by layer, possess unusual contemporary power to make readers think about their own families and the homes they try to sustain.

Dan, Luke, Jack, and Teddy are the Boughton boys. Faith, Hope, and Grace are

∽

Marilynne Robinson, who teaches at the University of Iowa Writers' Workshop, has written three acclaimed novels. Housekeeping *(1980) received a Hemingway Foundation/PEN Award for best first novel,* Gilead *won the 2005 Pulitzer Prize in fiction, and* Home *was a finalist for the 2008 National Book Award.*

∽

Glory's sisters. "The girls in this family," Glory remarks, "got named for theological abstractions and the boys got named for human beings." In the Boughton household, however, faith, hope, grace, and glory are not abstractions. In addition to being the names of daughters and sisters, those words shape the family's identity and its members' different responses to it.

Although the children have grown up and left, and one parent has been buried and the other is dying, the Boughton home remains a place where Scripture is respected, prayers are said, conversation about life's significance continues, the importance of forgiveness is affirmed, hope seems unending, and gratitude for good everyday things—the stuff that often constitutes grace—finds expression. However, despite Glory's presence, not much is glorious about the Boughton family, although some of them are successful enough. Teddy is a doctor. Following in his father's footsteps, Luke is a minister. Like Gloria, Dan is a teacher. Reverend Boughton has been revered as a pastor, and, for the most part, the now-scattered Boughton family enjoys esteem in Gilead. Nevertheless, the Boughtons—especially Glory, Jack, and their father—are hurting and grieving because love is often painful, life does not respect Scripture, prayers go unanswered, coherent meaning is elusive, forgiveness is no match for harm done and guilt felt or unacknowledged, hope harbors hopelessness, discouragement undermines faith, and grace, whether divine or human, may be insufficient. In the Boughtons' home, these disheartening experiences are linked to the fact that Jack's full name is John Ames Boughton. He was indeed named for a human being, Robert Boughton's best friend, Reverend John Ames.

The reflection that Robinson invites, intensified by her story's melancholy, does not depend entirely on *Gilead* (2004), the equally touching novel that preceded *Home*. These novels, however, are definitely companions; their narratives intersect and amplify each other as the lives of the Boughton and the Ames families unfold together. Readers who track both stories will appreciate all the more the brilliance of Robinson's prose, how perceptively she handles the secret contradictions and unspoken feelings of family life, how lucidly she interprets fundamental elements of Christian teaching, and how sensitively she probes the regret and heartache that engulf people when ties that bind are broken.

The yearnings found in both novels are specific to the Ames and Boughton homes, which are steeped in Christianity, but versions of those longings are widely shared by families everywhere. Narrated in the third person, Glory's perspective informs *Home*, while Reverend Ames's voice governs the first-person account in *Gilead*. At seventy-six, Ames is older than Robert Boughton, who has been his lifelong friend, but Ames's heart is failing, and he, too, is dying. Ames treasures books, including those on philosophy, and he loves writing and baseball, too. He has seen plenty of suffering and grief in Gilead. His life has included sorrow, which touched him deeply and forever when childbirth took his wife, Louisa, and then Rebecca, his newborn daughter, as well. Ames was out of town when the child was born six weeks early. She did not live long; Ames got home in time to hold her for only a few minutes before she died. Before Ames arrived, Boughton baptized the baby as Angeline, because nobody could tell him the name chosen for the infant. Eight years later, when the third Boughton son is born, he is named after Ames—probably, Ames thinks, as a way of making up for his own childlessness—and it is Ames who baptizes the boy who will come to be the cause of so much sadness.

In *Gilead*, Ames recalls these tender and heartbreaking experiences because he is writing a memoir for his seven-year-old son, Robby, who is named after Robert Boughton. Late in life, Ames unexpectedly found love again. Boughton performed the marriage between Ames and Lila, who is more than thirty years younger than her husband, and a boy was born to them. Ames longs to be remembered by his son, but he knows that he will die before his son really knows him. So the old man leaves behind a testament that one day may help to fill his absence. Ames writes intimately, lovingly, and in great detail to his child, although he cannot know if his son will ever read the words his father has written, let alone understand them as Ames intends. He expects that Robby will leave Gilead one day.

Ames, says Glory, has been like a second father to the Boughton family, and so it is no surprise that she shares news about the long-lost Jack's homecoming. Jack's return, however, is very surprising, for this man, now forty-three, has scarcely been heard from since he left home two decades earlier, the departure—an abandonment, really—provoked by his fathering a child out of wedlock. The young mother, Annie Wheeler, came from an impoverished family and a desolate rural home. It made no sense that Jack took up with her. The Boughtons, especially Glory, tried to help the abandoned child but to little avail. At the age of three, Jack's daughter died from an untreated infection. Though it is scant consolation, her grave is in the Boughton family plot in Gilead's cemetery. Ames correctly reflects that, despite this, Jack remains the most beloved among the Boughtons, a position that has everything to do with Jack's being the family's lost sheep, whose redemption is much desired by them all, and especially by his father.

Jack can be charming and considerate. Although he lacks religious faith, even when he seems to long for it, Jack knows the Bible, and his piano-playing repertoire contains well-loved hymns and gospel songs. He remains the wayward outsider, a self-described "lifelong exile from the ordinary world," his woebegone life scarred by the crime of robbery—prison included—and alcohol abuse. Jack's history, before and after his rejection of fatherhood's responsibilities, caused great disappointment to Ames and to Glory and the other Boughtons and gave little hope of change. Nothing, however, causes his father and the others more anguish than Jack's absence from home, which is amplified by a silence so prolonged that for years at a time the Boughtons did not know what Jack's circumstances were or even if he were alive. When at last Jack announces his homecoming and makes the promise good, glimmers of hope surround his return. His presence buoys his father's spirits.

Jack makes repairs to the Boughton house; he tends the flowers his mother planted long ago. Jack and Glory gradually share painful secrets of their lives, and they become good friends as well as caring siblings. Jack reestablishes his relationship with Ames, even attending his church a few times. Affection grows between Robby and Jack, who plays baseball with the boy, which Ames is too old to do. Not without Ames's concern, Lila—experience tells her that a person, indeed everything, can change—shows Jack hospitality. Jack even considers that he might be able to make a life in Gilead, a hope that includes the revelation that Jack has an African American wife named Della and a son. However, Jack is unemployed, and the daily news details racial violence in places such as Montgomery, Alabama. The chances are slim that he and his wife can make a home anywhere in a still-segregated America.

"I was clutching at a straw, coming to Gilead," Jack tells Glory, but it does not work. Jack's shame and self-loathing are redoubled by his drinking and by an Ames sermon that Jack takes—probably mistakenly—personally as condemning his irresponsibility. He tries to asphyxiate himself with exhaust fumes in the Boughton barn, but he is too drunk to start the motor on the car he has restored. Glory finds him before it is too late but not in time to forestall Jack's decision: "I have to go now."

Jack will not be home when his father dies. He kisses his father's brow before both of them depart, but the reconciliation between them stays incomplete. On his way to catch the bus out of town, Jack and Ames unexpectedly meet once more. Ames gives Jack some money and then asks if Jack would allow him to place his hand on Jack's brow and bless him. Jack agrees, thanks the old man, and then he is gone.

Both *Gilead* and *Home* recall hymns and gospel songs. One that Jack plays for his father has a beckoning refrain: "Come home, come home, You who are weary, come home; Earnestly, tenderly, Jesus is calling, Calling, O sinner, come home!" *Home* makes its readers wonder how that call works, if it does. As Robinson's storytelling draws people into such meditation, her readers may recall that the source of Gilead's name is biblical. Anticipating millennia ago that his people would be swept into Babylonian exile, the Jewish prophet Jeremiah asked his lamenting question, "Is there no balm in Gilead?" (Jeremiah 8:22) A song from the African American religious tradition remembers Jeremiah and affirms that "there is a balm in Gilead to make the wounded whole . . . [and] to heal the sin-sick soul."

Robinson also leaves her readers to ask if that song rings true, for at the end of *Home*, Glory decides that she may, after all, be home to stay. A few days after Jack's departure for destinations unknown, she meets his wife, Della, and their son, Robert. Their visit to Gilead can last only a few minutes, but clearly Della and the boy know and care about the Boughton home in ways that could only be explained by Jack's love for it and them. Della leaves Glory a phone number in case Jack calls home. In response to Glory's question about baseball, the young Robert Boughton says, "Yes, ma'am. I play some ball," and Della tells Glory that the boy "thinks he's going to be a preacher."

Is there a balm in Gilead? Can one truly come home and be at home to stay? As she provides Glory's last thought—"The Lord is wonderful"—Robinson aptly keeps her readers wondering and perhaps yearning, too.

John K. Roth

Review Sources

Booklist 104, no. 19/20 (June 1, 2008): 6.
Library Journal 133, no. 13 (August 15, 2008): 71-72.
New Statesman 137 (October 27, 2008): 54.
New York, September 1, 2008, p. 96.
The New York Review of Books 55, no. 18 (November 20, 2008): 45-46.
The New York Times Book Review, September 21, 2008, p. 16.
The New Yorker 84, no. 27 (September 8, 2008): 76-78.
Newsweek 152, no. 12 (September 22, 2008): 73.
O, The Oprah Magazine 9, no. 9 (September, 2008): 218.
People 70, no. 12 (September 22, 2008): 63.
Publishers Weekly 255, no. 26 (June 30, 2008): 159.
Time 172, no. 12 (September 22, 2008): 92.
The Times Literary Supplement, September 19, 2008, pp. 19-20.
Vogue 198, no. 9 (September, 2008): 662.
The Wall Street Journal 252, no. 69 (September 20, 2008): W8.

HOMECOMING

Author: Bernhard Schlink (1944-   )
First published: Die Heimkehr, 2006, in Germany
Translated from the German by Michael Henry Heim
Publisher: Pantheon Books (New York). 260 pp. $24.00
Type of work: Novel
Time: The 1940's to the early 2000's
Locale: West Germany, Switzerland, California, East
   Germany, New York City, upstate rural New York,
   unified Germany

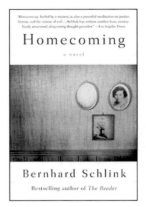

A German man born in 1945 and raised after World War II struggles to make a life for himself while pursuing clues that his supposedly dead Nazi father lives on, clues that eventually lead to the highest circle of American academia

Principal characters:
> PETER DEBAUER, also known as PETER GRAF and DR. FÜRST, a young
>   German law-book editor
> ELLA GRAF ("DEBAUER"), his single mother, a private secretary
> GRANDFATHER and GRANDMOTHER, his father's Swiss parents
> KARL, main character in a homecoming novel
> BARBARA BINDINGER, Peter's girlfriend, a teacher
> AUGIE MARKOVICH, her American husband whom she divorces
> VERONIKA, Peter's former girlfriend for eight years
> MAX, her son, in need of a father
> JOHANN DEBAUER, also known as VOLKER VONLANDEN, WALTER
>   SCHOLLER, and JOHN DE BAUR, Peter's father, an opportunist,
>   international con man, and deconstructionist
> GERDA WOLF, key West German informant for Peter
> ROSA HABE, key East German informant for Peter
> GOTTHOLD RANK, key Swiss informant for Peter

   A former judge in the Constitutional Court of North Rhine-Westphalia, a professor of public law and legal philosophy at Berlin's Humboldt University, an author of several detective mysteries, and an author of the best-selling novel *Der Vorleser* (1995; *The Reader*, 1997), Bernhard Schlink definitely has the necessary background to write *Homecoming*, a fictional investigation into modern history, identity, and legal theory. Besides that, *Homecoming* gets personal, drawing on autobiographical details and reflecting the fallout from Nazism from which Germans of Schlink's generation suffered, whereby the sins of the fathers were visited on the sons. *Homecoming* is centered around a son's search for such a father, unfortunately one who carries on his Nazi ways even in the United States and in highest academia, as shockingly demonstrated in the novel's climax.

Before its spectacular climax, however, the novel tends to drag a bit, depending, as it does, on the somewhat dull personality of its main character, Peter Debauer, a law student who never finishes his dissertation, drops out, and, after training to be a masseur, becomes an editor of law books and periodicals in a publishing house. Peter's personal life has a similar drift and malaise: His mother tries to

Bernhard Schlink, born in Bielefeld, Germany, is a former judge and an expert on law. He is author of a series of detective mysteries and the international best-selling novel The Reader *(1995).*

control him right into middle age, and his various affairs with women are either one-night stands or live-in disasters. For eight years he lives with the unstable Veronika, supporting her and her illegitimate son Max even as she continues to be unfaithful. Later he falls in love with and moves in with Barbara Bindinger, who turns out to be married to an American journalist absent for long periods on reporting assignments. Peter, however, has one saving obsession: He is driven to find out about his father, Johann Debauer, a Swiss citizen who supposedly died in Eastern Germany working for the Red Cross during World War II and whom Peter sorely missed growing up.

The mystery of Johann Debauer's fate and Peter's obsessive search to find out about him provide the other main interest in the first four of the novel's five sections. Readers cannot help but get caught up in this historical detective story, and luckily Peter is better as a detective of history than as manager of his own life. That is because his own life depends in some measure on unraveling the clues of history. Besides filling a void, the facts about his father might make him proud, since his father apparently died saving lives. In contrast to Peter, older Germans, including his mother, are depicted as being vague and not wanting to talk much about World War II, especially the Holocaust.

Although set mostly in unnamed West German towns, the novel begins with Peter recollecting his childhood summer stays in Switzerland with his grandparents. Their middle-class home in a little Swiss village beside a lake is idyllic compared to the shabby environment of postwar Germany where Peter spends the rest of the year with his then-impoverished mother. The peaceful Swiss scene lulls the reader as it does Peter, who has fond memories of the place and of photographs showing his father, also an only child, as a normal talented boy and young man: " . . . he had collected stamps, sung in the church choir, played handball, drawn, painted, and been a voracious reader." Although nearsighted, the father had been "a good pupil and law student, and never done military service."

Later, readers might look back and ask how such a peaceful, idyllic place could have produced such a monster as John de Baur. Even in the Swiss setting there are clues, and not just the "impatient," arrogant look on young Johann's face. The grandfather is a Germanophile full of stories from "Swiss or German history, especially military history." It is the grandfather, who has done his share of homesick wandering, who introduces the theme of homecoming in the novel through his theory that all Germans abroad suffer from angst for the fatherland. Homer's *Odyssey* (725 B.C.E.) becomes the prototype for a distinct genre of German homecoming stories.

Like Penelope, Peter's grandparents become busy at night—in their case editing a pulp-fiction series blandly titled Novels for Your Reading Pleasure and Entertainment. These four hundred or so sentimental books are full of German angst, heroic deeds, and homecomings. In short, the novels restore the banal German beliefs that supposedly got a reality check in World War II.

His grandparents will not let young Peter read the novels, but, because paper is expensive in Germany, they do allow him to take extra galleys home and use the backs of pages for homework. Only years later does the obedient Peter break down and read one of the galleys, followed by others. The first story is about a German soldier named Karl who escapes from a Siberian prison, makes his way across Russia and Eastern Europe, and after several years reaches home, only to open the door on his startled wife, two small children, and another man. The last few pages, however, are missing, used for homework, so the story's ending becomes another mystery for Peter to resolve, a mystery that turns out to be intertwined with his and his father's life.

Over the years, the mystery becomes harder to solve because his grandparents changed titles and authors' names, libraries and archives do not keep pulp fiction, and even the publishing house goes out of existence. Two decades later, when Peter moves to another city, he recognizes "a massive, gloomy, inhospitable building of red sandstone" as the home to which Karl returned. A visit to the building at 38 Kleinmeyerstrasse not only enables Peter to meet the love of his life, Barbara Bindinger, but puts him on the trail of the homecoming novel's author.

Some brilliant detective work by Peter (and plotting by Schlink) gradually leads to Volker Vonlanden, a Nazi propagandist during World War II; then to Walter Scholler (supposedly a Viennese Jew who survived Auschwitz), art editor for a Communist newspaper in East Germany; and finally to the homecoming novel's author—all of whom turn out to be different versions of Peter's father, now reincarnated as John de Baur, popular professor at Columbia University, family man, and leading American expert on the deconstruction of law.

All these revelations leave a reader's head spinning even before the novel's spectacular climax: a face-off between Peter and his father first at Columbia University and then at a wintry retreat in rural upstate New York. The revelations themselves raise questions. How could Peter's mother lie to him for so long? (It even turns out she was never married to his father, so he is illegitimate, legally Peter Graf.) How much did Peter's upstanding Swiss grandparents know? (Probably very little, but what they did know went to the grave with them.) Could Peter be the half-brother of Barbara's older sister? (It is bizarre to contemplate, but Peter's father apparently had an affair with Barbara's mother before the mother married.) Of most concern to Peter is how his father, who babysat him for ten weeks, could have so callously forgotten about him and his mother.

John de Baur recalls the case of Paul de Man (1919-1983), a Yale literary scholar and leading exponent of deconstruction in literature. During 1941 and 1942 in Nazi-occupied Belgium, his home country, the young de Man wrote almost two hundred articles for a collaborationist newspaper, including an anti-Semitic article titled "The Jews and Contemporary Literature." After de Man's death, the articles were rediscovered, causing quite a controversy in the literary world. When he immigrated to the United States in 1948, de Man abandoned his wife and three sons, then married an American girl without first getting a divorce.

Despite these similarities, the known sins of de Man pale in comparison to those of the fictional de Baur. If de Baur is modeled after de Man, Schlink exaggerated considerably for effect, maybe to avoid any lingering ambiguity such as that which surrounds de Man. De Baur's Swiss origin seems a rough parallel to de Man's Belgian origin, but again the Swiss origin eliminates any ambiguity about his Nazi sympathies: De Baur is not a reluctant, one-time recruit in an occupied country but a gung-ho volunteer from a neutral country. De Baur wants to be involved with the Nazi leadership, cozying up to a favorite of the führer, assuming the ridiculous pseudonym Volker Vonlanden ("Folk of the Land"), and writing Nazi propaganda.

Even after the fall of the Nazi regime, de Baur does not so much abandon his Nazi beliefs as cover them up, changing his outer colors like a chameleon to adapt to the powers that be. Caught in the Communist East, de Baur cozies up to the local military administrator, a Soviet Jew; takes on the identity of Walter Scholler, a Viennese Jew and Auschwitz survivor ("And he had a number tattooed on his arm"); and becomes art editor of a Communist propaganda newspaper. Soon he escapes to West Germany, then is not heard from for a while (which might be his homecoming novel period), and finally, according to him, gets a scholarship in 1950 to go to the United States. There, with his Nazi principles, his chameleon personality, his experience in writing propaganda for opposing sides, and his European accent, he is well prepared to assume leadership in the deconstruction movement. De Baur's résumé proudly lists Leo Strauss (a favorite philosopher of American neoconservatives) and Paul de Man as his teachers.

Homecoming is one of those rare novels that is both entertaining on a popular level and intellectually engaging. While Schlink's leanings as a scholar of law are apparent, he is able to explain deconstructionist theory and present both sides of the debate about it. He also makes it clear that Nazism was not just a German phenomenon, it might not be dead, and it might even have made inroads in the United States. The novel's frequent references to Homer's *Odyssey* become a little tedious and heavy-handed, but they do point to *Homecoming* as a kind of Germanic allegory, a reverse *Odyssey*.

Readers will obviously notice that de Baur, the slick Nazi Odysseus, does not return home. Instead, after helping mess it up, he flees it, in a mockery of the sentimental homecoming novels that he writes. He abandons his son and the son's mother and starts another family in a new land. Peter, the Germanic Telemachus, has to hunt down his father, comes to hate him, and finally has to confront him. If anything, it is Peter who experiences the homecoming: He is able to deal with his demons, find some peace, and return home to his beloved Barbara and the fatherless Max. *Homecoming* is an allegory for Schlink's lost generation.

Harold Branam

Review Sources

Booklist 104, no. 8 (December 15, 2007): 25.
Bookseller, February 1, 2008, p. 50.
The Economist 386 (January 12, 2008): 74.
Kirkus Reviews 75, no. 22 (November 15, 2007): 1175.
Library Journal 132, no. 20 (December 15, 2007): 102.
London Review of Books 30, no. 15 (July 31, 2008): 21-24.
The New York Times Book Review, January 13, 2008, p. 14.
The New Yorker 84, no. 7 (March 31, 2008): 129.
Publishers Weekly 254, no. 41 (October 15, 2007): 37.
The Spectator 306 (January 12, 2008): 29-30.
The Times Literary Supplement, February 8, 2008, p. 19.

HOSPITAL
Man, Woman, Birth, Death, Infinity, Plus Red Tape, Bad Behavior, Money, God, and Diversity on Steroids

Author: Julie Salamon (1953-   )
Publisher: Penguin Press (New York). 363 pp. $25.95
Type of work: Current affairs, ethics, medicine

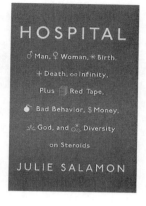

Salamon's account of a year in the life of Maimonides Medical Center in Brooklyn, told through the lives of administrators, doctors, staff, and patients, captures the day-to-day drama of large metropolitan hospitals, struggling to survive in a broken health care system

Principal personages:
> DR. ALAN ASTROW, associate director, medical oncology
> JO ANN BALDWIN, assistant vice president, community outreach
> PAMELA BRIER, president and chief executive officer
> DR. JOSEPH CUNNINGHAM, chair, department of surgery
> DR. DAVID GREGORIUS, emergency room resident
> MS. HERNANDEZ, patient
> DR. DOUGLAS JABLON, vice president, patient relations/special assistant to the president
> DR. ISRAEL JACOBOWITZ, cardiac surgeon
> DR. SAMUEL KOPEL, oncologist and medical director, cancer center
> MARTIN PAYSON, chairman of the board
> MR. ZEN, patient

Julie Salamon had little interest in hospitals until a series of coincidences—a "karmic connection" (*bashert* in Yiddish)—led her to write *Hospital*. First, Jo Ann Baldwin, an administrator at Maimonides Medical Center (MMC) in Brooklyn, asked to meet her after reading *Rambam's Ladder* (2003), Salamon's book about philanthropy and charity, based on the teachings of the medieval Jewish philosopher and physician Maimonides (known as Rambam to Hebrew scholars). They agreed to meet, and Salamon was impressed by Baldwin's vivid description of the 750-bed MMC, trying to meet the needs of a constantly changing, multicultural neighborhood. A few months later, Salamon was invited by Dr. Alan Astrow, a hematologic oncologist at St. Vincent's Hospital in Manhattan, to attend a series of lectures on the spiritual needs of patients. Astrow also had read *Rambam's Ladder*. Impressed by Astrow's sensitivity to patients, Salamon was drawn to him immediately. Soon afterward, she received an e-mail from a friend, suffering from ovarian cancer, who mentioned Astrow, a "smart and caring doctor," and informed her that he would be moving to the new cancer center at MMC. A year after meeting Baldwin, Salamon contacted her and asked to spend a year at Maimonides, using the opening of the can-

Julie Salamon, a former reporter and critic for The New York Times *and* The Wall Street Journal, *is a widely published essayist and best-selling author of six previous books, including the prize-winning* Rambam's Ladder *(2003), which deals with modern charity and philanthropy;* Facing the Wind *(2001), a crime account; and* The Devil's Candy *(1991), a Hollywood classic. She was named a Kaiser Media Fellow in 2006.*

cer center as the focus for a book. Pamela Brier, the president of the hospital, and Martin Payson, the chairman of the board, eventually agreed and encouraged staff to cooperate with her. They gave Salamon virtually unlimited access to personnel and patients, with the stipulation that she was to protect the privacy of patients.

Maimonides (originally Israel-Zion Hospital) had been founded a century earlier to meet the needs of Hasidic Orthodox Jewish immigrants in Borough Park, Brooklyn. Orthodox Jews still represent 20 to 25 percent of the hospital's patients and, because of their historic ties to the hospital, they demand and wield a powerful say in its politics and practices. However, the neighborhood has come to include many other ethnic groups, including Chinese, Pakistanis, Russians, Eastern Europeans, and Hispanics. At the center of social change in the United States after 9/11, the neighborhood reflects conflicts between Jews and Muslims, Muslims and Hindus, and modernists and fundamentalists. Cultural differences patients present—languages, customs, health beliefs, and different care expectations—as well as their immigration and health insurance problems make extraordinary demands on administrators, staff, and caregivers. There are also conflicting demands from big business, consumers, and environmentalists.

Hospital, the result of Salamon's year of virtual immersion in MMC, reads like a novel. Payson told her the hospital is like a film set, and Salamon has written a real-life medical drama, as vivid as any film or television series. Interactions between administrators and community; administrators and staff; and physician and staff and patients are depicted against the backdrop of their personal lives, exposing not only their strengths but also their problems, flaws, and errors. Salamon also explores the fears and heartaches of patients and families, dealing with serious illness. Her keen observations and skillful interviews—the direct quotes are excellent—reveal the acute and ongoing day-to-day personal and professional problems that dog dedicated hardworking people on the job. By focusing on selected colorful individuals—physicians, administrators, nurses, cleaners, social workers, technicians, and patients—Salamon, a consummate reporter, reveals the inner workings of the hospital, with its cross-cultural forces, its internal feuds, its situations of greed and comedy, its poignant life-and-death struggles, and its system's politics, ethics, bureaucracy, and "screw-ups." A helpful "cast of characters" sorts out the people through whom the story is told.

Drama in the emergency room focuses on lead character David Gregorius, a first-year resident from the Midwest and newcomer to New York City. His outgoing e-mails, "Suck Reports," provide comic relief as they reveal his "culture-shock" in battling with cockroaches, navigating the subway, and observing Brooklyn crime. They also document his demanding schedule, exhaustion, and dedication. His initial reaction to the emergency room (ER) is likened to landing in a Third World country. The ER boasts a sophisticated computer system for tracking patients, but it is an incredibly chaotic world, worse than most ERs in the United States. It is overcrowded with immigrants—including Hispanics, Russians, Eastern Europeans, Chinese, and Pakistanis—and it is extremely noisy, with the constant beeping of monitors and sounds of different languages, including Yiddish, Chinese, Urdu, and Arabic. The hospital has translators for sixty-seven languages. While she spends time in the ER, Salamon learns about Hatzolah, the Orthodox Jewish emergency medical service that mans volunteer ambulance squads. Hatzolah has real clout with MMC, because it decides which hospitals get their business, and hospital admissions bring in money. In the past, when Hatzolah was dissatisfied with the hospital, admissions fell. Demanding in its advocacy for its clients, Hatzolah can increase the stress on caregivers in the ER.

The new comprehensive cancer center was built to persuade Brooklynites that they did not have to travel to Manhattan to find good care. However, losses from the center are a serious drain on the hospital budget—its new linear accelerator and the subterranean room that houses it cost five million dollars. The medical director of the cancer center is Samuel Kopel, an oncologist, whose wife is dying of ovarian cancer. The intimate details of their personal battle with cancer provide a narrative thread in the book. The stories of Mr. Zen and Ms. Hernandez, two hospitalized patients, also give a human face to cancer. In discussing their care, Salamon explores questions about cultural and language problems, finances, and policies that drive access to health care. The hero at the center is Astrow, the new chief of hematologic oncology, who brought Salamon to Maimonides. His compassion and preoccupation with the ethical and spiritual aspects of care are inspiring. Nevertheless, it has been a hard first year for him; he is disheartened by the politics and feuds he encounters in his new position. Some wonder if he is tough enough for the job.

Bitter feuds provide the content for a chapter entitled "Insults and Injuries." One involves the rivalry between the chair of surgery, Joe Cunningham, and his former medical partner, Israel Jacobowitz, which is not discussed at any length, perhaps because Cunningham is wary of Salamon and refuses to be interviewed. Salamon has many interviews with various staff members on Kopel's ongoing feud with his former close friend and medical partner, Michael Bashevkin, but it never makes sense to her. It is generally agreed that they are both decent, caring men. However, their quarrel contributes to the hospital's financial crisis. The hospital depends on referrals from Bashevkin's huge practice to fill beds, and he is not sending his patients to Maimonides.

Salamon's impressive research of the health care system places MMC within the "big picture" of managed care in the United States, where greedy pharmaceutical companies and insurance companies, which put profit ahead of caring, dominate. The huge number of payers—Medicare, Medicaid, and insurance companies—require meticulous documentation and adherence to complex coding requirements and guidelines for hospital reimbursement. Since 1983, Medicare's Diagnosis-Related-Groups (DRGs), a formula based on about 500 categories of patients, has dictated the standard reimbursement for patients and made moving patients through the system a bureaucratic nightmare.

Salamon learns the challenges of hospital administration, as she interviews and shadows Pamela Brier, the chief executive officer (CEO) since 2003. The hospital is ranked high by the Joint Commission on the Accreditation of Healthcare Organizations: It has a first-class cardiology department, and in 2003 it delivered more babies than any other hospital in New York State. Brier wants to showcase these accomplishments. Despite MMC's impressive track record, Brooklynites cling to the idea that the best care is found in Manhattan. A major expansion, now underway at MMC, includes building a larger ER and increasing the number of inpatient beds. In transition from a neighborhood institution to a major medical center competing for patients, the hospital is always in a state of flux. Interviews with Brier and other administrators are amazingly candid. A successful leader of a New York City hospital, Brier came to MMC to assist the former CEO turn the hospital into a prosperous institution. Shortly after taking over as CEO, she sustained serious injuries in an auto accident that left her husband a semi-invalid. Brier was back on the job in record time. She sees the hospital as a microcosm of the world, dealing with universal issues, and although she is considered a "micro-manager" and somewhat quirky in interpersonal relationships, she is well equipped to deal with egos, community tensions, budget problems, and local politics. In addition to guiding the overall direction of MMC, she holds town-hall meetings, works to foster good relationships with the neighborhood and the Muslim community, and attends charity functions. She comes across as dedicated and driven, concerned with every aspect of care, from competence to cleaning to staff cooperation to patient treatment. Every patient who comes into the hospital must be treated with respect and made to feel safe.

This mission is reinforced by the vice president for patient relations and special assistant to the president, Douglas Jablon. Known as "the fixer," Jablon is very much in tune with the Orthodox community, and he heads a department of patient representatives who are notary publics, interpreters, and patient advocates. His training philosophy is simple: "First you gotta take care of patients. Number two, all this advertising is very important, but I believe the patient is the best advertising, especially over here . . . if you treat them very well, they'll talk good about us."

This is a first-rate book. Although Salamon includes petty details and at times seems to belittle people who have been candid in her interviews, *Hospital* succeeds in describing the hard work, politics, and relationships involved in running a hospital. It also portrays caring people, trying to do their best to help others. However, the book has nothing good to say about the current health care system. Payson, the Maimonides chairman, holds out the hope that eventually a single-payer system will solve the problems of the present "insane" system. This country cannot afford to wait for reform much longer.

Edna B. Quinn

Review Sources

Booklist 104, no. 18 (May 15, 2008): 9.
The Economist 387 (May 10, 2008): 94.
JAMA: Journal of the American Medical Association 300, no. 22 (December 10, 2008): 2679.
Kirkus Reviews 76, no. 6 (March 15, 2008): 293.
Mother Jones 33, no. 3 (May/June, 2008): 81.
The New York Times Book Review, July 6, 2008, p. 2.
Publishers Weekly 255, no. 13 (March 31, 2008): 48-49.
The Wall Street Journal 251, no. 116 (May 17, 2008): W8.

THE HOUSE ON FORTUNE STREET

Author: Margot Livesey (1953-   )
Publisher: Harper (New York). 311 pp. $24.95
Type of work: Novel
Time: The early twenty-first century
Locale: London

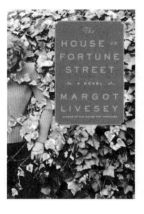

Two young women and two men are variously defeated in the pursuit of ideal love

> *Principal characters:*
> ABIGAIL TAYLOR, an actress and founder of a struggling theatrical repertory; owner of the house on Fortune Street in London
> SEAN WYMAN, a Keats scholar who left his wife to live with Abigail
> DARA MACLEOD, a therapist, Abigail's friend since college and downstairs tenant
> CAMERON MACLEOD, Dara's father

The House on Fortune Street is the story of two single young women who were close friends in college but have drifted apart. Their histories and circumstances are revealed in stages, at first through Sean, Abigail's live-in boyfriend, and Cameron, Dara's father. Their two points of view dovetail with later accounts from Dara and Abigail, exploring the distances that have grown between them in part due to secrets they have kept from each other. The novel begins with Sean, a scholar writing his dissertation on medical references in the poetry of John Keats (1895-1821). Sean's experiences to some degree parallel those of Keats, and the novel's four sections loosely echo the structure of Keats's poem *Endymion* (1817), while Cameron's, Dara's and Abigail's tales are each informed by a book or literary character. Sean's section ends with Dara's suicide; the following three sections shift from Cameron's memories of Dara's childhood, through Dara's work and the beginning of her doomed love affair with a married man, to Abigail's childhood, her career, and her relationships with her father, Dara, and Sean. Abigail's final, summing-up meeting with Cameron allows each of them to reveal secrets, confess failings, and bring Dara's story to a close.

As the novel opens Sean is living with Abigail, a beautiful theater actress who pursued him until he agreed to leave his wife; she owns the house on Fortune Street where the two share the upstairs flat. Abigail has asked him to pay rent, so he agrees to collaborate with his old friend Valentine on a book promoting assisted suicide. Abigail is launching a repertory theater company and constantly travels; when he receives an anonymous letter accusing Abigail of seeing another man he suspects she is involved with Valentine; as soon as their book is complete Valentine confirms the affair (later admitting to Abigail that he sent the anonymous letter) and Sean leaves the Fortune Street house.

In his last weeks at Fortune Street, Sean occasionally runs into Dara, Abigail's college friend who rents the downstairs flat. Dara has been waiting years for her lover Edward to leave his girlfriend and move in with her. Just before Christmas Sean talks with Dara, but he responds more to her natural gift for listening than to signs that Dara needs a sympathetic ear and tells her about the book on assisted suicide. Shortly after the holidays, Sean enters Dara's apartment, believing she spent Christmas with her family and intending to make her home more welcoming for her return. He finds Dara's body and a suicide note torn in small pieces and left in an envelope addressed to her parents. Sean hides the note to spare Dara's parents the pain of reading it. Recalling their last conversation, he realizes he overlooked her obvious distress and may even have validated her suicidal feelings with his talk of people who, he felt, had justifiably ended their own lives.

∼

Margot Livesey grew up in Scotland and holds a B.A. in English from the University of York. She is the author of five previous novels, including The Missing World *(2002),* Eva Moves the Furniture *(2001), and* Banishing Verona *(2004).*

∼

In the second section, Dara's father, Cameron, tells about his marriage to Fiona, and his realization that he was attracted to young girls. Cameron never acted upon his secret interests, but when Dara was ten years old he became obsessed with her best friend, a little girl named Ingrid. Cameron discovers that Charles Lutwidge Dodgson, the author of *Alice in Wonderland* (1865) under the name Lewis Carroll, photographed young girls—sometimes naked. An amateur photographer, Cameron feels an affinity for Dodgson that seems to somewhat justify his own feelings. When Fiona encourages Cameron to pursue photography as a hobby, he welcomes the opportunity to take photographs of Dara and Ingrid or of Ingrid alone. He tells himself that merely taking pictures of the girls is harmless; he can enjoy his passion without any negative effect on the children.

Cameron describes a camping trip Dara will later recall as her last happy childhood memory, involving the MacLeods and Ingrid's family, including Ingrid's mother Iris and her teenage sister Carol. During the trip, Cameron unthinkingly snaps a picture of Ingrid, half-naked, changing into a bathing suit. The trip ends in an angry nighttime confrontation on the beach involving Carol, Iris, and Cameron when Carol is found naked with a young man who was camping nearby. Later in recounting the incident to Fiona, Cameron does not tell her that Carol had accused him of an inappropriate interest in her little sister. Iris does not confront Cameron, but she does tell Fiona about Carol's remark, and Fiona immediately understands that Cameron failed to mention Carol's accusation because it was true. Fiona develops Cameron's film, and she finds the photograph of Ingrid that proves his guilt. Fiona divorces Cameron, agreeing to keep his attraction to girls a secret if he pays a large amount of alimony and agrees not to see his children again. Years later, she allows him visitation, but he can never explain why he left, and Dara is devastated by her father's sudden and unexplained desertion.

Cameron invites the adult Dara to an exhibition of Dodgson's photographs that includes portraits of little girls, hoping for an opportunity to tell her the truth, but the photographs disturb her; she insists the children were damaged by Dodgson's predilections, even if he never touched them. Later the same day Dara asks Cameron why he left the family when she was young, and Cameron tells her it was because his older brother Lionel's untimely death left him with unbearable fears for his own children's safety. Dara is relieved to think it was Cameron's love for the family that drove him away. Ironically, she remarks that psychological damage is passed along through generations unless families face the truth, and before the day is out she confides to Cameron that she and Edward are planning to move in together and have a baby.

Dara's point of view in the novel's third section is informed by Charlotte Brontë's novel *Jane Eyre* (1847). Dara is a counselor at a small center that works with abused and emotionally disturbed women. She first meets Edward when he trips and falls at her feet as she sits sketching by a canal (Edward has the same name as Jane Eyre's ill-fated love Mr. Rochester, and his fall mirrors their first meeting where Rochester falls from a horse). Conflict at her job and her own account of the visit to the Dodgson exhibit reveal her inability to read people, confirmed by her growing relationship with Edward.

Dara agrees to rent and renovate the vacant downstairs apartment in Abigail's house so she will have a place of her own where Edward, who refuses to share a bathroom with her housemates, can spend the entire night. The apartment is in poor condition, and Dara resents Abigail's assumption that it is good enough for Dara, even though Abigail would only live in it if she was broke. Nonetheless, Dara redecorates and waits eagerly for Edward's first visit—during which he confesses that he has a young daughter with another woman, with whom he still lives platonically for the child's sake. Dara, who from childhood could not understand or even recognize dishonesty in others, is only briefly angry and soon agrees to continue seeing Edward; they will move in together at some future time when his child is better able to cope. Dara expects Abigail to sympathize, thinking her situation is parallel to Abigail's persuading Sean to leave his wife. Abigail disappoints her again by pointing out that Sean had no children and never deceived her. Dara's section ends with her account of the Dodgson exhibit, her confusion about the lies people tell and live, and her innocent acceptance of her father's lie.

Abigail is central to Sean's and Dara's stories, but her point of view is only revealed in the novel's final section, with its echoes of Charles Dickens's *Great Expectations* (1860-1861). Abigail's parents were nomads, moving from job to job and town to town at a moment's notice; the adult Abigail longs for stability and has worked hard to become self-sufficient. She and Dara form a close friendship in college—Abigail is talented and beautiful but emotionally distant and financially poor; Dara is plain and studious, emotionally vulnerable but financially secure. A mysterious benefactor offers Abigail a stipend to support her studies; she assumes the money comes from Dara's mother, Fiona, but learns after Dara's death that Cameron had provided for her through college (which Dara had envied, unbeknown to either Abigail or Cameron).

Abigail's relationships are primarily sexual; in contrast, Dara is completely devoted to the young political activist she meets in college, and she breaks down and is briefly hospitalized when he ends the relationship. Dara is shocked at Abigail's promiscuity and surprised when Abigail suddenly focuses on Sean, convinced his marriage is empty and he belongs with her. Abigail uses an inheritance to buy the Fortune Street house, dumping the boyfriend who helps her renovate the upstairs apartment when a friend mentions offhandedly that he might someday be legally entitled to half the house. Once Abigail has won Sean, she quickly becomes disillusioned with him and is easily drawn into the affair that ends their relationship.

The novel ends with a chance meeting between Abigail and Cameron. Each admits to the other the ways in which they failed Dara: Cameron speaks about the borderline pedophilia that destroyed his family, while Abigail admits she had avoided Dara and shut down their friendship, weary of hearing about Edward and fearful of revealing that her own ideal love story was a sham. Cameron is carrying Dara's suicide note, which Sean had decided to give him after all, and allows Abigail to read it. The note reveals that Dara had accidentally seen Edward with his daughter and supposedly platonic—but obviously pregnant—girlfriend.

Although central to the novel, Dara—wan, prone to migraines, and defenseless when treated badly by family, friends, or lovers—is a less interesting character than Abigail. Edward's betrayal is unsurprising; the complete despair that seizes Dara as a result and her failure to seek help seem out of sync with her experiences as a therapist and her emotional reconciliation with Cameron. The writer builds anticipation for Abigail's entrance, raising questions about this talented and charismatic actress who hounded Sean to leave a happy marriage, casually cheated on him, and then treated her friend so shabbily. In spite of the intended theme—how young single women are affected by their secrets and histories—Cameron's is perhaps the most compelling of the four stories. Margot Livesey is effective in her risky portrait of a man who successfully avoids acting on his pedophilia, but the depth of Cameron's conflict and the yawning generation gap between him and the other protagonists make him seem out of place in this novel.

Maureen Puffer-Rothenberg

Review Sources

The Atlantic Monthly 302, no. 2 (September, 2008): 118-119.
Booklist 104, no. 13 (March 1, 2008): 47.
Kirkus Reviews 76, no. 5 (March 1, 2008): 6.
Library Journal 133, no. 3 (February 15, 2008): 93.
People 69, no. 18 (May 12, 2008): 64.
Publishers Weekly 255, no. 1 (January 7, 2008): 32.

HOW FICTION WORKS

Author: James Wood (1965-   )
Publisher: Farrar, Straus and Giroux (New York).
   288 pp. $24.00
Type of work: Literary criticism
Time: 350 B.C.E. to 2005

Rather than suggesting how aspiring fiction writers should write, Wood, by engaging in close, analytical readings of representative passages from their writing, analyzes how a broad spectrum of writers from ancient times to the current century write

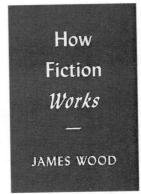

Principal personages:
   MIGUEL DE CERVANTES (1547-1616),
      Spanish novelist
   WILLIAM SHAKESPEARE (1564-1616), England's foremost playwright
   MOLIÈRE (1622-1673), French dramatist, born Jean-Baptiste Poquelin
   JANE AUSTEN (1775-1817), British novelist
   CHARLES DICKENS (1812-1870), British novelist
   GUSTAV FLAUBERT (1821-1880), French novelist
   HENRY JAMES (1843-1916), American novelist
   ANTON CHEKHOV (1860-1904), Russian novelist and playwright
   JAMES JOYCE (1882-1941), Irish novelist
   D. H. LAWRENCE (1885-1930), British novelist
   E. M. FORSTER (1889-1970), British literary critic
   SAUL BELLOW (1915-2005), Canadian American novelist, Nobel Prize
      in Literature, 1976
   MURIEL SPARK (1918-2005), Scottish novelist
   DAVID FOSTER WALLACE (1962-2008), American novelist and essayist

The term "genius" is bandied about so cavalierly that it is usually misapplied. It often confuses mere competence with genius rather than referring to the unique intelligence that is the mark of a William Shakespeare, a Jane Austen, or an Albert Einstein. Given this caveat, it is not out of line to call James Wood, based on his penetrating understanding of the dynamics of fiction writing, a genius in the field of literary criticism.

In this discerning book, whose title might erroneously suggest that it is a how-to book for people who hope to become novelists, Wood draws on his encompassing literary background and, in what becomes a thumbnail history of much of the Western world's greatest literature, analyzes the mystery of how notable writers of fiction have achieved their artistic outcomes. Wood's credentials for writing a book of this sort are impeccable; other distinguished critics have identified him as the most outstanding literary critic of his day.

In 1992, just short of his twenty-seventh birthday, Wood, still living in his native

Great Britain, became the chief literary critic of *The Guardian* of London, a publication for which he still writes regularly. He served for twelve years as a major literary critic and senior editor of *The New Republic* in New York, and during this time he taught classes in literature and literary criticism at Boston University (coteaching with Nobel laureate Saul Bellow), Kenyon College, and Harvard University, where he has been professor of the practice of literary criticism since 2003. A regular contributor of book reviews to *The New Yorker*, he left *The New Republic* in 2007 to become a staff writer for that prestigious magazine.

British-born James Wood is among the most celebrated contemporary literary critics in the English-speaking world. He has published one novel, The Book Against God *(2003). A staff writer for* The New Yorker *and professor of the practice of literary criticism at Harvard University, Wood has published two collections of essays,* The Broken Estate *(2000) and* The Irresponsible Self *(2004).*

Wood is controversial in that he spurns a narrow academic approach to literary criticism in favor of applying an aesthetic perspective to the fictional works he is reviewing. He assesses fiction by scrutinizing it closely and analytically, claiming "that there really is no such thing as irrelevant detail in fiction, even in realism, which tends to use . . . detail as a kind of padding, to make verisimilitude seem nice and comfy."

Were he to analyze the preceding sentence, Wood undoubtedly would fix his attention upon its last five words, pointing out that they progress—or, according to one's likes and dislikes—regress from the formality of "verisimilitude" to the downright familiar jargon of "nice and comfy." His contrast in those words is clearly aimed at drawing his readers into his camp immediately after the formality of verisimilitude may well have alienated them.

Although Wood never refers directly to Plato's theory of ideas (forms or shapes that are the essence of objects), he is concerned in many pages of this book with a quality that he chooses to call "thisness" and, in one instance, identifies as "quiddity." Thisness and quiddity refer to the essence of things. In writing about David Foster Wallace's story "The Suffering Channel," Wood notes that Wallace is writing about the decomposition of language, and that, by writing twenty or thirty pages in a style that may seem tedious and trying to read, he "prosecutes an intense argument about the decomposition of language in America, and he is not afraid to decompose—and discompose—his own style in the interests of making us live through this linguistic America with him." In doing so, Wallace creates a Platonic ideal, his prose capturing the thisness of his argument through a process that Wood terms the "full immersion method."

Wood contends that few books have appeared that consider how fiction works after the publication in 1927 of E. M. Forster's *Aspects of the Novel* (which Wood considers imprecise) and of three books by Milan Kundera on the art of fiction. He considers Kundera a novelist and essayist, not a literary critic in any practical sense.

Whereas Forster often eschews flat characters, preferring fiction populated by what he considers round characters, Wood defends flat characters. He likens them to caricatures and points out their artistic function of illuminating specific human traits or characteristics, often by exaggerating them and presenting them unilaterally. He considers roundness impossible in fictional characters because, he contends, they are not real people. He complains that the quest for roundness in fictional characters dominates (he says, "tyrannizes") readers, novelists, and critics, much to their critical disadvantage.

Wood discusses in fresh critical terms many of the warhorses of early twentieth century literary criticism, leveling his gaze upon most of the usual topics that have concerned critics: plot, metaphor, voice, and character development. He dismisses Forster's concepts of flat and round characters, preferring that fictional characters be studied in terms of what he terms "transparencies" and "opacities."

To illustrate this, he broaches a broad array of literary characters ranging from the soldier in Anton Chekhov's short story "The Kiss" to Becky Sharp in William Makepeace Thackeray's *Vanity Fair* (1848), from Prince Hal and Falstaff in Shakespeare's *Henry IV, Part I* (1597) to Isabel Archer in Henry James's *The Portrait of a Lady* (1881). Wood consistently draws on an enormous range of works of fiction by such novelists as those mentioned above as well as Gustav Flaubert (to whom Wood devotes considerable space and whom he considers sacrosanct), Honoré de Balzac, James Joyce, Ford Madox Ford, Saul Bellow, Fyodor Dostoevski, Sinclair Lewis, Don DeLillo, William Gass, Thomas Hardy, D. H. Lawrence, Iris Murdoch, Virginia Woolf, Beatrix Potter, Muriel Spark, Theodore Dreiser, and a host of others.

Wood details how a novelist such as Spark, in her novel *The Prime of Miss Jean Brodie* (1961), exercises what he calls a ruthless control over her fictional characters with her use of the flash-forward technique rather than the flashback. Spark surges forward from the main action of the plot to tell her readers what eventually happens to the characters about whom she is writing: Miss Brodie will die of cancer, Mary Macgregor will die at age twenty-three in a fire, and students mentioned in the text will enter into lackluster marriages or, in one case, will enter a convent.

Wood acknowledges that these flash-forwards, a technique also employed effectively by National Book Award winner Annie Proulx, may seem cruel to some readers because they make "summary judgments," but he contends that Spark uses them effectively to question whether Miss Brody ever actually had a prime herself. The primes of some of the schoolgirls with whom Spark populates her novel are behind them rather than skulking furtively in their respective futures. The chief virtue of Spark's flash-forwards is that they give Spark authorial control beyond any she could achieve were she simply to write within a purely temporally sequential context.

Among Wood's many perceptive discussions of how fiction writers handle the details of their composition is his discussion of temporality. Every writer of fiction is ultimately forced to come to grips with how to deal with time in unfolding their stories. Wood contends that, within any work of fiction, its creator must deal with elements of time and with the simultaneity of events that occur within the story.

A fictional character, for example, may be drowning, but, as his or her rowboat drifts away out of reach, children may be flying kites on a nearby beach, unaware of the drama being enacted within sight of them, or a cat may be climbing a nearby tree to attack a nest of toothsome fledglings. At any single moment in a story, a crucial event, central to the story, may be occurring while routine activities happen nearby. This is a temporal reality that authors writing realistic fiction must recognize and acknowledge for their fiction to achieve credibility.

Wood devotes thirty-one pages to a detailed discussion of language and follows it with eight pages concerning dialogue. In the former, he considers how skillful writers achieve rhythm and linguistic momentum by handling everyday speech in all its simplicity with the sort of deftness found in the writing of such complex stylists as Herman Melville, James, Woolf, and Lawrence.

Differentiating writing as an art quite distinct from music or painting, Wood notes that prose is always simple, no matter how difficult and extraordinary it may seem, because it is a medium used in commonplace communication. He accounts how Flaubert, who ranks at the top of Wood's list of exemplary stylists, labored over matters of style, agonizing over every word. He goes on to demonstrate how such intense labor characterizes the writing of such modern authors as Bellow and John Updike and how it is the offspring of such earlier literary stylists as Molière and Cervantes, who have been models for many of the noteworthy literary stylists following them.

Wood points out that Bellow, whom he identifies as one of the most effective stylists among modern novelists, eclipsing such notables as DeLillo, Updike, or Philip Roth, "read poetry: Shakespeare at first (he could recite lines and lines from the plays, remembered from his schooldays in Chicago), then Milton, Keats, Wordsworth, Hardy, Larkin, and his friend John Berryman. And behind all this, with its English stretching all the way back into deeper antiquity, the King James Bible."

The successful novelist, according to Wood, must be attuned to the rhythms and musicality of language. He also points to the difficulty of translating many of the rhythms of one language into another language, citing a Flaubert sentence from *Madame Bovary* (1857) as an example of this difficulty. The sentence in question is "L'idée d'avoir engendré délectait," which Wood translates as "The idea of having engendered delighted him," an accurate literal rendering of the French words. He notes that Geoffrey Wall, in his Penguin translation of *Madame Bovary*, renders the sentence thus: "The thought of having impregnated her was delectable to him." Again a worthy translation.

Wood then goes on perceptively to point out what is lost in both translations. "Say the French out loud as Flaubert would have done, and you encounter four 'ay' sounds in three of the words: 'L'id*ée*, engend*ré*, d*é*lect*ait*.'" He goes on to point out that an English translation that sought "to mimic the untranslatable music of the French . . . would sound like bad hip-hop: 'The no*tion* of procrea*tion* was a delecta*tion*.'"

Wood's uniquely fresh approach to interpreting literature makes *How Fiction Works* an intellectually challenging book that will bear reading and rereading by those seriously interested in literary criticism. The scope and depth of Wood's assessments consistently impress.

R. Baird Shuman

Review Sources

American Scholar 77, no. 4 (Autumn, 2008): 137-139.
The Economist 386 (February 9, 2008): 90.
Kirkus Reviews 76, no. 8 (April 15, 2008): 416.
Library Journal 133, no. 9 (May 15, 2008): 103-104.
The Nation 287, no. 19 (December 8, 2008): 46-52.
The New Republic 239, no. 1 (July 30, 2008): 35-37.
New Statesman 137 (February 11, 2008): 56.
New York, August 11, 2008, pp. 64-65.
The New York Review of Books 55, no. 18 (November 20, 2008): 85-88.
Newsweek 152, no. 5 (August 4, 2008): 60.
Publishers Weekly 255, no. 16 (April 21, 2008): 43.
Time 172, no. 4 (July 28, 2008): 60.
The Times Literary Supplement, February 8, 2008, p. 13.
The Writer 121, no. 10 (October, 2008): 43.

IDA, A SWORD AMONG LIONS
Ida B. Wells and the Campaign Against Lynching

Author: Paula J. Giddings (1947-   )

Publisher: Amistad/HarperCollins (New York). Illustrated. 800 pp. $35.00

Type of work: Biography, history, women's issues

Time: 1862-1931

Locale: The U.S. South, particularly Memphis, Tennessee; the U.S. North, particularly Chicago; Great Britain

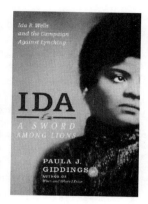

*A comprehensive biography of this journalist, lecturer,
feminist, reformer, and public intellectual, a forceful advocate of civil rights, social justice, woman suffrage, and the
antilynching cause, that provides an overview of Jim Crow
racial violence and African American citizenship and activism in the post-Reconstruction and Progressive eras*

Principal personages:

IDA B. WELLS-BARNETT, outspoken agitator for social change

THOMAS MOSS, proprietor of a Memphis grocery store who was brutally
murdered by a white lynch mob, spurring a black exodus from
Memphis to the Oklahoma Territory

T. THOMAS FORTUNE, editor of the *New York Age* and founder of the
Afro-American League, a key supporter of Wells's exposés of
Southern lynching

FREDERICK DOUGLASS, former abolitionist and proponent of African
American equality and women's rights, who championed Wells's
career as a public lecturer in the antilynching cause

FERDINAND BARNETT, progressive attorney and founder and editor of the
Chicago Conservator, who became Wells's husband in 1895

JOSEPHINE ST. PIERRE RUFFIN and MARY CHURCH TERRELL, Wells's
colleagues in the black woman's club movement

SUSAN B. ANTHONY and JANE ADDAMS, white women reformers with
whom Wells associated

WALTER WHITE and W. E. B. DU BOIS, leaders of the National
Association for the Advancement of Colored People (NAACP)

Ida B. Wells was a complex woman, and *Ida, A Sword Among Lions* by Paula J.
Giddings is a complex book that captures the full scope of her challenging and impressive life. It spanned from the Civil War into the "nadir" years of post-Reconstruction racial segregation, through the Progressive Era and World War I, and on to the
beginning of the Great Depression.

Wells was raised in the South. In the 1890's, when her newspaper office was destroyed and she received threats upon her life because of her determined political out-
spokenness on racial violence issues, she went into exile in the North. She spent the

~

A former journalist, Paula J. Giddings is the author of the acclaimed When and Where I Enter: The Impact of Black Women on Race and Sex in America *(1996) and* In Search of Sisterhood: Delta Sigma Theta and the Challenge of the Black Sorority Movement *(1988) and editor of* Burning All Illusions *(2002), an anthology of articles on race published in* The Nation. *She is the Elizabeth A. Woodson 1922 Professor in Afro-American Studies at Smith College.*

~

majority of her adulthood working and traveling for social-justice causes. In the last three decades of her life, she was based in Chicago, where she raised her family and became deeply involved in local social welfare and community politics as well as in more sweeping national reforms.

Wells was born in Holly Springs, Mississippi, the eldest daughter of former slaves who were ardent believers in education and work as means of uplift for African Americans. Her parents were early supporters of the Freedman's Aid Society's Shaw University (later Rust College), which Wells attended. Wells's happy family life was destroyed in 1878, when a yellow fever epidemic claimed the lives of both her parents. Orphaned at age sixteen, Wells set out on her own, with varying success, to supply financial support for her younger siblings and herself. Well-read and a lover of literature, she turned to the highly respectable profession of teaching, and she soon took up residence in Memphis, Tennessee. There she honed her oratorical and debating skills as a member of the Memphis Lyceum. As Giddings demonstrates, this was preparation for a lifetime of public speaking to come.

Giddings re-creates the social milieu of Memphis of the 1880's and the class, gender, and racial contradictions that faced a forthright young black woman such as Wells in a city where Jim Crow restrictions were taking hold. Wells would test those strictures with a lawsuit in 1883-1884, when she was discriminated against on the Chesapeake and Ohio Railway and she resisted moving to a segregated car. Teaching school, meanwhile, proved to be just the first of her professions. Gifted as a writer, she began to earn a name in freelance journalism. She wrote regular columns under the pen name "Iola," and in 1889, in association with the minister Taylor Nightingale and editor J. L. Fleming, became one-third owner and editor-in-chief of the *Memphis Free Speech and Headlight.* In doing so, Wells joined the ranks of other influential black male and female journalists working nationwide, and she began to travel extensively to promote the newspaper.

The violent murder of Wells's friend—grocer and postman Thomas Moss—by a white mob in 1892 was a turning point in her career, as well as in the lives of many of the African American residents of Memphis. In a pivotal editorial written after Moss's murder, Wells observed "that neither character nor standing avails the Negro if he dares to protect himself against the white man or become his rival." She then urged the black citizens of Memphis to observe Moss's dying words and leave the city, because no justice could be found for them there. Thousands responded, and they made their way to the Oklahoma Territory.

In a more pronounced way, the death of Moss launched Wells on an incredible arc as the nation's leading voice of protest against lynching. Her campaign to dispel myths and educate the public as to the true causes and intents of lynching took form through her editorials and later pamphlets. In the 1890's it would lead her from Memphis to New York and on to tours of Great Britain as an antilynching lecturer. Forced from the South, she worked for the *New York Age*, and in 1892 she produced her classic feature story based on her lynching investigations, "Southern Horrors: Lynch Law in All Its Phases." She was well received in Great Britain in 1892 and 1894, where, speaking before British audiences, she urged that international political pressure be exerted on the United States for an end to atrocities. Back in the United States, she joined with Frederick Douglass in decrying racism at the 1893 Chicago World's Fair, and she produced the famed protest pamphlet *The Reason Why the Colored American Is Not in the Columbian Exposition*. Gleaning personal insights from Wells's diary and her unfinished autobiography, as well as making copious use of detail from a wealth of African American newspapers from around the country, Giddings tells the story of these pivotal developments in Wells's activism with thoroughness and grace.

Most important, Giddings does an excellent job in explaining Wells's reeducation of the populace—and of other prominent reformers—on the issue of lynching. Through careful fieldwork investigations and compilation of sociological statistics, Wells disproved the popular belief that lynching was chivalrous retaliatory justice against licentious black men for the crime of rape. Wells demonstrated that more commonly consensual interracial relationships were involved; that white women's reputations were upheld at the cost of the lives of wrongly accused black men; and that white men who perpetuated lynching crimes were deeply hypocritical, as evidenced by the large number of mulatto citizens in the South. It was indeed black women who historically were victimized at the hands of white men, and Wells defended their honor. Wells pointed out that often, as in the torture and murder of Moss, lynching had nothing to do with sexuality at all. Moss in effect died because he was too successful as a black entrepreneur. After his funeral, ownership of his store ended up in the hands of a white commercial rival. In her lectures and writings on lynching, Wells particularly targeted prominent liberal and progressive whites who she felt perpetuated atrocity through their complacency and silence. For Wells, lynching was a moral outrage that compromised the status of the nation and mocked its stated ideals.

Despite the book's subtitle, Giddings's study ably demonstrates that the antilynching campaign was far from Wells's only field of reform. Wells also promoted woman suffrage, and she was an important figure in the black woman's club movement and the National Association of Colored Women. She was active as well in the early years of both the National Association for the Advancement of Colored People (NAACP) and the Universal Negro Improvement Association (UNIA). The first half of Giddings's narrative focuses on the portion of Wells's life leading up to 1895, when, at age thirty-two, she wed publisher Ferdinand Barnett of Chicago. While the young Wells battled against negative views of single women and of women in public, the wedded Wells faced new challenges in balancing continued activism with marriage and family life. Giddings captures the contradictory viewpoints on the issue in the elite urban black community: Was racial progress better served by women through devotion to domestic obligations or through public achievement? With a supportive husband, Wells-Barnett hyphenated her name, and she managed to meet both expectations: raising a family of four children and remaining an active force for social change.

In the last half of her book Giddings charts Wells's efforts to create interracial alliances, her political activism against residential and school segregation, and her role in founding social welfare agencies and political organizations, including the Frederick Douglass Women's Center, the Negro Fellowship League, and the Ida B. Wells Club and Alpha Suffrage Club in Chicago. Wells also took on the cause of labor, championing the organizing of black railway workers through A. Philip Randolph's Brotherhood of Sleeping Car Porters and Maids.

In the course of her perpetual activism, Wells was hindered by the sexism of men of her own race and by the racism (or overwillingness to compromise on issues of race) of white women reformers. Among the latter were the suffragists who attempted to bar Wells from marching with whites in the 1913 suffrage parade in Washington, D.C., for fear of alienating white supremacists in the South. Among black women, color consciousness and class biases could be divisive, as were petty or honest differences. Meanwhile, Wells had success working in alliance with others as divergent as Jane Addams and Marcus Garvey. As Giddings demonstrates, Wells's worst opponent could be her prickly personality, which even she realized was a force to conquer. Wells's belief in protest and direct action was also dismissed as problematic by those who favored more accommodating approaches and by other activists who feared loss of financial support from white philanthropists.

In her last years, Wells found herself marginalized in the causes to which she had dedicated her life. The NAACP grew in strength as it led action on the lynching issue, and the influence of women's groups declined. Wells helped win success in the 1915 campaign of Oscar DePriest, the first black alderman of Chicago, but her own independent efforts at winning office in the Illinois State Senate in 1930 failed. The East St. Louis riot and the racial violence that ravaged American cities at the end of World War I dismayed many who had long struggled for progress in racial rights. Wells was placed under surveillance and threatened with arrest on charges of treason for her organizing on the issue.

Readers of *Ida, A Sword Among Lions*—the title of which comes from Psalm 57:4—will be struck by how many of the dilemmas that faced Wells as a woman and as an African American citizen transcend time. Giddings's narrative of the unfolding events of Wells's personal and public life is encyclopedic. The biographical account is set in the context of the grassroots political history of the nation and the inner workings of organizations for social change. Despite its length, *Ida, A Sword Among Lions* encourages readers to follow up with more exploration into the life and impact of Wells-Barnett. Readers interested in greater scholarly analysis of Wells, especially the religious basis of her political outlook and the gendered aspects of her activism and the antilynching campaign, should turn to Patricia A. Schechter's brilliant biography, *Ida B. Wells-Barnett and American Reform, 1880-1930* (2001). Those who would like to enjoy Wells through her own words can delve into *Crusade for Justice: The Autobiography of Ida B. Wells* (1970), edited by Wells's daughter, Alfreda M. Duster, or some of Wells's many published essays.

Barbara Bair

Review Sources

Booklist 104, no. 11 (February 1, 2008): 20.
Kirkus Reviews 76, no. 2 (January 15, 2008): 74-75.
Library Journal 133, no. 3 (February 15, 2008): 112.
Ms. 18, no. 1 (Winter, 2008): 74-75.
The New York Times Book Review, May 18, 2008, p. 25.
O, The Oprah Magazine 9, no. 3 (March, 2008): 176.
The Wall Street Journal 251, no. 56 (March 8, 2008): W8.

I'M LOOKING THROUGH YOU
Growing Up Haunted—A Memoir

Author: Jennifer Finney Boylan (1958-   )
Publisher: Broadway Books (New York). 288 pp. $23.95
Type of work: Memoir
Time: The 1970's to 2006
Locale: Pennsylvania, Connecticut, and Maine

Boylan's touching but humorous account of growing up as a young male haunted by the secret knowledge of his true female identity

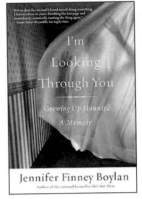

Principal personages:
  JIMMY/JENNY BOYLAN, transgendered
    writer, musician, college professor
  LYDIA BOYLAN, Jenny's once close, now
    estranged older sister
  H. S. and ELEANOR BOYLAN, Jenny's parents
  GRACE FINNEY, Jim Boylan's wife and Jenny Boylan's partner

Jennifer Finney Boylan has already written about her experience as a transsexual in the best-selling memoir *She's Not There: A Life in Two Genders* (2002), a book that recounts the story of a forty-year-old man, married with two sons, who finally embraces his true identity and begins the process that leads to gender-reassignment surgery and a new life as a woman. So while this new memoir, *I'm Looking Through You*, does not cover that ground (giving the basic information with real dispatch at several points), it nevertheless cannot help focusing on the issue of Boylan's gender identity, though it does so by placing this in the much more universal context of a coming-of-age tale. The declaration emblazoned on Jimmy Boylan's high school T-shirt, "I act different because I am different," could be the motto for all teenagers rebelling against parents and conventions as they struggle to come to terms with who they are and what that means for their future lives. Adolescence is turbulent, brutal, and comical, not just for boys who feel trapped in the wrong body, but for everyone, to some degree or another. Boylan's confusions and fears, however, are more specific; and it is this specificity that gives the book its uniquely haunted quality. Aware of his particular difference, young Boylan knows that "in order to survive, I'd have to become something of a ghost myself, and keep the nature of my true self hidden." It means haunting his own body, being "a wraithlike presence otherwise invisible to the naked eye—like helium, or J. D. Salinger, or the G-spot." In those few early sentences readers are introduced both to the memoir's principal metaphors (ghosts and hauntings) as well as to Boylan's principal tone: a voice that can turn on a dime from the serious to the comic. She is dead earnest about her haunted past; but as a fifty-year-old woman looking back on that time, she is also able to see and re-create the genuine comedy in it all.

A word about this act of looking back on the past: In a prefatory "Author's Note," Boylan makes it quite clear that her story, like all memoirs, is an impression, not a photographic record, and so it will "contain elements of invention, in keeping with the facts of my life." She will dramatize events, supply dialogue, and expand time frames in telling her story. Perhaps this is no more than a reminder that memories are personal and emotional constructs: They invite embellishment, insist on dilation or contraction, are powerful in their instability and suggestiveness, difficult to verify, and rarely shared exactly by others (when a friend at a thirtieth high school reunion, for instance, says that something Boylan wrote about never happened, she responds: "just because it never happened doesn't mean I can't remember it"). So long as she does not "shamelessly bamboozle the reader," Boylan believes that she is on safe ground in terms of presenting the truth. However, some

Jennifer Finney Boylan is a professor of English at Colby College, the author of several novels and short-story collections, as well as the best-selling memoir She's Not There *(2002). An increasingly public transgendered personality, she has appeared on* The Oprah Winfrey Show *and* Larry King Live, *and she has played herself on the ABC soap opera* All My Children.

readers may feel that proviso gives her a little too much leeway for creative elaboration. Before many pages have gone by, the reader confronts a family living in a crumbling haunted house: an affable father who asks his son to play piano pieces backward; a kimono-clad grandmother who dances atop barroom tables dispensing wisdom about the value of eating dirt; a visionary uncle who rides the rails scrawling utopian manifestos; an aunt with foot-long fingernails; a cousin who eats only plums; a dog, Matt the Mutt, that urinates on cue in fireplaces; and a friend who channels the Cowardly Lion. Then there is the narrator herself, who is electrocuted within the first few minutes of arriving at the family's "Coffin" House, who sees ghosts and hovering blue mists everywhere, who travels on trains that run over young girls, who sleeps in bat-ridden bell towers, and who wakes to play Rolling Stones songs on the college carillon. It all seems a little over the top, everything boosted into capital letters and day-glo colors—a sort of "can-you-believe-this?" hyperbole designed to rivet readers and boost sales.

Should the reader question any of this? Should the reader believe that a toilet left running overnight could actually flood three floors of a house, knocking down walls, taking out ceilings, and floating grand pianos? Should the reader simply understand that little Jimmy's mistake creates a mess for his family: an external image that makes concrete his internal condition? Is it just the nature of contemporary memoir to trade in this species of exuberant exaggeration? These questions do not exactly resolve themselves, but they do not finally undermine the tale, either. Even accounting for an imagination that may be cranking up the dial on drama and whipping up dialogue that has the tart, quippy feel of a novel (if hardly the feel of everyday human exchange), the reader quickly accepts the fact that Boylan's life really did unfold among some quirky personalities and in some amazing circumstances—a haunted house, spectres, floods, electrocutions—all on Philadelphia's Main Line. Most readers will indeed be riveted.

Questions of heightened dramatization aside, it is clear that Boylan tells the story she needs to tell. The motives are sound, transparent, and compelling. It may be surprisingly breezy and lighthearted, an account that refuses to be any more serious than it has to be (readers will sense early on that there is not much that will not be sacrificed for a laugh, and the book delivers many of them). Nevertheless, it is finally no joking matter: Growing up as she did was a perilous business and was painfully hard to understand. Boylan admits that while she has little use for transgender theory, finding the whole academic discourse that surrounds her situation not "especially helpful in terms of explaining what I felt," she does have faith in the power of a meaningful narrative. "To be honest, just about the only theory I trust is *story*, and I'm hoping that, before all is said and done, the tale I am trying to tell can stand in for the theory." It is in telling her story that she hopes to integrate her two lives, to live unhaunted by the past, able to see herself as connected to the confused young man she once was and to feel she has not betrayed him by moving toward a different gender. The memoir ends with the sense that this connection has been achieved, that Boylan's "transformative powers of blarney" have woven together all the stages of her life into a single fabric that contains past, present, and future.

However, it takes years to get there, with many bumps in the road and many frights along the way—frights that begin as the Boylans move into an *Addams Family* nightmare of a house that right from the start seems luxuriantly outfitted with the entire catalog of occult machinery: creaking stairs, closing doors, undulating curtains, ghostly footsteps, and the vaporous shrouded figures that only Jimmy can see. The teenager is visited by two distinct presences: one a young girl who lived in the house and is said to have drowned, the other a middle-aged woman clad in a nightgown who frequently appears when Jimmy is looking in the mirror. The latter most disturbs him, the vision seeming ominously to ask, "Who are you and what are you doing here?" Only decades later, when as a woman she is once again back in the "Coffin" House and looking into that same mirror, does it occur to her that the floating translucent old woman in white is not a ghost at all but simply her own reflection. As she says, "Against all odds, I had become solid." She begins to suspect it is far more often the case that hearts, not houses, are haunted; and by confronting the woman in the mirror she begins to understand what the message has been all along: "*Don't be afraid, Jenny*, she said. *It's only me.*" It is a moving scene, a crucial transformative moment, and, in many ways, the heart of the memoir—this acceptance of self in spite of difference and difficulty. However, it is characteristically edged with humor and permeated with a wry, hard-earned self-knowledge.

Boylan handles all of her scenes with this same poised expertise, knowing exactly how to launch them ("The train lurched a little as we ran over the girl") and keep them in the air. Chapters are divided into short, punchy sections, loaded with amusingly observed detail, and delivered in language unfailingly fresh and snappy. The scene revealing her father's cancer diagnosis—when this gentle droll man, a cigarette perpetually poised at his lips and smoke rings circling his head, tells young James that he'll need to be the man of the family now—is perfectly calibrated to demonstrate both a father's warm support for an unusual son and a son's private terror of being a disappointment to a beloved father. It is all handled with deft poignancy and real emotional tact. The scene of the trip to the Hershey chocolate factory with two school friends, on the other hand, is laugh-out-loud funny, a druggy, pop culture-riddled riff ripped from the pages of *Mad* magazine. Boylan's account of a summer job as a very ineffectual bank teller—who leaves wads of thousands by the water cooler, who gives patrons hundred-dollar bills instead of tens, who is more intent on finishing his epic poem "The Kiwi" than on reaching the end of the day with a balanced till—shows yet another kind of humor, a sweet pathos wrapping itself around the sitcom high-jinks. Boylan's pummeling at the hands of thuggish prep school boys who call him "faggot" and mock his willowy body and feminine manner is a vignette of a different sort, quick, graphic, heartbreaking in its depiction of bigotry festering into adolescent violence. Neverthless, Boylan survives all these skillfully rendered moments, living out his secret in the privacy of his bedroom, where he reads Betty Friedan's *The Feminine Mystique* (1963) in a bra stuffed with grapefruit and confronts the spirits that wander in and out and put to him the puzzling questions that, as Jenny, he will ultimately be forced to answer.

As Boylan says, when reflecting on the sad fact that his beloved sister has refused any contact since James became Jennifer, one cannot get a new history with a new body. Therefore, the task is to connect the new with the old, the present with the past. In this respect, Boylan's story transcends the narrative of one transsexual's journey and becomes a tale that speaks to all people, since they all carry on these negotiations with their past lives, coming to terms with events that have haunted them, with secrets that have occasionally turned them into masquerading, unreal figures, into ghosts. All people are faced with the need to accept themselves and go about the business of living and loving in the world as they find it. That is the story, related with great humor and admirable candor, that Boylan's memoir tells.

Thomas J. Campbell

Review Sources

Entertainment Weekly, January 18, 2008, p. 87.
Kirkus Reviews 75, no. 22 (November 15, 2007): 1184.
Lambda Book Report 16, nos. 1/2 (Spring/Summer, 2008): 11-12.
Library Journal 133, no. 2 (February 1, 2008): 68-69.
Ms. 18, no. 1 (Winter, 2008): 74-75.
People 69, no. 3 (January 28, 2008): 61.
Publishers Weekly 254, no. 47 (November 26, 2007): 42.
School Library Journal 54, no. 5 (May, 2008): 162.

IN DEFENSE OF FOOD
An Eater's Manifesto

Author: Michael Pollan (1955-   )
Publisher: Penguin Press (New York). 244 pp. $21.95
Type of work: Current affairs, science

Pollan offers a different way to think about food, and he exposes the belief system he calls "nutritionism," an ideology that benefits the food industry and the nutrition industry at the cost of human physical and spiritual health

Since the discovery in the late twentieth century of an American "obesity epidemic," scientists and journalists have explored the question of why the United States, one of the most prosperous and well-educated countries on the planet, should have such a difficult time providing nutritious food for its people or why its people are not making healthy food choices. Responses to this epidemic, and to the food industry that many believe fuels it, have included the international Slow Food movement, which supports small food producers whose work does not harm animals, workers, or the environment, and the so-called locavore movement, which encourages consumers to eat as much locally grown food as possible to avoid the damages caused by shipping, packaging, and mass production.

These movements have also produced dozens of books by well-known chefs, journalists, and activists exploring the question of how to eat responsibly. Barbara Kingsolver in *Animal, Vegetable, Miracle: A Year of Food Life* (2007) and Bill McKibben in *Deep Economy: The Wealth of Communities and the Durable Future* (2007) describe their family's determination to avoid industrially processed food and instead eat only food that has been produced locally by small farmers and businesses for a year or a season. Both found that eating this way was at first difficult and time-consuming, but both found new pleasures in growing and preparing food, working together as a family, and leaving a lighter footprint on the earth.

Longtime food writer Michael Pollan contributed fascinating information about where the food most Americans eat comes from in *The Omnivore's Dilemma: A Natural History of Four Meals* (2006). In that book, Pollan traced common foods back to their sources, focusing on industrially farmed food, organic food, and food he grew, hunted, and collected himself. He demonstrated that most of the processed and packaged foods available in a supermarket contain long lists of surprising ingredients (some form of corn, for example, turns up in almost everything), and that a lot of foods labeled "organic" or "natural" are also mass-produced industrial products.

The Omnivore's Dilemma, a best seller, presented enough unsettling information to make consumers wonder about the items in their grocery carts, but, as Pollan reports in the introduction to *In Defense of Food: An Eater's Manifesto*, it did not answer the question on many readers' minds: "Okay, but what should I *eat?*" *In Defense of Food* is a thoroughly researched, nonprescriptive response to that question, and the answer boils down to seven words that begin the book and appear frequently throughout its pages: "Eat food. Not too much. Mostly plants."

To explain what he means by "food"—not to be confused with the "other edible foodlike substances in the supermarkets"—Pollan devotes the first two of the book's three sections to exposing the ideology of "The Age of Nutritionism" and delineating "The Western Diet and the Diseases of Civilization." After 1977, he explains, when federal dietary guidelines first began to describe nutrients instead of food groups, food labels began touting supposed nutritional benefits. Claims of "high fiber," "low cholesterol," or "added vitamins" were featured prominently, and consumers came to believe that they could make healthy food choices by counting one nutrient or another. Today, consumers take for granted that counting calories or grams of particular kinds of fat, carbohydrates, or protein is the key to healthy eating, and they have lost sight of food itself. Even when the conventional wisdom about which nutrient to focus on changes every few years or even every few months, consumers willingly surrender their own good sense about eating to follow the advice of experts.

There are several things wrong with this approach, as Pollan argues. For one thing, the food experts do not know as much as they claim to. They observed, for example, that processing wheat into bleached white flour strips the grain of much of its iron, and they successfully reintroduced iron to create "enriched" flour. However, what hundreds of other micronutrients are removed with the wheat germ, and which ones are important to human health? The answer is, no one really knows.

Another problem is that consumers tend to focus on only one or two nutrients at a time, thinking of each ingredient as good or bad in itself. Someone counting fat grams might buy low-fat cookies and eat an entire box, ignoring the sugar, processed flour, and other harmful ingredients in those cookies. The result, as everyone has noticed, is thousands of new cases every year of obesity, diabetes, and heart disease. To Pollan it seems the more attention the American public pays to trying to eat healthy food, the sicker people become. In addition, most of the pleasure has been taken out of eating, which used to bring families and cultures together. Pollan reports that in one study, when people in France were shown a picture of chocolate cake and asked to comment on it in one word, their most common response was "celebration"; Americans shown the same picture mostly responded "guilt."

Pollan lays the blame for the resulting confusion at the feet of three groups: the federal government, whose shifting food groups and food pyramids promote the ideology of nutritionism; the food industry, which promotes processed and packaged food that promises to deliver on various health claims; and journalists, who report without question each new nutritional "discovery," from oat bran to omega-3 fatty acids. In

Michael Pollan has written five books and dozens of articles about gardening and food for national publications. His previous book, The Omnivore's Dilemma *(2006), was recognized by both* The New York Times *and* The Washington Post *as one of the ten best books of the year.*

lucid, often humorous, prose, Pollan describes competing and superseding health claims, market manipulations by the food industry, and sheeplike behavior on the part of consumers. In these analyses, Pollan demonstrates one of his great strengths as a writer: the ability to explain complicated science to a general audience. The way out of the mess Americans find themselves in, he concludes, is to get back to eating food—traditional, recognizable, satisfying, pleasurable food.

In "The Western Diet and the Diseases of Civilization," Pollan describes the typical American diet and reports on numerous studies linking this diet to so-called Western diseases, including diabetes and cardiovascular disease. He begins with an anecdote about a group of diabetic urban Australian Aborigines who returned to their isolated homeland, took up their traditional diet and way of life, and in only seven weeks dramatically improved their health. Other studies have shown not only that people who eat traditional diets low in processed foods have lower rates of the Western diseases, but that greatly reducing the amount of processed food in one's diet can reverse damage already done. As Americans have gradually moved from eating whole foods to eating processed and refined "foodlike substances," from simple foods to artificial and processed foods with dozens of unpronounceable ingredients, from small intensely flavored portions eaten slowly to large megameals devoured in the car, from a large variety of leafy and fruity plants to a few grains, they have sacrificed health for convenience and economy. As Pollan puts it succinctly, industrial agriculture has driven a change "from quality to quantity."

Americans eat more and more calories, sampling a small portion of the seventeen thousand new foods products brought to market each year, but they derive less and less nourishment from the foods they eat. While the food industry provides Americans with empty calories and new epidemics, and the nutrition industry presents a series of conflicting solutions, another industry steps up to the rescue: the medical industry, with its medications, procedures, and equipment aimed at treating the new diseases.

Pollan achieves a remarkable blend of passion and rationalism in this book; he is persuasive because he knows how to build a logical case and because he has lived the changes he wants to see. Still, it must be said that there are passages in the first sections of *In Defense of Food* that sound just like the books for which Pollan sees his work as an alternative. All of the popular diet books explain calmly why the books that came before have missed some essential truth about eating, and they all present a rational explanation for their own proposals. The smart ones take the time to show how their diet is more natural, or more traditional, or more like what the Europeans or Japanese eat, and they find a way to make following their advice seem virtuous, not just vain. Pollan accomplishes all of this and only occasionally sounds as though he is offering the latest scientific breakthrough diet, a testimony to the clarity of his vision and the preciseness of his language. In fact, his "Manifesto" aims much higher and much deeper than that of a diet book, and it nearly always hits its mark.

Having shown persuasively what is wrong with the way Americans eat, Pollan makes several modest proposals in his third section, "Getting over Nutritionism." At the heart of the proposals is his seven-word motto: "Eat food. Not too much. Mostly plants." He revisits the word "food," offering rules of thumb to help readers recognize food when they see it. One should not eat anything, he advises, that would be unknown to one's great-grandmother; in other words, one should stick to the outer walls of the grocery store and avoid most of the packaged, processed, enriched, preserved foodlike substances in the aisles. Even simple foods such as meat and dairy should be avoided if they contain more than five ingredients or ingredients that the ancestors would not recognize, including the ubiquitous high-fructose corn syrup.

Pollan advises avoiding foods that contain strange-sounding chemical ingredients, and he lists the few basic ingredients in the loaf of bread his grandmother would have baked and then the more than thirty-five ingredients in a loaf of Sara Lee Soft & Smooth Whole Grain White Bread. The contrast is sharp and persuasive. Next, Pollan offers advice that he admits sounds counterintuitive: "Avoid food products that make health claims." The analysis he has already presented in the first two sections of the book makes his comment that "health claims have become hopelessly corrupt" seem entirely reasonable.

At the end of *In Defense of Food*, Pollan returns to the ideas that concluded *The Omnivore's Dilemma*. Consumers should grow as much of their own food as they can and buy as much of the rest from farmers' markets and community-supported agriculture programs (CSAs). If most of what a person eats is food ("Eat food"), as Pollan defines it, and portions are reasonable ("Not too much"), then specific menus should not matter much, as evidenced by the wide variety of traditional diets found in healthy cultures around the world. For several reasons, including the health of the environment and a desire to make healthy food available equitably, Pollan encourages readers to eat "mostly plants," especially leafy plants. He also advises readers to learn about soils, drink wine, eat the best-quality food they can afford, cook at home—from scratch—and eat only full meals at a table.

Since the publication of *In Defense of Food*, Pollan has faced criticism for seeming to ignore the many people who lack the time and the money to follow his advice, and that criticism is partially fair. He acknowledges that many Americans eat poorly because sugar and fat have become so inexpensive, thanks to industrialized food processing and government indifference, but in this book he speaks more to individual choice than to political action. Pollan is calling for nothing short of a complete overhaul of the American way of eating, but his manifesto is addressed primarily to those educated and well-off readers who are already members of the choir.

Cynthia A. Bily

Review Sources

American Scientist 96, no. 3 (May/June, 2008): 243-245.
Booklist 104, nos. 9/10 (January 1, 2008): 30.
The Christian Science Monitor, April 1, 2008, p. 14.
Commentary 126, no. 1 (July/August, 2008): 68-73.

Entertainment Weekly, December 21, 2007, p. 87.
Food Management 43, no. 3 (March, 2008): 14.
Kirkus Reviews 75, no. 22 (November 15, 2007): 1194.
National Catholic Reporter 44, no. 12 (February 8, 2008): 7a.
The New York Review of Books 55, no. 4 (March 20, 2008): 23-24.
Newsweek 151, no. 4 (January 28, 2008): 48.
Publishers Weekly 254, no. 47 (November 26, 2007): 41.
The Saturday Evening Post 280, no. 3 (May/June, 2008): 18.
The Wall Street Journal 251, no. 27 (February 2, 2008): W8.

INDIGNATION

Author: Philip Roth (1933-   )
Publisher: Houghton Mifflin (Boston). 233 pp. $26.00
Type of work: Novel
Time: 1951-1952
Locale: Newark, New Jersey, and the fictitious
    Winesburg College in rural Ohio

*Setting his story against the background of the Korean
War, Roth tells of a young man whose single-mindedness,
ambition, and naïveté render him vulnerable to a series of
increasingly disastrous mishaps*

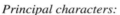

Principal characters:
    MARCUS MESSNER, the narrator, a nineteen-
        year-old, first-generation college student
        with dreams of being class valedictorian, avoiding the draft, and
        becoming a lawyer
    MR. MESSNER, Marcus's overprotective father, a kosher butcher living in
        Newark, New Jersey
    MRS. MESSNER, Marcus's stoical and loving mother, a homemaker
    OLIVIA HUTTON, a beautiful but deeply troubled sophomore transfer
        student whose sexual savvy both enthralls and baffles Marcus
    SONNY COTTLER, popular member of an all-Jewish fraternity who tries
        unsuccessfully to induce Marcus to pledge
    HAWES D. CAUDWELL, dean of men at Winesburg College and Marcus's
        chief nemesis

Indignation, Philip Roth's twenty-ninth novel, shares with his other recent fictional efforts, *Everyman* (2006) and *Exit Ghost* (2007), a spare narrative structure and a thematic concern with human frailty. Unlike those astringent, wintry novels, however, *Indignation* concentrates on the experiences of a young man, nineteen-year-old Marcus Messner, as he leaves his hometown college in Newark and transfers to Winesburg College, a conservative Christian liberal arts institution in rural Ohio. (The school's name alludes to Sherwood Anderson's classic *Winesburg, Ohio*, with its assortment of smothered provincial lives offered as a gallery of "grotesques.") Indeed, in this novel Roth seems to be going back to the period he mined so profitably in such earlier works as *Goodbye, Columbus* (1959) and *Portnoy's Complaint* (1969), both of which deal with the rites of passage undergone by a young Jewish man struggling to achieve independence from his overweening parents and to find his way among the Gentiles generally and shikses (WASP females) in particular. It was a period in the author's life also treated in his autobiography, *The Facts* (1988), in a section titled "Joe College."

It is instructive to compare the straightforward account of Roth's separation and initiation experience as presented in the autobiography with his protagonist's vicissi-

Philip Roth has won numerous literary awards, including National Book Awards for Goodbye, Columbus *(1959) and* Sabbath's Theater *(1995), the Pulitzer Prize for* American Pastoral *(1997), the PEN/Faulkner Award for* Operation Shylock *(1993), National Book Critics Circle Awards for* Patrimony *(1991) and* The Counterlife *(1986), the National Medal of Arts in 1998, and the Gold Medal in Fiction from the American Academy of Arts and Letters in 2002.*

tudes in *Indignation.* In *The Facts* Roth tells how he graduated from high school in 1950 at age sixteen, working for the next nine months as a stock clerk in a Newark department store, before enrolling at a downtown branch of Rutgers University while still living at home with his parents. Though an exemplary student, he felt increasingly "suffocated" by his father's inclination to control his private life, and so he determined to get away from home. "I didn't care where 'away' was—one college would do as well as another." As it happened, a neighborhood friend was then a student at Bucknell University, located in the small town of Lewisburg, Pennsylvania, and recommended it to Roth. A campus visit convinced him—despite the college's location in a small rural town, its Baptist roots, its requirement of weekly chapel attendance for underclassmen, and its paucity of other Jewish students—to enroll. Outwardly, these circumstances parallel those in which Marcus Messner finds himself in the novel. He, too, transfers from a state college in Newark after his freshman year in order to escape his father's strictures. The latter are much enlarged upon in the novel, for Mr. Messner's determination to keep a tight rein on his son's every move derives from an irrational and increasingly obsessive fear that, left to his own devices, Marcus could be victimized or even killed at any moment, a fear greatly exacerbated by the Korean War, which looms over the entire story like a malevolent Fate. In addition, Marcus's reasons for choosing the bucolic Winesburg College are more whimsical than Roth's for choosing Bucknell. Marcus is attracted not only by the college's distance from his home but also by its All-American, crew-cut and white-bucks image as depicted on promotional brochures, seemingly oblivious to the rigid restrictions and requirements that would later prove so troublesome.

Once they have matriculated at their new schools, Marcus's and Roth's careers follow different paths. For Roth, the college presented a series of opportunities to grow socially as well as academically. He pledged a fraternity (resigning from it after a year), formed close friendships with other students and several young faculty members, made the dean's list for academic achievement, coedited a campus literary magazine, and had a steady girlfriend during his junior and senior years. An article he wrote attacking the campus newspaper earned him a browbeating by the dean of men and censure from a board overseeing student publications, but such clashes with authority only validated his growing independence and self-confidence. In Marcus's case, the situation is far more desperate. From almost the beginning of the academic year he is effectively isolated, in short order rejecting two sets of roommates until finally securing a single room where he can study in peace. He spends most of his waking hours immersed in his studies, earning pocket money working part time as a waiter in a local watering hole (where he tries to ignore anti-Semitic slurs from fellow students). When approached by Sonny Cottler, a prominent member of the one Jewish fraternity at Winesburg, and encouraged to pledge, Marcus firmly rebuffs him. As this behavior suggests, Marcus's isolation is to a large extent self-imposed. To get straight A's and eventually become class valedictorian, to enroll in the campus ROTC program so as to enter the Army as an officer after graduation, to earn enough to lessen the financial burden on his family—these are his only goals and, with one exception, he doggedly refuses to consider various opportunities for personal growth made available by college life. His unwillingness to compromise his goals, which creates conflicts between Marcus and his roommates and the fraternity members, amounts to the kind of unconventional behavior that attracts attention from the bastions of conformity empowered to protect the status quo in a small college, especially in the 1950's.

The single exception to Marcus's willed isolation is his brief affair with an attractive coed, Olivia Hutton, whom he meets in American history class. On their first date, she startles him by her readiness to perform oral sex on him, an act so far beyond anything Marcus has before experienced that he is even more bewildered than he is inflamed with erotic desire. While his attraction to her is enhanced by her being a shikse, the long scar on her left wrist and revelations about a troubled past—including alcoholic binges, sexual promiscuity, a broken home, and a psychological breakdown—soon present Marcus with complications with which he is clearly ill prepared to deal. In effect, though she appears genuinely attracted to Marcus, her pathology and his tunnel vision are such that there is no real chance for them to establish an enduring relationship. When Marcus is hospitalized after an emergency appendectomy, Olivia visits his room and again provides sexual satisfaction. Instead of feeling transported by pleasure, however, he is burdened by guilt and confusion, and these are only compounded by a visit from his mother and her resolute opposition to Olivia as Marcus's girl. For her part, Olivia abruptly disappears from the college and from the novel, apparently after suffering another breakdown. Marcus never hears from her again.

He learns of Olivia's departure from the dean of men, Hawes D. Caudwell, who has been monitoring Marcus's behavior and twice calls Marcus into his office for accusatory talks. In the first meeting, the dean takes Marcus to task for changing roommates and refusing to pledge a fraternity or to try out for the baseball team, acts that go against the grain of college "tradition." Made increasingly angry by what seem to him trivial criticisms, Marcus takes the opportunity to voice his fervent objections to the mandatory chapel rule, which only makes him seem even more rebellious in the dean's eyes. Their second meeting takes place after Caudwell learns of Marcus's affair with Olivia (a nurse had walked in on them in the hospital room). He is only too willing to presume that the boy is responsible for her pregnancy, which precipitated the breakdown, though the reader knows he is not. Added to the "case" against Marcus is Caudwell's knowledge that Marcus has paid another student to take his place in chapel and forge his signature on the attendance sheet. These confrontations provide the dramatic fulcrum of the novel, resulting in Marcus's dismissal from the college for violating the student code of conduct. His understandable indignation at this climactic injustice elicits the emotion that gives the novel its title.

Marcus's encounter with the dean occurs on the same day as another kind of confrontation, a panty raid that quickly turns into a near riot. Though Marcus does not participate in this collective eruption of aggression, eighteen of his fellow students are dismissed afterward. The juxtaposition of these scenes carries the implication that both are somehow the result of the suppression of youthful energies characteristic of the period. To reinforce this suggestion, Roth appends a "Historical Note" in which he updates the picture of Winesburg College, pointing out that after student demonstrations of the 1960's, culminating in the week-long occupation of the dean's office, "the chapel requirement was abolished along with virtually all the strictures and parietal rules regulating student conduct that had been in force there for more than a hundred years. . . ." On a global level, the violent unleashing of pent-up urges is expressed in the ongoing war in Korea, which claimed the lives of some 54,000 Americans.

One of the book's biggest surprises is the offhand revelation, about fifty pages in, that Marcus, the narrator, believes he is dead. In "Out from Under," the brief final chapter narrated in the third person rather than by Marcus himself, the reader learns that Private Messner has indeed been mortally wounded—"bayonet wounds . . . had all but severed one leg from his torso and hacked his intestines and genitals to bits"— on the battlefield in Korea, some four months after his abrupt departure from Winesburg. The narrative preceding this disclosure, entitled "Under Morphine," is the drug-induced dream of his life, a fact that necessarily casts doubt on its veracity.

Such narrative legerdemain is typical of Roth's fiction, which is now grouped into the novels of Nathan Zuckerman, David Kepesh (both fictional alter egos of the author), Philip Roth, and "others." Whether the "postmortem" device succeeds in *Indignation* is an open question. The novel has received mixed reviews, some praising its narrative economy in rendering the protagonist's inexorable doom, others faulting it for sketchy characterization and thematic contrivance. Critical consensus may ultimately depend on whether readers recognize that *Indignation* is not intended as a fully represented fictional action, which would entail a cast of three-dimensional characters and a complex, "realistic" plot. Rather, it is most fruitfully read as a kind of moral fable or apologue, in which the fictional material is scrupulously selected and organized so as to convey, as powerfully as possible, a central truth. In this case that truth, which is formulated several times and repeated in the book's final lines, ironically confirms the basis of Mr. Messner's fears for his son's life: "the terrible, the incomprehensible way one's most banal, incidental, even comical choices achieve the most disproportionate result." Or, as the father warns his son at another point, "It's about life, where the tiniest misstep can have tragic consequences." Marcus's story embodies this perception with maximum force, inducing indignation in the reader as well as in Marcus. Indeed, indignation ("the most beautiful word in the English language," Roth calls it) is at once the cause and the consequence of Marcus's fate. Mutatis mutandis, it is a state of mind that animates virtually all of the author's literary output.

Ronald G. Walker

Review Sources

The Atlantic Monthly 302, no. 3 (October, 2008): 111-114.
Booklist 104, no. 17 (May 1, 2008): 6.
The Boston Globe, September 14, 2008, p. 5D.
Kirkus Reviews 76, no. 11 (June 1, 2008): 12.
Los Angeles Times, September 16, 2008, p. A7.
The New Republic 239, no. 7 (October 22, 2008): 32-35.
New Statesman 137 (September 22, 2008): 86-88.
The New York Review of Books 55, no. 15 (October 9, 2008): 4-8.
The New York Times Book Review, September 21, 2008, p. 1.
The New Yorker 84, no. 30 (September 29, 2008): 91.
Publishers Weekly 255, no. 19 (May 12, 2008): 37.
Time 172, no. 18 (November 3, 2008): 75-79.
The Washington Post, September 14, 2008, p. T6.

IROQUOIS DIPLOMACY ON THE
EARLY AMERICAN FRONTIER

Author: Timothy J. Shannon (1964-   )
Publisher: Viking Press (New York). 272 pp. $22.95
Type of work: History
Time: The eighteenth century
Locale: The Mohawk Valley and Finger Lakes district in
    what became New York State

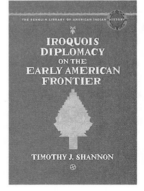

Shannon describes how this Indian Confederacy used diplomacy with the French and British to further its own interests

Principal personages:
JONCAIRE, a French Canadian who learned
    the Iroquois language as a Seneca
    captive, then became France's chief Indian agent until his death in
    1739
CANASATEGO, a chieftain who expanded Iroquois power in the 1740's
HENDRICK (TEE YEE NEEN HO GA ROW), a principal spokesman for the
    Mohawks during King George's War, who visited London in 1710
WILLIAM JOHNSON, an Anglo-Irishman who became the most important
    colonial intermediary with the Indians, 1746-1774
JOSEPH BRANT (THAYENDANEGEA), a Mohawk ally of Britain during the
    American war for independence
MOLLY BRANT, William Johnson's common-law wife and an advocate
    of war against the Americans
GEORGE CLINTON, the New York governor who worked to dispossess
    the Iroquois of their lands after 1783
CORNPLANTER, a Seneca war chief who sided with the British, then did
    what he could to save his people from the consequences of defeat
HENRY KNOX, Washington's secretary of war, who protected Indian
    rights by asserting federal authority over all relationships with the
    tribes

In *Iroquois Diplomacy on the Early American Frontier*, an elegantly written contribution to the Penguin Library of American Indian History, Timothy J. Shannon explains why Dutch, French, British, and American diplomats had such difficulties in negotiating treaties with the Iroquois. Europeans were accustomed to dealing with monarchs who could sign binding agreements. This was an inappropriate approach to tribes, which had no equivalents of kings, no hereditary succession, and, most important, no expectation that every individual would agree to promises made by their leaders. Indians believed that if any individual disliked a decision, he could move away or just ignore it. The idea that if one Sachem made a trade agreement that tribal members did not like, they could switch allegiance to a new Sachem essentially invalidated whatever agreements the first chief had made. Indians addressing a governor as "father" considered this only a recognition of his giving gifts to his children, not a symbol of subjection. Europeans, unwilling to believe that such anarchy was possible, persisted in trying to impose their schema on the Native Americans.

∾

Timothy J. Shannon earned a bachelor's degree at Brown University in 1986 and a doctorate in history from Northwestern University in 1993. He has published widely on American Indian history in the colonial era and is currently chair of the history department at Gettysburg College.

∾

The Iroquois were a confederation of five tribes (later six), which developed customs that minimized conflicts among themselves and maximized their military potential. At a time when disease was running rampant through all of America, but especially among the Indians, the Iroquois were able to use firearms obtained by trade in furs to drive their weakened competition out of the Ohio country, intrude into the pays d'en haut (Great Lakes), and take captives to replenish their diminishing numbers. They made themselves into a third force that could balance the French against the British and keep war at a distance. Although they may not have been as powerful as they thought, the colonial powers were reluctant to challenge their claims.

The Iroquois saw diplomacy as a continuing process that emphasized renewal and condolence ceremonies, not as a business transaction. Europeans misinterpreted Iroquois expectations of gifts as thoroughly businesslike—the exchange of gifts was so one-sided that Europeans assumed they were buying the Indians' alliance much as they rented mercenaries from minor German princes. The symbol of Iroquois practice was the Covenant Chain, a recitation of past discussions as recorded on wampum belts, the exchange of gifts, and the linking of arms. The long speeches around the council fire would be concluded with a drinking bout of considerable length and enthusiasm.

After the foundation of Montreal in 1642, the French extended their fur trade into Huron country, undermining the Iroquois monopoly of trade with the interior. The Iroquois attacked, successfully, until the arrival of French troops in 1666. Peace was reestablished, but a renewal of war in the 1680's ended with half the Iroquois warriors dead and the survivors divided, most looking to the British for trade and aid, a significant minority looking to the French.

By 1700, the balance of power had shifted to the Europeans, but the Europeans were such intense rivals that the relatively small number of Iroquois exercised enormous power, as long as war did not come to their homes and destroy them. Iroquois delegations visited Albany and Montreal frequently, trading furs for European products (knives, clothing, guns, and powder), taking home valuable gifts, and usually complaining that they were insufficient. The French won more friends because their governors were allotted more funds than were their British counterparts, and because their governors were both better informed by fur traders and missionaries and because they did not have the distractions of dealing with a growing and independent-minded populace. However, the British paid higher prices.

By 1720, Iroquois power had extended south as well as west. This was first apparent in Pennsylvania, where the Delaware were being tricked out of their lands by William Penn's descendants (the famous Walking Purchase), then coerced into acquiescence by the Iroquois. Some of the Pennsylvania tribes sank into poverty, and others turned to the Iroquois for protection. The Iroquois lorded it over these new dependents, taunting that they had made women of them and that they could do whatever they wished. At the same time, they informed Europeans that they were newcomers with no rights to the lands they currently held.

At a great conference in Lancaster in 1744, the Iroquois sold lands they did not possess. The governors were quite willing to assume that they had thereby acquired the equivalent of a title of those lands. Who was the greater swindler: the colonial governors or the Sachems? This alliance of native and newly arrived thieves angered more distant Indian tribes, driving them into the arms of the French.

Meanwhile, war parties were raiding south as far as the Carolinas. This led to more extensive diplomatic contacts with Virginia and the extortion of more gifts. By the 1750's, when Virginians were thinking of settling the Ohio country, the Iroquois influence was at its height because they were able and willing to sell lands belonging to the tribes living there, a practice that alienated the affected tribes, especially the Shawnee.

As the Western tribes sought help from the French, it seemed inevitable that the French would build forts to protect them. Fort Duquesne, constructed where the Allegheny and Monongahela Rivers joined to form the Ohio, was a direct challenge to Iroquois authority over the Ohio region, and other forts in the Lake Champlain region and around Niagara threatened to surround the Iroquois. If the British could not break this chain of fortifications, they would have to cede the interior to the French and probably the Iroquois, too. The result was the French and Indian War.

At the beginning of this contest, in 1754, there was a great conference at Albany. There Benjamin Franklin vainly proposed a union of the British colonies interested in the region. This led to a later myth that the American Constitution was based on Iroquois practices, which demonstrates a complete misunderstanding of the Iroquois Confederation as well as the process by which the Constitution was written.

William Johnson kept most Iroquois loyal to Britain and ignored the bloody campaign against Fort Duquesne; he and his supporters saw the challenge to the north as much more serious. Unfortunately for them, the French and their Indian allies were far too strong. The British sympathized little with the Iroquois and did not easily accept the correct explanation of why some Iroquois warriors had chosen to fight alongside the French: They could not control their young men. Nor could the Iroquois warriors see any point in sieges, toe-to-toe combat, or discipline. When denied the right to pillage and plunder captured towns, they went home.

When the string of British victories in 1759 ended French control of Canada, the British saw no reason to credit the Iroquois with having contributed to the triumph. Even Johnson subsequently negotiated directly with Western Indians, not through the Iroquois; and the Iroquois remained neutral during Pontiac's War.

The Proclamation of 1763 guaranteed the Indians possession of the lands west of the Allegheny Mountains, but there were already so many colonial settlers in western Pennsylvania that it took a treaty in 1765 to draw a more realistic boundary. There were no British troops stationed on the frontier to keep settlers out. Accepting trade goods for peace seemed to be all that the Indians could do. Not receiving the plentiful gifts of yore, the Iroquois now gladly sold more Western lands, lands they did not own. It fell to the Shawnee to lead the armed struggle against the newcomers.

Intervention in the American Revolution was inevitable: The British demanded it, the legacy of Johnson required it, and American migration across the Alleghenies had to be opposed. Joseph Brant used the crisis to advance his personal status, but an epidemic caused the Oneidas to declare that there was no longer a council fire, making it impossible to work out a united policy. Seneca women, led by Molly Brant, demanded war, and young men hired themselves out to the British. However, the British invasions from Canada failed. With greater Iroquois support, they might have succeeded, but the battle at Oriskany showed what the high cost in lives would be. The warriors had been told that they could sit down, smoke their pipes, and watch, but when the shooting started, it involved Iroquois against Iroquois. Mutually destructive raids drove many into Canada, and in 1779, when the American armies were free to turn to the West, the Senecas could only retreat ahead of them. The beautiful villages and fertile fields were abandoned to destruction, and the returning Seneca faced starvation.

There never had been a clear alternative. The Iroquois had been divided—some counseled peace, others war—and the wish of the majority for neutrality was impossible. Once the French had vanished, there was no way to play one party against another, and when the British realized that their allies were far weaker than they had expected, they abandoned them. Once the crown conceded American independence, the Iroquois were at the mercy of their recent enemies.

All the Iroquois could do was play the cupidity of delegations from Massachusetts, New York, Connecticut, and Pennsylvania against each other. Meanwhile, dispirited Indians turned to hard spirits. Worn down by alcoholism and poverty, they accepted cash, presents, and private pensions in return for their lands.

There had always been a chasm between those who wanted to learn American ways and those who preferred to live as before, even if that meant poverty and death. This chasm now deepened. Some Iroquois went to Canada, others accepted reservations, and some merged with other Indian groups. Cornplanter spoke for those wishing to accommodate the victors.

Meanwhile, new Indian nations had appeared in the West, nations that challenged American claims to the Ohio region. Even as those tribes inflicted defeats on American armies, the Iroquois firmly refused to join in the war. It was a wise decision, because the Americans were too strong and too numerous to be held back long. In the end George Washington's administration rewarded the Iroquois with new and more favorable treaties and, by enforcing its new constitutional authority, prevented the states from forcing them to give up their lands.

This friendship faded quickly as American attention was drawn farther west, but the principle that Indian tribes retained sovereign rights was maintained. The Iroquois remained a nation within a nation.

William L. Urban

Review Sources

Library Journal 133, no. 9 (May 15, 2008): 115.
Publishers Weekly 255, no. 12 (March 24, 2008): 59.

IT'S GO IN HORIZONTAL
Selected Poems, 1974-2006

Author: Leslie Scalapino (1947-   )
Publisher: University of California Press (Berkeley).
  241 pp. $16.95
Type of work: Poetry

A startling and distinctive selection of poetry from one of America's most innovative contemporary poets

Leslie Scalapino's *It's Go in Horizontal* introduces readers to one of the most challenging and provocative American poets currently writing. This collection is part of the New California Poetry Series, which is edited by Robert Hass, Calvin Bedient, Brenda Hillman, and Forrest Gander and which has published such thought-provoking poets as Mark Levine, Fanny Howe, Harryette Mullen, and Ron Silliman. Scalapino gained recognition for her experimental approach to writing during the 1970's in San Francisco, and over the length of her career, she has been linked to the Language poets, exhibiting her fascination in the different ways that language can be perceived.

Scalapino is a writer of many talents. While she has published several volumes of poetry since the mid-1970's, she also has found the time and energy to write plays, fiction, and nonfiction. As a student, she studied French poetry, becoming enamored with the works of Charles Baudelaire and Arthur Rimbaud. During this period, Scalapino also came under the influence of the poet Philip Whalen, who had studied Eastern religions. One of the central points of her writing is the necessity to sabotage what she considers a very male-dominant language. She considers it her duty to alter language in every way possible in order to neutralize this dominance. As the poet sees it, language can be used to either reinforce the power base or subvert it. Scalapino wishes to tip the language scales, to allow all female and minority voices to be heard.

Her first poetry collection, *O, and Other Poems*, published in 1976, was dedicated to the great modernist writer Virginia Woolf. It was obvious at the outset of her literary career that Scalapino was a multidimensional poet, clearly driven by philosophical, political, and spiritual ideas. She was determined to juggle linguistic complexities with a visual perspective, so that in reading her poetry the reader should internalize Scalapino's linguistic patterns and observe and inhale her words visually. The poet challenges both herself and the reader, and words and images tantalize those who encounter her on her own terms. Collaboration among various art forms plays a vital role in her approach to literary expression. On several occasions, the poet has combined her words with a visual artist in order to create a richer tapestry. Never less than provocative, Scalapino consistently has merged images with words. She has stated that it is imperative to express both a "social" as well as a "political" vision. The purpose of the literary journey is "to get to the inner relation of events," and in so doing,

~

Leslie Scalapino is an award-winning author who has established herself as one of the leading avant-garde poets of her generation. In addition to her poetry, she has published several important books of fiction, drama, and nonfiction.

~

the poet creates something fresh and unique. As Scalapino sees it, a sequence that may look similar to something from the past has essentially been pared down, made smaller and more particular.

During the 1970's, Scalapino published four small-press volumes of poetry. In 1982, she published her first major volume, *Considering How Exaggerated Music Is*, through North Point Press. This included poems that were first published in her earlier small-press volumes. *It's Go in Horizontal* opens with poems from the 1970's. Portions of the long poem "hmmmm" introduce the reader to the world of Scalapino. First published in the 1976 volume *The Woman Who Could Read the Minds of Dogs*, it was chosen also to be included in her 1982 North Point Press collection. The full poem is made up of a series of disjointed narratives that dwell on surreal sexual matters. There is much fantasy, while the tone of the poem remains neutral. The provocative elements are presented in a matter-of-fact manner, as in: "I mean I see a man/ (in a crowd such as a theatre) as having the body of a seal in the way/ a man should, say, be in bed with someone, kissing and barking,/ which is the way a seal will bark and leap on his partly-fused hind limbs." Throughout the series, the poet describes individuals as being other creatures and as having the attributes of these creatures. The bending of gender roles and of reality continues throughout the poem "Instead of an Animal." Scalapino turns the act of suckling into a surreal expression of identity. In the poem, there are many examples of alternate realities. There are two women "suckling at the teats of the nursing mother; the/ infant being left to whine while the mother endured these females/ feeding off of her." It even gets "[s]tranger when it is the male opening his shirt in public,/ and applying an infant to his chest as if he had breasts." The poet turns stereotypes upside down, proposing several alternatives for the reader to ponder, including: "Some children of seven to ten years of age or so/ were letting each other open their shirts and dresses/ and suck on each others' nipples." For the poet, gender roles definitely are worth questioning and looking at with new eyes. Scalapino wishes to take stock of what makes individuals truly human, and she refuses to accept cultural dictates at face value.

In her writing, the poet takes aim at all preconceived notions, even down to individual words and how they are placed on the page. She subverts the conventional lyrical approach to poetry. Heavily influenced by Eastern philosophy as she was growing up, Scalapino has attempted to present through her writing something other than a Western perspective of self. In her work, she has been described as being concerned not with "subject" or "ego" but with the "active self." This active self is revealed in the mere "seeing" of it. Out of this approach, Scalapino has come to value "relativism." The poet plays with experience and with convention. A person becomes an entity in physics that will reveal different characteristics, depending on which direction it takes. As a writer, Scalapino has been highly influenced by the visual arts, especially film and video. It is important for the reader to absorb her poetry visually. She will place sections of a poem on various spots on the page, and the reader must be alert to placement and to spacing. It is not possible for the reader to assume that there is an inherent wholeness to any of her poems. Part of her nonfiction work, *How Phenomena Appear to Unfold*, is included in *It's Go in Horizontal* in order to delineate some of her rationale for writing. In "Note on My Writing, 1985," Scalapino states that a "segment in the poem is the actual act or event itself" and that the "self is unraveled as an example in investigating particular historical events, which are potentially infinite." The point also is made that "[t]he self is a guinea pig," suggesting that the poet has created an artifice. She refuses to adhere to Western tradition, to be a pawn of the male-dominant culture or language, and to look for what can be termed "closure." At one point in *How Phenomena Appear to Unfold*, Scalapino drives home the point that perception of what is occurring at any particular moment is what is important. For the poet, history is created by what is perceived, what is seen in the moment. With that in mind, there is no beginning, middle, or conclusion. There is only what Scalapino has described as "a constant recurring and beginning."

While Scalapino shares elements with the Language poets, she is not limited by any school. Her avant-garde tendencies cannot be saddled by static thought patterns, and it is her intention to break all fixed patterns, whether social, cultural, or biological.

Through "poetic innovation," Scalapino supposes that it is possible not only to alter human identities but also to eliminate them altogether. In her 1985 collection *That They Were at the Beach*, the poet examines the nature of gender differences. For the poem "A sequence," Scalapino speaks of the sex act and how the private parts normally covered by clothes look, when exposed, leopardlike. The sex act itself has made flesh and organs become like those of a leopard. This poem appears in block paragraph form, including repetition for added impact. The same collection also includes what the poet calls the "chameleon series." Parts of this series, which have been selected for *It's Go in Horizontal*, are dramatically different in form from "A sequence." This is made obvious by the way in which the images are presented on the page, such as "men who're/ poor and aren't/ doing anything// standing in/ the sun/ by a housing project// their/ living in/ a motionless way// having been/ led later/ on// in the social/ world." These lines appear on one page. On other pages there may be fewer lines included. Such a spare page draws attention to the few words that inhabit the page. Each snapshot, each word, and each image, therefore, carry an immense weight.

While Scalapino's images may appear fragmented and her tone deadpan, she still produces quite jarring and provocative poetry. Her approach can be traced to such innovative writers as Gertrude Stein and Ezra Pound. Scalapino's poetic form has been called "serial" because of its use of "discrete units of text that are potentially infinite in number."

Some readers may struggle with Scalapino's flat and repetitive poems, devoid of an emotional link and, therefore, disorienting for the reader who may have been socially, politically, and culturally trained to respond to certain subjects and images in a certain way. Her erotic poetry may not elicit what the reader expects—such as excitement—from eroticism, leading to disappointment. For Scalapino, the erotic nature of the poem is not supposed to excite the reader.

The current collection includes a selection from many of the poet's most important volumes. Her 1988 book *Way* won an American Book Award, and *It's Go in Horizontal* features from it the "Bum Series," "The Floating Series," and the "Delay Series." In each of these, the poet provides the reader with snapshots of a reality that is altered with each snapshot. The "Bum Series" opens with "the men—when I'd/ been out in cold weather—were/ found lying on the street, having/ died—from the weather; though/ usually being there when it's warmer." This tragic setting is introduced matter of factly, without a sense that anything can be done to remedy the situation. Each fragment in the series serves as another part of the human fabric. It ends with "the bums—/ found later—in the whole setting/—though when the car/ hadn't been repaired—and so/ their grinding and/ movement in relation to it." Scalapino presents a "way" to see the world, to see how language can create its own social significance. *It's Go in Horizontal* includes poems and parts of poems from more than ten collections, and in so doing has presented a stimulating introduction to a leading innovator of contemporary American poetry. While some readers may take issue with being allowed to encounter only excerpts of several major works, this remains a striking volume that should be savored by those who value what modern poetry can deliver.

Jeffry Jensen

Review Source

Publishers Weekly 255, no. 16 (April 21, 2008): 38.

THE JEW OF CULTURE
Freud, Moses, and Modernity

Author: Philip Rieff (1922-2006)
Publisher: University of Virginia Press (Charlottesville).
  224 pp. $34.95
Type of work: Sociology

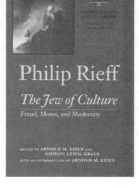

The final volume of Rieff's Sacred Order/Social Order trilogy, this book presents a selection of Rieff's writings from the early 1950's through the 1990's loosely organized around the theme of "the Jew of Culture" as an ideal type in Rieff's vision of the nature of social order

The Jew of Culture is a posthumous work by cultural theorist Philip Rieff. Presented as the final volume of Rieff's Sacred Order/Social Order trilogy, it contains selections of Rieff's work published from 1952 through 1982, plus a previously unpublished essay written about 1994. Before his death in 2006, Rieff agreed that his former student, Arnold M. Eisen, would assemble these writings around the concept of "the Jew of Culture." Eisen worked with coeditor Gideon Lewis-Krauss to shape a work that is essentially a retrospective on Rieff's intellectual career.

Rieff explicitly introduced the idea of "the Jew of Culture" in the 1970's, at the time when his writing style had taken a turn toward oracular pronouncements and his attitude toward modern culture had become sternly disapproving, if not condemnatory. By that period in his work, Rieff considered a culture a way of ordering and organizing individuals around principles and practices that had to be sacred if they were to be meaningful. Rieff was Jewish by heritage, and he saw Judaism as a primal culture of Western civilization. Christianity had emerged from Judaism, and Christianity had defined itself either as a continuation of Judaism or as an opposition to Judaism. Therefore, the Jew of Culture, in Rieff's perspective by the 1970's, was not just a Jewish intellectual or cultured individual, but a representative of the oldest tradition of sacred order underlying Western civilization.

The selections in this book can be read both as representatives of the Jew of Culture idea and as illustrations of the development of this idea in Rieff's thinking. The first piece, on British novelist and statesman Benjamin Disraeli, was written at the beginning of the author's career. Although Disraeli had been baptized into the Church of England when he was twelve years old, he had been born a Jew. Rather than deny his Jewish heritage in frequently anti-Semitic Victorian England, he took pride in it and often seemed to dwell on it, even after he rose to the position of prime minister. Rieff argues that Disraeli was able to conceive and pursue a vision of England as the New Israel because of his nostalgic attachment to the Old Israel. The Disraeli chapter introduces Rieff's view of religious tradition as the source of order and structure in life, bringing individuals into a social existence, and it hints at the special importance

~

Philip Rieff was a cultural theorist who received his doctorate from the University of Chicago. He taught at several universities but spent most of his career as the Benjamin Franklin Professor of Sociology and University Professor at the University of Pennsylvania. He was appointed professor emeritus at the University of Pennsylvania upon his retirement in 1992.

~

Rieff attributes to Judaism as a religious tradition.

The second chapter is a brief review of the book *Büchlein vom gesunden und kranken Menschenverstand* (1921; *Understanding the Sick and the Healthy*, 1953) by the little-known Jewish philosopher Franz Rosenzweig. The editors include it to demonstrate Rieff's interest in Jewish religious thought and to show the development of his thinking in preparing to write about a much greater influence on Western culture, Sigmund Freud.

Freud: The Mind of the Moralist, first published in 1959, was Rieff's first major work. In this key revisionist study of Freud, Rieff argued that the father of psychoanalysis occupied a position at the center of an intellectual revolution that shifted attention away from the perspective of society shaping the individual and toward that of the individual creating society out of instinctual conflicts. Although Rieff was ambivalent about the heritage of psychoanalysis in this work and critical of Freud's successors, Rieff regarded Freud as an intellectual pioneer. *The Jew of Culture* reprints the preface to the second edition of his book, followed by a section from the book entitled "The Religion of the Fathers." In these pages, Rieff wrote at length on the role of Judaism in Freud's life and thought. Religion, in Rieff's view, organizes the character of individuals by means of faith. Freud attempted to develop a new theory of culture, based on the idea of the primacy of the individual, to address the decline of religion as a source of social organization. However, Rieff maintained in this preface, Freud ignored the role of the Jewish tradition and of his own complex identification with Moses in making possible the rethinking of the relationship between the individual and society. In Freud as a "psychological Jew," Rieff found a basic contradiction. A heritage from a religiously based culture established the organization of Freud's personality and intellectual creativity, but that creativity turned the relationship around and began with the individual rather than with culture. Rieff praised Freud as a thinker, and specifically as a Jewish thinker, but he was pessimistic about the consequences of Freud's thought.

In Rieff's second major book, *The Triumph of the Therapeutic: Uses of Faith After Freud* (1966), the pessimism deepened. By making the individual, rather than the social order, the organizing principle of human society, Freud created what Rieff called "the therapeutic ethos." This ethos dictated that therapy, a set of techniques for promoting the well-being of the individual, replaced the cultural organization of personality, which shaped individuals around the idea of the pursuit of virtue. Rieff saw this ethos as undermining social order and the placement of individuals in the social order. He argued that it was therefore ultimately suicidal in character because only a social order can give life the necessary meaning and structure.

In this 1966 book, Rieff devoted chapters to analytical psychologist Carl Jung, radical psychotherapist Wilhelm Reich, and novelist D. H. Lawrence as advocates of various forms of the destructive therapeutic ethos. *The Jew of Culture* summarizes this argument about the therapeutic ethos by reprinting the first, introductory chapter of *The Triumph of the Therapeutic*, "Toward a Theory of Culture." In this selection, Rieff began with a meditation on the famous poem "The Second Coming," by William Butler Yeats, which opens: "Things fall apart; the centre cannot hold." Rieff maintained that the center of Western culture could not hold and that the things held together by it were indeed falling apart. He argued that a culture survives because of the ability of its institutions to direct people by sinking motivations so deeply into their thoughts that they would be held together in common understandings. The modern type of second coming, or search for salvation, appeared through the emergence of the psychological personality seeking individual well-being. The "Jew of Culture" theme behind this volume is least evident in this chapter, although Rieff does refer to Christian and Jewish cultures as connected ways of organizing character.

From the publication of *The Triumph of the Therapeutic* in 1966 to the early 1970's, Rieff's attitude toward contemporary society became much harsher, more judgmental, and more deeply conservative. This may have been a reaction to the tumults of the era as well as Rieff following the logic of his own argument about the therapeutic ethos. His writing style also changed. The Rieff of the early 1950's, who wrote the chapter on Disraeli, used a sharp, clear style and straightforward argument. The author of the books on Freud and the therapeutic dealt with sophisticated concepts but still used a fairly comprehensible vocabulary, introducing a limited amount of specialized jargon. By the opening of the 1970's, however, Rieff had adopted the knotty, enigmatic style and twisting, nonlinear form of exposition that characterized most of his late works.

In 1971, Rieff arrived at Skidmore College for an interview on the subject of "psychological man" that would later be published in a special issue of the journal *Salmagundi*. However, Rieff was dissatisfied with the transcript of the interview, which he thought did not adequately represent his views. In place of the interview, he wrote an essay that was later expanded into the slim book *Fellow Teachers* (1973). The editors of *The Jew of Culture* have put together excerpts from that book, under the title "Fellow Teachers," which can give the reader a feel for the complexity of the full version.

Rieff described contemporary America as a cultureless society, utterly given over to the anarchy of the therapeutic. While some of his work seems nostalgic for the order that he suggested premodern Christianity provided, in the passages of "Fellow Teachers" he portrayed Christianity as "transgressive," as a rebellion against its parent Judaism, as well as a continuation and transformation of the Jewish cultural order. He cast teachers as rabbis, in the position of carrying on the work of culture in a society that had turned against all culture.

Rieff made a brief return to some of his old clarity in an essay on Oscar Wilde published in *Salmagundi* in 1983 and later reprinted in the collection entitled *The Feeling Intellect: Selected Writings*, edited by Jonathan Imber and published in 1991. "The Impossible Culture: Wilde as a Modern Prophet" used the approach of *The Triumph of the Therapeutic* by presenting an intellectual figure as a representative of a cultural trend. After describing Wilde's trial for sodomy, Rieff discussed the wit's "The Soul of Man Under Socialism," written in 1891, which Rieff considered Wilde's greatest essay. Under socialism, according to Wilde, all the constraints on humanity would dissolve, and each human personality would grow to its perfection. Rieff argued that this was impossible because it is precisely the constraints that shape personality and give life to society. With the future dissolution of boundaries prophesied by Wilde, according to Rieff, people would not become innocent children but demons freed of the authority inherited from past systems of belief.

The final chapter—entitled "Is Not the Truth the Truth?"—is the only previously unpublished piece in *The Jew of Culture*. It is a commentary on Yosef Hayim Yerushalmi's *Freud's Moses: Judaism Terminable and Interminable* (1991). Yerushalmi had pondered Freud's considerations of Moses, a figure from Jewish history who had fascinated the psychoanalyst. In his late work *Der Mann Moses und die monotheistische Religion* (*Moses and Monotheism*, 1939), published in 1938, Freud maintained that Moses was actually not a Hebrew but an Egyptian who had adopted the monotheism of Pharaoh Akhenaten. Rieff, who by the time he wrote this was much more critical of Freud than he had been at the time of his first book, argued that in turning against Moses, Freud had also turned against Jewish culture. Rieff drew parallels to Adolf Hitler's attacks on the Jews in the war that began in that same year, 1939.

The linking of Freud and Hitler in this last piece should raise questions about whether the progression of thinking summarized in this book led Rieff to dramatic rhetorical overstatements in his writings after 1970. Readers might ask whether there really was any past time of social order shaped by religious culture that made life better or more meaningful than it is today or than it is likely to be in the future. Rieff made a valuable contribution in pointing out the rise of the therapeutic approach to life in modern society, and the focus on individual well-being instead of social order may pose some genuine problems. Still, these problems hardly seem to warrant condemning modern Western society as a suicidal anticulture.

Carl L. Bankston III

Review Source

Reference-Research Book News, August, 2008.

JOHN MILTON
Life, Work, and Thought

Authors: Gordon Campbell (1944-   ) and Thomas N.
    Corns (1949-   )
Publisher: Oxford University Press (New York). 496 pp.
    $39.95
Type of work: Literary biography
Time: 1608-1674
Locale: London and Cambridge, England

An exacting account of Milton's life that reshapes conceptions of the man, as a thinker, a political and religious activist, and a poet

Principal personages:

JOHN MILTON, a poet and activist
THOMAS YOUNG, a schoolmaster and
    clergyman, his early teacher and friend
CHARLES DIODATI, likely Milton's closest friend
EDWARD PHILLIPS, his nephew and pupil, chief amanuensis of Milton's
    Paradise Lost (1667) and his biographer
MARY POWELL, his first wife
CYRIACK SKINNER, his pupil, lifelong friend, and biographer
WILLIAM LAUD, the archbishop of Canterbury, 1633-1645
CHARLES I, the king of England, 1600-1649
OLIVER CROMWELL, the Lord Protector of England, 1653-1658
CHARLES II, the king of England, 1660-1685

John Milton: Life, Work, and Thought by Gordon Campbell and Thomas N. Corns significantly distinguishes itself from previous biographies of Milton because its account of the poet's life derives from firsthand inspection of all available contemporary documents and life records. It parallels the effort of David Masson in his seven-volume *The Life of John Milton: Narrated in Connexion with the Political, Ecclesiastical, and Literary History of His Time* (1859-1894). In addition, it builds upon the two major biographical works of the twentieth century, J. Milton French's five-volume *Life Records of John Milton* (1949-1958) and William Riley Parker's two-volume *Milton: A Biography* (1968), a work that Campbell revised in 1996. The quantity and complexity of material concerning Milton, so much of it discovered since the time of Masson, as well as French and Parker—not to mention the tasks of locating, digesting, and evaluating it—make the achievement of Campbell and Corns a landmark in Milton studies.

Furthermore, the authors examine the primary material in its immediate social and cultural setting. They note how the language of those sources, though perhaps ordinary in its time, is ambiguous today. Accordingly, they define and describe wide-

~

*Gordon Campbell, professor of
Renaissance Studies at the University
of Leicester, and Thomas N. Corns,
professor of English at Bangor
University, are both Fellows of the
Royal Historical Society. They were
appointed general editors of a
proposed eleven-volume* Oxford
Milton, *and both have been elected as
Honored Scholars of the Milton Society
of America.*

~

ranging implications that the factual record has for Milton's emergent personality and his daily life—goals, tasks, associations, conflicts, and developing skills as a writer of poetry and prose. They make the same scrupulous analysis of the accounts of the poet's life written by those who knew Milton or who acquired information from others who did—Edward Phillips, John Aubrey, Cyriack Skinner, Anthony Wood, and John Toland. They note, however, that the early studies of Milton owe much to his own prose writings. Consequently, they extend their detailed and comprehensive study of primary materials to the autobiographical passages in Milton's prose tracts, setting them in context as polemics. They scrutinize his habit of fashioning his life, actions, and persona to varying rhetorical demands. Further, since Milton reveals private aspects of himself in his poetry, the authors note how literary language, dependent upon layers of cultural assumptions, is even more ambiguous than nonliterary language. The authors probe connections between Milton's role as author in numerous genres and in his religious, artistic, and political views.

In addition, Campbell and Corns recognize that archival, verified, and confirmed facts and records represent only a fragment of the wide, unrolling panorama of the past. Accordingly, they distinguish their biography through the latest Stuart, Commonwealth, and Restoration historiography. They draw upon demographic, economic, commercial, legal, theological, and sociological scholarship. Through their attention to the language of the original sources and to its historical contexts, they not only describe Milton's life, work, and thought but also re-create it, step by step, contrasting expectations with outcomes. Readers look through Milton's eyes, becoming immersed in the pulse of his life. They observe his personal, public, artistic, and theological decisions amid the dynamics of Puritanism, republicanism, radicalism, and dissent, with the labels carefully reappraised. With the skill of novelists, they evoke Milton's present as it moves forward in time.

The sheer range of the assembled materials is astonishing. They tend, however, to avoid combining physical time with subjective or psychological time, the mysterious inner processes that accompany sequential acts of the observational world. The sharp clarity of a moment fades with the advance of other moments. The authors limit their probing of time's nonlinear effects upon Milton, keeping to the light of present awareness.

Campbell and Corns write that the stages of Milton's "radicalization" are the spine that runs through their study. With unrivaled precision, they describe Milton's progression as poet, political writer, and theologian, there being no final stasis, contrary to conventional views. Given aspects of Milton's life as scholar, family man, teacher, religious and political reformer, public servant, and poet, the authors describe influences of social organizations, such as higher education, art and culture, church and state. Their concerns—pressing, urgent, and direct—arise from the political texture of his actions and his writings. They focus on the revolutionary decades of the 1640's and 1650's, with Milton's support of Puritan church reform, the execution of King Charles I, the civil wars, and Milton's role in the Parliamentary government, largely under Oliver Cromwell. Prolific and versatile, Milton emerges in Campbell and Corns's work as a leading pamphleteer and political thinker. They indicate how the accumulated weight of Milton's revolutionary politics shaped *Paradise Lost* (1667), *Paradise Regained* (1671), and *Samson Agonistes* (1671). Further, they show that the major poems grew out of the creative and spiritual strength of his Christian belief, affirming his stance as poet-prophet unique in moral authority and exalted in function. The authors tend to underestimate, however, the practical effects of Milton's radical view of the church. For him, faith based on authority of Scripture and on personal, inward prompting of the Holy Spirit supersedes the visible church. The "paradise within thee, happier far," the reacquired paradise or inner Eden of *Paradise Lost*, results from the Holy Spirit's teaching alone. God prefers "[b]efore all Temples th' upright heart and pure," his anticlericalism remaining firm.

In depicting Milton's public life during his tumultuous times, Campbell and Corns make an incomparable analysis of the themes, language, and characteristics of Milton's political prose. They indicate, for instance, that Milton's emerging Christian theology gives humans, as God's creatures, self-evident and undeniable rights, and they explain reasons for his secular approach to attaining those rights. Moreover, they explore matters that appear only in hindsight of more than three centuries. Milton's political writings, they believe, sufficiently advanced the cause of freedom and human rights to label him a founding father of America. Still, they find that Milton's ideas of freedom, justice, and equality did not go far enough, limited to a few virtuous elite, similar to the Christian humanism of the medieval period, the Reformation, and the Enlightenment. The authors hesitate to resolve ambiguities of his role in the Commonwealth government, as with Cromwell's punitive military expedition to Ireland in 1649. They suggest, through his apparent silences, that at times Milton's official duties caused him either to separate his religious conscience from his politics or to realize that he must do what he could, given the world as it was, and leave the rest to God. His final years, in which he made a limited return to politics, suggest the latter course.

Campbell and Corns indicate that, in his duties as polemicist for the Commonwealth government, Milton did conform to political realities. He combined high learning and bold speculation with the need to descend to the level of opponents, to be poised and polished and yet harsh and sharp. He functioned as an attacker against all attackers. He knew that in politics what began as pure in motive can be tarnished in application. Politics involved, for instance, the ambiguities of the death of Charles I, the distinct agonies of civil war, the ever-shifting alliances of revolutionary leaders, and the eventual dissatisfaction with the Commonwealth. Campbell and Corns describe how Milton's challenges to the social norms—his commitments, his risks, and his consequences—made him into a pioneer who learns from pioneering, a true forerunner of the American experiment.

Campbell and Corns, while objective, find Milton flawed, self-contradictory, self-serving, ruthless, ambitious, and cunning, but they do not reconcile their conclusions with other features of Milton's personality. They reveal him as dauntless, moral, compassionate, resourceful, loyal, and genuine in spiritual matters. They also indicate his enthusiasms, for the culture of Italy, for music, for art, for mathematics, for literature (ancient and modern), for a Renaissance ideal made real, tender, and refined, but always human. To that list should be added Milton's devotion to political, religious, and intellectual liberty, all three then bound together. They meant self-sacrifice and uninhibited boldness, for which he would lose his sight in 1652 and nearly his life at the restoration of King Charles II in 1660. In addition, Campbell and Corns illustrate Milton's conviction that the poet must exemplify moral and religious integrity and universal learning, that wisdom, goodness, and justice can be the poet's themes only if they are the poet's life. They indicate how that idealism, a purity of mind and body, found expression in Milton's early poems, first published in 1645, such as "Arcades," "A Masque Presented at Ludlow Castle," and "Lycidas." Campbell and Corns, though seeking to judge him by his own values and those of his day, found in Milton awkward contradictions.

With more sympathy, Campbell and Corns chart Milton's preparation as epic poet, his questioning of career and abilities, especially given his impending blindness. They indicate patterns of stress, peculiar to people like Milton who, living a life of chastity and disciplined effort, believe they have extraordinary abilities they must use well, for the good of humanity, and yet not allow themselves to be destroyed by a crisis of emotion. Milton's concerns for that good, founded in a republican form of government, with wide religious toleration and civil liberties, delayed his intended vocation as author, his intuition of special, solemn poetic destiny. The authors describe how Milton's poetic hopes, long deferred, earnestly and uncommonly sought, reach fulfillment: The divine muse, with undiminished moral, imaginative, and spiritual energy, comes to the prepared mind of the blind Milton in his fifties, when he is beset by personal and public loss and poor health, surrounded by enemies. He writes the sacred epic for which he had been preparing his entire life, reconciling salvation history with the individual soul.

Campbell and Corns, finely detailing Milton's changing convictions and his fulfillment as self-declared poet-prophet, tend to underestimate the impression certain events had upon him early in his career. For example, they note that during his 1638-1639 trip to Europe, Milton met with Galileo Galilei, and they declare that Galileo's cosmology had little or no effect on Milton. For several reasons, their conclusion seems mistaken. Along with explorer Christopher Columbus, Galileo is among the few contemporaries of Milton cited in *Paradise Lost.* Moreover, in that poem, the archangel Raphael describes both the Ptolemaic and Copernican universe. The latter led the Inquisition to condemn Galileo, a fact Milton includes in *Areopapitica* (1644), his classic defense of the freedom of thought, learning, and utterance.

The conclusion that Campbell and Corns reach regarding Galileo appears to be indicative of their treatment of Milton's view of physical science. They see him as unsympathetic to its method of rational inquiry, even though Milton takes all knowledge for his province in *Paradise Lost*. Moreover, Campbell and Corns tend to overlook the intellectual daring, the open-mindedness, and the mistrust of institutions, religious and secular, that pervade Milton's poetry and prose—all of which, for Milton, Galileo may have symbolized.

Still, in *John Milton: Life, Work, and Thought*, Campbell and Corns, in faithfulness to an ever-expanding body of verifiable fact, have produced of biography of Milton that supersedes all others, full of new insights, observations, and invitations to reflection. Both well-proven Milton scholars, they know that the facts of Milton's wondrous life need no embroidery. Fittingly, their biography coincided with the four-hundredth anniversary of Milton's birth in December 1608.

Timothy C. Miller

Review Sources

Library Journal 133, no. 18 (November 1, 2008): 66.
Publishers Weekly 255, no. 44 (November 3, 2008): 53.

JOHNNY ONE-EYE
A Tale of the American Revolution

Author: Jerome Charyn (1937-)
Publisher: W. W. Norton (New York). 479 pp. $25.95
Type of work: Novel
Time: 1776-1784
Locale: In and around Manhattan, New York City

This novel depicts both imaginary and real characters of the Revolutionary War era, providing unique insights and three-dimensional characterizations of major historical figures

Principal characters:
> JOHN STOCKING (JOHNNY ONE-EYE), a teenage boy who spies for both sides in the war between the American colonies and the British monarchy
> GEORGE WASHINGTON, commander in chief of the American rebels and one-time lover of Johnny One-Eye's mother, Gertrude
> GERTRUDE JENNINGS, owner of a notorious Manhattan brothel, mother to Johnny-One Eye and spy for her great love, General Washington
> CLARA, a mixed-race prostitute with regal bearing, with whom men from both armies fall in love
> SIR WILLIAM HOWE, British general and commander in chief

An unusual and refreshingly human look at famous historical figures, *Johnny One-Eye* is an engrossing and readable novel. With the action concentrated largely in Manhattan, New York City, Jerome Charyn blends empirical evidence with interesting and entertaining fictional characters that fit believably into the customs and events of the time period.

The book opens with the narrator and primary character, John Stocking, also known as Johnny One-Eye, about to be hanged for attempting to poison General George Washington's soup. Intelligent and wily, seventeen-year-old Johnny believes he has outsmarted his captors. Though the "poison" he put in the general's soup was harmless, Johnny finds himself in a dreary dungeon of a jail nonetheless. Johnny is in fact a double agent, spying for both the British and the Americans during the early days of the Revolutionary War. He came by his nickname after losing an eye in battle under the command of American General Benedict Arnold. Hired as Arnold's secretary, Johnny was only briefly embattled before becoming wounded.

Johnny does not know who his father is; his mother, Gertrude Jennings, is the proprietress of a brothel named Holy Ground because of its proximity to a nearby Catholic church. Her workingwomen are thus referred to irreverently as "nuns." In addition to being a brothel, Holy Ground is a favorite meeting place for high-ranking American and British combatants, not least of which is General Washington, commander in chief of the rebels, and General William Howe, commander of the British forces. Washington is married to wealthy Martha Custis, who is home at Mt. Vernon, their famous Virginia plantation. A farmer and the highest-ranking American soldier, Washington is said to have come to Holy Ground merely to play cards. In fact, he has been in love with Gertrude since their meeting years earlier in a roadside tavern where she was a waitress. Becoming aware of the previous relationship between his mother and Washington, Johnny convinces himself that the general is his father; his mother neither denies nor confirms the veracity of her son's wishful deduction.

A Guggenheim Fellow, Jerome Charyn has authored more than thirty books. His novel Darlin' Bill *(1980) garnered the Rosenthal Award from the American Academy and Institute of Arts and Letters.*

In contrast to the wide and varied spectrum of Washington's historical legacy, ranging from hyperbolic praise for mythical qualities to debunking as emotionally weak and militarily bumbling, author Charyn portrays the general as kind, equitable, and humble, although he is strong and ruthless in battle. In short, he is an extraordinary human being who rose to the momentous challenge of fighting a revolution for his country and his fellow citizens.

The main protagonist of the book, John Stocking (Johnny One-Eye) is a teenager advanced beyond his years by the remarkable era and circumstances in which he lives. Raised in a brothel with a less-than-attentive mother, surrounded by prostitutes and their powerful clients amid the uproar of rebellion, Johnny is boyish and mature at the same time. In addition to his perilous and exciting existence as a double agent, Johnny's life is complicated by his desperate love for Clara, the most popular and elusive of the prostitutes at Holy Ground.

Fleeing her homeland and sexually abusive stepfather in Dominica, Clara was taken in as a homeless waif by Gertrude to be pampered at Holy Ground. An Octoroon (mixed race) with dark skin, blond locks, and piercing green eyes, Clara is at once enigmatic and profoundly practical. She becomes an obsession for love-struck, endlessly hopeful, and loyal Johnny.

Johnny occupies a precarious position among the intrigues and destruction of personal lives brought about by the war. Himself a "changeling," an ostensibly illegitimate boy with shifting loyalties, he received an education at King's College, where his tuition was paid by the British monarchy. His heart, though, leads him toward the cause of the American rebels, especially since he believes that General Washington is his father. At home in Holy Ground, Johnny is in close contact with high-ranking British and American officers who frequent the brothel—a unique position for a double agent. He is also in great danger of being killed by either side.

General Washington, in particular, has a great deal of use for Johnny. First encountering the boy as a result of the attempted soup poisoning, Washington sets up a ruse of hanging him, but what the general really wants, and gets, is Johnny's service as a dedicated spy for the American rebels.

Johnny becomes enamored of Washington. The general's integrity and resilience are impressive, but the possibility that he is Johnny's father is an irresistible force for the boy. Johnny hears an enticing tale by a British loyalist and frequent visitor to Holy Ground: Many years earlier, Washington was a young man returning to his farm after fighting in the Indian Wars. He was a striking and charismatic man, uncommonly tall, with impeccable manners and a melancholy air about him, having recently survived an unrequited love affair with his neighbor's wife. Having financial problems, George became engaged to wealthy Martha Custis; still, he was a lonely man, pining for his former lover. It was during this time that he met Gertrude Jennings, a waitress at a tavern in the Virginia Tidewater country. The two were sporadic lovers until George arrives one day to find Gertrude gone without a trace.

Gertrude had found her way to Manhattan, pregnant and impoverished. Her good looks, ample charms, and intelligence propelled her into prosperity as a brothel madame, and Holy Ground was launched. More than a decade passed before Washington discovered Gertrude's whereabouts. Having become wealthy and married in the intervening years, Washington, as leader of the Revolutionary army, was camped in New York, battling the British occupation of Manhattan. Holy Ground was recommended to him as the best place in town to socialize and to play vingt-et-un, a favorite card game. There he and Gertrude were reunited.

With British military personnel in charge of Manhattan, Washington and his troops are miserably outnumbered and poorly provisioned. Holy Ground is a good diversion, and it is an excellent place to pick up information and military plans. Unknown to Johnny for a long while is that his mother is also a spy—for Washington.

British commander General Sir William Howe also frequents Holy Ground, as does his brother, Admiral Dick Howe. Sir William takes for a mistress the wife of a scurrilous loyalist citizen, but he patronizes the brothel for social and military contacts. Dick becomes enchanted with the lovely Clara, much to Johnny's envious chagrin.

Johnny's loyalties shift for a time, but the more he is exposed to the legendary General Washington, whom he presumes to be his father, the more Johnny forms an allegiance to the American rebel cause. Washington is besieged by worries and seemingly insurmountable military odds, which he must face with a raggedy army of hungry and often-contentious men. Still, the good general is devoted to his men, doggedly determined to face and defeat the British occupiers of his beloved country. In a scheme to capture General Washington, British General Howe invites him to Holy Ground for a game of vingt-et-un, which is nearly an obsession for both men. Through brothel spies, Washington learns that the invitation is a trap. He attends anyway, wins the game, and leaves unharmed, because Admiral Dick Howe, who claims it is not an honorable way to vanquish an enemy, has shamed his brother William into letting Washington leave.

Johnny is in the thick of the action as events swirl around him. Imprisoned on a battleship under horrific and inhumane conditions, manipulated into overseeing his African American friends in backbreaking labor for the British Army, and generally running into mayhem and heartbreak at every turn, Johnny finds his life is exciting but constantly in danger. Though ridiculed as the bastard son of a notorious whore,

Johnny is more educated and chivalrous than most of his torturers. The constants in his life include his ambivalence toward his mother, his desire to know his paternity, and his deep love and respect for Clara.

In a surprisingly disappointing denouement, Johnny discovers his real father is a cutthroat thief, a lowlife whose character could not be less like the heroic figure of General Washington. Not so surprising is Johnny's eventual attainment of Clara, the woman of his dreams.

The battles and eventual outcome of the Revolutionary War are well known to most readers, and no searing revelations on that topic are offered in this novel. There is, however, a deeply poignant nostalgia and melancholy for the life of General Washington after the Revolutionary War and his extremely well regarded tenure as the first president of the newly formed United States of America.

Author Charyn's affection for the time period and for larger-than-life heroes is apparent in this work. Characterizations of real-life figures such as Arnold and Alexander Hamilton are neither revealing nor stirring. Washington is clearly Charyn's favorite founder; this is an empathetic and compelling portrayal of a man often regarded as stern, aloof, and annoyingly esoteric.

Although *Johnny One-Eye* occasionally and subtly veers off plot, it is a highly readable and enjoyable book. The colloquial dialect is applied unevenly, though consistently enough to create a word picture of the diverse backgrounds of the population of the fledgling American colonists and their British counterparts. Johnny, the main protagonist through whose "one-eye" is seen all other characters, appears as a likable, literate rogue who finally overcomes all odds, gets the girl, and enjoys a happy ending.

Johnny One-Eye: A Tale of the American Revolution makes a familiar historical saga come alive with a fresh look at well-known characters and events. While crowded with characters that sometimes seem a bit superfluous to the story, the dramatic dissection of the main players is riveting. Charyn's novel is a good choice for readers who enjoy historical fiction, with its compelling mix of factual data embellished with overt drama and satirical levity.

Twyla R. Wells

Review Sources

Booklist 104, nos. 9/10 (January 1, 2008): 42.
Entertainment Weekly, February 22, 2008, p. 100.
Library Journal 133, no. 1 (January 1, 2008): 81.
The New Yorker 84, no. 5 (March 17, 2008): 83.
Publishers Weekly 254, no. 45 (November 12, 2007): 32.
The Wall Street Journal 251, no. 39 (February 16, 2008): W10.

JUST AFTER SUNSET
Stories

Author: Stephen King (1947-   )
Publisher: Charles Scribner's Sons (New York). 384 pp.
  $28.00
Type of work: Short fiction
Time: The late twentieth and early twenty-first centuries
Locale: The United States

*A collection of thirteen stories by King, twelve of which
originally appeared in* The New Yorker, Esquire, Playboy,
Postscripts, The Magazine of Fantasy and Science Fiction,
*and other magazines and anthologies between 1977 and
2008 and one that first appears in this book*

Principal characters:
> WILLA, a young woman
> EMILY OWENSBY, a young mother whose baby daughter has recently
>   died
> HARVEY STEVENS, a sixty-year-old stockbroker
> JOHN DYKSTRA, a college English professor who writes hard-boiled
>   detective stories
> RICHARD SIFKITZ, a thirty-eight-year-old commercial artist
> SCOTT STALEY, a former insurance company employee
> JANICE GANDOLEWSKI, a high school student
> N., a psychiatric patient
> JOHN HALSTON, a professional killer
> ANNE, a widow
> MONETTE, a traveling salesman
> AYANA, a blind African American girl
> CURTIS JOHNSON, a stock investor

Stephen King prefaces his first short story collection since 2002's *Everything's
Eventual* with a quote from Arthur Machen's 1890 story "The Great God Pan." In
Machen's story, except for a scientist who appears at the beginning and at the end, the
characters are ordinary people living ordinary lives until they encounter Evil. King
sees horrors in mundane items such as port-a-potties and stationary bikes and at common places such as highway rest stops. King also finds terrors in the events of a normal life, such as the deaths of close relatives and pets, and his characters suffer from
high blood pressure and cholesterol, prostate cancer, and obsessive-compulsive disorder. Notes at the end of the book explain the circumstances surrounding the writing
of each story.

"The Things They Left Behind" (2005) concerns survival guilt in the aftermath of
the events of September 11, 2001, when hijackers crashed two passenger jets into the
World Trade Center in New York and a third into the Pentagon outside of Washing-

ton, D.C. The main character is Scott Staley, an insurance company employee who worked on the 110th floor of the World Trade Center but heard a voice in his head early on 9/11 telling him not to go into work. He paid attention to the voice and called in sick that day. A year later, the belongings of his deceased co-workers appear at his apartment, and he can hear the bits and pieces talk about the last day in their owners' lives. Although Staley tries to throw the items away, they keep reappearing.

In "Stationary Bike" (2003), Richard Sifkitz is a commercial artist diagnosed with high cholesterol. He buys a stationary bike, but he finds working out boring. He then paints a mural on the wall facing the bike and imagines that he is biking down a road leading through a forest to a mountain and populated by road workers that he names Berkowitz, Carlos, Freddy, and Whelan. Sifkitz then finds that he is inspired to create some pictures just

Stephen King has written more than two hundred short stories and forty novels, mostly in the horror genre. He received O. Henry and World Fantasy awards for his 1994 short story "The Man in the Black Suit," and he has edited the anthology The Best American Short Stories 2007.

for himself rather than merely executing commissions for others. Eventually, his day-dreams become more and more real, and Sifkitz gets the feeling that someone is following him. He finally discovers that the road workers have unique personalities and independent lives of their own. The premise is similar to one in King's novel *Duma Key* (2008), in which the process of painting gives the main character a kind of extra-sensory perception.

A dream disrupts the lives of Harvey Stevens and his wife in "Harvey's Dream" (2003). Of all the stories in this collection, it is the most literary, which is not surprising considering that it first appeared in *The New Yorker*. It is also the one that has had the best critical acceptance, being nominated for the Bram Stoker Award and selected for the 2003 *The Year's Best Fantasy and Horror* anthology. In his notes at the end of the book, King writes that it was inspired by one of his own dreams and that he wrote it in a single sitting.

"Graduation Afternoon" (2007) was inspired by another of King's dreams in which he envisioned a nuclear mushroom cloud over New York City. The main character, Janice, is dating a boy from a family much wealthier than hers and is visiting that family on the day he graduates from prep school. They live outside the city, so the bomb does not kill them immediately.

In "Mute" (2007), Monette, a middle-aged traveling salesman and lapsed Catholic, explains to a deaf-mute hitchhiker the demise of his twenty-six-year marriage, although it turns out that the hitchhiker is really not deaf. Monette later recounts the incident while confessing to a priest. This is the kind of story that used to appear on the old television series *Alfred Hitchcock Presents* that King watched when he was young. The hitchhiker thinks he is helping the salesman by killing his wife and her lover.

"Ayana" (2007) is a blind miracle worker that King uses to explore the question of why some people are cured of illnesses and others die. When the title character, a young African American girl, walks into the hospital room of the father of the story's narrator, the girl kisses the old man's cheek, and he miraculously recovers from terminal cancer. The girl also kisses the narrator, who later finds that he has received healing powers of his own. It is somewhat reminiscent of King's 1996 novel *The Green Mile*, in which the character John Coffey has mysterious healing powers.

In 1998, King and his wife Tabitha bought a winter home near Sarasota, Florida, and the state is turning up more and more as a setting for his fiction. *Duma Key* is set around Sarasota, and he also uses Florida settings in *Just After Sunset* with "A Very Tight Place" (2008), "Rest Stop" (2003), and "The Gingerbread Girl" (2007). The last story is the longest in this collection. Emily Owensby takes up running after the death of her baby daughter, then leaves her husband, and finally takes up residence in her father's house on Vermillion Key off Florida's Gulf Coast. She immerses herself in the fiction of John D. McDonald, Ed McBain, and Raymond Chandler, but she does not read a newspaper, turn on the television, or even power up her father's personal computer to surf the Web. After working up to running seven miles a day, she finds a dead body while on a run and quickly discovers that she has crossed paths with a serial killer.

A portable toilet is a plot device in "A Very Tight Place," and a rest stop becomes the site of a major event in a man's life in "Rest Stop." The former concerns a feud between neighbors over a piece of land, and the latter is about a man witnessing a crime. King once used a portable toilet on a Florida beach, and it almost tipped over. When it occurred to him that one could be used as a murder weapon, he wrote "A Very Tight Place." King has often said that he would not hesitate to gross out a reader if it made the story more effective, and he does his best in this combination of the first-person narration of Edgar Allan Poe's "The Premature Burial" (1844) and the way in which someone lures another person into a trap as in Poe's "The Cask of Amontillado" (1846). The two neighbors live on a barrier island off Florida's Gulf Coast. One wants to develop a piece of land on the island, but the other wants it left alone.

"Rest Stop" was inspired by an incident King witnessed while driving from St. Petersburg to Sarasota and is one of the many stories and novels King has written in his career in which the main character is a writer. John Dykstra, who writes suspense novels under the pseudonym of Rick Hardin, is a meek, mild-mannered college English professor. The story plays on King's habit of speaking of his pseudonym Richard Bachman as if he were a real person with an existence independent of King's. When Dykstra stops at a rest area on Interstate Highway 75 en route to Sarasota, he sees an abusive husband beating up his wife and has to decide whether to get involved and then what to do. His solution is to channel his Hardin personality and act like a private eye in a hard-boiled detective novel.

"The Cat from Hell" is the oldest story in this collection, first published in *Cavalier* in 1977, just after King's books started to appear on the best-seller lists. This is the first time it has been included in any of his short story collections. It concerns a hit man who accepts a contract to kill a cat, but finds that it is not so easy. The cat has supernatural powers.

A train derailment has stranded a group of passengers in the middle of Wyoming at the beginning of "Willa" (2006), but eventually this tale becomes a ghost story. The ghosts mean no harm to the living, and their existence can be pleasant if they can find a nice place to haunt, in this case a country music nightclub. At least Willa and her fiancé accept their deaths, unlike the others who died in the train accident and are still waiting for a rescue.

In *Danse Macabre*, King's 1981 informal study of horror in fiction, film, and television, he devotes ten pages to the old television series *The Twilight Zone*. "*The New York Times* at Special Bargain Rates" (2008) is the kind of story that would not have been out of place in that anthology television series, because the main character is a woman who has just lost her husband in a plane crash, but then receives a cell phone call from him.

In his notes, King explains that while he has abandoned the Methodist religion of his childhood, he still feels that somehow the soul will survive a person's physical death. In both "Willa" and "*The New York Times* at Special Bargain Rates," the recently dead find themselves in train stations, but they can choose to leave.

The single story that has never appeared elsewhere is "N.," and it is the one that connects most fully with King's earlier work and with some of his literary ancestors. King cites Machen's "The Great God Pan" in the story, and both that story and Charlotte Perkins Gilman's "The Yellow Wall Paper" (1890) in his end notes. N. lives in Castle Rock, a town in southwestern Maine that King created for much of his early fiction. (The town's name comes from William Golding's 1954 fiction *Lord of the Flies*, King's favorite novel.) The title character is a psychiatric patient suffering from obsessive-compulsive disorder, like the narrator of Gilman's story, but the underlying cause, N.'s therapist discovers, is that N. is holding back creatures from another dimension that want to invade our world. N.'s use of a camera is the inverse of a camera's function in King's 1990 novella, "The Sun Dog," another Castle Rock story. In "The Sun Dog," a camera provides a gateway for a demonic dog to come into this world, and in "N.," a camera helps the title character hold back the creatures. If N. had read some of the other stories in this collection, then he would have known that the demons are already among us.

Thomas R. Feller

Review Sources

Booklist 105, no. 2 (September 15, 2008): 5.
Entertainment Weekly, November 14, 2008, p. 77.
Kirkus Reviews 76, no. 17 (September 1, 2008): 908-909.
Library Journal 133, no. 15 (September 15, 2008): 51.

The New York Times, November 5, 2008, p. C1.
The New York Times Book Review, November 23, 2008, p. 17.
People 70, no. 21 (November 24, 2008): 53.
Publishers Weekly 255, no. 35 (September 1, 2008): 35.
San Francisco Chronicle, November 30, 2008, p. M7.
USA Today, November 11, 2008, p. D6.

KNOCKEMSTIFF

Author: Donald Ray Pollock (1954-   )
Publisher: Doubleday (New York). 206 pp. $22.95
Type of work: Short fiction
Time: The mid-1960's to the late 1990's
Locale: Knockemstiff, a hamlet in Ross County,
  southcentral Ohio

*Eighteen loosely connected stories about the desperate
underclass denizens of a backwater Appalachian town in
southern Ohio*

Most new American literary sensations tend to be young,
sophisticated, middle-class or upper-class graduates of elite
writing programs. Author Donald Ray Pollock comes from
a starkly different place: the desolate world of Appalachian rural poverty. A high
school dropout, Pollock worked at a paper mill in Chillicothe, Ohio, for thirty-two
grueling years before becoming a writer in his middle age—an almost unheard-of career trajectory that lends his debut story collection, *Knockemstiff*, an extraordinary degree of blue-collar verisimilitude.

In eighteen gothic stories set in and around Knockemstiff (a real though now mori-
bund township in southern Ohio), Pollock explores the crude, damaged, often gro-
tesque lives of the American backwoods poor. His choice of subject matter places him
in a long and distinguished literary tradition whose practitioners include Mark Twain,
Sherwood Anderson, Erskine Caldwell, William Faulkner, Flannery O'Connor, Harry
Crews, Breece D'J Pancake, Carolyn Chute, Russell Banks, Pinckney Benedict, Annie Proulx, Dorothy Allison, and many others. What is unique about Pollock's fiction
is its powerful blend of exceedingly grim (sometimes horrifying) content, economy
and precision of form, and utter neutrality of tone—a combination that makes these
stories vivid, enigmatic, Kafkaesque nightmares that linger in the imagination.

Though they feature a diverse array of characters, the stories in *Knockemstiff* share
some common themes and concerns. All of Pollock's characters are losers: poor, uneducated, venal, coarse, lonely, impulsive, despairing. Woefully ill equipped to cope
in modern society, the denizens of Knockemstiff devote their energies not to improving themselves—a prospect that seems remote if not impossible—but to escaping
their miseries any way they can, without regard to consequences. The prime means of
escape are the usual ones chosen by the dispossessed in every land and epoch: cathar-
tic violence, cheap sex, chronic drug and alcohol abuse, and inane wish-fulfillment
fantasies (often centered on revenge of some sort). Moreover, many of Pollock's dis-
solute characters eventually succumb to what psychiatrists rather euphemistically
term decompensation, the functional deterioration of mental health with attendant
loss of cognition and memory. In sum, a gradual but ineluctable entropy rules in
Pollock's universe; in every instance, things go from bad to worse as polluted minds

~

A native of Knockemstiff, Ross County, Ohio, Donald Ray Pollock quit high school at seventeen to work in a meatpacking plant. He spent thirty-two years employed by the Mead Paper Mill in Chillicothe, Ohio, and battled drug and alcohol addictions until he achieved sobriety in 1986. In 1994, Pollock earned a B.A. in English from Ohio University-Chillicothe and started writing fiction in 1999. Knockemstiff *is his first book.*

~

and bodies weaken, wither, and die. However, Pollock's aim is not to wallow in depravity and ruin. A closer examination of these stories reveals a deep interest in the vagaries of human psychology. Pollock's characters suffer all manner of humiliation, deprivation, and trauma—conditions that give rise to unpredictable forms of displacement (the term in psychology for an unconscious defense mechanism whereby the mind redirects affect from an object felt to be dangerous or unacceptable to an object felt to be safe or acceptable). It might be said that displacement is the subject of Pollock's book.

Violence against the weak, unsuspecting, and vulnerable is the most common form of displacement practiced by Pollock's down-and-outers. In "Real Life," an ignorant father thinks he is doing his son a service by infecting him with the worst legacy imaginable: mindless, reactive aggression. Bobby, the first-person narrator, recalls an incident he witnessed when he was seven: his brutal, alcoholic father, Vernon, beating a man half to death in the men's room of a drive-in motion-picture theater after the man admonished him for cursing in front of his son. If that were not enough, Vernon encouraged Bobby to attack and beat up the man's son, which Bobby did, to his father's great pride and delight.

In "Schott's Bridge" neediness collides with predation when Todd Russell, a lonely, timid gay man, forms an ill-advised friendship with Frankie Johnson, a local homophobic tough who displaces his own masculine insecurities by visiting numerous acts of physical and emotional sadism on Todd, culminating in a particularly vicious beating and rape, and the theft of Todd's car and all of his money. At the end of the story, Todd, drugged, ravaged, and dazed, contemplates jumping off Schott's Bridge—a man destroyed only because he dared to want love.

"Assailants" also deals with displacement. Delbert "Del" Murray's mentally impaired wife, Geraldine (also known as "The Fish Stick Girl" because she carries fish sticks in her purse), has developed agoraphobia and panic attacks after being assaulted and nearly strangled in front of Tobacco Friendly by a man with a paper sack over his head. Flirting shamelessly with a young female clerk at the local Quikstop, Del mentions his wife's assault, but the clerk dismisses her as "some kind of nutcase, homeless person or something." To displace his own embarrassment, shame, and rage Del returns to the store with a paper sack over his own head to frighten the clerk. Unfortunately, his ruse is too effective: Startled, she pitches from her stool, hits her head on a display case, and is knocked unconscious, perhaps dead. Thus, ironically, Del takes the violence visited upon his wife and carries it forward onto another innocent victim.

"I Start Over" deals with a somewhat similar case of displacement and its violent effects. Big Bernie Givens, "fifty-six years old and sloppy fat and stuck in southern

Ohio like the smile on a dead clown's ass," cannot deal with the fact that his adult son, Jerry, has been permanently rendered a drooling vegetable after a three-day booze-and-drug binge. Displacing his intense sorrow and frustration causes Givens to lose his job when he assaults a coworker. Now homicidal and suicidal, Bernie again engages in displacement when he viciously assaults some teenagers who make fun of him and Jerry at a drive-through restaurant. As the story ends, the police are pursuing Bernie's car after the incident; he will most likely "start over" as a convicted felon.

Not all violence in *Knockemstiff* is a result of displacement. Sometimes it is merely self-serving or opportunistic. In "Dynamite Hole," the first-person narrator, Jake Lowry, a half-demented, middle-aged hermit who lives in an abandoned school bus, confesses to two heinous acts. In the first instance, Jake—who was evading the draft in World War II by hiding in the hills—deliberately leads two pursuing soldiers into a swarming nest of copperhead snakes; one of them is fatally bitten. In the second, more recent instance, Jake comes upon fifteen-year-old Truman Mackey copulating with his own sister. After murdering Truman with a rock to the skull, Jake rapes and murders the boy's sister. He then hides the bodies in an underwater cave, and they are never found. No one suspects that he is a killer. What is particularly chilling is that the rape and double-murder do not come out of malice or rage; they are only the banal results of Jake taking advantage of a convenient opportunity to end his own virginity, no doubt rationalizing that the incest he discovered gave him moral carte blanche.

A different kind of displacement—expressed through desperate, perverse sex—is another hallmark of Pollock's stories. A glaring feature of "Dynamite Hole" and "Schott's Bridge," predatory sex is the central theme of "Hair's Fate." Daniel, a fourteen-year-old boy with "old-people glasses and acne sprouts and a bony chicken chest," resorts to sex in the outhouse with "Lucy," his sister's carnival doll. As punishment, Daniel's father brutally cuts off his prized long hair with a knife, a crushing humiliation that prompts Daniel to run away from home. A fat, slovenly trucker named Cowboy Roy picks up Daniel while he is hitchhiking and takes him back to his grimy house trailer. There, Cowboy Roy feeds Daniel amphetamines and, as the story closes, is about to molest him. In "Fish Sticks" Del recounts an incident that happened almost thirty years before. In the mid-1970's, Del (age fifteen) develops a case of wanderlust after reading a trashy paperback, Jack W. Thomas's *Reds* (1970), about young drug addict drifters. Del convinces his friend, Randy, to escape Knockemstiff and take a bus to Florida. In St. Petersburg they meet Leo, a fat, sloppy street hot dog vendor who promises to pay the boys for fellatio. After a dispute about compensation, Del swings a lamp at the fat man's head, perhaps killing him. As is typical in these stories, sex and violence often merge and become indistinguishable.

If dangerous affect cannot be displaced onto harmless objects, it can always be anesthetized. Illicit drugs are on a par with sex and violence for ubiquity in *Knockemstiff*. Almost unbelievably, the first-person narrator in "Bactine" recalls regularly huffing Bactine, the topical antiseptic-anesthetic that, inhaled in spray form, is a deadly, mind-twisting toxin. The unnamed first-person narrator of "Blessed" recounts his precipitous downward spiral after becoming addicted to OxyContin (also known as "Hillbilly heroin"). Illegal anabolic steroids destroy Randy, Del's friend in

"Fish Sticks," and Sammy Coburn in "Discipline." Avid bodybuilders, Randy and Sammy sacrifice their health and ultimately their lives for the dubious, short-term benefits of macho narcissism. In "Pills" middle-aged Robert "Bobby" Shaffer recounts an incident that occurred when he was sixteen. He and his friend, Frankie Johnson, steal four bottles (240 pills) of Black Beauties (pharmaceutical amphetamines) from Wanda Wipert, the bartender at Hap's Bar and a drug dealer on the side. Their plan is to drive to California in Frankie's "muscle car," a 1969 Dodge Coronet Super Bee, but they end up staying in Knockemstiff, high on speed for five solid days and nights.

"Pills" nicely illustrates another abiding theme in *Knockemstiff*: the endless desire to escape from the town and the hideous life it affords, juxtaposed by the endless futility would-be escapists encounter. Alcohol, drugs, sex, violence, travel, and fantasy—all produce a temporary release that leaves the person who partakes further weakened and more deeply trapped, like one who struggles in quicksand only to hasten the sinking process. What becomes clear as these incredibly bleak but fascinating stories unfold is that Knockemstiff is much more than a geographic or a socioeconomic trap; it is a state of mind probably best described as unconscious (and therefore ineluctable) nihilism. In other words, Pollock's grotesques—to borrow a term from Sherwood Anderson—have unwittingly but quite understandably equated the depredations of a brutal society with the nature of life itself. Their total loss of faith in the fundamental goodness of life probably pervades a terrifyingly sizable portion of the American underclass. Nevertheless, Pollock does not caricature or condemn the fictive citizens of Knockemstiff; his tone is scrupulously even-tempered and nonjudgmental. The deeply unsettling effect rendered is akin to what psychoanalyst Sigmund Freud termed "the uncanny" (German *Das Unheimliche*—literally "un-home-ly"), the concept that something is at once both vividly familiar and foreign, recognizable yet also strangely unrecognizable. While Pollock is never overtly political, these stories, in all of their horror, stand as a searing indictment of an entire civilization.

Robert Niemi

Review Sources

Entertainment Weekly, March 21, 2008, p. 65.
Kirkus Reviews 76, no. 1 (January 1, 2008): 12.
Los Angeles Times, April 6, 2008, p. F7.
Minneapolis Star Tribune, March 16, 2008, p. F14.
New Statesman 137 (July 14, 2008): 59.
The New York Times Book Review, March 23, 2008, p. 17.
Publishers Weekly 254, no. 46 (November 19, 2007): 31.
USA Today, March 20, 2008, p. 7D.
The Wall Street Journal 251, no. 33 (February 9, 2008): W1.

THE LAST DAYS OF OLD BEIJING
Life in the Vanishing Backstreets of a City Transformed

Author: Michael Meyer (1972-   )
Publisher: Walker (New York). Illustrated. 355 pp.
$25.99
Type of work: Memoir, history
Time: 1995-2007
Locale: Beijing, China

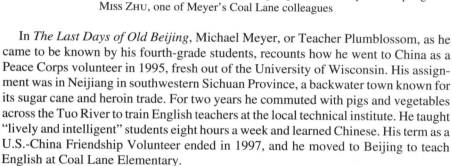

The experiences of a Peace Corps teacher who stayed on in Beijing and witnessed the preparations for the Olympics in 2008

Principal personages:
MICHAEL MEYER, the author, a fourth-grade English teacher at Beijing's Coal Lane Elementary School
THE WIDOW, the author's neighbor who lives in a cloud of smoke from her Flying Horse cigarettes and pampers him with pork dumplings
MISS ZHU, one of Meyer's Coal Lane colleagues

In *The Last Days of Old Beijing*, Michael Meyer, or Teacher Plumblossom, as he came to be known by his fourth-grade students, recounts how he went to China as a Peace Corps volunteer in 1995, fresh out of the University of Wisconsin. His assignment was in Neijiang in southwestern Sichuan Province, a backwater town known for its sugar cane and heroin trade. For two years he commuted with pigs and vegetables across the Tuo River to train English teachers at the local technical institute. He taught "lively and intelligent" students eight hours a week and learned Chinese. His term as a U.S.-China Friendship Volunteer ended in 1997, and he moved to Beijing to teach English at Coal Lane Elementary.

Meyer describes Beijing's facelift for the Olympics with a rueful realization that "no one should have to live in poverty, no matter how picturesque." Sixty Starbucks, a couple hundred McDonald's, a matching number of Kentucky Fried Chickens, and dozens of Pizza Huts accommodate the hungry citizens, who have been accustomed to such local dishes as Feng's boiled tripe and Chen's stewed intestines at Langfang Second Lane. Other Beijing culinary favorites include "knife-shaved" noodles, broad strands of pasta boiled in pork broth, and vermicelli with shredded pork and peppers known more colloquially—and mysteriously—as "ants climbing trees."

As more and more cars pour onto the streets every day, the site of his school amid luxury homes and strip malls convinces Meyer to move to the Dazhalan community in central Beijing in 2005, where he is ideally positioned to witness the intense preparations for the Summer Olympics of 2008. He lives in a two-room apartment in a *hutong*, one of the many ancient lanes crisscrossing Beijing's center, an area of prime real estate for developers. Dazhalan's 114 *hutong* are home to fifty-seven thousand residents in its

~

Michael Meyer is a teacher and a writer who has won the Lowell Thomas Award for travel writing. His work has been published in Time, Smithsonian, *and other magazines. In China he trained the nation's UNESCO World Heritage site managers in preservation practices.*

~

half-square-mile area; the shortest *hutong* is ten yards long, the narrowest is fifteen inches. Red Bayberry and Bamboo Slanted Street, where Meyer lives, runs eight hundred yards through the neighborhood. Life in Dazhalan is colorful. On his way to the men's latrine, Meyer passes a vegetable stand, a hairdresser, and a gathering of mah-jongg players. The latrine presents four slits in the floor and the admonition No Spitting, No Smoking, No Coarse Language, No Missing the Hole.

The campaign to "Say Farewell to Dangerous Housing" means the end for the crowded *hutong* as more and more neighborhoods are razed. Everyone dreads the Hand, the symbol pronounced *chai* that means "raze." When it appears on a dwelling, the residents have to move. Meyer tells the story of Mr. Yang and his family, who bo ght their courtyard in 1945, but after the Liberation (Mr. Yang's word) in 1949 they subdivided the rooms and sold them for fear of being labeled capitalists. Then during the Cultural Revolution, the rooms were divided again and given to workers, leaving Mr. Yang's parents one small room. The end comes when the Hand paints *chai* on the wall one night. The authorities offer about one thousand dollars per square meter for an apartment, much of which is stolen by a conspiracy between the evaluator and the omnipresent developers. Mr. Yang cries when he describes the razing of his home to make way for rubble-bordered office towers christened Investment Plaza and Corporate Square. A Ritz-Carlton hotel was in the *hutong*'s future.

Another family victimized by the Hand was the Hans, owners of a small shop on Langfang First Lane. Mrs. Han tended the shop while Mr. Han repaired cell phones at the back of the store. They worked twelve hours a day and lived in one small room in Meyer's courtyard. The Hans had left their six-year-old son with his grandparents and migrated from China's northeast a year earlier and had used their life savings to buy a new store on a busy location and were saving money when the Hand left its mark in spring of 2006.

Meyer gives a colorful account of the *Evening News*, his favorite tabloid among Beijing's eight daily newspapers. For five mao (seven cents) he gets at least fifty pages, much smaller than the record 208-page issue that the publisher discontinued when the vendors learned it was worth more for scrap. The *Evening News* enjoyed a circulation of 1.2 million and was "fattened" by supplements advertising "health powders" and other miracle products touted as guaranteeing a woman's sexual success. The paper's contents remind Meyer of the weekly community paper he grew up reading in Minnesota, with announcements plastered on the front page and the inside stuffed with stories of crimes and other misdeeds. The police section in the *Evening News* always features shocking incidents such as "Girl lights gasoline on sleeping boyfriend" and "Forty prostitutes arrested at karaoke club." Guns were outlawed but crimes with knives were a regular feature of the *Evening News*, with such items as a foot-massage-parlor operator who fatally stabbed a customer for sexual harassment and a woman who sliced up her mother-in-law's head during an argument.

Meyer confesses to studying the missing person ads every day, "despite knowing better." Some of the missing are elderly people with physical problems or alcohol addiction; many are children (the paper ran seventeen ads one day); and one mentally retarded couple ran away together. Meyer judges the rewards surprisingly low, the highest being ten thousand yuan ($1,333) for finding an eighty-two-year-old woman with Alzheimer's disease. Missing dogs generally bring in three thousand to five thousand yuan. Many of the stories recount bizarre events, such as those about a woman who got her hand stuck in a latrine hole for an hour, a man who strangled a neighbor's cat after it ate his bird worth one thousand dollars, and a man who offended his fellow passengers by airing his smelly shoes and socks out an open window on the bus.

Meyer describes his Beijing friends fondly. The eighty-year-old Widow who lives next door comes and goes freely, looking after him and feeding him his favorite pork and chives dumplings. They have lived side by side for two years, but one day she tells Meyer she is to be relocated in a high-rise. At that time, Meyer coaxes the Widow's remarkable life story out of her. She was born in Port Arthur, now Dalian, on the Yellow Sea, where her father was a railroad engineer. When she was fifteen, the family moved to Beijing, living first near Fresh Fish Junction and then on Big Ear *hutong*. Life under the Japanese was spartan, but it got worse when her father married her off to an army officer who abandoned her during her second pregnancy. The People's Liberation Army arrived in 1949 and gave her more than a hundred pounds of rice, a sack of noodles, and eleven pounds of flaxseed oil. "The Communist Party welcomed me with an open door. The Party's great kindness to me is something I can't ever completely express or finish attempting to." When Chairman Mao died, the Widow cried; when Zhou Enlai died, she not only cried but could not eat for the entire day.

One of Meyer's most stubborn *hutong* acquaintances is Old Zhang, whom he meets in the street one cold night and who tells him of witnessing a young woman being brutally evicted and hauled away in cuffs. Old Zhang is seventy-three and teaching himself English. After almost fifty years of living in Fresh Fish Junction, he wakes one morning to find the Hand has left the *chai* symbol on his wall. Old Zhang continues to live in his house, fighting the Heavenly Street Development Company and insisting that he can survive on cabbages and radishes. In the final showdown with the arbitrator, Old Zhang accepts 580,000 yuan ($77,333), not the 800,000 yuan he had asked for but a good deal under the circumstances.

Meyer's chapter on "Springtime" yields some observations about the new Wal-Mart opening near Dazhalan. Old people like the moving ramps because escalators make them nervous, but on the ramps "grandmothers balanced like surfers." Spring also brings ten dust storms to Beijing, dumping 330,000 tons of sand on the city. The worst storm produced an air pollution index of a toxic 500, whereas 150 is judged so dangerous people should stay indoors. After the dust storms the city is "blanketed" by allergy-breeding willow and polar seeds. Since 2001, only male species have been planted, but one million female species live on.

Frustrated by the unimaginative rote lessons at Coal Lane Elementary, Meyer takes his fellow English teachers to the International School of Beijing to observe the more demanding teaching methods used there. Coal Lane relies on a reading primer featuring a character named Mocky, whose simple activities are summed up in a chant. When he carries a plate of greens, for instance, the children chant: "We'll go and visit uncle. It's very, very far. We'll take some salad with us, and go there in a car."

Miss Zhu observes the teaching strategies closely and changes her approach to include more individual initiative in reaching answers. A visit to China's largest bookstore, Book Mansion, with 230,000 titles taking up 172,000 square feet, wins the full attention of Meyer's students: "a seated bundle of green, hand-knit sweaters, black pigtails, and bowed heads" concentrating on Calvin and Hobbes and a Garfield English-Chinese dictionary. Translations of Dan Brown's *The Da Vinci Code* (2003) and Robert C. Atkins's *Dr. Atkins Diet Revolution* (1972) nudge up against Woody Allen's *The Whore of Mensa* (1974), and a book on love in the English language explains that "'I'm bored' really means 'Do you want to have sex?'" When Meyer sees Allen Ginsberg's *Howl* (1956) among Book Mansion's offerings, he calls the translator, Wen Chu'an, who teaches Beat Studies at Sichuan University and asks why the Beats are so popular. Wen explains that young readers are inspired by the Beats' "ardent love of freedom in action and speech." Jack Kerouac's *On the Road* (1957) sold thirty thousand copies, but translations of management guides such as Larry R. Donnithorne's *The West Point Way of Leadership* (1994) swamped all the Beat works. Meyer's thirty-fourth birthday is celebrated with a "spongy yellow cake" complete with a yellow cardboard crown, hand-drawn cards, and a jar of Nescafé Gold instant coffee from Miss Zhu.

Meyer cites Jane Jacobs's book *The Death and Life of Great American Cities* (1961) and Herbert Gans's description of Boston's West End as not a slum but a "stable, low-rent area." For Meyer, Dazhalan and Fresh Fish Junction are just such stable neighborhoods, and he sympathizes with Jacobs's claim that they are doomed because nobody is exploiting them for fortunes. The *hutong*, in Meyer's view, are like the New York sidewalks in the safety that comes from all eyes being on them, in the feelings of community they foster, and in the lessons in living they teach children.

Whenever there is anything comic in his situation, Meyer can see it. One morning he awakes in the dark with a spider as large as his hand probing his ear. He crushes the creature, jumps for the tap, and knocks over a row of empty beer bottles before tragedy strikes: "My dinner of braised fatty pork and twice-fried spicy green beans awoke within; I needed a toilet." He runs in "minced, clenching steps" for the toilet down the lane, but he does not make it in time. He kicks his boxer shorts into the pit and goes home thinking that perhaps he would be glad to see the Hand painted on his door.

Meyer has a sharp eye for character and incident, and he presents it in a fresh and irresistible prose style.

Frank Day

Review Sources

Booklist 104, nos. 19/20 (June 1, 2008): 26.
The Economist 388 (August 2, 2008): 85.
Kirkus Reviews 76, no. 11 (June 1, 2008): 93.
Library Journal 133, no. 7 (April 15, 2008): 96.
New Statesman 137 (August 18, 2008): 50-51.
Newsweek 151, no. 24 (June 16, 2008): 63.
Publishers Weekly 255, no. 14 (April 7, 2008): 5.
The Wall Street Journal 251, no. 150 (June 27, 2008): W10.

THE LAST FLIGHT OF THE SCARLET MACAW
One Woman's Fight to Save the World's Most Beautiful Bird

Author: Bruce Barcott (1967-   )
Publisher: Random House (New York). 313 pp. $26.00
Type of work: Environment, history, natural history, nature
Time: 2002-2005
Locale: Belize

An exploration of the environmental, economic, and political forces involved in an attempt to save a river, its valley, plants, and wildlife from a dam and the lake it would impound

Principal personages:
SHARON MATOLA, manager of the Belize Zoo and primary opponent of the dam
SAID MUSA, prime minister of Belize during the planning and building of the dam
RALPH FONSECA, finance minister of Belize during the planning and building of the dam
TONY GAREL, Matola's long-time assistant at the zoo
JACOB SCHERR, a lawyer working with the Natural Resources Defense Council
ARI HERSHOWITZ, member of the Natural Resources Defense Council
STAN MARSHALL, chief executive officer of Fortis, the Canadian company that contracted to build the dam

The book's title, *The Last Flight of the Scarlet Macaw*, may be somewhat misleading since the scarlet macaw (*Ara macao*) is neither endangered nor threatened. It is widespread in Central and South America, and it is not on the verge of extinction. Author Bruce Barcott knows that fact and says so, although he also makes the point that the Belizean subspecies (*Ara macao cyanoptera*) is endangered in some ranking systems. That is the bird about which he is writing, and this dual classification introduces the question of whether subspecies should be considered for protection under endangered-species legislation or whether such laws should concern only species. In response to that question, Barcott explores some related aspects of biological taxonomy (the classification and naming of animals and plants). He employs a strategy similar to this throughout the book. He is telling a story, but when the story line comes to a topic he thinks needs explanation, he interrupts to fill the reader in on the tangential topic, which is always interesting and important.

Working under the assumption that this subspecies is worthy of special conservation efforts, the book details the attempt of an American woman to block construction of a dam that would flood the valley in which the overwhelming majority of the scarlet macaws in Belize live. Sharon Matola runs a zoo in Belize, and, esoteric as it may seem, the taxonomic question posed above becomes a real problem for her. She uses the local subspecies's status to argue against the dam, arguing that you cannot flood the only habitat in Belize that supports this endangered subspecies. Stan Marshall, chief executive officer (CEO) of Fortis, the Canadian company that wants to build the dam, challenges her on the basis of the International Union for the Conservation of Nature and Natural Resources

~

Bruce Barcott lives in Seattle with his wife and two children and writes for Outside *magazine,* The New York Times, Sports Illustrated, Mother Jones, *and other magazines. A former Ted Scripps Fellow in Environmental Journalism, Barcott has also written* The Measure of a Mountain *(1997) and* Northwest Passages *(1994).*

~

(IUCN) Red Data Book, which considers the species and not the subspecies. This publication, a gold standard in endangered-species listings, recognizes the scarlet macaw as a widespread and abundant species, and so it is not one requiring special treatment in planning a dam or other environment-disrupting activity.

Barcott describes Matola as a maverick who is not afraid to rock the boat, even when it is clear that she is the one most likely to be spilled overboard. She chooses to enter the fight over the dam to be built on the Macal River, and her opposition triggers the cascade of events explored in the book. Barcott's exploration involves economic as well as ecologic problems and the trade-offs inherent in questions such as the effects of dams and other situations in which conservation and economics seem at loggerheads. These questions are particularly troublesome in developing countries such as Belize. Barcott also explores the political intrigue that often accompanies such problems, wherever they occur.

In setting the stage, Barcott outlines the history of Belize (formerly British Honduras) and makes a point of describing the resentment that natives of Belize hold against the British for the way they stripped the natural resources from the country and left nothing in exchange. Belize was the last Latin American country to achieve independence, one that is still incomplete in some ways. This resentment extends to foreigners in general, which made it impossible for Matola (a citizen of the United States) to lead a grassroots opposition to the dam. It also weakened the impact of Jacob Scherr and Ari Hershowitz of the Natural Resources Defense Council (NRDC), as they joined in the fight against the dam. Tony Garel, a native Belizean who worked at the zoo, and others tried to fill the native-leadership role in Matola's place.

In keeping with his proclivity to fill in the background for his story, Barcott outlines the history of dams and dam building, including a historical sketch of the North American dam-building era. In the "Epilogue," he compares the story he tells in the book with John Muir's attempt to save Hetch Hetchy Valley in Yosemite National Park from a dam. He suggests that the massive development of dams was not a good thing, because dams often do not pay for themselves (even in strictly economic terms), and they often collect silt so rapidly that they become worthless and fall into disuse or must be restored, at great expense, in just a few years. Barcott's bottom line: Dams kill rivers. Still, dams have been built for many different reasons: for flood control, for hydroelectric power, for a reliable water supply for human consumption and irrigation, and for recreation, such as boating and fishing, on the lake formed. He acknowledges disagreements about the usefulness of dams, though his convictions are quite clear. The dam on the Macal, called Chalillo, was primarily planned to generate electricity, converting the kinetic energy in the flow of water into electrical energy. Barcott outlines the science and history of hydroelectric power.

Barcott explores the projected electrical production and economic contribution of the Chalillo dam and the alternative options for producing the electricity without the dam. The alternatives included burning oil purchased from Mexico and burning the organic material left over from the production of sugar. Analysis suggested that the dam would not solve Belize's shortfall in electric energy, although it would contribute to the electricity supply of the country. He explains Matola's argument for an alternative economic contribution of the Macal valley. Recognizing that the Belize economy is based on tourism, especially ecotourism, she suggested that a pristine, wildlife-filled Macal valley with the ecotourist income it would produce might be a more significant contribution to the economy of Belize than a dammed, water-filled valley and the electricity it would produce.

Barcott reports that studies on the structural integrity of the valley walls did not suggest that it was a good site for a dam. Although the valley walls were said to be granite in the site's Environmental Impact Assessment (EIA), which was commissioned by the parties determined to build the dam, independent surveys demonstrated that there was no granite in the area. In addition, some of the rock present was soft and susceptible to shifting and collapse under the weight of the dam. However, the most damning indictment of the EIA concerned a map that accompanied the report. A fault line found on the original geological map of the Macal valley was missing on the map turned in as part of the EIA. Earthquakes develop along fault lines, and fault lines do not spontaneously disappear from maps, so this was clear evidence of dishonesty and a callous disregard for human life. If the dam failed, anyone living downstream would be exposed to a flash flood.

Duke Energy, a company based in the United States, was indirectly contracted by the Belizean government to build the dam when it bought a host of Latin American contracts from another American power company. The above disclosures, a letter-writing campaign directed at Duke Energy, and a statement adopted by the IUCN, all playing on the company's desire to improve its environmental image, gave Duke Energy second thoughts. When it hesitated, Fortis, a Canadian company that primarily did small hydroelectric projects and that had purchased Belize Electricity Limited (BEL), jumped at the chance to take on the project. Stan Marshall, Fortis CEO, assured the interested parties that Fortis would not build a dam that was not economically, structurally, and environmentally sound. However, the contract between the company and the government of Belize freed Fortis from all liability even if the dam failed, not an encouraging sign of corporate responsibility.

Political intrigue resulted in the dam going forward despite these warning signs. Barcott appears to be evenhanded in reporting on the struggle, and he clearly believes that corruption in the Belizean government and Fortis, the Canadian firm contracted to build the dam, was involved in the decision to go ahead, with little consideration of the potential problems discussed above.

Additional evidence of corruption is found in the heavy-handed tactics employed by the Belizean government. When it became clear that Matola was determined to fight the dam, the government planned to construct a landfill adjacent to the zoo, and the landfill's drainage would contaminate the zoo's water supply. In addition, the proximity of the landfill would detract from the zoo's desirability as a recreational destination. As with the dam, the location was far from ideal for a landfill even if the zoo were not there. There were better locations available on the basis of landfill requirements alone. The plan to locate the landfill next to the zoo was a ploy attributed to Said Musa, the Belizean prime minister, and Ralph Fonseca, another official of the government; both were supporters, and presumed beneficiaries, of the dam site in the Macal valley. The proposed location of the landfill was thought to be their response to Matola's opposition to the dam and an attempt to neutralize her.

Other evidence of the heavy hand of the Belizean government, suggesting how serious the authorities were about constructing the dam, occurred when an antidam rally Matola planned was poorly attended, although disenchantment with the dam was known to be widespread. The simple explanation for the poor attendance was that the same power brokers spread the word that things would not go well for those seen at the rally. In another context in the book, a native Belizean made the point that because Belize is such a small country, everyone knows everyone, and he declared that to be one of the good things about Belize and simultaneously one of the bad things about Belize. In this context, it played out as a bad thing; Belizeans did not want to be subject to governmental reprisals because they attended the rally.

In the end, the landfill was established at another location, not next to the zoo. However, the dam was built, despite an intriguing attempt to block its construction through a British court. It was intriguing because Belize had been independent of Great Britain since 1981, but it still had laws that allowed appeal to a British court called the Judicial Committee of the Privy Council. Barcott explains that situation, the events related to the appeal, and the court's judgment.

Barcott weaves this and more together into an entertaining story, interspersed with brief but informative histories and scientific fundamentals related to Belize, taxonomy, endangered species, dams, hydroelectricity, and the Privy Council.

The book is well written and carefully edited; any errors escaped notice in this reading. There is a helpful map of Belize, and the description of sources is thorough and helpful to the reader looking for more detail on a topic. However, there is no index, an unfortunate omission in a book as full of information as this one. The reader wishing to revisit a topic is reduced to a haphazard search through the book. Chapter titles would have helped in this regard, and the abbreviated table of contents is as useless as the absent index. Though poorly served by these shortcuts, the book is an excellent addition to the library of anyone interested in environmental problems, politics, Belize, or the other topics considered in the book. Reviews of the book have been enthusiastic.

Carl W. Hoagstrom

Review Sources

Audubon 110, no. 2 (March, 2008): 154-156.
Booklist 104, no. 11 (February 1, 2008): 10.
Discover 29, no. 2 (February, 2008): 72.
The International Herald Tribune, February 16, 2008, p. 15.
Kirkus Reviews 76, no. 1 (January 1, 2008): 19.
Natural History 117, no. 3 (April, 2008): 52-53.
The New York Times Book Review, February 17, 2008, p. 1.
Orion, March/April, 2008, p. 76.
Publishers Weekly 254, no. 47 (November 26, 2007): 38-39.
Scientific American 298, no. 3 (March, 2008): 100.
The Washington Post Book World, March 2, 2008, p. BW09.

LAVINIA

Author: Ursula K. Le Guin (1929-   )
Publisher: Harcourt (New York). 279 pp. $24.00
Type of work: Novel
Time: Several years after the fall of Troy, traditionally
    dated to 1184 B.C.E.
Locale: the region of Latium (modern Lazio) in Italy

A back story from Vergil's Aeneid *is transformed into
the fictional autobiography of the Italian princess who became the bride of the Trojan Aeneas after a bitter war for
her hand on Italian soil*

Principal characters:
> LAVINIA, the only surviving child of an
>   Italian king
> LATINUS, Lavinia's father and king of Laurentum in Latium, Italy
> AMATA, Latinus's wife and queen who has gone insane because of the
>   death of her young sons
> TURNUS, prince of the neighboring Rutulians and suitor for Lavinia
> AENEAS, leader of a band of Trojan exiles
> ASCANIUS, Aeneas's son by his Trojan wife Creusa
> THE POET, the ghost of Vergil, author of the *Aeneid*

Ursula K. Le Guin, a prolific writer of fantasy, generally directs her great storytelling skills to worlds such as Earthsea, created entirely in her own imagination. In these
fantasy worlds, Le Guin is able to examine issues of gender and spirituality from
unique and unusual perspectives. Her protagonists, such as Luz Marina Falco Cooper
in *The Eye of the Heron* (1983), are often strong females who must deal with difficult
moral and intellectual issues amid societies in conflict.

As she did with Tenar in *Tehanu: The Last Book of Earthsea* (1990), and with the
women in *Searoad: The Chronicles of Klatsand* (1991), Le Guin creates in *Lavinia*
another strong, independent female protagonist who struggles to find her way in a
world dominated by men. Like many of Le Guin's protagonists, Lavinia responds
with regret, determination, and hope as the familiar world of her childhood is transformed into a very different place by war and by time.

In *Searoad* Le Guin used the Greek myth of Persephone to tell the stories of several
generations of women in the fictional town of Klatsand, Oregon. In *Lavinia* Le Guin
turns for inspiration to Roman myth and tradition and especially to Vergil's *Aeneid*,
the great first century B.C.E. epic poem about the journey of the Trojan Aeneas to
found a new kingdom in Italy after the Trojan War.

Vergil's poem provides only a bare frame for Le Guin's tale, which centers around
a key but silent character from the Roman epic. While nearly half of the twelve books

The American writer Ursula Le Guin is best known for her series about the fantasy world of Earthsea, especially Wizard of Earthsea *(1968). She was the recipient of a Library of Congress Living Legends award in 2000 and the Science Fiction and Fantasy Writers of America Grand Master Award in 2003.*

of the *Aeneid* deal with the war fought between Aeneas and the Italian prince Turnus for the hand of an Italian princess, Lavinia plays only a passive role in the Roman story. In the *Aeneid* she is at the mercy of her father, who, by custom, must choose her husband. She is also at the mercy of the Fates and of her gods, who prophesy that she is destined to marry not a native Italian but a foreigner. Lavinia's parents both play important speaking roles in Vergil's poem, but Lavinia says nothing. Her most dramatic appearance is a scene in which her hair catches fire at a religious sacrifice—an event understood by Vergil and his readers as an omen supporting Aeneas's claim. Vergil ends his poem with Aeneas's frenzied slaying of Turnus on the battlefield, not with the marriage that would inevitably follow this victory.

From these few details, Le Guin weaves Lavinia's fascinating tale. Le Guin's Lavinia gains her own voice as she tells her life story and puts the events described in Vergil's *Aeneid* into the larger context of her autobiography. Le Guin's Lavinia narrates her life from the perspective of old age and approaching death. In addition to her post-*Aeneid* life as wife, mother, and widow, Lavinia describes the joys and sorrows of her youth. Her childhood friendships, delightful romps in the Italian countryside, and, especially, her close relationship with a loving father are contrasted with the early deaths of her two younger brothers and the growing insanity of her mother Amata, who responds to the death of her sons with increasing resentment toward her daughter. Amata's madness has some support from Vergil's poem, but the other details of Lavinia's childhood are, for the most part, drawn from Le Guin's own imagination and powerful narrative skills. So, too, are substantial portions of the novel that deal with events following those described in the *Aeneid*, namely, Lavinia's marriage to Aeneas, her difficult relationship with her stepson Ascanius, her worries about her fatherless son Silvius, and her decision to withdraw at the end of her life to a secluded spot in the country.

Unlike Vergil, Le Guin creates in Lavinia a strong-willed woman who is able to find personal freedom and self-identity even within the confines of a traditional society, in which daughters must obey their fathers and accept husbands chosen for them. Le Guin's princess is no passive pawn. With the support of her father, she uses and even manipulates religious signs to avoid marriage with the unappealing Rutulian prince Turnus, despite strong maternal pressure to accept Turnus's offer of marriage. Instead, Lavinia herself chooses marriage with the Trojan prince Aeneas, even though it will mean leaving the home of her beloved father and even though she knows from prophecy that her marriage with Aeneas will be cut short by his untimely death. As a widow, Lavinia works out an uneasy relationship with her stepson Ascanius, while ensuring the safety and position of her son Silvius (who will be the ancestor of Romulus and Remus, the twin founders of Rome).

In *Lavinia* Le Guin has captured the deep Italian respect for tradition, custom, and values. Lavinia understands and affirms the obligations that society imposes on her as daughter of the king. She shares with her Trojan husband a strong piety, that is, a compelling sense of duty or obligation to one's gods, fathers, and fatherland. A close bond with ancestors and an intense love for the Italian countryside permeate not only Le Guin's novel but also Vergil's *Aeneid*, as well as much of Roman literature. Le Guin's Italian princess is rarely happier than when she is wandering as a girl in the fields and the sacred woods of her beloved Latium. It is in these woods that she chooses to end her days after the death of Aeneas and the majority of their son Silvius.

Lavinia's story is steeped in the religious traditions of early Italy, which Le Guin has researched carefully. Lavinia's religion begins in the home, where she, as her father's only daughter, has the responsibility for maintaining the household gods and their daily worship. Upon her marriage to Aeneas, Lavinia must abandon her father's gods for those of her new husband, but she makes this transition freely and willingly, guarding Aeneas's Trojan household gods as religiously as she had those of her father.

Le Guin describes in detail many traditional Roman beliefs and religious practices, including omens, prophecies, agricultural rites, and, especially, animal sacrifices, which will seem strange to many modern readers. In traditional Roman religion, the whole world is sacred and the gods permeate all aspects of life. Not only does Lavinia perform daily religious obligations in her father's or her husband's houses, but also she sets out on many pilgrimages to worship in the countryside. In particular, she frequents an ancient grove of trees in Albunea, where her ancestors have worshiped from time immemorial. It is here, on pilgrimages with her father, that she meets, first, her divine ancestor Faunus and, later, her "poet," a shadowy figure whom Lavinia realizes comes from the future and who will tell her story. It is near this sacred spot that she chooses to return to spend her final days.

This poet, unnamed in *Lavinia*, is Vergil (70-19 B.C.E.), who will not live for many centuries following the events described in *Lavinia*. At the time of his conversations with Lavinia, the *Aeneid* has already been written and Vergil is facing death from illness. From her poet, Lavinia learns in detail about the savage war that will be fought for her hand and of her marriage to Aeneas (destined to last only four years because of the hero's death). From his conversations with Lavinia, the poet comes to realize that he did not do justice to the strong-minded Italian princess in the *Aeneid* and regrets that his impending death leaves him no time to revise his depiction. On his deathbed, Vergil is said to have directed that the *Aeneid* be burned. Readers of *Lavinia* are perhaps intended to imagine that Vergil's supernatural encounter with Lavinia in Le Guin's novel led the poet to this brutal request, so fortuitously countermanded by the emperor Augustus.

The poet empowers Lavinia. With her knowledge of the future, she is able to understand and to navigate the many challenges of her life. She is able to embrace Aeneas as her husband the first time she sees the hero. She understands the inevitability of the war that follows Aeneas's arrival. She accepts with resignation the shortness of their marriage, and for this reason, she relishes with delight every sweet moment with her husband, even as she hopes that somehow she has misunderstood the poet's words and that her husband will not die so prematurely.

Lavinia's knowledge of the future is also a great burden. She cannot change what is fated. She is unable to warn her husband of his impending death. Rather, she must live with the inevitability of that death silently in her heart. She alone can understand the mysterious scenes engraved on her husband's great shield, made, according to Vergil, by the blacksmith god Vulcan at the request of Aeneas's divine mother Venus. These scenes depict future events made possible by Aeneas's victory in Italy, including the founding of Rome and the great battle of Actium, in which the future Augustus defeated Mark Antony and Cleopatra and became sole ruler of the Roman Empire in 31 B.C.E. Lavinia recognizes the meaning of all these scenes, but she is unable to share them with those around her, just as she cannot warn Aeneas of his death.

Lavinia's foresight also cannot help her console Aeneas regarding the savage war fought for her hand and especially regarding the brutal slaying of Turnus, with which Vergil had ended the *Aeneid*. Aeneas's instinct had been to spare his antagonist's life; however, seeing around Turnus's waist a sword belt that the Rutulian prince had plundered from the body of Pallas, one of Aeneas's Italian allies, Aeneas angrily thrusts his sword into Turnus's chest. Lavinia had had Turnus's death foretold to her by Vergil, but this knowledge is of little use, as she watches her husband agonize over his brutal action on the battlefield and over his conflicting loyalties toward virtuous action, which would have spared Turnus, and toward piety, which demanded the Rutulian prince's death. Aeneas died without resolving this conflict, which also remains unresolved in Vergil's *Aeneid*.

In *Lavinia* Le Guin thus merges the present time of Lavinia's life with the future time of her poet, Vergil. As she did with Pandora, the protagonist in *Always Coming Home* (1985), who lives both in the past and in the future, Le Guin enables Lavinia to live not only in the present but to anticipate future events. In this way, Lavinia's future is not only the Roman future of Vergil's Augustan world but also a more timeless future in which she seeks to avoid oblivion and gain immortality through the words of Vergil. For Lavinia, physical death is less important than obliteration of her memory. In Vergil's poem, and perhaps even in Le Guin's novel, Lavinia has gained that immortal fame.

Thomas J. Sienkewicz

Review Sources

Booklist 104, no. 14 (March 15, 2008): 28.
Bust 51 (June/July, 2008): 104-104.
Entertainment Weekly, April 25, 2008, p. 121.
Kirkus Reviews 76, no. 4 (February 15, 2008): 166.
Library Journal 133, no. 4 (March 1, 2008): 74.
Publishers Weekly 254, no. 51 (December 24, 2007): 24.
School Library Journal 54, no. 5 (May, 2008): 161.
Science Fiction Studies 35, no. 2 (July, 2008): 349-352.

THE LAZARUS PROJECT

Author: Aleksandar Hemon (1964-   )
Publisher: Riverhead Press (New York). 294 pp. $24.95
Type of work: Novel
Time: 1908 and the present
Locale: Chicago, Ukraine, Moldova, Romania, and
Bosnia

Hemon's second novel uses alternating chapters to tell
the story of a Jewish refugee killed by the chief of police in
Chicago in 1908 and a contemporary Bosnian immigrant
who retraces the young Jew's steps through Eastern Europe

Principal characters:
VLADIMIR BRIK, a writer and Bosnian
   immigrant
LAZARUS AVERBUCH, a nineteen-year-old Jewish immigrant
OLGA AVERBUCH, Lazarus's sister
GEORGE SHIPPY, Chicago chief of police
AHMED RORA, Brik's friend, a photographer
MARY BRIK, Brik's wife, an American-born neurosurgeon
ISADOR MARON, Lazarus's friend
WILLIAM P. MILLER, a reporter for the *Chicago Tribune*
HERMANN TAUBE, a prosperous Jewish lawyer
RAMBO, a guerrilla leader during the siege of Sarajevo
MILLER, an American journalist posted in Sarajevo
IULIANA, Brik's guide to the Jewish history of Chisinau
SERYOZHA, a pimp who drives Brik and Rora from Chisinau to
   Bucharest
AZRA HALILBAŠI, Rora's sister, a surgeon in Sarajevo

Aleksandar Hemon's *The Lazarus Project* begins dramatically, with a factual account of how, on March 2, 1908, Lazarus Averbuch, an impoverished nineteen-year-
old Jew, was shot seven times when he showed up unexpectedly at the home of
George Shippy, the Chicago chief of police. Why the indigent young outsider was
calling on Shippy at his affluent address remains a mystery, though the chief's assumption that Averbuch was an anarchist intent on violence became the official verdict. Though he is not Jewish (or, for that matter, Muslim, Serb, or Croat), Vladimir
Brik, a sparsely employed writer who left Bosnia for Chicago in 1992, before the war
that finally put an end to Yugoslavia as a federated republic, becomes intrigued by the
enigmas of the century-old case. Financed by a grant, he determines to write a book
that will bring the immigrant Lazarus, like his Biblical namesake, back to life again.

As accomplice in his Lazarus project, Brik recruits a former classmate in Sarajevo,
a photographer named Ahmed Rora, just as Hemon appropriates the photographs of
Velibor Bozovic to accompany his text. Rora, an extroverted, energetic fellow, is

fond of telling jokes and yarns and uses his camera to insert himself into the lives of others. Brik determines that in order to understand and write about Lazarus, who had fled anti-Semitic violence in Europe, he will retrace Lazarus's steps before arriving in the United States. "I needed to follow Lazarus all the way back to the pogrom in Kishinev, to the time before America," he explains. "I needed to reimagine what I could not retrieve; I needed to see what I could not imagine. I needed to step outside my life in Chicago and spend time deep in the wilderness of elsewhere." During the eventful journey through Eastern Europe, Rora, who came to Chicago

Aleksandar Hemon was visiting the United States in 1992 when the war in Bosnia prevented him from returning home. He settled in Chicago and began mastering English. His first book was the short-story collection The Question of Bruno *(2000), and his first novel,* Nowhere Man *(2002), was a finalist for the National Book Critics Award. Hemon was awarded a Guggenheim Fellowship in 2003 and a MacArthur Foundation grant in 2004.*

after the Balkan wars, provides Brik with lurid details of violence and duplicity during the siege of Sarajevo. Rora claims he fought in a guerrilla group under the command of a flamboyant bully who called himself Rambo.

Himself an immigrant to Chicago from Serbia who was determined to learn English well enough to forge a literary career in it, Hemon deftly deploys his adopted language to create a complex fiction about storytelling, identity, and survival. In chapters that alternate between 1908 and the present, the novel suggests parallels in bloodshed and xenophobia. In each era, a dishonest reporter named Miller provides a distorted version of events. In 1908, William P. Miller, reporting for the *Chicago Tribune*, sensationalizes the death of Lazarus Averbuch, concocting inflammatory prose that heightens communal mistrust. During the siege of Sarajevo, a war reporter also named Miller is a journalistic buccaneer more intent on getting scoops than getting the story right. Lazarus Averbuch's killing occurs on the eve of a visit to Chicago by the notorious anarchist leader Emma Goldman, and those with power and privilege, still smarting from the destructive turmoil of the Haymarket Riot of 1886, are suspicious of outsiders, especially if they are poor, Jewish, and freethinking. For most of Chicago, the stranger's death is framed as a victory over anarchy.

Olga Averbuch, however, is devastated by the death of her beloved younger brother, whose move to America she had encouraged and had sponsored. Though the authorities decide to dispose of his body unceremoniously in a pauper's grave, she stubbornly insists on having him reburied in a respectful Jewish ceremony. She refuses consolation from radicals who, claiming him as a martyr useful to their cause, are indifferent to his individual human life. She is approached by Hermann Taube, an urbane lawyer representing the prosperous, assimilated Jews of Chicago, who urges her to cooperate with the police in order to avert an outbreak of anti-Semitism. Like her brother Lazarus, Olga has survived the deadly Kishinev massacre of 1903, three days of anti-Semitic rioting in which hundreds of houses were looted and destroyed and dozens of Jews were murdered, and Taube warns her that, unless she cooperates, the incident with her brother could incite a similar pogrom in Chicago. However,

Olga mistrusts him and allows her brother's friend, Isador Maron, whom the police are pursuing as a dangerous accomplice of the dead Jew, to hide in her apartment.

Meanwhile, Brik's journey through Eastern Europe immerses him in a shabby, squalid world populated by gangsters, cheats, and prostitutes. In the Moldovan capital Chisinau, formerly known as Kishinev, he visits the Jewish cemetery, where a local resident named Iuliana tells him about the atrocities committed against the Jewish community a century ago. He imagines the ordeal that young Lazarus, traumatized by the violence in his native town, experienced as he fled his home for a refugee camp and then moved on, passing through the same route Brik takes, on his way to Chicago. Brik breaks his hand helping Rora beat up an unsavory Romanian pimp named Seryozha who drives them from Chisinau to Bucharest and plans to sell an attractive young woman into prostitution. In addition, Brik witnesses a shooting, with seven bullets, that is every bit as shocking, senseless, and deadly as the shooting that puts an end to Lazarus's life.

"My country's main exports are stolen cars and sadness," says Brik, who is a sad specimen of Bosnia's exports to the United States. He also becomes uncertain of just what his nationality is. Brik's opening statement (at the beginning of the second chapter, which is the first chapter set in the present tense) announces his divided identity: "I am a reasonably loyal citizen of a couple of countries." Crosscutting between 1908 and 2008 and between Chicago and Eastern Europe, the structure of Hemon's novel emphasizes the theme of duality. Ill at ease in Chicago, where he fails to find a satisfying job or way of life, Brik travels back to Europe, describing himself as "ready to enter the parallel universe of iniquity and murder."

When he first settled in the United States, Brik had embraced a vision of human good will. Marrying the American-born Mary, a neurosurgeon who is by profession committed to benevolence, he had tried to share her belief in fundamental goodness. Her conviction, according to Brik, is that: "Humans could not be essentially evil, because they were always infused by God's infinite goodness and love." However, though his wife contends that the Americans who tortured prisoners at Abu Ghraib were decent but misguided kids, he argues that they were instead sadists who reveled in power over others. Rejecting her willful naïveté, he reports: "I told her that to be American you have to know nothing and understand even less, and that I did not want to be American." It is in part Brik's disgust with American innocence that sends him to Europe to confront traces of unmitigated evil, while his wife stays behind in Chicago. Brik's strained phone calls to Mary indicate that his marriage to her—and to America—is disintegrating, even as he remains estranged from Europe.

Rora never abandoned his Bosnian cynicism. "Nobody deserves death, yet everybody gets it" is his blunt verdict. However, despite—or because of—his grim subject matter, Hemon's writing style is playful. An example of the dark humor often generated by the linguistic cunning of an author still in awe of a language he has learned as an adult occurs one morning in Chicago. Entering his kitchen in order to make himself some coffee, Brik recalls: "I spotted a can in the corner whose red label read SADNESS." Nevertheless, after quickly realizing that the word on the label is not SADNESS but SARDINES, he does not feel relieved to discover his error: "It was too late for recovery, for sadness was now the dark matter in the universe of still objects around me: the salt and pepper shakers; the honey jar; the bag of sun-dried tomatoes; the blunt knife; a desiccated loaf of bread; the two coffee cups, waiting."

The Lazarus Project is ultimately a self-begetting novel, a work that recounts its own genesis; it tells the story of how Brik becomes ready to write a work very much like *The Lazarus Project*. However, it also undermines the credibility of narrative. Scattered throughout the novel are several examples of storytelling that are exposed as shams—the sensational journalism of the two reporters named Miller; the letters that Olga writes to her mother back in Europe to reassure her that everything is fine with Lazarus; Rora's fabricated adventures in Sarajevo during the war. Can readers trust any storyteller, including Hemon?

A parable on how to read *The Lazarus Project* is inserted in the form of Brik's recollection of his blind Uncle Mikhal, who used to ask his young nephew to read nonfiction to him. Brik reveals that he delighted in embroidering passages with contrivances of his own, about nonexistent subatomic particles and miraculous survivals of shipwreck. "I would experience a beautiful high," he recalls, reflecting the exhilaration of authorship, "because I was constructing a particular, custom-made world for him, because he was in my power for as long as he listened to me." Brik feels guilty about this deception, until he realizes "that my uncle might have been aware of my deception, that he might have been complicit in my edifice-building." Brik realizes, too, that such complicity can create even richer fictions than those of a mendacious storyteller manipulating a gullible listener. In the larger story that he presents his reader, Brik never solves the mystery of Lazarus nor resolves the dichotomies between America and Europe, past and present. However, in laying bare its own artifice, *The Lazarus Project* invites a careful reader to participate in an uncommonly invigorating inquest into human malevolence and fallibility.

Steven G. Kellman

Review Sources

Bookforum 15 (April/May, 2008): 23.
Booklist 104, no. 15 (April 1, 2008): 26.
Esquire, May, 2008, p. 36.
Kirkus Reviews 76, no. 5 (March 1, 2008): 211.
Library Journal 133, no. 6 (April 1, 2008): 76.
New Statesman 137 (August 11, 2008): 50-51.
New York 41, no. 17 (May 12, 2008): 70-71.
The New York Times Book Review, May 25, 2008, p. 13.
The New Yorker 84, no. 22 (July 28, 2008): 82-85.
Poets & Writers 36 (July/August, 2008): 61.
Publishers Weekly 255, no. 12 (March 24, 2008): 53.
The Times Literary Supplement, August 8, 2008, p. 19.

LIBERTY OF CONSCIENCE
In Defense of America's Tradition of Religious Equality

Author: Martha C. Nussbaum (1947-   )
Publisher: Basic Books (New York). 406 pp. $28.95
Type of work: Law, religion, philosophy, current affairs

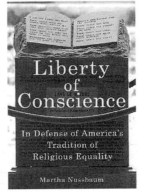

In a wide-ranging study of the sources and results of the First Amendment's guarantee of religious freedom, a noted philosopher finds a guiding principle in the dual concepts of fairness and of respect for the demands of each individual citizen's conscience

Each era of American history has been wracked by controversy over the limits of religious liberty. Although this matter was supposedly settled by the First Amendment to the Constitution, multiple questions arise over interpretation of its provisions. Although many issues tend to recur regularly in slightly different form, the book's author, Martha C. Nussbaum, believes that the twenty-first century has seen a subtle trend toward national endorsement of a religious worldview. *Liberty of Conscience* sprang from the author's wish to counteract this trend.

The First Amendment proscription against the entanglement of church and state is contained in two clauses—the establishment clause ("Congress shall make no law respecting an establishment of religion") and the free exercise clause ("or prohibiting the free exercise thereof"). By and large these provisions have served the nation well. However, the relationship between government and faith has always been more problematic than the simple phrase "separation of church and state" implies. This book explores the philosophical basis for these unique American principles and for the conflicts that occur around their margins.

Roger Williams is known to most Americans as the founder and first governor of colonial Rhode Island. In a persuasive opening to the book, however, Nussbaum lays out a case for Williams's thought as the core philosophy behind American thought on the proper relationship between state power and the individual.

In his early life, Williams received a classical education and took priestly orders in the Church of England. Uneasy with the treatment being meted out to English dissenters in the 1630's, he migrated to the New World. At first he found a welcome and a congregation in Salem, but his beliefs got him into trouble with the Massachusetts Bay Colony, too. He was forced to flee to Rhode Island, where he formulated guidelines for a new colony with true religious freedom.

Williams's basic concern was protection for the individual conscience. He equated conscience with the soul, counting it the most distinctive human trait. He had spent much of his early life in settings where not only religious practice but also belief was prescribed by civil authorities. Such compulsion, he said, was "soule rape"—worse than the foulest crimes. Nussbaum notes that this high valuation for individual conscience grew out of Protestant thought, but she adds that most religions hold a similar respect for each human's moral faculty. This tradition goes all the way back to the Romans. A central feature of Stoic philosophy was its belief that every human, regardless of gender, education, or station in life, contains a spark of the divine in the capacity to make moral choices.

Under Williams's leadership, Rhode Island was the only American colony that allowed complete religious liberty. In a century when the principle was very much an exception, the colony received two successive royal charters granting such freedoms. It is noteworthy that Charles II, having come to the English throne after unprecedented political-religious chaos, would not risk such leeway in Britain. However, he seems to have harbored some willingness to experiment elsewhere, and faraway Rhode Island benefited.

~

Martha Nussbaum holds a Distinguished Service Professorship at the University of Chicago, with joint appointments in law, philosophy, and divinity, and she has written numerous books on topics related to these fields. Her book The Clash Within *(2007) deals with democracy and religious violence in India.*

~

The scope of Williams's respect for conscience was unusual for his time. He had spent much time with the Narragansett Indians, and hence he realized that religious diversity extended further than the differences that brought English settlers to the New World. The colony's charter protected not only belief and its expression in opinion but also in acts of worship and other practices, as long as the adherents behaved "peaceablie."

Although Williams was alone among influential colonists of his generation in his concern for everyone's religious liberties, the colony's example and Williams's extensive writings percolated through the intellectual life of all the American colonies. Most settlers of the Middle and Northern colonies had immigrated at least partly for religious freedom, so they could relate to Williams's sentiments if not to the details. In the century and a half of British presence in North America before nationhood, American political philosophy came to diverge more and more from the European model. Kings and nobles were far away. The church establishments that bolstered their status became increasingly irrelevant. Instead, the concept of equality flourished. A state could not logically support equality if certain citizens were "more equal than others" because of religious affiliation.

Williams's core ideas found an especially receptive audience in the men who framed the Constitution. Their personal belief systems varied widely—the author makes sure to point this out—but all were strongly committed to the ideals of liberty and equality. Even under the relatively weak established churches existing in some colonies, events occurred to show their incompatibility with American values. "Dissenters" could be—and occasionally were—jailed for refusing to pay taxes to support the church. They were routinely excluded from office-holding and also from university entrance.

After giving this illuminating background, Nussbaum examines the writing of the First Amendment. She gives little attention to Thomas Jefferson's part in the Virginia

Act for Establishing Religious Freedom. Rather, she presents an in-depth study of James Madison's thought, expressed most powerfully in his "Memorial and Remonstrance Against Religious Assessments" (1785). In this essay, Madison argued against any state support for religions, no matter how broadly based or "non-preferential" it is. The mere fact of state support has the subtle effect of making citizens who belong to religions outside the enumerated ones or to none at all feel excluded. Madison also argued that automatic support tends to make any religious group static, indolent, and bureaucratic. His reasons carried the day, in Virginia against Patrick Henry's proposal and later on the national scene, when the Bill of Rights was being written in 1789.

Madison's thinking was not entirely incorporated into the First Amendment, however. Nussbaum outlines its various drafts and the issues involved. She notes that the final text is a committee construct. Compromises had to be made with advocates for states that still had established churches. She suggests that its framers left many matters on the margin of church-state relations deliberately vague, relying on the judgment of history to sort them out.

The remaining chapters of *Liberty of Conscience* examine some of the major church-state controversies and court cases that have dotted American history. Nussbaum's approach is more topical than chronological. Unlike the early section, which is hard if rewarding going for readers not versed in political philosophy, the cases she discusses are likely to ring a bell with the general reader who has an interest in church-state issues.

"Accommodation" is a term for cases where the law may have to bend when it conflicts with citizens' informed conscience. In a society where matters of employment, education, and military service are increasingly surrounded by regulations with the force of law, such clashes occur often.

Nussbaum examines the *Sherbert* case, a Supreme Court ruling in which unemployment benefits were ultimately granted to a Seventh Day Adventist textile worker who refused to work on Saturday. She also looks at *Employment Division v. Smith*, a 1990 ruling that denied similar benefits to a Native American drug counselor fired for his sacramental use of peyote during religious rites. The latter decision outraged such a wide cross section of American society that Congress passed the Religious Freedom Restoration Act. Subsequently the Supreme Court took umbrage at this end-run around its decision, and it attempted to nullify the act's applicability to the states. The issue remains in flux. Accommodation issues have also arisen over Amish schooling, the sanctity of the confessional, and other knotty issues.

Under "Fearing Strangers," the author analyzes controversies pitting "minority" religious groups against the prevailing culture. One example given is Roman Catholic parents' objections to public school practices, which in the nineteenth and early twentieth centuries often included the pro forma recitation of Protestant prayers and versions of the Bible. In discussing this issue, Nussbaum states that Catholics have been subjected to the most long-lasting and virulent mistreatment of any group in the United States. She mentions only one relevant case in support of this statement—a school disciplinary case that never reached a court—and gives little other documentation. In light of the country's past mistreatment of African Americans, American Indians, and other minority groups, this is an astounding statement to find in an otherwise well-reasoned book. In any event, Roman Catholics solved the immediate problem of their children's indoctrination by creating a system of parochial schools. The persistence of fear-based prejudice ebbed as Catholic immigrants achieved economic power and social status, a process that Mormons are now also undergoing.

Mormonism is discussed at length, almost entirely in terms of the late nineteenth century struggle over polygamy. There was a Supreme Court case about Mormon polygamy, *Reynolds*, brought in 1874. Nussbaum shows that it was argued on chauvinistic and racist grounds that would not be admissible in any court today. She does not note, however, that the Mormons' status was part of a larger debate about the future of the Western states, only solved by political compromise some two decades later. She also makes a somewhat bizarre argument for the Mormon polygamists on feminist grounds, saying the plight of Mormon plural wives was no worse than that of other married women of the era, who likewise had no independent rights or property. Although in strictly legal terms this may be true, this argument ignores the greater power imbalance in polygynous marriages supported by religion.

In subsequent chapters Nussbaum takes a brief look at many recent, recurring controversies. School prayer, public display of religious symbols, and evolution versus creation narratives in public schools are all discussed, with Nussbaum's analysis usually matching the conclusions of Supreme Court cases and mainstream opinion. One partial exception is her study of the *Kiryas Joel Village District* case in 1994. This was the episode in which a public-school district was drawn to coincide with a village of the Satmar Orthodox Jewish sect. Many scholars found this an impermissible breach of the separation principle. Nussbaum, on the other hand, describes the extreme problems faced by autistic or otherwise handicapped Satmar children in coping with a regular public-school environment that made no allowance for their naïveté, strange (and hence mockable) dress, and mannerisms, and which thoroughly confused them. Since the law requires public support for disabled children's education, and since special education teachers cannot be paid from public money while working at parochial schools, Nussbaum concludes that such districting provided equal treatment to children for whom nothing else has worked. At minimum, this is an illuminating sidelight on a difficult case.

Liberty of Conscience brings a scholarly perspective on church-state issues to a general audience. Even those not well versed in legal or philosophical arguments can follow the author's clear explanations and appreciate the "facts behind the headlines" which she offers in discussing newsworthy cases. Her attempt to find a unifying principle to the unique American relationship between church and state is not totally successful, but the effort throws light on its very complexity. Overall, the book is a good introduction to the constantly shifting landscape of church-state jurisprudence.

Its main failure is its neglect of historical or sociological factors in the conflicts it explores. This is magnified by some over-the-top statements made without documentation, such as those about Mormon polygamy or about the persecution of Roman Catholics. The text is meticulously documented in the sections on philosophy and on

Supreme Court decisions, so this lack is strange. It would also have been interesting to read the author's impressions of current issues, such as the evangelistic presence at the U.S. service academies or present-day Mormon polygamists, but space limitations probably account for such gaps.

In a concluding chapter, the author deplores the attacks on religious liberty that have appeared in American politics in recent years. As she has shown, they are nothing new, and on balance Nussbaum is optimistic. She believes that the American people have maintained, and even grown, in their respect for fellow citizens' rights to follow their own beliefs in a diverse society.

Emily Alward

Review Sources

America 198, no. 17 (May 19, 2008): 22-23.
The American Prospect 19 (May, 2008): 37.
Booklist 104, no. 12 (February 15, 2008): 17.
First Things 180 (February, 2008): 35.
Kirkus Reviews 75, no. 23 (December 1, 2007): 1235.
Library Journal 133, no. 3 (February 15, 2008): 110.
The Nation 286, no. 22 (June 9, 2008): 42-48.
The New York Review of Books 55, no. 8 (May 15, 2008): 24-27.
Publishers Weekly 254, no. 51 (December 24, 2007): 48.